VIVA - FACTS ON FILE

GUIDE TO RESEARCH

VIVA - FACTS ON FILE

GUIDE TO RESEARCH

JEFF LENBURG

New Delhi | Mumbai | Chennai | Kolkata | Bangalore | Hyderabad | Kochi | Guwahati

First Indian Edition 2007
Reprinted 2010

VIVA BOOKS PRIVATE LIMITED

- 4737/23 Ansari Road, Daryaganj, New Delhi 110 002
  E-mail: vivadelhi@vivagroupindia.net, Tel. 42242200
- 76, Service Industries, Shirvane, Sector 1, Nerul, Navi Mumbai 400 706
  E-mail: vivamumbai@vivagroupindia.net, Tel. 27721273, 27721274
- Jamals Fazal Chambers, 26 Greams Road, Chennai 600 006
  E-mail: vivachennai@vivagroupindia.net, Tel. 28290304, 28294241
- B-103, Jindal Towers, 21/1A/3 Darga Road, Kolkata 700 017
  E-mail: vivakolkata@vivagroupindia.net, Tel. 22836381, 22816713
- 7, Sovereign Park Apartments, 56-58, K. R. Road, Basavanagudi, Bangalore 560 004
  E-mail: vivabangalore@vivagroupindia.net, Tel. 26607409, 26607410
- 101-102 Mughal Marc Apartments, 3-4-637 to 641, Narayanguda, Hyderabad 500 029
  E-mail: vivahyderabad@vivagroupindia.net, Tel. 27564481, 27564482
- First Floor, Beevi Towers, SRM Road, Kaloor, Kochi 682 018, Kerala
  E-mail: vivakochi@vivagroupindia.net, Tel: 0484-2403055, 2403056
- 232, GNB Road, Beside UCO Bank, Silpukhuri, Guwahati 781 003
  E-mail: vivaguwahati@vivagroupindia.net, Tel: 0361-2666386

www.vivagroupindia.com

Published by arrangement with

Facts on File, Inc.
132 West 31st Street
New York 10001
USA

ISBN 978-81-309-0539-6

Published by Vinod Vasishtha for Viva Books Private Limited, 4737/23, Ansari Road, Daryaganj, New Delhi-110 002. Printed and bound by Anand Sons, Delhi - 110092.

To my aunt Violet, aunt Joan, and uncle Andy,
and to my former journalism professor Lew Barrett,
for all of your love and support over the years,
this one is in your honor.

CONTENTS

Expanded Table of Contents ix
Acknowledgments xxix
Introduction xxxi

SECTION I RESEARCHING YOUR TOPIC

1 Developing Your Subject 3
2 Gathering Your Information 10
3 Evaluating Your Sources 28

SECTION II FINDING SOURCES OF INFORMATION

4 Finding Archives and Archival Collections 37
5 Finding Associations, Societies, and Organizations 54
6 Finding Biographical Information 74
7 Finding CD-ROM Collections 95
8 Finding Electronic Databases 110
9 Finding Electronic Journals, Zines, and Newsletters 136
10 Finding E-mail Discussion Groups and Newsgroups 161
11 Finding General References 171
12 Finding Government Publications and Agencies 200
13 Finding Libraries: Academic, Government, Research, Public, School, State, and Special Libraries 226

14 Finding Newspapers, Magazines, Journals, and Radio and Television News 248
15 Researching on the Web 276
16 Finding Search Engines 303

SECTION III FINDING SOURCES BY SUBJECT

17 Aging 319
18 Business and Economics 328
19 Criminal Justice 338
20 Ecology and the Environment 351
21 Film and Television 361
22 Health and Medicine 377
23 History 386
24 Law 396
25 Literature and Literary Criticism 406
26 Music 422
27 Nursing 430
28 Politics and Public Policy 440
29 Psychology 450
30 Religion and Theology 459
31 Science and Technology 469
32 Sports 481
33 Theater and Dance 492
34 Women's Studies 506

SECTION IV USING YOUR SOURCES

35 Citing Your Sources 519
36 Creating Your Bibliography, Works Cited, or References 528

APPENDIXES

Appendix I APA Style 533
Appendix II MLA Style 537
Appendix III *The Chicago Manual of Style* 539

Selected Bibliography 541
Index 542

EXPANDED TABLE OF CONTENTS

Acknowledgments xxix
Introduction xxxi

SECTION I RESEARCHING YOUR TOPIC

1 Developing Your Subject **3**
Choosing Your Topic 3
Searching Your Topic 5
Effectively Searching Your Topic 5
Options for Searching 6
Methods of Searching 6
Defining and Narrowing Your Topic 8
Doing Preliminary Research 9

2 Gathering Your Information **10**
Planning Your Research 10
Setting an Agenda for Your Research 10
Listing Your Tools and Strategies 11
Creating a Timetable/Schedule 11
Finding Your Sources 13
Using Libraries 13
Online Catalogs 14
Popular References 15
Periodicals 17
Electronic Databases 19

Microforms: Microfilm and Microfiche 21
Interlibrary Loans 22
Other Library Resources 23
Using the Internet 23
Using CD-ROM Collections 25
Using Video and DVD Resources 25
Using Specialized Sources 25
Knowing When to Stop 26
3 Evaluating Your Sources **28**
Understanding Your Source 28
Considering the Source 28
Considering Who Said It 29
Considering the Facts 30
Purpose 30
Accuracy 31
Authority 31
Relevancy 32
Timeliness 33
Objectivity 33
Coverage 33

SECTION II FINDING SOURCES OF INFORMATION

4 Finding Archives and Archival Collections **37**
Types of Archives 37
Researching Archives and Archival Collections 38
Library Catalogs 38
Finding Aids 38
Online Databases 39
Free Sites 39
Subscription Sites 40
Overseas Sites 41
Printed References 42
Local Archives 42
Internet Archives 43
African-American Studies Archives 44
Agricultural and Farm Archives 45
American History Archives 45
American Jewish Archives 46
Art Archives 47
Congressional Archives 47

Ethnic Archives 48
Government Archives 48
Historical Archives 48
Labor Archives 49
Medicine Archives 49
Newspaper Archives 49
Performing Arts Archives 49
Recordings Archives 50
Space Exploration Archives 51
Television News Archives 51
Women's History Archives 51
Special Collections 52

5 Finding Associations, Societies, and Organizations **54**
Researching Associations 54
Print and CD-ROM 55
On the Web 55
Associations on the Net 56
African Americans 56
Alternative Medicine 57
Architecture 57
Chemistry 59
Computer Science 59
Criminal Investigation/Forensic Science 60
Dance 61
Disabilities 61
Drama 62
Environmental Health 62
Gerontology 63
Health and Medicine 63
Consumer Associations 63
Professional Associations 65
Human Rights 65
International/Regional Associations 65
Nongovernmental Associations 66
Language 67
Literature 67
Mathematics 68
Music 69
Nutrition 70
Philosophy 71

Physics 72
Religion and Theology 73
Women's Studies 73

6 Finding Biographical Information **74**
Researching Biographical Information 74
Biographical Indexes 75
Popular Biographical References 76
Books 76
Magazines 79
References for Regional Figures 79
References for International Figures 80
References by Subject 80
Aerospace 80
Art 80
Business 81
Education 81
Film, Theater, and Television 81
Law 82
Literature 82
Medicine and Health Care 83
Music 83
Politics 85
Science 86
Specific Ethnicities 86
African Americans 86
Arabs 87
Asian Americans 87
Hispanics/Hispanic Americans 87
Native Americans 88
Sports 88
Women 89
Biographical Information in Electronic Form 90
Biographical Information Online 91

7 Finding CD-ROM Collections **95**
Researching CD-ROM Collections 95
Locating CD-ROM Collections 95
Popular Titles by Subject 96
Biography 96
Business and Economics 97

Demographic Studies and Statistics 98
Encyclopedias 100
General References 101
Law and Government 102
Health and Medicine 103
History 103
Literature 105
Performing Arts (Drama, Film, Music, Television, and Theater) 106
Phone Directories 107
Religion 108
Science 108
Women's Studies 109

8 Finding Electronic Databases **110**
Researching Electronic Databases 110
General Databases 111
Academic 111
K–12 111
Databases by Subject 113
Agriculture 113
Anthropology 113
Biography 113
Biology 114
Business and Economics 114
Chemistry and Physical Sciences 116
Communications 116
Controversial and Cultural Issues 116
Criminal Justice and Law 117
Dictionaries, Directories, and Encyclopedias 118
Earth and Environmental Sciences 119
Education 119
Engineering Sciences 119
Ethics 120
Ethnic and Area Studies 120
General References 120
Government Publications 121
Health and Medicine 122
History 123
Humanities and Fine Arts 124
Journal and Magazine Article Indexes 124
Library Science/Books and Publishing 126

Literature 127
Newspaper Article Indexes 129
Performing Arts (Film, Music, Television, and Theater) 130
Philosophy 131
Political Science and Public Administration 131
Psychology 132
Religion 132
Sciences 132
Social Sciences 133
Sociology and Social Work 133
Sports and Exercise Sciences 134
Technology 134
Visual Arts and Architecture 134
Women's Studies 135
VHS and DVD Collections 135

9 Finding Electronic Journals, Zines, and Newsletters **136**
Researching Electronic Journals 136
Subscription-Based Journal Article Index Databases 137
Free Journal Article Index Databases 138
Multiple Subject Directories of E-Journals 139
Single-Subject Directories of Journal Collections 141
Architecture 141
Art 142
Astronomy 142
Biology 142
Business and Economics 142
Education 142
History 143
Journalism and the Media 143
Law 143
Medicine 143
Music 143
Philosophy 144
Psychology 144
Sociology and Social Sciences 144
Religion 145
Free E-Journals on the Web 145
Aging 145

Agriculture 145
Anthropology 146
Art 146
Biochemistry 146
Biology 147
Business 148
Chemistry 148
Computer Science 148
Computing 149
Consumer Information 149
Criminal Justice 149
Current Events 149
Economics 149
Education 150
Engineering 150
English 150
Environment 151
Ethnic Studies 151
Film Studies 151
Foreign Languages 152
Geological Sciences and Mining 152
History 152
Human Development and Family Studies 152
Journalism 152
Law 153
Library Science 153
Mathematics 154
Medicine 154
Military Science 157
Music 157
Nursing 157
Nutrition 158
Philosophy and Religion 158
Physics 158
Political Science 158
Psychology 159
Science/Technology 159
Social Work 159
Sociology 159
Speech and Communication Studies 160
Theater 160
Women's Studies 160

10 Finding E-mail Discussion Groups and Newsgroups **161**
Researching Discussion Groups 161
Understanding Discussion Groups 161
Deciding to Join a Discussion Group 162
Joining a Discussion Group 162
Finding Discussion Groups 163
Mailing List Search Engines and Directories 163
Mailing List Archives 165
Using Discussion Groups for Research 165
Finding Further Information on Discussion Groups 165
Researching Newsgroups 166
Understanding Newsgroups 166
Deciding to Join a Newsgroup 168
Joining a Newsgroup 168
Finding Newsgroups 169
Newsgroup Search Engines 169
Newsgroup Directories 169
Newsgroup Archives 170
Using Newsgroups for Research 170

11 Finding General References **171**
Researching General References 171
Almanacs 172
Atlases 173
Bibliographies 174
Chronicles: By Eras and Decades 175
Chronologies and Daybooks 176
Chronologies 176
Daybooks 177
Dictionaries 177
English Language Dictionaries 177
Specialized Dictionaries 178
Directories 178
Encyclopedias 179
Guides to Books and References 180
Microform Collections 181

Periodical and Newspaper Indexes 181
Agriculture 181
Anthropology 181
Art and Humanities 182
Bibliography 182
Biography 182
Biology 182
Books and Book Reviews 183
Business and Economics 183
Chemistry 184
Computers 184
Criminal Justice 184
Demography 184
Dissertations 184
Education 185
Engineering 185
Environment 185
History 186
Language and Literature 186
Law 187
Medicine 188
Minorities 189
Motion Pictures 189
Music 189
Newspapers 190
Philosophy 192
Physical Education 192
Political Science 192
Psychology 193
Public Opinion 193
Science and Technology 194
Social Sciences 194
Sociology 194
Statistics 195
Women's Studies 195
Popular Quotations 195
Public Opinion Polls 195
Statistical Abstracts 196
Yearbooks 198
Additional References 198
Web References 198

12 Finding Government Publications and Agencies **200**
Researching Government Publications and Agencies 200
Government Guides and Catalogs 201
Federal Government Information 203
On the Web *203*
In Print *204*
State and Local Government Information 205
On the Web *205*
In Print *206*
Foreign Government Information 207
On the Web *207*
In Print *207*
Government Journals and Publications 207
Government Sources Online 221
Other Government Documents 225

13 Finding Libraries: Academic, Government, Research, Public, School, State, and Special Libraries **226**
Researching Libraries 226
Academic Libraries 227
Government Libraries 228
Departmental Libraries *229*
Military Libraries *231*
Other Governmental Libraries *232*
Presidential Libraries *234*
Independent Research Libraries 236
Public Libraries 238
School Libraries 239
Special Libraries 240
State Libraries 240
Library Directories 244
In Print *244*
On the Web *245*
Library Online Public Access Catalogs 245
Virtual Libraries 246

14 Finding Newspapers, Magazines, Journals, and Radio and Television News **248**
Researching Newspapers, Magazines, and Journals 248

Microfilm and Microfiche Periodicals 249
U.S. Newspapers by State 251
Foreign Newspapers 256
Canada 256
England 256
France 256
Soviet Union and Russia 256
Magazines and Journals 256
Advertising 256
Aeronautics and Space Flight 256
African Americans 256
Aging 257
Agriculture 257
Anthropology 257
Archaeology 257
Architecture 257
Art 257
Astronomy 257
Automobiles 257
Biology 257
Broadcasting 257
Business 257
Chemistry 258
Children and Youth 258
Communication 258
Computers 258
Consumer Education 258
Dance 258
Ecology 259
Education 259
Electronics 259
Engineering 259
Fashion 259
Foreign Language 259
Forestry 259
Future 260
Gardening and Horticulture 260
General Interest 260
Geography 260
Health and Medicine 260
History 260
Home Economics 261

Law 261
Literature and Language 261
Literature and Politics 261
Motion Pictures 261
Music 261
Nursing 261
Photography 261
Political Science 262
Population 262
Psychiatry 262
Psychology 262
Recreation and Sports 263
Religion and Theology 263
Science 263
Social Sciences 263
Sociology 263
Sound Recordings 263
Speech 264
Technology 264
Theater 264
Travel 264
Women's Periodicals 264
Zoology 264
News Digests 264
Newspaper and Magazine Indexes, Databases and Directories 265
Publication Web Sites 270
Researching Radio and Television News 272
15 Researching on the Web **276**
Narrowing Your Focus 276
Research Sites by Category 276
African-American Studies 277
Aging 277
Agriculture 277
Art History 278
Associations and Organizations 278
Astronomy 279
Business, Economics, and Finance 279
Chemistry 280
Computers and Cyberspace 280
Consumer Issues 281

Country Directories 281
Demographic Data 282
Education 283
Environment 283
Ethics 284
Film and Theater 284
Forensic Science 285
General Reference Sources 285
Geology and Earth Science 286
Government and Politics 286
Health and Medicine 288
History and Culture 288
International Affairs/International Studies 290
Law and Criminal Justice 291
Media Studies 292
Military and Defense 292
Physics 293
Public Opinion Surveys 293
Rankings and Awards 294
Religion and Theology 294
Science and Technology 295
Social Issues 295
Speeches 296
Subject Guides and Directories 297
Web Searching 299
Best References on the Web 300
Finding Other Web Databases 302
16 Finding Search Engines **303**
Researching Search Engines 303
Using Search Engines 303
Categories of Search Engines 304
Web Search Engines 304
Web Metasearch Engines 306
Web Directories 308
Topical Search Engines 309
Arts and Entertainment Search Engines 309
Business and Financial Search Engines 309
Computers and Technology Search Engines 310
Country and Region Search Engines 310
Australia and New Zealand 310
Europe 311

France 311
Germany 311
Government Search Engines 311
Health and Medicine Search Engines 311
Kid-Safe Search Engines 312
Legal Search Engines 312
News Search Engines 312
Major News Search Engines 312
Other News Search Engines 313
Question-and-Answer Search Engines 313
Science Search Engines 314
Web Search Engine Tutorials 315

SECTION III FINDING SOURCES BY SUBJECT

17 Aging 319
Selected Books and References 319
Selected Article Indexes and Abstracts 321
Printed Indexes and Abstracts 321
Web Indexes and Abstracts 321
Selected Full-Text Article Databases 322
Selected Periodicals 323
Selected Web Sites 326
18 Business and Economics 328
Selected Books and References 328
General Resources 328
Handbooks, Directories, and Yearbooks 329
Selected Article Indexes and Abstracts 332
Printed Indexes and Abstracts 332
Web Indexes and Abstracts 333
Selected Full-Text Article Databases 333
Selected Periodicals 335
Selected Web Sites 336
19 Criminal Justice 338
Selected Books and References 338
Selected Article Indexes and Abstracts 339
Printed Indexes and Abstracts 339
Web Indexes and Abstracts 340

Selected Full-Text Article Databases 342
Selected Periodicals 344
Selected Web Sites 348
General Information 348
Statistics—Comprehensive Sources 349
Statistics—Individual Sources 350

20 Ecology and the Environment 351
Selected Books and References 351
Selected Article Indexes and Abstracts 354
Printed Indexes and Abstracts 354
Web Indexes and Abstracts 355
Selected Full-Text Article Databases 356
Selected Periodicals 357
Selected Web Sites 359

21 Film and Television 361
Selected Books and References 361
General Resources 361
Film and Television Studies and Criticism 364
Filmographies 367
Selected Article Indexes and Abstracts 367
Printed Indexes and Abstracts 367
Web Indexes and Abstracts 369
Selected Full-Text Article Databases 370
Selected Periodicals 372
Selected Web Sites 374

22 Health and Medicine 377
Selected Books and References 377
Selected Article Indexes and Abstracts 378
Printed Indexes and Abstracts 378
Web Indexes and Abstracts 380
Selected Full-Text Article Databases 382
Selected Periodicals 383
Selected Web Sites 384

23 History 386
Selected Books and References 386
General Sources 386

U.S. History 386
World History 388
Selected Article Indexes and Abstracts 389
Printed Indexes and Abstracts 389
Web Indexes and Abstracts 390
Selected Full-Text Article Databases 391
Selected Periodicals 393
Selected Web Sites 394
24 Law **396**
Selected Books and References 396
Selected Article Indexes and Abstracts 399
Printed Indexes and Abstracts 399
Web Indexes and Abstracts 400
Selected Full-Text Article Databases 402
Selected Periodicals 403
Selected Web Sites 404
25 Literature and Literary Criticism **406**
Selected Books and References 406
Anthologies 406
Biography and Literary Criticism 407
Encyclopedias 410
General References 411
Selected Article Indexes and Abstracts 411
Printed Indexes and Abstracts 411
Web Indexes and Abstracts 413
Articles and Literature 414
Print Indexes 414
Web Indexes and Abstracts 415
Selected Full-Text Article Databases 417
Selected Periodicals 418
Selected Web Sites 421
26 Music **422**
Selected Books and References 422
Selected Article Indexes and Abstracts 424
Printed Indexes and Abstracts 424
Web Indexes and Abstracts 424

Selected Full-Text Article Databases 427
Selected Periodicals 427
Selected Web Sites 428

27 Nursing 430

Selected Books and References 430
Selected Article Indexes and Abstracts 431
Printed Indexes and Abstracts 431
Web Indexes and Abstracts 433
Selected Full-Text Article Databases 436
Selected Periodicals 438
Selected Web Sites 438

28 Politics and Public Policy 440

Selected Books and References 440
Almanacs 440
Encyclopedias 440
General References 441
Selected Article Indexes and Abstracts 443
Printed Indexes and Abstracts 443
Web Indexes and Abstracts 444
Selected Full-Text Article Databases 445
Selected Periodicals 446
Selected Web Sites 448
Public Policy Organizations 448
Federal Organizations 449
International Organizations 449

29 Psychology 450

Selected Books and References 450
Selected Article Indexes and Abstracts 451
Printed Indexes and Abstracts 451
Web Indexes and Abstracts 452
Selected Full-Text Article Databases 454
Selected Periodicals 455
Selected Web Sites 456

30 Religion and Theology 459

Selected Books and References 459
Selected Article Indexes and Abstracts 460

Printed Indexes and Abstracts 460
Web Indexes and Abstracts 463
Selected Full-Text Article Databases 464
Selected Periodicals 465
Selected Web Sites 467
31 Science and Technology 469
Selected Books and References 469
Dictionaries 469
Encyclopedias 471
General References 472
Selected Article Indexes and Abstracts 473
Printed Indexes and Abstracts 473
Web Indexes and Abstracts 474
Selected Full-Text Article Databases 477
Selected Periodicals 479
Selected Web Sites 480
32 Sports 481
Selected Books and References 481
Almanacs 481
Dictionaries 482
Encyclopedias 482
General References 483
Handbooks 483
Selected Article Indexes and Abstracts 483
Printed Indexes and Abstracts 483
Web Indexes and Abstracts 484
Selected Full-Text Article Databases 486
Selected Periodicals 487
Selected Web Sites 490
33 Theater and Dance 492
Selected Books and References 492
General References 492
Reviews/Criticism 495
Selected Article Indexes and Abstracts 497
Printed Indexes and Abstracts 497
Web Indexes and Abstracts 498

Selected Full-Text Article Databases 500
Selected Periodicals 502
Selected Web Sites 504

34 Women's Studies 506
Selected Books and References 506
Bibliographies 506
Chronologies, Encyclopedias, and Histories 506
Statistical References 508
Selected Article Indexes and Abstracts 508
Printed Indexes and Abstracts 508
Web Indexes and Abstracts 510
Selected Full-Text Article Databases 513
Selected Periodicals 513
Selected Web Sites 515

SECTION IV USING YOUR SOURCES

35 Citing Your Sources 519
Avoiding Plagiarism 519
Quoting, Paraphrasing, and Summarizing 521
Creating In-Text Citations 525
Finding Online Guides and Tutorials 526

36 Creating Your Bibliography, Works Cited, or References 528
APA Style 529
MLA Style 529
The Chicago Manual of Style 529
Online Bibliography Creators 531

Appendix I APA Style 533
Appendix II MLA Style 537
Appendix III *The Chicago Manual of Style* 539

Selected Bibliography 541
Index 542

ACKNOWLEDGMENTS

Given the breadth and scope of this project, I have so many individuals, groups, institutions, and organizations that I want to thank who have made this book possible.

Very special thanks to the staffs and members of the following library trade associations for providing vital information and guiding me to countless valuable sources consulted in writing this book. They include the American Library Association, the American Association of School Librarians, the Association of Library Collections and Technical Services, the Public Library Association, and the Association of College and Research Libraries.

I also wish to thank the many fine university and college libraries for their assistance in providing many other sources of information. They include Arizona State University West, Birmingham Southern College, Columbia University, County College of Morris, Delta State University, Duke University, Estrella Mountain Community College, Harvard University, Las Positas College, and Loyola University Chicago. My thanks as well to Ohio State University, Purdue University, Princeton University, Stanford University, Texas A&M University, Tufts University, the University of Central Florida, the University of North Carolina, the University of Lethbridge, the University of Vermont, and Yale University.

My sincere gratitude especially to Dennis Isbell, Academic Program Support Librarian Humanities & Fine Arts of Arizona State University West Library, for assisting me with various research requests, in addition to handling so many other important tasks. Also my heartfelt thanks to many other ASU West library specialists for their efforts in compiling many useful subject guides used in researching this volume: Deg Farrelly, Bee Gallegos, Hank Harken, Carolyn Johnson, Lisa Kammerlocher, and Leslee Sheel.

I also would like to recognize the many fine and talented researchers, librarians, scholars, professors, teachers, and writers, too numerous to mention, who have written or created countless printed and online research guides, Web sites, or recommended lists of research which were helpful in the course of writing this book.

Finally, I would like to thank my editor Jeff Soloway for understanding the importance of this book and believing in this project from day one, and for his support and encouragement along the way. Also to my wife Debby, love and kisses for her many sacrifices in allowing me to pursue my dreams.

INTRODUCTION

The success of every essay, term paper, or written project depends not only on the quality of your writing but also on the quality of your research. With the vast explosion in growth of electronic technology, virtual libraries, the Internet, and traditional libraries, researching any topic has never been easier than it is today, so long as you understand the process, and know where to find and how to access such sources.

The Facts On File Guide to Research is a general introductory volume that explains the art and methods of research and researching any topic, for any given purpose. Featuring valuable tips for beginners and more experienced students of all ages, this long-overdue compendium is divided into four sections for easy use.

Section I: Researching Your Topic explains general strategies and methods of research, everything from ways to choose, search, and test your topic, to planning your research and finding your sources, to evaluating the accuracy, credibility, and reliability of your sources.

Section II: Finding Sources of Information extensively details various outlets of research. Discussed at length is how to find archives and archival collections; associations, societies, and organizations with research; biographical information; electronic databases with full-text articles; and electronic journals, zines, and newsletters. Also highlighted are e-mail discussion groups and newsgroups; general references (almanacs, bibliographies, periodical and newspaper indexes, yearbooks, and more); government agencies and publications, libraries (academic, government, public, school, research, special, and state libraries); newspapers, magazines, journals, and radio and television stations; and research on the Web on virtually any subject.

Section III: Finding Sources by Topic conveniently surveys the most recommended information sources by librarians and researchers, with detailed listings of selected books and references, print and Web article indexes, periodicals and Web sites, to research any subject or field of interest, from aging to women's studies.

Section IV: Citing Your Sources provides examples of proper style and techniques for avoiding plagiarism, quoting, paraphrasing, and summarizing your research, and creating text citations and a bibliography, works cited, or list of references, including Web sites to create your bibliography electronically.

Finally, this book features an easy-to-use section of American Psychological Association (APA), Modern Language Association (MLA), and *Chicago Manual of Style* guides, including many different examples on listing sources in your bibliography, works cited, or list of references.

In writing this book, the author consulted with countless library and trade association professionals, faculty members and instructors, fellow researchers and authors, and a wide variety of sources to deliver this highly informative reference.

Every effort was made to verify sources, to confirm the accuracy and reliability of information, and to research as much as humanly possible all aspects of this reference work. The author selected what are considered the best sources of research on the planet today.

Section I

RESEARCHING YOUR TOPIC

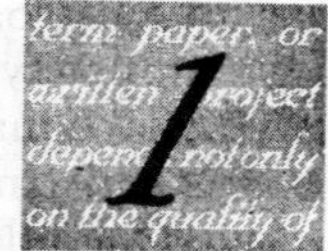

1 Developing Your Subject

Knowing whether your subject is researchable is the most important first step to developing your essay, term paper, or written project. Fortunately, with the dramatic boom in technology today, vast resources exist to research almost any topic of interest. From the Internet, to schools, to colleges and universities, to public libraries, to museums, never before in the history of humankind has so much information been so readily accessible for the greater good. You don't have to be an experienced researcher to find what you want or what you want to know. Of course, understanding the art and methods of research will help you achieve your objective more successfully.

The term *research* suggests a purpose. The whole idea behind doing research is to pry more fully, to dig more deeply, and to examine more closely something that piques your curiosity. Whether you need to research for practical, personal, or academic reasons, whether you are researching a school paper, your family history, or a subject of great personal interest, the manner in which you develop your topic is important to finding what you want.

CHOOSING YOUR TOPIC

Your success as a researcher depends on the nature of your topic—what you are writing about, what you are seeking, or what you hope to answer. Most students conduct research for the purposes of writing an essay or research paper assigned by their instructor. In most cases, your instructor will assign you a topic to write about, suggest some suitable possibilities or ask you to develop a topic of your choice.

Your subject should be timely and appropriate for research. Topics that generate the most press coverage (such as abortion, domestic violence, or gay marriage) and dominate the public's consciousness are more easily researchable since so much published material from a variety of different sources is available. Conversely, subjects that are more specialized require a more concerted effort to uncover background information, relevant facts, and source material. In this case, unearthing this information may prove more difficult. Avoid settling on any topic without checking out its research potential first.

Developing a topic that is researchable isn't as difficult as you think. To expedite the process, first take stock of those immediate resources that can aid you in the development of your idea and guide you in the right direction. To zero in on the most interesting or most suitable angle for your paper, check out the most promising resources. Three successful strategies can help you achieve this goal:

1. **Check your library.** Never underestimate your school or public library as a major source for ideas. Do some quick reading to learn more about topics you have in mind, or you have been assigned. Books, periodicals, newspapers, and electronic media head the list of potential resources you can review. One useful source for finding ideas or topics for written projects is *10,000 Ideas for Term Papers, Projects, Reports and Speeches,* 5th ed., by Kathryn Lamm (New York: Arco, 1998).

Browse the headings in your library's catalog, keeping potential topics in mind. The library reference staff can assist you in determining the plausibility of your topic. Reference librarians know a wide range of resources and strategies, and also may spot problems with your topic that you never considered. They can direct you to the best places to look for preliminary information on your topic.

Consulting general encyclopedias or general references, like the *Columbia Encyclopedia* or the *Encyclopaedia Britannica,* that cover a variety of subjects or disciplines will help you realize the potential of your topic, or help you consider ideas to write about. Encyclopedias are the common background sources used in libraries for specific topics. They provide a broader context for your research and tell you in general terms what is known about your topic. General references achieve the same objectives and, much like encyclopedias, feature entries that include complete bibliographies of additional sources you can check later.

Online databases, often offered free through your school or public library, are another important tool for generating ideas as well. Equipped with search engines, they allow you to research any subject or topic. Many include links to full-text articles and preliminary source material. (See "Options for Searching" for more details.)

2. **Check the Internet.** Doing a general search of the Internet can also help you develop your topic or come up with topical ideas. Various Web search engines, from AltaVista to Google, will lead you to a wide range of suitable Web pages, providing overviews, background material, and other potential resources.

Another great venue of ideas is Questia.com, the world's largest online library of books and journals. Rich in scholarly content, the site contains a variety of research paper resources, including links to more than 5,000 popular paper topics in art history, biography, economics, education, health, history, music, philosophy, psychology, and religion, as well as controversial topics.

When researching your topic, be careful of Web sites not sponsored by established groups, companies, and organizations, or those that appear biased in nature, such as lobbyist and advocacy groups. Also avoid articles that are outdated and those that have no author's name attached to them. (For more information regarding using Web sites, see Chapter 3, "Evaluating Your Sources.")

3. **Check with others.** Sometimes it pays to bounce your ideas off other people you know, or brainstorm with those who may be more experienced or more knowledgeable than you are. As noted earlier, you may want to talk with your class instructor for his or her constructive input. Or talk with friends, family members, or classmates who will freely express their ideas and can provide a good creative "think tank" approach for you in finding a topic.

Still stuck on a topic? Reading current newspapers and magazines or watching or listening to news on radio and TV programs that cover "hot button" issues of the day can be beneficial. Every day they report important stories on topics of national, state, and local interest and can be a natural source of ideas. (For a more complete discussion of sources, see "Finding Your Sources" in Chapter 2, "Gathering Your Information.")

Whatever you decide, don't select a topic just for the sake of getting your assignment done. Choose a topic that you are passionate about, and that you will enjoy spending considerable time and energy researching. Possessing enthusiasm for your subject is essential to keep you driven through every stage of your project to completion.

Also keep in mind that developing your topic will be an ongoing process. As you undertake the process, in your search for more specific information, you may find the need to change, broaden, narrow, refine, or tweak your topic if the depth of material you need to define your topic does not fully exist.

SEARCHING YOUR TOPIC

How well you search your topic and the way you search it is very important to developing your idea. Whether you decide to use the Internet or online periodical and article databases, using search engines is the fastest possible way to retrieve information on a variety of subjects or topics.

Effectively Searching Your Topic

To effectively search your topic, first you need to clearly define it. Write a clear, short sentence that summarizes your search topic. In other words, say what you want to find your information on. *Example:* I would like to write about the increasing problem of teenage pregnancy in the United States.

Having summarized your topic, pick out the keywords that best describe your concept and that make up your search topic. In the case of the above example, three concepts reflect the main idea of your paper: *teenage, pregnancy,* and *United States*. Using these terms, you want to enter these exact words to search your topic on various search engines or online databases. Your search results will list every available Web page or document featuring your three terms in their description. The sources listed will include links to each described Web site. By reviewing the summary of the Web sites listed, you can visit those sites that seem relevant and determine if they apply to your subject or not. (Note: Often, sites will contain links to other related Web sites and resources that you also can review).

When searching your topic, remember this: No search engine covers everything online. They allow you to search for different things in different ways, and they all produce different results. That is because search engines index only portions of the Internet or, for electronic databases, certain kinds of periodicals, and not necessarily the same pages or publications. Therefore, if you can't find what you are looking at one site or one database, it's important to try another.

In both cases, most search engines produce comprehensive and relevant results based on the keywords that appear in the context of your field of inquiry. Others produce results in the order of popularity by the number of other sites linked to a site, or the popularity of the linking sites on that particular search engine, or by relevancy. This is mostly the case with Internet search engine sites.

Options for Searching

Google (www.google.com) is by far the best search engine on the Web today for finding leading sites on a particular topic. Pages listed first are the ones that other sites link to most often and, unlike other search engines, Google stores Web pages in its database, allowing you to see expired pages that otherwise would not be available. Yahoo! (www.yahoo.com) is another popular search engine site. It indexes pages by topic, producing a list of links appropriate to your topic. To narrow your search for a specific time period, Hot Bot (www.hotbot.com) is another great choice. Using its advance search, you can specify date limits with your search like "in the last month" or "in the last three months," so your search won't produce a list of sites that are irrelevant to your topic.

Other places to start your search are Excite (www.excite.com), Lycos (www.lycos.com), and Northern Light (www.northernlight.com), which rank sites by relevancy, or AltaVista (www.altavista.com), which allows you to state your search in the form of a question.

If you don't find what you want using a single search engine, then try one of the metasearch engines. They simultaneously search through multiple search engines, directories, or other Web collections for documents related to your subject. Leaders in this category include AlltheWeb (www.alltheweb.com), Ask Jeeves (www.ask.com), Dogpile (www.dogpile.com), Metacrawler (www.metacrawler.com), and Webcrawler (www.webcrawler.com). (For a complete roundup of search engines, metasites, and search directories, see Chapter 15.)

Besides using Internet search engines, if you decide to try online databases at your library, you no doubt will have a variety of choices from which you can search full-text books, newspapers, magazines, and journals on virtually any subject or topic. These licensed databases feature articles on current events, individual and specific subjects, and social and controversial topics that all may be instrumental in helping you search for a topic. They include Academic Search Elite, CQ Researcher, InfoTrac, Issues and Controversies Opposing Viewpoints, and many others. (For a complete list of databases, see Chapter 7, "Electronic Databases.")

Methods of Searching

In the beginning, when searching your topic using either Web search engines or electronic databases, problems may arise from matching the keywords of your searches with what is used in search engine or database. Applying many proven techniques will alleviate this problem in your quest to find an appropriate topic and plenty of information about it. Two common methods of searching are:

1. **Phrase Searching.** Phrase searching requires you to use a proper name or distinct phrase enclosed in double quotations (for example: "affirmative action," "mental health organizations," or "John Ritter.") Before commencing with your search, you need to think of the proper name, phrase, or organ-

ization that you want to search to direct you to Web pages or documents most associated with your subject or topic.

2. **Boolean Searching.** The Boolean method allows you to use common words with many meanings and contexts with what are called "search connectors," such as AND, OR, or NOT, to achieve the best search results. (Most major search engines, such as AlltheWeb, Google, and many others, put AND between words by default.)

Adding AND to your keywords will limit your search to the topic you have defined. Let's say you want to research "censorship" and "media." By combining these keywords with AND (*censorship AND media*) in your search, you would retrieve Web pages or documents containing those identical words. The same would apply if your topic is teenage pregnancies. Simply by connecting "teenagers" and "pregnancies" with AND, your search will retrieve only specific records found in that search engine's database containing those words.

Unlike AND, using OR in combination with your keywords will actually broaden your search and result in more "hits" that mention either word. In this case, if your subject this time is automobile emissions and pollution, to retrieve the most documents related to your subject and mentioning those words, you would search your subject thusly: *automobiles OR emissions OR pollution.*

Less popular than other search connectors is NOT. Combining NOT with your keywords will actually *exclude* certain concepts and terms from your search, and thus exclude certain documents not containing the specified term. For example: *advertising NOT television.* Using this method, the search engine will retrieve only those documents that mention "advertising" and not television. One major problem with NOT as a search connector is that it may discard articles that are important. Therefore, you may want to restrict your usage of OR if this handicaps your search for material.

In addition to phrase or Boolean searching, you can apply a variety of other proven methods to effectively search your topic, namely:

1. **Nested Searches.** A nested search is another technique often used for searching a topic. It combines the use of AND and OR in the same search statement. Unlike search connectors, nested searches use parentheses to enclose the "or" part of the search. If cloning is your topic and you want to examine the ethical considerations and legal ramifications, your nested search statement would be *cloning and (morals or laws).* The results of your search will focus on any document featuring this combination of words.

2. **Truncated Searches.** A truncated search, a second common method, uses an asterisk (*) symbol to retrieve any variation of your topic search. For example, using our previous topic, "cloning," by adding an asterisk at the end ("clon*"), you would find everything in that search engine's database with that root word, such as "cloning" and "clones."

3. **Subject Heading or Descriptor Searches.** The final search method uses subject headings or descriptors commonly contained in library catalogs or electronic databases. These databases apply a unique set of subject headings, such as Library of Congress Subject Headings (a classification system for books, references, periodicals, and so on), that describes each item in its database, from A to Z—(for example, "Animals" or "Sports." Subject headings often differ from database to database, so knowing the right subject headings

will make your search more precise. Familiarizing yourself with the subject headings or descriptors used by search engines and how to use them in your search will help you to uncover many more relevant documents and narrow your search, if needed.

In the meantime, start by doing a keyword search using words that best describe your topic to see what subject headings or descriptors work. Next, browse through your search results and make a list of the subjects or descriptors found in your Web pages or documents that more precisely identify your subject or concept. Redo your search using the new subjects or descriptors that you identified.

DEFINING AND NARROWING YOUR TOPIC

After conducting your initial search for ideas, if you haven't found enough information on your topic, then you may need to focus your idea more sharply to fulfill the purpose of your assignment (and possibly get that "A" you've dreamed of). With a well-crafted topic, you can focus your research and hunt for relevant facts and information that will flesh out your idea and make your project successful. The following are common tips that will help you more favorably achieve your objective:

1. Avoid Being Too General. When developing your topic, try not to be too general in your approach, but be more specific. For example, if you decide to research "alcoholism and teenagers," doing your preliminary research with a topic as general this will result in finding more information than you bargained for. That's because any preliminary research you conduct will be too broad and your findings so widespread that you won't know what information is usable, necessary, or dispensable. Conversely, topics that are too new can be troublesome as well. That's because often few sources exist, making the task of research that much more difficult.

2. Make Sure Your Topic Is Well Defined. You'll have an easier time researching your topic if you formulate a well-defined researchable question or well-focused topic to answer what will be the thrust of your essay, paper, or written project. If you rush ahead too quickly with a topic you have not defined, you may fail to develop your topic effectively. Your research question will provide the focus of your research and your paper, so when you are conducting your research, the information you gather will answer and support your paper's point of view or central theme. Your question should be clear, concise, detailed, and focused. By taking this time-tested approach, you will not only know the topic you will be specifically researching but also the point you want to take in your paper.

Let's say your topic is television violence. What exactly do you want to know? Are you interested in the effect of violent television content on viewers in general, on adults, or on children? If your interest is children, then you want to frame your question thusly: "What effect does television violence have on children?" Your research—and ultimately your paper—will now focus on answering this important question, and depict how violence in television affects the behavior of children who watch these influential programs.

Another example might be secondhand smoke, one of those "hot button" issues. Again, what is the point of view or theme of your paper going to be? Do you want to focus on secondhand smoke and its damaging effect on teenagers? Do you want to argue that it poses no serious health risk at all? Since so much has been written and published about this subject, the latter may be hard to prove. Conclusive evidence may not exist to support this viewpoint. Certainly, an easier topic to research would be "secondhand smoke and its damaging effect on teenagers." Ask yourself what you want to focus on in the form of a question. It could be simply, "What is the long-term effect of secondhand smoke on teenagers?"

DOING PRELIMINARY RESEARCH

Once you have found a topic that works favorably in your search, you then need to conduct more preliminary research to determine if ample research exists for your topic. Like a great explorer uncovering uncharted territory or a great archaeologist undertaking an important dig for unknown artifacts, you need to get your explorer shoes on and dig deeper.

Doing more preliminary research will provide you with the additional facts, opinions, and details to assess the overall feasibility of your topic. The more you research and the more dedicated you are to this task, the more fully you will be able to assess your topic's viability.

During this phase of the operation, you want to consult as many sources as possible. This may involve keyword searching on Internet search engines, Web directories, specialized Web sites, or online databases at your library to find more information relevant to your topic.

As an active researcher, you want to constantly evaluate your research, its purpose and its relevancy by asking yourself, "How does it relate to my topic?" "What ideas support my topic?" "From where does the author draw his or her ideas?"

The last question is vitally important for two reasons. First, most published articles—mostly in scholarly journals, specialty publications, books, and popular references—will feature a bibliography of sources at the end offering additional avenues to research for your topic later. Secondly, the author of the article may have used only a fraction of material from that listed "source." Therefore, you should always consult the original article to see if other important details were covered that the writer left out.

Another important tip: Remember, many of the books and articles that you find in periodical indexes also will have bibliographies. You can check these for additional relevant sources for your research.

At this stage of your project, your search may yield a bumper crop of information that precisely addresses your paper's concept. If so, you are in good shape. Or you may find that potential sources for your topic are few and far between, or that there are hundreds of sources, far too many to list. If either is the case, then pick a question that a dozen or so of the sources you have found focus on and restate the theme of your paper appropriately. Don't be married to your original idea if it will be too restrictive or cumbersome. Otherwise, you are setting yourself up for more frustration than it is worth.

Now that you have successfully found your topic, you are ready for the next task: Finding all the information and sources needed for your written project and, more important, developing a plan that will ensure your success.

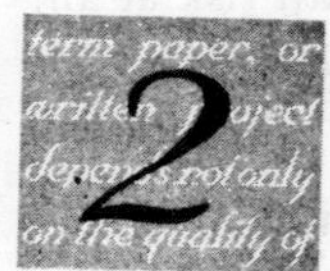

Gathering Your Information

Your success rate in researching your topic, subject, or idea will dramatically improve if you plan appropriately, develop a timetable to achieve your objective, and take the right course of action to gather information for your project.

The quality of the information you gather is more important than the quantity. Assembling a large mass of material through your research does not mean that all of it will be useful or, for that matter, necessary. Therefore, carefully planning what you need to research is imperative.

PLANNING YOUR RESEARCH

All undertakings, whether throwing a 50th-anniversary party for your grandparents, buying a new car, moving into your first apartment, or moving to another state, have one thing in common: They all take careful planning. The same goes with researching your paper. A well-developed plan will mean the difference between completing your project on time or ahead of schedule.

Three logical steps you should take before digging for more information and to fulfill your research are:

1. Set an agenda for your research
2. Develop a list of the research tools and strategies
3. Create a timetable or schedule for completion

Setting an Agenda for Your Research

Planning in advance what you need to research can save you a tremendous amount of time and energy. You need a road map to take you in the right direction. Otherwise, you will be spinning your wheels and getting nowhere fast. To avoid this problem, you need to set an agenda for your research.

Accomplishing this task is easy. Consider the purpose of your topic and the expectations that your instructor has for your paper. What should your paper look like? What do you hope to learn about your topic? What characteristics should your paper reflect? Is your paper supposed to examine a highly debatable political, cultural, or scholarly issue? Is your paper supposed to take a position or weigh both sides of the issue? Who will your audience be? If you're not sure what the requirements are, always ask your instructor so you are heading down the right path.

Following this exercise, determine what methods of research will be appropriate to meet those expectations. What kind of sources are you allowed to use? How much evidence is needed to shape your paper? What variety of sources are required reflecting different viewpoints?

Finally, look at what combination of research will help you fulfill the objective of your assignment. Decide which tools and references you should use to balance your research and that you plan to explore. The tools and strategies you select will guide you to finding the research you need to accomplish your assignment.

Listing Your Tools and Strategies

Now that you have successfully set an agenda, you need a shopping list. Your list should cover those research tools and strategies you decided upon that are most suitable and most appropriate for your project.

In doing your preliminary research to test your topic, you probably only scratched the surface. Consulting encyclopedias, newspapers and magazines, and the Internet probably fulfilled your initial needs, but now you need to broaden the scope of your research to other mediums to fully research your topic before writing your paper.

Consequently, list other print and electronic research tools that you want to explore in earnest, and check them off after you've completed this task. Your list might be something like this:

___ Check almanacs
___ Check biographical dictionaries
___ Check electronic databases
___ Check master bibliographies
___ Check microfilm indexes
___ Check scholarly journals
___ Check specialized subject references
___ Check other sources (such as government documents, statistical abstracts, and the like)
___ Check with a librarian (for helping you find any of the above or other relevant sources)

Your list may look different from the above example, but, nonetheless, it will help you focus on your needs and help you to achieve them.

As you embark on this phase of research, be diligent. Take notes of what research you have completed, including citations—particular information that gives proof of what you have researched—for each source you plan to use, such as the author, title, publisher, year, and Web address, and what you have left to finish. This information will be useful to you later, when you compile your bibliography or works cited page for your essay, term paper, or written project.

Creating a Timetable/Schedule

Nearly everything in life is scheduled or involves some kind of rigid routine. You may wake up at the same time every morning, have breakfast at the same time (or skip breakfast every morning—your choice), go to school at the same time, or do your school work at the same hour every day. While it may be redundant and suffocating at times, the fact is that having a schedule works best to allow you to accomplish all that you need to do.

When embarking on your research project, how well you manage and schedule your time is equally important. Researching an essay, term paper, or written project involves many critical stages, each of them completed successfully and on schedule, if your project is to be successful, too.

To accomplish your research with ease, establish a schedule that breaks your project into small, manageable tasks. Your research won't be completed in one day, and it shouldn't be. Researching your paper is a process that encompasses the commitment of time and energy of a scheduled period of time to attain your goals. Students may spend a day or so or up to two weeks, depending on the scope and nature of the assignment, first searching for a topic, then defining and narrowing it before gathering the necessary research to begin writing their project.

Depending on the time you have to complete your project, you should develop a schedule that addresses your time constraints and pending deadline for your project. For example, if you have only two weeks, then you really should complete your research in the first week so you can spend the second week writing your paper. If you have a month, you may have the luxury of more time, but you should plan on completing all of your major research within the first two weeks.

Following are examples of two schedules, based on the above scenarios, which you can adapt or change to fit your needs:

Research Schedule #1

Day One: Actively begin researching your topic on the first day. Locate what you consider will be the best resources to uncover useful information for your paper. Keep a log of the sources you have visited and what resources you need to check the next day.

Day Two: Keep researching your topic. Check more sources on your list and make notes of what new sources you have found.

Day Three: Continue down your list of potential resources. Keep accumulating relevant information from your other sources. Make notes of the sources you have reviewed.

Day Four: Now review all your research. Evaluate what you have and organize your research for your paper. After organizing your research, prepare an outline for your paper, indicating what research you plan to use in your paper and to determine if you have everything you need for your project or still need more information.

Day Five: If necessary, use this day to acquire any last-minute research that will be important to writing your paper.

Research Schedule #2

Week One: Aggressively research your topic and commit as much time as possible during that first week. Find the most promising sources to unearth the most meaningful material for your paper. Keep a running account of your success and make notes of the research that you completed, what sites or resources you have checked, and, by week's end, what research you have not completed.

Week Two: Continue researching your topic. Find and evaluate more sources. Create a preliminary outline for your paper, based on your research, in the order of what you plan to cover. To accomplish this task, carefully review and organize all of your research by the subtopics you want to discuss that are relevant to your main topic. By organizing your research and also outlining your paper, you can determine if you need any additional research. If necessary, you should acquire it before the end of the week so you can start writing your paper.

FINDING YOUR SOURCES

Every paper that you write for a class or school has one major characteristic in common: They require sound, credible evidence to support your paper's point of view, or topic. Now that you have narrowed and defined your research topic and are ready to research your paper, you want to examine every conceivable source and form of research for your topic, from print to electronic material, from the Internet to your local library. Books, magazines, newspapers, journal articles, popular references, and CD-ROMs are just a few of the potential sources you should explore and consider.

To examine your topic more fully, the following traditional and electronic sources (explored in depth in Section II) will offer new perspective, new insights, and new evidence that will be vital to your success in researching your topic and, therefore, should not be overlooked.

USING LIBRARIES

While the Internet has become the chosen portal for information most preferred by students, school and public libraries offer substantial resources, not available on the Web or found in a single place, that you should use when conducting research for your paper. Using this wonderful resource will pay big dividends in the rich material that you will unearth.

Approximately 93,000 school libraries and 3,658 college and university libraries exist in the United States alone. That includes 100 of the largest university libraries that describe themselves as "research libraries."

Academic libraries differ in the services they offer to the general public. However, most colleges and universities allow public use of their facilities. You don't have to be enrolled as a student to utilize their computer databases, electronic catalogs, and Internet resources. Largely funded and tax-supported, major universities generally offer many more electronic resources than do most public libraries. For student use only, school libraries, from kindergarten through high school, also offer similar services and a wide range of computer databases that are invaluable instruments for research.

Your local public library is another good choice. With more than 9,000 public libraries in the United States, each branch serves the community by providing reading material, recordings, videotapes, and basic reference and research collections. Public libraries also feature a vast collection of electronic databases, free of charge, which they license for public use. These include electronic periodical indexes, bibliography indexes, encyclopedias, general references, and special collections and archival material not found anywhere else.

As an added bonus, most public libraries offer high-speed Internet access over a local network that can rapidly advance your process of doing research electronically—with one limitation: Most libraries limit use of the Internet to 30 minutes or less. But, given the rapidity by which you can acquire your research, it is well worth the effort.

Whether you visit your school or public library, you will find some fantastic tools to get you started on your way to finding the research you need to complete your project. The following will help you locate relevant information for your project.

Online Catalogs

Card catalogs, at one time the primary source for finding every book available in your library, have become a thing of the past. They have been replaced by an online catalog, also known as Online Public Access Catalogs (OPACs), that does the same thing, only much faster. These computerized catalogs feature information on what books, periodicals, special collections, and databases are available to use, to check out, or to research.

Most online catalogs are easy to search. You can search your information by author, title, or subject, cross-referenced for easy use, and most libraries permit remote access to look up items in their catalog without making a trip to the library. You can access or locate quickly the holdings or items at your library or other libraries, any hour or day of the week. In addition, when using online catalogs, you can download or print records of titles you want check out, and renew or place material on hold. (For more information regarding OPACs, see Chapter 12, "Finding Libraries.")

Problems can arise in finding appropriate titles. This depends on the nature of your topic—how current or old it is, and whether the library carries books about that subject. Searching by title requires knowing the title you want to locate. The same applies when searching for a particular author. This does not mean you won't be successful in producing a list of titles that are relevant if you search a title using a common keyword. The only problem is if the words you choose are not compatible with how the titles are listed. In that case, you may not produce a complete listing of titles appropriate to your search.

You don't have to know the author or title of the book to use the online catalog to find what you want. As with keyword searching on the Internet, the subject heading category allows you to enter the keywords of what you are interested in researching, and the online catalog will retrieve a listing of those titles the library currently has available. This includes popular reference titles that are unavailable for checkout but that can be useful nonetheless.

When searching the online catalog, you should have a clear idea of your topic or at least have narrowed your topic. If your topic is too broad, you may find too many sources and not all of them pertinent.

If you have trouble locating a specific title or subject, ask the reference librarian or a library staff member for help.

As noted earlier, most libraries use the Library of Congress classification system—beginning with "A" and ending with "Z"—for organizing and shelving books in subject order. Every book that comes up in your search will have certain call numbers next to the title, author's name, place of publication, publication date, and other relevant bibliographic information. Depending on what books you use as your source material, you will want to keep a copy of this information for your bibliography.

To locate the book in the library, write down or print out a copy of the results of your search. You will need to know the call numbers so that you can track down the titles you are interested in perusing or checking out. The call numbers will correspond with those listed on the spine of the books and also tell you their location in the library. Libraries generally organize titles by topic.

Popular References

Popular references are a great resource of information and can help you thoroughly investigate your topic. Found in the reference room of your library, they can provide valuable background information and statistical data on almost every subject.

As noted earlier, consulting the online catalog is the fastest and simplest way to find a title of interest. Sometimes you may find a title that you were unaware of by browsing the library shelves. More often than not, however, using the online catalog is your best bet to quickly locate newly published titles, specialty titles, or reference books, including specialized references, those that specifically cover the subject you are researching. (One great source for finding general and subject references is Robert Balay's *Guide to Reference Books, 10th ed.* [Chicago: American Library Association, 1996], which lists 10,000 reference books by subject area.)

Another good method for locating other titles is to check out published bibliographies in your library that index books published on a specific subject. (There is more about bibliographies later in this chapter.) Or try the Library of Congress Subject Headings, a comprehensive A-to-Z catalog of subjects offered in any library using this system. To locate additional reference materials, you may also want to consult *The New York Times Guide to Reference Materials* by Mona McCormick (New York: Times Books, 1985), which features information on various reference sources.

Reference works can provide droves of usable information for your paper. Some of it may be useful, supporting research focusing on a specific aspect, or a few helpful facts worth gleaning. When selecting a potential title for research, you should spend some time evaluating its content to determine how useful it will be. Reviewing the table of contents will help you see whether the general content matches the purpose of your research. That is something you will need to decide. Whether a book is useful or not will become obvious once you go through the process.

Many general references, available in print and electronic form, may be useful to your research in a variety of ways. Your school or public library should have numerous popular reference titles covering most commonly written about subjects and specialties. Generally, eight types of references are available from your school or public library for research use only: general and specialized encyclopedias, biographical dictionaries and almanacs, dictionaries and handbooks, and bibliographies and statistical abstracts.

Consulting general and specialized encyclopedias to obtain background and specific information about a specific field or topic s highly recommended. Encyclopedias exist on dozens of fields of interest, such as a biographical encyclopedia of American authors or a guide to legal and medical terms. They can be valuable tools in your research.

Encyclopedias such as *Encyclopaedia Britannica* and *Encyclopedia Americana* function as primary sources for background information and general overviews on current topics. Entries are usually footnoted and include a bibliography of sources, used to write the information presented, that may be worth checking out on your own for additional material on your subject.

Biographical dictionaries offer profiles of well-known figures and important people in culture, history, and world events from all walks of life. Many contain brief accounts, personal data, and biographical overviews examining the life and work of the individual that are well written and documented.

Some of the best biographical references available today include *Current Biography,* detailing persons of various professions and nationalities; *Dictionary of American Biography,* offering brief biographies of more than 15,000 deceased Americans representing many professions; and *Who's Who in America,* featuring biographies of many living notables.

Numerous other print and electronic subject-specific and regional "who's whos" list prominent individuals in particular fields of interest, covering the full spectrum of subjects. Titles in this category range from *Who's Who in American Art* to *Who's Who in Rock & Roll.* (For detailed coverage of biographical references, see Chapter 6.)

Almanacs offer a collection of miscellaneous facts, statistics, tables, charts, lists, and quick answers to questions you may have regarding different subjects of interest, including education, health, geography, sports, and countless others. Popular almanacs include *Information Please Almanac* and *The World Almanac and Book of Facts.*

Dictionaries may be unabridged—very large dictionaries that enable you to check the meaning of virtually any word—or subject dictionaries that cover specialized terminology of a particular discipline. Examples include *The Oxford English Dictionary* to *The Facts On File Dictionary of Music.*

Subject handbooks and bibliographies are two more valuable sources. Handbooks covering a variety of subjects are available through most libraries and provide a comprehensive overview on the concepts, procedures, techniques, and facts of specific topics. Examples range from *Violent Children: Research Handbook* to *Social Change in America: The Historical Handbook.*

Bibliographies list other available sources most pertinent to your topic. These resources index articles and books in your subject area. They can be the quickest way to locate additional sources for you to use. Dozens of published bibliographies dot library reference shelves, such as *An Annotated Bibliography of 20th Century Critical Studies of Women's Literature* to *Subject Guide to Books in Print.*

One of the best general print bibliographies is H. W. Wilson's *Bibliographic Index,* which lists bibliographies that have been published separately or in books or journals. The index is also available in electronic form and indexes more than 350,000 bibliographies published in English and other languages. You can also find bibliographies on almost any topic on the Web for easy access as well. Libraries often post collections of bibliographies on their Web page.

Statistical abstracts offer statistical information that can be important to your essay, term paper, or project. *Statistical Abstracts of the United States,* prepared by the U.S. Bureau of the Census and published by the Government Printing Office, is the one of the best resources of its kind, containing vital facts and figures about Americans and the United States. (For a detailed look at general references, see Chapter 10.)

Periodicals

Besides finding relevant books and references for your research, you also should consult printed newspapers, magazines, and scholarly journals. Periodicals are continuous publications published daily, weekly, monthly, or quarterly. Your school or public library is a great place to hunt down popular periodicals. Most libraries have reading rooms that display the latest issues of national publications, local newspapers, regional magazines, consumer magazines, general interest publications, and trade magazines written for the public, as well as scholarly journals written by and for professionals in various fields. Many of these publications will be invaluable in providing you with in-depth, specific information appropriate for your topic.

Newspapers range from local newspapers that serve a city, town, or state, such as *The Boston Globe* or *The Los Angeles Times,* to nationally published newspapers, like *USA Today,* offering general coverage. Popular periodicals lining library shelves mostly include weekly or monthly magazines that provide articles on timely subjects written by staff reporters or freelance writers. Common titles include *Ebony, People Magazine, Reader's Digest, Sports Illustrated, Time,* and *Vogue.*

For substantive coverage of issues of vital importance to a broad, general audience, general interest publications, such as *Christian Science Monitor, Economist,* and *National Geographic,* are the answer. The information is presented in an easily readable manner, and articles are geared to any educated audience.

Many scholarly journals, providing specialized treatment of important issues with articles written by scholars or experts in a specific field, also populate most reading rooms. Most journals contain articles based on new research and include references and bibliographies, or a list of sources, used to research and write them. Some scholarly titles are *American Economic Review, JAMA: The Journal of American Medical Association, Journal of Marriage and Family,* and *Modern Fiction Studies.*

Trade journals cover a plethora of specialized subjects focusing on the practice, art, or technique of a profession or field with articles written by reporters or industry professionals. Most publications report the latest news and new developments, from breaking issues to new products, for their readership. Titles range from *American Small Farm Magazine* to *Utility Week.* (For extensive coverage of newspapers, magazines, and journals, see Chapter 10.)

Current issues of popular periodicals are usually displayed in the reading room of your library, arranged alphabetically by title, for easy access. Once a new issue arrives, back issues are relegated to reference shelves, where they are stored along with copies of other previous issues of each periodical, still accessible for research and reference purposes. Libraries vary on their policy allowing students or patrons to check out periodicals. Always check with your library regarding their policy and availability. If restrictions exist, you can always photocopy an important article that you need for future use.

To find periodicals on your subject, most libraries offer both print and electronic periodical indexes, either on CD-ROMs or over the Internet, that you can use to locate titles, abstracts, or articles related to your topic. Printed indexes are updated and published annually. Indexes published on CD-ROM or available online are updated more frequently, so the information is more current.

The best index to check first is the *Readers' Guide to Periodical Literature.* Found in your library's reference room and available in print and electronic form, this comprehensive directory lists articles, primarily from magazines, written on a particular subject. Articles are listed by the author and subject, the title and publication, and by the year published.

Additional indexes to consult include the *Alternative Press Index,* covering non-mainstream publications, *Essay and General Literature Index,* which indexes essays, essay anthologies, and essay collections, and the *Popular Periodical Index,* which covers many magazines not listed in the *Readers' Guide.* Other sources include *Standard Periodical Directory,* which lists titles of periodicals; and *Ulrich's International Periodicals Directory,* which covers thousands of serials, periodicals, annuals, and newspapers worldwide.

To access more scholarly articles, you will need to use specialized indexes, also located in the library's reference room. Similar to the *Readers' Guide to Periodical Literature,* they contain abstracts or short summaries of articles published in journals in one specific field. Indexes include: *American History and Life, Art Index, Biological Abstracts, Business Periodicals Index, Communications Abstracts, Criminal Justice Periodicals Index, Education Index, General Sciences Index, Humanities Index, Index Medicus, MLA International Bibliography of Books and Articles on the Modern Languages and Literatures, Music Index,* and *Social Sciences Index.* Check with your library regarding access and availability.

Libraries also provide computer access to other popular indexes, such as SearchBank and FirstSearch. Published by Dialog, a leading provider of online-based information, both indexes include abstracts and some full-text articles from various publications.

In addition, major newspapers, such as *The New York Times* and *The Washington Post,* publish online and printed indexes to articles that appeared in past editions that you can peruse. In most cases, older articles, not accessible electronically, are available on microfilm or microfiche and are part of your library's collection of microform periodicals.

CD-ROM and online indexes have a clear advantage over printed editions. Search engines enable you to find the article or issue that you want, quickly and painlessly. Subsequently, from the results of your search, you can print a copy of the abstract or article (if full text). With the abstract information, you can find a copy of the publication in your library to check out. If the publication is unavailable, you can check out other libraries in your area to see if they have the issue you are seeking.

Electronic Databases

Besides enlisting periodical sources and browsing library catalogs for books and references, countless electronic databases, including periodical indexes and abstracts, are an effective tool for locating magazine and journal articles by subject, and for researching clearly defined subjects. Located in the reference area of your library, they serve as a guide to the contents of selected periodicals, published primarily in journals, magazines, and newspapers, in the United States and around the world.

Most indexes and abstracts today are published in either book or electronic form, and exist for almost every subject or field of interest. Print volumes cover a specific period when the articles are published, either annually or monthly. Content of print indexes often includes references to newspaper articles, articles in books, monographs, and government documents. In some cases, print indexes cover topics not featured on electronic indexes.

Electronic indexes are available via CD-ROM and online. Found on computer workstations in the reference area of your library, they come complete with searchable databases, and have a distinct advantage over their printed counterparts. While covering the same content, most electronic indexes offer "full text" versions of articles listed, though not in all cases, and the information is often more current.

Most electronic indexes feature subject headings or keyword searching. Specific information about each entry in its database is listed, including article title, author, publication name, date published, and other abbreviated information that requires use of the index's abbreviation key to understand. You will want to write down the information as listed, so you can see if your library carries the magazine or journal you desire.

Abstracts are similar to an index. They act and work like an index in the sense that they are subject oriented and offer specific information with each entry, including a brief description of what each article is about, which can help you decide whether the article is relevant to your research or topic.

Like indexes, abstracts are available in CD-ROM form or in bound printed versions in the reference area of your library. Book abstracts list entries by subject, and therefore you will need to find your subject in the index to see if what you need is included. Each entry has a number or identifying code that you will use to find the article you want and its description in the abstract portion of the book.

CD-ROM abstracts are much easier to use. You can instantly search your subject using a keyword search to produce a list of abstracts of relevant articles.

Keep in mind that indexes often overlap in their coverage, so some periodicals may be listed in several different databases. Even so, depending on your topic, it is worth checking out many different indexes and abstracts that are relevant to your subject to uncover the best and most appropriate information for your paper.

Indexes and abstracts cover a wide variety of subjects and types of periodicals. As noted earlier, the *Readers' Guide to Periodical Literature* is a major index for general interest magazines (also available in the printed version). But to research many different disciplines, several outstanding indexes and databases, available at most school or public libraries, fulfill this purpose more than adequately. Tops in this category is Academic Search Elite (EBSCOHost), which covers a wide range of academic subjects from 1985 to the present. This online database features full-text articles from more than 3,000 scholarly journals and mainstream publications, including *The Christian Science Monitor, The New York Times,* and *The Wall Street Journal.* Another excellent resource is Expanded Academic Index (also known as InfoTrac), which thoroughly indexes the contents of both popular magazines and prominent scholarly journals, covering the full spectrum of subjects. Equally useful is the Expanded Academic Index ASAP. This massive database indexes articles dating back to 1980 from nearly 3,000 journals and 1,900 other periodicals, including full-text versions of many articles.

When locating full-text articles in newspapers, NewsBank InfoWeb is one of the best databases of its kind. This large database contains articles from more than 500 newspapers. Another highly recommended database for tracking newspaper articles is National News Five, which indexes stories and provides full-text access to stories originally published in *The Christian Science Monitor, The Los Angeles Times, The New York Times, The Wall Street Journal,* and *The Washington Post.*

For full-text articles of selected newspapers, legal publications, scholarly journals and trade publications, LexisNexis Academic Universe is the best choice. Another highly esteemed database is ProQuest Newspapers, which provides full-text access to more than 500 newspapers published in the United States and around the globe and articles indexed from 1996 to the present.

Many other periodical databases are more specialized and cater to different fields of interest. CQ Researcher reports on current controversial, social, political, economic, and international issues, including summaries, opposing viewpoints, bibliographies, and more. Another alternative, A Matter of Fact, features commentary and statistics on topical social, economic, political, health, environmental, and public policy issues, including excerpts from speeches and written works, derived from congressional sources and general interest and specialized publications.

Ethnic Newswatch offers full-text articles from ethnic, minority, and Native press newspapers, magazines, and journals representing a diversity of perspectives and viewpoints. For more pointed commentary and viewpoints, Alt-Press Watch features articles from alternative press journals and magazines, while Left Index covers political, economic, social, and cultural issues from leftist media around the world.

Other subject-specific indexes provide unlimited access to abstracts or full-text articles in business, social science, general science, education, and more. For example, ABI/Inform indexes business periodicals and business-related articles. American History and Life is a popular journal index on the topic of history, and CINAHL covers nursing and nursing periodicals.

Indexes also cover scholarly journals in other specialized fields. PsycINFO indexes several thousand articles published in behavioral science periodicals only. The British Humanities Index lists articles published in this field only, and the Social Sciences Index is geared specifically toward this individual discipline. If you are studying art, then the Art Index would be appropriate. Or, if you desire more scholarly and academic articles, then electronic indexes, such as LexisNexis Academic Universe or Academic Search Premier, are well worth your time. (For a more comprehensive listing of electronic databases, see Chapter 7.)

One of the best educational electronic indexes, available free of charge to anyone that has access to the Internet, is ERIC (the Educational Resources Information Center). The largest educational database of its kind in the world today, ERIC consists of 16 subject-specific information databases, or clearinghouses, providing full access to article abstracts, curriculum guides, and professional journals in education and related fields.

Microforms: Microfilm and Microfiche

Today, more often than not, most libraries also house older back issues of popular newspapers on microforms—a general term for microfilm and microfiche. Many complete collections of major metropolitan newspapers, popular magazines, journals, and retrospectives of historical newspapers from various towns throughout the United States dating back to the 1800s are available in this form, arranged alphabetically and stored in chronological order in the reference area of your library. Collections also include dramatic works, dissertations, manuscripts, government publications, pamphlets, and other materials of great value to researchers.

Subjects represented in microform collections are also wide ranging. They include histories of African Americans, art, diplomacy, economics, labor, military, religion, theater, and women, as well as oral and photographic histories.

Most titles or collections will be listed in your library's online catalog, and guides to major collections are also available in the reference area of your library. To search the item of interest, you need to use the relevant title in combination with the search term "microform" (*New York Times* AND microform). If your library possesses that publication in microform, your search will produce a citation listing all pertinent information. Unfortunately, since libraries do not always fully catalog microform titles, your subject search may produce less than desirable results. When in doubt, consult the reference staff of your library for further assistance.

When locating microforms of older published newspaper and magazine articles not found on the electronic databases discussed earlier, your best source to find many more articles related to topic is the *Readers' Guide to Periodical Literature,* available in print or electronic form through your library. This valuable index lists article citations for previously published stories in major magazines, newspapers, and journals, by subject. Information provided includes the title of the article, the author's name, the publication name, section and page numbers, and the month, day, and year of publication. Using the article citations you have found, you can check with your library to see if they have microform sets—either microfilm or microfiche—of the past newspapers, magazines, or journals corresponding with the back issues you need.

For additional source material, you also should consult individual printed indexes to microform collections of major newspapers, such as *The New York Times* or *The Washington Post,* and magazines and other periodicals. Each index features citations of additional articles that you research.

Indexes also exist for historical publications, such as the *Index to American Periodicals of the 1700s* and *Index to American Periodicals of the*

1800s. Combined, both directories index 400 periodicals published on microfilm in the American Periodicals Series. (Also available is an electronic database corresponding with both editions.)

Major public and university or college libraries usually feature extensive collections, and the size and scope of collections vary. For additional information on other microform titles or holdings held by other libraries throughout the United States, check with your library regarding printed resources to aid your search.

To find descriptions of all microform publications in print today, also check the *Subject Guide to Microforms in Print.* This popular reference lists 10 classes and 400 subheadings of microform titles published and sold to libraries around the world, covering such topics as religion, language/linguistics, geography, history, and more.

Various directories also list information about other newspapers published in microform. In this case, you should consult *Newspapers in Microform, United States, 1948–1972* and *Newspapers in Microform, Foreign Countries, 1948–1972.* Each directory lists thousands of microform U.S. and foreign newspaper titles held by libraries around the United States.

Another solid source of information is *Union List of Microfilms,* which catalogs 25,000 microform titles housed by 197 institutions. (For more extensive coverage of microfilm collections, see Chapter 13.)

Microfilm is stored on plastic spools, kept in boxes, and marked by the respective dates of when the issues were originally published. Arranged alphabetically by title, each spool is a long, continuous 35-millimeter filmstrip of every complete issue of whichever newspaper you choose to research. It is viewed on an electronic reader that enables you to see the text of the article you are looking for. The "forward" and "reverse" buttons enable you to scan through a number of articles and issues quickly, until you locate the article you want. For a small fee, you can print positive or negative copies of articles that you find.

By comparison, microfiche is individual flat sheets of cut film. While smaller in size than microfilm, it is capable of preserving a considerable number of pages and printed text in reduced form. Photographic images of articles and entire issues are stored on small cards that can be viewed on a separate machine. The viewer not only allows you access to articles you want, but also the option to print copies of the article, again for a small fee.

If you haven't used a microfiche or microfilm reader before, ask for help from a nearby reference staff member.

Interlibrary Loans

Nothing is more frustrating than identifying a book, magazine, or journal you need and finding that your library does not carry it. Requesting an interlibrary loan can often be the right solution. If your library is part of a network of libraries, or shares materials with other libraries in your area, you can request an interlibrary loan, and that periodical or book will be forwarded to your branch for your use. This is where it helps to plan ahead. Some interlibrary loans can take three to four weeks before the material you requested has been received by your library from the other library or branch.

To request an interlibrary loan, you will need to provide the reference librarian or a library staff member with the specific information about the material you need. When requesting books, you need to provide the author, title, publisher, and date of publication; for articles, the article title, journal title, author, volume, date, page numbers, and the name, year, and page number of the reference source (where you found the article listed), will do. Without this vital information, your library would be hard pressed to fulfill your request. So write it down.

OTHER LIBRARY RESOURCES

With most libraries becoming more technologically driven, many, especially larger academic and public libraries, offer a vast amount of other resources for research that complement the more traditional methods described above. Among them are the Internet, CD-ROM, and video collections, featuring information on a variety of subjects.

Using the Internet

Because of its unlimited resources and scope, the Internet (also commonly known as the World Wide Web, or the Web) is the obvious first choice as a preliminary research tool for most researchers today, mostly because so many people have access, 24 hours a day, seven days a week. Connecting millions of users through thousands of networks in more than 50 countries, the Internet provides the ability to research your topic in the privacy of your home or, if high-speed access is something you lack, at your local school or public library. One disadvantage is that some libraries have only a few computers with Internet connections, so sometimes you need to sign up for them in advance. Others limit use to 30-minute or one-hour blocks so that everyone can enjoy the rich benefits of the Internet. Of course, if you have other traditional research to do, you can work around this potential snag until a computer becomes available.

Researching on the Internet can be a rewarding experience. For researchers, one of greatest advantages of the Internet is the large and growing number of potential resources it offers. From uncovering the truth about Alzheimer's disease to learning more about the benefits of space research, this information superhighway boasts not only an abundance of Web sites but also large amounts of data and information on practically any subject. Internet research can be time consuming, mostly because the Web offers such a wide array of choices and potential sites to research. Therefore, when researching your topic on the Internet, you should allow ample time in your schedule to utilize this great wonder of the world.

Using the Internet to research your topic has many advantages. You can use it to access online catalogs to see what types of books are available at your library or other libraries in your area. You can also access books and references, plus special collections. You can also check on availability of a book or periodical, or request one to check out.

Beside these basic privileges that can expedite the process of your research, the Internet offers many other pluses. Whether you use your library's Internet connection or your own, you can tap boundless other outlets from which you can find and retrieve information pertinent to your topic or paper.

Standard reference sources, such as almanacs, dictionaries, directories of people and places, encyclopedias, and other great references, also reside on the Web. Many are accessible through a popular reference site, Refdesk.com, which features links to a wide assortment of online references.

The Internet offers countless straightforward directories that group Web sites into categories and subcategories. Directories are an excellent place to research general or more specific groups or subgroups for types of information. Yahoo! is one of the most popular of all directories on the Web (www.yahoo.com), featuring a myriad of directories on a wide range of topics. Yahoo!'s directories are well organized and list links to numerous sites relevant to your topic or subject that you can individually research. Another remarkable site, with a searchable database, is Libdex Open Directory (www.libdex.com), featuring thousands of directories for all kinds of subjects and categories, including online references, such as almanacs, books, bibliographies, and encyclopedias.

Literally thousands of major metropolitan, regional, out-of-state, and small-town newspapers—more than 4,000 and counting—in the United States alone also publish online. Newspaper Web sites offer either full or limited access to previously published stories dealing with important issues, and can be accessed from any place at any time of day. One popular resource, with links to seemingly every online newspaper throughout the world, is Linkname: Steve's Online Newspapers, or http://www.mediainfo.com:4900/ephome/npaper/nphtm/online.htm). Many daily, weekly, or monthly newspapers and magazines that specialize in a specific field, likewise have a presence on the Web and offer searchable directories. (See Chapter 13, "Finding Newspapers, Magazines, Journals, and Radio and Television News," for more details.)

Thanks to the Internet, millions of data sites and popular source materials are completely accessible to explore. They can provide perspective and information on national, state, and local issues relevant to your topic. This includes everything from state and local public records, to vital records and facts (from the latest U.S. Census to economic data), to federal, state and local government Web sites, to government agencies and government documents. (See Chapter 11, "Finding Government Publications and Agencies," for more information.)

In addition, virtual libraries populate the World Wide Web, many with databases you can use to search contents of their sites for archives and archival collections, corporation profiles, crime statistics, electronic journals, health and safety information, medical information libraries, polls and surveys, and more, if you know how. These and many other resources, including how to access them, are discussed in the next section.

With all that the Internet has to offer, with its alluring possibilities and potential sites, it is important to note that the Internet is not a perfect research device. Not all Web sites are reputable, credible, accurate, or reliable in terms of content. Personal Web pages abound and should be avoided since they often contain information that is either incorrect or misleading. It is important to rely on sites that are operated by a recognized entity, government, group, or agency, or a credible news source. To avoid using poor resources, part of your research should include evaluating the resources you find. If you feel a site that you found may not be credible or worthy, don't use it. Many techniques to properly evaluate electronic sources are discussed later in this book.

Using CD-ROM Collections

With more than 16,000 titles in circulation, CD-ROM collections represent another popular source of information and research. Like books and references, most collections cover a specific discipline. Government documents, census data, genealogy, historical information, and vital statistics are among the many subjects available in this format that have great value to researchers.

Either preloaded directly onto the computers or transmitted over a network to your library's computers, CD-ROM collections are often mixed with online databases, listed on a menu by subject or title, in most cases. In the case of large databases, libraries pay an annual license fee allowing them to offer these databases, accessible on computers available to their patrons. One primary advantage of the online versions is they are updated much more frequently than their CD-ROM compatriots.

To access these databases, you may require help from the reference librarian, who may have to key in a password before you can use them. Depending on the size and nature of your library, plus its annual budget, the selection of titles varies.

Using Video and DVD Resources

Another form of electronic media that holds tremendous potential for research is VHS and DVD collections.

More than 4,000 titles or virtual databases are available for home use—from dictionaries, to encyclopedias, to other mainstream reference—that combine audio, graphics and animation in addition to text, and put millions of pieces of data and images at your fingertips. (See Chapter 10, "Finding General References," for more details regarding video and DVD resources.)

USING SPECIALIZED SOURCES

To fully complement your research, you should also check out specialized sources, described in Section II. Many, but not all, of these sources are available at your local school or public library. While researching at your library may be more convenient, you might also consider, if your research warrants it, visiting other libraries, archives, or associations specifically dedicated to your topic or field of interest, including government libraries, independent research libraries, special libraries, and state facilities.

Topping the list is a host of archives and archival collections on many subjects, including local and Internet-based collections, throughout the United States. Featuring historical and rare material covering the history or life of an individual, group, or organization, they range from private papers and manuscripts, to letters and diaries, to personal photographs and other unique artifacts. Specialized associations and societies can also offer a wealth of information.

Finding and researching biographical information about notable figures can be accomplished with ease at your local library. Among your library's specialized sources you'll find many resources—biographical indexes, popular biographical references, volumes on regional figures, references on international figures, references by subject, biographical information in electronic form and online—covering people of every trade and profession.

In addition to standard publications discussed earlier in this chapter, electronic databases, CD-ROM collections, specialty electronic journals, zines, and newsletters are also vital tools in your research. This includes subscription-based journals, accessible at a library, and free journals on the Web.

So are e-mail discussion groups and newsgroups, which are fast becoming an acceptable source for research. Comprised of professionals, experts, and enthusiasts, these online groups regularly exchange ideas and information covering many fields of interest. You can access these groups in the privacy of your own home simply by joining. Membership is usually free.

General references are also useful and widely available. Beyond the books and references highlighted earlier, your library most likely features other, more specialized references, including atlases, bibliographies, chronicles by eras and decade, chronologies and daybooks, dictionaries and directories, encyclopedias and guides, and references on popular quotations, public opinion polls, and statistics.

Sources also can be found at your library to research most state, local, federal, and foreign governments and agencies. These include printed guides and catalogs, in addition to free online sources.

Newspapers, magazines, and radio and television news are also important sources of information. If you research them only at your local library, you may only touch the surface. While most public and academic libraries offer sizable collections of print and electronically published publications, both popular and academic, finding the right publication often involves knowing where to find it. Chapter 14 details numerous magazine indexes, databases, and publication Web sites addressing a specific topic or research.

To aid you in your research, the Web itself also offers a bevy of references and research sites on virtually every subject. With so many Web sites available, the task of researching the Web at times may seem daunting—unless, of course, you have this book. Chapter 15 highlights the best research sites, references, and databases on the Web that are accessible free of charge.

Finding and using the right search engines on the Web can mean the difference between success and failure in researching your topic. To greatly improve your chance of success, Chapter 16 discusses search engines, including traditional search engines, metasearch engines, and search engine directories.

KNOWING WHEN TO STOP

As important as researching your topic and reading and organizing all the evidence you have retrieved for your written assignment is knowing when to stop researching. You can determine this by asking yourself a few key questions:

- Does your research fulfill the intended focus of your paper?
- Do you have any unresolved questions? Did you answer all the questions you set out to research?

- Have you answered the "who," "what," "where," "when," "why," and "how" for your topic?
- Is your research balanced or does it only present one point of view?
- Are you confident in your research? Does it do the job and provide all the evidence needed?

If you can say "yes" to all of the above questions, then your job is done. If you are unable to answer yes in every case, then review what you still need to research and seek the material you need to satisfy your assignment and—more importantly—your instructor.

Evaluating Your Sources

With so many sources to choose from when researching your paper, how can you be certain that the material you have gathered is reliable, appropriate, and accurate? Whether you derive your information from books, periodicals, the Internet, or radio and television, it is always important to critically analyze and evaluate your sources and judge their quality before using them.

Because of today's heavy reliance on the Internet, never before has evaluating your sources been more critical. News organizations, government agencies, reference and encyclopedia publishers, and electronic publishers are generally considered more accurate and reliable since most have developed a high standard of accuracy over the years that researchers can count on.

However, as mentioned in the previous chapter, not all source material is credible or accurate. Specifically, the Internet has raised serious concerns regarding the accuracy and authenticity of material. The rapid rate of growth of this medium has resulted in a huge proliferation of errors, inconsistencies, innuendoes, rumors, and misinformation reported by sites operated by individuals who are concerned less with accuracy and more with promoting a personal agenda. Several proven methods can help you evaluate your sources, no matter where they come from, to ease such concerns.

UNDERSTANDING YOUR SOURCE

First, you need to understand what type of source you are using to determine its overall credibility. In the world of research, there are two types of sources: Primary sources and secondary sources.

Primary sources are published material, such as novels, speeches, eyewitness accounts, letters, interviews, and autobiographies, featuring the writer's original words, opinions and viewpoints, with no opposing view.

Secondary sources consist of works written by a third party, providing objective commentary, interpretations, criticism, evaluations, and analysis published in books, government documents, journals, newspaper reports, newsletters, magazine articles, and others, about the individual or subject you are researching.

CONSIDERING THE SOURCE

It can be difficult to decide what is a reliable or unreliable source. In some cases, this depends on the type of source, where the information was published, and who published it. Therefore, you must consider your sources carefully. Journalists are trained to take this methodical approach. When covering a story, they examine both sides and, to be as accurate as possible, interview several sources representing differing viewpoints. It is important, then, to consider where your information comes from.

Most researchers lessen this concern by using many popular sources, including books, magazines, newspapers, journals, government publications, indexes, databases, and reference works, and the original source of information for their research. The material is usually authoritatively written and well sourced, so you don't have to defend the credibility of the information cited.

General reference works, like encyclopedias, usually carry the same stamp of approval. They cover a wide spectrum of topics and provide summaries of large areas of research that are well documented and include bibliographies of sources used. Encyclopedias cover what is generally known about a subject and provide basic information based on considerable research done by members of its staff to compile such overviews for public use.

One common mistake, however, is to believe after reading the encyclopedia entry that it provides complete coverage of your subject. Information may at times be too general, outdated, or not completely accurate. That is why most researchers use encyclopedias only in the early stages of their research, consulting a multitude of other current and popular sources to bridge the gap.

CONSIDERING WHO SAID IT

As important as the source of your information is who is saying it. Experts are those who are believed to have extensive knowledge on a given subject. Even so, experts are known to make mistakes, and you should never accept what they say at face value without documented evidence. While the credentials of experts are important, they are no shortcut for finding answers to what you are researching. They should be evaluated just as you would any other source.

For example, in April 2004 the U.S. State Department announced to the news media that a new federal report had shown that terrorism activities in the United States had dramatically decreased since the Bush administration had launched its global war on terror. In June of that year, Secretary of State Colin Powell learned that mistakes were made in the reporting of such information—that terrorism activities had actually increased—and he apologized to the country for the error.

Another example is the Enron scandal. Prior to the scandal, if people could choose between quoting former Enron CEO Kenneth Lay or a lower-level employee, they would want to hear from Lay, since he seemed more qualified to talk about the company earnings and the company's overall success. Few realized that when Lay claimed that Enron's profits were up dramatically, and that the future was rosy that the opposite was true.

Don't take a person's word at face value. Verify the facts. Examine other sources relevant to what was said to see how accurate or how true the statement really is. If you can't verify what's been said, then don't use it.

CONSIDERING THE FACTS

Facts have a way of dominating research. Everything you research needs to be factual—based on published facts that support your topic and help you prove what you are exploring without the shadow of a doubt. Every remarkable piece of daunting data, fascinating fact, and timely tidbit you find has a purpose in your research and, with any evidence you uncover, you want to corroborate your findings. In other words, you want to find other documents that have reported the same information as the original source, so you can verify that the information you will be reporting is true. There's nothing worse than reporting factual information that appears correct, only to find out later that it isn't.

Some published "facts" may not be facts at all and should not be misconstrued as such. Statements of facts are generally used in all documents, perhaps used to draw some conclusion or make a substantial statement based on evidence given elsewhere. Again, such statements should be factually based, and be sure that such statements attribute an original source that you can verify.

In the mainstream media today, assumptions, inferences, opinions, and editorializing are rampant and confused with fact. This is often the case when politicians make a key statement to the press or a special guest tries to persuade viewers of a certain position on a cable news program. Many times they will make statements that are mere opinion or twisted versions of the truth. Assumptions, inferences, opinions, and editorializing can be unrelated to the truth if you find no evidence in your research to support such claims.

Beware of biased reporting as well. Many popular publications publish slanted, biased articles to promote their viewpoints. This practice is common in magazines, such as *The New Republic,* which promotes a liberal point of view, or *National Review,* which promotes a staunchly conservative point of view. Articles that appear in these publications tend to focus on issues and causes near and dear to these factions.

Similarly, be suspicious of documents that overgeneralize and lack sufficient evidence or reach conclusions too quickly. Weigh the importance of the material and form your own judgment of whether it offers sound reasoning based on solid evidence instead of hasty generalizations. Remember that evidence of truth matters the most when considering facts in your research.

Scholarly journals offer more reliable evidence than popular magazines because the writers fully document all sources, and their articles are published through university presses and publishers that rigorously screen their articles to meet specific standards of evidence.

The above steps are very important to evaluating your research. Remember the following criteria to be sure that the information you have accumulated can be used.

Purpose

The purpose of the information is critical to the success of your research and your paper. Does the purpose of the material you have uncovered fit the purpose of your topic? Also, what is the purpose of the document? It is it to inform? To persuade? To present opinions? To report research? To demonstrate any bias?

You should always question the motives of the author. Why did the author write the article on this particular subject? Did he or she have some hidden agenda? Was the article or material published by an organization with a particular purpose? Is the intention to promote a particular point of view or a cause? Is the material fair and balanced in its view?

Critically analyzing the purpose of your research will help you define what will be critical to your paper, and what will not.

Accuracy

When analyzing the materials you have found, you want to examine every document closely to see that the author supports his or her statements with facts, data, and references to research. Are the facts verifiable? Is there a bibliography? Documentation adds to the authenticity of the material, and also makes the author's claim credible.

It's important, then, to examine every statement made by the author and verify that his or her statements are not just opinion, but substantiated fact. When an author makes reference to a source, check out the bibliography to see if that source is listed. If you are doubtful about the credibility of the statement made, you can then check that source yourself to see if the evidence cited is actually presented.

Evaluating Web documents is equally important. To determine accuracy, check the document to see if an author's name is listed or is credited, and what qualifies them to write about your topic. There is a big difference between author and webmaster. The author is the person who researched and wrote the document; the webmaster is responsible for creating, updating, and overseeing the Web site and is not liable for its content.

When credit is not provided, you should find out more about the group, company, or organization that sponsors the site by clicking on the "About Us" icon to determine if they are reputable and trustworthy. If you cannot locate this information anywhere on the site and no site map exists, then consider e-mailing the author. You can locate an e-mail address and other contact information, by clicking on the "Contact Us" icon. If this is unsuccessful, as a last resort you can e-mail the webmaster.

With Web documents, as with any published document, consider the purpose of the document and why it was produced in the first place.

Authority

When reviewing a book, article, Internet site, or any published reference, you should question the authority of the material as part of your critical analysis. You want to consider the expertise of the author and question his or her credentials. Who published the document? Does the author have the expertise on the subject? What makes him or her qualified?

The answers to your questions will emerge if you dig a little. Review the material and see if it tells you anything about the author's credentials. Perhaps the author has written several articles about the subject or has credits that indicate he or she is an authority in that particular field. If you are still unconvinced, check a bibliographical source—one noted in the document and referred to in the bibliography—to determine the authenticity of the article. Another step is to critically review the material and see if the evidence presented is authoritative and appropriately cited—in other words, relevant facts and testimony are credited—throughout to support its point of view.

This third step can be problematic when analyzing many Internet sources. Not all Internet sites provide the identity, credentials of the author, or producer of the page. If you are not sure where the Web document was published, simply check the URL for the Web address and location. You should question the reliability of a source that does not give you this information and not use it as a source if it does not pass this important test.

Relevancy

Besides the authority of your research, you want to examine its relevance. How relevant is your research? Is it appropriate to your topic? Does it address your objective? Is the content vital to your topic?

When researching your topic, you will find some research more suitable than others, and need to decide which is appropriate to your topic. Determining the value of your research can help you to pinpoint what's important, what to keep, and what to cast aside.

To evaluate the relevance of books, magazines, and journal articles, simply read through the document to see if it looks promising. With books, you can tell right away by reading the introduction and table of contents. The introduction provides a complete overview of what the book offers; the table of contents, a complete list of topics. The index, in the back pages of the book, also can be a valuable resource. It gives names, terms, and page numbers of topics and items detailed in the book.

If you require more information about the book that you are considering, examining book reviews will shed further proof of the book's value, reputation, and validity. Reviews, published in hundreds of popular magazines and journals, can found by searching several indexes offered through most libraries.

Book Review Digest (1905–present) features reviews of thousands of books annually. Book Review Online is a bimonthly index of reviews from 225 magazines and journals. *Index to Book Reviews in Humanities,* another annual index, offers reviews published in humanities periodicals. *Index to Book Reviews in Social Sciences* is a yearly index of reviews published in social science periodicals; *Current Book Review Citations* features book citations of reviews published in more than 1,000 periodicals, updated annually. *Booklist* is a monthly periodical that reviews new books published throughout the year. Check with your library for availability.

With magazine and journal articles, read the first few paragraphs of the article to determine if the article focuses on your subject in the manner you had hoped. If you are still uncertain, then examine the entire article and see what the author highlights in each paragraph and look for keywords that sum up the topic of each paragraph and, more importantly, the points the author is covering in the article. You will know in a short amount of time whether the article is worthwhile or not.

Abstracts of articles and books provide brief overviews or summaries about the contents of an article and reading them can speed up the process to determine which books and articles are most relevant to your cause.

Timeliness

The timeliness of your research is also important. How current is your material? The more current your source material is, the more relevant it can be to your topic. Older material may be just as valuable. It can provide a historical perspective and transformation of your topic over a specific period of time. But, generally, when researching and writing about a topic, you want to find the most recent evidence to support your claim.

To critically analyze the currency of your material, first look at the date of the publication. When was your material published? How old is this material? Is it timely and relevant? Online catalogs, indexes, or abstracts usually list the date when a book, newspaper or magazine article, journal article, or other reference work was published. Reliable Web sites also provide this information, albeit differently. The date an item was published or when the information was last updated may be posted on the Web site. This information usually is at the end of the document.

Be careful using old and outdated Web sites where information has not been updated regularly. If a site has too many dead links, it is a clue that the site is not updated. The information itself may be not current enough for your needs and the site less reliable as a potential source.

Objectivity

The role of a researcher is to remain objective and unbiased at all times, which can be difficult. The point in researching your topic is to present a balanced view of the subject you are exploring and to inform others of your findings with the same objectivity and impartiality.

Analyzing your research involves judging its objectivity. It's important never to take the information you read from your research as the absolute truth. Instead, question your research as you review it. How objective is it? What is the tone of the document? Is it reasonable, logical, and presented fairly? Are opposing views offered? Is there any noticeable bias?

Be careful of documents that offer no opposing view. Bias and lack of objectivity is often a problem with Web sites where the information is a mask for advertising or promoting a particular product or cause. In such cases, the opinions expressed may be positioned for the purpose of selling on you on their service, cause, or whatever they are advocating. Material such as this may demonstrate a hostile tone and be highly opinionated.

Overresearching one side of your topic presents the same danger. You will end up creating an imbalance in your research. Sometimes a researcher creates bias in their research accidentally.

Research featuring broad claims or sweeping statements with no strong facts to support the claims should also be carefully scrutinized. The more objective your research is, the more balanced your topic will be in the end. Even when taking a stance on a particular issue, you can always strengthen your topic by examining the opposing view.

Coverage

How well does the document cover your subject? Is the material too general or not specific enough?

Research that offers more in-depth coverage is generally more useful than articles that skimp on details and simply provide a basic overview or condensed view of your topic. The more compelling evidence, quotable sources, and supporting material that you can glean from your research, the more authoritative your paper will be on the subject.

Following these steps will not ensure that your source material is appropriate, accurate, and solid, but that it provides the necessary evidence to make your essay, term paper, or written project a success.

Section II

FINDING SOURCES OF INFORMATION

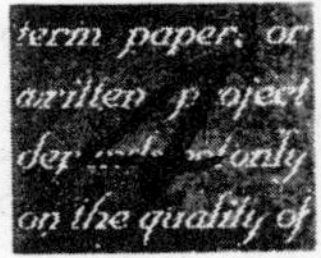

Finding Archives and Archival Collections

Archives are windows to the past, to history, and to everything of historical value that once shaped the world and human culture. Thousands of libraries, museums, and historical societies house archival collections, many available to researchers by appointment. They include a wealth of rare and unusual items—notes, minutes, manuscripts, correspondence, photographs, audio and videotapes, and other materials in different subject areas.

TYPES OF ARCHIVES

Depending on the nature of your research, archival collections can be a rich resource of information. General and cultural archives offer preserved documents about a specific subject or discipline, and can be found at historical societies, presidential libraries, genealogical societies, independent research libraries, museums, or specialized archival repositories.

Institutional archives are an equally vital resource. Public records, such as those maintained and preserved by government archives, are one example. Others include associations, colleges and universities, elementary and secondary schools, health care organizations, religious organizations, and others that maintain their own institutional or general archives.

Most archival resources, whether general, cultural, or institutional, offer some kind of inventory list or catalog of what archival records are available to the public for research. Descriptions of these collections vary, and not all catalog descriptions are alike. They may describe the extent of the collection—what records it houses, when it was created, and what each box or folder of the collection contains.

Not all archives describe which individual items make up a collection. For example, if a site owned the papers of Mark Twain, every item in the collection may be listed and described, but not all archives provide this information equally. Sometimes a printed catalog describing the contents of a special collection may be available but may only serve as a descriptive inventory of what the collection contains.

Accessing archival collections may involve some travel on your part, or you may be able to access them (or some portion of them) online. That all depends on the nature and size of the collection, and whether electronic access is an option.

Over the years, many major archival sites have made certain materials available online, such as items from special exhibits, or established regional centers that provide public access to their materials.

RESEARCHING ARCHIVES AND ARCHIVAL COLLECTIONS

Locating archives and relevant archival collections, including special collections, held at archives, libraries, and other institutions takes a little work on your part, but can be well worth the effort. Four methods exist for finding archives and archival collections; they are described below.

Library Catalogs

Most public or college/university libraries feature archival collections, and information about them is usually listed in their online catalog under the subject, person, or place you are researching. Combining the words of your topic in your keyword search with popular terms, such as "archives," "bibliography," "manuscripts," "records," and "sources," will produce results that identify archival collections relevant to your subject. Listed next to the entry information from your search results will be subheadings, like "Archives" or "Manuscripts," referring to material from a special collection owned by the library that is available for research purposes.

The reference library staff can also help you find information about archival collections that are available for public review. In addition, most reference desks have special directories and indexes that you can review featuring general descriptions of archival collections available throughout the United States. Most references include vital information, including archives by subject, by location, and how to access them.

Finding Aids

"Finding aids" are inventories, registers, indexes, or guides to archival collections held by archives and manuscript repositories, libraries, and museums. With their detailed descriptions, they serve as guides to collections of papers, publications, and personal materials, complete with background about the person who created the materials in the collection and an overview of the collection.

Finding aids help librarians, researchers, scholars, and students determine whether the content of a collection will satisfy their needs. Numerous college and university libraries have made their finding aids available online. They include searchable online databases and holdings of their archival collections.

California university and research center archival collections can be accessed, without charge, through the University of California, Berkeley's Online Archive of California (http://www.oac.cdlib.org).

Other universities in the United States that offer finding aids online through their reference libraries include:

- Columbia University (www.columbia.edu/cu/lweb/)
- Harvard University (http://lib.harvard.edu/)
- University of North Carolina at Chapel Hill (http://www.lib.unc.edu/)
- Yale University (http://www.library.yale.edu/)

In addition, the Library of Congress (http://www.loc.gov/rr/ead/) offers finding aids to primary source material.

You can find more information on finding aids and other resources by using any search engine (enter the keywords: "finding aids and archival collections").

Online Databases

Using Internet search engines to locate archival material can often be futile. Descriptions of archival materials, books, and nonprint materials held in libraries and archives, culled from the records of research libraries around the globe, are accessible through several national and international online databases that compile such information for researchers and librarians.

The frustration of reviewing printed catalogs, directories, and guides or combing multiple search engines can be avoided by using these well-respected sites, which gather and store information about repositories and collections, including mostly free access to home pages of archives, libraries, and historical societies.

FREE SITES

The following are the most popular free Internet sites for finding repositories, collections, and archives:

Ready, 'Net, Go (http://www.tulane.edu/~/miller/ReadyNetGo.html)
Provides links to major indexes, lists, and databases of archival resources available on the Web.

Repositories of Primary Sources (http://www.uidaho.edu/special-collections/Other.Repositories.html)
Maintained by Terry Abraham of the University of Idaho, with more than 5,250 Web sites, this site describes worldwide holdings of manuscripts, archives, rare books, historical photographs, and other primary sources for researchers. Entries are divided by nine categories: Western United States and Canada; Eastern United States and Canada: States and Provinces A–M; Eastern United States and Canada: States and Provinces N–Z; Latin America and the Caribbean; Europe A–M; Europe N–Z; Asia and the Pacific; Africa and the Near East; and Additional Lists.

Entries cover national, state, and local historical collections, centers, museums, societies, and associations; college, university, and public library archives; and state and county archives. Also highlighted are institutes and museums, from Baseball's Hall of Fame to presidential museums, and special collections of every discipline, such as health and medicine, performing arts, rare books, and Russian culture. Home page URLs of each entry are also listed, providing immediate access to more information.

UNESCO Archives Portal: An International Gateway to Information for Archivists and Archives Users (http://www.unesco.org/webworld/portal_archives/pages/Archives/)
This international gateway to information features more than 5,000 links to archives of every kind: architectural archives, literature and art archives, military archives, state and regional archives, and many others. Entries feature brief descriptions of each site.

SUBSCRIPTION SITES

Many subscription sites are also available that are wonderful resources. They include:

ArchivesUSA (http://archives.chadwyck.com/)
A comprehensive online directory of 5,500 repositories and 141,178 collections of primary source material located throughout the United States. Repositories include college, university, library, and historical society archives.

This Web site combines information and records from *The National Union Catalog of Manuscript Collections* (NUCMC), from 1959 to the present, which covers pertinent details of 93,100 collections gathered and indexed by the Library of Congress. This collection is only fully searchable on this site. Also tracked on this site are names and subjects of more than 58,600 records published separately in National Inventory of Documentary Sources in the United States (NIDS), a microfiche series produced by ProQuest. ArchivesUSA's database also includes 93,100 NUCMC records, more than 4,250 submitted records, more than 2,350 links to repository home pages and more than 5,000 links to online finding aids.

Using ArchivesUSA's Collection Search, collections can be searched by keyword, collection name, repository name, city and state, NIDS fiche number, and NUCMC number, if known. Repositories themselves can be searched individually, using the site's Repository Search engine. Searches produce detailed information about each repository and collection, including descriptions of collection holdings, phone and fax numbers, hours of service, e-mail address and home page URLs. It is available by annual subscription; check with your library regarding the availability of this service.

National Union Catalog of Manuscript Collections (NUCMC) (http://www.loc.gov/coll/nucmc/nucmc.html)
Begun in 1997, this electronic database contains detailed descriptions of more than 72,000 collections held by repositories throughout the United States from 1986 to the present. Collections are indexed by topic, personal, family, corporate, and geographic names, and are searchable via the Library of Congress Web site.

OCLC WorldCat (Online Computer Library Center) (http://www.oclc.org/worldcat/)
Considered the world's largest database, with more than 52 million bibliographic records, OCLC WorldCat catalogs books and other materials held by more than 9,000 member institutions. Records exist for everything from stone tablets to electronic books, wax recordings to MP3s, DVDs to Web sites. OCLC WorldCat is also a good place to find corporate archives, church

records, historical society records, and more. Using this Web site requires special access through a library that subscribes to its service.

RLG Archival Resources (http://www.rlg.org)
Provides access to online finding aids, citations, actual collection guides or inventories that reveal where collections came from, how they are organized, and what they contain. Records describe collections in the RLIN AMC (see below) database, and feature catalog records and detailed collection guides to digitized archival materials throughout the United States and the United Kingdom.

RLG Cultural Materials Database (http://www.rlg.org)
A multidisciplinary set of online catalogs with millions of records describing collections of high-quality digital versions of rare and unique materials, including ancient maps, books, drawings, handwritten letters, moving images, paintings, sound recordings, and more, donated by archives, libraries, and museums around the world.

RLG Union Catalog (http://www.rlg.org)
Reflecting collections of major research libraries, academic, public, corporate and national libraries, and archives, museums, and historical societies, this comprehensive database describes a wealth of cataloged material, including books, serials, archival collections, manuscripts, maps, musical scores, sound recordings, films, photographs, posters, computer files, electronic resources, and more.

RLIN AMC (Archives and Mixed Collections File) (http://www.rlg.org)
RLIN (Research Libraries Information Network) is an online bibliographic database focusing on the holdings of most university and research libraries in the United States. This large database stores records for literally millions of archival collections, books, computer files, films, maps, music scores, photographs, and sound recordings of libraries, museums, state archives, and historical societies throughout North America. Records are searchable by personal or organization names, or by subject. Access to records listed in RLIN's database requires special access or assistance by a reference librarian.

OVERSEAS SITES

Databases covering overseas and international repositories, archives, and collections are also accessible on the Web. They include:

European Archival Network (www.european-archival.net)
Repositories and archives for 49 European countries are referenced on this Web site, including links to sites to find more information about the archives found in its database.

Overseas Archival Repositories on the Internet (www.archivesinfo.net/overtop/html)
This well-organized, easy-to-navigate Web site provides links to archival web pages, directories, and repositories from more than 20 countries and territories, including Australia, Bahamas, Canada, Chile, China, Denmark, Dominican Republic, Egypt, Finland, France, Germany, Hong Kong, Ireland, Israel, Italy, Japan, Malaysia, Namibia, Netherlands, New Zealand, Norway, Singapore, South Africa, Switzerland, Thailand, and Zambia.

PRINTED REFERENCES

Although the quality and content can vary, numerous catalogs, directories, encyclopedias, and guides all provide references to archival materials and collections. To thoroughly research potential archival collections that fit your purpose, several popular references—printed counterparts to available electronic or online versions through your library—will do the trick:

Articles Describing Archives and Manuscript Collections in the United States: An Annotated Bibliography, compiled by Donald L. DeWitt, 458 pages (Westport, Conn.: Greenwood Press, 1997)
Listed are more than 2,000 annotated entries of archive and manuscript collections, including some foreign archives, under 13 topical categories, including art, theater, film and television, business, education, history, librarianship, literature, religion, and other fields.

Directory of Archives and Manuscript Repositories in the United States, Second Edition, 853 pages (Phoenix: Oryx Press, 1988)
Published by the National Historical Publications and Record Commission, this massive hardbound book lists general descriptions of archives and information about any published guides describing such collections, arranged by state with a subject index.

Guide to Information Resources in Ethnic Museum, Library and Archival Collections in the United States, compiled by Lois J. Buttlar and Lubomyr R. Wynar, 369 pages (Westport, Conn.: Greenwood Press, 1996)
This comprehensive reference describes collections about some 70 American ethnic groups, arranged alphabetically by category, from 786 cultural institutions.

National Inventory of Documentary Sources in the United States (NIDS) (Teaneck, N.J.: Chadwyck-Healey, 1983–)
Available on microfiche, this directory covers registers, guides, and indexes to collections in academic libraries, historical societies, state archives, university archives, plus federal records, the Manuscript Division of the Library of Congress, and many others. A cumulative index of the entire directory is also available on CD-ROM.

National Union Catalog of Manuscript Collections (NUMC) (Washington, D.C: Library of Congress, 1959–1993)
Unlike its online counterpart, this printed directory contains detailed descriptions of thousands of additional collections held at repositories throughout the United States. The book comes complete with an easy-to-use index for collections by topic, personal, and family, corporate, and geographic names.

LOCAL ARCHIVES

Whether you are researching the history of your state, your family, or a special subject, most major metropolitan areas, cities, and small towns have historical archives, historical societies, or university archives of some kind. These groups can be useful for tracking vital background or filling in the gaps for information that otherwise is difficult to find.

Most historical societies are listed in your local Yellow Pages but there are other ways to collect this information. Many national societies provide information and links to state and local history archives, historical societies, or genealogical societies, and are worth checking out.

For a complete directory of historical societies in the United States, Canada, and Australia, one of the best sites on the Web is Daddezio.com (www.daddezio.com/society/hill/). Societies are indexed and listed alphabetically by state, and can be searched by name. You can also click on any state and jump to the page of any historical society listed.

If you are looking for historical societies and state archives, two recommended sites are U.S. State Historical Societies and State Archives Directory (http://web.syr.edu/~jryan/infopro/hs.html), compiled by Joe Ryan, and State Archives and Historical Societies, sponsored by the Ohio Historical Society (http://www.ohiohistory.org/textonly/links/arch_hs.html). Each lists state archives and historical societies, from A to Z.

For a one-stop resource on state archives, the Office of the Secretary of State in Georgia also has compiled a complete Web list (www.sos.state/ga.us/archives/rs/sarl.htm). The site features every state archive department, division, library, or museum, including addresses, phone numbers, and Web addresses, with links to related pages.

A complete and updated directory of genealogy libraries in the United States is available online at Golden West Marketing (www.gwest.org/gen_libs.htm). This well-maintained and updated site lists every national genealogical library, local genealogical center, and public library with collections of genealogical material for every state, city, and town, including vital contact information, such as name, address, and phone number.

Another highly recommended genealogical Web site is Genealogy.org. The site has many links to searchable online databases for ancestry information, birth records, marriage records, death records, census records, military records, court/land records, and state records. Genealogy and family histories are also searchable by state. The site also features a complete listing of genealogy Web sites around the world and other potential resources for researchers.

The USGenWeb Project (www.usgenweb.org.) provides information on Web sites for genealogical research in literally every county and every state of the United States. Run entirely by volunteers, this noncommercial project links to state pages, census projects, specialized genealogical and historical projects, and a digital library offering transcriptions of public domain records, including census records, marriage records, wills, and other public documents.

Countless universities throughout the United States and Canada house special archives whose holdings include catalogs, chronologies, biographies, books, letters, manuscripts, personal records, photographs, and other resources. To locate university archives near you, one of the best sources on the Web is the Libdex Open Directory. For a complete listing of university archives, visithttp://pscontent.com/od2/opendirectory.php?browse=/Reference/Archives/University/.

INTERNET ARCHIVES

During the last decade, due to the tremendous growth of the Internet, dozens of archives and archival collections, for nearly all subject areas or disciplines, can now be found on the World Wide Web. These Web sites can be tremendous assets when researching your topic. In some cases, archival material is readily accessible, viewable, and printable; in others, access is limited and only general information about the archive or its collection is provided. Even so, having so many archival sites available at your fingertips may outweigh any inconvenience. The following is a partial list of Internet archival sites by subject that are generally useful to researchers.

African American Studies Archives

African-American Collections (www.lib.auburn.edu/archive/find-aid/afam.htm)
A repository of church meeting agendas, bulletins, personal papers, photographs, and oral histories documenting the history of blacks in Alabama, held by Auburn University, with some documents viewable online.

African-American Women—Online Archival Collections (www. http://scriptorium.lib.duke.edu/women/digital.html)
Scanned images of manuscript pages and full-text writings of African-American women are presented on this site from the Special Collections Library at Duke University.

The Amistad Research Center (www.tulane.edu/~amistad/amfirst.htm)
One of the nation's largest repositories specializing in African-American history, the archive features a collection of art and manuscripts charting African-American history and race relations. The center's other holdings include documents on Native Americans, Puerto Ricans, Chicanos, Asian Americans, European immigrants, Appalachian whites, and records related to Protestant denominations, Roman Catholicism, Judaism, and many other collections that are secular in nature. Located at Tulane University's Tilton Hall in New Orleans, Louisiana, this repository also includes a digital photograph collection.

Archives of African American Music and Culture (AAAMC) (www.indiana.edu/~aaamc/index2.html)
Features one the largest collections in the nation of oral histories, photographs, musical and print manuscripts, audio and video recordings, and educational broadcast programs. Established in 1991, AAAMC houses materials covering various musical idioms and cultural expressions from the post–World War II era. Housed at Indiana University in Bloomington, Indiana, the popular music collections cover the individual work of artists Harry Allen, Johnny Griffith, Johnny Otis, as well as the history of Motown Records and more than 200 black popular music radio programs from the 1970s and 1980s.

Atlanta University Center Archives (www.auctr.edu/arch.htm)
Documenting the history of African Americans, mostly in the southeastern United States, this archive houses books by and about people of African descent, archival records, and manuscript collections, including official university records, publications, theses, and dissertations from schools in the Atlanta University Center. Manuscript collections also include personal papers,

library manuscripts, and organizational records. The complete inventory of the center's archival and manuscript collections is available for use online.

Black Archives of Mid-America (www.blackarchives.org)
Another specialized repository featuring diaries, newspapers, records, and oral histories of African Americans in Iowa, Kansas, Missouri, and Oklahoma. A collaboration between the Black Archives of Mid-America and the Kansas City Public Library, the archive, founded in 1974 by Horace M. Peterson III, covers every facet of African-American culture, music, art, theater, education, the military, medicine, sports, religion, and community affairs. The center's Web site enables users to browse the archival galleries and search its database for archival holdings.

Agricultural and Farm Archives

Agricultural and Farm Collections (www.lib.auburn.edu/archive/find-aid/agriculture/htm)
Maintained by Auburn University's Archives and Manuscripts Department, the archive Web site contains inventory links to each of its more than 100 individual collections, including records, personal papers, extracts, interviews, court decisions, oral histories, and some photographs viewable online, dating back to the early 1800s.

U.S. National Agricultural Library (NAL) (http://www.nalusda.gov/)
In cooperation with the U.S. Department of Agriculture, this impressive site features an extensive catalog of searchable books, serials, audiovisuals and other resources, and an article citation database to easily locate journal articles, book chapters, short reports, and reprints (called AGRICOLA) on topics related to agriculture in the United States. NAL publications and databases can be accessed, downloaded, or printed, including agricultural images, annual reports, newsletters, and more, and agriculture information on the Internet can be searched or browsed by subject under AgNIC (Agriculture Network Information Center).

American History Archives

AARC: The Assassination Archives and Research Center (http://www.aarclibrary.org)
Founded in 1984, the Assassination Archives and Research Center, the largest private archives in the world on political assassinations, features an extensive electronic library of approximately 50,000 pages of reports, transcripts, and documents relating to political assassination. Documents include all 26 volumes of the Warren Commission Report on the assassination of President John F. Kennedy.

American Life Histories (www.memory.loc.gov/ammem/wpaintro/wpahome.html)
Containing manuscripts from the Federal Writers Project compiled during the period 1936–40, the entire collection, maintained by the Library Congress Manuscripts Division, is viewable online and includes 2,900 documents representing the work of more than 300 writers from 24 states. Documents con-

sist of drafts of various lengths and various forms, from narratives to case histories. They reflect the attitudes, perspectives, and beliefs of a different time and each describes the writer's family history, including education, income, occupation, political views, religion, and more.

American Memory (http://memory.loc.gov/)
Offering more than 7 million digital items from more than 100 historical collections, viewable and playable online, this archive covers all subjects relating to the history and culture of the United States. Agriculture, art and architecture, business and economics, geography and history, languages and literature, philosophy and religion, political science and law, recreation and sports, social sciences and technology—all these and more are represented. Collections are arranged by decade (from the 1400s to the present) and region (Northeast, South, Midwest, West). Digital items include rare books, sound recordings, films, high-resolution images, and text with enhanced navigation. Sound recordings are offered in four formats: RealAudio, MPEG 2, Layer 3 (.mp3) and WaveForm (.wav).

Library and Archival Exhibitions on the Web (http://www.sil.si.edu/SILPublications/Online-Exhibitions/)
A project of Smithsonian Institution Libraries, this site features online exhibitions created by libraries, archives, and historical societies drawn from library and archival materials, including books, manuscripts, photographs, audio and video recordings, and more. An online guide lists exhibitions alphabetically by title. A keyword search engine enables you to access individual exhibitions by geographic location, institution, or subject.

National Council on Public History Resources (http://www.ncph.org/links.html)
Offers an extensive listing of history organizations, historical societies, museums and sites, with Web links, on a variety of historical subjects.

Wisconsin Historical Society Archives (www.wisconsinhistory.org/archives/index.html)
The oldest continuously funded American historical society, the Wisconsin History Society serves as the archive of the state of Wisconsin, collecting and preserving manuscript collections, books, periodicals, maps, relics, newspapers, audio and graphic materials documenting Wisconsin and U.S. history. Based in Madison, Wisconsin, the society maintains an online catalog describing its manuscript and government record collections and a searchable database of its holdings with about 5 percent of its collection online as of 2004.

American Jewish Archives

American Jewish Archives (www.americanjewisharchives.org)
One of the largest collections committed to preserving American Jewish history in the United States. Located at the Jacob Rader Marcus Center at Hebrew Union College in Cincinnati, Ohio, the archive houses more than 10 million pages of documentation, including manuscripts, photographs, audio and videotapes, microfilm, and genealogical materials covering the religious,

organizational, economic, cultural, personal, society, and family life of American Jewry.

Research requests are welcome and all inquiries are required in writing, either by fax, e-mail, or regular mail. E-mail requests can be made using an online request form. Nominal fees are charges for photocopying, copies from microfilm, audio or videotape duplicating, photograph reproductions, and copying of other images. Complete guidelines to making research requests and a price list for reproduction services can be found on the archive's Web site.

The American Jewish Historical Society Archives (www.ajhs.org/research/Archives.cfm)

The society houses another vast collection on Jewish history. About 1,000 collections are divided into two categories: personal papers, including artifacts of individuals and families, and institutional records, containing the records of schools, synagogues, orphanages, and other organizations related to Jewish life in America. Collections include correspondence, journals, administrative records, clippings, manuscripts, and other memorabilia, with the oldest document being a court record dated 1572, during the Mexican Inquisition. Other collections represent many notable 18th- and 19th-century American and political and communal Jewish leaders and notable 20th-century figures.

The archive is headquartered in New York, with reading rooms in New York's Center for Jewish History and facilities at Hebrew College in Newton, Massachusetts. None of the archive's collection is viewable online. However, staff members will assist researchers who are interested in the society's archives, museum, and photographic collections. Questions can be e-mailed to ajhs@ajhs.org.

Art Archives

Archives of American Art, Smithsonian Institute (AAA) (http://archivesofamericanart.si.edu)

The world's largest collection of visual arts in America, the collection spans the centuries since the founding of America to the present day, with more than 14 million items. More than 5,000 collections are represented, including letters, diaries, sketches, sketchbooks, photographs, exhibition catalogs, scrapbooks, business records, art periodicals and other documents. In addition, the archive features more than 3,000 interviews with artists, and nearly 1,000 photographs. The collections and archives can be accessed online through AAA's online catalog, finding aids and guides and research section on the Web.

Congressional Archives

Congressional Collections at Archival Repositories (http://www.archives.gov/records_of_congress/repository_collections/)

Maintained by the Center for Legislative Archives National Archives and Records Administration (NARA), this site covers the history of the U.S. Congress in official records of Congress, private and personal papers of members of Congress, and other collections located in repositories around the country. Collections are indexed alphabetically by archival institutions and by member of Congress name.

Ethnic Archives

Immigration History Research Center (IHRC) (http://www.ihrc.umn.edu)
The IHRC, located at the University of Minnesota, preserves and maintains a library and archival collection covering the history of the American immigrant experience.

Government Archives

The National Security Archive (NSA) (http://www.gwu.edu/~nsarchiv/)
This independent, nongovernmental research institute and library collects and publishes declassified documents acquired through the Freedom of Information Act (FOIA), a public interest law defending and expanding public access to government information. Founded in 1985 by a group of journalists and scholars, the archive, a tax-exempt public charity supported by donations that receives no government funding, has become the world's largest nongovernmental library of declassified documents.

Located on the seventh floor of George Washington University's Gelman Library in Washington, D.C., the archive's holdings include more than 2 million pages of material in more than 200 separate collections, most of which are accessible on the archive's major databases of released documents. It is open to the public without charge. Staff members process more than 2,500 requests for documents and information every year.

Researchers can search for documents on the NSA's Web site and gain access to the full-image versions of thousands of documents. Researchers can learn more about the site's published document collections that can be reviewed online through ProQuest, a subscription publication service, or the Digital National Security Archive, subscribed to by university libraries.

In addition, information about other collections of published documents is available only to researchers who visit the archive in person. For guidelines to using the archive, check out the "Guide for Researchers" page at http://www.gwu.edu/~nsarchiv/nsa/archive/resguide.htm.

All queries or requests should be sent to the archive via e-mail (nsarchiv@gwu.edu) or mailed to the following address: The National Security Archive, The George Washington University, Gelman Library, Suite 701, 2130 H Street N.W., Washington, DC 20037. The archive does not accept telephone inquiries.

U.S. National Archives and Records Administration (NARA) (http://www.archives.gov)
Overseeing the management of federal records, this independent federal agency provides access to a selection of nearly 50 million historical electronic records created by more than 20 federal agencies. With the help of AAD (Access to Archival Databases System), an online search engine, you can search approximately 350 data files with millions of records. Also available are descriptions of NARA's nonelectronic records, and an online catalog.

Historical Archives

Historical Text Archive (http://historicaltextarchive.com/)
This online archive contains a wide range of primary sources, including articles, books, essays, documents, historical photos, and Web links for a broad range of historical subjects.

Internet Archive (http://www.archive.org/)
This digital library of Internet sites and other cultural artifacts in digital form, dating back to 1996, offers free access to researchers, historians, scholars, and the general public. Books, audio, and moving images are represented.

Labor Archives

Directory of Labor Archives (Society of American Archivists) (http://www.archivists.org/saagroups/stchc/labor_archives_directory.asp)
Hosted by the Society of American Archivists, this site lists archives with important holdings regarding the history of workers and labor in America.

Medicine Archives

History of Medicine (http://www.nlm/nih.gov/hmd/)
Maintained and operated by the National Library of Medicine, this site features one of the world's great history of medicine collections on the Web, including general information on collections, finding guides and fact sheets, and research resources, such as locators, publications, and images from the history of medicine.

Newspaper Archives

NewspaperARCHIVE.com (http://www.newspaperarchive.com/DesktopDefault.aspx)
Requiring free registration to access, NewspaperARCHIVE.com contains more than 13 million searchable, full-size newspaper pages of many North American major and local newspapers from 1748 to the present. You can conduct your search by location (country, state, or city) and by date (year, month, and day). Free membership provides access to the archive's "free" newspapers; paid subscribers have unlimited search, view, and download access to site's entire archives. (Paid membership as of 2005 is $17.95 monthly; $99.95 annually.) To take full advantage of the site's services, your browser must be Internet Explorer version 5.0 or later, or Netscape Navigator version 4.7 or later, or America Online version 5.0 or greater.

Performing Arts Archives

Chicago Jazz Archive (www.lib/uchicago.edu/e/su/cja/)
Extensive collection of sheet music, recordings, photographs, and stock arrangements, held at the University of Chicago's Regenstein Library. Established in 1976, the collection has become a major resource for jazz researchers worldwide. Primarily focusing on Chicago style jazz, the archive Web site provides online guides introducing users to the archive holdings, scope of collections, accessing material online, and obtaining research assistance.

Shubert Archive (www.shubertarchive.org)
This collection archives every aspect of the careers of the famed Shubert brothers as producers and managers. Documents include general correspondence, business records, music, scripts, press materials, photographs, posters and window cards, architectural plans, costume designs, set designs, and other objects, held by the Shubert Foundation at the Lyceum Theatre in New

York City. The bulk of the collection focuses on the first four decades of the Shubert brothers' careers. The earliest records date back to the 1890s.

Unfortunately, no material from this collection is available for viewing online. The Shubert Archive is open to qualified researchers, serious scholars, writers/historians, and theater professionals by appointment only. Queries regarding the archive can be mailed to the Shubert Archive, 149 West 45th Street, New York, NY 10036, or e-mailed to: information@shubertarchive.org.

UCLA Film and Television Archive (http://www.cinema.ucla.edu/)
Second only to the U.S. Library of Congress in size and scope, this internationally renowned film and television repository houses one of the largest collections of film and television material, with more than 220,000 motion picture and television titles and 27 million feet of newsreel footage. None of the materials in UCLA Film and Television Archive are accessible online, but contents are searchable by using several online databases offered on its Web site. Individuals can arrange viewing appointments through the archive's Research and Study Center (ARSC) by phone (310) 206-5388, by fax (310) 206-5392, or by e-mail: arsc@ucla.edu.

William Ransom Hogan Archive of News Orleans Jazz (www.tulane.edu/~lmiller/JazzHome.html)
A renowned resource for New Orleans jazz research, this collection, held at Tulane University and part of the Special Collections Division of Howard-Tilton Memorial Library, features oral histories, recorded music, photographs and film, sheet music and orchestrations, ephemera and memorabilia, research notes, manuscripts, clippings, and bibliographic references. Vintage and contemporary books, periodicals, and special collections complement its holdings. The archive Web site features online tools enabling visitors to use a comprehensive index of its extensive oral histories, recorded sound, printed and manuscript music, graphics, and other files. For further information, or to submit a request, you can call the archive at 504-865-5688.

The Wisconsin Center for Film and Theater Research (http://www.wisconsinhistory.org/wcftr/filmlist/)
One of the largest repositories of manuscripts, films, photographs, and graphics related to the entertainment industry, featuring more than 15,000 American and international films and television programs. Twenty percent of its holdings are feature films. The archive's films and programs, except feature films, are catalogued in the center's Film and Photo Archive catalog. Researchers can search the center's feature film collection separately on its Web site. Information listed includes title, production company, date, country, format, and call number.

Recordings Archives

The National Sound Archive Catalogue (http://cadensa.bl.uk/)
Containing nearly 2.5 million sound recordings from pop, jazz, and world music, this stunning collection, held by the British Library National Sound Archive (NSA), features a vast array of material. Covered are early 19th century recordings, CDs, DVDs and minidisc recordings, commercial recordings

from the United Kingdom and overseas, BBC radio broadcasts, recordings by popular artists and composers, musical works, interviews, recordings of plays, and more. The online catalog has a searchable database and includes information on all of the archive's published and unpublished recordings. It should be noted that some recordings from the collection are not included in the catalog. Users can place orders of copies of recordings from the collection for a slight fee. As of 2005, only a few recordings can be listened to online. Inquiries are accepted by mail, phone, fax, or e-mail: The British Library Sound Archive, 96 Euston Road, London NW1 2DB, United Kingdom; phone: +44 (0)20 7412 7440; fax: +44 (0)20 7412 7441; e-mail: soundarchive@bl.uk.

Space Exploration Archives

NASA Historical Archive (http://science.ksc.nasa.gov/history/history.html)
Space history from 1958 to the present, including such popular topics as manned missions, Project Mercury, and the Space Shuttle, is covered on this, the official NASA Web site.

Television News Archives

Vanderbilt Television News Archive (http://tvnews.vanderbilt.edu/)
Located in Nashville, Tennessee, the Vanderbilt Television News Archives is the most extensive and complete archive of network news broadcasts for ABC, CBS, CNN, NBC, and PBS from 1968 to the present. A nonprofit organization created by Nashville insurance executive and Vanderbilt University alumnus Paul C. Simpson, the Vanderbilt Television News Archive records, indexes, and preserves network television news for further study and research. This expanding collection houses more than 30,000 individual network evening broadcasts and more than 9,000 hours of special news-related programming. Special reports covering such national and international events as political conventions, presidential press conferences, the Watergate hearings, and the Persian Gulf War, are also included.

For a fee, copies of videotapes are provided on a library loan basis. Loan requests can be completed online, and the length of the loan is usually for 30 days. A charge of $50 is assessed for any videotape that is not returned. Video duplications cover a single news broadcast or a compilation of multiple news segments onto a single videotape. The cost of duplication is based on the number of news segments requested. Each compilation is limited to one hour. Fees for duplication range from $25 to $100 per half hour, and payment must be made before the item will be shipped. Researchers can contact the archive by phone, 615-322-2927, or by e-mail: tvnews@library.vanderbilt.edu.

Women's History Archives

Archives of Women in Science and Engineering (http://www.lib.iastate.edu/spcl/wise/wise.html)
Held at Iowa State University, this archive, devoted to women in science and engineering, features personal papers of women scientists and engineers and records of related organizations.

A Guide to Uncovering Women's History in Archival Collections (http://www.lib.utsa.edu/Archives/WomenGender/links.html)
A project of the Archives for Research Center on Women and Gender at the University of Texas, San Antonio, this comprehensive guide features a geographic index to Web pages of archives, libraries, and other repositories featuring primary source materials about women.

The History of Women in America (http.//www.radcliffe.edu/schles/)
Unique collection of manuscripts, books, and other materials, including thousands of records, photographs, oral histories, and audiovisual materials, housed in the Arthur and Elizabeth Schlesinger Library at Radcliffe College. Materials from the collection are not available on the Web, but the site (under the link "Research Guides") provides links to a variety of women's research.

The Woman's Collection (www.twu.edu/library/woman)
Represents a major research history of American women. Since its founding in 1932, the collection has grown to more than 42,000 cubic feet of manuscript collections, 19,000 photographs, more than 2,000 periodical titles, and major book collections on microform. Located at the Blagg-Huey Library at Texas Woman's University in Denton, Texas, the archive also contains material about women's education in Texas. A searchable online catalog, database, and subject guide to the archive's holdings is available on the Web.

SPECIAL COLLECTIONS

Hundreds of public, university, and research libraries throughout the United States house special collections ranging from dozens to thousands of individual pieces. Items include rare books, manuscripts, historical records, drawings, photographs, maps, newspaper clippings, personal letters, films, audio and videotapes, and assorted unusual artifacts covering the gamut of subjects and disciplines.

When considering special collections, the collection size, geographic location, and institutional history can provide clues to the collection strengths and usefulness. To locate special collections, you can use traditional print guides or check your library's online catalog. Don't underestimate the importance of your library's online catalog. The online catalog is the most important and most powerful tool that libraries have to organize and present information on items cataloged in their system in appropriate categories. They can be gateways to various other information sources, such as bibliographies, library guides, or other relevant databases.

In addition, you can access online public access catalogs for any major library near you to search for special collections on a given topic. Some previously described databases, such as OCLC WorldCat, also can be used to locate other buried treasures found in library catalogs. Check with your school librarian or reference librarian at your local public library for additional resources.

Major university or college libraries and research libraries often have special collections related to their region. Some collections are accessible and viewable online, or offer a complete inventory and description of items.

Other collections are available for viewing only at the physical site where they are held.

The following is a selected list of some of the most notable university, public, and research library and museum special collections throughout the United States that provide assistance and are open to visiting researchers:

- ASU Special Collections Beinecke Rare Book and Manuscript Library, Yale University
- Bucknell University Edna M. Sheary Charitable Trust Project
- Burton Historical Collection, Detroit Public Library
- Getty Research Institute Research Library
- Haverford College Quaker and Special Collections
- Indiana State University Rare Books and Special Collections, Cunningham Memorial Library
- Kent University Libraries Special Collections and Archives
- Long Island Division at the Queens Borough Public Library
- Los Angeles Public Library—Rare Books Department
- Louis B. Mayer Library—Library of the American Film Institute
- Margaret Herrick Library—Academy of Motion Picture Arts and Sciences
- San Francisco Performing Arts Library and Museum
- San Francisco State University J. Paul Leonard Library Special Collections and Archives
- The Sherer Library of Musical Theatre at Goodspeed
- Texas Tech University Southwest Collection/Special Collections Library
- UCLA Department of Special Collections
- University of Arizona Library Special Collections
- University of California, Irvine Special Collections and Archives
- University of California, Santa Barbara Department of Special Collections
- University of Florida Department of Special and Area Studies Collections
- University of Michigan Bentley Historical Library
- University of Michigan Special Collections Library
- University of North Dakota Elwyn B. Robinson Department of Special Collections
- University of Southern California Special Collections
- University of Virginia Special Collections Library
- Vanderbilt University Special Collections and University Archives

Further information and links to above Web sites can be accessed at the following Web site: http//pscontent.com/od2/opendirectory.php?browse=/Reference/Libraries.Special_Collections/.

Columbia University's library also maintains one of the best Web sites for locating archives and manuscript collections. The site lists dozens of academic institutions, in alphabetical order, throughout the United States, complete with links to Web pages of each institution (http://www.columbia.edu/cu/lweb/eguides/speccol.html).

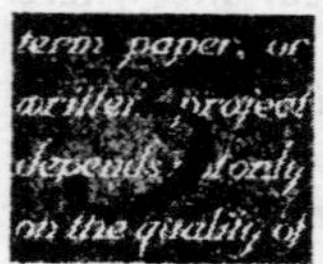

Finding Associations, Societies, and Organizations

Countless associations, institutes, societies, organizations, and other scholarly groups serve a vital purpose in the discussion and dissemination of critical facts, information, opinion, research, and other collaborations to inform and educate the general public on a large variety of political, social, and cultural issues. Most of these associations are nonprofit groups comprised of professionals in a given field.

When researching your topic, it is wise to expand your horizons and explore the many different public entities dedicated to your field of study. Many of these organizations are accessible on the Web and offer easy access to a vast number of educational and instructional resources, including online guides, article databases, current and past issues of scholarly journals, newsletters and other publications, reports and position papers, press releases, and much more.

Fortunately, most public, school, and university libraries subscribe to many popular references and online databases that can help you locate an association, society, or other organization relevant to your subject or topic. This also includes a broad selection of multiple and single-subject Web directories that list dozens of other potential sites for you to explore.

RESEARCHING ASSOCIATIONS

To easily locate and access associations, societies, and other organizations in the United States and around the globe, your library no doubt offers one or more directories on the subject in print or electronic form. Most of these directories offer detailed information about thousands of nonprofit groups listed in alphabetical order and indexed by subject. To find an association, society, or organization that suits your needs, check out the following recommended resources:

Print and CD-ROM

Associations Yellow Book (New York: Leadership Directories, 2005)
Published semiannually, this 1,300-page directory covers major trade and professional associations, including organizational details and current contact information.

The Directory of Associations (Scottsdale, Ariz.: Concept Marketing Group, 2003)
A comprehensive source of information on more than 34,000 professional, business, and trade associations, 501c nonprofit organizations, chambers of commerce, and other charity and community institutions available in print, CD-ROM, and online formats.

Encyclopedia of Associations: International Organizations, 41st Ed., 3 vols. (Detroit, Mich.: Gale Research, 2004)
Published in print and on CD-ROM, this classic three-volume reference provides detailed information on international and national membership organizations, including U.S.-based organizations.

Encyclopedia of Associations: Regional, State and Local Organizations, 16th Ed., 5 vols. (Detroit, Mich.: Gale Research, 2005).
This five-volume general reference, sold as individual volumes or a set, provides unparalleled coverage of regional, state, and local nonprofit membership organizations without duplicating information from Gale's primary guide, *The Encyclopedia of Associations*. This title is available in both print and CD-ROM editions.

The Foundation Directory (New York: The Foundation Center, 2003–)
In print since 1960, this comprehensive directory, also available online through its publisher, includes addresses, financial data, interest areas, and more on over 20,000 foundations, in all fields, throughout the United States.

On the Web

ASAE's Gateway to Associations (http://info.asaenet.org/cda/asae/associations_search/1.3200,MEN3.00.html?AlliedSocietyCode=ALL&submit=GO%21)
A free service of the American Society of Association Executives, this directory is keyword searchable by name, category, and location, complete with Web links.

Associations Unlimited (www.GaleNet.com/servlet/AU)
Web database available by subscription to libraries featuring more than 144,000 detailed entries for organizations worldwide, including 23,000 U.S. national associations, 19,000 international associations, and 112,000 U.S. regional, state, and local associations culled from Gale's *Encyclopedia of Associations*.

Infoplease: U.S. Societies and Associations Directory (http://www.infoplease.com/ipa/A0004878.html)
Partial directory of U.S. societies and associations of general interest derived from the printed edition of Gale's *The Encyclopedia of Associations.*

Internet Public Library Associations on the Net (http://www.ipl.org/div/aon/)
Provided by the Internet Public Library, this is the best guide to prominent associations and organizations on the Web. Listed by discipline and described is nearly every association in the arts and humanities, business, education, entertainment, health and medicine, law and political science, and science and technology.

ASSOCIATIONS ON THE NET

Thousands of associations, academies, societies, institutes, leagues, and other special organizations of every purpose and nature offer Web access to a plethora of timely information and rich resources. That includes online and electronic versions of annual reports, journals, newsletters, special publications, member surveys, president's messages, as well as multiple links to other related sites. For your convenience, the following is a sample list, culled from many credible sources, of some of the most notable associations accessible on the Web by category:

African Americans

African-American Organizations (http://www.aawc.com/aao.html)
This Web page lists links to many African-American fraternal and social organizations and political and social advocacy groups.

National Association for the Advancement of Colored People (NAACP) (http://www.naacp.org)
The official homepage of the NAACP, this site offers an abundance of resources, including text of speeches by the association's president, Kweisi Mfume, and direct links to pages of other minority and advocacy organizations.

National Association of Black Journalists (http://nabj.org/index2.html)
The homepage for the "largest media organization for people of color in the world," this site offers information about the organization's events and purpose, with few links to other sites.

The National Bar Association (NBA) (http://www.nationalbar.org)
Considered the African-American counterpart to the American Bar Association, the NBA provides access to law-related Internet resources covering African-American issues.

National Council for Black Studies, Inc. (http://www.usccr.gov)
Hosted by Eastern Illinois University, this organization's Web page presents many useful links to African-American studies.

The National Urban League (NUL) (http://www.nul.org)
Assisting African Americans in the achievement of social and economic equality since 1910, the NUL offers a wide selection of Internet resources and programs relevant to African-American interests.

U.S. Commission on Civil Rights (http://www.usccr.gov)
Investigating, studying, and collecting information concerning discrimination or a denial of equal protection of the laws under the Constitution, the

U.S. Commission on Civil Rights, through its Web site, offers general information on filing discrimination complaints, press releases, and downloadable PDF versions of publications dealing with civil rights issues.

Alternative Medicine

Acupuncture and Oriental Medicine Alliance (http://www.acupuncturealliance.org/)
Reflecting the philosophy, goals, and missions of its founders, this social welfare organization features press releases, free and nominally priced publications, and links to other organizations and journals.

Alternative Medicine Foundation (http://www.amfoundation.org/)
Providing alternative choices to consumers and health care providers, the Alternative Medicine Foundation offers a variety of online resources and databases featuring evidence-based information on alternative medicine therapies: HerbMed, covering herbal medicine treatments, TibetMed, devoted to Tibetan medicine, and online guides. Also highlighted are recommended books and journals, links to professional organizations, and various Web resources.

American Alternative Medicine Association (http://www.joinaama.com/)
This association for alternative medicine practitioners includes links to many online resources related to this field.

American Association for Health Freedom (formerly the American Preventive Medical Association) (http://www.apma.net/index.htm)
Founded as a political voice for health care practitioners who use nutritional and complementary therapies in patient care, this national association offers detailed information covering legal and legislative matters related to patient management and medical care. This site features the latest news and articles on the subject, as well as many online resources, such as position papers and links to other medical resources endorsed by the AAHF.

American Chiropractic Association (http://www.amerchiro.org)
Featured on this association's Web site is an overview of chiropractic medicine, health tips, news, and a fact sheet.

National Center for Homeopathy (http://www.homeopathic.org)
This homepage for this national association includes basic information on homeopathy and sections devoted to news, research, and clinical studies.

Architecture

American Society of Architectural Illustrators (http://www.asai.org/toc.htm)
Open to architects, designers, students, and others, this nonprofit, international professional organization offers Web access to publications, directories, showcases, and history.

Architecture Research Institute (http://www.architect.org/)
Devoted to creating more compact, ecologically sustainable, more walkable, and less car-dependent cities, this national think tank group publishes many useful resources that are accessible online, including a bibliography of works on architecture, design, and urban planning.

Architectural League of New York (http://www.archleague.org/)
More than 100 years old, this distinguished league, which aids architects and the public, provides information on symposia, lectures, gallery exhibitions, and other events that it sponsors.

The Association for Computer-Aided Design in Architecture (ACADIA) (http://www.acadia.org/)
A forum for discussion of theory, research, and applications in architectural computing, ACADIA provides many helpful links to conferences and a searchable conference paper database.

Center for the Built Environment (CBE) (http://www.cbe.berkeley.edu/)
Established in 1997 at the University of California, Berkeley, to provide timely, unbiased information on promising new building technologies and design techniques, this official homepage offers full-text reports and publications and links to other resources.

DOCOMOMO—Documentation and Conservation of the Modern Movement (http://www.docomomo.com/)
With chapters in 40 countries, DOCOMOMO, committed to preserving and conserving important architectural buildings and monuments of the modern era, publishes a host of material on its Web site, including journals and information on conferences and symposia.

The National Register of Historic Places (http://www.cr.nps.gov/nr/)
Authorized under the National Historic Preservation Act of 1996 to identify, evaluate and protect the United States's historical and archeological resources, the National Register of Historic Places provides free access to a searchable database of properties and links to National Register publications.

National Trust for Historic Preservation (http://www.nthp.org/)
Chartered by Congress in 1949, this private organization dedicated to the preservation of historic buildings sponsors this searchable Web site of information on historic home ownership, at-risk sites, historic site travel, public policy issues, and a calendar of preservation-related events.

The Society of Architectural Historians (http://www.sah.org/)
Promoting scholarly research and the preservation of architectural monuments, the society, founded in 1940, features on its Web site information about chapter events, meetings, and conferences, as well as links to relevant resources on the Internet.

Theatre Historical Society of America (THSA) (http://www.historictheatres.org/)
The only U.S. organization devoted exclusively to recording and preserving the architectural, cultural, and social history of American theaters, THSA,

through its archives and publications, provides information on more 7,000 theaters nationwide, as well as the latest news.

World Monuments Fund (http://wmf.org/)
Dedicated to the preservation of art and architecture, the World Monuments Fund lists the 100 most endangered sites, information on current projects and events, and links to other conservation resources on the Web.

Chemistry

American Chemical Society (ACS) (http://www.acs.org/)
Furthering the understanding of chemistry and chemical sciences, the ACS offers information on careers in chemistry and chemical sciences, programs, and meetings, plus a separate section for educators and students featuring articles and educational Web sites for K–12 and college students and graduates.

ChemSoc (http://www.chemsoc.com/)
An online directory of worldwide chemistry societies, this searchable Web site lists names, addresses, contact information, and Web addresses on all major national chemistry societies.

Royal Society of Chemistry (RSC) (http://www.rsc.org/)
The largest organization in Europe for advancing chemical sciences, the RSC features a vast array of links and information useful to educators and students in the study of chemistry and chemical sciences. Included are online journals, books, and databases, and science activities for visitors.

Computer Science

American Association for Artificial Intelligence (AAAI) (http://www.aaai.org/)
The AAAI was founded in 1979. Its Web site contains information on artificial intelligence, AAAI books, journals, conference proceedings, and technical papers, conferences, workshops, and symposia.

Association for Computing Machinery (ACM) (http://info.acm.org/)
ACM is the world's first educational and scientific computing society, established in 1947. Its Web site hosts information about ACM activities, conferences, and publications. The site also includes the ACM Digital Library, available by subscription, featuring full-text articles and papers from past journals, magazines, and proceedings. Only abstracts and tables of contents are viewable by nonsubscribers.

IEEE Computer Society (http://www.computer.org/)
This is considered the world's oldest and largest professional association of its kind. The IEEE was founded in 1947, and its Web site includes information about standards, certification, education and employment, plus access to its subscription-based digital library of full-text journal articles.

Resources of Scholarly Societies: Computer Science (http://www.scholarlysocieties.org/compsci_soc.html)
Listed on this Web site, sponsored by the University of Waterloo Library, are links to Web sites of scholarly computer science societies around the world.

Society for Industrial and Applied Mathematics (SIAM) (http://www.siam.org/)
Formed in 1952 to advance the application of mathematics to science and industry, this professional society for computer scientists, mathematicians, engineers, statisticians, and engineers offers a Web site with information about conferences, meetings, publications, and subscription access to its online journals.

Criminal Investigation/Forensic Science

American Academy of Forensic Sciences (AAFS) (http://www.aafs.org/)
Publishers of the *Journal of Forensic Sciences,* the AAFS provides access to a searchable online index from 1981 onward of past articles and issues. The site also includes information about career and educational opportunities, including a special page called the "Young Forensic Scientists Forum," for aspiring forensic scientists.

American Academy of Psychiatry and the Law (http://www.emory.edu/AAPL/)
This national forensic psychiatry academy, with a subspecialty in legal and legislative matters, features a code of ethics, the table of contents to its *Journal of the American Academy of Psychiatry and the Law,* and selected articles from the academy's newsletter.

American Board of Forensic Document Examiners (http://www.abfde.org)
Covering the application of allied sciences and analytical techniques used in forensic document examination, this site offers articles about the process of document examination, as well as a searchable database to locate certified document examiners by state.

American Board of Forensic Odontology (http://www.abfo.org/)
For greater insight into forensic odontology, this site features dental identification and bite mark standards, guidelines, and policies, among other resources, including many other organizations and individual practitioners.

American Society of Crime Laboratory Directors (ASCLD) (http://www.ascld.org/)
Dedicated to the improvement of crime laboratory operations, this nonprofit society features a list of accredited forensic science laboratories and other educational and forensic links.

Association of Firearm and Tool Mark Examiners (AFTE) (http://www.afte.org/)
The AFTE offers a variety of resources covering the area of ballistics, including access to its *AFTE Journal,* and other resources, including individual trigger pull, firearm brand/manufacturer cross-reference search, ammunition manufacturers and distributors, firearm manufacturers and distributors databases, and other links.

The Forensic Science Society (FSS) (http://www.forensic-science-society.org.uk/)
This United Kingdom forensic science society features a keyword-searchable database of articles to its journal of the Forensic Science Society, *Science & Justice,* plus book reviews, and other Web site links.

International Association for Identification (IAI) (http://www.theiai.org/)
Providing training and educational opportunities in the identification aspects of forensic science, the association features on its Web site information about training opportunities, certifications, conferences, and history, links to other forensic science or law enforcement documents and Web sites, and a list of publications, including the subscription-based bimonthly *Journal of Forensic Identification.*

Dance

The American Dance Therapy Association (http://www.ADTA.org/)
This national professional support organization for dance/movement therapists provides contacts, articles, dance therapy definitions, and links to related sites and training.

Dance USA (http://www.danceusa.org/)
Dedicated to the advancement of professional dance, Dance USA, founded in 1982, offers programs and information including facts and figures, journals, monthly member bulletins, specialized listservs, advice for young dancers, and a collection of studies and booklets.

Disabilities

ADDA: National Attention Deficit Disorder Association (http://www.add.org/)
This official Web page features information about research, treatment, and support groups.

American Association of People with Disabilities (http://www.aapd.com/)
A not-for-profit advocacy organization, the AAPD offers information and resources focusing on all aspects of people with disabilities.

Disabled People's International (http://www.dpi.org/)
Dedicated to the cause of human rights of people with disabilities, Disabled People's International (DPI) features a separate resources section of informative articles by region and by topic on disability issues worldwide.

Learning Disabilities Association of America (http://www.ldanatl.org/)
Featuring 50 state affiliates and more than 775 local chapters, this national disabilities association offers a broad spectrum of available resources covering problems and issues of those with learning disabilities, including attention deficit disorder, dyslexia, transitional concerns, and testing.

NAD (National Association of the Deaf) (http://www.nad.org/)
Offers information on conference workshops and publications.

National Organization on Disability (http://www.nod.org/)
Promoting equality for millions of American men, women, and children with disabilities, the National Organization on Disability features information on community involvement, economic participation, and access to independence for people with disabilities, as well links to other agencies and organizations, disability information, and additional resources.

Drama

The Drama League (http://www.dramaleague.org/)
In existence for more than 75 years, this membership association for drama professionals offers useful information for those studying and researching the dramatic arts, including annual surveys and the history and listings of the league's annual Drama League Awards.

The Dramatists Guild of America (http://www.dramaguild.com/)
This professional association of American playwrights provides access to information on literary managers, competitions, publications and newsletters, and resources directories.

Dramaturgy Pages (http://www.dramaturgy.net/dramaturgy/)
Covers a variety of resources on the Internet and elsewhere examining the works of theater and performance.

Drama West (http://members.iinet.net.au/~kimbo2/Dramawest/)
Promoting drama education and its practice, this western Australian association features several online resources, including a "Swap Shop" for teachers with resources and ideas, and a directory of related links.

Institute of Outdoor Drama (http://www.unc.edu/depts/outdoor/)
A public service agency of the University of North Carolina at Chapel Hill, the institute, established in 1963, offers resources on the planning and production of outdoor drama, including information on conferences, auditions, newsletters, festivals, and directories.

New Dramatists (http://newdramatists.org/)
Founded in 1949, this not-for-profit service organization has a Web site that contains information on fellowships and programs for playwrights.

Environmental Health

American Public Health Association (http://www.apha.org/)
Including researchers, health services providers, teachers, and administrators among its members, this association, called "the oldest and largest organization of public health professionals in the world," features a variety of resources, including full-text access to the association's publications, *American Journal of Public Health* and *The Nation's Health*.

American Water Resources Association (AWRA) (http://www.awra.org/)
Covering everything related to life's most precious resource, this Web site provides reports on water from states and conferences, and access to publications.

National Environmental Health Association (NEHA) (http://www.neha.org/)
Founded in 1937 to advance the cause of environmental health, this association offers links on its Web site to information and materials covering food protection, hazardous waste, and materials, including books, online resources, and links to its popular journal, the *Journal of Environmental Health*.

Natural Resources Defense Council (NRDC) (https://www.nrdc.org/)
Safeguarding the interests of people, plants, and animals, this national council through its Web site offers links to information on issues of global warming, environmental legislation, nuclear waste, nuclear war, and wildlife and fishery. Also included is a timeline of major environmental events in history.

Society of Environmental Toxicology and Chemistry (SETAC) (http://www.setac.org/)
Publishers of the Society of Environmental Toxicology and Chemistry newsletter, this nonprofit society devoted to environmental management, conservation, education, and research and development features a membership area for students that provides access to an online journal, newsletter, and membership directory.

Gerontology

AARP: American Association of Retired Persons (http://www.aarp.org)
As the largest advocacy organization in the world for people age 50 and over, AARP's Web site is one of the most informative when it comes to issues of aging. The site covers legislative, health and wellness, money and work, and life transition issues with sections on each, as well as research and reference sources, such as news articles and print and online resources.

American Geriatrics Society (http://www.americangeriatrics.org)
Dedicated to improving the lives and well-being of America's senior citizens, the American Geriatrics Society provides educational and research opportunities for the elderly, gerontology professionals, and the public with consumer and patient materials, such as publications, online resources, and a student section containing additional information and useful links on geriatric issues.

Gerontological Society of America (http://www.geron.org)
With more than 5,000 members in the field of aging, this nonprofit professional organization dedicated to the study and research of aging provides educational resources for students and the general public. The society's Web site includes data resources for gerontology, online resources on aging, searchable online professional journals, including *The Gerontologist* and *Journals of Gerontology Series* (A & B), plus links to a student organization with activities for students.

Health and Medicine

CONSUMER ASSOCIATIONS

Alzheimer's Association (http://www.alz.org)
Supporting families and individuals affected by this debilitating disease, the Alzheimer's Association homepage offers a great menu of topical information. Included are separate pages for "People with Alzheimer's," "Family Caregivers & Friends," "Physicians & Health Care Professionals," "Researchers," and "Media," along with an online glossary of terms and the Benjamin B. Green-Field Library and Resource Center, which lends materials on Alzheimer's and provides information to professionals and the general public.

American Cancer Society (ACS) (http://www.cancer.org)
Whether you want facts about specific kinds of cancer or information on treatment, prevention, and early detection, the American Cancer Society Web site covers it all. The site contains separate sections with facts and figures, publications, answers to basic questions about living and coping with cancer, research programs, as well as links to additional Web sources with additional and more in-depth information.

American Diabetes Association (http://www.diabetes.org)
With more than 18 million Americans suffering from one form of diabetes or another, the American Diabetes Association offers the latest information, education, and research in the field today. Visitors to the site can access diagnostic information about the disease, advice on nutrition and exercise, basic meal planning guidelines for diabetics, and information on advocacy, legal resources, and community programs and events.

American Heart Association (AHA) (http://www.americanheart.org)
With heart disease reigning as the number-one killer in America today, this Web site contains general and consumer information on all forms of heart disease. Included is information on the warning signs for heart attacks and stroke, diseases and conditions, children with heart disease, nutrition and exercise, sample recipes, publications and resources, as well as the "Heart and Stroke A–Z Guide," an online alphabetical index to information related to these diseases.

American Stroke Association (http://www.strokeassociation.org)
A division of the American Heart Association, the American Stroke Association provides information directly related to the topic of stroke, including a consumer guide on risk management, prevention, treatment, and recovery, resources specifically for affected families, information for caregivers, and more.

Asthma and Allergy Foundation of America (AAFA) (http://www.aafa.org)
For the more than 60 million Americans who suffer from asthma or allergies, the AAFA offers a host of resources on its Web site. Contents include free online information about asthma and allergies, education programs for consumers and health professionals, a question-and-answer section called "Ask the Allergist" with past questions archived, and a section with information suitable for kids and teens.

National Multiple Sclerosis Society (http://www.nmss.org)
To learn more about prevention and treatment, the latest research, and education related to this devastating disease, the National Multiple Sclerosis Society's official Web page offers a wide range of information for patients, families, and individuals. Sections include "Just the Facts," featuring answers to the most frequently asked questions; "Living with MS," offering basic information, tips, and personal stories; headlines about new clinical trials of promising treatments and legislation; and an online library containing accurate, current, and comprehensive information about those living with MS.

PROFESSIONAL ASSOCIATIONS

American Academy of Pediatrics (AAP) (http://www.aap.org/family/)
Dedicated to the health and well-being of children, the AAP features many valuable resources for parents and the public, including free articles and information on a variety of important health issues, such as obesity, sudden infant death syndrome (SIDS), safety and injury, and a list of child care guides and publications.

American Dental Association (ADA) (http://www.ada.org/)
Vital information covering all aspects of oral health is available through the ADA's Web site. A separate section, "Your Oral Health," contains many different resources, such as oral health news, a list of topics from A to Z, interactive learning tools, links to frequently asked questions, and additional related Web sites.

American Medical Association (AMA) (http://www.ama-assn.org/)
This professional association dedicated to serving the interests of physicians throughout the United States is a great resource of information. The AMA's Web site offers the latest medical headlines and news affecting physicians and the medical community, access to free articles from the AMA's leading professional journals in dermatology, facial plastic surgery, family medicine, and more (http://pubs.ama-assn.org/), and patient health information provided by the nation's leading medical societies.

Human Rights

INTERNATIONAL/REGIONAL ASSOCIATIONS

Council of Europe's Human Rights Web (http://www.coe.int)
Founded in 1949, the Council of Europe, the continent's oldest political organization comprised of 45 countries, offers a variety of resources on its Web site that are relevant to human rights issues, including legal judgments and pending cases, equality between men and women, and more.

International Labour Organization (http://www.ilo.org)
Developing and promoting international labor standards, this special United Nations agency offers numerous databases with direct access to documents, standards, national labor laws, and other resources of interest.

Organization of American States (http://www.oas.org)
This portal to the Web pages of the Inter-American Commission on Human Rights and the Inter-American Court of Human Rights (click on "Human Rights" under "Sectors & Topics" at the top of the page) includes texts, speeches, annual and country reports, and judgments on human rights cases.

United Nations High Commissioner for Human Rights (UNHCHR) (http://www.unhchr.ch)
Promoting human rights and providing access to human rights information, the UNHCHR offers an extensive collection of UN human rights documents produced by these and other UN organs, as well as international human rights instruments, news, and other publications.

NONGOVERNMENTAL ASSOCIATIONS

Amnesty International (http://www.amnesty.org)
This international organization, with 1 million members in 162 countries, offers a wealth of information covering human rights in many different countries, including full-text reports, surveys, and links to other Web pages.

Fédération Internationale des Ligues de Droits de l'Homme (http://www.fidh.org/)
Comprised of more than 100 organizations in 86 countries, this organization—the first international nongovernmental association to promote human rights—offers selected full-text country reports and abstracts from its monthly publication, *La Lettre de la FIDH,* available in English, French, and Spanish.

Human Rights First (http://www.humanrightsfirst.org/)
Human Rights First, formerly the Lawyers Committee for Human Rights, works to advance justice, human dignity, and respect for the rule of law and the guarantee of human rights. The homepage features news on the latest court cases, legal decisions and legal acts, and selected full-text publications.

Human Rights Internet (http://www.hri.ca)
This Canadian-based association that promotes the exchange of information within the human rights community provides a selection of resources, including full-text articles, UN documents, international treaties, and a human rights Internet directory.

Human Rights Watch (HRW) (http://www.hrw.org)
An independent nongovernmental organization supported by contributions from private individuals and foundations worldwide, HRW covers the human rights movement around the world. The site features human rights information by country, full-text annual world reports and individual country reports, information on global issues, and more.

HURIDOCS (http://www.huridocs.org/)
Established in 1982 as a global network of human rights organizations concerned with human rights information, the Human Rights Information Documentation System disseminates timely information and provides many other helpful resources covering human rights. The association's main Web page features the latest news as well as free articles from its official newsletter, *HURIDOCS.*

International Committee of the Red Cross (ICRC) (http://www.icrc.org)
Providing aid and protection to millions of victims of worldwide conflicts and violence, the ICRC offers on its Web site articles, texts of relevant treaties, and information the ICRC's activities in other countries relevant to human rights.

International Helsinki Federation for Human Rights (http://www.ihf-hr.org)
Protecting human rights in the Central Asian Republics, Europe, and North America, the International Helsinki Federation for Human Rights, an impor-

tant international organization, offers access to full-text reports, information on current projects, lists of the individual committees, and links to related Web pages.

Minority Rights Group International (http://www.minorityrights.org)
Working to secure the rights of ethnic, religious, and linguistic minorities worldwide, this international nongovernmental organization provides access to news and events, international statements, international instruments, minority rights and developments, and publications and resources on human rights.

Language

Modern Language Association (MLA) (http://www.mla.org/)
Founded in 1883 by teachers and scholars, this not-for-profit membership organization devoted to study and teaching of language and literature publishes an assortment of books and journals useful to teachers, students, and researchers, including the *MLA Handbook for Writers of Research Papers* and the *MLA International Bibliography.* For students writing essays and research papers, the site provides direct links to frequently asked questions and print and electronic formats of MLA style guides.

SIL International (http://www.sil.org/)
This leading Christian service organization, whose sole mission is to study, develop, and document the world's lesser-known languages, offers several vital resources, among them: *The Ethnologue,* a catalog of more than 6,700 languages spoken in 228 countries, and SIL Bibliography, a searchable database of academic works only. In addition, the site features links to publications, activities, and training programs of interest to linguists, anthropologists, and language teachers.

Literature

American Comparative Literature Association (ACLA) (http://www.acla.org/)
The American Comparative Literature Association, founded in 1960 for scholars whose work involves several literatures and cultures as well as cross-cultural literary study itself, offers a host of resources in the areas of research. The ACLA's Web site includes journal listings with links to a broad selection of literary journals, and general research links offering a list of general research sites and links to research libraries online.

American Folklore Society (AFS) (http://www.afsnet.org/)
Founded in 1888 for people involved in folklore work, the American Folklore Society, whose members include scholars, teachers, and professionals in the arts, is a rich resource of information on folkloric subjects. The AFS homepage provides access to documents, position statements on cultural, educational, and professional issues, information on national and international folklore projects, and the tables of contents of the society's quarterly journal, *The Journal of American Folklore.*

American Literature Association (http://www.calstatela.edu/academic/english/ala2/)
Devoted to the study of American authors, this nonprofit organization, established in 1989, contains information on news, events, activities, upcoming conferences, and affiliated societies with contact names and e-mail addresses.

Electronic Literature Organization (http://www.eliterature.org/)
Promoting the writing, publishing, and reading of electronic literature, this site includes news, information tools for electronic publishing, links to publishers, and a searchable directory of electronic literature on the Web.

Poetry Society of America (http://www.poetrysociety.org/)
This leading poetry association provides essential sources for poets and students interested in the art of poetry, including extensive lists of poetry colonies, conferences, and festivals, literary organizations and resources, and poetry journals and literary magazines with links.

Society for the History of Authorship, Reading and Publishing (http://www.sharpweb.org/)
This relatively young (founded in 1991) global network for book historians, scholars, professors of literature, librarians and publishing professionals covers all aspects of the printed culture, selected scholarly journals, and much more.

Mathematics

American Mathematical Society (AMS) (http://www.ams.crg/)
The AMS was established in 1888 to further mathematical research and scholarship. Its Web site has information of interest to members, authors, and visitors and contains information on what's new in mathematics, government affairs, publications, reference tools, survey data, math guides, and a library of online scholarly journals, some accessible for free.

Mathematical Association of America (MAA) (http://www.maa.org/)
Called "the world's largest organization devoted to the interests of collegiate mathematics," this 30,000-member society, including college and university faculty, high school teachers, government and corporate workers, research mathematicians, and graduate and undergraduate students, provides another great online resource in its Web site, which features news, book reviews, interactive columns, and numerous scholarly journals.

Society for Industrial and Applied Mathematics (SIAM) (http://www.siam.org/)
Founded to advance applied mathematics and computational science, SIAM hosts an ideal Web site for students with research needs in the field of science and technology. The society's home page contains a variety of resources, including news, books, and a comprehensive library of online journals, such as *SIAM News, SIAM Review,* and *Theory of Probability and Its Applications,* plus 11 peer-reviewed research journals.

Music

American Federation of Musicians (AFM) (http://www.afm.org/public/home/index.php)
The largest musicians' union in the world, the AFM, established in 1896, provides an extensive collection of resources covering the musical arts. This includes articles on labor issues, entertainment news, music magazines, and facts on how to hire a musician, plus additional information on conferences and organizations, products, and technology.

American Guild of Organists (http://www.agohq.org/)
Covering the field of organ and choral music, this national guild features educational and professional materials for members and nonmembers. The site offers information on education and professional development opportunities, competitions and conventions, and a guide to the organ for young people.

American Music Conference (http://www.amc-music.org/)
Founded in 1947, this nonprofit educational association offers on its Web site a great menu of resources related to all aspects of music, from breaking news to different kinds of music research.

American Music Therapy Association (AMTA) (http://www.musictherapy.org/)
Recognizing the importance of music therapy in rehabilitation, special education, and community settings, the AMTA's Web site offers insight into this specialized topic, including details about what music therapy is and careers in this vital profession.

The American Musicological Society (http://www.sas.upenn.edu/music/ams/)
Established to advance research in various fields of music, this unique society offers a laundry list of educational resources and links, including newsletters, journals, and other publications.

The American Society of Composers, Authors and Publishers (ASCAP) (http://www.ascap.com/)
This longstanding organization (created in 1914) is an essential resource for anyone researching the composing and publishing side of the music business. This site includes a searchable database of performed music, interviews with composers and authors, several online guides, and a newsletter.

Country Music Association (http://www.countrymusic.org/)
The people behind the annual CMA Awards, the Country Music Association is the world's best resource for anything and everything about country music. The association's Web site offers information on educational seminars, facts on country artists, online articles from its publications, *Communique* and *Close Up*, and more.

The Creative Musicians Coalition (http://www.aimcmc.com/)
Dedicated to the advancement of new music and the success of the independent musician, this nonprofit organization features publications, artist's pages, and online magazines.

The Galpin Society (http://www.music.ed.ac.uk/euchmi/galpin/)
This is one of the oldest professional music societies dedicated to researching the history, construction, development and use of musical instruments. Its Web site provides access to links to musical instrument collections and published journal.

International Alliance for Women in Music (http://music.acu.edu./www/iawm/home.html)
An international alliance for women composers and all women in music, this nonprofit organization, celebrating the contributions of all women musicians, provides a host of resources. The site contains events listings, audio samples of women composers's work, and links to journal articles.

The International Association for the Study of Popular Music (http://www.iaspm.net/)
A forum for interdisciplinary research on popular music, the site of this international association provides links covering a wide range of related disciplines, including bibliographies and journals.

Jazz Composers Collective (http://www.jazzcollective.com/)
This nonprofit organization for musicians and composers offers selected materials of interest to students, including jazz history, special projects, current and past newsletters, and links to recordings and CDs by composers-in-residence and other members.

Medieval Music and Arts Foundation (http://www.medieval.org/)
Dedicated to the advancement and understanding of medieval music and related subjects, this national foundation offers access to composer discographies, lively discussions about early music, and news on upcoming concerts and events.

National Music Publishers' Association (http://www.nmpa.org/)
Representing more than 600 American music publishers, the NMPA has worked to interpret copyright law and educate the public about matters pertaining to music publishing. The Web site contains news and articles about the latest legislative, legal, and educational initiatives concerning the protection of music copyrights across all media.

The Society for Music Theory (http://smt.ucsb.edu/smt-list/smthome.html)
Promoting fruitful discussion of music theory between music theorists, musicologists, performers, and scholars in other fields, this society, established in 1977, features a variety of resources on its Web site for those interested in the fundamentals of music theory. They include electronic resources, such as newsletters and journals, and links to regional, graduate student, and international organizations devoted to the study of music and music theory.

Nutrition

American Society for Clinical Nutrition (ASCN) (http://www.nutrition.org/)
Publishers of *The Journal of Nutrition,* this national organization for clinical nutritionists in the United States provides some great information and resources on the subject of nutrition. On its main Web site, contents include

position papers, press releases, House testimony, and Web links to other organizations and resources, as well as access to current and past articles of its journal from 1997 to the present.

American Dietetic Association (ADA) (http://www.eatright.org)
Considered the largest group of food and nutrition professionals in the United States, the ADA offers many useful resources for students studying diet and nutrition, including bibliographies, food pyramids, nutrition fact sheets, and position papers, many full text, plus links to professional societies and much more.

Food and Agriculture Organization of the United Nations (FAO) (http://www.fao.org)
Since its founding in 1945, this United Nations organization has lead international efforts to defeat hunger, helping both developed and developing countries. The FAO's Web site is a source of knowledge and information, including a multilingual database called FAOSTAT that offers a collection of statistics on nutrition and agriculture. The site also features many other statistical and nutrition-specific databases, country information and country profiles, and publications focused on food quality and nutrition.

International Food Information Council (IFIC) (http://www.ific.org/)
Created for the purpose of communicating science-based information about food and nutrition by food and beverage companies, the IFIC provides online access to a variety of full-text resources about food safety and nutrition. The site offers separate sections, such as fast facts on food and nutrition, a glossary of food-related terms, consumer research and opinion, a directory of other organizations, agencies, and associations, and .PDF versions of its bimonthly *Food Insight* newsletter from 1997 to the present.

International Vegetarian Union (IVU) (http://www.ivu.org)
Comprised of vegetarian societies around the world, the IVU, founded in 1908 to advance the cause of vegetarianism, sponsors a Web site for information related to vegetarianism. This multilingual site contains an article index of vegetarian articles written by its members, a listing of vegetarian phrases in different languages, and links to famous vegetarians, a museum of vegetarianism, recipes, news, events, special-interest groups, and youth pages.

Vegetarian Resource Group (VRG) (http://www.vrg.org/)
Providing information about vegetarianism and related issues, this nonprofit organization is another rich resource of information on the subject. The VRG's Web site offers immediate access to numerous full-text documents about vegetarian nutrition and lifestyles, including guides and handouts, polls, and recipes. Also accessible is information about restaurant and travel choices for vegetarians. Many publications produced by the VRG are available through this site, including *The Vegetarian Journal,* a print magazine, and *The VRG-NEWS,* a free e-mail newsletter.

Philosophy

The American Philosophical Association (http://www.apa.udel.edu/)
Promoting the exchange of ideas among philosophers and scholarly activity in philosophy, this professional association, founded in 1900, offers some

useful reference and resource materials for the study of philosophy on its Web site. Included are "Philosophy in the News," an extensive collection of links to news articles and radio programs featuring philosophy and philosophers, separate sections with direct links to other organizations of related interests, and Web resources, such as associations and societies, bibliographies, electronic texts, and philosophical guides and journals.

The American Philosophical Society (http://www.amphilsoc.org/)
Since its formation in 1743 by Benjamin Franklin, this eminent scholarly organization, America's first learned society, has played a major role in promoting excellence in the humanities and sciences through scholarly research and community outreach programs. With more than 700 members worldwide, most of them distinguished scholars in the humanities and social sciences, the Web site of this legendary society is a great source of knowledge and information for scholars and students with a strong interest in philosophy. The site offers direct access to online journals, catalogs, and guides, including finding aids and subject guides on all related fields, manuscript guides, and a list of publications, other archives, and cultural institutions.

Human Behavior and Evolution Society (HBES) (http://www.hbes.com/)
Offering a healthy exchange of ideas and research findings about human and animal behavior and evolution, this international, interdisciplinary scholarly society, comprised of members from a variety of fields of study, features many beneficial resources for students. The site includes overviews of human behavior and evolution on the Web, a free searchable articles database, and access to full-text articles published in scholarly journals, including the HBES's official academic journal, *Evolution and Human Behavior,* links to Web-based research studies, and more.

The Philosophy of Science Association (PSA) (http://scistud.umkc.edu/psa/)
Engaged in the study and discussion of the philosophy of science from many different viewpoints, the Philosophy of Science Association, which sponsors conventions and meetings and publishes many periodicals in the field, offers a number of instruments on its Web site of use to students. This includes a searchable archive of the PSA newsletter, featuring informative and thought-provoking articles by scholars, information about the association's journal, *Philosophy of Science,* and numerous links to science studies resources.

Physics

American Institute of Physics (AIP) (http://www.aip.org/)
Founded in 1931, this national organization, comprised of 10 member societies, including the American Physical Society (http://www.aps.org/), the Optical Society of America (http://w3.osa.org/), and the American Association of Physics Teachers (http://www.aapt.org/), offers a wealth of information and resources about physics and all related fields. Free access is provided to AIP's *Physics Today,* featuring timely articles, book reviews, a readers' forum, and Web guides; information on 14 scholarly journals, such as *Applied Physics Letters* and *Virtual Journals in Science and Technology,* and extensive links to education and student sites in the field of physics are also provided.

Institute of Physics (IOP) (http://www.iop.org/)
With more than 26,000 members worldwide, this U.K.-based institute, publishers of more than 40 prestigious journals in physics and related disciplines, provides free public access to the tables of contents of its journals.

Scholarly Societies Project—Physics (http://www.lib.uwaterloo.ca/society/physics_soc.html)
This alphabetical list, regularly maintained and updated by the University of Waterloo, features links to physics professional and scholarly societies around the world.

Religion and Theology

American Academy of Religion (http://www.aar-site.org/)
Examining religion's critical role in social, political, and economic events and in the lives of individuals and communities, this 8,000-member professional association of academically trained religious scholars provides public information on a variety of issues. The academy's Web site offers a vast collection of links to scholarly and religious alliances, societies, and organizations, and other scholarly resources for students of religion and theology.

Women's Studies

Institute for Women's Policy Research (IWPR) (http://www.iwpr.org/)
An organization devoted to advocating public policy issues of critical importance to women and their families, the IWPR offers research, information, and reports focusing on poverty and welfare, employment and earnings, work and family issues, health and safety, and women's civic and political participation.

League of Women Voters (http://www.lwv.org/)
Considered the United States's premier grassroots citizen organization for women, the League of Women Voters' offers up-to-date information and tools on its Web site to engage women in the democratic process at the federal, state, and local levels.

National Organization for Women (NOW) (http://www.now.org/)
The largest organization of feminist activists in the United States, with more than 500 000 members and 50 chapters nationwide, the National Organization for Women features an extensive collection of articles (under the section titled "Issues") on many key issues for women, from abortion rights to women in the military.

National Women's Studies Association (NWSA) (http://www.nwsa.org/)
Promoting feminist teaching, research, and community service with a vision that all people can develop their fullest potential, the NWSA, with chapters throughout the United States, provides information on women's caucuses, task forces, interest groups, and access to NWSA publications in .PDF form.

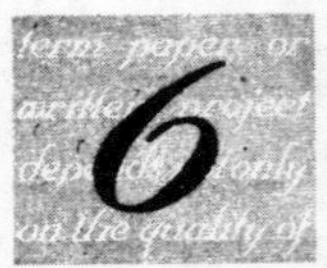

Finding Biographical Information

Finding useful biographies of newsworthy individuals from around the world, such as famous people, world figures, headline makers, corporate leaders, and other notables, has never been easier. Today, biographical material on millions of subjects is available: resources of every type and format, from printed volumes to electronic databases. Most popular references compile biographical data, personal information, citations, or full-text articles culled from thousands of credible sources and periodicals.

As with any form of research, having a better understanding of what types of biographical resources are available—how they differ and what they offer—will greatly improve your odds of finding the research you need for your project.

RESEARCHING BIOGRAPHICAL INFORMATION

Perhaps the easiest way to locate biographical information is to conduct a keyword search of your subject on your library's online catalog. Your library's online catalog will list those biographical sources—and in what form, print or electronic—that it carries about the individual subject you are researching.

To do a subject search, enter the individual's name. For example, if you wanted to find out more about actress Cameron Diaz, you would type: *"diaz cameron"* (last name followed by first name). Your subject search would produce a listing of all references—books, references, videos, and so on—held at the library that contain her name.

To locate only a biography or biographical references for Cameron Diaz, your keyword search would combine "biography" in the first space, and in the next space: *"cameron diaz."* In this case, the search results would specifically list biographical sources your library offers.

On the other hand, to locate biographical sources for people in a certain subject area or profession, your keyword search would combine the words describing the profession/subject with the terms "biography" and "dictionaries." For example, if you were interested in finding biographical information about key figures in politics, you would type: "politics and biography and dictionaries." Your search will probably produce a current list of books, references, or periodicals for further research.

In addition to this method, your library offers many other resources through which you can search or access information about your subject.

BIOGRAPHICAL INDEXES

Biographical indexes are a great place to find preliminary biographical data, biographical information, and citations to various published sources offering in-depth coverage of people from all professions. The most popular indexes for this purpose are:

Abridged Biography and Genealogy Master Index, 3 vols. (Detroit, Mich.: Gale Group, 1988–).
Although it was last updated in 1995, this solidly written and researched three-volume set is still useful. It contains biographical data and sources selected from 266 reference works for further study on approximately 2,000 subjects. Citations include biographee's name, birth date, and death date, if applicable.

Biography and Genealogy Master Index, 8 vols. (Detroit, Mich.: Gale Group, 1980–)
One of the most popular indexes for researching biographical and bibliographic information. In print since 1980, this authoritatively written compendium is the most comprehensive compilation of biographical citations and biographical information available. More than 12 million citations culled from 2,500 published works and 1,500 biographical retrospectives, including biographical dictionaries, "who's who" lists, subject encyclopedias, literary criticisms, history publications, and other indexes, are offered on more than 4 million contemporary and historical figures, past and present, known throughout the world. Spanning more than 1,000 years of biographical names, entries are updated and more than 450,000 new entries are added annually to this intriguing resource.

Biography Index (New York: H.W. Wilson Company, 1946–)
Indexing public figures in more than 5,500 publications, more than 336,000 records on biographical information about prominent people in every field, this long-running reference features information from 3,000 periodicals, including more than 2,000 individual and collective works published annually on famous or well-known people, including autobiographies, bibliographies, interviews, memoirs, and more. An online version is available, covering 1984 to the present.

Current Biography Cumulated Index 1940–2000 (New York: H.W. Wilson, 1940–)
This comprehensive guide lists all the profiles and obituaries originally published in H.W. Wilson's *Current Biography* series. Subjects are listed alphabetically and the index is cross-referenced for easy use. Many researchers start with this hardcover volume to determine if a profile has been published about their subject of interest.

World Biographical Index (München: K.G. Saur, 1982–)
Also of great value, this latest edition contains 3.5 million short biographical entries on prominent individuals from North and South America, Western and Central Europe, Africa, Australia and New Zealand, and Oceania. Bibliographic information is included, as are complete indexes to many biographical archives, with descriptions of the archives, their contents, and locations throughout the world.

POPULAR BIOGRAPHICAL REFERENCES

When it comes to finding biographies, brief accounts, and information of famous men and women who have made headlines in the past or are making headlines today, many popular biographical references are also available through your library. The following are highly recommended:

Books

Current Biography (New York: H.W. Wilson, 1940–)
Drawing its information from newspaper and magazine articles, books, and some personal interviews, *Current Biography,* a valuable source for researchers, students, and libraries, is published in four forms: a comprehensive monthly magazine, annual yearbook, international yearbook, and a cumulated index of every profile and obituary published from 1940 through 2000. Most libraries subscribe to the magazine and have the above volumes available on reference shelves for research. In addition, H.W. Wilson offers two online versions of this time-honored reference: *Current Biography Illustrated* and *Current Biography 1940–Present.*

Current Biography Yearbook (New York: H.W. Wilson, 1940–)
This annual hardcover compilation of biographies published in the previous year usually covers more than 200 personalities in arts and entertainment, business and industry, literature, music, politics and government, sports and science, and more. It comes complete with a cumulated index for articles and obituaries published in the current decade. An alternative to this series is *Current Biography International Yearbook,* a new annual publication featuring profiles exclusively on international figures of prominence outside the United States.

Who's Who in America, 3 vols. (Chicago: A.N. Marquis, 1899–)
In print since 1899, *Who's Who in America* has been the premier biographical dictionary of prominent men and women in the United States, used by researchers, librarians, journalists, and students. Updated every year, the three-volume set chronicles more than 100,000 high-achieving leaders and individuals. *Who's Who in America, 59th Edition 2005,* features 70,000 updated entries and 27,000 brand new listings. Libraries usually have the latest edition and previous volumes available in the reference area for research.

Who's Who in 20th Century America (New Providence, N.J.: Marquis Who's Who, 2000–).
Less expansive but still useful, this one-of-a-kind reference encompasses those individuals responsible for unforgettable human achievement and who brought significant changes in the world in the 20th century. They include

innovators and inventors, Nobel Peace Prize winners, award-winning writers, artists, entertainers, U.S. presidents, and more. The achievements and successes of 3,800 individuals are captured in in-depth biographies.

Who Was Who in America, 16 vols. (New Providence, N.J., Marquis Who's Who, 1896–)
Features biographies of many history makers who are now deceased. The 16-volume chronological set covers more than 130,000 subjects, from 1607 to 2002, from the Queen Mother to race car driver Dale Earnhardt. Each biographical profile is meticulously documented and highlights such details of the subject's life as family relationships, political affiliations, key positions held, awards, published writings, and vital statistics.

Other highly recommended volumes for looking up biographical information include:

Abridged Encyclopedia of World Biography, 6 vols. (Detroit, Mich.: Gale Group, 1999)
Six-volume set offering condensed biographies of contemporary and multicultural figures abridged from the original printed edition of the *Encyclopedia of World Biography.*

The Almanac of Famous People, 8th Edition, 2 vols. (Detroit, Mich.: Gale Research, 2003)
Titled *Biography Almanac* from 1981 to 1987, this updated two-volume reference features more expanded coverage of 30,000 famous individuals, including dates and places of birth, nationality, nickname, and best-known name.

American National Biography, 24 vols. (New York: Oxford University Press, 1999)
A 24-volume collection of brief biographies of 17,500 major figures who influenced the course of American history. Published to replace Oxford's *The Dictionary of American Biography,* this critically acclaimed historical work, 10 years in the making and available online by subscription, provides a wealth of research and information about significant individuals from America's past.

Cambridge Dictionary of American Biography, edited by John Stewart Bowman (New York: Cambridge University Press, 1995)
One of the most comprehensive single-volume biographical references, this 941-page hardcover edition, written by more than 40 scholars, features brief biographies of prominent individuals deemed important to the development of American society. This massive work contains nearly 9,000 entries addressing all periods of American history and people from all fields, including politics, the military, science, academia, the arts and humanities, sports, and more. Entries include figures both living and deceased.

Chambers Biographical Dictionary, 7th Ed., edited by Una McGovern (Edinburgh: Chambers, 2002)
Provides biographies of worldwide figures of public or historical importance. Revised and updated, this comprehensive and authoritative single volume extensively covers more than 17,500 international figures representing a cross-section of human achievement in areas such as the arts, business,

philosophy, politics, science, technology, and sports. Spanning the centuries, notables covered include Boudicca, Nelson Mandela, Maya Angelou, Isaac Newton, David Beckham, and Bill Clinton.

Concise Dictionary of American Biography, 5th Ed., 2 vols. (New York: Scribner, 1997)
Abridged two-volume edition providing significant coverage of American notables, from 1971 through 1980. Entries feature birthplaces, occupation, and more.

Dictionary of American Biography (Detroit, Mich.: Gale Group, 1990–)
Updated in 2001, this 20-volume set features biographical overviews of the lives of celebrated men and women, from 1928 to the present, who made significant contributions in American history. Highlighted are business leaders, diplomats, explorers, political figures, scientists, and others from more than 700 fields.

Encyclopedia of World Biography, 2nd Ed., 23 vols. (Detroit, Mich.: Gale Group, 1998–)
This 23-volume masterful reference provides complete, fully illustrated biographies of contemporary and multicultural figures. Highly informative biographies cover almost 7,000 important individuals. In 1999, Gale Group published a CD-ROM edition.

Newsmakers (Detroit, Mich.: Gale Research Co., 1985–)
Hardbound annual formerly titled *Contemporary Newsmakers* (1985–88) featuring profiles of the people making today's news headlines. Reprinted from Gale's quarterly publication of the same name. Includes references to other biographical sources, separate obituary section, and four indexes to locate entries by name, nationality, occupation, and subject.

The Oxford Dictionary of National Biography edited by H. C. G. Matthew and Brian Harrison (New York: Oxford University Press, 2004)
Offering quick sketches of famous subjects, this revised collection, available in 60 printed volumes and online (www.oup.com/oxforddnb/info/), provides biographies of 50,000 prominent British historical figures, both men and women, who shaped all aspects of the British past and present.

The Scribner Encyclopedia of American Lives, 6 vols. (New York: Charles Scribner's Sons, 1998–)
Each volume in this six-volume set presents scholarly biographies of more than 500 notable Americans who made significant contributions to U.S. history. Detailed, in most cases, are the individual's family heritage, education, marriages and divorces, residences, and cause of death and place of burial. Subsequent volumes cover a five-year period and entries contain biographical references.

U-X-L Encyclopedia of World Biography, 10 vols. (Detroit, Mich: Gale Group, 2002)
This first edition, 10-volume set offers biographical profiles of 750 notable current and historical figures, selected from entries originally published in the *Encyclopedia of World Biography.*

Who's Who: An Annual Biographical Dictionary (Hampshire, U.K.: Palgrave Macmillan, 2002)
Published in London since 1849 and previously published in the United States by St. Martin's Press, this is an annual biographical dictionary of famous English men and women.

Magazines

Biography (New York: A&E Television Networks, 1997–)
Carried by most libraries, this former monthly, now quarterly magazine chronicles the notables from the worlds of business, politics, sports, and show business. Unfortunately for research purposes, there is no cumulative *Biography* index. Instead, researchers may look up names in *The Readers' Guide to Periodicals* (New York: H.W. Wilson, 1890–) to see if a previous issue of *Biography* is listed.

Current Biography (New York: H.W. Wilson, 1940–)
Published 11 times a year, each issue profiles 18 to 20 subjects representing a wide range of professions. Each issue is well written and researched and also contains obituaries of figures discussed in previous issues, plus a cumulative index in each issue listing those profiled in the current year. Profiles from back issues are added annually to the printed and online editions of *Current Biography*.

REFERENCES FOR REGIONAL FIGURES

Regional *Who's Who* volumes, also published by Marquis, provide quick access to biographical profiles of individuals in specific territories of the United States and Canada. Academic, business, cultural, government, medical, political, scientific leaders and professional athletes, in cities and states are among those represented in each volume. Volumes include:

Who's Who in the East (Boston: Larkin, Roosevelt & Larkin; New Providence, N.J.: Marquis, 1943–)
Features more than 21,000 profiles of noteworthy figures in the eastern region of the United States and Canada.

Who's Who in the Midwest (New Providence, N.J.: Marquis, 1949–)
Contains more than 15,000 biographies of the most influential men and women from the Midwest United States.

Who's Who in the South and Southeast (Chicago, Ill.: A.N. Marquis, 1950–)
Chronicles more than 16,000 major personalities from across the U.S. South and Southeast.

Who's Who in the West (Chicago, Ill.: A.N. Marquis, 1949–)
Reviews more than 15,000 prominent individuals from the western region of the United States.

REFERENCES FOR INTERNATIONAL FIGURES

Volumes that are international in scope:

International Who's Who (London: Europa Publications, 1935–)
Covers the lives and achievements of nearly 22,300 of the most distinguished men and women from almost every country, from heads of state, politicians, religious leaders and ambassadors, to notables in business, finance, technology, film, music, fashion, literature, performing arts, and sports. An online version is also available by subscription.

Who's Who in the World (Wilmette, Ill.: Marquis Who's Who, 1972–)
This all-inclusive annual volume provides access to more than 57,000 personal profiles of important leaders from 230 countries and territories. Coverage includes leaders of large corporations, heads of educational, religious, scientific, humanitarian and professional organizations, ambassadors and ministers, high-ranking military officers, writers, musicians, artists, actors, dancers, filmmakers, and much more.

REFERENCES BY SUBJECT

In addition to the above biographical forms, you also can find biographical material on subjects from specialty fields of interest in assorted printed volumes and Web sites. Examples include:

Aerospace

NASA Astronaut Biographies (www.jsc.nasa.gov/Bios/astrobio.html)
Every NASA astronaut on active duty since 1995 is chronicled, along with former NASA astronauts, including those now deceased, and international astronauts, including cosmonauts assigned to joint U.S. and Russian projects, plus those individuals from international space agencies who have trained and served as mission specialists with NASA.

Art

Artists' Biographies (http://www.artnet.com/library/index.asp?N=1)
Considered one of the most informative online references on the world of art and artists, Artnet offers more than 16,000 basic biographies of painters, sculptors, photographers, architects, designers, ceramicists, graphic artists, and other artists from around the world. Some 15,000 entries are culled from articles originally published in the award-winning reference *The Grove Dictionary of Art.*

Who's Who in American Art (New York: R.R. Bowker, 1937–)
Includes more than 11,000 biographies of artists, critics, curators, administrators, librarians, historians, collectors, educators and dealers from the field of visual arts in the United States. Profiles are listed in an A–Z format and cross-referenced in a separate geographical index in this exhaustive tome, which also includes a special index of all previously profiled artists who have died since 1953.

Business

Inventors Hall of Fame (http://www.invent.org/hall_of_fame/1_0_0_hall_of_fame.asp)

This official site for the Inventors Hall of Fame features biographical information on inventors—men and women responsible for great technological advances—searchable by name or by invention.

Who's Who in Finance and Industry (New Providence, N.J.: Marquis Who's Who, 1971–)

Comprehensively lists biographical data on more than 18,000 professionals and leaders in business and industry. Covered throughout this 884-page volume are senior executives, presidents and CEOs, federal department and commission heads, directors, administrators, professors, and many others.

Education

Who's Who in American Education (Owings Mills, Md.: National Reference Institute, 1988–)

Surveys the careers of more than 20,000 men and women recognized for their excellence and dedication to the highest standards of American education. Educators from all levels are highlighted in this 1,000-page volume. They include accomplished professionals from adult education, association administration, counseling/career planning, gifted and talented/special education, government administration, higher education, libraries, preschool education, and more.

Film, Theater, and Television

International Dictionary of Films & Filmmakers, 4th Ed. (Detroit, Mich.: St. James Press, 2000)

Provides complete biographical coverage of the most studied actors, actresses, directors, writers, and production artists in cinema history. Biographical details, filmographies, and information regarding productions and awards are included with each entry.

MovieActors.com (http://www.movieactors.com)

Updated and maintained by Video Producers, Inc., this extensive online database features numerous biographies of movie stars from the 1930s, 1940s, 1950s, 1960s, 1970s, 1980s, 1990s, and 2000s. Separate categories include award-winning actors, character actors, and sci-fi actors, plus individual databases for best actor, best actress, best supporting actor, and best supporting actress awards.

Screen World, Vol. 55 by John Willis and Barry Monush (New York: Applause Books, 2004)

Previously published by Crown Books, this popular film annual series features biographical entries to more than 2,250 living stars, including real name, school, place, and date of birth. Also included are overviews of every major U.S. and international film release during the previous year, with complete filmographies for each production (cast, credits, company, month released, rating, running time, and so on).

Theatre World, Vol. 59 by John Willis with Ben Hodges and Tom Lynch (New York: Applause Books, 2004)
Annually highlights the year in theater on Broadway, off-Broadway, and other professional stage productions, complete with cast listings, opening and closing dates, song titles and other production information, throughout the United States. Biographical data on actors, producers, directors, and others, obituary information, and major drama awards are included. This latest title covers the 2003–04 theater season. It has been published by various companies since 1944. Previous editions were published by Crown Publishers from 1966 to 1991. In 1992, Applause Books acquired the series.

What a Character!.Com (http://www.what-a-character.com/)
Biographical information is archived on hundreds of character actors from the worlds of film and television. Subjects are indexed alphabetically, and each entry includes a photograph. They are searchable by name or title of film or program in which the actor appeared.

Who's Who In Entertainment, 7th Ed. (Detroit, Mich.: Gale Group, 2002)
Provides complete biographical information on 19,000 entertainment notables in all major fields within the industry: motion picture, television, theater, music, and radio. Examples include animation technicians, lighting specialists, photographers, writers, and others.

Who's Who in Hollywood: The Largest Cast of International Film Personalities Ever Assembled, by David P. Ragan (New York: Facts On File, 1998)
This exhaustive reference incorporates capsule biographical information on some 35,000 actors, living or deceased, including bit players and character actors as well as major film stars.

Law

Who's Who in American Law (New Providence, N.J.: Marquis Who's Who, 1978–)
Offers biographies of almost 15,000 leading attorneys and other legal professionals. Entries cover their personal and career histories, specialties, education, and achievements.

Supreme Court Justices (http://www.oyez.org/oyez/portlet/justices/)
The most comprehensive site on the Web for information about Supreme Court justices, this site offers detailed biographical information on every Supreme Court justice, past and present. Content includes basic biographical overviews, background, lengthy biographies, and other resources for each subject listed. Subjects can be sorted and viewed in alphabetical or chronological order as well.

Literature

American Literature (http:/xroads.virginia.edu/~HYPER/hypertex.html)
This well-organized and easy-to-use Web site offers full text biographies and commentaries on famous authors, such as Henry Adams, Edgar Allan Poe, Constance Rourke, Harriet Beecher Stowe, Mark Twain, and many others.

Contemporary Authors (Detroit, Mich.: Gale Research Co., 1962–)
Multivolume hardbound edition and online database (www.gale.com) presenting complete biographical and bibliographical information, frequently updated and revised, on more than 120,000 U.S. and international authors, including journalists, nonfiction writers, novelists, playwrights, poets, and scriptwriters, the most-studied literary figures of the 20th century. The Web site provides a fully searchable database providing fast access to biographical data on contemporary writers.

Dictionary of Literary Biography (Detroit, Mich.: Gale Research Co., 1978 –)
Career biographies of major writers are represented in this large, 25-volume reference. Two supplementary series are intended as companions to the above: *Dictionary of Literary Biography Documentary Series* (Detroit, Mich.: Gale Group, 1982–) concentrates on the major figures of a particular literary period, movement, or genre in each annual volume. *Dictionary of Literary Biography Yearbook* (Detroit, Mich.: Gale Group, 1980–) is an annual compendium that includes material covering a given year's literary highlights.

The Pulitzer Prizes (http://www.pulitzer.org)
In addition to covering the history of this prestigious prize, this site features full-text biographies, photographs, and cartoons for past Pulitzer Prize winners (from 1995 to the present) for achievements in American journalism, letters, drama, and music. Names and citations, for every year the Pulitzer Prize has been awarded (since 1917), can be searched by category or year.

Medicine and Health Care

Who's Who in Medicine and Health Care (New Providence, N.J.: Marquis Who's Who, 1996 –)
This 985-page book offers vital biographical information on more than 27,000 leaders in the teaching, practice, planning, financing, and delivery of health care. Included are medical professionals, administrators, educators, researchers, clinicians, and industry leaders from throughout the medical and health care industries.

Music

All Music Guide (www.allmusic.com)
Online guide offering biographies of music artists, including background information on albums and songs, covering a wide range of musical styles, including bluegrass, blues, classical, contemporary Christian, country, folk, gospel, reggae, and rock.

Biographical Encyclopedia of Jazz, edited by Leonard Feather and Ira Gitler (New York: Oxford University Press, 1999)
Highlights the careers of 3,300 jazz musicians from around the world, such as Miles Davis, Duke Ellington, Dizzy Gillespie, and Charlie Parker. Alphabetically arranged and thoroughly researched, each biography details the background and career of each musician. This is considered the most comprehensive jazz encyclopedia.

Composer Biographies (www.cl.cam.ac.uk/users/mn200/music.composers.html)
Brief general biographies are provided on major composers, including date of birth and death, and summaries of their achievements with relevant links to composer Web pages.

The New Grove Dictionary of Jazz, 2nd Ed., edited by Barry D. Kernfield, 3 vols. (New York: Grove, 2002)
The most comprehensive three-volume reference ever produced on jazz performers and jazz history, featuring more than 4,500 articles and 1,800 discographies on seemingly every performer. Copiously illustrated and cross-referenced for easy use, this edition also covers jazz terms, topics, instruments, styles, festivals and clubs, record labels, and much more.

The New Grove Dictionary of Music and Musicians, 2nd Ed., edited by Stanley Sadie, 29 vols. (New York: Grove, 2001)
Revised and updated, this 29-volume set profiles more than 20,000 20th-century composers and performers of music, covering many genres, including jazz, rock, pop, and world music, spanning all continents and cultures. Detailed bibliographies accompany each profile. Encyclopedic coverage is also provided on the history of various popular instruments and styles, terms, and genres.

New Rolling Stone Encyclopedia of Rock and Roll, edited by Patricia Romanowski, Holly George-Warren, and Jon Pareles (New York: Fireside, 1995)
Offers 2,200 meticulously researched essays examining the work, history, and influence of rock and roll figures, from the famous to the almost forgotten.

PBS Jazz Biographies (http://www.pbs.org/jazz/biography/)
A companion Web site to the critically acclaimed PBS TV documentary *Jazz*, by filmmaker Ken Burns, this site lists nearly 100 famous jazz musicians, including detailed biographies and audio samples of their work. Biographies are derived from *The New Grove Dictionary of Jazz*, published by Oxford University Press.

Rock and Roll Hall of Fame Inductees (http://www.rockhall.com/hof/allinductees.asp)
Complete biographical overviews and time lines are provided on each rock star inducted into the Rock and Roll Hall of Fame since 1986. Subjects can be searched by name or year inducted.

The Rock Who's Who, 2nd Ed. by Brock Helander (New York: Schirmer Books; London: Prentice Hall International, 1996)
Features biographical sketches on 395 innovative performers, personalities, and groups in rock 'n' roll. Although somewhat outdated, this prodigious work includes complete discographies, including original issue information, for recordings by each artist.

Unofficial Encyclopedia of the Rock & Roll Hall of Fame, by Nick Talevski (Westport, Conn.: Greenwood Publishing, 1998)
Provides career biographies of 149 Hall of Fame inductees, including artists, producers, record company founders, and deejays. Bibliographic information included.

The Virgin Encyclopedia of Popular Music, Concise 4th Ed. (London: Virgin in association with Muze, Inc., 1997)
Authoritative compendium featuring biographical profiles of more than 384 artists, from award winners to one-hit wonders. Completely revised and updated, biographies review each artist's musical work. Album and video information and suggested readings accompany each profile.

Politics

The American Presidency (http://ap.grolier.com/)
Online articles and biographies of every U.S. president, vice president, and first lady from the *Encyclopedia Americana.* Separate articles are linked with fast access to relevant subjects, including the Congress, elections, and the Constitution.

Biographical Dictionary of the American Congress, 1774–1996 edited by Joel D. Treese, Dorothy J. Countryman, and Wayne P. Walker (Washington, D.C.: CQ Press, 1996)
This popular resource features more than 11,400 individual biographies of current and former members of the U.S. Congress since 1774. Entries detail party affiliation, personal information, and background.

Biographical Directory of the U.S. Congress (http://bioguide.congress.gov/biosearch/biosearch.asp)
Biographical information is summarized on all members of the U.S. House of Representatives and U.S. Senate from 1774 to the present. Biographies of all current and former congressional representatives and senators are searchable by name, position, and state.

Encyclopedia of the American Presidency by Michael Genovese (New York: Facts On File, 2004)
Provides an array of information about U.S. presidents, including presidential and vice presidential biographies; sketches of key figures important to each president, such as relatives, political opponents, press secretaries, and cabinet members; and accounts of historical events that occurred during each president's administration.

National Governors Association (http://www.nga.org/)
This official association Web site, features under the section entitled "Governors" a searchable database of biographical information on all U.S. governors dating back to the colonial days.

Who's Who in American Politics (New York: R.R. Bowker, 1968–)
This critically acclaimed reference documents the lives and careers of more than 29,000 American political decision makers and leaders at all levels of government. Biographies of individuals in this two-volume, 2,600-page set are listed alphabetically by name and by state.

Science

American Men and Women of Science, 21st Ed. (New York: R.R. Bowker, 1989–)

Exhaustively covers more than 129,000 active scientists in seven hefty volumes. Alphabetically arranged by name, this respected resource examines key players in the biological, physical, and related sciences throughout North America.

Biographical Dictionary of Scientists, 3rd Ed., 2 vols. (New York: Oxford University Press, 2000)

Recounts the lives, theories, discoveries, landmark contributions, and artistic, personal, political, social, and religious concerns of 1,200 of the world's great scientists.

Concise Dictionary of Scientific Biography, 2nd Ed. (New York: Scribner's, 2000)

Comprehensively details more than 5,400 scientists from all areas of history and from throughout the world. Entries are indexed by nationality and by field, highlighting place and date of birth, areas of research, and major career achievements.

4,000 Years of Women in Science (http://www.astr.ua.edu/4000WS/4000WS.html)

Features biographies, listed by discipline, on more than 125 of the most notable women in science and technology. Some biographies are illustrated on this site, authored by Deborah Crocker and Sethanne Howard of University of Alabama.

Notable Scientists, 1900 to the Present, 2nd Ed. (Detroit, Mich.: Gale Group, 2000)

Highlights the accomplishments and careers of nearly 1,600 scientists, including men, women, minority, and international scientists, since the beginning of the 20th century.

Who's Who in Science and Engineering (Wilmette, Ill.: Marquis Who's Who, 1992–)

Authoritatively profiles more than 30,000 leading scientists and engineers, including the world's foremost inventors, discoverers, and industry executives. Highlighted in this 1,200-page volume are leaders from all areas of science and engineering, including architecture, chemical engineering, computer science, electrical engineering, information science, life sciences, materials engineering, mathematics, medicine, physical sciences, social sciences, and system engineering.

Specific Ethnicities

AFRICAN AMERICANS

Contemporary Black Biography, Vol. 25 (Detroit, Mich.: Gale Research Co., 1997)

Documented are the extraordinary lives of 65 notables of African heritage in full-length biographies, arranged alphabetically. Details include date and place of birth, educational and career information, memberships and awards, and complete source citations for each entry.

Notable Black American Women, 3 vols., edited by Jessie Carney Smith (Detroit, Mich.: Gale Group, 1992–2003)
Extensively profiled are approximately 300 black American women that have made major contributions to American society and the world. Personal background and personal achievements are chronicled for each subject in this fully illustrated three-volume set.

Who's Who Among African Americans, 16th Ed. (Detroit, Mich.: Gale Group, 2003)
This expertly written reference profiles the personal lives and careers of notable African Americans, including leaders from the arts, business, religion, sports, and more.

ARABS

Who's Who in the Arab World, 16th Ed. (Beirut: Publitec Editions, 2002)
This comprehensive directory features 6,000 biographical sketches of the most important people in 19 Arab counties from all fields of industry.

ASIAN AMERICANS

Distinguished Asian American Business Leaders by Naomi Hirahara (Westport, Conn.: Greenwood Press, 2003)
This illustrated reference is an inspiring collection of engagingly written biographies of 96 Asian men and women who have enjoyed successful careers in business. Each biographical entry concludes with references for further reading.

Notable Asian Americans edited by Helen Zia and Susan B. Gall (Detroit, Mich.: Gale Group, 1995)
The lives of 250 prominent past and present Asian Americans are highlighted, including their personal, career, and educational backgrounds and their significant achievements.

HISPANICS/HISPANIC AMERICANS

Biographical Dictionary of Hispanic Americans, 2nd Ed. by Nicholas E. Meyer (New York: Facts On File, 2001)
Chronicling more than 250 Hispanic Americans, in A-to-Z format, representing more than 500 years of achievement, biographical essays highlight the backgrounds and careers of notable Hispanic Americans in arts and entertainment, business, health and medicine, literature, science, religion, and other fields.

Dictionary of Hispanic Biography edited by Joseph C. Tardiff and L. Mpho Mabunda (Detroit, Mich.: Gale Group, 1996)
Profiling Hispanic notables from the 15th century to the present from Latin America, Spain, and the United States, this biographical dictionary represents key figures from a variety of fields, including business, education, entertain-

ment, religion and sports. The 700 entries are arranged alphabetically and include a list of selected works (books, films, recordings, and so on) of each biographee.

Notable Hispanic American Women, Book I (Detroit, Mich.: Gale Research, 1993)
Exhaustively profiling more than 300 Hispanic-American women of national and international prominence, this useful volume, though not up to date, features detailed biographical, educational, and career data, major achievements, and more for each entry.

NATIVE AMERICANS

A to Z of Native American Women by Liz Sonneborn (New York: Facts On File, 1998)
Fascinating look at more than 100 notable Native American women, from the 1500s to the present, including artists, educators, filmmakers, performers, political activists, professionals, scholars, spiritual leaders, traders, warriors, and writers. Each profile includes biographical sketches covering each woman's achievements and challenges. Subjects range from the well known to the lesser known, such as singer Buffy Sainte-Marie and leader/activist Wilma Mankiller.

Native American Women: A Biographical Dictionary, 2nd Ed. edited by Gretchen M. Bataille and Laurie Lisa (New York: Routledge, 2001)
Although somewhat outdated, this reference examines the lives and achievements of almost 250 Native American women born between 1499 and 1965. This reference, written by more than 70 contributors, examines Native American women of diverse roles who may be lesser known.

Notable Native Americans (Detroit, Mich.: Gale Group, 1995)
Outdated but still worthwhile compilation of biographical and bibliographic information on more than 265 prominent Native American men and women in art and literature, athletics, education, entertainment, journalism, law, medicine, politics, religion, and science.

Sports

Biographical Dictionary of American Sports edited by David L. Porter (Westport, Conn.: Greenwood Press, 1987–)
This outstanding reference series offers detailed biographies on distinguished sports personalities in baseball, basketball, football, and other outdoor sports. Profiles cover more than the usual personal information and career statistics. Titles in the series (available in print and online, by subscription) include:

Biographical Dictionary of American Sports: Baseball, Revised and Expanded Edition, A–F (Westport, Conn.: Greenwood Press, 2000)

Biographical Dictionary of American Sports: Baseball, Revised and Expanded Edition, G–P (Westport, Conn.: Greenwood Press, 2000)

Biographical Dictionary of American Sports: Baseball, Revised and Expanded Edition, Q–Z (Westport, Conn.: Greenwood Press, 2000)

Biographical Dictionary of American Sports: Basketball and Other Indoor Sports (Westport, Conn.: Greenwood Press, 1989)

Biographical Dictionary of American Sports: Football (Westport, Conn.: Greenwood Press, 1987)

Biographical Dictionary of American Sports: Outdoor Sports (Westport, Conn.: Greenwood Press, 1988)
In addition to the publisher's online database, two supplements published by Greenwood, *Biographical Dictionary of American Sports, 1992–1995*, and *Biographical Dictionary of American Sports, 1989–1992*, provide updated information on all entries from the previous editions. To cross-reference entries in the series from 1987 to 1992, Greenwood has also published *A Cumulative Index to Biographical Dictionary of American Sports*, which lists all items alphabetically..

International Encyclopedia of Women and Sports edited by Karen Christensen, Allen Guttmann, and Gertrud Pfister, 3 vols. (New York: Macmillan Reference USA, 2001)
Written by scholars and specialists, this book profiles the top women athletes, such as Olympic speed skater Bonnie Blair and figure skater Katarina Witt. Also included are extensive articles about each sport, current social and cultural issues, health and fitness issues, and much more.

Notable Sports Figures edited by Dana Barnes, 4 vols. (Detroit, Mich.: Gale Group, 2003)
This top-notch reference spotlights more than 600 sports figures throughout history from around the world who have greatly influenced, dominated, or changed their sport. Each profile examines the awards, career statistics, and subject's life chronologically

Women

National Women's Hall of Fame (www.greatwomen.org)
More than 150 American inductees into this prestigious hall of fame are individually profiled, along with information about the museum and educational resources.

Notable Women in American History: A Guide to Recommended Biographies and Autobiographies by Lynda G. Adamson (Westport, Conn.: Greenwood Press, 1999)
This easy-to-read reference recognizes 500 remarkable women, from every walk of life, in American history, from colonial America through 1998. Annotated biography and autobiography offerings published since 1970 are provided for each entry.

Notable Women in World History: A Guide to Recommended Biographies and Autobiographies by Lynda G. Adamson (Westport, Conn.: Greenwood Press, 1998)
Offered throughout is biographical data and annotated lists of recommended biographies, autobiographies, letter collections, and journals relating to the

lives of 500 of the most notable women in world history, from 1503 B.C. to the present.

Significant Contemporary American Feminists: A Biographical Sourcebook, edited by Jennifer Scanlon (Westport, Conn.: Greenwood Press, 1999)
This biographical reference recounts the lives and work of 50 leading feminists—grassroots organizers, playwrights, poets, politicians, scientists and theologians, among others—who have helped to develop the feminist movement in the United States. Coverage extends from the late 1960s into the 1990s.

Who's Who of American Women (Chicago: A.N. Marquis, 1959–)
More than 33,000 notable women and their professional accomplishments are profiled in this 1,172-page volume, including high-level federal officials, mayors, business leaders, elected and appointed state officials, and outstanding educators.

Women's Biographies: Distinguished Women of Past and Present (www.distinguishedwomen.com)
Biographical information, bibliographies, and links to related sites covering prominent women of cultural and historical significance are presented on this site, created and maintained by Danuta Bois. Profiled are artists, civil rights crusaders, entertainers, educators, heads of state, politicians, scientists, writers, and others. Sources can be searched by name or by subject.

BIOGRAPHICAL INFORMATION IN ELECTRONIC FORM

Many popular references, including biographical indexes, dictionaries, encyclopedias, and compilations, are also available in electronic form on CD-ROM through your library. (For additional titles, see Chapter 7, "Electronic Databases," under the heading "Biography.") CD-ROM creates a whole new world of possibilities for exploring biographical data, biographical essays, or biographical profiles of famous or relatively obscure figures.

Like their printed counterparts, the CD-ROM editions are authoritatively written and researched by professionals, including archivists, biographers, historians, genealogists, journalists, and scholars. The quality of these time-honored resources is only enhanced through the computerization of the material. Allowing instant access, most electronic versions enable you to quickly locate articles or interviews, browse indexes, search for records, and save or print results. They have proven to be essential reference and research tools for students and researchers.

In researching your subject, you may want to consider using the following CD-ROM editions offered through most libraries that subscribe to these services:

- Biography and Genealogy Master Index (CD-ROM), Gale Group, 1993
- Biography Indexing: A Cumulative Index to Biographical Material in Books and Magazines (CD-ROM), H.W. Wilson 1984–

- The Complete Marquis Who's Who Plus (CD-ROM), Reed Publishing, 1994–
- Dictionary of National Biography (CD-ROM), Oxford University Press, 1996–

BIOGRAPHICAL INFORMATION ONLINE

With the rapid expansion of the Internet has comes an explosion of virtual biographical Web sites, offering large and expandable databases, featuring biographies written on nearly every subject, from famous personalities to newsmakers to historical figures.

The evolution of this electronic form has caused many mainstream reference publishers to produce electronic versions of many of their traditional references that offer fast, easy access for researching your favorite subjects. Most publishers offer such databases for a fee by subscription, while others allow use of their online databases free of charge. To avoid paying a fee, check with your library to see if it offers the database that interests you.

Certainly, this technology is still evolving, but someday online information may be the norm for publishers and researchers, as printed volumes are much more costly to produce and distribute.

No matter what your subject or interest, you are likely to find the following online databases useful:

A&E's Biography (http://www.biography.com)
This, the official Web site for A&E's *Biography* series, features a massive searchable database called "Bio Search," that holds more than 25,000 short profiles and basic biographical information of famous and notable persons past and present. A complete alphabetical listing of names in the database is also provided. The site also includes an online store from which you can purchase videos of past broadcasts of *Biography* episodes.

American National Biography Online (ANB Online) (www.anb.org/)
Based on the award-winning reference book of the same name, the online version features 18,000 fully searchable biographies, thousands of illustrations, and 80,000 hyperlinked cross-references on subjects in its database. New biographies are added quarterly (January, April, July, and, October), including articles on recently deceased figures who were not subjects in the print edition. Biographies and bibliographies are regularly updated to incorporate new facts and sources used. You can search the contents of ANB Online by full text, subject name, gender, occupation, birth date, birthplace, death date, and contributor name, if known. This easy-to-use database also includes hypertext links to other subjects within ANB and to select non-ANB Web sites relevant to your subject.

Biographical Dictionary (http://www.s9.com/biography/)
This award-winning online dictionary contains biographies of more than 28,000 notable men and women since the earliest days of humankind to the present day. Subjects can be searched by year of birth, year deceased, professions and positions held, literary and artistic works, achievements, and other keywords.

Biography and Genealogy Master Index (www.gale.com)
Like its long-running printed counterpart, this subscription service database is a good place to start looking for biographical material on people from all time periods, geographical locations, and fields of endeavor. Entries include current sources and retrospective works of individuals, both living and deceased, with citations from published sources, including dictionaries, who's whos, subject encyclopedias, literary criticism, and other sources.

Biography Index (www.hwwilson.com)
Available by subscription, this searchable database features biographical information originally published in more than 2,700 English-language periodicals, in all subject areas, contained in indexes published by H.W. Wilson.

Biography Reference Desk (http://www.hwwilson.com)
Offering access to full-text articles on more than 400,000 people, this subscription-only site contains the online content of Wilson Biographies Plus Illustrated and the complete Biography Index database.

Biography Resource Center (www.gale.com/BiographyRC/)
Easily accessible to subscribers are full-text biographies, personal facts (such as gender, ethnicity, occupation, nationality, and so on), and quick reference information on more than 300,000 noteworthy individuals from all disciplines—arts, business, entertainment, government, history, literature, politics, sports, and more—from around the world. Contents are culled from more than 760 volumes of Gale Group reference sources, including 90 of the most consulted biographical references. Among the references used are *The Complete Marquis Who's Who, Contemporary Artists, Contemporary Authors, Contemporary Dramatists, Dictionary of American Biography, Scribner's Encyclopedia of American Lives,* and *Encyclopedia of World Biography,* plus newspaper and magazine articles. Fully reprinted articles from more than 250 magazines, covering a broad range of subject areas, are also featured. You can search subjects based on one or more personal fact, such as birth and death year, ethnicity, gender, nationality, or occupation, or combine criteria to create a custom search.

BUBL LINK (www.bubl.ac.uk/link/types.biographies.htm)
Catalogs more than 100 international subjects, ranging from famous bohemian authors, to popular composers, to presidents, to memorable women mathematicians, with links to Web sites devoted to each, free of charge.

Current Biography Illustrated (http://www.hwwilson.com)
Searchable database, available by subscription, of more than 25,000 articles on figures from 1940 to the present, plus more than 19,500 photographs, originally published in *Current Biography* magazine. Biographies averaging 2,500 words cover celebrities, politicians, businesspeople, writers, actors, sports figures, artists, scientists, and many others. Article sources and references accompany each profile, providing opportunities for further research. Each year another 450 new profiles are added to the database, which is updated monthly.

Current Biography, 1940–Present (http://www.hwwilson.com)
By-subscription online version of the library reference series, offering the same content, without illustrations, with searchable database.

Dictionary of Literary Biography (www.gale.com)
Online companion available by subscription to the printed edition that provides fast, easy access to biographical information on the world's most influential literary figures, culled from the series' more than 280 bound volumes. Written by recognized scholars in their respective fields, entries offer biographical and analytical coverage of each subject and their literary achievements. Online tools enable researchers to examine writers in relation to their work as well as in a historical context. Profiles are continuously updated for currency.

Encyclopaedia Britannica Online (http://www.eb.com/)
Current biographies of famous and historical figures and hundreds of articles not found in the printed edition on virtually any subject. The online edition, available by subscription, also includes the complete *Merriam-Webster's Collegiate Dictionary* and the *Britannica Book of the Year* (1994–), plus thousands of Web links selected, rated, and reviewed by *Britannica* editors.

Grove Dictionary of Art (http://www.groveart.com)
Offered by subscription, this dictionary includes information on notable artists and all aspects of the visual arts, covered in full-text journal articles and entries in standard reference works. Updated monthly, coverage also includes information on artistic techniques, worldwide art, and other related topics.

Grove Music (www.grovemusic.com)
Provides comprehensive coverage of music and biographies of artists from all genres, past and present. You can browse articles or search subjects by name. Links are also provided to related Web sites.

InfoPlease (www.infoplease.com)
This popular free online almanac features 30,000 searchable biographies on people in the news from all walks of life.

Literature Resource Center (www.gale.com)
Provides access by subscription to biographies, bibliographies, and critical analysis on 2,500 of the most studied authors from more than 70 literary periodicals. Included are full-text articles, essays, and links to Web sites. Content is derived from such long-standing published references as *Contemporary Authors, Dictionary of Literary Biography* and others.

Lives, the Biography Resource (http://amillionlives.com)
Claiming distinction as the largest guide to biography sites on the Web, Lives features extensive indexes and links, free of charge, to thousands of biographical materials, including biographies, autobiographies, memoirs, diaries, letters, oral histories, and more on individual lives of the famous, the infamous, and the not famous, now deceased.

Oxford Dictionary of National Biography (http://www.oup.com)
Online companion to the printed edition, available by subscription, featuring 50,000 biographies of men and women who have shaped all aspects of the British past from the printed edition.

Wilson Biographies Plus Illustrated (http://www.hwwilson.com)
One of the most comprehensive databases of its kind, available by subscription, featuring the entire content of *Current Biography Illustrated,* the database contains profiles of more than 110,000 well-known figures and 32,000 images.

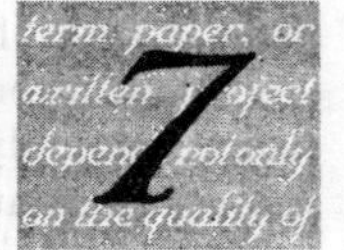

Finding CD-ROM Collections

Any book about research would be considered incomplete unless it contained a chapter about popular CD-ROM collections. Even though CD-ROM isn't the revolutionary force it once was to collect and store data, sounds, and images, since many databases today are being produced over the Internet and accessed by libraries by subscription, CD-ROM remains a viable format used by many libraries and the public. Compatible with all computers, CD-ROM is still a fast, efficient way to access a multitude of facts, information, and multimedia images combined on one or many discs.

RESEARCHING CD-ROM COLLECTIONS

Working with CD-ROM collections is very similar to working with Internet databases licensed by your library. In most—but not all—cases, depending on the product, you can search by keyword or subject for full-text articles, maps, drawings, photos, or historical time lines, to support your essay, term paper, or written project. As with any electronic database, searching a CD-ROM collection has its limits. Enter a query and work with different keyword or subject combinations when searching them. More than likely, your search will produce favorable results so long as you use keywords that are compatible with the system. (For more information on searching, see the category, "Searching Your Topic," in Chapter 1.)

As with any licensed database or collection, some CD-ROM collections are available only for patron or student use. Check with your library regarding restrictions or limitations regarding access and use.

LOCATING CD-ROM COLLECTIONS

With so many thousands of CD-ROM collections offered today, finding a relevant source is easy. Just as you would to find a popular book, the best way to locate any CD-ROM title is to search your library's online catalog.

When accessing the catalog, to search by keyword, simply enter "CD-ROM" with the subject (with AND as a search connector) to retrieve records in the library's database (example: "aviation AND CD-ROM"), then hit enter. Your search will retrieve records of any interactive CD-ROM titles that your library offers in your area of interest.

In addition to the library's online catalog, several other sources are published annually or semiannually in print and CD-ROM form that provide more information on CD-ROM collections and databases. This includes information about specific CD-ROM titles that your library may not carry but which are used by libraries around the world. They include:

CD-ROM Finder: The World of CD-ROM Products for Information Seekers (Medford, N.J.: Learned Information, Inc., 1993–)
This annually updated directory contains overviews of new CD-ROM products.

CD-ROMs in Print (Westport, Conn.: Meckler, 1987–)
Updated semiannually and available in both print and CD-ROM editions (the latter called CD-ROMs in Print Plus), this resource reviews more than 16,000 CD-ROM titles of every discipline, including multimedia, laserdisc, and electronic products.

Gale Directory of CD-ROM Databases (Detroit: Gale Research, 2004–)
Profiles more than 4,000 CD-ROM database products updated semiannually.

POPULAR TITLES BY SUBJECT

Whether you're interested in finding out more information about a developing-world country, a popular U.S. president, or current statistical data, your library no doubt will offer many CD-ROM collections to suit your particular need. Widely available at most libraries is the following list of popular titles by subject (excluding major licensed online or CD-ROM indexes and databases offering citations, abstracts, and full-text articles featured in Chapter 8).

Biography

Finding biographical information about famous people, including actors, authors, politicians, and sports figures, is a snap, thanks to a remarkable selection of CD-ROM titles, such as:

Complete Marquis Who's Who (New Providence, N.J.: Marquis Who's Who, Inc., 1999)
Multimedia collection encompassing 20 volumes of the *Marquis Who's Who's* library providing access to more than 768,000 biographies of major figures in all areas and fields—active, retired, or deceased—from 1607 to the present.

Contemporary Authors (Detroit, Mich.: Gale Research, 1997–)
Also available as a Web database, this annual CD-ROM edition of the long-running book series includes biographical and bibliographical information on more than 100,000 contemporary writers.

Current Biography (New York: H.W. Wilson, 1996)
This CD-ROM delivers full-text biographies and obituaries of famous actors, artists, businesspeople, journalists, politicians, scientists, sports figures, and

other prominent people in the news that have appeared in the print version of *Current Biography Yearbook* since 1940.

Dictionary of American Biography (New York: Charles Scribner's Sons, 1995)
This 21-volume set includes full-text biographical information on nearly 19,000 notable Americans who died before December 31, 1980.

Encyclopedia of World Biography (Detroit: Mich.: Gale Research, 1999)
Based on the popular print edition, this multimedia disc features biographical information on 7,200 individuals, including world-renowned personalities in all fields, from ancient times to the present.

Business and Economics

Whether you are interested in obtaining financial data, company profiles, company history, or ownership information on thousands of American businesses or statistical and economic data by industry, manufacturer, or country you may want to try the following choices:

Compact Disclosure (Bethesda, Md.: Disclosure Inc., 1989–)
Updated monthly, this CD-ROM edition, also available via the Internet, features profiles and information on more than 12,000 public companies mostly compiled from data filed with the Securities and Exchange Commission (SEC). Covering data for the past five years, records include business descriptions, ownership data, subsidiary names, financial data, and more.

DRI/McGraw-Hill Encyclopedia of World Economics (New York: McGraw-Hill Professional Book Group, 1995)
Comprehensively covers all major world economies, including those of post-communist nations; updated semiannually.

Dun's Business Locator (Dun & Bradstreet, current)
Contains more than 10 million name listings and comprehensive business information on major companies, including company name, address, phone number, and much more.

Economic Census CD-ROM (Washington, D.C.: U.S. Department of Commerce, Bureau of the Census, Data User Services Division, 1995–)
First published in 1995, this annually updated source covers U.S. Census figures from 1992 to the present.

The Illustrated Book of World Rankings (New York: M.E. Sharpe, 2001)
This essential resource, last updated to the year 2000, evaluates and compares the position of each country to its counterparts by various rankings—geography, climate, population, religion, politics, and more, including hard-to-find statistics and international data.

International Financial Statistics (New York: International Monetary Fund, 1948–)
Based on the print copy published monthly since 1948, this CD-ROM version reports international statistics for more than 200 International Monetary Fund member countries on all aspects of international and domestic

finance. Data covered include inflation, deflation, exchange rates, interest rates, production, prices, national accounts, and international transactions, including tables of this information by country. Also offered in a printed edition.

UNIDO Industrial Statistics Database (New York: UNIDO, 2003)
Provides industrial statistics for 29 industries in the manufacturing sector. Presented by country, year, and the International Standard Industrial Classification of All Economic Activities (SIC) category, information includes number of establishments, employment, number of female employees, wages and salaries, output, and production indexes.

Demographic Studies and Statistics

Demographics and statistics, such as birth and death rates or population and life expectancy data can be useful in any research paper. Census data, state and county data, government spending figures, regional and national economic statistics, and more are accessible on CD-ROMs. Among them:

Budget of the United States Government (Washington, D.C.: Executive Office of the President, Office of Management and Budget: Superintendent of Documents, U.S. Government Printing Office, 1995–)
Presents all data and information regarding the annual budget for the U.S. federal government, including historical tables and spreadsheets for comparisons.

Consolidated Federal Funds Report (Washington, D.C.: U.S. Department of Commerce, Bureau of the Census, Data User Services Division, 1994–)
Lists federal government expenditures and expense obligations of state, county and subcounty areas throughout the United States. The CD-ROM version is compatible with the printed version, available to consumers.

County and City Data Book (Washington, D.C.: U.S. Department of Commerce, Bureau of the Census, Data User Service Division, 1989–)
Features demographic, economic, and governmental data for the U.S. federal government and private agencies.

Demographic Yearbook Historical Supplement 1948–1997 (New York: United Nations, 2000)
This first electronic version of *Demographic Yearbook* is the single most complete source of official demographic statistics for all countries and areas of the world. Statistics cover 50 years of data for 229 countries or areas from 1948 to 1997. Fully annotated data covers population, birth, life expectancy, death, and other vital statistics, plus easy-to-use data tables for analysis.

Historical Statistics of the United States (Washington, D.C.: Bureau of the Census, 1949–)
CD-based product providing statistics in full text on the United States from colonial times to 1970 covering population, health, labor, income, price indexes, and much more.

National Economic, Social & Environmental (NESE) Data Bank (Washington, D.C.: NESE Databank/U.S. Department of Commerce, 1992–95)
Includes on CD-ROM complete data on the U.S. budget, economics, education, justice, and population, among others. This data bank also offers text

versions of popular government publications, including *The Economic Report of the President* and *Health United States.*

National Trade Data Bank (NTDB) (Washington, D.C.: U.S. Department of Commerce, Economics and Statistics Administration, Office of Business Analysis, 1990–)
Features two separate databases—NTDB (Reports) and NTDB (Foreign Traders). The Reports database provides full text and data from more than 100,000 U.S. government publications covering the subject of international trade. The Foreign Traders database offers information on more than 12,000 U.S. companies interested in exporting and foreign importers. Also covered are agents and distributors of interest to U.S. companies who want to export.

REIS: Regional Economic Information System (Washington, D.C.: U.S. Department of Commerce, Economics and Statistics Administration, Bureau of Economic Analysis, Regional Economic Measurement Division, 1990–)
This disc provides economic data, including industry earnings, employment, and personal income for local areas from 1969 to 1992.

School District Data Book (U.S. Department of Education, 1990)
Features data culled from the 1990 census, the National Center for Education Statistics Common Core of Data, and the Census Survey of Local Government Finance on CD-ROM.

Statistical Abstract of the United States (Washington, D.C.: U.S. Department of Commerce, Economics and Statistics Administration, Bureau of the Census, Data User Services Division, 1993–)
Annually updated collection of statistics and tables that are not available in the print edition.

U.S. Census of Population and Housing (Washington, D.C.: U.S. Department of Commerce, Economics and Statistics Administration, Bureau of the Census, 1992–)
The census is conducted every 10 years by the U.S. Census Bureau. This CD-ROM collection features the latest data and statistics on the characteristics of the population of the United States.

USA Counties (Washington, D.C.: U.S. Department of Commerce, Bureau of the Census, Data User Services Division, 1992–)
Highlights data on every county and 15 federal and private agencies from June 1992 to the present.

USA Trade (Washington, D.C.: STAT-USA and U.S. Bureau of the Census, Foreign Trade Division, Department of Commerce, 1998–)
Contains data including statistics and economics concerning the value and quantity of commodities imported or exported, from 1991 to 1995, in this historical database produced by the U.S. Census Bureau.

World Data (Washington, D.C.: The World Bank, 1994)
Features economic data on more than 200 countries through 1995. Information concerning debt, finance, natural resources, social resources, and trade,

along with current social indicators of development and world debt tables data are included.

Encyclopedias

In addition to their printed volumes, many publishers of encyclopedic works have made CD-ROM versions available through most libraries. Thanks to technology, these electronic versions, offer many more research choices, with cross-reference links and search options, than their printed counterparts ever could. They include:

Britannica CD (Chicago: Encyclopaedia Britannica, 1997–)
Latest CD version of this award-winning encyclopedia containing the full 44-million-word text of the multivolume hardcover version.

Deluxe Compton's Interactive Encyclopedia (Cambridge, Mass.: The Learning Company, Inc., 1997–)
Includes more than 40,000 articles and information on important events, more than 8,000 photos, 600 sound clips (including music and historic speeches), 100 videos, animations, and slide shows. Special features include Exploratorium Interactive Science Activities, offering links to 22 Web-browser based science lessons, San Francisco's acclaimed children's science museum, and 360 IPIX Views, providing 360-degree virtual tours and panoramic views of noted places such as the ancient ruins at Machu Picchu and the International Space Station. Another added feature is Planetarium, which provides spectacular views of the night sky from any location on any date of the year. Other unique features are multimedia explorations of ancient civilizations, outer space, and beyond, a feature called "On This Date" that taps into a treasure trove of historical information, and "Neighborhood Resources," which offers information on nearby museums, zoos, libraries and more. Also included is a 100,000-word dictionary and thesaurus.

Encyclopedia Americana (Danbury, Conn.: Grolier, 1996–)
Contains the complete, updated contents of the 30-volume, more-than-25-million-word printed version of the *Encyclopedia Americana,* featuring more than 45,000 articles and 2,000 illustrations in black-and-white and in color. Also offered is the complete *Merriam-Webster's Collegiate Dictionary,* providing definitions for more than 15,000 words, lists of common abbreviations, signs and symbols, lists of foreign terms, biographies, and more. Other CD-ROM components include Helicon Publishing Company's *Chronology of World History,* covering ancient, medieval, and modern periods of world history; and the Academic Press *Dictionary of Science & Technology,* offering more than 130,000 entries covering 124 fields of science. In addition to this CD-ROM edition, there is an online version that is equally comprehensive.

Infopedia 2.0 (Cambridge, Mass.: SoftKey, 1995–)
One of the most complete multimedia encyclopedias and references available, featuring the entire 29-volume *Funk & Wagnalls New Encyclopedia,* plus seven essential reference books. They include *Roget's 21st-Century Thesaurus, Hammond World Atlas, 1995 World Almanac & Book of Facts, Merriam-Webster's Dictionary, Merriam-Webster's Dictionary of Quotations, Merriam-Webster's Dictionary of English Usage,* and *Webster's New Biographical Dictionary.* More than 200,000 entries are covered, featuring more than 5,000 photo-

graphs, 150 videos and animations, more than 2,100 maps, flags, charts, and tables, and more than 450 sound clips.

Grolier Multimedia Encyclopedia (Danbury, Conn.: Grolier Electronic Pub., 1995–)
Intelligently organized two-CD-ROM set that complements the multivolume hardcover version. A plethora of engaging pictures, videos and sounds, from actual recordings to musical excerpts, accompanies more than 39,000 informative articles, divided into basic categories such as geography, history, language and literature, performing arts, and others. Numerous time lines, and links to online sources are also provided, including online versions of *Grolier's Encyclopedia Americana* and its *Book of Knowledge.* Researchers using this CD-ROM edition can access Grolier's Research Center to choose a topic, organize research, write the paper, and find article links and lists of supporting resources for 140 of the most frequently researched subjects for all grade levels. In addition, an Internet index lists more than 108,000 online resources. Other easy-to-use tools include a built-in atlas with 1,200 maps, a dictionary, and a thesaurus.

Microsoft Encarta 2004 Encyclopedia Deluxe (Redmond, Wash.: Microsoft, 2003)
Contains the full text of *Funk & Wagnalls New Encyclopedia,* plus 1,000 additional articles, multimedia images, and search engine.

Webster's New International Encyclopedia (Oxford, U.K.: Attica Interactive, Helicon Publishing, Ltd.,; Chatsworth, Calif.: Cambrix Publishing Inc., 1998)
Placing greater emphasis on global topics and personalities, this new international edition features more than 39,000 hyperlinks, thousands of photos, videos, and illustrations, more than 13,000 time lines of world history, and a wide range of subjects, including global cultures, international business, natural history, science, sports, technology, and world history. Also contained on this useful multimedia reference is a complete world atlas.

World Book Encyclopedia 2003 Ultra-Deluxe Edition (Chicago: World Book, 2003)
A suite of six publications on seven discs, this collection includes the full content of the 22-volume *World Book Encyclopedia,* the *World Book Encyclopedia of People and Places,* and the *World Book Encyclopedia of Science.* This user-friendly, interactive resource boasts 22,300 easy-to-use articles, 1,400 maps, more than 9,600 illustrations, 117 videos, 781 audio clips, and 129 panoramic views covering global and historical topics, headline-making personalities, and useful, up-to-date information from the beginning of ancient civilization to the present. In addition, more than 1,850 tables and time lines with charts can be created. A fully interactive *World Book Dictionary* with more than 245,000 definitions and a searchable database is included, along with online encyclopedia updates to access the most current information.

General References

Many general reference works, including almanacs, dictionaries, encyclopedias, and books of quotations, are offered on CD-ROM, sometimes bundled with other well-known reference titles. Some common titles are:

Microsoft Bookshelf (Redmond, Wash.: Microsoft, 1999)
Offers popular general references, including the *American Heritage Dictionary, Concise Columbia Encyclopedia, Columbia Dictionary of Quotations, The People's Chronology, Roget's Thesaurus,* and *The World Almanac and Book of Facts.*

Multimedia World Factbook (Parsippany, N.J.: Bureau Development, 1991)
Presents information and vital statistics on the people, geography, government, communications, defense forces, and economy of every country in the world. Featuring an advanced user interface and powerful search and retrieval engine, content is divided into 10 major regions, with maps, flags, and national anthems of each country, and facts and statistics that you can print or cut and paste into a word processor program. An extensive database with query tool that allows you to export information is also featured, along with the complete text of the *CIA World Factbook.*

The Penguin Hutchinson Reference Library (Oxford, U.K: Helicon Publishing Ltd.; Chatsworth, Calif.: Cambrix Publishing Inc., 1998)
Offers seven general references on a single CD-ROM, providing access to a vast array of encyclopedia articles (25,000 in all), facts, figures, information, quotations, word definitions, and global historical events facts. Handsomely illustrated, this reference pack includes 13,500 time lines, thousands of cross-referenced links, more than 8 million words, and a full word search of all seven titles. Featured on this disk are the *Hutchinson Encyclopedia,* a complete cross-reference resource; the *Longman Dictionary of the English Language,* with more than 220,000 definitions; *The New Penguin Dictionary of Quotations,* featuring 10,000 quotations and 2,000 sources; and *The Chronology of World History,* from 10,000 B.C. to the present). Also included are *Roget's Thesaurus; Usage and Abusage,* a guide to correct usage of words; and the *Helicon Book of Days,* covering important events for each day of the year.

The Way Things Work (New York: Dorling Kindersley Multimedia, 1994)
Electronic version of a visual dictionary of more than 70,000 inventions; based on the best-selling book of the same name.

The World Reference Pack (New York: Dorling Kindersley Multimedia, 1995)
This three-CD-ROM reference set provides a portrait of the world, its people, and history, past and present. Three other references are included: *Cartopedia: The Ultimate World Atlas* offers interactive digital maps and worldwide demographic and statistical information; *Chronicle of the 20th Century* covers day-by-day the people, places, and events in history; *Eyewitness History of the World* uncovers the human history, including different civilizations, historical events, and people from the first humans to present key figures.

Law and Government

Laws, facts, figures, and historical documents of governments throughout the world are accessible in a wide range of sources by subject area. They include:

CIA World Factbook (Minneapolis, Minn.: Quanta Press, 1998)
Revised annually; contains facts and figures on more than 200 countries and territories.

The Constitution Papers (United States: Reflective Arts International, 1987)
Includes visual representations of the most famous documents in U.S. history, including the Articles of Confederation, the Constitution, the Declaration of Independence, the Federalist Papers, the Mayflower Compact, the Magna Carta, and much more.

Exegy: The Source for Current World Information (Santa Barbara, Calif.: ABC-CLIO, 1994–)
Features biographies and information on countries, events, and organizations with up-to-date versions issued bimonthly.

U.S. Code Annotated (St. Paul, Minn.: West Pub. Co., 1996–)
Provides complete text of the U.S. Constitution, court rules, decisions, federal regulations, legislative notes, and references.

Health and Medicine

Health issues and medical topics are detailed in a number of popular electronic resources. Among them are:

Family Medical Reference Library (New York: Dorling Kindersley, 2000)
Provides fast access to medical information, from symptoms to diagnosis of more than 650 diseases and disorders. Includes practical health information, nutrition and wellness tips, and a glossary of more than 700 prescription drugs. Also features three-dimensional human skeleton focusing on bones and joints.

Mosby's Medical Encyclopedia: The Complete Home Medical Reference (Cambridge, Mass.: The Learning Company, 1997)
Offers essential information on nearly 20,000 medical definitions and a wide range of health care topics, including health problems and treatments, pregnancy, pediatrics, and prescription and over-the-counter drugs, plus thousands of charts, illustrations, audio clips, and videos.

History

An unbelievable wealth of electronic resources documenting world and U.S. history, including culture, historical events, world conflicts, political, religious, and social issues both past and present, are well represented on CD-ROM. As there are far more resources to list than space will allow, the following is a starting point:

American History Explorer (Mountain View, Calif.: Parsons Technology, 1996)
This multimedia CD-ROM collection contains more than 1,300 articles, 85 historical documents (the Articles of Confederation and presidential addresses) and more than 1,000 photos, drawings, paintings, and cartoons,

culled from libraries and historical sites, covering early American history through the post–Civil War period. Some historical presentations are supplemented with film and music. The main menu item, "Source Book," enables access to 1,300 definitions and brief articles. Most articles concern places, events, and political figures in history. Special attention is given to the history of African Americans, business, culture, Native Americans, and women. Copious links are included among articles and between articles and pictures. The "Time Trek" feature makes time lines accessible for eight periods in history, from "Exploration" through "Reconstruction," along with links to relevant articles, maps, and documents for each year. A searchable index is also included.

CD Sourcebook of American History (Mesa, Ariz.: Candlelight Publishing and Infobases International, 1992)
Award-winning reference tool containing 20,000 pages of historical documents and illustrated histories, covering the pre-Columbian voyages through World War I.

Chronicle Encyclopedia of History (New York: DK Multimedia, 1997)
A collection of 4 million years of articles, films, music, quotation, animations, artworks, and themed overviews chronicling the history of humankind. Every civilization and culture, dynasty and disaster, discovery and breakthrough, industry and empire, revolution and republic, triumph and travesty, and global conflict of the modern world is fully documented. Built-in links, search screens, browsable highlights in history, popup screens to read history by era, by decade, by month, or by year, and moment-by-moment updates of world history as it happens are among the outstanding research tools on this disk. Biographies of history's "100 most influential" figures, time lines, three-dimensional interactive tour of world history, animated maps, sound clips, videos, photographs, and artworks are likewise included.

Chronicle of the 20th Century (New York: DK Multimedia, 1996)
Based on the best-selling book of the same name, this complete interactive guide covers the century's people, places, events, fads and fashions, politics and personalities, wars, sports, science, and cinema. More than 6,000 stories, including biographies and themed articles, combined with 3,000 photos, scores of video and audio clips, and a host of interactive features, highlight this informative and entertaining volume. Written in a lively, "you are there" style, news entries for every single day (all 34,000 of them) of the century detail the major events of the past century. For additional research, built-in links take you to the publisher's Web site where you can look up more related articles and information on subjects of 20th-century life.

The Complete National Geographic: 108 Years of National Geographic Magazine (Washington, D.C.: National Geographic Interactive; Novato, Calif.: Distributed by Mindscape, 1997)
Features 9,400 fascinating articles and more than 192,000 pages of photographs that you can browse, search, and print, covering the most memorable moments and discoveries of the 20th century as reported by *National Geographic* magazine. This 32-disk, 10-volume set, arranged by decade, details more than 100 years of newsmakers and newsmaking events, from the 1906

San Francisco earthquake to the aftermath of the Gulf War. Users also have access to *National Geographic's* online resource center.

Famous American Speeches: A Multimedia History, 1850 to the Present (Phoenix, Ariz., Oryx Press, 1996–)
Multimedia collection, searchable by subject, of hundreds of famous speeches, speakers, and time lines, combining audio clips, photographs, and video clips in United States history from 1850 to the present.

Freedman's Bank Records (Salt Lake City, Utah: Intellectual Reserve, Inc.: Church of Jesus Christ of Latter-day Saints, 2000)
Contains documents, names, and information on African-American ancestry on approximately 480,000 freed slaves during and after the Civil War from 1864 to 1871.

Keesing's Record of World Events (Harlow, Essex: Longman Information & Reference; New York: Stockton Press, 1960–1972)
Keyword-searchable electronic digest on events of global importance, 1960 to the present, including assassinations, coups, economic trends, elections, natural disasters, political appointments, and wars.

Multimedia World History (Parsippany, N.J.: Bureau of Electronic Pub., 1994)
Comprehensively covers selected texts, narration, audio clips, animations, photographs, moving pictures and still graphics, biographies of the greatest figures in world history and the most important events in the history of world civilization. With an advanced user interface and powerful search engine, this multimedia reference also features five videos of world events exclusively produced for this CD-ROM edition.

20th Century Day by Day (New York: DK Interactive Learning, 1999)
Features more than 6,000 news stories, 110 biographies, 90 archival videos, and 70 video clips.

World History: 20th Century (New York: MultiEducator, Inc.)
Examines the tragedies, triumphs, regional conflicts, progress, and peace of the 20th century. Included are six fully narrated regional chronologies, featuring time lines and entries on major events in different parts of the world. Other features include biographies of 200 important historical figures of the 20th century, bibliographical references, a world chronology, and nearly 100 video clips.

Literature

Whether you are trying to find examples of classic literature, poetry, or great quotations, the following resources should do the trick:

Bookscope (Woodbridge, Conn.: Primary Source Media, 1995)
Searchable database of more than 350,000 current book titles with direct access provided to table of contents information on each entry.

Books in Print with Book Reviews Plus (New Providence, N.J.: Bowker Electronic Pub., 1998–)
A CD-ROM companion to the printed library edition, updated monthly, listing more than 840,000 books currently in print and 85,000 book reviews.

Columbia Granger's World of Poetry (New York: Columbia University Press, 1995)
Features a complete text of 10,000 poems and popular quotations, with a searchable index.

Gale's Quotations: Who Said What? (New York: Gale Research, 1995)
A collection of more than 117,000 quotations, from ancient times to the present, searchable by author, speaker, and more.

Greatest Books Collection (Irvine, Calif.: World Library, 1996)
Features full text of 150 works from history, literature, philosophy, poetry, religion, and science.

Performing Arts (Drama, Film, Music, Television, and Theater)

Everything you want to know about your favorite actor, composer, musician, movie or television show, are among the bevy of information available through countless electronic resources, from indexes and abstracts to full-text articles. Some top choices in the field are:

The Hutchinson Encyclopedia of Music (Oxford, U.K.: Helicon Publishing Ltd.)
Considered the most comprehensive, authoritative, interactive music encyclopedia ever published on CD-ROM, this encyclopedia covers all genres and performers from all decades of music. Enhanced by 200 photographs, more than 500 music clips, and more than 400 musical quotations, approximately 11,000 entries with 1,000 hyperlinks are presented, in A-to-Z format. Of these, 1,800 focus on early music, 3,000 on opera, and 4,000 on the greatest 20th-century music personalities. Topics cover a wide range of musical interests, including chamber music, composer and musician biographies, instrument families, musical terms and translations, operas, and solo works. Summaries of stage and concert works, as well as chronologies of more than 2,500 music landmarks covering the developments and performers from the 20th century are also included. Links to photographs, musical instrument sounds, orchestral clips and recorded music staves are provided.

Microsoft Cinemania (Redmond, Wash.: Microsoft, 1995)
This entertaining multimedia interactive guide on movies and moviemakers contains filmographies of more than 10,000 personalities and profiles of more than 4,500 directors, writers, and other movie professionals. Also featured are more than 1,000 photographs from some of the great moments in film history, 150 movie dialogue clips, 30 video clips, 800 in-depth reviews, and more than 90,000 extensive cast and credit listings of classic and contemporary movies from Cinebooks' *Motion Picture Guide.* In addition, articles are reprinted from Baseline's *The Encyclopedia of Film,* James Monaco's *How to Read a Film,* and Ephraim Katz's *The Film Encyclopedia.* Critical reviews of thousands of films are also provided, written by well-known critics Roger Ebert, Pauline Kael, and Leonard Maltin.

Total Television CD-ROM (New York: Byron Preiss Multimedia/Simon & Schuster Interactive/Penguin Putnam, 1996)
Based on the book by Alex McNeil, this CD-ROM version exhaustively chronicles more than 7,000 daytime, prime time, syndicated, and cable programs complemented by video clips and still photos. Supplementary material includes the history of the Emmy Awards (reprinted from Thomas O'Neill's book, *The Emmys*), a year-by-year, night-by-night grid of each network's prime time line-up of shows from 1948 through the end of the 1995–96 season, and indexes cross-referencing nearly every series that ever aired. This fully searchable interactive edition also features a fun and informative multimedia tour of television history, hosted by Ron Simon, curator of television for the Museum of Television and Radio. All performers, writers, directors, and producers in the electronic version are conveniently indexed and information is easily retrievable simply by clicking on their name.

Phone Directories

Even though the Internet has become a popular method for looking up phone numbers and addresses of individuals and businesses, many CD-ROM resources, available to libraries, offer instant access to millions of residential and business listings. Most are searchable by name or type of business. They are:

American Yellow Pages (Omaha, Nebr.: American Business Information, 1994–)
Lists complete addresses, phone numbers, and fax numbers for 10 million U.S. businesses. Searchable by type of business or company name. Updated monthly.

11 Million Businesses Phone Directory (Omaha, Nebr.: American Business Information, 1995–)
Presents business listings that can be searched by company name and phone number. Database does not include complete addresses of each entry.

PhoneDisc Business Pro (Bethesda, Md.: Digital Directory Assistance, 1996–)
Features 9.5 million businesses listed by company name, SIC code, street address, and telephone number, updated quarterly.

PhoneDisc PowerFinder (Bethesda, Md.: Digital Directory Assistance, 1996–)
This powerful database features 91 million business and residential listings. Updated quarterly, entries can be searched by name, portions of address, telephone number, and type of business.

PhoneDisc USA Residential (Bethesda, Md.: Digital Directory Assistance, 1994–)
Contains 81 million residential listings searchable by name only.

70 Million Households Phone Book (Omaha, Nebr.: American Business Information, 1994–)
Features residential phone numbers verified using public records.

Religion

History, doctrine, formation, theology, theories, viewpoints, perspectives, and every other aspect of most religions throughout the world are well documented in a number of electronic resources. They include:

The Encyclopedia Judaica CD (New York: Macmillan, 1997)
Fully integrates all the text, articles, and information of the original 16-volume edition, with powerful search capabilities and an interactive time line covering the legacy of the Jewish people. Jewish existence is chronicled by 2,200 contributing authors and 250 editors around the world in 25,000 articles that provide a comprehensive picture of Jewish life. Thousands of photos and additional graphic elements, including videos, slide shows, music, maps, charts, and tables, plus 100,000 hyperlinks to information, round out this presentation of the Jewish world and civilization.

The Encyclopedia of Religion (New York: Macmillan Library Reference, 1996)
Emphasizing "religion's role within everyday life and as unique experience from culture to culture," this keyword-searchable multimedia version of the 16-volume reference series includes 2,734 articles on religion.

Master Christian Library V.8 (AGES Software, 1996–)
Offers a wealth of information on Christian literature, from great historical books to reference works—more than 500 resources in all, including Bibles, biographies, commentaries, dictionaries, histories, maps, quotations, and word studies. Text and pages can be copied and pasted into word processing documents, printed from the screen, and material is searchable using keywords or phrases.

Science

Scientific discoveries, new research, and the latest developments in all sciences are thoroughly covered on several highly acclaimed CD-ROM collections, including:

The Hutchinson Science Library (Oxford, U.K.: Helicon Publishing Ltd.)
Contains six multimedia references highlighting the great scientific discoveries and latest developments in every scientific field: *The Hutchinson Chronology of Science, The Hutchinson Dictionary of Science, The Hutchinson Dictionary of Scientists, The Hutchinson Natural History Dictionary, The Hutchinson Concise Dictionary of Medicine,* and *The Hutchinson Concise Dictionary of Computing and Multimedia*. Published in association with the Science Museum of London, this unique resource offers 13,000 biographies of scientists from the past and present, highlighted by more than 1,000 illustrations. Time lines of more than 2,500 key events and discoveries are easily accessible, and more than 1 million words and 10,000 dictionary entries are fully searchable. All six books can be searched individually or together in any combination as well.

Multimedia Encyclopedia of Science & Technology (New York: McGraw-Hill, 1999)
Containing 7,300 articles, 105,100 scientific terms, study guides for biology, chemistry, engineering, geosciences, health sciences, and physics, 550 illustrations from the McGraw-Hill *Encyclopedia of Science & Technology, 7th Edition,* and scientific terms from the McGraw-Hill *Dictionary of Scientific and Technical Terms, 5th Edition.* Includes additional material created especially for this CD-ROM edition.

Women's Studies

Resources for women's studies, cover a wide range of issues important to women. Recommended are:

United Nations Women's Indicators and Statistics Database (New York: United Nations, 1991–)
Authoritatively compiles international statistics covering 212 countries in all areas of the world. Some 1,600 statistical series, covering 1970–93, are represented.

Women's Studies on Disc (New York, N.Y.: G.K. Hall & Co., Macmillan Library Reference, 1995–)
Covers a broad range of periodical literature and topics, including education, gender issues, feminist art, literature, and popular culture of interest to women. Approximately 20,000 journal citations are covered, mostly from American publications. This includes material such as scholarly articles, book reviews, and many others.

Finding Electronic Databases

Another popular tool used for research is electronic databases delivered on CD-ROM or over the Internet. Licensed or sold to public, school, and university libraries, these databases store large amounts of electronic data, including abstracts, full-text articles, graphics, audio and video files, for easy reference. Due to their substantial content and easy accessibility, full-text databases appeal to a wide range of students. Special-interest bibliographic databases are also heavily used.

The importance of CD-ROM as a type of delivery system for databases has diminished somewhat since its inception. Databases using HTML and PDF formats and direct Web links to source content have become the preferred choice at the moment, allowing users to download or print content. Electronic journals and e-books are also fast becoming a secondary carrier of information, with publishers creating many electronic reference titles in language, health, business, and other disciplines.

Companies that produce electronic databases, particularly full-text databases reprinting original newspaper, magazine, or journal articles in their entirety, license this material from the original publishers. They, in turn, license libraries to carry their products online or in other forms, such as CD-ROM.

RESEARCHING ELECTRONIC DATABASES

One of the greatest assets of electronic databases is that the content is fully searchable. Similar to searching your library's online catalog or an Internet search engine, through keyword or subject searches you can find relevant abstracts, citations, or full-text articles with ease as supporting evidence for your essay, term paper, or written project.

The trick to finding appropriate material is to narrow your search and make it more specific to the subject matter that you are searching. Remember, as discussed in Chapter 1 (under "Searching Your Topic"), the keywords or combination of words you use in your search will directly impact your success, so choose your keywords wisely. For instance, if you are researching the NASA space program, your subject by itself is too broad. If you focus on the failures of the NASA space program instead, then by combining these words ("NASA space program" and "failures"), your search should produce results more relevant to your subject.

At most college and university libraries, off-campus access to electronic databases is available. To take advantage of this service, you need to be enrolled and have a student I.D. Check with your library regarding the terms and conditions of such use.

Much like other resources, electronic databases may be placed into the following two categories: General databases, providing information on a variety of subjects from popular and academic sources, and databases by subject, featuring mostly academic source material specific to a certain discipline.

GENERAL DATABASES

Most school and public libraries offer academic databases that index abstracts and full-text articles from literally thousands of popular and general-interest periodicals, including newspapers, magazines, and scholarly journals. Keep in mind that your library may carry a variation of the products listed or some derivative thereof. Most databases cover a broad spectrum of subjects and are keyword searchable. Popular databases include:

Academic

InfoTrac Expanded Academic ASAP (Gale Group, 1980–) WEB
The best general database of its kind, InfoTrac abstracts and indexes more than 3 million articles, with complete text to more than 1 million articles.

LexisNexis Academic (LexisNexis, 1977, most 1990s–) WEB
Superb source for finding full-text business, company, financial, general, government, legal, medical, and political news from scholarly journals and major metropolitan newspapers.

MasterFILE Premier (EBSCO Publishing; abstracts: 1984– , full-text: 1990–) WEB
Multidisciplinary abstract and index of more than 3,100 primary sources, and articles from nearly 1,950 general publications covering nearly all subject areas.

K–12

EBSCOHost MAS Ultra—School Edition (EBSCO Publishing, abstracts: 1984– , full text: 1990–) WEB
Archives full text of more than 515 high-school-level general interest and current event magazines.

EBSCOHost Middle Search Plus (EBSCOHost, 1984–) CD, WEB
Provides unlimited access to more than 145 magazines covering general topics appropriate for middle school students. Also includes the *Funk & Wagnalls New Encyclopedia, The Encyclopedia of Animals, Essential Documents in American History,* and the *CIA World Factbook.*

EBSCOHost Primary Search (EBSCO Publishing; current) WEB
Consists of full text for more than 65 popular magazines and almanacs and encyclopedias for elementary school students.

eLibrary (ProQuest, current) WEB
Delivers comprehensive periodical and digital media content with full-text magazine and newspaper articles, designed specifically for students.

InfoTrac Junior Edition (Gale Group, current) WEB
Features titles and full-text coverage designed for junior high and middle school students.

InfoTrac K-12 Series (Gale Group, current) WEB
This database provides age-appropriate research and information covering multiple disciplines for students K–12.

InfoTrac OneFile (Gale Group, 1980–) WEB
A one-stop source for news and periodical information, including more than 4,200 full-text articles and five newspaper indexes, for students of all grade levels.

InfoTrac Student Edition (Gale Group, current) WEB
This easy-to-use collection features a variety of general references and full-text sources for secondary school students.

Junior Edition—K-12 (Gale Group, current) WEB
Designed for middle school students, this database provides access to a variety of indexed and full-text magazines, newspapers, and reference books on current events (formerly called *SuperTom Junior*).

JuniorQuest (ProQuest, 1988–) WEB
Online database, designed for middle school students, offering full-text articles about popular topics from nearly 100 age-appropriate magazines and newspapers.

KidQuest (ProQuest, 1988–) WEB
This popular database offers full-text articles from publications for elementary and middle school students.

Kids Edition—K-12 (Gale Group, current) WEB
Like others in its class, this K–12 database offers easy access for elementary school students to full-text magazines, newspapers, and reference books (formerly called *Primary TOM*).

Kids InfoBits (Gale Group, 1992–) WEB
Multisource abstract and index database designed for students in kindergarten through fifth grade featuring full-text children's and general interest magazines, reference books, and thousands of newspaper articles.

Student Edition—K-12 (Gale Group, current) WEB
Designed for high school students and featuring a broad selection of full-text magazines, newspapers, and references (formerly called *SuperTOM*).

DATABASES BY SUBJECT

A vast collection of electronic databases is widely available at libraries. With so many thousands of potential electronic resources offered today, the following is a select list, not complete by any means, of the most popular databases by subject, produced and licensed by the top U.S. information systems companies to libraries around the world:

Agriculture

AGRICOLA (FirstSearch) (OCLC, 1970–) WEB
This leading agricultural database contains substantial citations to articles on agricultural topics.

Biological and Agricultural Index (FirstSearch) (OCLC, 1983–) WEB
Offers article citations on the entire range of sciences related to biology and agriculture.

CAB Abstracts (CAB International, 1984–) WEB
Premier index abstracting agriculture and related subjects.

Anthropology

Anthropological Index Online (Royal Anthropological Institute, 1957–) WEB
Complete index of more than 800 anthropological journals by the Museum of Mankind Library (London), including bibliographies and obituaries.

Anthropological Literature (Research Libraries Group, 1984–) WEB
Indexes articles in journals and more than 1,400 edited works.

Biography

Biography and Genealogy Master Index (Gale Group, current) WEB
This master database indexes available reference sources and important retrospective works of more than 13 million individuals, both living and deceased, from every field of activity and from all areas of the world.

Biography Index (H.W. Wilson, 1984–) WEB
Cites biographical articles from more than 3,000 English-language periodicals, in all subject areas, covered by H.W. Wilson indexes.

Biography Resource Center (Gale Group, current) WEB
This online resource combines comprehensive biographies on hundreds of thousands of notable people in all disciplines from nearly 80 Gale biographical reference works, and full-text magazine and newspaper articles.

The Complete Marquis Who's Who (Gale Group, 1985–) CD, WEB
Provides access to more than 1 million biographies of men and women in every significant field of endeavor from Marquis's library of "Who's Whos."

Current Biography Illustrated (H.W. Wilson, 1940–) WEB
Web-based database of more than 15,000 illustrated full-text biographies and more than 9,400 obituaries of famous individuals.

World Biographical Index (K.G. Saur, 1998–) WEB
Features brief biographical overviews and citations on notables in Australia, New Zealand, North and South America, Oceania, and Western and Central Europe.

Biology

Aquatic Sciences and Fisheries (CSA, 1978–) WEB
Worldwide coverage of citations and abstracts of literature in aquatic science, including published journals, monographs, dissertations, hard-to-obtain "gray" literature, and conference proceedings.

Biological Abstracts (Ovid Technologies, 1951–) WEB
Comprehensively abstracts articles covering agriculture, biochemistry, biomedicine, biotechnology, botany, ecology, microbiology, pharmacology, and zoology.

Biological and Agricultural Index Plus (H.W. Wilson; indexing: 1983– , full text: 1997–) WEB
Complete indexing and full-text articles of popular and professional scientific journals.

Biology Digest (FirstSearch) (OCLC, 1989–) WEB
Features abstracts and summaries of articles on all of life sciences.

BioOne (BioOne Amigos Library Services, abstracts: 1971– , full text: 1991–) WEB
Collection of 60 full-text bioscience research journals from 49 publishers.

BIOSIS (BIOSIS, 1969–) WEB
This online service offers more than 13 million citations and abstracts of life and biological science literature from around the globe.

Business and Economics

ABI/INFORM (UMI, abstracts: 1971– , full text: 1991–) WEB
Abstracts and indexes articles from more than 1,600 leading business and management publications, including full-text articles from more than 800 publications.

Business and Company Resource Center (Gale Group, 1979–) WEB
Details global company and business news, including company profiles, industry rankings, industry statistics, investment reports, marketing data, and articles on more than 300,000 companies.

Business and Industry (FirstSearch) (OCLC, 1994–) WEB
Searchable international database of 600 leading trade magazines, newsletters, general business press and business dailies, and business sources, with full-text articles.

Business Full Text (H.W. Wilson, abstracts: 1990– , full text: 1995–) WEB
Part of WilsonWeb's OmniFile, this database covers leading business magazines and business topics.

Business NewsBank (NewsBank, 1980–) WEB
Catalogs selected information and full-text articles from more than 500 newspapers, newswires, and business journals.

Business Source Premier (EBSCO Publishing, 1965–) WEB
This business database contains abstracts and full text of more than 2,680 business periodicals, including nearly 2,140 business journals. Also available as Business Source Elite with full text for nearly 1,060 journals.

D&B Million Dollar Database (Dun & Bradstreet, current) WEB
Provides access to information on 1.6 million U.S. and Canadian public and private businesses.

Disclosure (FirstSearch) (OCLC/Disclosure Inc., most recent five years) WEB
Offers comprehensive profiles and information on more than 12,000 public companies, mostly compiled from data filed with the Securities and Exchange Commission (SEC).

EconLit (American Economics Association, 1969–) WEB
Indexes and abstracts more than 450 international economic journals, including articles, essays, research papers, books, and more.

Factiva (Dow Jones & Reuters, current) WEB
Access to full text of 8,000 international business and general publications.

General BusinessFile ASAP (EBSCO Publishing, 1996–) WEB
Contains citations to articles in more than 800 local and regional journals and newspapers and business-related articles from more than 3,000 publications (formerly called *IAC Business Index*).

Hoover's Online (Hoover's Inc., current) WEB
This leading business database offers business news, lists, stock quotes, and global industry overviews, with advanced searching, for 50,000 public and private enterprises worldwide.

Mergent (Mergent Inc., current) WEB
Formerly called FIS Online, this service includes U.S. and international company data, including archival data, annual reports, insider trading data, institutional holdings, and more.

ProQuest Newspapers (ProQuest, 1982–) WEB
Indexes, with some full text, various business and finance news publications, including *Barron's, Asian Wall Street Journal, Wall Street Journal Europe,* and others.

ReferenceUSA (infoUSA Inc., current–) WEB
Detailed directory of more than 12 million businesses throughout the United States.

Standard & Poor's Net Advantage (Standard & Poor's, current) WEB
Primary source for economic and financial information on more than 50 U.S. industries, including statistics, comparative analysis, and industry portfolios.

STAT-USA (U.S. Department of Commerce, current) WEB
Presents extensive data on U.S. and international business and economics, including market research, trade data, and analyses for each country, with material from the *National Trade Data Bank*.

Wall Street Journal (ProQuest, Online: 1984– , CD: 1989–) CD, WEB
Offers complete in-depth coverage of national and international financial news.

Wilson Business Full Text (H.W. Wilson, abstracts: 1990– , full text: 1995–) WEB
Full-text articles from leading English-language business magazines.

Chemistry and Physical Sciences

ACS Journals Online (ACS, current) WEB
Database of full-text online journals produced by the American Chemical Society.

Chemical Abstracts (SciFinder Scholar, 1907–) WEB
Searchable abstracts, data, reports, and statistics combining several databases.

Chemical Channel (DIALOG, current) WEB
Full-text database covering current chemical and industry news.

Merck Index (Merck & Co., current) CD, WEB
Online version of this popular printed encyclopedia of chemicals, drugs, and biologicals providing records on a single chemical entity or small group of related compounds.

Ullmann's Encyclopedia of Industry Chemistry (Wiley-VCH, current) WEB
Fully covers all areas of science and technology with nearly 1,000 articles written by experts in their fields.

Communications

ComAbstracts (Communication Institute For Online Scholarship, 1966–) WEB
Indexes and abstracts articles published in the primary professional literature of the communications field.

Controversial and Cultural Issues

CQ Researcher (CQ Press, 1991–) WEB
Reports on current and controversial issues in the news, including background information, a chronology, opposing viewpoints, statistics, and a bibliography with each report.

Ethnic Newswatch (ProQuest, 1991–) WEB
Comprehensive collection of more than 830,000 full-text articles from 240 publications reflecting ethnic, minority, and Native viewpoints.

GenderWatch (ProQuest, 1970–) WEB
Full-text database of diverse publications focusing on gender-related subjects.

Issues and Controversies On File (Facts On File News Services, 1995–) WEB
Provides supporting and opposing views on 250 current and controversial issues with full-text articles.

Opposing Viewpoints Resource Center (Gale Group, current) WEB
Collection of more than 2,000 full-text viewpoint articles from magazines and newspapers, including tables, charts, graphs, and links to Web sites.

Pro and Con Online (Congressional Digest, current) WEB
Archives complete full-text articles from the *Congressional Digest, Supreme Court Debates,* and *International Debates.*

Criminal Justice and Law

Criminal Justice Abstracts (SilverPlatter, 1968–) WEB
Abstracts articles covering such subjects as the courts, crime prevention, juvenile justice, and punishment.

Index to Legal Periodicals and Books (FirstSearch) (OCLC/H.W. Wilson, 1993–) WEB
Cites articles from 620 publications and law books covering all areas of jurisprudence, including court decisions and legislation.

LegalTrac (Gale Group, indexing: 1980– , full text: 1990–) WEB
Indexes approximately 800 of the most highly regarded legal publications.

LexisNexis Academic (Legal Research) (LexisNexis, indexing: 1975– , full text: 1990–) WEB
Archives articles from legal newspapers, magazines, and law reviews, including all federal court, state high court, and appellate decisions, tax laws, patent research, plus listings from the *Martindale-Hubell Law Directory.*

SIRS Government Reporter (SIRS Publishing, abstracts: 1971– , full text: 1991–) WEB
Features full-text government and historic documents, U.S. Supreme Court decisions, and complete congressional, federal agency, and Supreme Court justice directories.

Westlaw (West Group, 1980–) WEB
Online legal database designed to research law-related issues.

Dictionaries, Directories, and Encyclopedias

Associations Unlimited (Gale Group, current) WEB
Details a great number of nonprofit organizations in the United States and the world, including professional societies, religious organizations, trade associations, and others.

Encyclopedia Americana (Grolier, 1997) CD, WEB
Complete, updated contents of the 30-volume printed edition, featuring more than 45,000 articles and 2,000 illustrations in black-and-white and color, plus the complete *Merriam-Webster's Collegiate Dictionary, Chronology of World History,* and *Dictionary of Science and Technology.*

Encyclopaedia Britannica Online (Encyclopaedia Britannica, current) CD, WEB
Full version of this award-winning encyclopedia featuring more than 72,000 encyclopedic articles, links to more than 130,000 Web sites, *Merriam-Webster's Collegiate Dictionary,* and the *Britannica Book of the Year.*

Funk & Wagnalls New World Encyclopedia (EBSCO Publishing, current) WEB
Annually updated online version featuring 25,000 encyclopedic entries covering a wide range of topics.

Grolier Multimedia Encyclopedia Online (Grolier, current) CD, WEB
Highly respected reference featuring more than 36,000 articles, time lines, bibliographies, and Web links.

Merriam-Webster's Collegiate Dictionary (Merriam-Webster, 1994–) WEB
Includes full contents of the printed edition, including terms and definitions, abbreviations, foreign words and phrases, biographical names, and more.

Microsoft Encarta (Microsoft Corporation, 1994–) CD, WEB
First launched on CD-ROM, this multimedia encyclopedia, also available on the Web, includes significant content—more than 26,000 articles—covering a broad range of subjects. Also features sounds, pictures, and videos.

Oxford English Dictionary (Oxford University Press, current) WEB
Complete online version of this authoritative English-language dictionary.

Oxford Reference Online: The Core Collections (Oxford University Press, current) WEB
Brings together 100 language and subject dictionaries and reference works—more than 60,000 pages—covering varied subjects into one cross-searchable resource.

Ulrich's International Periodicals Directory (R.R. Bowker, 1974–) WEB
Current comprehensive source of information on selected periodicals and serials published in the United States and throughout the world.

World Almanac (World Almanac, 1998–) WEB
This fundamental reference combines material from *The World Almanac and Book of Facts, The World Almanac of the U.S.A., The World Almanac of*

U.S. Politics, The World Almanac for Kids, and *Funk & Wagnalls New Encyclopedia* with more than 32,000 records to create a huge database.

World Book Encyclopedia (World Book, current) WEB
Offers the full content of the 22-volume *World Book Encyclopedia, The World Book Encyclopedia of People and Places,* and *The World Book Encyclopedia of Science,* with 22,300 articles, including maps, illustrations, videos, audio clips, and more.

World News Digest (Facts On File News Service, 1940–   ) WEB
Online version of printed edition highlighting major news events from 1940 to the present. Also includes a collection of biographies, historical documents, and selected topical editorials.

Earth and Environmental Sciences

Environmental Science and Pollution Management (Cambridge Scientific Abstracts, 1984–   ) WEB
Abstracts published material covering important areas of environmental science.

GEOBASE (FirstSearch) (OCLC, 1980–   ) WEB
This online service abstracts and indexes more than 2,000 journals in physical and human geography, earth and environmental sciences, ecology, and related disciplines.

LexisNexis Environmental (LexisNexis, 2002–   ) WEB
Offers a diverse collection of sources on key environmental issues.

Education

Education Full Text (H.W. Wilson, abstracts: 1994–   , full text: 1996–   ) WEB
Presents abstracts and full-text articles covering contemporary education issues.

ERIC (OCLC, abstracts: 1966–   , full text: 1996–   ) WEB
Provides full access to journal articles from *Resources in Education* and *Journals in Education* and documents from *the Educational Resource Information Center*—92 percent of them in full text. The database is also available online through Cambridge Scientific Abstracts and EBSCO-Host.

Engineering Sciences

Applied Science and Technology Full Text (H.W. Wilson, abstracts: 1983–   , full text: 1997–   ) WEB
Abstracts and indexes periodicals, with some full-text articles.

Engineering Index (Engineering Information Inc, 1970–   ) WEB
Provides abstracts to journals, technical reports, society publications, books, conference proceedings, and papers. (Also known as Compendex Plus.)

INSPEC (OCLC/IOP Axiom, 1969–   ) WEB
Large database of abstracts in engineering and related fields.

McGraw-Hill Encyclopedia of Science and Technology (McGraw-Hill, 1998–) CD, WEB
Complete online version of the printed edition, including 7,000 full-text articles, thousands of definitions, and biographies of 1,200 notable scientists.

Ethics

Ethics Index (American Theological Library Association, 1990–96) WEB
Interdisciplinary resource covering literature on ethics; selected from general, popular, and scholarly journals and from prominent newspapers.

Ethnic and Area Studies

Black Studies on Disc (G.K. Hall, 1988–) CD
This ethnic studies database cites articles, books, book reviews, videos, and other materials covering African American and African diaspora studies, plus other racial and minority groups.

Ethnic NewsWatch (Softline Information Inc., 1980–) CD, WEB
Comprehensive database of full-text articles from newspapers, magazines, and journals of the ethnic and minority press.

HAPI (Hispanic-American Periodicals Index) Online (EBSCO Publishing, 1970–) WEB
Includes 210,000 citations indexing Hispanic periodicals, articles, books, and reviews, literary works, and other documents.

International Index to Black Periodicals Full Text (G.K. Hall, abstracts: 1902–91; full text: 1990–) WEB
Provides bibliographic citations, abstracts, and selected full-text of articles from more than 150 international scholarly and popular journals, newspapers, and newsletters.

General References

FactSearch (FirstSearch) (OCLC, 1984–) WEB
Comprehensive guide to statistical statements on current social, economic, political, environmental, and health issues, derived from 300 sources, including newspapers, periodicals, newsletters, and government documents with Web links to free full text.

FirstSearch (OCLC, current) WEB
Provides electronic access to a rich collection of reference databases and more than 10 million full-text illustrated articles, as well as up-to-date bibliographic records from the WorldCat database.

General Reference Center (Gale Group, 1980–) WEB
General interest database used to search magazines, reference books, and newspapers for information on current events, popular culture, the arts and sciences, sports, and more.

Ingenta (Ingenta, 1988–) WEB
Claims to be the world's largest Web site for the search and delivery of research articles, including article summaries from more than 20,000 publications with full text of more than 4,500 titles.

LexisNexis Reference (LexisNexis, current) WEB
General electronic reference featuring country profiles, quotations, polls and surveys, state profiles, brief biographies of business executives, politicians, and others, and an almanac.

SIRS Knowledge Source (SIRS, current) WEB
Provides integrated online access to full-text articles and resources from four reference databases: SIRS Researcher, SIRS Government Reporter, SIRS Renaissance, and SIRS NetSelect.

Student Resource Center (Gale Group, current) WEB
Contains a wide range of cross-curricular material including literary, science, history, and biographical databases, reference material, critical essays, primary source documents, and full-text articles from newspapers and popular periodicals.

Government Publications

American FactFinder (U.S. Census Bureau, 2000–) WEB
Free online source of information for population, housing, economic, and geographic data based on the latest U.S. Census.

Catalog of U.S. Government Publications (U.S. Government Printing Office, 1988–) WEB
Abstracts U.S. government publications, including books, maps, reports, serials, and more, covering all subjects.

CIA World Factbook (Central Intelligence Agency, 2003–) WEB
Contains facts and figures, revised annually, on more than 200 countries and territories.

FirstGov (U.S. Government Printing Office, current) WEB
Free centralized site offering information on more than 20,000 local, state, and federal agency Web sites.

GPO Monthly Catalog (U.S. Government Printing Office, 1976–) WEB
Features more than 522,000 bibliographic records for all types of U.S. government documents. Also offered as GPO MARCIVE (1976–) and GPO on SilverPlatter (1976–).

Index to Current Urban Documents (Greenwood, current) WEB
This comprehensive online guide features more than 2,400 government documents indexed each year from more than 500 major U.S. and Canadian cities.

LexisNexis Congressional (LexisNexis, 1970–) WEB
Provides easy access to full-text detailed information about Congress, including member biographies, committee assignments, voting records, financial data, and the full text of key regulatory and statutory resources.

LexisNexis State Capital (LexisNexis, current) WEB
Single source covering bills and laws, constitutions, proposed and enacted regulations, legislature membership, and newspapers of record for all 50 states.

LexisNexis Statistical (LexisNexis, 1971–) WEB
Fully indexes tables and statistical information produced by the U.S. government, state governments, international organizations, and some private and academic sources.

Military and Government Collection (EBSCO Publishing, current) WEB
Covers military titles, newsweeklies, and trade publications.

Health and Medicine

Alt-HealthWatch (EBSCO Publishing, 1990–) WEB
A leading database devoted to alternative health and medical treatment and wellness with full-text articles from more than 170 journals.

CINAHL (Cumulative Index in Nursing and Allied Health Literature) (CINAHL Information Systems, Citations: 1982– , abstracts: 1986–) WEB
Authoritative resource for nursing and allied health professionals providing indexes and abstracts to more than 1,600 journals, available through EBSCO Host and FirstSearch.

Clinical Pharmacology (EBSCO Publishing, current) WEB
Provides current and clinically relevant drug monographs for all U.S. prescription drugs, including new and investigational drugs, over-the-counter products, and herbal and nutritional supplements.

Clinical Reference Systems (Clinical Reference Systems, current) WEB
Indexes more than 7,000 reports on various medical topics available through EBSCOHost.

Cumulated Index to Nursing and Allied Health Literature (Ovid Technologies, 1982–) WEB
Contains abstracts, cited references, and some full-text articles for nursing and allied health topics from more than 500 nursing and 600 biomedical journals (84 in consumer health).

Health and Wellness Resource Center (Gale Group, current) WEB
An authoritative database of medical journal, magazine, and newspaper articles, plus pamphlets and medical encyclopedias and dictionaries covering a wide range of health topics.

Health Source: Consumer Edition (EBSCO Publishing, abstracts: 1984– , full text: 1990–) WEB
Searchable database on many health topics, including general health, food sciences and nutrition, medical sciences, and sports medicine, with full-text articles from more than 190 journals.

Health Source: Nursing/Academic Edition (EBSCO Publishing, 1974–) WEB
Provides 600 full-text scholarly journals covering many medical disciplines. Also abstracts and indexes more 850 journals.

HighWire: Library of the Sciences and Medicine (HighWire Press, current) WEB
Indexes more than 12 million articles in more than 4,500 MEDLINE journals.

IAC Health Reference Center (InfoTrac, current) WEB
Full-text access to more than 200 allied health and medical journals, consumer magazines, and pamphlets.

MEDLINE (PubMed/U.S. National Library of Medicine, 1950–) WEB
This premier medical database contains 9 million citations from more than 3,500 international journals with links to participating online journals and many other related databases. Alternative version: MEDLINEPlus (National Institutes of Health, current).

Nursing Journals Full Text (ProQuest, 1988–) WEB
Offers full-text coverage of more than 270 professional nursing journals.

PubMed (U.S. National Library of Medicine, mid-1960s–) WEB
Online service providing direct access to more than 12 million MEDLINE citations.

TOXLINE (U.S. National Library of Medicine, 1965–) WEB
Includes information on biochemical, pharmacological, physiological, and toxicological effects of drugs and other chemicals.

History

America: History and Life (ABC-CLIO, 1964–) WEB
Comprehensive bibliography covering the history and culture of the United States and Canada from prehistory to the present, featuring abstracts and citations for some 8,000 articles and more than 2,100 journals, published worldwide.

CultureGrams (Axiom Press, current) WEB
This online database produces reports on every country and on 180 world cultures highlighting their customs, history, lifestyle, people, and society, including maps, statistics, and photographs.

Daily Life through History (Greenwood, current) WEB
Historical database featuring detailed portrayals of ordinary life in different cultures throughout history.

Historical Abstracts (ABC-CLIO, 1954–) CD
Covers entire world history, from 1450 to present, through article abstracts and bibliographic citations of books and dissertations on all aspects of world history from more than 2,100 leading journals. Also available in expanded printed edition.

Historical Index to The New York Times (UMI, 1851–1922) CD, WEB
Bibliographic resource of American history as covered in this metropolitan daily.

History Resource Center (Gale Group, current) WEB
Integrates important historical documents, references, scholarly journals, and newspaper and magazine articles in a single interface.

International Medieval Bibliography (International Medieval Institute, 1967–) WEB
Leading interdisciplinary bibliography of the Middle Ages featuring more than 300,000 articles published in more than 4,000 journals and periodicals and 5,000 miscellaneous volumes.

Humanities and Fine Arts

Arts and Humanities Citation Index (Thomson ISI, 1975– , 1999–) CD, WEB
Provides access to bibliographic information and cited references in nearly 1,130 leading arts and humanities journals, and relevant items from approximately 7,000 top science and social sciences journals. Author abstracts are from 1999 to the present and back files to 1975.

Arts and Humanities Search (FirstSearch) (OCLC, 1980–) WEB
Indexes more than 1,300 of the world's leading arts and humanities journals, with some articles, from more than 5,800 social science and science journals.

Humanities Abstracts (FirstSearch) (OCLC, 1984–) WEB
Searchable directory providing abstracts to more than 400 periodicals, including some of the best-known journals.

Humanities and Social Sciences Index Retrospective (H.W. Wilson, 1907–84) WEB
Indexes nearly 1,200 periodicals with citations to more than 1 million articles covering a century of research.

Humanities Full Text (H.W. Wilson, indexing: 1984– , full text: 1995–) WEB
Comprehensively indexes and abstracts the most noted scholarly and specialized magazines, including full-text articles.

Journal and Magazine Article Indexes

Academic Search Premier (EBSCO Publishing, abstracts: 1984– , full text: 1990–) WEB
Indexes and abstracts nearly 3,930 scholarly journals in various disciplines.

Alt-Press Watch (ProQuest, 1995–) WEB
Full-text database providing access to alternative publications, including newspapers, magazines, and journals.

ArticleFirst (FirstSearch) (OCLC, 1990–) WEB
Describes items listed on the table of contents pages of 12,600 journals in business, the humanities, science, social science, technology, and others.

Electronic Journals Service (EBSCO Publishing, 1990s–) WEB
Offers complete access to thousands of electronic journals and millions of articles, all on one site.

Expanded Academic ASAP (EBSCO Publishing, 1980s–) WEB
Academic index of current events, the humanities, general sciences, and social sciences from scholarly journals and the latest six months of *The New York Times*, with full-text articles (formerly called IAC Academic Index).

IDEAL (Elsevier, 1993–) WEB
Electronic library of 174 journals formerly published by Academic Press with full text in the sciences and social sciences.

JSTOR (JSTOR, 1800s–latest 3–5 years) WEB
Contains back files of scholarly journals, some full text, in the arts, anthropology, Asian studies, ecology, economics, education, finance, history, mathematics, philosophy, political science, population studies, sociology, and more.

Kluwer Online (Kluwer Academic Publishers, 1997–) WEB
Includes full text to a variety of scholarly journals.

Magazine Article Summaries Full Text (EBSCO Publishing, 1980s–) WEB
Magazine database featuring abstracts and full-text articles from 450 general magazines.

Magazine Express (ProQuest, 1988–) CD
Covers more than 190 top consumer publications, including general-interest magazines and specialized titles.

Magazine Index Plus/ASAP (Gale Group, 1998–) CD
Indexes and abstracts full-text articles from general interest and popular publications.

NewsBank Popular Periodicals Premier (NewsBank, 1980s–) WEB
Offers full-text coverage of 12 magazines; also available with NewsBank NewsFile.

Periodical Abstracts (ProQuest, 1971–) CD, WEB
Abstracts and indexes full-text articles from academic journals, popular magazines, and business publications; also available through OCLC FirstSearch.

Periodicals Abstracts Research II (UMI, abstracts: 1971– , full text: 1986–) WEB
General database spotlighting academic journals, popular magazines, and trade publications in most disciplines.

Periodicals Contents Index Full Text (Chadwyck-Healey, 1970–91) CD, WEB
Fully indexes more than 200 years of articles from journals in the arts, humanities, and social sciences.

ProjectMUSE (Johns Hopkins University Press, 1990–) WEB
Full-text database providing access to thousands of articles from more than 100 scholarly journals in the arts, humanities, mathematics, and social sciences.

ProQuest General Periodicals (ProQuest, 1986–) CD
Abstracts and indexes full images of articles from hundreds of leading magazines and journals.

Readers' Guide Full Text Mega Edition (H.W. Wilson, 1983–) WEB
Comprehensively abstracts and indexes, with full text, popular and general-interest magazines covering all subjects, published in the United States and Canada. The database is also available as Readers' Guide Full Text (1994–).

Resource/One (ProQuest, 1986–) CD, WEB
Covers more than 170 general-reference periodicals and two popular newspapers with full-text editions available.

SIRS Researcher (ProQuest, 1988–) CD, WEB
Contains select full-text articles covering a broad range of topics, including economic, historic, global, political, social, and scientific issues, from 1,600 publications.

TOC Premier (EBSCO Publishing, 1960s–) WEB
Database of the tables of contents for more than 23,000 scholarly journals.

Ulrichsweb.com 2.0 (R.R. Bowker, current) WEB
Bibliographic database detailing more than 250,000 periodical titles.

Wilson OmniFile Full Text (H.W. Wilson, indexing: 1982– , full text: 1994–) WEB
Combines six of Wilson's full-text periodical databases (Education, General Science, Humanities, Readers' Guide, Social Sciences, and Business) and five additional databases covering disciplines such as applied science and technology and literature.

Wilson Select Plus (OCLC/H.W. Wilson, 1994–) WEB
Indexes and abstracts full-text periodical articles in science, humanities, education, and business from 800 journals, magazines, and newspapers.

Library Science/Books and Publishing

ARBAOnline (Libraries Unlimited/ARBA Online, 1995–) WEB
This leading library science database covers 9,500 reviews of print and electronic reference works from more than 400 publishers in 500 subject areas.

Books in Print with Book Reviews Plus (R.R. Bowker/Reed Reference, current) CD
Companion to the printed library edition, updated monthly, listing more than 840,000 books currently in print and 85,000 book reviews.

Choice Reviews (American Library Association, 1988–) WEB
Provides Web access to significant reviews of current books and electronic resources by subject experts in more than 40 disciplines.

Ebrary (Ebrary, Inc., current) WEB
Collection of more than 20,000 electronic books in key academic areas.

eLibrary (ProQuest, Periodicals: 1981– , Multimedia: historical to the present) WEB
Delivers periodical content from than 1,500 full-text books, magazines, newspapers, transcripts, and more. Academic/public library and elementary curriculum versions also available.

Global Books in Print (R.R. Bowker/Reed Reference, current) CD
Comprehensive source of information on more than 5 million books, including full-text reviews.

NetLibrary (NetLibrary, current) WEB
Broad collection of more than 4,500 electronic books online.

Literature

Bibliographic Index (H.W. Wilson, 1984–) WEB
Indexes more than 271,000 bibliographies from periodicals and books.

Columbia Granger's World of Poetry (Columbia University Press, current) WEB
Includes 250,000 poem citations, 13,000 poems in full text, 7,500 excerpts, biographies of leading poets, and bibliographies on hundreds of poems and poets.

Contemporary Authors (Gale Group, current) CD, WEB
Major biographical resource on the lives and works of more than 100,000 contemporary writers, including bibliographies.

Contemporary Literary Criticism (Gale Group, 1973–) WEB
Database, also available in print, offering literary criticism since 1959.

Critical Companions to Popular Contemporary Writers (Greenwood, current) WEB
Full access to hundreds of titles by 46 of the most widely read contemporary writers, including analysis, selected reviews, criticism, and complete bibliographies.

Dissertation Abstracts Online (UMI, 1861–) CD, WEB
Available through FirstSearch, this searchable index and abstracts covers more than 1.6 million doctoral dissertations and master theses from 1,000 accredited institutions.

Essay and General Literature Index (FirstSearch) (OCLC, 1985–) WEB
Indexes nearly 65,000 essays contained in 5,300 anthologies and collections and other works published from more than 300 volumes and 20 annual or serial publications published in the United States, Britain, and Canada. Index is also available through SilverPlatter.

Gale Literary Index (Gale Research, current) CD, WEB
Master index of all 31 literary series published by Gale Research, cross-referencing more than 110,000 author names and more than 120,000 titles.

The Horn Book Guide Online (Greenwood, current) WEB
Complete electronic version of this renowned guide to critical reviews of nearly every hardcover trade book published in the United States for young people.

Literature in Context (Greenwood, current) WEB
Unlimited access to a rich collection of primary source material, collateral readings, and commentary for classic literature.

Literature Resource Center (Gale Group, 1983) WEB
Integrates several literary resources covering every literary discipline, including journalism, fiction, and poetry, with full-text articles, including biographies, bibliographies, and critical analysis.

Lit Finder (Roth Publishing, current) WEB
Three-part database including Essay Finder, a database of full-text essays; Poem Finder, the largest, most comprehensive database of current poetry; and Story Finder, providing thousands of full-text short stories.

MLA International Bibliography (FirstSearch) (OCLC/Modern Library Association, 1963–) WEB
Contains more than 1 million citations to books, dissertations, essay collections, working papers, and proceedings derived more than 4,000 journals published worldwide.

MagillOnLiterature (EBSCO Publishing, indexing: 1984– , full text: 1990–) WEB
Definitive online source compiled by Salem Press featuring critical analyses and brief plot summaries of the most studied works in the history of literature.

PapersFirst (FirstSearch) (OCLC, 1993–) WEB
Searchable database with access to individual papers presented at worldwide conferences, meetings, workshops, and symposia.

ProceedingsFirst (OCLC, 1993–) WEB
Contains thousands of records of every published conference proceeding, meeting, symposia, workshop, and more.

Scribner Writers Series (Gale Group, current) WEB
This online resource offers access to 1,600 original and descriptive critical essays on the lives and works of important authors from around the world.

Twayne's Author Series (Gale Group, current) WEB
Full content of nearly 600 books by authors from the United States, England, and throughout the world.

Newspaper Article Indexes

DIALOG OnDisc Papers (DIALOG, 1986–) CD
CD-ROM database, updated quarterly, providing text of articles from major metropolitan newspapers such as *The Boston Globe, The Detroit Free Press, The Philadelphia Inquirer,* and others.

Facts On File World News Digest (Facts On File News Services, 1940–) WEB
Presents full-text newspaper and journal articles, plus biographies, chronologies, government documents, speeches, statistics, and more, covering current and world events and political news from around the world.

FirstSearch (OCLC, current) WEB
This interactive online information system features more than 35 multidisciplinary periodical databases.

General Periodicals OnDisc (UMI, 1986–97) CD
Contains abstracts and more than 350 scanned images from more than 1,000 popular periodicals. Offers monthly updates.

Global NewsBank (NewsBank, 1996–) WEB
International articles database, translated into English, from newspapers, magazines, wire services, government documents, and news agencies.

The Los Angeles Times (ProQuest, 1985–) WEB
Provides extensive coverage of national, international, and local news in current and past editions of this major daily newspaper.

National News 5 (ProQuest, 1986–) CD, WEB
Full-text access to *The New York Times, The Los Angeles Times, The Washington Post, The Wall Street Journal,* and *The Christian Science Monitor.*

The New York Times (ProQuest, 1851–three years before current date) CD, WEB
Complete articles and images covering regional, national, and international news starting with the first issue of this major metropolitan daily.

NewsBank CD-News (NewsBank, 1983–) CD
A comprehensive resource of news coverage, updated quarterly, with full-text articles from nearly every major newspaper.

NewsBank Newsfile (NewsBank, 1980s–) WEB
Includes more than 70,000 articles, some full text, from more than 500 newspapers and news wire services, including regional, national, and international sources.

Newspaper Abstracts with Full Text (ProQuest, 1989–) WEB
Online service of selected full-text articles, reviews, editorials, and more from newspapers such as *The Wall Street Journal, The New York Times,* and others.

Newspaper Source (EBSCO Publishing, 1984–) WEB
This full-text news source covers more than 140 U.S. and international newspapers.

ProQuest Historical Newspapers (ProQuest, 1851–2001) WEB
Cover-to-cover digital reproductions in PDF files of every page from every issue of *The New York Times, The Wall Street Journal, The Washington Post, The Christian Science Monitor, The Los Angeles Times,* and *The Chicago Tribune.*

ProQuest News and Magazines (ProQuest, 1986–) WEB
Offers current information on popular magazines, journals, national newspapers, and local papers.

ProQuest Newspaper Abstracts (ProQuest, 1986–) CD, WEB
Abstracts and indexes the top U.S. and international publications.

SIRS Discoverer (ProQuest, 1988–) CD, WEB
Delivered on CD-ROM and on the Web, this database offers full-text articles and images from more than 1,600 national and international newspapers, magazines, and government documents.

UMI Newspapers OnDisc (UMI, 1988–) CD
Presents complete text versions of articles from the following four newspapers, updated monthly: *The New York Times* (1988–present); *USA Today* (1990–present); *The Wall Street Journal* (1989–present); and *The Washington Post* (1989–present).

The Washington Post (ProQuest, 1989–) CD, WEB
Full online version of one of America's most respected newspapers.

World News (DIALOG, current) WEB
Covers hundreds of news items daily from around the globe.

USA Today (ProQuest, Online: 1987– , CD: 1990–) CD, WEB
Entire online editions of this popular newspaper abstracted and indexed.

Performing Arts (Film, Music, Television, and Theater)

Film Index International (British Film Institute, 1930–) WEB
Directory of scholarly written information on approximately 90,000 films—including silent movies, art house classics, and blockbusters from more than 170 countries—and 30,000 film personalities from around the world, 1930 to the present.

Grove Music Online (Oxford University Press, current) WEB
Online service featuring comprehensive articles and biographies of music and musicians in all genres, based on the print edition of *The New Grove*

Dictionary of Music and Musicians and *The New Grove Dictionary of Opera.*

International Film Archive (International Federation of Film Archives, 1972–) CD
Provides access to two periodical indexes—*The International Index to Film Periodicals* (1972–93) and *International Index to Television Periodicals* (1979–82) containing more than 325,000 records.

International Index to Music Periodicals Full Text (Chadwyck-Healey, abstracts: 1900– ; full text: 1997–) WEB
Current indexing for more than 300 international music periodicals, both scholarly and popular, with full-text articles for more than 40 titles.

International Index to the Performing Arts Full Text (ProQuest, indexing: 1864– ; full text: 1998–) WEB
Indexes and abstracts more than 210 international journals covering the full spectrum of performing arts, including full-text articles, biographical profiles, discographies, events, interviews, obituaries, and reviews.

Music Index Online (Harmonie Park Press, 1979–) WEB
Online index of articles in more than 640 international music periodicals related to all aspects of classical and popular music.

Philosophy

Philosopher's Index (SilverPlatter, 1940–) WEB
Also published in hardcover, this thorough index of journal literature in philosophy and related fields features abstracts to books and articles from more than 300 major journals in 15 fields of philosophy.

Routledge Encyclopedia of Philosophy (Routledge, 1998–) CD, WEB
Unsurpassed database of articles, some full text, on subjects ranging from contemporary, cross-cultural, ethical, interdisciplinary, and political philosophy.

Political Science and Public Administration

Congressional Research Service Index (University Publications of America, 1916–98) CD
Comprehensively indexes studies and reports conducted by the Congressional Research Service from 1916 to 1998; also available in microfilm and microfiche with printed guides. Material includes in-depth policy analysis and research, background analyses, economic, legislative, and scientific analyses, legal arguments, legislative histories, and pro and con arguments on almost every subject of interest to the U.S. Congress.

PAIS International (FirstSearch) (OCLC/Public Affairs Information Service, 1971–) WEB
Lists more than 400,000 records covering articles, books, conference proceedings, government documents, and statistical directories focusing on public policy.

Psychology

PsycARTICLES (American Psychological Association, 1988–) WEB
Comprehensive database featuring more than 25,000 full-text articles on current issues in psychology from 42 respected journals, published by the American Psychological Association and available on several platforms, including EBSCO, OCLC FirstSearch and Ovid. Journals included in this database are indexed in PsycINFO.

PsycINFO (EBSCO Publishing, abstracts: 1887– , full text: 1967–) WEB
Extensively covers psychological literature from more than 1,300 journals, as well as selected dissertations and books.

PsycLIT (EBSCO Publishing, 1887–) WEB
Consists of two databases covering international literature of psychology and behavioral sciences, the first with more than 1.2 million abstracts of journal articles in 30 languages from more than 45 countries (1887 to the present); the second indexing English-language books and book chapters published worldwide since 1987.

Religion

ATLA Religion Index (OCLC/American Theological Library Association, 1949–) WEB
Master index of five searchable databases for religious and theological research and study with more than 1.1 million records in more than 30 languages from 1,400 international journals and 14,000 multiauthor works.

Religion and Philosophy Collection (EBSCO Publishing, 1975–) WEB
Unparalleled collection representing more than 300 journals covering a broad spectrum of topics.

Religion and Theological Abstracts (Religion and Theological Abstracts, 1958–) CD, WEB
Lists articles from more than 400 scholarly journals published worldwide, covering areas such as theology and world religions. Also available in printed edition.

Sciences

AccessScience (McGraw-Hill, current) WEB
Science database featuring more than 7,100 articles, 115,000 dictionary terms, and more than 2,000 biographies of notable scientists.

Encyclopedia of Astronomy and Astrophysics (Nature Publishing Group, current) WEB
Definitive reference with 3,000 articles covering 30 different subject areas.

Encyclopedia of Life Sciences (Nature Publishing Group, current) WEB
Full access to more than 3,000 continually updated peer-reviewed articles on the life sciences.

General Science Full Text (H.W. Wilson, indexing: 1984– , full text: 1995–) WEB
Indexes and abstracts full-text articles covering a full range of science topics.

Life Sciences Collection (Ovid Technologies, 1982–) WEB
Online compilation of more 2 million citations and abstracts to 25 life science disciplines from more than 5,000 articles, books, journals, monographs, and other sources.

Science Citation Index (Thomson ISI Web of Science, 1980–) CD, WEB
Current bibliographic information, author abstracts, and citations to articles published in 3,700 major scholarly science and technical journals covering 100 scientific disciplines. Also contains back-file article abstracts dating back to 1991. A larger online version, Science Citation Index Expanded, covers more than 5,900 journals in all.

ScienceDirect (Elsevier Science, 1995–) WEB
Leading science database with access to text from more than 1,800 scientific, technical, medical, mathematical, management, and social science journals.

Social Sciences

Social Science Citation Index (Thomson ISI, 1997–) CD
This social science database features citations to articles originally published in more than 1,400 journals and 50 related disciplines.

Social Sciences Full Text (H.W. Wilson, abstracts: 1994– , full text: 1995–) WEB
Fully covers the fields of anthropology, criminology, economics, law, political science, sociology, and more.

Social Sciences PlusText (ProQuest, 1971–) WEB
Integrates index from H.W. Wilson's Social Sciences Index with entire articles from more tnan half of the publications.

Sociology and Social Work

Social Work Abstracts (SilverPlatter, 1977–) WEB
Abstracts social work and human services in the areas of theory and practice and service, social issues, and social problems.

Sociological Abstracts (FirstSearch) (OCLC, 1963–) WEB
Indexes information from more than 2,600 journals in the areas of anthropology, gerontology, psychology, sociology, and more.

Sociological Collection (EBSCO Publishing, 1965–) WEB
This comprehensive database features nearly 580 full-text, peer-reviewed titles with information covering all areas of sociology.

UNESCO Databases (UNESCO Publishing, 2002) CD
Provides direct access to 100,000 bibliographic references, entries including 10,500 research institutes and information services, and 4,650 periodical titles in the social sciences.

Sports and Exercise Sciences

Physical Education Index (Cambridge Scientific Abstracts, 1970–) WEB
Abstracts articles from a broad range of publications covering physical and health education, sports medicine, and more.

SBRnet: Sports Business Research Network (Sports Business Research, 1993–) WEB
This Web-delivered database includes an array of articles, market research reports, government data, news releases, statistics, and other references related to the sports and recreation industries.

SPORT Discus (Sports Information Resource Centre, 1830–) WEB
Indexes articles covering the full range of sport, physical fitness, sport science, and recreation.

Technology

ACM Digital Library (Association for Computing Machinery, abstracts: 1985– , full text: 1991–) WEB
This informative database offers full text of ACM journal publications and selected conference proceedings.

Computer Source: Consumer Edition (EBSCO Publishing, 1984–) WEB
Features full text of 139 periodicals and abstracts and indexing for more than 160 titles, covering valuable market information on computers, telecommunications, electronics, and the Internet.

Internet and Personal Computing Abstracts (FirstSearch) (OCLC, 1989–) WEB
Provides citations and summaries of personal computer publications.

Visual Arts and Architecture

Art Abstracts (First Search) (OCLC/H.W. Wilson, 1994–) WEB
Indexes and abstracts published articles from almost 400 periodicals covering all aspects of the visual arts.

ARTBibliographies Modern (Cambridge Scientific Abstracts, 1974–) WEB
Abstracts current literature of modern art from journal articles, books, dissertations, essays, exhibition catalogs, and exhibition reviews.

Art Full Text (H.W. Wilson, abstracts: 1984– , full text: 1997–) WEB
This leading art database cites and abstracts more than 400 leading international art publications, with full-text articles from 98 periodicals.

Avery Index to Architectural Periodicals (Research Libraries Group, indexing: 1930– , coverage: 1860s–) WEB
Comprehensive listing of articles in scholarly and popular literature and professional association publications published worldwide.

Grove Dictionary of Art (Oxford University Press, current) WEB
This entire 34-volume dictionary online features more than 45,000 articles on art, international in scope with links to more than 22,000 images.

SIRS Renaissance (FirstSearch) (OCLC, 1988–) WEB
Selected full-text coverage of articles on architecture, cultures, philosophy, religion, and visual arts.

Women's Studies

Contemporary Women's Issues (FirstSearch) (OCLC, 1992–) WEB
Indexes journals, newsletters, reports and other publications, with full-text articles, covering timely and relevant women's issues.

Women's Studies Encyclopedia (Greenwood, current) WEB
Features more than 700 alphabetically arranged entries covering women and society throughout history and around the world.

Women's Studies International (NISC International, 1972–) WEB
Fully indexes women's studies material from around the globe covering a myriad of subjects.

VHS AND DVD COLLECTIONS

In addition to the above subject electronic databases, it is also worth checking into your library's collection of VHS and DVD titles. They can be a secondary source of information, including popular educational titles and documentaries on various subjects.

Finding Electronic Journals, Zines, and Newsletters

The field of electronic journals, zines, and newsletters, including online versions of traditional printed journals and other publications that exist purely in electronic form on the Web, is an ever-expanding form providing well-written and credibly researched articles by scholars, researchers, and leading authorities on a host of subjects and disciplines. Most electronic journals (also known as e-journals) offer full and unfettered access to selected articles from recent and past issues, including tables of contents.

As is the case with most major newspapers and popular magazines today, not every publisher of electronic versions of traditional academic and scholarly journals offers free and unlimited access. In some cases, access to back issues and previously published material is restricted to authorized users or available only by subscription. Other publishers post only tables of contents online for viewing.

Fear not. There are ways around this problem. Many traditional academic and scholarly journals are accessible without charge through a variety of licensed databases available through school and university libraries that you can access as a visitor or as a student on campus. If you are unable to tap into your local school or college university library's resources, a growing number of sites and resources on the Web provide easy access to many e-journals in all subjects.

RESEARCHING ELECTRONIC JOURNALS

Electronic journals come in two forms: online editions of print titles, and electronic only. Online editions are simply reproduced versions of current issues. Electronic-only journals are those exclusively published on the Web.

Your best sources for researching electronic journals are college and university libraries. Many provide free title listings or directories with links on their library Web sites to a myriad of electronic journals in all major disciplines. By simply clicking on the link of the journal title, you will taken to the journal home page where all available issues are listed or can be accessed. Other college or university library Web pages list e-journals under "subject guides" by topic, also with links. In many cases, full-text stories are freely accessible; in some cases, unless you have student access or are a subscriber, only access to thousands of e-journals will be free. Many independently operated multiple- or single-subject Web sites, listed elsewhere in this chapter, also provide free access to many different journals.

In addition to browsing through college or university library Web sites, directories, or subject guides, you also can research the availability of electronic journals using your library's online catalog. You search by keyword for your topic and electronic resources (type "literature and electronic resources (journals)"), or by subject (type "electronic resources (journals)").

Depending on the publisher, you can view not only full-text articles but also the tables of contents and archives of previous issues, and search by keyword for articles or individual titles. Plus you can save, e-mail, or print articles that you find in either HTML or PDF format. An added advantage of e-journals is that usually the full text of nearly every story is also searchable, even graphics.

SUBSCRIPTION-BASED JOURNAL ARTICLE INDEX DATABASES

Journal article index databases have become popular on school and university campuses. They allow free access to millions of article abstracts, citations, and full-text articles in academic and scholarly journals. For students, many databases are accessible on campus and off with the use of a student I.D. Visitor access is usually restricted to on-campus use. Examples of subscription-based index databases include:

BioOne (BioOne, coverage dates vary)
Full-text articles from 33 journals, published primarily by scholarly societies, focused on the biological, ecological, and environmental sciences.

Cambridge Journals Online (Cambridge University Press, coverage dates vary)
Citations, abstracts, and full-text journals in the areas of humanities, sciences, and social sciences published by Cambridge University Press.

GenderWatch (Softline Information, Inc., 1970–)
Primarily full-text database with abstracts of feminist and gender studies periodicals, including scholarly journals and newsletters, mostly from 1990 to the present.

IDEAL (Academic Press, 1993–)
Full-text articles from more than 170 scholarly journals in all disciplines published by Academic Press.

JSTOR (JSTOR, from volume 1 excluding the past 3–5 years)
Contains full-text articles from more than 322 scholarly journals in varied subjects.

Kluwer Online (Kluwer Academic Publishers, coverage dates vary)
Direct access to citations, abstracts, and full-text academic, legal and human science journal articles from the Kluwer family of publishers.

ProjectMUSE (Johns Hopkins University, 1990–)
Features full-text articles from more than 100 scholarly journals in the humanities, the social sciences, and the sciences. Includes journals published by Johns Hopkins University since 1995 and others published by Carnegie Mellon, Duke, Indiana, MIT, Oxford, and Penn State university presses, as well as the presses of the Universities of Hawaii, Texas, and Wisconsin.

ScienceDirect (Elsevier Science, coverage dates vary)
Full-text articles and abstracts to more than 1,000 Elvesier Science journals in all major scientific disciplines.

Scientific American Archive Online (Scientific American, Inc., 1993–)
Electronic database of full-text journal articles covering science and technology, including photographs, graphics, and advertising.

Synergy (Blackwell Science Ltd., coverage dates vary)
Provides full-text access to more than 250 full-text science, technology, and medical journals.

University of Chicago Press Journals Online (University of Chicago, coverage dates vary)
Features full-text articles from more than 40 scholarly journals in humanities, law, science, and social science published by the University of Chicago Press.

Wiley InterScience (Wiley InterScience, coverage dates vary)
Offers full-text access to journals in science and all related disciplines.

FREE JOURNAL ARTICLE INDEX DATABASES

Opportunities exist to access some of the same journals and same material on virtually every topic as you would in licensed databases as well as hundreds of other online e-journals and traditional paper journals in electronic form without leaving your home or office computer. Index databases for journal articles available free on the Web include:

Ingenta (http://www.ingenta.com/)
Formerly called UnCover, this database contains millions of article citations. Articles are available for purchase but require you to complete a user profile.

Northern Light (http://www.nlsearch.com/)
As part of its "Special Collection," Northern Light features a searchable database of 3,400 publications, including journals, reviews, books, magazines, and newswires. Titles appear in alphabetical and subject category lists.

MULTIPLE SUBJECT DIRECTORIES OF E-JOURNALS

The World Wide Web likewise offers many comprehensive subject directories developed by libraries, organizations, and individuals of e-journals on multiple subjects and specialties. Among the most notable are:

ARL Directory of Electronic Journals, Newsletters and Academic Discussion Lists (http://www.arl.org/scomm/edir/)
Based on the Association of Research Libraries' most recent edition of the *Directory of Electronic Journals, Newsletters and Academic Discussion Lists* (1997), this online database includes more than 7,000 listings of journals, newsletters, zines, and professional e-conferences accessible on the Internet. Searching the directory requires users to register and obtain a login and password.

Australian Journals On-Line (National Library of Australia) (http://www.nla.gov.au/ajol/)
Lists more than 900 Australian journals, magazines, and zines on the Internet.

The BUBL Information Service: Electronic Journal and Texts (http://bubl.ac.uk/journals/)
This electronic journal section of the BUBL (Bulletin Board for Libraries), funded by JISC (Joint Information Systems Committee) of the Higher Education Funding Councils of England, Scotland, Wales, and Northern Ireland, provides a selected listing of e-journals and directories of e-journals and other related information.

E-Journals (http://www.columbia.edu/cu/lweb/eresources/ejournals/)
A service of Columbia University's LibraryWeb, this page features electronic journals that can be accessed by title, by subject index (A–Z), or by general subject category.

E-Journals.org (http://www.e-journals.org/)
Via the World Wide Web Virtual Library, this directory offers links to several hundred electronic journals, including humanities, scientific, technical, and medical publications.

Electronic Journal Miner (http://ejournal.coalliance.org/)
Directory in association with the Colorado Alliance of Research Libraries (CARL) with links to more 3,000 e-journals, arranged by title and by subject, using Library of Congress subject headings, with brief descriptions of each journal.

Electronic Journals and Magazines (http://www.usg.edu/galileo/internet/electronic/elecjour.html)
Compiled by the Main Library Reference Department at the University of Georgia, this superb site lists e-journal publishers, including "Multiple-

Subject Journal Collections," "Single-Subject Journal Collections," and "General Interest Magazines." Also featured is an excellent directory of some 3,000 science journals accessible on the Web, arranged by title and subject.

Electronic Journals and Magazines (http://www2.fmg.uva.nl/sociosite/)
This directory of sociological journals, mostly Dutch and European titles, was created by Albert Benschop at the Sociological Institute of the University of Amsterdam.

Electronic Journals and Periodicals (University of Tennessee, Knoxville) (http://www.lib.utk.edu/ej/)
Contains a listing of "Collections of Other Sites" and a selected listing of e-journals, magazines, and newspapers by title and subject.

E-ZINE-LIST (http://www.e-zine-list.com/)
This list, originally compiled by John Labovitz, features almost 1,000 electronic zines from around the world that are accessible via the Web, gopher, ftp, e-mail, and other services.

Film/TV/Media Journals (http://www.screensite.org/link-12.html)
Directory of popular film, television, and media journals with Web links, sorted by date, rating, or popularity.

Full-Text Publications of Scholarly Societies (http://www.lib.uwaterloo.ca/society/full-text_soc.html)
Sponsored by the University of Waterloo Library, Scholarly Societies Project, this Web page covers newsletters or publications similar to newsletters, and a few research publications.

Genamics JournalSeek (http://journalseek.net/)
The largest fully categorized database of free journal information available on the Web today, this database contains nearly 65,000 titles, including descriptions, homepage links, and more.

Internet Public Library: Online Serials (http://www.ipl.org/div/serials/)
A searchable site of more than 2,300 title links maintained by the Internet Public Library arranged alphabetically by title and by topic category.

jake (Yale University School of Medicine) (http://jake.openly.com/)
Started as a project at Yale University in 1999, jake ("jointly administered knowledge environment") is an online reference source that manages and links online journals and journal articles from 154 databases for students, researchers, and librarians.

Lists of Newspapers and Periodicals, and News Resources Online (LC) (http://lcweb.loc.gov/rr/news/lists.html)
Available through the Library of Congress (LC), this resource page contains electronic journal directories and catalogs, not actual listings of the actual e-journals themselves.

NewJour: Electronic Journals & Newsletters (http://gort.ucsd.edu/newjour/)
This is the Web archive of the newjour listserv, a collaboration of many librarians at many different institutions that is maintained at the University of California, San Diego (UCSD). It offers a daily listing of new e-journals and newsletters on the Web.

Penn Library: E-Journals (http://www.library.upenn.edu/cgi-bin/res/sr.cgi?resourcetype=17)
Produced by the University of Pennsylvania library, this well-organized directory provides links to more than 1,600 e-journals listed by title and by 40 subject categories, arranged alphabetically and by topic.

Scholarly Journals Distributed via the World Wide Web (http://info.lib.uh.edu/wj/webjour.html)
A service of the University of Houston, this Web page provides direct links to more than 100 Web-based scholarly journals.

Serials in Cyberspace: Collections, Resources, and Services (www.uvm.edu/~bmaclenn)
Developed and maintained by Birdie MacLennan of the University of Vermont, this site includes listings of Web sites with electronic journal collections in the United States and abroad, selected e-journal titles, and other useful resources.

Voice of the Shuttle: Journals & Zines Page (http://vos.ucsb.edu/browse-netscape.asp?id=2714)
This site, developed and maintained by Alan Liu of the University of California, Santa Barbara, includes many popular electronic journals and zines in humanities.

The World Wide Web Virtual Library: Electronic Journals (http://scholar.lib.vt.edu/ejournals/vpiej-l.html)
Offered by the World Wide Web Virtual Library, this site comprehensively lists electronic journals, newsletters, and newspapers accessible via the Internet.

SINGLE-SUBJECT DIRECTORIES OF JOURNAL COLLECTIONS

In addition to researching general index databases and multiple subject directories, single-subject journal collections may provide what you need. Individual online collections of e-journals, e-zines, magazines, and newsletters are available via the World Wide Web, as follows:

Architecture

Architecture Journals (http://www.architectstore.com/magazine.html)
Links to more than 100 architecture magazines and journals.

Art

FineArt Forum Resource Directory: Journals, Zines, Newsletters (http://www.msstate.edu/Fineart_Online/art-resources/journals.html)
An A-to-Z directory of fine art journals, e-zines, and newsletters.

Astronomy

Astronomy Related Electronic Resources (http://www.cwru.edu/UL/Subjects/ASTR/elect.htm)
Provided by the Case Western Reserve University Library, this site contains extensive links to astronomy e-journals and bibliographic sources.

Biology

BioMed Central (http://www.biomedcentral.com/)
Open access to more than 100 scholarly journals covering all areas of biology and medicine, arranged by title or by subject.

Business and Economics

bizjournals (http://www.bizjournals.com/journals.html)
Provides an extensive list of major metropolitan business journals by city, with direct links to each publication.

BizLink: Business Journals (http://www.bizlink.org/bizjournals.asp)
This online business resource contains a collection of popular and international business magazines and journals, with full-text articles, from such publications as *American Banker, Business Week, Economist, Fortune, Kiplinger's Personal Finance Magazine,* and *Occupational Outlook Quarterly.* The database can be keyword-searched by company name, industry, subject, place, and personal name.

Economic Journals on the Web (http://www.oswego.edu/~economic/journals.htm)
Provided by the State University of New York at Oswego, this directory provides a complete list of economic journals with links, arranged alphabetically.

WebEc (http://www.helsinki.fi/WebEc/journals.html)
In addition to indexing journal-related information in economics, from research to working papers, this Web page also provides a list of leading economic journals, arranged by title.

Education

Newsletters and Journals from ED (U.S. Department of Education) (http://www.ed.gov/newsletters.html#top)
Administered by the U.S. Department of Education, this Web page offers links to nine electronic publications on a variety of educational topics.

TRACE Electronic Journals (http://www.adm.uwaterloo.ca/infotrac/edujournals.html)
Directory of links available through the University of Waterloo's TRACE (Teaching Resources and Continuing Education) Web site, to journals related to teaching, learning, and education that are published electronically.

History

Electronic Journals for History (http://ejw.i8.com/histe-j.htm)
Easy-to-follow alphabetical listing of electronic historical journals with links and e-mail addresses.

History Cooperative (http://www.historycooperative.org/)
This pioneering nonprofit humanities resource features a top-level collection of current volumes with full text of 12 scholarly historical journals, including *American Historical Review* (1999–), *The History Teacher* (2000–), and *Journal of American History* (1999–).

The History Journals Guide: The World Wide Web Virtual Library (http://www.history-journals.de/)
This site features a directory of periodicals with information about 5,400 history journals worldwide.

Journalism and the Media

Journalism Electronic Journals (http://ejw.i8.com/journe-j.html)
Links to more than two dozen journalism electronic journals available on the Web.

Journalism Library Electronic Journals (http://www.columbia.edu/cu/lweb/indiv/jour/ejournals.html)
A small but useful listing of trade and scholarly electronic journals and newsletters with links available through Columbia University's Journalism Library.

Law

CASE Free Electronic Journals (http://case.leeds.ac.uk/journals.html)
Funded by a grant from the Higher Education Funding Council for England, this legal information gateway project of Yorkshire and Humberside includes a directory of electronic law journals, listed in alphabetical order, including full text, abstracts, and tables of contents.

Law Journals (http://www,washlaw.edu/lawjournal.html)
A service of the Washburn University School of Law, this site lists titles and descriptions of electronic legal journals, arranged alphabetically.

Medicine

PubMed Central (http://www.pubmedcentral.nih.gov/)
Free and unrestricted access to the U.S. National Library of Medicine's digital archive of life sciences journal literature, listed by title and start date, with searchable database. Currency and age varies by journal. Service was launched in February 2000.

Music

Electronic Music Journals and Newspapers (http://www.music.indiana.edu/collections/e-journals.html)
This music resource list provided by the William and Gayle Cook Music Library at the Indiana University School of Music covers selected electronic

music journals available on the World Wide Web, including titles, coverage dates, and Web addresses.

Music Electronic/Online Journals (http://library.wustl.edu/~music/internet/online_journals.htm)
Maintained by Washington University in St. Louis's Gaylord Music Library, this directory lists about a dozen electronic and online music journals with descriptions and links.

Philosophy

EpistemeLinks.com Philosophy Resources on the Internet (http://www.epistemelinks.com/Main/MainJour.aspx)
Includes links to more than 700 print and electronic journals, searchable by title, by topic or philosopher area, or by selected publishers.

Genamics JournalSeek Philosophy (http://journalseek.net/phil.htm)
This ever-growing database features links to hundreds of philosophy electronic journals.

Journals in Philosophy (http://homepages.ed.ac.uk/pmilne/links_html/journals.html)
Compiled and maintained by Peter Milne of the University of Edinburgh, this directory features information about journals in philosophy in all related fields, listed alphabetically or by subject.

Psychology

Electronic Journals and Periodicals (http://psych.hanover.edu/Krantz/journal.html)
Alphabetical index of psychology-related electronic journals, conference proceedings, and other periodicals, with Web links.

Electronic Journals Psychology (http://www-library.st andrews.ac.uk/External/Journals/psychology.html)
Alphabetical list of free and subscription-based academic and scholarly journals with links through St. Andrews University Library.

Psychology WWW Virtual Library Journals (Electronic and Print) (http://www.clas.ufl.edu/users/gthursby/psi/journals.htm)
Features a complete list of psychology and behavioral science electronic and print journalism and lists of journals by publisher, arranged alphabetically.

Sociology and Social Sciences

Social Science Online Periodicals (Full Text) (http://www.uvm.edu/~bmaclenn/)
This comprehensive list developed and maintained by the UNESCO Social and Human Sciences Documentation Centre (SHS/DC) features e-journals in social science and all related disciplines.

Social Sciences E-Journals (http://www.clas.ufl.edu/users/gthursby/socsci/ejournal.htm)
Part of the World Wide Web Virtual Library, this directory features links to more than 100 journals in the social sciences, arranged by title.

SocioSite (http://www2.fmg.uva.nl/sociosite/)
This global information system of the University of Amsterdam features more than a dozen individual databases, including article, journal and newsletters databases arranged by subject and country.

Religion

Electronic Journals for Religion (http://ejw.i8.com/rele-j.htm)
Extensively lists multifaith religious studies, Christian, and general theology journals and links to several dozen electronic publications.

Religious Studies Web Guide (http://www.ucalgary.ca/~lipton/journals.html)
Maintained by Saundra Lipton at the University of Calgary, this directory includes a specific title listing of religious journals with direct links.

FREE E-JOURNALS ON THE WEB

No matter what your subject or your interest, e-journals, including many online electronic journals and traditional paper journals delivered in electronic form, are accessible on the Web without charge. Access to some journals is provided through centralized archives by publishers featuring multiple titles, such as the American Physical Society (APS), BioMed Central (BMC), Highwire Press, the Institute of Electrical and Electronics Engineers (IEEE), Oxford University Press (OUP), PubMed Central, and the Scientific Electronic Library Online (SciELO). Other individual titles are accessible directly from the publisher's Web site.

The University of Reno Libraries (http://www.library.unr.edu/ejournals/free.html) provides direct access to thousands of free electronic journals on all subjects. The following is a list of journals available through its Web site, cross-referenced by subject for easy use:

Aging

Arthritis Research (1999–)

Agriculture

AgBioForum (1998–)
Agriculture 21 (1998–)
Applied and Environmental Microbiology (1998–)
Aquaculture Outlook (1995–)
Arid Lands Newsletter (1994–)
BMC Biotechnology (2001–)
BMC Plant Biology (2001–)
Botanical Electronic News (1995–)

Economic Research of Interest to Agriculture (1951–)
FDA Consumer (1989–)
Florida Buggist (1917–20)
Florida Entomologist (1920–)
Genetics (1988–)
Issues in Science and Technology Online (1996–)
Journal of Bacteriology (1998–)
Journal of Biological Chemistry (1980–)
Journal of Extension (1984–)
Journal of Insect Science (2001–)
Journal of Range Management (1948–98)
Plant Cell (2000–)
Plant Physiology (1998–)
U.S. Agricultural Trade Update
Wheat Yearbook (1995–)

Anthropology

Anthropoetics (1995–)
British Archaeology (1995–)
Ethnomusicology OnLine (1995–)
Internet Archaeology (1996–)
Mana (1997–)
Revista de Antropologia (1997–)

Art

Architronic (1992–99)
Documentary Box: Online Journal of the Yamagata International Documentary Film Festival (1994–)
DoubleTake Magazine (1995–)
Gadfly (1998–)
Journal of Design Research (2001–)
Jouvert (1997–)
M/C: A Journal of Media and Culture (1998–)

Biochemistry

Antimicrobial Agents and Chemotherapy (1998–)
BioMedical Engineering OnLine (2002–)
Biophysical Journal (1976–)
BMC Biochemistry (2000–)
BMC Chemical Biology (2001–)
EMBO Journal (2001–)
Embo Reports (7/00–)
Eukaryotic Cell (2002–)
Issues in Science and Technology Online (1996–)
Journal of Biochemistry (1996–)
Journal of Biological Chemistry (1980–)
Journal of Biomedicine and Biotechnology (2001–)
Journal of Insect Science (2001–)

Lipids in Health and Disease (9/02–)
Molecular Cancer (2002–)
Nucleic Acids Research (2000–)
Physiological and Biochemical Zoology (1997–)
Proceedings of National Academy of Sciences of United States of America (1990–)
Recent Progress in Hormone Research (2001–)

Biology

Advances in Physiology Education (1989–)
American Journal of Respiratory Cell and Molecular Biology (7/97–)
Applied and Environmental Microbiology (1998–)
Biophysical Journal (1976–)
BMC Bioinformatics (2001–)
BMC Cell Biology (2000–)
BMC Chemical Biology (2001–)
BMC Developmental Biology (2001–)
BMC Ecology (2001–)
BMC Evolutionary Biology (2001–)
BMC Genetics (2000–)
BMC Genomics (2000–)
BMC Immunology (2000–)
BMC Microbiology (2001–)
BMC Molecular Biology (2000–)
BMC Neuroscience (2000–)
BMC Physiology (2001–)
BMC Plant Biology (2001–)
BMC Structural Biology (2001–)
Botanical Electronic News (1995–)
Cell and Chromosome (2002–)
Cell Biology Education (2002–)
Cell Growth and Differentiation (1999–2002)
Christmas Bird Count (1997–)
Clinical Science (1998–)
EMBO Journal (2001–)
Eukaryotic Cell (2002–)
Genetics (1988–)
Genetics and Molecular Biology (1998–)
Genome Biology (2000–)
Issues in Science and Technology Online (1996–)
Journal of Bacteriology (1998–)
Journal of Biology (2002–)
Journal of Clinical Microbiology (1998–)
Journal of General Virology (1967–)
Journal of Insect Science (2001–)
Journal of Range Management (1948–98)
Journal of Virology (1998–)
Kinetoplastid Biology and Disease (2002–)
Lipids in Health and Disease (9/02–)

Microbial Cell Factories (2002–)
Microbiology and Molecular Biology Reviews (1998–)
Molecular and Cellular Biology (1998–)
Molecular Biology of the Cell (1997–)
Nucleic Acids Research (2000–)
Physiological and Biochemical Zoology (1997–)
Plant Cell (2000–)
Plant Physiology (1998–)
Proceedings of National Academy of Sciences of United States of America (1990–)
Respiratory Research (2000–)
Scientist (2000–)
Stem Cells (1996–)

Business

Asia Inc Online (1992–)
At Issue (1995–)
B Quest (Business Quest) (1996–)
BusinessWoman Magazine (1999–)
CIO Online (1994–)
Cotton, World Markets and Trade (1996–)
CPA Journal (1989–)
E Law (1993–)
Electronic Business (1998–)
Intel Technology Journal (1997–)
Journal of Information, Law and Technology (1996–)
Journal of the International Academy of Hospitality Research (1990–98)
Monthly Labor Review (1991–)
Risk Management Magazine (1995–)
World Bank Research Observer (1998–2000)

Chemistry

Electrochemical and Solid-State Letters (1998–)
Issues in Science and Technology Online (1996–)
Journal of the Electrochemical Society (1999–)
Nucleic Acids Research (2000–)
Proceedings of National Academy of Sciences of United States of America (1990–)

Computer Science

Intel Technology Journal (1997–)
Issues in Science and Technology Online (1996–)
J.UCS: Journal of Universal Computer Science (1994–)
Journal of Artificial Intelligence Research (1994–)
Journal of Functional and Logic Programming (1995–99)
Journal of the Brazilian Computer Society (1997–2000)
RLE Currents (1999–)
Software Focus (2000–01)

Computing

ALN Magazine: Asynchronous Learning Networks Magazine (1997–2000)
Boardwatch Magazine (1995–)
Byte (1999–)
CIO Online (1994–)
Computer-Mediated Communication Magazine (1994–99)
Currents in Electronic Literacy (1999–)
Cyberlaw Informer (1999–2001)
DB2 Magazine (1996–)
DM Direct (1997–)
Electronic Business (1998–)
First Monday: Peer Reviewed Journal on the Internet (1996–)
Intel Technology Journal (1997–)
IPCT-J: Interpersonal Computing and Technology (1993–99)
Journal of Electronic Publishing (1997–)
Journal of Information, Law and Technology (1996–)
LAN Times Online (1997–98)
NCSA Access (1992–96)
PC Magazine Online (2000–)
Scout Report (1994–)
Tele.Com (2001–)

Consumer Information

Consumer News and Reviews (2000–)
FDA Consumer (1989–)

Criminal Justice

Alaska Justice Forum (1993–)
Crime Times (1995–)
Journal of Credibility Assessment and Witness Psychology (1997–)
Journal of Criminal Justice and Popular Culture (1993–)
Journal of Prisoners on Prisons (1988–)
Justice Policy Journal (2001–)
Western Criminology Review (1998–)

Current Events

Atlantic Monthly (1857–)
Central Europe Review (1999–)
Gadfly (1998–)
Helsinki Monitor (1995–97)
Reason Online (1993–)
Reproductive Freedom News (1997–)

Economics

Cotton, World Markets and Trade (1996–)
Monthly Labor Review (1991–)
OECD Observer (1996–)

World Bank Economic Review (1997–2000)
WTO Focus (1996–)

Education

Currents in Electronic Literacy (1999–)
Early Childhood Research and Practice (1999–)
Education Policy Analysis (1993–)
Education Statistics Quarterly (2000–)
Electronic Journal of Science Education (1997–)
Journal of Industrial Teacher Education (1994–)
Journal of Interactive Media in Education (1996–)
Journal of Statistics Education (1993–)
Journal of Vocational and Technical Education (1994–99)
Journal on Excellence in College Teaching (1990–)
Nevada Kids Count Data Book (2000–)
Source: A Journal of Education (1999–)
State Indicators of Science and Mathematics Education (1997–)

Engineering

AGC News and Views (1999–)
AMPTIAC Newsletter (1997–2001)
AMPTIAC Quarterly (2002–)
Architronic (1992–99)
BioMedical Engineering OnLine (2002–)
Energeia (1995–)
EPRI Journal (2001–)
IEEE Standards Bearer (1995–)
Issues in Science and Technology Online (1996–)
Journal of Design Research (2001–)
MCEER Bulletin (Multidisciplinary Center for Earthquake Engineering Research) (1994–)
RLE Currents (1999–)
Technology Interface (1996–2000)
TeraWord (2003–)
WSSPC Newsletter/EQ Earthquake Quarterly (1996–)

English

ALAN Review: Assembly on Literature for Adolescents (1996–2001)
Atlantic Monthly (1857–)
Boston Review (1975–)
Children's Bookwatch (2001–)
Common Place (2000–)
Culture Machine (1999–)
Currents in Electronic Literacy (1999–)
Documentary Box: Online Journal of the Yamagata International Documentary Film Festival (1994–)
DoubleTake Magazine (1995–)
Early Modern Literary Studies (1995–)

Electronic Antiquity: Communicating the Classics (1993–2001)
Electronic Journal for Computer Writing, Rhetoric and Literature (1994–)
Gadfly (1998–)
Heroic Age (1999–2001)
Internet Writing Journal (1997–)
Jenda: A Journal of Culture and African Women's Studies (2000–)
Journal of Electronic Publishing (1997–)
Journal of International Women's Studies (2000–)
Journal of Religion and Film (1997–)
Journal on Excellence in College Teaching (1990–)
Jouvert (1997–)
Language Learning and Technology (1997–)
M/C: A Journal of Media and Culture (1998–)
Mississippi Review (1995–)
Notes from the Windowsill (1993–98)
Oklahoma Review (2000–)
Online Journal of Distance Learning Administration (1998–)
Studies in Bibliography (1948–99)
TESL-EJ: Teaching English as a Second or Foreign Language (1994–)
Women in Literature and Life Assembly (1992–)

Environment

Acclimations: Newsletter of the U.S. National Assessment of the Potential Consequences of Climate Variability and Change (1998–)
Antarctic Journal of the United States (1993–99)
Applied and Environmental Microbiology (1998–)
Arid Lands Newsletter (1994–)
Berkeley Lab Research Review (1994–)
Consequences: the Nature and Implications of Environmental Change (1995–99)
Conservation Ecology (1997–)
Electronic Green Journal (1994–)
Energeia (1995–)
Ethics in Science and Environmental Politics (2001–)
Journal of Bacteriology (1998–)
Journal of Range Management (1948–98)
Proceedings of National Academy of Sciences of United States of America (1990–)

Ethnic Studies

Ethnomusicology OnLine (1995–)

Film Studies

Documentary Box: Online Journal of the Yamagata International Documentary Film Festival (1994–)
Gadfly (1998–)
Journal of Film Preservation (1995–)

Journal of Religion and Film (1997–)
Language Learning and Technology (1997–)

Foreign Languages

DELTA: Documentação de Estudos em Lingüística Teórica e Aplicada (1997–)
Estudios Filológicos (1998–)
Language Learning and Technology (1997–)
Literatura y Lingüística (1997–)

Geological Sciences and Mining

Antarctic Journal of the United States (1993–99)
EERI Newsletter (Earthquake Engineering Research Institute, selected articles) (2000–)
GeoDrilling International (abridged) (1996–)
Geotimes (1996–)
Gold Bulletin (London, England) (1998–)
GSA Today (1995–)
ICMM Newsletter (2001–)
Issues in Science and Technology Online (1996–)
No-dig International (abridged) (1996–)
PEER Center News (Pacific Earthquake Engineering Center) (1998–)
Pennsylvania Geology (1995–)
Western States Seismic Policy Council Newsletter (1996–)
WSSPC Newsletter/EQ Earthquake Quarterly (1996–)
Health Ecology
Advances in Physiology Education (1989–)

History

British Archaeology (1995–)
Common Place (2000–)
CROMOHS: Cyber Review of Modern Historiography (1997–)
Intersections: Gender, History and Culture in the Asian Context (1998–)
Journal of International Women's Studies (2000–)
Journal of Multimedia History (1998–2000)

Human Development and Family Studies

Forum for Family and Consumer Issues (1996–)
Nevada Kids Count Data Book (2000–)

Journalism

American Communication Journal (1997–)
Columbia Journalism Review (1991–)
Computer-Mediated Communication Magazine (1994–99)
Currents in Electronic Literacy (1999–)
Federal Communications Law Journal (1993–)

First Monday: Peer Reviewed Journal on the Internet (1996–)
International Journal on Media Management (1999–)
JMM (International Journal on Media Management) (1999–)
Journal of Electronic Publishing (1997–)
Journal of Information, Law and Technology (1996–)
Journal of Interactive Media in Education (1996–)
Journal of Religion and Film (1997–)
Journal of Technology Studies (1996–)
Newspapers and Technology (1997–)
Research Information (2002–)
T.H.E. Journal (1994–)
Tele.Com (2001–)
Web Journal of Mass Communication Research (1997–)

Law

Asian-Pacific Law and Policy Journal (2000–)
Cyberlaw Informer (1999–2001)
Federal Communications Law Journal (1993–)
Reproductive Freedom News (1997–)

Library Science

ALAN Review: Assembly on Literature for Adolescents (1996–2001)
Ariadne (1996–)
ARL Newsletter (1995–)
Associates: the Electronic Library Support Staff Journal (2000–)
Boston Review (1975–)
Bulletin of the Medical Library Association (1911–2001)
CLIR Issues (1998–)
Computer-Mediated Communication Magazine (1994–99)
Cultivate Interactive (1999–)
Currents in Electronic Literacy (1999–)
Cyberlaw Informer (1999–2001)
Cybermetrics (1997–)
D-lib Magazine: the Magazine of Digital Library Research (1995–)
E Law (1993–)
Educause Review (1994–)
Exploit Interactive (1999–2000)
First Monday: Peer Reviewed Journal on the Internet (1996–)
Information Research (1995–)
Information Technology and Libraries (2001–)
International Journal on Media Management (1999–)
Internet Writing Journal (1997–)
IPCT-J: Interpersonal Computing and Technology (1993–99)
Issues in Science and Technology Librarianship (1991–)
JMM (International Journal on Media Management) (1999–)
Journal of Electronic Publishing (1997–)
Journal of Information, Law and Technology (1996–)
Journal of Interactive Media in Education (1996–)
Journal of Library Services for Distance Education (1997–99)

Journal of Technology Education (1989–)
Journal of Technology Studies (1996–)
Journal of the American Medical Informatics Association (1997–)
Journal of the Medical Library Association (2002–)
LAN Times Online (1997–98)
Learned Publishing (1997–2002)
LIBRES: Library and Information Science Research (1996–)
MC Journal: Journal of Academic Media Librarianship (1993–2002)
Online Journal of Distance Learning Administration (1998–)
PC Magazine Online (2000–)
Prism (1999–)
Public Access Computer Systems Review (1990–98)
Research Information (2002–)
RLG DigiNews (1997–)
Scout Report (1994–)
Studies in Bibliography (1948–99)
T.H.E. Journal (1994–)
Techne: Journal of the Society for Philosophy and Technology (1995–)
Telecommunications Electronic Review (1994–)

Mathematics

Electronic Journal of Combinatorics (1994–)
Electronic Journal of Differential Equations (1993–)
Electronic Research Announcements of the American Mathematical Society (1995–)
Electronic Transactions on Numerical Analysis (1993–)
New York Journal of Mathematics (1994–)
Pacific Journal of Mathematics (1997–)
Proceedings of National Academy of Sciences of United States of America (1990–)

Medicine

Academic Medicine (2000–)
ACP Journal Club (1992–)
Advances in Physiology Education (1989–)
Advances in Psychiatric Treatment (2000–)
American Journal of Pathology (1998–)
American Journal of Respiratory Cell and Molecular Biology (7/97–)
Annals of Clinical Microbiology and Antimicrobials (2002–)
Annals of General Hospital Psychiatry (9/02–)
Annals of Internal Medicine (1993–)
Antimicrobial Agents and Chemotherapy (1998–)
Applied and Environmental Microbiology (1998–)
Archives of General Psychiatry (1998–)
Archives of Pathology and Laboratory Medicine (1999–)
ASH Education Program Book (2000–)
BioMedical Engineering OnLine (2002–)
Biomedical Library Acquisitions Bulletin (BLAB) (1992–)
Biophysical Journal (1976–)

BMC Anesthesiology (2001–)
BMC Biochemistry (2000–)
BMC Bioinformatics (2001–)
BMC Biotechnology (2001–)
BMC Blood Disorders (2001–)
BMC Cancer (2001–)
BMC Cardiovascular Disorders (2001–)
BMC Cell Biology (2000–)
BMC Chemical Biology (2001–)
BMC Clinical Pathology (2001–)
BMC Clinical Pharmacology (2001–)
BMC Complementary and Alternative Medicine (2001–)
BMC Dermatology (2001–)
BMC Developmental Biology (2001–)
BMC Ear, Nose and Throat Disorders (2001–)
BMC Ecology (2001–)
BMC Emergency Medicine (2001–)
BMC Endocrine Disorders (2001–)
BMC Family Practice (2000–)
BMC Gastroenterology (2001–)
BMC Genetics (2000–)
BMC Genomics (2000–)
BMC Geriatrics (2001–)
BMC Health Services Research (2001–)
BMC Immunology (2000–)
BMC Infectious Diseases (2001–)
BMC International Health and Human Rights (2001–)
BMC Medical Education (2001–)
BMC Medical Ethics (2001–)
BMC Medical Genetics (2001–)
BMC Medical Imaging (2001–)
BMC Medical Informatics and Decision Making (2001–)
BMC Medical Research Methodology (2001–)
BMC Microbiology (2001–)
BMC Molecular Biology (2000–)
BMC Musculoskeletal Disorders (2000–)
BMC Nephrology (2000–)
BMC Neurology (2001–)
BMC Neuroscience (2000–)
BMC Nuclear Medicine (2001–)
BMC Ophthalmology (2001–)
BMC Oral Health (2001–)
BMC Palliative Care (2002–)
BMC Pediatrics (2001–)
BMC Pharmacology (2001–)
BMC Physiology (2001–)
BMC Plant Biology (2001–)
BMC Pregnancy and Childbirth (2001–)
BMC Psychiatry (2001–)
BMC Public Health (2001–)

BMC Pulmonary Medicine (2001–)
BMC Surgery (2001–)
BMC Urology (2001–)
BMC Women's Health (2001–)
bmj.com (1998–)
British Journal of Ophthalmology (1997–)
British Journal of Psychiatry (2000–)
British Journal of Radiology (1997–)
Bulletin of the Medical Library Association (1911–2001)
CA: A Cancer Journal for Clinicians (1990–)
Canadian Journal of Anesthesia (2000–)
Canadian Medical Association Journal (1997–)
Cancer Cell International (2001–)
Cancer Epidemiology, Biomarkers and Prevention (1999–)
Cancer Research (1999–)
Cardiovascular Diabetology (2002–)
Cell Biology Education (2002–)
Cell Growth and Differentiation (1999–2002)
Centres of Excellence for Women's Health Research Bulletin (2000–)
Clinical and Diagnostic Laboratory Immunology (1998–)
Clinical Cancer Research (1999–)
Clinical Microbiology Reviews (1998–)
CMAJ: Canadian Medical Association Journal (1997–)
Contemporary Surgery (2000–)
Dermatology Online (1995–)
Diabetes (1998–)
Diabetes Spectrum (2001–)
Dynamic Medicine (10/02–)
eHealth International (2002–)
EMBO Journal (2001–)
Embo Reports (7/00–)
Emerging Infectious Diseases (1995–)
Endocrine Reviews (1992–)
FDA Consumer (1989–)
Genetics (1988–)
Heart Surgery Forum (1998–)
Infection and Immunity (1998–)
Injury Prevention (1998–)
International Journal for Equity in Health (2002–)
International Journal of Health Geographics (2002–)
Issues in Science and Technology Online (1996–)
Journal of Antimicrobial Chemotherapy (1997–)
Journal of Bacteriology (1998–)
Journal of Biological Chemistry (1980–)
Journal of Clinical Investigation (1996–)
Journal of Clinical Microbiology (1998–)
Journal of Experimental Medicine (1996–)
Journal of General Virology (1967–)
Journal of Molecular Diagnostics (1999–)
Journal of Neurology, Neurosurgery, and Psychiatry (1997–)

Journal of the American Medical Informatics Association (1997–)
Journal of the Medical Library Association (2002–)
Journal of Virology (1998–)
Journal Watch Online (1987–)
Learning and Memory (1998–)
Malaria Journal (2002–)
Microbiology and Molecular Biology Reviews (1998–)
Molecular Biology of the Cell (1997–)
Molecular Cancer Therapeutics (2001–)
Molecular Endocrinology (1992–)
Molecular Interventions (2001–)
Morbidity and Mortality Weekly Report (1982–)
Nephrology Dialysis Transplantation (1997–)
News in Physiological Sciences (1986–)
Oncologist (1996–)
Physiological and Biochemical Zoology (1997–)
Physiological Genomics (1999–)
Proceedings of National Academy of Sciences of United States of America (1990–)
Psychiatric Bulletin (2000–)
Psychosomatics (1999–)
RadioGraphics (1999–)
Radiology (1998–)
Recent Progress in Hormone Research (2001–)
Stem Cells (1996–)
Texas Heart Institute Journal (2000–)
Thorax (1998–)

Military Science

Airman (1995–)
NATO Review (1991–)

Music

EOL (Ethnomusicology Online) (1995–2000)
Ethnomusicology OnLine (1995–)
Gadfly (1998–)
Journal of Seventeenth-Century Music (1995–)
M/C: A Journal of Media and Culture (1998–)
Music Theory Online (1993–)
Notitiae Cantus (1994–97)

Nursing

BMC Complementary and Alternative Medicine (2001–)
BMC Emergency Medicine (2001–)
BMC Family Practice (2000–)
BMC Geriatrics (2001–)
BMC Health Services Research (2001–)
BMC International Health and Human Rights (2001–)

BMC Medical Ethics (2001–)
BMC Medical Informatics and Decision Making (2001–)
BMC Medical Research Methodology (2001–)
BMC Nursing (2002–)
BMC Palliative Care (2002–)
BMC Pregnancy and Childbirth (2001–)
BMC Public Health (2001–)
BMC Women's Health (2001–)
Canadian Women's Health Network (1996–)
Diabetes Spectrum (2001–)
Emerging Infectious Diseases (1995–)
Infection and Immunity (1998–)
International Journal for Equity in Health (2002–)
Morbidity and Mortality Weekly Report (1982–)

Nutrition

Diabetes Spectrum (2001–)
FDA Consumer (1989–)

Philosophy and Religion

Culture Machine (1999–)
First Things: A Journal of Religion and Public Life (1992–)
Journal of Buddhist Ethics (1994–)
Journal of Religion and Film (1997–)
Journal of Southern Religion (1998–)
Jouvert (1997–)
Mathesis Universalis (1996–98)
Techne: Journal of the Society for Philosophy and Technology (1995–)
Women in Judaism (1997–)

Physics

Berkeley Lab Research Review (1994–)
Issues in Science and Technology Online (1996–)
MRS Internet Journal of Nitride Semiconductor Research (1996–)
Optics Express (1997–)
Proceedings of National Academy of Sciences of United States of America (1990–)
RLE Currents (1999–)
Science and Technology Review (1995–)

Political Science

Asian-Pacific Law and Policy Journal (2000–)
Boston Review (1975–)
Central Europe Review (1999–)
Comparative Connections—East Asian Bilateral Relations E-Journal (1999–)
Dispatch Magazine (1993–99)
Governing (1990–)

Helsinki Monitor (1995–97)
Journal of Political Ecology (1994–)
MOST Journal on Cultural Pluralism (UNESCO) (1999–)
NATO Review (1991–)
Reason Online (1993–)
Tobacco Control (1992–)
WTO Focus (1996–)

Psychology

APA Monitor (1998–)
Current Research in Social Psychology (1995–)
Early Childhood Research and Practice (1999–)
Issues in Science and Technology Online (1996–)
Journal of Credibility Assessment and Witness Psychology (1997–)
Laboratory Primate Newsletter (1984–)
MPR Online: Methods of Psychological Research (1996–)
Perspectives: A Mental Health Magazine (1996–)
Prevention and Treatment (1997–)
Proceedings of National Academy of Sciences of United States of America (1990–)
Psychosomatics (1999–)
Psynopsis: Canada's Psychology Newspaper (1995–)

Science/Technology

DRI News (1995–)
Ethics in Science and Environmental Politics (2001–)
Journal of Technology Education (1989–)
Journal of Technology Studies (1996–)
Proceedings of National Academy of Sciences of United States of America (1990–)
Technology Source (1997–)

Social Work

Advocate's Forum (1995–)
Community Services Catalyst (1991–94)
Current Research in Social Psychology (1995–)
Future of Children (1999–)
Journal of Prisoners on Prisons (1988–)
Nevada Kids Count Data Book (2000–)
Perspectives: A Mental Health Magazine (1996–)

Sociology

Current Research in Social Psychology (1995–)
Electronic Journal of Sociology (1994–)
First Things: A Journal of Religion and Public Life (1992–)
Journal of Buddhist Ethics (1994–)
Journal of Mundane Behavior (2000–)
M/C: A Journal of Media and Culture (1998–)

MOST Journal on Cultural Pluralism (UNESCO) (1999–)
Reason Online (1993–)

Speech and Communication Studies

American Communication Journal (1997–)

Theater

Didaskalia: Ancient Theater Today (1994–)
M/C: A Journal of Media and Culture (1998–)
Parabasis (1997–2000)

Women's Studies

BusinessWoman Magazine (1999–)
Canadian Women's Health Network (1996–)
Centres of Excellence for Women's Health Research Bulletin (2000–)
Intersections: Gender, History and Culture in the Asian Context (1998–)
Jenda: A Journal of Culture and African Women's Studies (2000–)
Journal of International Women's Studies (2000–)
On Campus With Women (2002–)
S&F Online: The Scholar & Feminist Online (2003–)
Womanist Theory and Research (1994–99)
Women in Judaism (1997–)
Women in Literature and Life Assembly (1992–)
Women'space (1995–)

Finding E-mail Discussion Groups and Newsgroups

The Internet holds untold possibilities and many more sophisticated applications for research worth exploring. Among these are discussion groups and newsgroups. These electronic forms of communication have advantages and disadvantages, but they can be helpful sources of information for your research paper, report, or written project—as long as they are used wisely.

RESEARCHING DISCUSSION GROUPS

There are thousands of discussion groups on the Web, so it can be difficult to find the appropriate one. Fortunately, information about most groups is collected and indexed on the Web and on discussion group Web sites. To find the right discussion group, you can try some general methods:

1. Search the Net. Discussion group information is retrievable using most major search engines, such as Google or Yahoo! Type in words describing the kind of newsgroup you want to find (example: "biology discussion groups") and your search will produce a long list of related sites that you can visit to determine their appropriateness or relevancy.

2. Visit Web directories. Many discussion group search engines and directories, listed elsewhere this chapter, featur^e annotated listings of discussion groups, often arranged by subject or in alphabetical order. Simply searching "discussion group directories" will direct to you an extensive list of relevant groups or Web sites.

UNDERSTANDING DISCUSSION GROUPS

Discussion groups, also known as "listservs" or "mailing lists," are virtual gathering places on the Internet that allow subscribers to discuss a particular topic and exchange information and ideas via e-mail. Some groups deliver messages one at a time; others bundle them and deliver them once or twice a week. As with a newspaper or magazine subscription, subscribers can place subscriptions "on hold" for a specific period of time.

Under this form of communication, any message sent to one member of the mailing list is dispatched to all subscribers. In some cases, the owner of the group may control which messages go through to members; other groups are simply "free-for-all" discussions without a moderator, or someone who is filtering the messages. Members of the group can join in on the conversation or begin a new topic if they wish. Besides distributing messages to members, some discussion groups or listservs also distribute edited electronic or "e-journals" and newsletters to those on the list.

DECIDING TO JOIN A DISCUSSION GROUP

Before joining a discussion group, you may first want to do a background check. You need to ask yourself one basic question: "Is the discussion group or mailing list relevant to my subject or topic?" Another question you can ask is "Will there be any advantages to joining the group?"

One strong indicator is the description of the list found at Web directories of discussion groups or mailing lists. Since many host their own Web sites, another method to determining the usefulness and relevancy of the group is to visit its Web site. In particular, check out the archives, if any, and read previous postings. This will give you a more in-depth view of the mailing list, its purpose and scope, and whether it is popular, scholarly, or commercial. By reviewing past postings, you also can determine if the group appeals to you and is well suited for your subject.

Some groups provide FAQs (frequently asked questions) pages that will also tell you more about them: when they were formed, how they operate, what their privacy policy is, whether they process junk mail or advertisements, and how active the group really is. Furthermore, this section may answer other important questions, such as how many e-mails are posted per day, per week, or per month; what volume of e-mails are posted overall; and, finally, who moderates the group and is responsible for overseeing the quality of the discussion.

JOINING A DISCUSSION GROUP

To join a discussion group or mailing list, simply send an e-mail to the administrative address of the group that interests you, with the body of the message containing only "subscribe," the list name, and your full name. You don't need to put anything into the subject area of your message or include your e-mail address, as it will automatically be included in the head of your e-mail. Once received, your e-mail address will be added to the list of every subscriber on the mailing list. Usually in less than 24 hours, you should receive a message validating your subscription, saying that you have been successfully added to the group. Your e-mail notification also will contain detailed information explaining how to send messages to the list, how to unsubscribe, how to retrieve any files, and how to obtain additional help from the list owner. In addition, you will receive a list of what commands to use when entering and exiting the list or storing messages in a separate file on your computer.

To leave or unsubscribe from the group, you simply send a new e-mail to the administrative address of the group that you joined, following the same steps you did to subscribe. First you address the e-mail. Next you type in the body of the message "unsubscribe UFOS-L" without listing your full name again. Then hit "send."

Joining a group does not give you the right to act irresponsibly. Most discussion groups or mailing lists have strict rules of etiquette or behavior every subscriber must follow. Known as "netiquette," these rules cover everything from how to post or send a message to the group and write a response, treat others with respect and courtesy, and use sarcasm and humor. Check with the administrator or leader of your group regarding the rules before freely participating.

While individuals or groups own most mailing lists, they are computer-generated, so you need to master various commands in order to subscribe, unsubscribe, and for general access and use of the list, especially during and after your research is completed. The following lists some commonly used listserv commands and their meanings:

Info	Access detailed information files
List	Find a description of all mailing lists
Query	Personal distribution options for list name
Get filename	Obtain a file from the mailing list filetype
REGister	Instruct Listserv about your name full_name OFF
Review	Review the list of subscribers
Statslistname	Review list of statistics
SET listname	Set personal distribution options (options)
SUBscribe	Subscribe to a list listname (full_name)
SIGNOFF	Signoff from a list

Several Web sites offer tutorial guides on mailing list commands offering online instruction on proper usage. One excellent site, by James Miles of Case Western Reserve University Law Library, features a comprehensive list with examples at http://learn.ouhk.edu.hk/~u123/unit2/mirror2/mailser.html.

FINDING DISCUSSION GROUPS

Many Web search engines and directories are available today, offering direct link access and searching capabilities of listerv, mailing lists, or discussion groups, plus e-mail newsletters and ezines. In addition, the Web offers several easily accessible and searchable archives of past listservs, mailing lists, or discussion groups on every conceivable subject or topic. The following is a partial list of the most widely used and recognized search engines, directories, and archives currently active on the Web:

Mailing List Search Engines and Directories

CataList (http://www.lsoft.com/catalist.html)

Fully browsable "official" catalog of listservs by L-Soft International featuring approximately 70,843 public lists on the Web. Lists are searchable for topics of interest.

Coollist (http://www.coollist.com/)

A free A-to-Z directory offering mailing lists on virtually every subject area, and the ability to join or start a mailing list.

Cumuli Ezine Finder (http://www.cumuli.com/ezine/)
Premier directory of e-zines and e-mail newsletters in a variety of different categories, including a list of top rated e-zines and recent additions.

DiscussionLISTS.com (http://www.discussionlists.com)
A comprehensive directory of e-mail discussion groups and communities that match your unique interests. Subject areas include arts and humanities, business and economy, computers and Internet, education, entertainment, government, health, lifestyle, news and media, recreation, reference, and society and culture.

EzineArticles.com (http://www.ezinearticles.com/)
Offers free content of articles from various e-zines. Categories include arts and humanities, business and finance, health and education, lifestyle, recreation and sports, and women.

Ezine-Universe (http://ezine-universe.com/)
Email newsletter directory listing nearly 8,000 titles available on the Web.

EzineSeek (http://www.go-ezines.com/Detailed/555.html)
Calling itself "the coolest ezine directory on the Web," this e-mail newsletter directory offers access to e-zines, articles, tips and advice, tutorials on ezine publishing, and a newsletter search engine.

Free Lists (http://www.freelists.org/)
Hosted site of free mailing lists, all Internet and technology-related, as well as portals to many other lists by subject.

I Want Newsletters (http://www.iwantnewsletters.com/)
Online resource offering free newsletters on a myriad of subjects, including arts and crafts, business, cultures, current events, education, entertainment, health and fitness, news, politics, and science.

John Labovitz's E-Zine-List (http://www.e-zine-list.com/)
Lists more than 4,000 electronic zines worldwide, accessible via the Web, FTP, e-mail, and other services.

Koolemail (http://www.koolemail.com/)
Free directory of e-mail newsletters in business, entertainment, health, and news, and special interest e-zines.

Law Lists (http://www.lib.uchicago.edu/~llou/lawlists/info.html)
Covers electronic legal discussion groups, newsletters, and journals.

ListQuest.com (http://www.listquest.com/)
Search from hundreds of mailing lists in a variety of categories.

List-Resources.com (http://list-resources.com/)
Entirely searchable directory of mailing lists, also arranged alphabetically by topic and subtopic, with access to different lists, information, and resources.

ListTool.com (http://www.listtool.com/)
Free online tool for subscribing, unsubscribing, and sending commands to 878 mailing and discussion lists in such categories as art, business, computers, law, music, and news.

Liszt (http://emailuniverse.com/)
This popular site offers searching of mailing lists on all subjects.

NewsLettersForFree.com (http://www.newslettersforfree.com/)
High quality source of newsletters, mailing lists, and e-zines organized by topic.

TILE.NET—Email Lists (http://www.tile.net/lists/)
Comprehensive Internet reference covering discussion and information lists.

Topica (http://lists.topica.com/)
Neatly organized searchable directory of thousands of Internet newsletters and discussion groups covering all major categories.

WebScoutLists (http://www.webscoutlists.com/)
Complete Web index of discussion lists, e-mail newsletters, and e-zines with online form to subscribe and unsubscribe.

Yahoo! Groups (http://groups.yahoo.com/)
Searchable directory of discussion groups on current events, health, sports, and more.

Mailing List Archives

The Mail Archive (http://www.mail-archive.com/)
An easy-to-use archiving service featuring more than 1,800 electronic mailing lists.

Mailing List Archives (http://www.askeric.org/plweb-cgi/fastweb?searchform+listservs)
Part of the AskEric database, this archive allows users to search mailing lists of every kind or format.

USING DISCUSSION GROUPS FOR RESEARCH

Articles or postings found at discussion groups or mailing lists can used as part of your research and quoted as you would any other electronic source of information. As with any form of research, you should always question the authority of the information given and verify its accuracy.

FINDING FURTHER INFORMATION ON DISCUSSION GROUPS

Several Web sites offer further information on discussion groups or mailing lists in the form of easily accessible articles and "how-to" guides. Among some of the best choices are:

Discussion Lists: Mail Server Commands (http://learn.ouhk.edu.hk/%7Eu123/unit2/mirror2/mailser.html)
An excellent, informative online article written by James Milles that reviews how to work with mailing list or discussion group commands, with examples.

How to Find an Interesting Mailing List (http://www.webliminal.com/search/arcdocs/wouters)
Written by Arno Wouters, this insightful article discusses several sources of lists and other information on discussion groups or mailing lists.

Internet Discussion Groups (http://www1.mwc.edu/~ernie/dgroups.html)
Developed and maintained by Ernest Ackermann, this site covers all the basics, including tips on how to join, communicate, or contribute, find names and addresses of lists, and leave a list.

Internet Mailing Lists: Guides and Resources (http://www.ifla.org/I/training/listserv/lists.htm)
Features general information and specific guides and other Internet resources discussing how mailing lists function, how to find them, types of commands, things to avoid, and common "netiquette," with links to other related Web sites.

The Net: User Guidelines and Netiquette (http://www.fau.edu/netiquette/net/)
Award-winning site by Arlene Rinaldi at Florida Atlantic University offering detailed guidelines on discussion group or mailing list "dos" and "don'ts," including "The Ten Commandments" of "netiquette" from the Computer Ethics Institute.

RESEARCHING NEWSGROUPS

Much like discussion groups, newsgroups are indexed by most search engines on the Internet today and, as a result, are easily searchable by subject or by directory. It helps to know what your subject area is before commencing your search. As explained later, Internet newsgroups are listed by "hierarchy"—a term that describes the nature of the group, such as biz. (business products or services), rec. (recreational topics, such as sports, hobbies, games, music, etc.), and talk. (discussion and debate of serious issues). The formal descriptions resulting from your search will help you determine what groups are right or not.

UNDERSTANDING NEWSGROUPS

Newsgroups, also called Usenet (User's Network) newsgroups, are open forums like bulletin boards arranged by subject, or hierarchy, accessible through an Internet connection. As in a public open forum, participants in the group freely express their thoughts and ideas.

As in discussion groups, participants exchange information, tips, and techniques in the form of posted messages, or articles. Postings are grouped by topic. Copies of each article are stored on the news server until you are ready to read them. You can read as many articles as you want, and articles are stored for a certain period of time before they are deleted.

Newsgroups can be used in various ways:

- To find help with a problem
- To post messages of items for sale or requests
- To track down items wanted
- To participate in online discussions with many people

In many respects, newsgroups are like an online support group. They allow you to network with others for many of the above reasons, including researching the same topic, or same issue that you are. Newsgroups are arranged in hierarchies, consisting of the following main seven categories:

comp.	Computer hardware, software, consumer information
news.	Usenet news and announcements
rec.	Hobbies, games, sports, music, and other recreations
sci.	Pure and applied sciences
soc.	Social science, social issues, and various cultures
talk.	Current issues, debates, and discussions
misc.	Any topic that doesn't have its own category

Other popular hierarchies also used include:

alt.	Any topic, silly or controversial
bionet.	Topics of interest to biologists
biz.	Business products and services
clarinet.	Online daily newspaper and wire services for a fee
hepnet.	High energy physics research
humanities.	Fine arts, literature, and other humanities, including philosophy
info.	A collection of mailing lists or newsgroups
k12.	Topics for elementary and high school students and teachers
relcom.	Russian-language newsgroups

Dozens of other local, regional, institutional, and special-interest groups are likewise available. For a complete listing of newsgroup hierarchies, check out the following Web sites:

The Master List of Newsgroup Hierarchies (http://www.magma.ca/~leisen/mlnh/)
Features the largest and most comprehensive alphabetical list of local and regional newsgroup hierarchies, including obsolete hierarchies, available on the Web and in other versions.

The Daily News (http://www.newsguy.com/hier.htm)
Lists every top-level Usenet newsgroup hierarchy with descriptions and related groups accessible by simply clicking the hierarchy name.

DECIDING TO JOIN A NEWSGROUP

Finding the right newsgroup to suit your needs can be difficult. Fortunately, search engines (listed below) allow free online searching of newsgroups in virtually every field. Since most sites extensively index every kind of newsgroup, by simply keyword-searching your subject topic, you should produce a list of relevant newsgroups to research and determine if they are a good fit or not. If searching becomes fruitless, then visit any number of newsgroup directories that feature an alphabetical list of newsgroups of hierarchy that you can also check.

As with a mailing list or discussion group, ask yourself, "Is this group relevant to my subject or topic?" and "Are there any advantages to joining?" If you end up answering "yes" to both questions after doing a thorough examination of the group in question, then by all means give it a try and join. You can always join a different group if that one doesn't work out.

Before joining, also read any rules relating to the newsgroup regarding what's allowed and not allowed, especially with posting articles. After you join, the administrator or maintainer of the group will usually send you the group's rules, and you're responsible for abiding by them. It would be embarrassing to have the administrator of the group reprimand you for your behavior or, worse, kick you out of the group.

JOINING A NEWSGROUP

As with mailing lists or discussions, there's no cost to join a newsgroup. You simply subscribe to the ones you want to visit. You can join and read what everyone else has to say, or join an existing discussion. Once you join, how much you participate is entirely up to you.

Some newsgroups involve the use of additional software called a newsreader, that comes bundled with your browser and e-mail software, such as Microsoft Internet Explorer and Outlook Express. Setup takes just a few minutes to complete, and instructions are usually provided with your browser software.

To begin the process of subscribing to a group, you can access the group's Web address directly through your browser. Simply type in the Web address in the address bar at the top of your browser, click "enter," and you will be transported in seconds to the group you want to join.

Once you arrive at your destination, simply follow the online instructions explaining how to join. It usually involves setting up a password in combination with your e-mail address. You will use this e-mail address and password in the future anytime you want to log on to the group. Once you are successfully set up, you will receive e-mail verification of your membership. It's that simple.

When you have gotten everything you need out of the group, you can unsubscribe. Usually this entails e-mailing the group, and you will be removed from the list of subscribers. Just because you terminate your subscription doesn't mean you can't resubscribe. You can resubscribe as many times as you need.

FINDING NEWSGROUPS

With more than 300,000 newsgroups in existence today, there are many ways to find a group that interests you. One of the best ways to track down potential sources is through newsgroup search engines. These sites show you which groups are relevant to your subject area and help connect you with others discussing similar interests online. A second resource is newsgroup directories that index newsgroups on virtually any topic. The following is a list of recommended newsgroup search engines and directories for your use:

NEWSGROUP SEARCH ENGINES

Forum One (http://www.forumone.com/)
Subscription site offering online searching of more than 300,000 Internet discussion groups in existence.

Google Groups (http://groups.google.com/)
Acquired by Google in 2001, this search engine, formerly known as Deja News, provides searching of newsgroup postings over various years and online participation in Usenet discussion groups from such hierarchies as alt.(any topic), biz. (business), comp. (hardware, software, consumer info), humanities. (fine arts, literature, philosophy), misc. (employment, health, and more), news. (Usenet news), rec. (games, hobbies, and more), sci. (sciences), soc. (social issues), and talk. (current issues and debates).

Newsgroup Search (http://newsgroups.langenberg.com/)
A single-site search engine providing access to multiple search engines, such as Google's UseNet, Yahoo's eGroups, and Aims Group.

Reference.com (http://www.reference.com/)
This searchable site offers direct access to more than 13,000 newsgroups and newsgroup directories and archives.

Tile.Net Newsgroups (http://tile.net/news/)
Online search engine of newsgroups also featuring a very comprehensive directory of groups listed by index, description, or hierarchy.

NEWSGROUP DIRECTORIES

CyberFiber Newsgroups (http://www.cyberfiber.com/)
This directory is one of the most comprehensive sources of newsgroups on the Web, listing thousands of main topics and subtopics.

Newsgroups -1 (http://www.newsgroups-1.com/)
Features a categorized list of Usenet, Google, and Yahoo! groups with links.

Searching for Groups (http://www.ibiblio.org/usenet-i/search.html)
Basic and advanced keyword search engine matching desired newsgroups pertaining to many different interests.

Usenetguide.com (http://www.usenetguide.com/)
Lists of groups, divided into text and binary.

Usenet Service (http://www.usenetservice.org)
Searchable directory of newsgroups covering a variety of hierarchies with access to articles by news server name.

NEWSGROUP ARCHIVES

Internet FAQ Archives (http://www.faqs.org/faqs/)
This site features Usenet frequently asked questions indexed by newsgroups, by category, and by multipage digests.

USING NEWSGROUPS FOR RESEARCH

With so many newsgroups in existence, you have to be selective about which newsgroups you use to answer a particular research question. The most reliable newsgroups should include experts, researchers, academicians, or professionals. Most newsgroups are geared toward nonbusiness discussions, but some focus on highly technical subjects for scientists and engineers or subjects of interest to business professionals, scholars, or educators.

From the above list of newsgroups, two of your best sources for locating qualified newsgroups are Google Groups and Yahoo! Groups. Google is by far the best source of newsgroups on the World Wide Web, making it easy to search, view, and post messages to newsgroups. Yahoo! Groups features more limited sites of interest, but sometimes offers more resources than Google does in this regard. Also see Finding Newsgroups, a Web site available at http://www.ii.com/internet/messaging/newsgroups/.

As always, critically evaluate and verify any information obtained from any newsgroup.

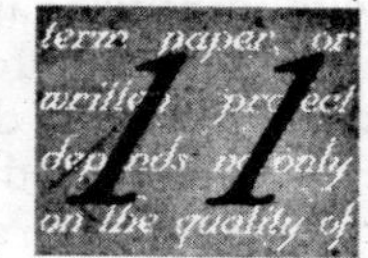

Finding General References

Published reference materials such as almanacs, yearbooks, encyclopedias, and indexes are indispensable resources of information that can be vital to your success in researching almost any topic. Other references can include memoirs and autobiographies, bibliographies, diaries, journals, speeches, interviews, letters, memos, manuscripts and other papers, information collected by government agencies or organizations, microfilm collections, public opinion polls, photographs, audio recordings, and moving pictures or video recordings. When visiting your school or public library, you will find many other useful reference books covering a wide range of information and used across all areas of research. (Many titles discussed in this chapter are also offered as electronic databases. For more information, see Chapter 7.).

RESEARCHING GENERAL REFERENCES

Finding general references suitable to your topic can be difficult, but there are ways to make it easier. Start with keyword searches of the online library catalog. Your keyword search should combine the general term that describes your subject with relevant terms (for example: "illegal immigration"). This keyword search will retrieve records of any book or reference covering this subject.

A second method of finding pertinent references is to consult the Library of Congress Subject Headings in your library's online catalog. This A-to-Z classification system assigns subject headings to all items in your library's catalog, such as books, references, periodicals, audiocassettes, videos, and other titles. Items are referenced by main subject headings and linked to broader, narrower, or related terms in the system. For example, under the main heading of "Animal Psychology," broader, narrower, or related terms would include psychology, animal behavior, or animal memory.

All subjects are fully searchable in the catalog. For example, by searching "smoking," a list of entries or categories of references ("Smoking Abstracts Periodicals," "Smoking Anecdotes," "Smoking Directories," "Smoking History," etc.), available at your library will appear on the screen in alphabetical order. Opposite each category will be a notation of the number of references available. After you click on a category, a listing of titles with identifying information will appear.

A third approach is to do a direct subject search, or do a new keyword search using the distinctive words or phrases on your library's online catalog. For example, a direct subject search of "smoking cessation" would retrieve records of any and all references—print and electronic—that deal with tobacco dependence, related diseases and treatment, and local or federal legislative action to reduce tobacco use.

On the other hand, a new keyword search might use a different combination of terms than before, such as "smoking and disease," and would find references specifically focused on the health consequences of smoking.

In addition to these more common methods, another way is to find a good general reference and use it to find more related references. Most major reference works include extensive bibliographies listing information on other pertinent references that were consulted in researching the subject. You can make a list of those other sources that sound worthwhile, then cross search them in the online catalog of your library, or other libraries, should they not have what you desire.

Finally, you should also consult your library's CD-ROM databases and online databases. They can provide access to other general references in electronic form.

The following is an overview of the best general reference sources recommended by researchers and librarians.

ALMANACS

When researching facts, statistics, and basic information, almanacs are an excellent source. Most yearly almanacs recap important events that occurred during the previous year and include data on major subject areas, such as business, arts and entertainment, and sports. Examples include:

The Americana Annual (New York, Chicago: Americana Corporation, 1924–)
Covers the preceding year with feature articles on newsworthy topics. Illustrated and indexed.

The Annual Register: A Record of World Events (Detroit, Mich.: Gale Group, 1958–)
This popular reference annually surveys current and political events by country and features chapters on such disciplines as the arts, law, religion, and science, plus statistics, obituaries, and a year-in-review chronology.

Encyclopedia Americana Annual (Danbury, Conn.: Grolier, annual)
A source of general information covering a wide range of subjects. Geared towards advanced high school students, college students, and adults.

Encyclopaedia Britannica Almanac (Chicago: Encyclopaedia Britannica, 2005)
Covers current events, history, geography, health, money, religion, science, and sports, and includes statistics on many topics in one compact volume.

Famous First Facts (New York: H.W. Wilson, annual)
Literally thousands of fascinating firsts are detailed in a wide range of subject areas, including education, entertainment, nations, history, politics, science, sports, and much more. Also offered in online and CD-ROM editions.

Guinness Book of World Records (New York: Time, annual)
This reference book chronicles more than 700 records in sports, science and technology, feats of engineering, and much more.

Information Please Almanac, Atlas & Yearbook (Boston: Houghton Mifflin, 1960–98)
A veritable treasure trove of facts and figures, plus news and current events. The title was changed to *Time Almanac* in 1999 after the publisher teamed with Time, Inc., to produce a "new almanac" (see *Time Almanac* for details). Meanwhile, *Information Please* lives on via the World Wide Web with current almanacs found at its official Web site: (http://www.infloplease.com/almanacs.html).

Time Almanac (New York: Time Almanac, 2002)
Formerly the *Information Please Almanac,* this volume comprehensively covers facts, statistics, dates, and information highlighting countries, world statistics, and many general subjects.

The World Almanac and Book of Facts (Chicago: World Almanac Books, 1868–)
An all-around reference, available in print and electronic editions, useful for researching hundreds of statistics and facts, including data on politics, economics, science, technology, sports, and entertainment, and offering comparative statistics from current and past editions.

In addition, several almanacs focused on specific subjects are published annually to provide relevant details and information. Examples include:

Almanac of Architecture and Design, 2004, 5th Ed. (Norcross, Ga.: Greenway Communications, 2004)
The Old Farmers' Almanac 2005 (Dublin, N.H.: Yankee Publishing, 2004)
ESPN Sports Almanac 2005 (New York: 2004)
Florida Almanac, 2004–2005, 16th Ed. (Gretna; La.: Pelican Publishing Co., 2004)
People Almanac 2004, 10th Ed. (New York: Time, 2003)
2005 International Television and Video, 50th Ed. (La Jolla, Calif.: Quigley Publishing Co., 2004)

ATLASES

Like almanacs, atlases can be a great asset. They accurately discuss aspects of a country or a region, including topographic information, or include maps and graphics on the environment, population, or other topics. Most atlases feature short articles, tables, statistics, and other important information. They include:

Atlas of the World, 10th Ed. (New York: Oxford University Press, 2002)
Handsomely illustrated atlas that features complete political and physical maps for each area of the world and maps of some of the world's greatest cities. Updated annually.

DK World Atlas, 2nd Ed. (New York: Dorling Kindersley, 2000)
First published in 1997, this atlas features more than 80,000 entries, with text, photos, charts, and thematic maps.

Hammond Atlas of the World, 4th Ed. (Stamford, Conn.: Hammond Publishing, 2002)
Strikingly beautiful atlas with detailed maps covering countries, continents, territories, and many other geographical areas of the world.

National Geographic Atlas of the World, 7th Ed. (Washington, D.C.: National Geographic, 1999)
Impressive visual and text resource covering the world and all its beauty, including its oceans, stars, climate, natural resources, and more; with full-page spreads and physical maps.

The New International World Atlas, 25h Anniversary Ed. (Skokie, Ill.: Rand McNally, 1999)
This international atlas is the only major atlas to offer introductory text in five languages (English, French, German, Spanish, and Portuguese). Content includes legends, thematic maps and diagrams, country maps, political maps of regions and continents, and locator maps on each page. Maps explain terrain formation, climate, population patterns, natural resources, environment, transportation, commerce, communications, and much more.

The Times Atlas of the World, 10th Ed. (New York: Crown Publishing Group, 1999)
Detailed, extensively indexed reference provides unparalleled coverage of all parts of globe. Includes a chronological history of cartography and stunning satellite images of the continents and oceans.

The World Book Atlas (Chicago: World Book, 2001)
Offered in conjunction with *The World Book Encyclopedia,* this atlas features 60 detailed Rand McNally maps similar to those published in *The New International Atlas,* and an index of 54,000 places.

BIBLIOGRAPHIES

General bibliographies—and specialized bibliographies, catering to a specific topic or a full range of topical ideas—are important tools for locating information. Most bibliographies contain primary and secondary sources that you can consult and from which you can develop a list of resources to use for your own research. Sources such as books, articles, and other materials are cited that cover a wide range of subjects. Two of the best general bibliographies in print today are:

Bibliographic Index: A Cumulative Bibliography of Bibliographies (New York: H.W. Wilson, 1938–)
This annually updated guide lists books and journals that include bibliographies on various subjects.

MLA International Bibliography of Books and Articles on the Modern Languages and Literatures (New York: The Modern Language Association of America, 1921–)
Also available online (from 1963 to the present), this comprehensive resource features more than 1 million citations of items from journals and series published worldwide, indexes, books, essay collections, working papers, proceedings, dissertations, and bibliographies, and includes information about the libraries that own such material.

Specialized bibliographies abound on a variety of individual subjects. Titles vary by library, so check with your library regarding the availability of bibliographies relevant to your subject area.

CHRONICLES: BY ERAS AND DECADES

Profusely illustrated and well-written chronicles of American and world history likewise have much to offer in terms of research. Covering different eras and decades, these massive volumes review major milestones, headline makers, different cultures, and more. Printed editions are available, as well as some electronic versions. Examples include:

American Chronicles: Year by Year Through the Twentieth Century by Louis and Alan Gordon (New Haven: Yale University Press, 1999)
Provides overviews of each decade, including major events in the news and facts and figures.

American Eras, 1600–1754: Colonial Era (Detroit, Mich.: Gale Group, 1998)

American Eras, 1783–1853: Development of a Nation (Detroit, Mich.: Gale Group, 1998)

American Eras, 1850–1977: Civil War and Reconstruction (Detroit, Mich.: Gale Group, 1998)

American Eras, 1879–1899: Development of the Industrial U.S. (Detroit, Mich.: Gale Group, 1998)
Each volume covers the individuals, world events, arts, communication, education, government and politics, and science and medicine from the colonial era onward.

American Decades: 1900–1909 (Detroit, Mich.: Gale Group, 1996)

American Decades: 1910–1919 (Detroit, Mich.: Gale Group, 1996)

American Decades: 1920–1929 (Detroit, Mich.: Gale Group, 1995)

American Decades: 1930–1939 (Detroit, Mich.: Gale Group, 1996)

American Decades: 1940–1949 (Detroit, Mich.: Gale Group, 1995)

American Decades: 1950–1959 (Detroit, Mich.: Gale Group, 1994)

American Decades: 1960–1969 (Detroit, Mich.: Gale Group, 1994)

American Decades: 1970–1979 (Detroit, Mich.: Gale Group, 1995)

American Decades: 1980–1989 (Detroit, Mich.: Gale Group, 1995)

American Decades: 1990–1999 (Detroit, Mich.: Gale Group, 2000)
Each volume examines the changes in American civilization from the beginning of the 20th century to the present, including important events, biographies of major figures for each decade, and subjects such as arts, education, politics, and more.

Chronicle of the World (New York: Dorling Kindersley, 1996)
This beautifully illustrated reference summarizes the history of humanity thus far, in chronological order from 3.5 million years B.C. to the present day.

20th Century Day by Day (New York: Dorling Kindersley, 1999)
This visual history features capsule summaries of the people, places, and events of the past 100 years in chronological order.

CHRONOLOGIES AND DAYBOOKS

Chronologies and daybooks vary widely in content. Some are available in both print and CD-ROM editions. Check with your library regarding availability. Popular titles include the following:

Chronologies

Encyclopedia of World Facts and Dates by Gorton Carruth (New York: HarperCollins, 1993)
This single-volume reference, covering prehistory to the present, features more than 50,000 significant facts, dates, and events that shaped world history in all aspects.

Chronology of the Ancient World—10,000 B.C. to A.D. 799 by H.E.L. Mellersh (New York: Simon and Schuster, 1994)

Chronology of the Medieval World—800 A.D. to 1491 by R.L. Storey (New York: Simon and Schuster, 1994)

Chronology of the Expanding World—1492–1792 by R.L. Storey (New York: Simon and Schuster, 1995)

Chronology of the Modern World—1763–1992 by Neville Williams (New York: Simon and Schuster, 1995)
Considered the best chronologies of the modern world, each is divided by time periods and by category. Sections thoroughly cover general events, politics, literature, entertainment, and births and deaths.

Daybooks

American Book of Days, 4th Ed. by Stephen G. Christianson (New York: H.W. Wilson, 2000)
Cross-referenced and indexed for easy use, this popular reference features more than 1,000 essays exploring significant events on the anniversaries or on the birthdays of individuals involved with in-depth treatment of military, scientific, ethnic, and cultural events.

Born This Day: A Book of Birthdays and Quotations of Prominent People through the Centuries by Robert A. Nowlan (Jefferson, N.C.: McFarland & Co., 1996)
Comprehensively lists authors, scientists, actors, poets, rulers, philosophers, playwrights, and others born on each day of the year.

Day by Day: The Forties by Thomas M. Leonard (New York: Facts On File, 1978)

Day by Day: The Fifties by Jeffrey D. Merritt (New York: Facts On File, 1980)

Day by Day: The Sixties by Thomas Parker and Douglas Nelson (New York: Facts On File, 1983)

Day by Day: The Seventies by Thomas Leonard, Cynthia Crippen and Marc Aronson (New York: Facts On File, 1988)

Day by Day: The Eighties by Ellen Meltzer and Marc Aronson (New York: Facts On File, 1995)

Day by Day: The Nineties by Smita Avasthi (New York: Facts On File, 2004)
Each volume highlights key daily events in the areas of world affairs, U.S. politics, culture, economy, and environment, culture and lifestyles, social issues, science and technology, and more.

Dictionary of Dates by Cyril Leslie Beeing (New York: Oxford University Press, 1997)
Presents a history of events and birthdays for each day of the month.

DICTIONARIES

Dictionaries offer substantive information enabling you to quickly check spelling, pronunciation, and word division. Like most printed references today, dictionaries are offered in multiple forms, both printed and electronic. Commonly found titles include:

English Language Dictionaries

The American Heritage Dictionary, 4th Ed. (Boston: Houghton Mifflin, 2000)
Contains more than 70,000 entries, including, the publisher claims, more biographical and geographical entries than any other paperback dictionary on the market today. Also has more than 400 images.

Funk & Wagnalls New International Dictionary of the English Language (New York: World Publishing, 2001)
Two-volume set that is sometimes regarded as the most comprehensive international encyclopedic dictionary in the world.

The Oxford English Dictionary (Oxford, U.K.: Oxford University Press, 2000)
One of the most authoritative, comprehensive English-language directories published, with coverage of the English language, its history, and cultural, political, and social influences. Also offered online.

Random House Webster's Unabridged Dictionary (New York: Random House, 1999)
One of the most complete dictionaries available, featuring more than 315,000 entries, including definitions, maps, illustrations, famous people, places, historical events, and much more.

Webster's New International Dictionary of the English Language (New York: Merriam-Webster, 1961)
This edition includes more than 450,000 words, including 10 million usage examples, biographical and geographical names, foreign words and phases, and word histories. Also available on CD-ROM.

Specialized Dictionaries

Your library may have specialized dictionaries as well. Specialized dictionaries are composed for a limited audience, like computer programmers or psychologists. You can locate these titles by searching your library's catalog by subject or title.

DIRECTORIES

Whether you are trying to uncover a listing of names and addresses of people associated with a particular company or organization, or information about a local, state, or regional organization, nonprofit association or international group, a number of published directories offer this information. Examples include:

Directories in Print, 25th Ed., 3 vols. (Detroit, Mich.: Gale Group, 2005)
Describes approximately 15,500 directories in all subjects.

Encyclopedia of Associations, 42nd Ed. (Detroit, Mich.: Gale Group, 2005)
Available in print, CD-ROM, and online, this comprehensive directory, arranged by subject, offers complete details on seemingly every national association and nonprofit group.

Encyclopedia of Associations: International Organizations, 41st Ed., 3 vols. (Detroit, Mich.: Gale Group, 2004)
Details countless international organizations.

Encyclopedia of Associations: Regional, States and Local Organizations, 16th Ed., 5 vols. (Detroit, Mich.: Gale Group, 2005)
Features contact and descriptive information about U.S. nonprofit membership organizations as part a multivolume set or in regional volumes divided by region.

The Foundation Directory (New York: The Foundation Center, 2003)
This popular reference includes addresses, financial data, interest areas, application requirements, and other information on various foundations located throughout the United States.

ENCYCLOPEDIAS

Useful facts on many topics covering all of human knowledge, including socioeconomic statistics, scientific information, sports records, and other data, can be found in general encyclopedias, most of which are revised and updated annually and may be available in electronic form. Encyclopedias are comprehensive and authoritative, the kind of general reference that should not be overlooked. Among the best are:

Academic American Encyclopedia, 21 vols. (Danbury, Conn.: Grolier, Inc., annual)
Contains more than 30,000 engagingly written articles by some 2,500 contributors, including bibliographies of sources.

Collier's Encyclopedia, 24 vols. (New York: Collier's, 1950–97)
Among the finest multivolume encyclopedias published in North America, featuring authoritative, essay-length articles and short entries on a broad range of topics written by some 4,500 academic specialists, aimed at adult readers and junior and high school students.

The Columbia Encyclopedia, 6th Ed. (New York: Columbia University Press, 2002)
The oldest and most prestigious single-volume general encyclopedia in the English language, this print edition offers more than 50,000 article entries on current and contemporary topics.

Compton's Encyclopedia and Fact Index, 26 vols. (Chicago: Encyclopaedia Britannica, 2002)
Published since 1922, originally by Compton's Learning, this reference contains more than 37,000 articles, profiles, and time lines covering many different topics and curriculum areas. It is designed for students in the upper elementary grades through high school. Also available on CD-ROM.

Encyclopedia Americana, 30 vols. (Danbury, Conn.: Grolier, Inc., annual)
A standard in school and public libraries, this encyclopedia, written by authorities in their fields, provides in-depth coverage and research on worldwide current affairs, American history, covering many major fields of interest, complete with bibliographies and indexed for easy reference. Grolier also publishes an online version that includes more than 45,000 searchable articles and 100,000 full-text periodical articles provided by EBSCO Publishing.

The New Book of Knowledge (Danbury, Conn.: Grolier, Inc., annual)
For elementary students and up, this easy-to-use encyclopedia offers more than 9,000 age-appropriate articles and 5,000 periodical articles on a variety of subjects.

The New Encyclopaedia Britannica, 15th Ed., 32 vols. (Chicago: Encyclopaedia Britannica, annual)
Intended for high school and college students, this popular source features entries covering a wide range of subjects. The series consists of three parts: the *Micropedia* (volumes 1–12), a twelve-volume set offering more than 60,000 short entries; the *Macropedia* (vols. 13–29), a seventeen-volume set featuring expanded articles complete with bibliographies; and the *Propaedia* (vol. 30), a one-volume book of knowledge. The set is accompanied by a two-volume index. Also available on CD-ROM as the Britannica 2004 Ultimate Reference Suite.

World Book Encyclopedia, 22 vols. (Chicago: World Book, annual)
Totaling 14,000 pages, this appealing 22-volume set, written in a clear, direct style, is said to be the most up-to-date encyclopedia offered, with almost 20 percent of its content revised annually. Combining relatively basic and advanced articles that are written by more than 3,000 expert contributors in collaboration with *World's Book's* editors and researchers, the entire series is offered online by subscription.

In addition to the above titles, most libraries carry specialized encyclopedias that cover a particular topic or discipline, such as art, business, history, law, medicine, music, psychology, religion, science, technology, and other specialties. They can be more thorough, since they are entirely focused on one subject. For a list of available titles, consult your library's catalog.

To find more information about additional dictionaries and subject encyclopedias, two recommended sources are *American Reference Books Annual* (Englewood, Colo.: Libraries Unlimited, 1970–) and *ARBA Guide to Subject Encyclopedias and Dictionaries, 2nd Ed.* (Englewood, Colo.: Libraries Unlimited, 1997).

GUIDES TO BOOKS AND REFERENCES

To locate a variety of popular references and books, a wide range of information sources used across all areas of research will help you find what you need:

Books in Print, 10 vols. (New York: R.R. Bowker, 1948– , annual)
Lists by author and title more than 1 million books available from U.S. publishers, updated annually with midyear supplements. Includes price and availability. Also published on CD-ROM and available online by subscription.

Subject Guide to Books in Print, 5 vols. (New York: R.R. Bowker, 1957– , annual)
Annually indexes more than 2 million nonfiction titles from *Books In Print*, arranged by subject.

MICROFORM COLLECTIONS

With the explosive growth of online databases and electronic resources, the popularity of microform collections is sometimes overlooked as a general reference source. However, they can still be helpful. Libraries throughout the United States offer microform collections, comprised of microfilm and microfiche, containing the entire of contents of catalogs, newspapers, magazines, historical publications, and special single documents.

Collections as well as the contents of each collection vary by library. To ascertain the availability of microform collections, check with library reference staff, who should have a listing of which microfilm and microfiche materials are available for public use. (For additional information on newspapers and magazines on microfilm and microfiche, see Chapter 13.)

PERIODICAL AND NEWSPAPER INDEXES

Printed subject indexes to periodicals are yet another important tool that you can use to find magazine, newspaper, and journal articles. Most libraries offer many outstanding printed volumes covering all disciplines, some of which have been in print for more than 50 years (and also are available in most cases in electronic versions. See Chapter 7 for details). This includes historical indexes covering the contents of major newspapers published during a specific time period, from the late 1700s through the 1990s. (For a complete roundup of historical newspaper indexes, see Chapter 13.) The following is an example of the kinds of subject and periodical indexes offered by school and public libraries:

Agriculture

Biological and Agricultural Index (New York: H.W. Wilson, 1964–)
Formerly *The Agricultural Index* (1916–), this popular reference series indexes more than 300 journals in agriculture and related fields.

Anthropology

Abstracts in Anthropology (Westport, Conn.: Greenwood Press, 1970–)
Published eight times a year, indexing and abstracting articles on archaeology, physical anthropology, cultural anthropology, and linguístics. Several hundred scholarly journals from February 1970 to the present are arranged by subject heading, subheading, and primary author. Also includes author and subject indexes.

Anthropological Literature (Pleasantville, N.Y., Redgrave Pub. Co., 1979–87)
Quarterly indexes of journal articles and essays, alphabetically arranged by author, under the headings of archaeology, biological and physical anthropology, cultural and social anthropology, and linguistics, and secondary disciplines, such as demography, history, geography, human genetics, international development, and sociology, published between 1979 and 1987. A supplementary section was added in 1992, indexing reviews of books, exhibits, films, journals, sound recordings, videos, and other materials and events. An online version indexes material from 1979 to the present.

Art and Humanities

The American Humanities (Troy, N.Y.: Whitston Pub. Co., 1975–

Published quarterly with an annual cumulation, this print index covers nearly 400 journals in the arts and humanities, including "creative, critical, and scholarly journals," indexed by author or subject, from spring/summer 1975 to the present. Short stories, poetry, and reviews are included. A list of journals indexed accompanies each issue.

Art Index (New York: H.W. Wilson, 1929–)

This outstanding reference indexes publications in all areas of art, including archaeology, architecture, art history, city planning, design, graphic arts, landscape architecture, photography and film, and other related subjects.

Arts and Humanities Citation Index (London: Institute for Scientific Information, 1975–)

A cumulative index covering more than 6,000 journals in the fields of the arts and humanities.

Humanities Index (New York: H.W. Wilson, 1974–)

This leading humanities index includes subject field indexes to archaeology, classical studies, folklore, history, language, literature, performing arts, philosophy, religion, theology, and relevant subjects.

International Index to Periodicals (New York: H.W. Wilson, 1907–65)

Originally published as the *Readers' Guide to Periodical Literature Supplement* (1907–19), this 18-volume set, retitled in 1920, indexes periodicals from around the world. Publication ceased with the April 1964/March 1965 edition.

Social Sciences and Humanities Index (New York: H.W. Wilson, 1966–74)

Nine-volume reference set that indexes citations to a wide range of important social sciences and humanities journals published between April 1965 and March 1974.

Bibliography

Bibliographic Index (New York: H.W. Wilson, 1937/42–)

Long-running reference that indexes more than 272,000 bibliographies from books, pamphlets, and more than 2,800 periodicals.

Biography

Biography Index (New York: H.W. Wilson, 1984–)

Indexes biographical information from books and magazines.

Biology

Biological Abstracts (Philadelphia: BioSciences Information Service, 1926–97)

Indexes and abstracts periodicals in agriculture, biology, and related sciences; continued as an online database since 1997.

Books and Book Reviews

American Book Publishing Record (ABPR) (New York: Bowker, 1960–)
Since the introduction of the first volume in February 1960, annually catalogs thousands of books published or distributed in the United States in Dewey Decimal System sequence, with separate sections for adult and juvenile fiction. Author, title, and subject indexes offer easy cross-referencing of entries.

Book Review Digest (New York: H.W. Wilson, 1905–)
This annual digest indexes book reviews that appeared in nearly 75 English and American general interest periodicals.

Book Review Index (Detroit, Mich.: Gale Group, 1969–)
Indexes book reviews published in almost 450 periodicals.

Cumulative Book Index (CBI) (New York: H.W. Wilson, 1908–2000)
Cumulative bibliographic reference with citations of English-language books, both fiction and nonfiction, published throughout the world from 1908 to 1999.

An Index to Book Reviews in the Humanities (Williamston, Mich.: P. Thomson, 1961–90).
Thirty-one-volume annually published series of citations to some 700 popular and scholarly periodicals, arranged by the author of the work reviewed.

Business and Economics

Business Education Index (New York: Delta Pi Epsilon Fraternity, 1940–2000)
Published by Delta Pi Epsilon, the national honorary professional graduate society for business educators at New York University, this annual reference indexes current business education publications.

Business Periodicals Index (New York: H.W. Wilson, 1958–)
In print since 1958, this annual compendium indexes 350 journals in business, finance, investment, advertising and public relations, accounting, economics, insurance, labor, and management.

Economic Literature Index (Nashville, Tenn.: American Economic Association, 1969–)
Comprehensively indexes citations to articles found in journals on economics and related industries.

Index of Economic Articles (Homewood, Ill.: R.D. Irwin, Inc., 1961–)
Formerly titled *Index of Economic Journals,* this annually published bibliographic reference, prepared under the auspices of the American Economic Association, covers current-year journal articles and essays, books, conference proceedings, and more than 350 research and scholarly journals on economics indexed by subject and author from 1886 to 1983. An online version from 1969 to the present is also offered.

Chemistry

Chemical Abstracts (Columbus, Ohio: American Chemical Society, 1907–)
Descriptive abstracts of documents featured from publications in more than 50 languages.

Computers

Computer Literature Index (Phoenix, Ariz.: Applied Computer Research, 1971–2003; EBSCO, 2003–)
This subject-specific index covers all computer trade publications, general business publications, and periodicals of computer and management professional societies. EBSCO Publishing in 2003 acquired the index, offering its contents online as part of its library of periodical databases.

Criminal Justice

Criminal Justice Abstracts (Monsey, N.Y.: Willow Tree Press, 1977–)
Printed resource that indexes criminal justice journals.

Demography

Population Index (Washington, D.C.: Population Association of America, 1936–37; Princeton, N.J.: Office of Population Research, Princeton University 1937–99)
First called *Population Literature,* this 65-volume quarterly reference, renamed in 1937, indexes citations to literature in the areas of demography and population, including books, doctoral dissertations, journal articles, serial publications, working papers, and nearly 400 journals covering all geographic regions and subject areas. Content is arranged by subject, then alphabetically by author. A special edition, *Governmental and International Serial Publications Containing Vital Statistics,* covers "routine official statistical publications" that are not included in regular issues. Each volume includes an author index and a geographical index arranged by country or region. A cumulative index of author and geographic indexes is published periodically. Print and online version coverage is from March 1935 to 1999.

Dissertations

Comprehensive Dissertation Index (Ann Arbor, Mich.: University Microfilms International, 1861–2001)
Produced by University Microfilms International (UMI), this series includes citations to virtually every doctoral dissertation accepted in North America since 1861. UMI also produced an electronic version in 1987.

Dissertation Abstracts International (Ann Arbor, Mich.: University Microfilms International, 1938–99)
Indexes dissertations from accredited North American educational institutions and more than 200 other institutions.

Education

Current Index to Journals in Education (CIJE) (Phoenix, Ariz.: Oryx Press, 1969–2000)
This education database indexes articles in more than 800 journals in association with the U.S. Office of Education's Educational Resources Information Center (ERIC).

Education Index (New York: H.W. Wilson, 1929–)
Indexes more than 400 English-language educational periodicals and yearbooks and related articles by author/subject covering the field of education, from preschool through college, including special education. Also indexes book reviews.

Higher Education Abstracts (Claremont, Calif.: Claremont Graduate School, 1984–)
Timely resource (formerly *College Student Personnel Abstracts*) featuring abstracts for almost 120 scholarly journals, conference papers, and monographs.

Resources in Education (Washington, D.C.: U.S. Government Printing Office, 1975–)
Abstracts nearly 400,000 papers, government documents, research reports, and related material, plus items from the ERIC collection.

Engineering

The Engineering Index (New York: Engineering Magazine, 1896–1906; American Society of Mechanical Engineers, 1907–68; Engineering Index, Inc., 1969–86)
First published in 1896, this annual index provides bibliographic citations and abstracts covering the world's technological literature in all engineering disciplines, indexing more than 3,500 scholarly journals, books, conference papers, reports, and other publications in the field of engineering through 1986. Entries are arranged under broad subject headings with an author index.

INSPEC (London: Institution of Electrical Engineers, 1969–)
Leading engineering index focusing on literature in the fields of computing, electrical engineering, electronics, and physics.

Environment

Environment Abstracts (Cambridge, Mass.: Environment Information Center, Inc., 1970–99)
Authoritative index with abstracts of both print and nonprint materials, including journal articles and reports, on a variety of environmental issues.

Pollution Abstracts (Bethesda, Md.: Cambridge Scientific Abstracts, 1970–)
Abstracts scientific research and government policies as reported in conference proceedings, journals, and other documents.

Water Resources Abstracts (Bethesda, Md.: Cambridge Scientific Abstracts, 1967–)
Combines citations with abstracts to printed literature on many water-related topics.

History

America: History and Life (Santa Barbara, Calif.: ABC-CLIO, 1964–)
This publication abstracts thousands of articles in 40 languages on the history of the United States and Canada, published worldwide. Although this series is now out of print, previous volumes can be found in libraries and online. (See listing in Chapter 7 for details.)

Combined Retrospective Index to Journals in History, 1838–1974 (Washington, D.C.: Carrollton Press, 1977)
An 11-volume set that provides retrospective indexing of 243 English-language periodicals on "all periods and areas in the field of history" from 1838 to 1974. Citations are arranged by subject in the first nine volumes and by author in the final two volumes. Index articles are listed chronologically under subject or author headings.

Facts On File World News Digest with Index (New York: Facts On File, 1940–)
Long a staple in libraries, this weekly digest highlights important current and news events.

Historical Abstracts (Santa Barbara, Calif.: ABC-CLIO, 1955–2000)
Print equivalent to the online database of the same name (1960–), with abstracts of scholarly journals and dissertations on world history (except United States and Canadian history) from 1450 to the present, including social and cultural history.

Language and Literature

Abstracts of English Studies (Boulder, Colo.: National Council of Teachers of English, 1958–91)
Thirty-four-volume index with abstracts of print and microfiche literary journals from January 1958 to 1991 organized by subject and by literary time period, and subdivided by topic or author studied.

Essay and General Literature Index (New York: H.W. Wilson, 1934–)
Also known as the *Essay Index,* this well-written volume indexes articles published in the humanities and social sciences.

Language and Language Behavior Abstracts (New York: Appleton-Century Crofts, 1967–84; La Jolla, Calif.: Sociological Abstracts, Inc., 1985–)
Covers all aspects of the study of language, including phonetics, phonology, morphology, syntax, and semantics. Abstracts articles from 1,200 serials published around the world.

Magazine Index (London: Thomson/Information Access Corporation, 1976–)
Indexes some 435 general-interest and popular periodicals.

MLA International Bibliography of Books and Articles on Modern Languages and Literature (New York: Modern Language Association of America, 1884–1999)
At times called *MLA Bibliography* and *Modern Language Association Annual Bibliography,* this ongoing bibliographic series indexes scholarly books, covering literary criticism, modern languages, literature, drama, folklore, and linguistics. Also available online.

NewsBank Index (Naples, Fla.: NewsBank, Inc., 1982–)
Indexes articles from 100 newspapers covering international, political, scientific, and socioeconomic fields.

Poole's Index to Periodical Literature (New York, London, G. P. Putnam, 1848; New York: C. B. Norton, 1853; Boston: J. R. Osgood & Co., 1882; Boston and New York: Houghton, Mifflin and Co., 1899; New York: P. Smith, 1938–)
A comprehensive subject index, also available online, to articles, book reviews, fiction, poetry, plays, and 479 American and English general periodicals listed by subject, by author, or the first word of the title of an article, first published in 1848 and then followed by additional annual installments and supplements. A cumulative index, *Cumulative Author Index for Poole's Index to Periodical Literature 1802–1906,* published in 1971, lists all personal names that appeared in the original index. To find the date and volume number of a specific article, consult *Poole's Index Date and Volume Key,* listing all 479 titles indexed by Poole and volume numbers to the years in which they were published.

Readers' Guide to Periodical Literature (New York: H.W. Wilson, 1900–)
In print since 1900, this popular reference features author and subject indexes to more than 230 general-interest magazines and *The New York Times.*

Law

Index to Canadian Legal Periodical Literature (Montreal: Canadian Association of Law Libraries, 1956–)
Bilingual subject-and-author index to English and French legal periodicals and articles from law journals, reports, and essay collections.

Index to Foreign Legal Periodicals (Berkeley: University of California Press/American Association of Law Libraries, 1960–).
Annually published multilingual index of articles and book reviews published in more than 500 legal journals worldwide listed by author, subject, country, or region since 1958.

An Index to Legal Periodical Literature (Boston: Boston Book Co.; Los Angeles: Parker and Baird Co.; Buffalo: Dennis, 1786–1937)
Otherwise known as the *Jones-Chipman Index to Legal Periodical Literature* (named after its editors), this six-volume index covers American legal periodicals to 1937.

Index to Legal Periodicals and Books (New York: H.W. Wilson, 1908–)
The most prominent index of legal literature offering citations to 600 legal periodicals (except legal newspapers, newsletters, and a few journals) and books by subject.

Index to Periodical Articles Related to Law (Dobbs Ferry, N.Y.: Glandville, 1958–)
This yearly compendium, first published in 1958, indexes articles on all subjects and topics related to law.

Shepard's Law Review Citations, 2 vols. with supplements (Colorado Springs, Colo.: Shepard's Citations, 1968–)
Annually updated index of federal court cases featuring comprehensive citations, listed in alphabetical order by title, to articles published in legal periodicals.

Medicine

Abstracts of Hospital Management Studies (Ann Arbor, Mich.: Health Administration Press for the Cooperative Information Center for Health Care Management Studies, the University of Michigan, 1965–1987)
Originally called the *Abstracts of Health Care Management Studies,* this index features abstracts to journals in hospital management, planning and public policy, and the delivery of health care.

Consumer Health and Nutrition Index (Phoenix, Ariz.: Oryx Press, 1985–97)
Quarterly index of consumer and health articles published in more than 60 major newspapers and popular magazines, including such titles as *Prevention, Harvard Medical School Letter,* and many others.

Cumulated Index to Nursing and Allied Health Literature (CINAHL) (Glendale, Calif.: Seventh-Day Adventist Hospital Association, 1956–1976; Glendale Adventist Medical Center, 1977–2000)
Comprehensively indexes hundreds of nursing, allied health, and health-related journals for nurses, allied health professionals, and those with an interest in health care.

Hospital Literature Index (Chicago: American Hospital Association, 1950–2000)
A subject-and-author index to English-language journals focused on hospital administration, planning, and delivery of services in hospitals and other health care institutions.

Index Medicus (Bethesda, Md.: National Library of Medicine, 1966–)
Highly regarded as a comprehensive index to biomedical literature, it features citations to articles from 3,100 biomedical journals with contents arranged by subject and author, and a bibliography of medical reviews.

Nursing Studies Index, 4 vols. (New Haven, Conn.: Yale University School of Nursing, 1900–1959)
The first annotated index of nursing research covering nursing literature published between 1900 and 1959.

International Nursing Index (New York: American Journal of Nursing, 1966–2000)
Ceased with v. 35, no. 2 (Dec. 2000).

Minorities

Chicano Index (Boston, Mass.: G.K. Hall, 1981–89)
Originally called the *Chicano Periodical Index,* this hardcover volume indexes literature "written by and about Chicanos (Mexican-Americans) and other Latinos in the United States," including nearly 50 journals, books, anthology articles, reports, and other documents from 1967 to 1988. A CD-ROM version, offered since 1990, covers the same content from December 1967 to the present.

Hispanic American Periodicals Index (HAPI) (Los Angeles: UCLA Latin American Center Publications, University of California, 1970–)
Hardcover index, also available on the Web, featuring comprehensive citations of more than 400 social science and humanities journals worldwide. Coverage includes articles, book reviews, and original literary works from Central and South America, the Caribbean, Mexico, and the United States.

Index to Black Periodicals (Boston, Mass.: G.K. Hall & Co., 1950–99; Detroit: Gale Group, 2000–)
Originally called *Index to Selected Periodicals, Index to Periodical Articles By and About Negroes,* and *Index to Periodical Articles By and About Blacks,* this annual reference indexes by subject or by author up to 40 general interest and scholarly African-American periodicals in each issue.

Motion Pictures

Film Literature Index (Albany, N.Y.: Filmdex, 1973–)
The only source of its kind featuring author-and-subject indexes to nearly 300 international film publications, including film criticism and film and television history from 1974 to the present.

Music

Music Article Guide (Philadelphia, Pa.: Information Services, 1966–96)
Discontinued quarterly index to 150 American music periodicals arranged by author, title, and subject from winter 1966 to fall 1996.

The Music Index: A Subject-Author Guide to Music Periodical Literature (Warren, Mich.: Harmonie Park Press, 1949–)
Premier index to more than 700 international musical periodicals representing all genres. Published annually since 1949 with quarterly updates. A complete online version of the index was introduced in 1999.

Newspapers

The Alternative Press Index (College Park, Md.: Alternative Press Center, 1969–)
Fully indexes articles written and published by more than 200 U.S. alternative and radical periodicals.

The Atlanta Journal, the Atlanta Constitution Index (Atlanta: 1971– ; Ann Arbor, Mich.: University Microfilms International, 1982–2000)
Originally called *The Atlanta Constitution: A Georgia Index* (1971–79), this hardcover reference series indexes and abstracts the entire contents of *The Atlanta Journal* and *Atlanta Constitution.* Items covered includes news, features, editorials, commentaries, business and financial news, sports, and reviews of books, art exhibitions, dance, movies, music, restaurants, and television programs. In 1997, the publisher dropped abstracts from the index. Entries list the author, article type (feature article, editorial, etc.), headline, and the subject terms under which the article is indexed, and are arranged alphabetically by subject heading (personal names are included). Publication of the printed index ceased in 2000. An online index covers 1985 to the present; full text is available for 1990 to the present.

Canadian News Index (Toronto: Information Access, 1977–79: Micromedia, 1980–92, 1993–)
Formerly known as the *Canadian Newspaper Index,* this bibliographic volume selectively indexes by subject or personal name the full contents of seven Canadian daily newspapers: *Calgary Herald, Globe and Mail, Halifax Chronicle Herald, Montreal Gazette, Toronto Star, Vancouver Sun,* and *Winnipeg Free Press.* Includes crime reports, general business news, editorials, feature stories, government news, major international news, sports events, and reviews of the arts. Renamed the *Canadian Index* in 1993, the *Canadian Newspaper Index* covers material from 1977 to the 1979; the *Canadian News Index* from 1980 to 1992; and the *Canadian Index* from 1993 to the present.

The Chicago Tribune Index (Wooster, Ohio, Newspaper Indexing Center, Micro Photo Division, Bell & Howell Co., 1972–78; New York: New York Times Co., 1982–)
Fully indexes articles from *The Chicago Tribune,* including several regional versions. Abstracts cover news, features, editorials, and commentaries, business and financial news, obituaries, sports articles, and the arts from 1972 to 1978, and from 1982 to the present. Abstracts were eliminated from the index beginning in 1997. Entries instead offer such information as author, article type, and headline, arranged alphabetically by subject. Also offered is an online version with coverage from 1985 to the present.

The Christian Science Monitor Index (Boston: Christian Science Pub. Soc., 1960–79; Wooster, Ohio: The Center, 1979–87; Ann Arbor, Mich.: Published under agreement with the Christian Science Pub. Society by University Microfilms International, 1987–)
Printed index of articles published in *The Christian Science Monitor* from 1950 to 1993. Articles are available online through *LexisNexis* from 1980 to the present.

The Left Index (Santa Cruz, Calif.: Left Index, 1982–)
Quarterly index of Marxist and radical leftist periodicals.

The Los Angeles Times Index (Wooster, Ohio: Bell & Howell Co., Newspaper Indexing Center, 1972–78; Ann Arbor, Mich.: University Microfilms International, 1984–)
Abstracts and indexes news, features, editorials, commentaries, business and financial news, sports, and reviews of books, movies, music, theater, television programs, and much more from the pages of *The Los Angeles Times* from 1972 to 1978, and from 1984 to the present. As with other indexes, abstracts were dropped in 1997 and entries were alphabetically arranged by subject instead listing the author, article type, and headline with each entry. An online full-text version is also available from 1985 to the present.

The New York Times Index (New York: New York Times Co., 1851–99)
Lists stories under subject headings using phrases instead of article titles. Useful for cross-referencing microfilm articles and older editions.

Times Index (London) (London: Times Pub. Co., 1957–72; Reading, England: Newspaper Archive Developments, 1973–)
Indexes article citations to the final editions of *The Times, The Sunday Times and Magazine, The Times Literary Supplement, The Times Educational Supplement, The Times Higher Education Supplement,* and *The Times Scottish Educational Supplement,* arranged by proper name or subject. Several variations and titles of the index are available, including *Palmer's Index to The Times Newspaper, Annual Index to The Times, The Official Index to The Times,* and *The Times, London Official Index.* Coverage is from 1785 to the present in print; online from 1900 to 1985; and in full text from 1990 to the present.

USA Today Index (Wooster, Ohio : The Center, 1983–87; Ann Arbor, Mich.: University Microfilms International, 1987–)
Abstracts and indexes the complete contents of this nationally published daily alphabetically by subject heading and personal names, by topic or geographical area from September 1982 to the present. Format changed in 1997, dropping abstracts from the index and featuring entries instead, with author, article type, and headline. Online version with full text covers 1989 to the present.

Wall Street Journal Index (New York: Dow Jones & Co., 1957– ; Wooster, Ohio: Newspaper Indexing Center, Micro Photo Division, Bell & Howell Co., 1976–)
Indexes abstracts to the contents of this leading business daily by corporate names (alphabetically arranged by company name) and general news by subject headings, personal names, organization names, product names, and geographic location from 1955 to the present. An online version indexes past editions from 1973 to the present, with full-text availability from 1984 to the present.

The Washington Post Index (Wooster, Ohio: Newspaper Indexing Center, Micro Photo Division, Bell & Howell Co., 1971–78; Woodbridge, Conn.:

Research Publications, 1979–89; Ann Arbor, Mich.: Published under agreement with the Washington Post by University Microfilms International Co., 1989–)
Renamed *The Official Washington Post Index* in 1979, this long-running hardcover reference features abstracts of news items, feature articles, editorials, business and financial news, sports articles, book and entertainment reviews, and more, alphabetically arranged by subject and further divided by topic or geographical area from 1971 to the present. Full-text articles from *The Washington Post* from 1977 to the present are also available online through LexisNexis Academic Universe. Articles are also searchable online at *The Washington Post* archives from September 1986 to the present.

Philosophy

Philosopher's Index (Bowling Green, Ohio: Bowling Green State University, 1967–)
Abstracts and indexes books, dissertations, monographs, and periodicals in the field of philosophy.

Physical Education

Physical Education Index (Cape Girardeau, Mo.: BenOak Pub. Co., 1970–97)
Annual index featuring citations with abstracts to more than 300 scholarly journals, including fitness and sports medicine, from 1970 to 1997.

Physical Fitness/Sports Medicine (Washington, D.C.: The President's Council on Physical Fitness and Sports, 1978–94)
Contains detailed citations to more than 3,000 periodicals, including *Physical Fitness/Sports Medicine,* a publication of the President's Council on Physical Fitness and Sports published from 1978 to 1994, and selected congressional papers.

Political Science

ABC Pol Sci: A Bibliography of Contents (Santa Barbara, Calif.: ABC-CLIO, 1969–2000)
Primarily indexes the tables of contents of nearly 300 international journals in their original languages covering political science and government, as well as law, economics, and sociology from 1969 to 2000. Subject and author indexes cumulated annually with each issue; separate five-year indexes are published separately. CD-ROM and online versions are also available.

Air University Library Index to Military Periodicals (Maxwell Air Force Base, Ala.: Air University Library, 1949–)
Formerly titled *Air University Periodical Index,* this hardcover reference, renamed in 1963, covers more than 75 English-language military and aeronautical periodicals, including news, articles, editorials, and book reviews, published by the government and private organizations searchable by subject or author. Volumes are published quarterly with an annual cumulative index from 1949 to the present. In 1994, EBSCO Publishing began offering an online version indexing articles from 1990 to the present.

The Combined Retrospective Index Set to Journals in Political Science, 1866–1974 (Washington: Carrollton Press, 1977–)
Eight-volume retrospective index of English-language periodicals that covers "all periods and areas in the field of political science." Arranged by subject and keyword in the first six volumes and by author in the last two volumes. Articles are listed chronologically under subject or author headings.

International Political Science Abstracts (IPSA) (Montreal: International Political Science Association, 1951–)
Preceding the online database of the same name, this bimonthly compendium offers comprehensive abstracts of selected articles published in more than 1,000 international journals and yearbooks.

PAIS Bulletin (New York: Public Affairs International Service, 1939–)
Interdisciplinary index providing easy access to citations of articles, books, and many other documents published worldwide on political, economic, and social issues. Through 1990, the index was called *PAIS Bulletin.* In 1991, it was renamed *PAIS International in Print.*

Psychology

Psychological Abstracts (Washington, D.C.: American Psychological Association, 1927–)
Indexes more than 1,200 periodicals and literature of psychology.

Public Opinion

American Public Opinion Index (Louisville, Ky.: Opinion Research Service, 1981–2001)
Twenty-volume annual indexing national, state, and local surveys and opinion polls and more than 250 polling sources, arranged by polling question, sources of polling results, and public opinion data from 1981 to 2000.

The Gallup Poll (Wilmington, Del.: Scholarly Resources, 1971–)
Annual index, beginning with the 1935–71 volume, of Gallup opinion polls on important political and social issues, arranged chronologically. Entries cover the date, question, and polling results and analysis by age, race, sex, income, geographic region, education, political affiliation, and much more. A full-text CD-ROM version is also offered, including a cumulative index for the years covered, from 1935 to 1997.

Index to International Public Opinion (Westport, Conn.: Greenwood Press, 1978–99)
Covers current-year statistics, polls, and opinion survey data of 68 countries. Subjects include consumer issues, crime, health care, politics, recreation, taxation, and welfare, and "trends and changes in public opinion" from 1978 through 1999. The index covers single-nation and multinational surveys, and three indexes are arranged by topic, by the country in which the poll was taken, and by countries and regions referenced in the survey questions.

Science and Technology

Applied Science and Technology Index (New York: H.W. Wilson, 1958–)
This annual volume indexes approximately 335 periodicals in the fields of aeronautics, automation, chemistry, computer technology, electricity, mathematics, physics, space science, telecommunications, and related disciplines.

General Science Index (New York: H.W. Wilson, 1978–)
This subject-specific volume covers more than 100 general science periodicals not generally covered by other indexes of its kind.

Science Abstracts (London: Institution of Electrical Engineers, 1967–)
Includes abstracts of books, conference papers, dissertations, patents, and periodicals in various sciences.

Science Citation Index (Philadelphia, Pa.: Institute for Scientific Information, 1961–94)
Interdisciplinary index, originally published bimonthly with annual cumulations, presenting citations to literature in science, medicine, agriculture, technology, and the behavioral sciences from 1961 through 1994. The index is now available in several electronic formats.

Social Sciences

Social Science Citation Index (London: Thomson ISI, 1973–)
This international index highlights published literature in behavioral and social science.

Social Sciences Index (New York: H.W. Wilson, 1974–)
Indexes by author and subject articles published in leading social science journals.

Sociology

Combined Retrospective Index to Journals in Sociology, 1895–1974 (Washington: Carrollton Press, 1978)
Comprehensive six-volume reference set retrospectively indexing periodicals in all periods and areas in the field of sociology by subject and keyword in the first five volumes, then by author in the final volume. Articles are likewise listed chronologically under subject or author headings from 1895 to 1974.

Social Work Research and Abstracts (National Association of Social Workers, 1972–)
Features extracted information from the quarterly journal *Social Work Abstracts,* which reviews some 400 U.S. and international journals with approximately 450 abstracts in each issue. With the March 1994 edition, the index was renamed *Social Work Abstracts.*

Sociological Abstracts (San Diego, Calif.: Sociological Abstracts, Inc., 1953–)
Abstracts and indexes published source material worldwide on sociology and related subjects.

Statistics

Statistical Reference Index (Washington, D.C. Congressional Information Service, 1981–)
Indexes by subject and names and by category previous-year U.S. statistics published by associations, institutes, corporations, publishers, research organizations, state governments, and university research centers (excluding information from the federal government's *American Statistical Index*) from 1980 to the present. Abstracts cover printed materials and the contents of publications published in the *Statistical Reference Index* microfiche collection (1984–). A full-text version of *Statistical Reference Index* is available online in LexisNexis Statistical Universe.

Women's Studies

Women Studies Abstracts (Rush, N.Y.: Rush Publishing Company, 1972–)
Provides abstracts to articles published in 35 popular and scholarly journals, along with book and media reviews and special issues, covering a broad range of subjects.

POPULAR QUOTATIONS

Popular quotations often spruce up an essay or research paper. Countless abstracts, enjoyable for browsing, offer quotations of every kind and every subject.

Bartlett's Familiar Quotations, 17th Ed., by John Bartlett (Boston, Mass.: Little Brown & Company, 2002)
This popular general anthology, originally published in 1855 as *A Collection of Familiar Quotations,* contains more than 25,000 quotations from 2,500 notables from ancient and modern times, presented in chronological order and indexed by author and thematic keywords.

The International Thesaurus of Quotations, 2nd Ed. by Eugene H. Erhlich (New York: HarperResource, 1996)
Arranged by topic, this thoroughly updated edition contains 16,000 timely, poignant, and brief quotations and proverbs indexed by category, keyword, and author.

The Oxford Dictionary of Quotations, 5th Ed. (Santa Monica, Calif.: Getty Center for Education in the Arts, 1999)
Arranged alphabetically by author, this revised edition offers 17,500 quotations from more than 3,000 authors, including famous writers, thinkers, and public figures from around the globe. Restored from past editions are sections on proverbs and nursery rhymes.

PUBLIC OPINION POLLS

Public opinion polls document the attitudes, mentality, view or popular understanding of an event or condition in society or the world today. Polls offer evidence that can help drive home a point in your paper.

A number of leading polling organizations publish their poll results:

Gallup Poll Public Opinion: Cumulative Index 1935–1997 (Wilmington, Del.: Scholarly Resources, Inc., 1999)
Billing itself as "the preeminent source on the attitudes and opinions of Americans since the New Deal," this well organized and highly useful reference indexes 25 volumes of nearly 10,000 surveys conducted and published by Gallup since 1935. Topics include major news events, politics, and social issues.

American Public Opinion Index, 1983–Present (Opinion Research Service, 2000)
A comprehensive index to microfiche collections of hundreds of scientifically conducted opinion polls at the national, state, and local levels arranged in three parts: an index of actual polling questions under alphabetical subject, sources of polling results, and a companion microfiche set providing responses to the polling questions. More than 250 polling sources are indexed, including many well-known polling organizations, such as Gallup, Harris, Roper, ABC, CBS, NBC, and California/Field.
For access to additional polls, surveys, and public opinion, see Chapter 11, "Research on the Web."

STATISTICAL ABSTRACTS

Statistical information collected by U.S. government agencies and private organizations, including social, political, and economic data, is widely available. Among the best published references are:

American Statistics Index (Bethesda, Md.: LexisNexis, 1974–)
Indexes and abstracts every type of statistical publication (periodicals, series, special reports, annuals and biennials, etc.) issued by the U.S. Government Printing Office or individual agencies archived in the ASI microfiche collection.

County and City Data Book (Washington, D.C.: Bureau of the Census, published every five years)
This valuable reference provides statistics for all U.S. counties, cities, and towns with 2,500 or more inhabitants, including official population and housing data, based on the most recent U.S. census.

Demographic Yearbook (New York: United Nations, 1962–)
This annual compendium summarizes demographics, including mortality, natality, marriage and divorce, population census, international migration, household composition, and more for about 230 countries and regions.

Directory of Trade Statistics Yearbook (Washington, D.C.: International Monetary Fund, 1981–)
Collection figures on the value of merchandise exports and imports by trade partners, as well as area and world aggregates showing trade flows between major areas of the world and 186 countries. Also published on CD-ROM.

Energy Statistics Yearbook (New York: United Nations, 1952–)
Annually compiles statistics on energy for some 210 countries and regions.

Gale Country and World Rankings Reporter, 2nd Ed. (Detroit, Mich.: Gale Group, 1997)
Unique reference that provides statistical charts and tables and physical, social, business, cultural, economic, demographic, governmental, and leisure information for more than 235 countries around the world.

Industrial Statistics Yearbook (New York: United Nations, 1974)
Contains industrial statistics covering almost 200 countries and regions.

International Marketing Data and Statistics (London: Euromonitor Publications, 1988–)
Covers business and marketing statistical data spanning 24 years from 161 non-European countries around the globe, including the United States, Asia-Pacific, and Latin America.

International Yearbook of Industrial Statistics (Vienna: United Nations Industrial Development Organization, 1996–)
General handbook of industrial statistics issued by the Industrial Development Organization.

State and Metropolitan Area Data Book, 5th Ed. (Washington, D.C.: Bureau of the Census, annual)
Highlighted in this collection are statistics on social and economic conditions in the United States and at every state and metropolitan level, including component counties and central cities of metropolitan areas.

Statistical Abstract of the United States (Washington, D.C.: Bureau of the Census, annual)
Available in print and on CD-ROM, the Abstract is a guide to sources of data from the Census Bureau, other federal agencies, and private organizations.

Statistical Abstract of the World, 3rd Ed. (Detroit, Mich.: Gale Group, 1997)
Offers statistical facts on a wide array of subjects from nearly 200 countries.

Statistical Reference Index (Bethesda, Md.: LexisNexis, 1980–)
Indexes U.S. statistics published by associations, corporations, institutes, publishers, research organizations, state governments, and university research centers.

Statistical Yearbook (New York: United Nations, 1948–)
Compiles international statistics covering a broad range of topics, such as culture, the economy, population, and more.

UNESCO Statistical Yearbook (New York: UNESCO, 1963–)
Last revised in 1999, this major reference book series provides key statistical information on education, science, technology, and communication in more than 200 countries.

World Economic Survey (New York: United Nations, 1955–)
Covers current trends, projections, and policies in the world economy.

YEARBOOKS

Information found in encyclopedias can be supplemented by consulting the most recent annual yearbook. Yearbooks feature articles, charts, and tables covering events of the past year, including the latest trends and statistics. Examples include:

Britannica Book of the Year: 1911 to the present (Chicago: Encyclopaedia Britannica, 1938–   , annual)
Highlights world news, conditions, events, fads, and trends mostly covering the United States through words and pictures.

Keesing's Record of World Events (London: Keesings, 1931–   , annual)
Covers world affairs with brief summaries, including excerpts of documents and an annual index. This yearbook is now available online.

ADDITIONAL REFERENCES

Besides the above-mentioned references, most libraries feature additional essential reference titles that you may wish to consult when researching your topic. These references may cover arts and entertainment, business, education, film and television, health and medicine, history and current events, law, literature, literary criticism, media and publishing, politics, religion, science, sports, or other topics. For the most current references in your subject area, consult your library's online catalog or library reference staff for a list of titles.

WEB REFERENCES

Besides traditional printed references, countless Web sites offer immediate access to online collections of many of the above popular references, including almanacs, bibliographies, dictionaries, encyclopedias, handbooks, and much more. The following is a partial list of the best ready reference sites on the Web:

Bartleby.com (http://bartleby.com)
Extensive online collection featuring more than 20 references, including encyclopedias, dictionaries, thesauri, quotations, and more.

Bibliomania: Free World Literature and Reference Books (http://www.bibliomania.com/)
Featuring an extensive library of reference books, biographies, classic nonfiction, and religious texts, Bibliomania's reference section includes fully searchable online versions of dictionaries, books of quotations, a thesaurus, literary sources, and other reference books. The site also includes a vast collection of biographies of famous people in politics, sports, culture, and science.

Encarta (http://encarta.msn.com/)
Created by Microsoft Network, this Web site offers a collection of online reference tools. Included is a searchable encyclopedia of more than 4,000

articles covering art, language, literature, history, geography, life science, performing arts, physical science and technology, religion and philosophy, social science, and sports. This is in addition to a Web-based dictionary and thesaurus, maps of all regions and countries, plus subject guides, news archives, lists and rankings, and a "This Day in History" section.

Ready References: The University Center Library (http://www.tuc.edu/lrc/readyref.htm)
This comprehensive reference page features links to numerous online resources, including almanacs, calendars, atlases, gazetteers, biographical sources, consumer information, calculators and currency converters, dictionaries and thesauri, and acronyms, and translators. Also featured are directories by subject, encyclopedias, yearbooks, fact books, handbooks, maps, news and media sources, quotations, poetry, statistics and data, and much more.

Refdesk.com (http://refdesk.com/fastfact.html)
An exhaustive resource of information, this site offers search options and indexes on many subjects, including high-quality almanacs and maps, dictionaries and thesauri, directories of people and places, virtual encyclopedias, libraries of data, magazines and news sources, quotations, and statistics.

ReferenceDesk.org (http://www.referencedesk.org)
Includes a large categorized collection of reference links to more than 600 different sites.

Yahoo! Education (http://education.yahoo.com)
Offers a small but helpful collection of references, suitable for any purpose, including searchable online versions of *The American Heritage Dictionary of the English Language, The Columbia Encyclopedia, Roget's II: The New Thesaurus, Bartlett's Familiar Quotations,* and the *CIA World Factbook,* among others.

yourDictionary (http://www.yourdictionary.com)
This site features the largest collection of links to online dictionaries of all kinds—more than 2,500 in more than 300 languages.

This chapter has covered some basic suggestions to get you started with researching your subject. Other titles may exist covering your subject or genre. To get the most out of your research, it is recommended that you consult with your library's reference staff for suggestions of additional titles that will also serve your purpose.

12

Finding Government Publications and Agencies

Federal, state, and local government agencies, publications, and other sources can be a gold mine of statistical, demographic, and up-to-date information. Most agencies are specialized and collect information, conduct research, or perform ongoing studies. Directories available through your local library can help you determine which agency has the exact information you are seeking. In many cases, obtaining this information is as easy as going online, making a phone call, or writing a letter to the right bureau or agency.

RESEARCHING GOVERNMENT PUBLICATIONS AND AGENCIES

Your first step to researching government publications and agencies is to determine which level, branch, or body of government is most relevant to your subject. Are the publications and agencies you are seeking federal, state, local, or foreign? Is the information you need related to the executive, legislative, or judicial branch of the U.S. government?

Your answers to these questions will depend on your topic, of course. If you are researching any agricultural topic, for instance, a good source would be a federal agency, such as the U.S. Department of Agriculture, which offers many publications and resources on the subject. Or, to research the environment, you would want to contact an agency like the U.S. Environmental Protection Agency.

As with any research, you can start searching for background information and government publications via your library's online catalog by simply keyword-searching your subject. For example, if your subject is "federal environmental regulations," keying in those words most likely will produce a list of publications not necessarily all government-produced related to that subject.

In addition, many libraries, including public, college, and university, offer navigational Web sites that assist you with the retrieval of government information. By simply keyword-searching "library government sources," you should find suitable sites from some of the top libraries around the country.

Besides the above methods of research, the following additional sources will take you in the right direction:

GOVERNMENT GUIDES AND CATALOGS

Locating experts and government agencies at both the federal and state levels is as easy as consulting several published guides and catalogs featuring comprehensive listings of nearly every agency, bureau, or office.

One of the best resources available for free online is the Government Guide (http://www.government.guide.com). This virtual directory provides links to seemingly every official federal, state, and local resource. Among the links provided is another important gateway of information, FedStats (www.fedstats.gov/), featuring vital statistics from more than 100 U.S. federal agencies. Agencies are listed alphabetically or by subject, with descriptions of the statistics they offer, plus links to their Web sites, contact information, and key statistics.

FedStats also features links to statistical data, plus statistics by geographical region from various U.S. agencies, including international, national, state, county, and local comparisons. Another valuable link is MapStats (http://www.fedstats.gov/qf/), which offers statistical profiles of counties, states, congressional districts, and federal judicial districts. In addition, this worthwhile site offers links to federal statistical policies, including budget documents, working papers, and Federal Register notices, and other statistical sites and general government locator sites of interest.

The U.S. Government Printing Office (GPO) is the largest federal depository of government information products. For more than 140 years, this agency has provided public access to government information by producing printed publications that serve the needs of the U.S. Congress, federal agencies, and the American public. Established by Congress, the GPO's Federal Depository Library Program (FDLP) disseminates information products from all three branches of the government to nearly 1,300 libraries nationwide. They include public libraries, college and university libraries, and law schools.

Not every depository library carries the same U.S. government publications. A library may offer only the publications best suited to their patrons. Find the depository library in your area that best meets your needs.

Every library arranges its collection of government publications differently, and how they are accessed also differs. Sometimes they are listed in the library catalog, or in special catalogs, and their location can vary. When in doubt, consult with the reference library staff.

You can also acquire copies of publications directly from the GPO. For quick searching of U.S. government publications, the GPO's *Catalog of U.S. Government Publications* is accessible through its official Web site, GPO Access (www.gpoaccess.gov). The site features an index to all print and electronic publications created by federal agencies, as well as an online bookstore and links to the full text of all government publications. In addition, a library locator allows you to find libraries and federal depositories in your area code or state that carry federal publications and other information products for your use. Publications listed are dated from January 1994 to the present, with new titles added daily. A search engine enables you to search publications by title or keyword phrase.

An additional resource is the U.S. General Services Administration Federal Citizen Information Center (formerly the Consumer Information Center), or in FCIC, Pueblo, Colorado. For many years, FCIC has been a gateway of information to questions about the federal government and everyday consumer issues.

One of its most popular publications is the *Consumer Information Catalog*. Downloadable from the FCIC's Web site in .PDF form (www.pueblo.gsa.gov/aboutus.htm), this free catalog lists consumer publications covering all topics that are available at little or no cost. Publications can also be purchased online. For questions, you can call the FCIC toll-free at 1-800-FED-INFO.

Several current government publications, available at most depository libraries, feature comprehensive listings and cumulative subject indexes of publications offered in print. They include:

Catalog of Government Publications (U.S. Government Printing Office, 1994–)
(See GPO Monthly Catalog).

Government Documents Catalog Service (AutoGraphics, 1976–)
Featuring the same contents as MarciveWeb DOCS and Catalog of United States Government Publications (MoCat), this online catalog service provides author, title, subject, keyword, and number indexing to U.S. government publications. Catalog service is also available under *Impact Access GDCS, Impact/ONLINE WebPAC, Monthly Catalog of U.S. Government Publications, MoCat, and WebPAC GPO Services.*

Government Publications Index (Information Access, 1976–)
This Internet-delivered database indexes articles appearing in periodicals published by federal agencies.

GPO Monthly Catalog (GPO) (http://www.gpoaccess.gov/cgp/index.html)
Available from the U.S. Government Printing Office's Web site, this catalog, also known as the Catalog of U.S. Government Publications (CGP), indexes all print and electronic publications created by federal agencies from 1994 to the present, including links to full text of some online titles.

MarciveWeb DOCS (San Antonio, Tex.: Marcive, 1976–)
Featuring similar content to the Catalog of Government Publications (CGP), this online database indexes every government publication cataloged by the U.S. Government Printing Office.

Monthly Catalog of United States Government Publications (Washington, D.C.: U.S. Government Printing Office, 1895–)
First published in 1895 and undergoing seven name changes since, the Monthly Catalog of the United States Government Publications, also known as MoCat, was originally printed as a catalog indexing thousands of government documents published each year. The original printed volumes dated from 1985 to June 1976. In July 1976, the format changed, and since then entries have resembled card catalog records. In addition to its semiannual indexes, the GPO issues cumulative indexes covering every five- and 10-year

period. The online database consists of bibliographic records that describe government information products produced by the U.S. Government Printing Office, available through the Federal Depository Library Program. Updated daily, records cover every U.S. government publication since January 1994.

Subject Bibliographies Index (Washington, D.C: U.S. Government Printing Office, current)
Complete index to approximately 150 subject bibliographies that are used to categorize the publications, subscriptions, and electronic products for sale by the Superintendent of Documents of the U.S. Government Printing Office (GPO), available through the GPO's online bookstore (http://bookstore.gpo.gov/sb/sale180html). Links are provided to the current list of products, and you can obtain free printed copies online of the GPO's subject bibliography catalogs.

U.S. Government Online Bookstore (U.S. Government Printing Office)
Publications available for purchase can be found at the GPO's online bookstore (http://bookstore.gpo.gov), including CD-ROM collections, electronic products, and catalogs.

In addition to the above government sources, another useful commercially published guide, listings thousands of government resources and programs, is:

Lesko's Info-Power III by Matthew Lesko (Detroit: Visible Ink, 1994–)
This excellent reference lists every government specialist, publication, hotline, or program—more than 45,000 and counting.

FEDERAL GOVERNMENT INFORMATION

Many Web sites, electronic databases, and printed directories can direct you to general information about government agencies, congressional leaders, federal government staffs, key contact information, and more. Invaluable research tools in this case are:

On the Web

The World Wide Web offers a variety of choices for easily locating this information. Among the best sites are:

FedWorld (http://www.fedworld.gov)
From this Web portal, offering links to a half-dozen information Web sites, you can search and access government agencies and Web sites, scientific and technical publications (published since 1990), full-text Supreme Court decisions from 1937 to 1975, and government science and technology web resources. The most powerful is FirstGov, the official U.S. government portal to 30 million government web pages.

LexisNexis Congressional Universe (Bethesda, Md.: LexisNexis, 1988–)
This subscription-based, Internet-delivery database provides comprehensive access to U.S. legislative histories, subject and author indexes, and abstracts of congressional publications from the Congressional Information Service, as

well as links to approximately 170 magazines and newspapers with substantial research value published by the U.S. government.

Thomas Legislative Information on the Internet (http://thomas.loc.gov/)
Another fine legislative portal, this comprehensive site, a service of the Library of Congress named in honor of Thomas Jefferson, contains full text of all versions of House and Senate bills (101st–107th Congress), Committee Reports (104th–107th Congress), Bill Summary and Status (93rd–108th Congress) and Public Laws (93rd–108th Congress). Also featured is full text of *The Congressional Record* (101st–107th Congress) including text search (101st–108th Congress) and roll call votes (101st–108th).

In Print

Additional published resources providing vital information include:

Congressional Staff Directory, 72nd Ed. by Joel Treese (Washington, D.C.: CQ Staff Directories, 2005)
Contains detailed information and listings, including biographies, committee appointments, county, city, state, and district representation, and important contact information, for every member of the U.S. Congress. Subscription to this annual printed edition includes Web access. Daily updates made to Web version.

Congressional Yellow Book (Washington, D.C.: Leadership Directories, Inc., 2005)
Published as fully updated quarterly editions, this indispensable guide, also available as part of The Leadership Library on the Internet (updated daily), provides the most current information available on members of Congress, key staff, and legislative responsibilities. Three indexes allow you to find entries by name, subject, or organization.

Federal Regulatory Directory (Washington, D.C.: CQ Press, 1979–)
Provides comprehensive information about 15 regulatory agencies, their powers and functions, plus facts on 63 other agencies, including contacts and telephone numbers. Updated annually.

Federal Staff Directory, 42nd Ed. by Paul Wayne Walker (Washington, D.C.: CQ Staff Directories, 2004)
Lists complete contact information and biographies for persons in the White House, the Department of Homeland Security, cabinet departments, independent agencies, and other organizations. Annual printed edition includes Web access with a year's subscription. The Web version is updated daily.

Federal Yellow Book (Washington, D.C.: Leadership Directories, Inc., 2005)
Considered the leading U.S. directory of the executive branch of the federal government, fully updated editions feature contact information for more than 40,000 federal offices, including the White House, cabinet-level federal departments, and independent federal agencies, complete with fax numbers, e-mail addresses and Internet addresses. Three indexes—subject, organization, and name—are included. *The Federal Yellow Book* is also available as part of The Leadership Library on the Internet and is updated daily.

Judicial Staff Directory by Claudia Driggins-Henley (Washington, D.C.: CQ Staff Directories, 2004)
Features judge and staff contact information and biographies for federal and state courts, federal circuit, district, and bankruptcy courts, and court administration, complete with Web access, updated daily, by subscription.

Official Congressional Directory, 2003–2004: 108th Congress (Washington, D.C.: U.S. Government Printing Office, 2003)
This annual directory provides key contact information for members of Congress and executive and judicial branches.

The United States Government Manual (Washington, D.C.: National Archives and Records Administration, 2003)
Edited by Raymond A. Mosley and John W. Carlin, this annually updated reference lists general information about every government agency, including top agency contacts, addresses, and telephone numbers.

STATE AND LOCAL GOVERNMENT INFORMATION

A plethora of guides, registries, yearbooks, and Web sites offering essential information on every major state and local official, agency, and department, are published and updated throughout the year and available for public use. Listing everything from basic contact information to detailed descriptions, each of these resources is helpful when researching your state and local governments.

On the Web

The Internet offers an assortment of fast and easy options for finding information about state and local governments. Among them:

The Council of State Governments (http://www.csg.org/csg/default)
News about current issues and links to state web pages can be found on this nonpartisan Web site that promotes excellence in state government. Information, research, and publications on critical state issues are also featured on the Web site for the National Conference of State Legislatures (www.ncsl.org)

State and County Quick Facts (http://quickfacts.census.gov/qfd/)
Operated by the U.S. Census Bureau, this searchable Web site is a source of comparative information on local government with facts about people, business, and geography.

State and Local Governments (http://lcweb.loc.gov/global/state/stategov.html)
On this Web site, the Library of Congress comprehensively indexes state and local government information, with direct links to those sites listed.

State and Local Government on the Net (http://www.statelocalgov.net/index.cfm)
The most comprehensive and current guide of its kind, this site provides immediate access to Web sites of thousands of state agencies and city and county governments. Drop-down menus allow you to view directory pages by

state or topic. You can view Web sites in any given state, county, or town and access lists of Web sites of state government constitutional officers, stage legislatures, state judiciaries, and departments throughout each state listed.

Stateline.org (http://www.stateline.org)
Founded and operated by the Pew Center on the States to help journalists, policy makers, and citizens become better informed, this site features state-by-state news, including headlines and full-text articles, plus statistics and other resources.

In Print

Many other authoritative resources are available in print (also online in some cases) through most academic and public libraries. They include:

Municipal Yearbook (Washington, D.C.: International City/County Management Association, 1934–)
Besides being a directory of officials, this annual reference, last published in 1998–99, also provides comparative statistical data on city government.

Municipal Yellow Book (Washington, D.C.: Leadership Directories, Inc., 2005)
Offers complete contact information for more than 37,000 elected and administrative officials of city and county governments and local authorities in semiannual editions. Listings for local governments include all agencies, branches, departments, and subdivisions, with names, titles, addresses, and telephone and fax numbers. Web access is offered through The Leadership Library, a subscription Internet service.

State Yellow Book (Washington, D.C.: Leadership Directories, Inc., 2005)
Published quarterly, this directory lists all governors, lieutenant governors, department heads, and chairs of state boards and commissions, senior staff at all levels of state government, and state Senate and House leaders, plus contact information, including direct-dial telephone numbers, postal and e-mail addresses, and Web sites, for officials in executive and legislative branches of the 50 state governments. Also available online, by subscription, through The Leadership Library.

In addition to the above directories, most states publish a reference guide called a "blue book" that lists every major official in their government and other essential information. Although these publications vary from state to state, your local library should carry them. If your library offers them, they would be listed in the library catalog under one of three subject headings: "Politics and government—Handbooks and manuals"; "Registers"; or "Officials and employees."

Another valuable resource that lists "blue books" published around the country is:

State Legislative Sourcebook: A Resource Guide to Legislative Information in the 50 States (Topeka, Kans: Government Research Service, 2000) by Lynn Hellebust.
This annual directory describes the different state legislatures and their publications.

FOREIGN GOVERNMENT INFORMATION

To access various kinds of foreign government publications and information about individual countries, several useful guides and directories are suggested.

On The Web

The Web offers information at your fingertips on every foreign government and country. One such site is:

Foreign Government Resources on the Web (http://www.lib.umich.edu/govdocs/foreignnew.html)
This well-organized and up-to-date site, created and maintained by the University of Michigan Library, hosts an extensive collection of links to foreign government information, organized by geographic area. Also featured are direct links to related foreign government resources, including biographies of officials; country background; constitutions, demographics and statistics; laws, and treaties; embassies; foreign policy; human rights; national symbols; foreign news sources; and additional Web pages for international agencies.

In Print

Printed directories can be equally helpful in tracking down specific information about a foreign government or country. Two top references are:

Guide to Country Information in International Governmental Organization Publications (Bethesda, Md.: Congressional Information Service, 1996)
Published in association with the Government Documents Roundtable (GODORT), a division of the American Library Association, this convenient volume contains a detailed annotated bibliography of International Governmental Organization (IGO) serials, monographs, and periodicals, plus relevant information about each country, indexed by title and country.

Guide to Official Publications of Foreign Countries, 2nd Ed. (Bethesda, Md.: Congressional Information Service, 1997)
Lists country-by-country official publications covering 19 categories, including bibliographies and catalogs, central bank publications, census, court reports, development plans, budgets, economic affairs, education, government directories and organization manuals, health, human rights, labor, legislative proceedings, regulations and constitutions, and more. Includes title index.

GOVERNMENT JOURNALS AND PUBLICATIONS

Electronic journals and federal publications, published by government agencies and commercial publishers, can be suitable sources of information for your paper as well. Published daily, monthly, or quarterly, they cover current and topical issues in all areas and branches of the government and military. Currently, more than 100 electronic journals, mostly government publications, are accessible free of charge on the Web. Several major university libraries, including those at the University of Louisville (http://

library.louisville.edu/government/periodicals/periodall.html), Oregon State University (http://ouslibrary.oregonstate.edu/research/govpubs.html), and Rutgers University (http://www.libraries.rutgers.edu/rul/rr_gateway/ejournals/ej-alpha.shtml)offer a complete alphabetical list with direct links or searchable database with links to publications including:

Access America (Washington, D.C.: National Partnership for Reinventing Government, October 1998–)
Access Currents (Washington, D.C.: U.S. Access Board, March/April 1999–)
Acquisition Review Quarterly (Defense Systems Management College, Fort Belvoir, Va., 1994–)
ADA Magazine Online (Fort Bliss, Texas: U.S. Army Air Defense Artillery School, 1998–)
Administrative Notes: Newsletter of the Federal Depository Library Program (Washington, D.C.: U.S. Government Printing Office, August 1996–)
Aerospace Power Journal (Maxwell AFB, Ala.: The College of Aerospace Doctrine Research, and Education, 1987–)
Aerospace Technology Innovation (Washington, D.C.: NASA, September/October 1993–)
AFIO Weekly Intelligence Notes (McLean, Va.: Association of Former Intelligence Officers, 1998–)
Africa Recovery Online (New York: Department of Public Information, United Nations, December 1996–)
AgExporter (Washington, D.C.: U.S. Department of Agriculture, Foreign Agricultural Service, 1996–)
Agricultural Outlook (Washington, D.C.: U.S. Department of Agriculture, Economic Research Service, 1995–)
Agricultural Research Magazine (Washington, D.C.: U.S. Department of Agriculture, Agricultural Research Service, May 1996–)
Aids to Navigation Bulletin (Yorktown, Va.: U.S. Coast Guard RTC, National Aids to Navigation School, Winter 1996/97–)
Air and Space (Washington, D.C.: Smithsonian Institution, 1991–)
Air Force Comptroller, The (Washington, D.C.: Assistant Secretary of the Air Force, Financial Management & Comptroller, 1998–)
Air Force Journal of Logistics (Washington, D.C.: U.S. Air Force, Air Force Logistics Management Agency, 1997–)
Air Land Sea Bulletin, The (Langley AFB, Va.: Air Land Sea Application Center, 1995–)
Air Travel Consumer Report (Washington, D.C.: U.S. Department of Transportation, Office of Aviation Enforcement and Proceedings, 1998–)
Air University Review (Maxwell AFB, Ala.: Air University, 1984–87)
Airman: Magazine of America's Air Force (Kelly AFB, Tex.: Air Force News Agency, Secretary of the Air Force Office of Public Affairs, 9/1995–)
Airpower Journal (Maxwell Air Force Base, Ala.: Air University, 1987–)
Alcohol Research and Health (Bethesda, Md.: National Institute on Alcohol Abuse and Alcoholism, 1994–)

Alcohol Tobacco and Firearms Quarterly Bulletin (Washington, D.C.: U.S. Department of the Treasury, Bureau of Alcohol, Tobacco and Firearms, June 1998–)

All Hands: Magazine of the U.S. Navy (Washington, D.C.: Naval Media Center, Publishing Division, Naval Station Anacostia, August 1922–)

Alternative Fuel News (Washington, D.C.: U.S. Department of Energy, Alternative Fuels Data Center, October 1997–)

American Rehabilitation (Washington, D.C.: U.S. Department of Health, Education, and Welfare, Rehabilitation Services Administration, 1997–)

Animal Welfare Information Center Bulletin (Beltsville, Md.: U.S. Department of Agriculture, National Agricultural Library, The Animal Welfare Information Center, 1990–)

Annals of Congress (The Debates and Proceedings in the Congress of the United States) (Washington, D.C.: Library of Congress, 1789–1824)

Antarctic Journal of the United States (Washington, D.C.: National Science Foundation, Office of Polar Programs, 1993–)

Approach: The Naval Safety Center's Aviation Magazine (Washington, D.C.: U.S. Naval Safety Center, 9/1999–)

Arctic Research of the United States (Washington, D.C.: National Science Foundation, Interagency Arctic Research Policy Committee, 1997–)

Armor (Fort Knox, Ky.: U.S. Army, Armor Branch, July/August 1997–)

Army Acquisition, Logistics and Technology Magazine (Washington, D.C.: U.S. Army, Office of the Assistant Secretary of the Army, Acquisition, Logistics and Technology, September/October 1995–)

Army Communicator/AC Online: The Army Signal Regiment's Professional Magazine (Fort Gordon, Ga.: U.S. Army Signal Center, Fall/1995–)

Army Logistician: the Professional Bulletin of United States Army Logistics (Fort Lee, Va.: U.S. Army Logistics Management Center, 1996–)

Ashore (Washington, D.C.: U.S. Naval Safety Center, Winter 1998/99–)

Asia-Pacific Population Journal (Bangkok: United Nations, Economic and Social Commission for Asia and the Pacific, 1986–)

Astro News (Los Angeles: U.S. Air Force, Space and Missile Systems Center Office of Public Affairs, 1998–)

Background Notes (Washington, D.C.: U.S. Department of State, Bureau of Public Affairs, Office of Public Communications, most recent only)

Battlefield Update (U.S. National Park Service, Heritage Preservation Services, Summer 1998–)

Beacon, The (Washington, D.C.: U.S. Department of Justice, National Domestic Preparedness Office, November 1998–)

Beam Line (Stanford, Calif.: Stanford Linear Accelerator Center, Fall/Winter 1994–)

Biofuels News (Washington, D.C.: U.S. Department of Energy, Alternative Fuels Data Center, Winter 1998–)

BISNIS Bulletin (Washington, D.C.: U.S. Department of Commerce, International Trade Administration, 1995–)

Bond Teller, The (Washington, D.C.: U.S. Department of Treasury, Bureau of Public Debt, 1997–)
Braille Book Review (Washington, D.C.: Library of Congress, National Library Service for the Blind and Physically Handicapped, 1994–)
Bulletin of the European Union (Brussels—Luxembourg: European Commission, 1996–)
Bulletin of the World Health Organization (Geneva: World Health Organization, 1999–)
Bulletin of the Global Volcanism Network (Washington, D.C.: Smithsonian Institution, 1990–)
Caribbean Currents (Washington, D.C.: U.S. Environmental Protection Agency, INFOTERRA/USA, March 1995–)
Catalog of United States Government Publications (MOCAT) (Washington, D.C.: U.S. Government Printing Office, 1994–)
CDC Surveillance Summaries Electronic Edition (Atlanta, Ga.: Centers for Disease Control and Prevention, 1983–)
Census and You (Washington, D.C.: U.S. Department of Commerce, Census Bureau, 1996–)
Census Briefs (Washington, D.C.: U.S. Department of Commerce, Census Bureau, 1996–)
Center for Building Science News (Washington, D.C.: Lawrence Berkeley National Laboratory, Environmental Energy Technologies Division, 1993–98)
Checklist of Official Publications of the State of New York (Albany, N.Y.: New York State Library, June 1989–)
Chemicals in Our Community (Washington, D.C.: U.S. Environmental Protection Agency, Office of Pollution Prevention and Toxics-IMD, Fall 1998–)
Child Care Bulletin (Vienna, Va.: National Child Care Information Center, 1995–)
Child Support Report (Washington, D.C.: Office of Child Support Enforcement, November 1994–)
Chips (Norfolk, Va.: U.S. Naval Computer and Telecommunications Area Master Station, LANT, 1982–)
Choices Magazine (Geneva: United Nations Development Programme, August 1999–)
Chronic Disease Notes and Reports (Atlanta, Ga.: National Center for Chronic Disease Prevention and Health Promotion, Summer 1996–)
Citizen Airman: Official Magazine of the Air Force Reserve (Robins AFB, Ga.: U.S. Air Force Reserve Command, Office of Public Affairs, 1997–)
City Limits: New York's Urban Affairs News Magazine (New York: City Limits Magazine, November 1996–)
City Record, The (New York: New York Department of Citywide Administrative Services, current only)
City Review, The (New York: City Review, 1997–)
Cityscape: a Journal of Policy Development and Research (Washington, D.C.: U.S. Department of Housing and Urban Development, 1994–)
Civil Engineer, The (Washington, D.C.: U.S. Air Force, Air Force Civil Engineer Support Agency, Summer 1996–)

Coast Guard (Washington, D.C.: U.S. Coast Guard, October 1998–)
Combat Edge, The (Langley AFB, Va.: U.S. Air Force Air Combat Command, 1998–)
Commerce Business Daily (CBDNet) (Washington, D.C.: U.S. Department of Commerce, December 2, 1996–)
Common Perspective, A (Washington, D.C.: U.S. Department of Defense, Joint Chiefs of Staff, September 1995–)
Community Update (Washington, D.C.: U.S. Department of Education, November 1994–)
Compensation and Working Conditions Online (Washington, D.C.: U.S. Department of Labor, Bureau of Labor Statistics, 1996–)
Congressional Quarterly Weekly Report (Washington, D.C.: Congressional Quarterly, 1983–)
Congressional Record (Washington, D.C.: Library of Congress, Thomas Legislative Information on the Internet, 1995–)
CONSERline: Newsletter of the CONSER Program (Washington, D.C.: Library of Congress, 1994–)
Consumer Product Safety Review (Washington, D.C.: U.S. Consumer Product Safety Commission, 1996–)
CSCE Digest (Washington, D.C.: Committee on Security and Cooperation in Europe, 1996–)
Cultural Resource Management (Washington, D.C.: National Park Service, 1978–)
Current Business Reports: Monthly Wholesale Trade: Sales and Inventories (BW) (Washington, D.C.: U.S. Census Bureau, 1996–)
Current Construction Reports: Expenditures for Residential Improvements and Repairs, C-50 (Washington, D.C.: U.S. Census Bureau, 1995–)
Current Construction Reports: Housing Completions, C-22 (Washington, D.C.: U.S. Census Bureau, 1996–)
Current Construction Reports: Housing Starts, C-20 (Washington, D.C.: U.S. Census Bureau, 1996–)
Current Construction Reports: Housing Units Authorized by Building Permits, C-40 (Washington, D.C.: U.S. Census Bureau, 1995–)
Current Construction Reports: New One-Family Houses Sold, C-25 (Washington, D.C.: U.S. Census Bureau, 1996–)
Current Construction Reports: Residential Improvements and Repairs Statistics, C-50 (Washington, D.C.: U.S. Census Bureau, 1995–)
Current Construction Reports: Value of New Construction Put in Place, C-30 (Washington, D.C.: U.S. Census Bureau, 1996–)
Current Housing Reports: Housing Vacancies and Homeownership, H-111 (Washington, D.C.: U.S. Census Bureau, 1994–)
Current Industrial Reports (Washington, D.C.: U.S. Census Bureau, 1992–)
Current Population Reports: Consumer Income, P-60 (Washington, D.C.: U.S. Census Bureau, no.187, 1995–)
Current Population Reports: Household Economic Studies, P-70 (Washington, D.C.: U.S. Census Bureau, no. 43, 1995–)
Current Population Reports: Population Characteristics, P-20 (Washington, D.C.: U.S. Census Bureau, no. 482, 1995–)

Current Population Reports: Population Estimates and Projections, P-25 (Washington, D.C.: U.S. Census Bureau, no. 1127, 1995–)

Current Population Reports: Special Studies, P-23 (Washington, D.C.: U.S. Census Bureau, no. 188, 1995–)

Daily Digest (Federal Communications Commission) (Washington, D.C.: Federal Communications Commission, 1994–)

Daily Treasury Statement (Washington, D.C.: U.S. Department of the Treasury, Financial Management Service, 199?–)

Defense Horizons (Washington, D.C.: U.S. National Defense University, Center for Technology and National Security Policy, 2001–)

Defense News (Washington, D.C.: Center for Technology and National Security Policy, National Defense University, 1993–)

DESA News (New York: United Nations Department of Economic and Social Affairs, October 1997–)

Development Update (New York: United Nations Department of Public Information, 1996–)

Diplomatic List (Washington, D.C.: U.S. Department of State, Office of the Chief of Protocol, 1994–)

Direct Loans Bulletins (Washington, D.C.: U.S. Department of Education, Office of Student Financial Assistance, 1997–)

DISAM Journal, The (Wright-Patterson AFB, Ohio: Defense Institute of Security Assistance Management, Spring 1999–)

Dispatch (Washington, D.C.: U.S. Department of State, Office of Public Communication, Bureau of Public Affairs, 1993–)

Domestic Airline Fares Consumer Report (Washington, D.C.: U.S. Department of Transportation, Office of Aviation and International Economics, 1996–)

DTIC Review, The (Fort Belvoir, Va.: Defense Technical Information Center, 1997–)

Earth System Monitor (Silver Spring, Md.: National Oceanographic Data Center, March 1995–)

Economic Indicators (Washington, D.C.: U.S. Council of Economic Advisers, April 1995–)

Economic Perspectives (Washington, D.C.: U.S. Department of State, International Information Programs, April 1996–)

ED Initiatives (Washington, D.C.: U.S. Department of Education, August 1995–)

Education Statistics Quarterly (Washington, D.C.: U.S. Department of Education, National Center for Education Statistics, 1999–)

EFTA Bulletin (Geneva: European Free Trade Association, September 2000–)

Election Notes (Richmond, Va.: Klipsan Press, 1996–)

Electric Power Monthly (Washington, D.C.: U.S. Department of Energy, Energy Information Administration)

Emerging Infectious Diseases (Washington, D.C.: U.S. Department of Health and Human Services, National Center for Infectious Diseases, 1995–)

Employment in New York State (Albany, N.Y.: New York State Department of Labor)

Employment Situation (Washington, D.C.: U.S. Department of Labor, Bureau of Labor Statistics)

Endangered Species Bulletin (Washington, D.C.: U.S. Fish and Wildlife Service, May/June 1995–)

Energy and Technology Review (Livermore, Calif.: Lawrence Livermore National Laboratory, March 1994–April 1995)

Energy Matters (Washington, D.C.: U.S. Department of Energy, Office of Industrial Technologies, 1999–)

Engineer: The Professional Bulletin for Army Engineers (Fort Leonard Wood, Mo.: U.S. Army Engineer School, Directorate of Training and Doctrine, December 1994–)

Environmental Energy Technologies Division News (Washington, D.C.: Lawrence Berkeley National Laboratory, Environmental Energy Technologies Division, 1999–)

Environmental Health Perspectives (Washington, D.C.: U.S. Department of Health and Human Services, Environmental Health Information Service, 1993–)

Environmental Notice Bulletin, The (Albany, N.Y.: Department of Environmental Conservation, November 10, 1999)

Epidemiological Bulletin (Washington, D.C.: Pan American Health Organization, 1995–)

Eurasia Bulletin (Washington, D.C.: U.S. Census Bureau, International Programs Center, 1996–)

Export Finance Newsletter (Washington, D.C.: Export-Import Bank of the United States, 1997–)

FA Journal: A Professional Journal for Redlegs (Fort Sill, Okla.: Field Artillery School)

Family Economics and Nutrition Review (Washington, D.C.: U.S. Department of Agriculture, Center for Nutrition Policy and Promotion, 1998–)

Fathom (Washington, D.C.: U.S. Naval Safety Center, 1999–)

FBI Law Enforcement Bulletin (Washington, D.C.: Federal Bureau of Investigation, 1989–)

FCA Newsline (Washington, D.C.: Farm Credit Administration, 1999–)

FDA Consumer (Washington, D.C.: U.S. Food and Drug Administration, April 1989–)

FDA Enforcement Report (Washington, D.C.: U.S. Food and Drug Administration, 1990–)

FDA Medical Bulletin (Washington, D.C.: U.S. Food and Drug Administration, 1996–).

FDA Veterinarian Newsletter (Washington, D.C.: U.S. Food and Drug Administration, November/December 1995–)

FDIC Banking Review (Washington, D.C.: Federal Deposit Insurance Corporation, Division of Research and Statistics, June 1995–)

FDIC Consumer News (Washington, D.C.: U.S. Federal Deposit Insurance Corporation, Fall 1996–)

Federal Register (Washington, D.C.: National Archives and Records Administration, 1995–)

Federal Reserve Bulletin (Washington, D.C.: Board of Governors of the Federal Reserve Board, 1997–)

Finance and Development (Washington, D.C.: International Monetary Fund, March 1996 -)

Finance and Economics Discussion Series (Washington, D.C.: Board of Governors of the Federal Reserve Board, 1996–)

Fish and Wildlife News (Washington, D.C.: U.S. Department of the Interior, Fish and Wildlife Service, 1997–)

Fishery Bulletin (Seattle, Wash.: U.S. Department of Commerce, NOAA, NMFS Scientific Publications Office, October 1998–)

Flying Safety (Kirtland Air Force Base, N.M.: Air Force Safety Center, 1997–)

FOIA Post (Washington, D.C.: U.S. Department of Justice, Office of Information and Privacy, 2001–)

FOIA Update (Washington, D.C.: U.S. Department of Justice, Office of Information and Privacy, 1979–2000)

Food and Nutrition Research Briefs (Washington, D.C.: U.S. Department of Agriculture, Agricultural Research Service, 1995–)

Food, Nutrition and Agriculture (Rome: FAO Food and Nutrition Division, 1991–)

Food Review (Washington, D.C.: U.S. Department of Agriculture, Economic Research Service, December 1996–)

Foreign Media Reaction Issue Focus (Washington, D.C.: U.S. Information Agency, Office of Public Liaison, November 1994–)

Forensic Science Communications (Washington, D.C.: U.S. Department of Justice, Federal Bureau of Investigation, April 1999–)

GAO Reports and Testimony (Washington, D.C.: General Accounting Office, 1995–)

Global Issues (Washington, D.C.: U.S. Department of State, International Information Programs, April 1996–)

Gotham Gazette (New York: Citizens Union Foundation)

Government Executive: The Independent Business Magazine of Government (Washington, D.C.: National Journal, August 1996–)

Gridpoints (Moffett Field, Calif.: NASA, NAS Systems Division, Winter 1999–)

Ground Warrior (Washington, D.C.: U.S. Naval Safety Center, Winter 1998–)

Hazardous Substances & Public Health (Atlanta, Ga.: Department of Health and Human Services, Public Health Service, Agency for Toxic Substances and Disease Registry, 1995–)

HCFA Health Watch (Washington, D.C.: U.S. Health Care Financing Administration, June 1996–)

Hill, The: the Capitol Newspaper (Washington, D.C.: The Hill)

HIV/AIDS Surveillance Reports (Atlanta, Ga.: U.S. Department of Health and Human Services, Centers for Disease Control and Prevention, National Center for HIV, STD, and TB Prevention, Division of HIV/AIDS Prevention, 1982–)

HIV Impact (Washington, D.C.: U.S. Department of Health and Human Services, Office of Minority Health, 2000–)

HRA Facts (New York: New York City Human Resources Administration, 1999–)

Human Genome News (Oak Ridge, Tenn.: U.S. Department of Energy, Oak Ridge National Laboratory, Spring 1989–)

Humanities (Washington, D.C.: National Endowment for the Humanities, November–December 1996–)

IAEA Bulletin, Quarterly Journal of the IAEA (Vienna: IAEA, March 1994–)

ICAO Journal (Montreal: International Civil Aviation Organization, December 1996–)

Industry, Trade, and Technology Review (Washington, D.C.: U.S. International Trade Commission, Office of Industries, 1997–)

Innovative Finance Quarterly (Washington, D.C.: U.S. Department of Transportation, Federal Highway Administration, Fall 1997–)

INS Communiqué (Washington, D.C.: U.S. Department of Justice, Immigration and Naturalization Service, April 1997–)

Internal Revenue Bulletin (Washington, D.C.: U.S. Department of the Treasury, Internal Revenue Service, 1996–)

International Briefs (Washington, D.C.: U.S. Census Bureau, International Programs Center, 1995–)

International Economic Review (Washington, D.C.: U.S. International Trade Commission, Office of Economics, 1997–)

International Finance Discussion Papers (Washington, D.C.: U.S. Federal Reserve Board, 1996–)

International Population Reports (Washington, D.C.: U.S. Census Bureau, International Programs Center, 1996–)

Issues in Labor Statistics (Washington, D.C.: U.S. Department of Labor, Bureau of Labor Statistics, 1996–)

Issues of Democracy (Washington, D.C.: U.S. Department of State, International Information Programs, May 1996–)

JED Online (Journal of Electronic Defense) (Electronic Warfare Association, 1992–)

Job Safety and Health Quarterly (Washington, D.C.: U.S. Department of Labor, Occupational Safety and Health Administration, 1999–)

Joint Force Quarterly: JFQ (Washington, D.C.: Institute for National Strategic Studies, National Defense University, 1993–)

Journal of Agricultural Genomics (Washington, D.C.: National Center for Genome Resources, 1995–2000)

Journal of Humanitarian Assistance (Cambridge, U.K.: Faculty of Social and Political Sciences, University of Cambridge)

Journal of Legal Studies (Colorado Springs, Colo.: Department of Law, U.S. Air Force Academy, 1996/97–)

Journal of Rehabilitation Research and Development (Washington, D.C.: Veterans Administration Rehabilitation Research and Development Service, 1998–)

Journal of Research of the National Institute of Standards and Technology (Washington, D.C.: U.S. Department of Commerce, Technology Administration, National Institute of Standards and Technology, 1995–)

Journal of the Executive Proceedings of the Senate of the United States of America (Washington, D.C.: Library of Congress, 1789–1805)

Journal of the House of Representatives of the United States (Washington, D.C.: Library of Congress, 1789–1805)

Journal of the House of Representatives of the United States (Washington, D.C.: U.S. House of Representatives; GPO, 1991–94)

Journal of the National Cancer Institute (Bethesda, Md.: Journal Editorial Office, National Cancer Institute, U.S. Department of Health and Human Services, 1997–)

Journal of the Senate of the United States of America (Washington, D.C.: Library of Congress, 1789–1805)

Journal of Transportation and Statistics (Washington, D.C.: U.S. Department of Transportation, Bureau of Transportation Statistics, 1998–)

Journals of the Continental Congress (Washington, D.C.: Library of Congress, 1774–89)

Juvenile Justice (Washington, D.C.: U.S. Department of Justice, Office of Juvenile Justice and Delinquency Prevention, 1993–)

Labor Area Summary (Albany, N.Y.: U.S. Department of Labor, Division of Research and Statistics, latest only)

Language and Civil Society: A Forum Electronic Journal (Washington, D.C.: U.S. Department of State, Office of English Language Programs, April 1999–)

LC Cataloging Newsline: Online Newsletter of the Cataloging Directorate, Library of Congress (Washington, D.C.: Library of Congress, 1993–)

Leading Edge (Wright-Patterson AFB, Ohio: U.S. Air Force Matériel Command, 1997–)

Library of Congress Information Bulletin (Washington, D.C.: Public Affairs Office, 1992–)

Logos: a Magazine About Research at Argonne National Laboratory (Argonne, Ill.: Office of Public Affairs, Argonne National Laboratory, Winter 1996–)

MANPRINT Quarterly (Washington, D.C.: U.S. Army, Personnel Technologies Directorate, Winter 1997–)

Marine Fisheries Review (Seattle, Wash.: NMFS, Scientific Publications Office, 1998–)

Marines Online: Official Magazine of the Marine Corps (Washington, D.C.: Division of Public Affairs, Media Branch, HQMC, 1996–)

Mass Layoffs (Washington, D.C.: U.S. Census Bureau, 1996–)

MDA Update (Washington, D.C.: National Technology Transfer Center, Winter 1994–)

Mech (Washington, D.C.: U.S. Naval Safety Center, 1999–)

Metal Industry Indicators (Washington, D.C.: U.S. Geological Survey, 1998–)

Microgravity News (Hampton, Va.: NASA Marshall Space Flight Center in conjunction with Hampton University, 1993–)

Military Intelligence Professional Bulletin (Fort Huachuca, Ariz.: U.S. Army Intelligence Center and Fort Huachuca, 1995–)

Military Review (Fort Leavenworth, Kan.: U.S. Army Command and General Staff College, 1997–)

Mineral Industry Surveys (Washington, D.C.: U.S. Geological Survey, 1997–)

MMWR: Morbidity and Mortality Weekly Report Electronic Edition (Atlanta, Ga.: Centers for Disease Control and Prevention, 1982–)

MMWR Recommendations and Reports Electronic Edition (Atlanta, Ga.: Centers for Disease Control and Prevention, 1983–)

MMWR Supplements Electronic Edition (Atlanta, Ga.: Centers for Disease Control and Prevention, 1985–)

Mobility Forum, The (Scott AFB, Ill.: HQ Air Mobility Command, Directorate of Safety)

Monthly Energy Review (Washington, D.C.: U.S. Department of Energy, Energy Information Administration, 1973–)

Monthly Labor Review (MLR) Online (Washington, D.C.: U.S. Department of Labor, Bureau of Labor Statistics, 1990–)

Monthly Product Announcement (Washington, D.C.: U.S. Census Bureau, 1997–)

Monthly Statement of the Public Debt (Washington, D.C.: U.S. Department of the Treasury, Bureau of the Public Debt, 1997–)

Monthly Treasury Statement of Receipts and Outlays of the United States Government (Hyattsville, Md.: U.S. Department of the Treasury, Financial Management Service, October 1997–)

NASA Spinoff Online (Washington, D.C.: NASA, Center for Aerospace Information, Technology Transfer Office, 1996–)

National Institute of Justice Journal (Washington, D.C.: U.S. Department of Justice, Office of Justice Programs, National Institute of Justice, August 1995–)

National Space Science Data Center Newsletter (Greenbelt, Md.: NASA Goddard Space Flight Center, September 1994–)

National Vital Statistics Reports (NVSR) (Hyattsville, Md.: National Center for Health Statistics, 1995–)

Natural Gas Monthly (Washington, D.C.: U.S. Department of Energy, Energy Information Administration, May 1996–)

Naval Aviation News (Washington, D.C.: U.S. Department of the Navy, Naval Historical Center, 1996–)

Naval War College Review (Newport, R.I.: Naval War College, 1996–)

NCO Journal, The: A Quarterly Forum for Professional Development (Fort Bliss, Tex.: U.S. Army Sergeants Major Academy, Summer 2000–)

NCUA News (Alexandria, Va.: National Credit Union Administration, 1997–)

News from the Front (Fort Leavenworth, Kan.: Center for Army Lessons Learned, December 1993–)

New York Affairs (New York: New York University, Taub Urban Research Center)

New York State Preservationist, The (Albany, N.Y.: New York State Parks Recreation and Historic Preservation, Spring/Summer 2000–)

Occupational Outlook Quarterly Online (Washington, D.C.: U.S. Department of Labor, Bureau of Labor Statistics, Spring 1999–)

OCHA News (New York: United Nations Office for the Coordination of Humanitarian Affairs, December 1998–)

OECD Observer (Paris: OECD, 1997–)

OERI Bulletin (Washington, D.C.: U.S. Department of Education, 1993–)

Official Journal of the European Communities (Luxembourg: Office for Official Publications of the European Communities)

OMB Circulars (Washington, D.C.: U.S. Office of Management and Budget, 1952–)

OMH Quarterly (Albany, N.Y.: New York State Office of Mental Health, September 1999–)

OPICNews (Washington, D.C.: U.S. Overseas Private Investment Corporation, January 2001–)

Parameters: Journal of the U.S. Army War College (Carlisle Barracks, Pa.: U.S. Army War College, 1996–)

Park Science (Washington, D.C.: National Park Service, 1981–)

Patent Abstracts (Washington, D.C.: Scientific and Technical Information Branch, National Aeronautics and Space Administration, July 1995–)

Peace Watch Online (Washington, D.C.: U.S. Institute of Peace, June 1996–)

People, Land, and Water (Washington, D.C.: U.S. Department of the Interior, Fish and Wildlife Service, December 1997–)

Pollution Prevention News (Washington, D.C.: U.S. Environmental Protection Agency, Office of Pollution Prevention and Toxics-IMD, October/November 1994–)

Postal Bulletin, The (Washington, D.C.: U.S. Postal Service, 1995–)

Postal Life (Washington, D.C.: U.S. Postal Service, July/August 1996–)

Preservation Briefs (Washington, D.C.: U.S. Department of the Interior, Technical Preservation Services Division)

Producer Price Indexes (Washington, D.C.: Department of Labor, Bureau of Labor Statistics, 1989–)

Profile, Life in the Armed Forces (Norfolk, Va.: U.S. Department of Defense, High School News Service, November 1998–)

Program Manager (Fort Belvoir, Va.: Defense Systems Management College, 1993–)

PS Online: The Preventive Maintenance Monthly (Redstone Arsenal, Ala.: U.S. Army Matériel Command, Logistics Support Activity, 1999–)

PTO Bulletin, The (Washington, D.C.: U.S. Patent and Trademark Office, Office of Public Affairs, May 1998–)

PTSD Research Quarterly (White River Junction, Vt.: U.S. Department of Veterans Affairs, National Center for Post-Traumatic Stress Disorder, 1990–)

Quarterly Banking Profile (Washington, D.C.: U.S. Federal Deposit Insurance Corporation, December 1994–)

Quarterly Financial Report for Manufacturing, Mining, and Trade Corporations (Washington, D.C.: U.S. Census Bureau, 1996–)

Quarterly Journal (Washington, D.C.: Office of the Comptroller of the Currency, 4th Q/1997–)

Record, The: The FEC's Monthly Newsletter (Washington, D.C.: U.S. Federal Election Commission, 1996–)

Recovery Times (Washington, D.C.: U.S. Federal Emergency Management Agency, 1995–)

Red Thrust Star (Fort Irwin, Calif.: U.S. Army, 11th Armored Cavalry Regiment, 1986–)
Regional Commissions Development Update (New York: United Nations Regional Commissions, New York Office, November 1996–)
Regional Outlook (Washington, D.C.: U.S. Federal Deposit Insurance Corporation, 1997–)
Research Reports (Washington, D.C.: Smithsonian Institution, Summer 1995 [no. 81]–)
Roll Call Online (Washington, D.C.: The Economist Group, most recent only)
Rural Conditions and Trends (Washington, D.C.: U.S. Department of Agriculture, Economic Research Service, 1996–)
Rural Development Perspectives (Washington, D.C.: U.S. Department of Agriculture, Economic Research Service, 1996–)
Sandia Technology (Albuquerque, N.M.: Sandia National Laboratories, Winter 1999–)
Science and Technology Review (Livermore, Calif.: Lawrence Livermore National Laboratory, 1995–)
Scientific and Technical Aerospace Reports (STAR) (Washington, D.C.: Scientific and Technical Information Branch, National Aeronautics and Space Administration, 1996–)
Searchlight on the City Council (New York: Citizens Union, most recent only)
SEC News Digest (Washington, D.C.: Securities and Exchange Commission, December 1998–)
Secrecy and Government Bulletin (Washington, D.C.: Federation of American Scientists, December 1993–June 2000)
Secrecy News (Washington, D.C.: Federation of American Scientists, 2000–)
Small Farm Digest (Washington, D.C.: U.S. Department of Agriculture, Cooperative State Research, Education, and Extension Service, Fall 1997–)
Smithsonian Magazine (Washington, D.C.: Smithsonian Institution, current issue only)
Social Security Bulletin (Washington, D.C.: U.S. Social Security Administration, Office of Research, Evaluation and Statistics, 1999–)
Soldiers (Alexandria, Va.: Department of the Army, July 1994–)
Space Research (Washington, D.C.: U.S. NASA, Office of Biological and Physical Research, Fall 2001)
Spokesman On-line (Kelly AFB, Tex.: HQ Air Intelligence Agency, April/May 1999–)
State Magazine (Washington, D.C.: U.S. Department of State, 1996–)
Strategic Forum (Washington, D.C.: National Defense University, Institute for National Strategic Studies, 1994–)
Studies in Intelligence (Washington, D.C.: U.S. Central Intelligence Agency, 1992–)
Survey of Current Business (Washington, D.C.: U.S. Department of Commerce, Bureau of Economic Analysis, 1998–)
Survey of Real Estate Trends (Washington, D.C.: U.S. Department of Commerce, Bureau of the Census, October 1995–)

Third Branch, The (Washington, D.C.: Administrative Office of the U.S. Courts, 1995–)

Trade and Employment (Washington, D.C.: U.S. Department of Commerce, Bureau of the Census, 1994–)

Traffic Safety Digest (Washington, D.C.: U.S. National Highway Traffic Safety Administration, Spring 1996–)

Treasury Bulletin (Washington, D.C.: U.S. Department of the Treasury, 1996–)

UN and Conflict Monitor (West Yorkshire, U.K.: University of Bradford, Centre for Conflict Resolution, 1994–)

United Nations Chronicle Online (New York: UN Department of Public Information, 1997–)

United States Attorneys' Bulletin (Washington, D.C.: U.S. Department of Justice, Executive Office for United States Attorneys, 1996–)

Urban Research Monitor (Washington, D.C.: U.S. Department of Housing and Urban Development, September/October 1999–)

USAID Developments (Washington, D.C.: U.S. Information Agency, 1996–)

U.S. Foreign Policy Agenda (Washington, D.C.: U.S. Department of State, International Information Programs, May 1996–)

U.S. Geological Survey Bulletin (Washington, D.C.: U.S. Geological Survey, Department of the Interior)

U.S. Geological Survey Circular (Washington, D.C.: U.S. Geological Survey, Department of the Interior)

U.S. Geological Survey Professional Papers (Washington, D.C.: U.S. Geological Survey, Department of the Interior)

U.S. Housing Market Conditions (Washington, D.C.: U.S. Department of Housing and Urban Development, Office of Policy Development and Research)

U.S. International Trade in Goods and Services (Washington, D.C.: U.S Census Bureau, Foreign Trade Division, 1994–)

USPTO Today (Washington, D.C.: U.S. Patent and Trademark Office, 2000–)

U.S. Society and Values (Washington, D.C.: U.S. Department of State, International Information Programs, June 1996–)

Vital and Health Statistics Series Reports (Hyattsville, Md.: U.S. Department of Health and Human Services, National Center for Health Statistics)

Weekly Compilation of Presidential Documents (Washington, D.C.: National Archives and Records Administration, 1993–)

Weekly Epidemiological Record (Geneva: World Health Organization, 1996–)

Weekly Weather and Crop Bulletin (Washington, D.C.: U.S. Department of Commerce, NOAA, and U.S. Department of Agriculture, November 1997–)

Women in Development (Washington, D.C.: U.S. Census Bureau, International Programs Center, 1995–)

World Agricultural Supply and Demand Estimates (Washington, D.C.: USDA Economics and Statistics System; Ithaca, N.Y.: Albert R. Mann Library, Cornell University, 1995–)

World Animal Review (Rome: FAO, 1991–)
World Bank Economic Review (Washington, D.C.: World Bank, 1992–)
World Bank Research Observer (Washington, D.C.: World Bank, 1992–)
Writ (Mountain View, Calif.: FindLaw, 2000–)

GOVERNMENT SOURCES ONLINE

Various other online sources published by federal agencies can provide documented evidence, essential facts and figures, and other vital data and statistics relevant to the topic you are researching. Highly recommended are:

Air Quality Data (http://www.epa.gov.air/data/index.html)
AIRSData offers air pollution data for the entire United States based on two EPA databases: AQS (Air Quality Systems), which monitors air pollution in cities and towns, and NEI (National Emission Inventory), which provides estimates of annual emissions and hazardous air pollutants from all types of sources. The Web site also enables you to produce reports and maps of air pollution data based on criteria that you provide.

American Workforce Issues (http://www.bls.gov/opub/rtaw/rtawhome.htm)
Published online and in print by the U.S. Department of Labor, the "Report on the American Workforce" analyzes a broad range of issues facing American workers in the workforce, including economic changes and conditions, job competitiveness, labor trends, and more.

Aviation Safety (http://www.faa.gov/safety/index.cfm)
Offers access to databases published by the Federal Aviation Administration, featuring the latest government reports covering aviation accidents, collisions, traffic, and safety.

Child and Family Statistics (http://www.childstats.gov)
This, the official Web site of the Federal Interagency Forum on Child and Family Statistics, offers easy access to federal and state statistics and reports on children and their families, including population, family characteristics, behavior and social environment, economic security, education, and health.

Comparative Statistics by Country (http://cyberschoolbus.un.org/infonation/index.asp)
Part of the United Nations's global and educational outreach project called Cyberschoolbus, this site, also known as InfoNation, is based on information published in the United Nations Statistical Yearbook. Users can compare statistical data of UN member countries, up to five countries at once. Statistical tables cover the population, economy, environment, health, and technology for each country selected. Using a special feature called "Country at a Glance," users also can look up information profiles of individual countries.

County and City Data (http://www.census.gov/statab/www/ccdb.html)
Viewable online, via .PDF files, is the latest edition of the *County and City Data Book* published by the U.S. Census Bureau. It provides population and

housing data from the most recent census for all counties, cities, and localities with more than 2,500 inhabitants, in addition to business and economic data by county and city.

Crime Statistics (http://www.fbi.gov/ucr/ucr.htm)
Offers the latest crime reports and crime statistics published by the Federal Bureau of Investigation.

Demographics and Statistical Information (http://www.census.gov)
Operated by the U.S. Census Bureau, this site contains the latest statistical and demographic information by national, state, county, and city level, based on the most recent census.

Economic Data (http://www.census.gov/econ/www/index.html)
Provided by the Census Bureau, this is a broad collection of business and economic data organized by industries and regions covering such vital data as leading economic indicators, income, labor, and poverty statistics.

Economic Statistics (http://www.whitehouse.gov/fsbr/esbr.html)
Current federal economic estimates and indicators and updated statistics are provided by a number of federal agencies, with links to information, including color charts.

Environmental Information (http://www.epa.gov)
Maintained by the Environmental Protection Agency, this official federal agency Web site features two important databases for researchers. The first is that of the Center for Environmental Information and Statistics (CEIS), a one-stop source of data and information on the environment, including state, country, and territory profiles, graphs, descriptions, and summaries on environmental hazards. The second is Envirofacts Data Warehouse, containing environmental information from EPA databases on Superfund sites, drinking water, hazardous waste, and more.

Federal Budget (http://www.whitehouse.gov/omb/budget/)
Presents facts, figures, analytical perspectives, historical tables, and spreadsheets for comparisons for the annual federal budget reported by the Office of Management and Budget.

Federal Laws and Regulations (http://www.access.gpo.gov/nara/index.html)
Contains full text of federal regulations, public laws, presidential orders, and other federal legal sources provided by the U.S. National Archives and Records Administration.

Government Expenditures (http://www.census.gov/govs/www/cffr.html)
Searchable database covering federal budget expenditures and expense obligations of state, county, and subcounty areas throughout the United States, published by the U.S. Census Bureau.

Government Statistics (http://www.fedstats.gov)
This site, maintained by the Federal Interagency Council on Statistical Policy, provides access to a full range of statistics and information from more than 70 agencies in the U.S. federal government for public use.

Health and Medicine (http://www.nih.gov)
Provided by the National Institutes of Health, this site features health information and the MEDLINE database of medical journals by the National Library of Medicine.

Health Data and Information (http://www.hrsa.gov/)
Created by the U.S. Department of Health and Human Services Health Resources and Services Administration (HRSA), this Web page features selected demographic data, graphs, tables, and other health-related information, including the top five causes of death and rates of infectious disease, for each state, with links to other HRSA programs and valuable health-related Web sites.

Healthcare Statistics (http://www.ahcpr.gov/hcupnet)
This site, part of the Healthcare Cost and Utilization Project (HCUP) of the Agency for Healthcare Research and Quality, provides access to national statistics, trends, and selected state statistics regarding hospital stays and patient care in the United States.

Highway Safety (http://www-fars.nhtsa.dot.gov)
Published by the U.S. Transportation Department, this Web site includes timely data on fatal vehicle accidents throughout the United States, searchable by state and county. Information can be searched by age of drivers, type of accident, and use of alcohol or speeding.

Law and Justice (http://www.usdoj.gov)
Provides access to information on civil rights, community policing, and agencies of the Department of Justice.

National Health Statistics (http://www.cdc.gov/nchs)
Features current health data and statistics provided by the Centers for Disease Control and Prevention.

National Resources Data (http://www.nrcs.usda.gov/technical/NRI/)
Conducted by the U.S. Department of Agriculture, the National Resources Inventory (NRI) is a statistical database of conditions and trends of soil, water, and related resources on nonfederal lands in the United States (nearly 75 percent of the nation's total land area). More than 800,000 scientifically selected sample sites in all 50 states are covered.

Railroad Safety (safetydata.fra.dot.gov/OfficeofSafety)
Features accident and inspection reports by county, published by the Federal Railroad Administration.

School District Demographics (http://nces.ed.gov/surveys/sdds/)
Sponsored by the National Center for Education, this Web site offers geographic and demographic data that describes and analyzes characteristics of school districts, children, and K–12 education.

Social Statistics (http://www.whitehouse.gov/fsbr/ssbr.html)
Available through the White House Briefing Room, this site provides easy access to current federal social statistics and links to information produced by a number of federal agencies. Includes color charts.

State and Metropolitan Data (http://www.census.gov/statab/www/smadb.html)
Contains many statistics on economic and social conditions for every state and metropolitan area in the United States, viewable online in .PDF form, from the fifth edition of a popular printed reference, *The States and Metropolitan Area Data Book*, published by the U.S. Census Bureau.

State Health Profiles (http://www.cdc.gov/epo/shp/)
The Centers for Disease Control and Prevention (CDC) has published state health profiles annually for all 50 states since 1987. The State Health Profile series (also available in print) focuses on key information regarding U.S health status, demographics, and distribution of federal health-care expenditures and services.

State Health Workforce Profiles (http://bhpr.hrsa.gov/healthworkforce/reports/profiles)
Developed by the U.S. Department of Health and Human Services, the State Health Workforce Profiles, also available on CD-ROM and in print, reports on supply, demand, distribution, education, and use of health personnel and per capita ratios for comparison with other states and the nation. Each profile includes brief overviews of residents' health status, services, and demand for health workers; health care employment by place of work, and health care employment in more than 25 health professions and occupations.

State of the Cities Data (http://socds.huduser.org)
The U.S. Department of Housing and Urban Development provides fully searchable key data for metropolitan areas, central cities, and suburbs, including detailed demographic and economic characteristics, latest unemployment rates, information on jobs, businesses and average pay (in the 1990s), violent and property crime, and more.

Statistical Resources on the Web (http://www.lib.umich.edu/govdocs/statsnew.html)
Statistical information of every kind for the United States and foreign countries, organized by subject, is easily accessible through this site, produced by the University of Michigan library. Featuring a comprehensive listing of statistical resources and links, categories include agriculture, business and industry, cost of living, demographics, education, energy, environment, finance, foreign economics, foreign trade, health, housing, labor, military, politics, and transportation.

Statistics on Aging (http://www.agingstats.gov)
Features the Federal Interagency Forum on Aging-Related Statistics, including data on older Americans for the year 2000.

Transportation Data (http://transtats.bts.gov)
Features a broad collection of transportation data by mode, subject, or agency, collected by various agencies within the U.S. Department of Transportation and other federal agencies, such as the U.S. Bureau of the Census.

U.S. Mortality Rates (http://www.cdc.gov/nchs/products/pubs/pubd/other/atlas/atlas.htm)
Offered online, in print, and on CD-ROM, the *Atlas of United States Mortality Rates,* published by the National Center for Health Statistics, documents all 18 leading causes of death, organized by race and sex, for small U.S. geographic areas.

Workplace Safety (www.osha.gov/oshstats)
Provides full access to workplace inspection reports, fines, and violations searchable by institution published by the Occupational Safety and Health Administration.

OTHER GOVERNMENT DOCUMENTS

Depository libraries throughout the United States function as centers of government information. They include the National Technical Information (NTIS), the Educational Resources Information Center (ERIC), and many others. Also available are documents and indexes from other levels of government.

One of the largest depositories of U.S. federal documents is at Columbia University. Since 1882, the university has served in this capacity, and it is a chief depository of New York State documents (1983–94). Held in the Lehman Library, the university's collection of U.S. government documents includes federal documents cataloged by subject, with many available on the Internet or CD-ROM, in addition to paper and microfiche.

Columbia University offers complete subject guides to material located in the U.S. Government Documents collections, Lehman Library, and other Columbia University libraries, including those accessible worldwide via the Internet. Guides cover U.S. federal government documents, international documents, state and local documents, major databases, U.S. senators and representatives, and more.

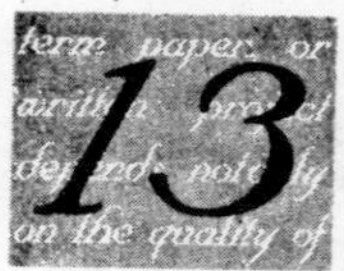

Finding Libraries

Academic, Government, Research, Public, School, State, and Special Libraries

Despite the tremendous growth of the Internet and electronic research, libraries still distinguish themselves as curators of various kinds of information and material in a single place. Every library, no matter its type or location, has something for those seeking research: books, periodicals, microforms, sound recordings, manuscripts, audio and video recordings, and materials in many other forms.

School and public libraries are generally the best places to conduct research for your essay, term paper, or written project, but other libraries are equally worthwhile for research and information. Heading the list are government and state libraries, independent research libraries, museums, special libraries, and special collection libraries.

RESEARCHING LIBRARIES

Researching the best library for your cause and subject isn't as difficult as it sounds. To locate the closest public library in your area, consult the Yellow Pages under the heading "Libraries—Public." For listings of college and university libraries, check under "Schools—Universities and Colleges (Academic)."

By calling the reference desk of the library that interests you, you can find out more about what kinds of reference materials, in print and electronic form, they offer, in addition to their hours and policies for restrictions and usage. By visiting the library's Web page, you can access the same information, search its online catalog, and check out whether it has everything you need. For that matter, you can research practically any library, anywhere in the world, on the Web via online public access catalogs (OPACs). This searchable database indexes the entire holdings of any library. (Read more about OPACs later in this chapter.)

Virtual libraries are also a convenient way to research your topic. They offer free, unrestricted access to many authoritative and credible references, including almanacs, anthologies, dictionaries, encyclopedias, and more, all in electronic form. These sites are fully searchable, too. (See "Virtual Libraries" for additional information.)

You may also find libraries by name or location by using several Internet resources. Many of them list not only public libraries but also school and state libraries throughout the United States and abroad. A few include:

Ask a Librarian . . . (http://www.loc.gov/rr/askalib/local-library.html)
A free online reference service of the Library of Congress listing a variety of online library locators to "respond to your specific and ongoing needs."

Libweb (The Library Index) (http://www.libdex.com/)
This international directory of library Web sites can be searched by keyword or browsed by region.

Public Library Locator (http://nces.ed.gov/surveys/libraries/librarysearch/)
Provided by the U.S. Department of Education, this directory offers keyword searching of U.S. public libraries by name, state, size of collection, number of staff members, and other criteria.

School Libraries on the Web (http://www.sldirectory.com/)
Worldwide directory of elementary and high school library Web pages that can be viewed by country or by state.

State Libraries (http://www.loc.gov/global/library/statelib.html)
In partnership with the Library of Congress and the American Library Association, this site lists state library Web sites throughout the country.

Additional Web directories to access other libraries, such as government, research, or special libraries, are also available. They accompany the sections about these types of libraries later in this chapter.

Of course, before proceeding with your research, knowing more about the different libraries you can access in your area can help. Among the potential sources of research to consider are:

ACADEMIC LIBRARIES

There are more than 3,400 academic libraries, including 1,300 two-year and 2,100 four-year college libraries, throughout the United States. Academic libraries, also known as research libraries, feature extensive collections of print material, plus a large variety of video, audio, and other forms of media. Other resources include archival and special collections on a wide range of subjects.

Most academic libraries are accessible online, and have Web sites that contain general information and access to online catalogs, magazine and newspaper databases (with access to some databases restricted to students only), electronic journals and books, and other useful Internet resources. As a registered student with I.D., you can use your academic library to check out materials and request interlibrary loans of titles from other campus libraries.

Visitor access by nonstudents varies, as do policies allowing public access to materials. Many academic libraries allow public use of their computers and online databases, though visitors are often required to obtain a guest pass or register at the reference desk. Unless you are an active or registered student of that college or university, checking out books or periodicals is not allowed. Policies regarding public use and public access are generally posted on most library Web sites. You also can call the library's reference desk regarding its policies before visiting the campus.

Many major four-year universities have other libraries on campus dedicated to certain areas of study, such as art, medicine, law, or science and technology, offering even more resources and more choices for further study and research.

According to the Association of Research Libraries in its latest annual rankings, the "Top 25" rated academic libraries in the United States and Canada today, in terms of sheer volume, are:

1. Harvard University
2. Yale University
3. University of Illinois, Urbana
4. University of Toronto
5. University of California, Berkeley
6. University of Texas
7. Stanford University
8. University of Michigan
9. Columbia University
10. University of California, Los Angeles
11. Cornell University
12. University of Chicago
13. Indiana University
14. University of Washington
15. University of Wisconsin
16. Princeton University
17. University of Minnesota
18. University of Alberta
19. Ohio State University
20. University of North Carolina
21. Duke University
22. University of Pennsylvania
23. Arizona State University
24. University of Virginia
25. University of British Columbia

Several online directories feature complete listings of academic libraries on the Web, with searchable databases. They include:

Libweb: USA Academic Libraries (http://sunsite.berkeley.edu/Libweb/)
This directory contains a listing of individual academic libraries accessible on the Web. Libraries are listed by region—Northeast, Midwest and Great Lakes states, Southeast, Southwest, Mountain and Plain states, and West—and by state, in alphabetical order.

lib-web-cats (http://www.librarytechnology.org/libwebcats/),
A directory of libraries worldwide, this database lists more than 3,000 academic libraries, from A to Z, in all specialties. Under search options, click on library type and highlight "academic" to produce a complete list. Otherwise, you can search for academic libraries by city, state, or country.

GOVERNMENT LIBRARIES

There are more than 1,350 government libraries throughout the United States. Government libraries are ideal sources for legal, historical, and local information, with many offering access to online resources, catalogs, and physical collections. They include department libraries sponsored by federal agencies, the Library of Congress, the Smithsonian Institution Libraries, and military and presidential libraries. (For a complete listing of departmental libraries and other governmental libraries, visit the following Web page: http://campus.umr.edu/library/gov/libr.html.) Examples of libraries in the above specialties include:

Departmental Libraries

Environmental Protection Agency RTP Library, 109 T.W. Alexander Drive, Research Triangle Park, NC 27709, 919-541-2259; http://www.epa.gov/rtp/library/

With a primary focus on air pollution, emphasizing chemical toxicity and the basic sciences, the Environmental Protection Agency RTP Library offers a large collection of resources including more than 400 journal titles, more than 4,000 books, and an extensive documents collection. The library's Web site offers access to the online catalog, EPA testing methods, EPA publications, and the Technology Transfer Network, a directory of links, facts, and information on related subjects.

National Agricultural Library, 10301 Baltimore Avenue, Beltsville, MD 20705, 301-504-5755; http://www.nalusda.gov/

As the nation's primary source for agricultural information and the research arm of the U.S. Department of Agriculture, the National Agricultural Library makes available an abundance of agricultural information for researchers, educators, policy makers, and the public. The library offers the Internet's most accessible agricultural research library supporting research, education, and applied agriculture. This includes a comprehensive article citation database, reference center, special collections, nutrient database, and guide to agriculture on the Web.

National Institute of Environmental Health Sciences Library, 111 Alexander Drive, Building 101, Research Triangle Park, NC 27709, 919-541-3426; http://library.niehs.nih.gov/

Providing access to research and information in the advancement of environmental health, the National Institute of Environmental Health Sciences (NIEHS) Library meets the needs of consumers, educators, and researchers through a variety of resources. Assets include an online library catalog, books and encyclopedias, published literature and scientific databases, journals including online access to 2,000 titles, research and consumer health links, and official NIEHS publications.

National Institute of Standards and Technology, 100 Bureau Drive, Stop 3460, Gaithersburg, MD 20899-3460, 301-975-6478; http://www.nist.gov/

Sponsored by this nonregulatory federal agency within the U.S. Commerce Department's Technology Administration, this site features general and specific information for researchers, kids, and the general public, including online databases, publications, and research on applied technology, measurements, and standards.

National Institutes of Health Library, Building 10, Room 1L-25, Bethesda, MD 20892-1150, 301-496-5612; http://nihlibrary.nih.gov/

A leading biomedical research library and a division of the U.S. Department of Health and Human Services, the National Institutes of Health Library provides a variety of useful resources for researchers, including online journals, databases, books, and other resources.

National Library of Education (NLE), 400 Maryland Avenue SW, Washington, DC 20202, 800-424-1616; http://www.ed.gov/NLE/index.html
Calling itself "the world's largest federally funded library devoted solely to education," the NLE, sponsored by the U.S. Department of Education, contains a wealth of resources and information for students, teachers, and researchers. The center's general collection consists of more than 100,000 books, about 850 periodical subscriptions, and more than 450,000 microforms all related to education, and several online tools, including ERIC, a national information system providing access to education literature and resources.

National Library of Medicine, 8600 Rockville Pike, Bethesda, MD 20894, 888-346-3656; http://www.nlm.nih.gov/
A provider of health-related library and information services, the National Library of Medicine is the world's leading biomedical library and publisher of the MEDLINE online information catalog. This online site features health research, databases, and publications.

The National Transportation Library, 400 Seventh Street SW, Room 7412, Washington, DC 20590, 800-853-1351; http://ntl.bts.gov/
Established in 1998 through the Transportation Equity Act for the 21st Century, this U.S. repository of transportation-related information features a broad range of resource and tools. They include online reference sources, such as a reference shelf consisting of U.S. Department of Transportation publications and a directory of transportation libraries, and digital collection on everything from aviation to safety and security.

U.S. Department of Energy Library, Germantown, MD (301) 903-6333; Washington, DC, 202-586-9534; http://www.ma.mbe.doe.gov/me40/library/index.html
Founded in 1947 when the Atomic Energy Commission was established, the Energy Library houses more than 1 million volumes of energy-related information, including government documents, monographs, series and periodicals, and an extensive collection of technical reports on microfiche and journals on microfilm. Materials emphasize physics, chemistry, biology, engineering, environment, economics, social issues, administration, and management. The library's technical book collection contains more than 41,000 titles and 85,000 volumes from the 1950s to the present. The Web site offers access to an energy library catalog, electronic journals, Web resources, a Department of Energy law library, and links to other related sources.

U.S. Department of the Interior Library, MS 1151, 49 C Street NW, Washington, DC 20240, 202-208-5815; http://library.doi.gov/
Providing the full gamut of professional reference and research services, the U.S. Department of the Interior Library features documents originally produced by the department, as well as a wide variety of books, journals, and other resources on U.S. natural and cultural heritage. Only an online catalog, enabling you to search its collection, and bibliographies of source material

are accessible at this site. Despite this limitation, the library's Web site provides a starting point for researching relevant subjects.

Military Libraries

Air Force Historical Research Agency, 600 Chennault Circle, Building 1405, Maxwell AFB, AL 36112-6424, 334-953-2395; http://www.au.af.mil/au/afhra/

Providing research assistance to military students, visiting scholars, and the public, the Air Force Historical Research Agency features the world's largest collection of documents on U.S. military aviation—more than 70 million pages. Among its holdings, accessible online, are popular topics on U.S. Air Force history, books and publications, historical reports and documents, photo albums, and more. Also featured are useful links to other libraries and museums, and military and government sites of interest.

Air Force Institute of Technology Library, Building 642, 2950 Hobson Way, Wright-Patterson AFB, OH 45433-7765, 937-255-3005; http://library.afit.edu/

Based in Ohio, the Air Force Institute of Technology Library offers access to its online catalog and research tools, including extensive bibliographies and subject guides to Web resources.

The Marine Corps University Library, 3250 Catlin Avenue, Quantico, VA 22134-5000, 703-784-4411; http://www.mcu.usmc.mil/MCRCweb/library.htm

Assisting students, faculty, and staff of the Marine Corps University (MCU) as well as the public with academic studies and research, the MCU Library offers free access to a mix of online collections and resources. Among them are student papers and theses, military publications, electronic text collections, references and search engines, subject bibliographies, and links to other Web pages.

Pentagon Library, 6605 Army Pentagon, Washington, DC 20310-6605, 703-695-1997; http://www.hqda.army.mil/library/

Primarily formed to serve the research needs of Pentagon personnel, the Pentagon Library Web site offers access to reference sources of military interest, including bibliographies, briefing guides, hot topic lists, and a host of related Web references and links.

U.S. Air Force Academy Libraries, Academic Library, 2354 Fairchild Drive, Suite 3A10, USAF Academy, Colorado Springs, CO 80840-6214; 719-333-2590; http://www.usafa.af.mil/dfsel/

The U.S. Air Force Academy Libraries Web site provides access to various reference, research, and reading collections through its three main libraries with links to related sites and resources.

U.S. Army Armor School Research Library, Harris Hall, 2368 Old Ironsides Avenue, Fort Knox, KY 40121-5200, 502-624-6231; http://www.knox.army.mil/school/ops/library/

Open to the general public and individuals interested in serious research, this full-service library, with emphasis on military subjects, offers online listings of library holdings, information, and links of military interest, including bibliographies of resources for major battles, access to digital libraries and magazines, and veteran's groups.

U.S. Army Center of Military History, 1099 14th Street NW, Washington, DC 20005-3402; e-mail: CMHOnline@hqda.army.mil; http://www.army.mil/cmh-pg/
The historical arm of the U.S. Army, the U.S. Army Center for Military History offers a vast number of online resources suitable for researchers of any age. Included is historical artwork and photographs, army unit histories, reference topics with access to individual materials, Medal of Honor citations, and the complete history of the U.S. Army.

U.S. Army War College Library, 122 Forbes Avenue, Carlisle, PA 17013-5220, 717-245-3660; http://carlisle-www.army.mil/library/
Offering high-quality research and military resources, this award-winning library's Web site offers library information, access to the online catalog, military reading lists and official military publications, bibliographies, and lists of print resources.

U.S. Coast Guard Academy Library, 31 Mohegan Avenue, New London, CT 06320-8103, 860-444-8444; http://www.cga.edu/academics/library/library.htm
The primary facility for research and study at the U.S. Coast Guard Academy, the academy's library Web page features a host of government documents, bibliographies of resources, and access to its online catalog.

U.S. Marine Historical Center, 1254 Charles Morris Street SE, Washington Navy Yard, Washington, DC 20374-5040, 202-433-3483; http://hqinet001.hqmc.usmc.mil/HD/
This museum and research library offers access through its Web site to information about Army divisions and the histories and traditions of the U.S. Marine Corps. Featured are historical and general information resources, including a "who's who" in Marine Corps history, and article overviews of special interest.

U.S. Naval Research Laboratory, Ruth H. Hooker Library, 4555 Overlook Avenue SW, Washington, DC 20375, 202-767-7323; http://infoweb2.nrl.navy.mil/
Named in honor of the Naval Research Laboratory's first librarian, this official Web site contains databases, reference tools, subject guides, and access to the library's online catalog.

Other Governmental Libraries

The Library of Congress, 101 Independence Avenue SE, Washington, DC 20540, 202-707-5000; http://www.loc.gov/
Serving the U.S. Congress and all U.S. residents, The Library of Congress is the nation's oldest federal cultural institution and also the largest library in the world, with nearly 128 million items on approximately 530 miles of bookshelves. Among its collections are more than 29 million books and other

printed materials, 2.7 million recordings, 12 million photographs, 4.8 million maps, and 57 million manuscripts.

Several useful online resources are available through the Library of Congress Web site. They include American Memory, a primary source of archival materials covering American culture and history; America's Library, featuring stories and facts celebrating the library's 200th anniversary; and Country Studies: Area Handbook Series, including studies of 100 countries. Among its other resources are State and Local Governments, a reference guide and index of links to various agencies and branches of state and local governments; the National Library Service for the Blind and Physically Handicapped, a free library program of Braille and recorded materials circulated to eligible borrowers.

Los Alamos National Laboratory Research Library, MS-P362, P.O. Box 1663, Los Alamos, NM 87545-1362, 505-667-5809; http://lib-www.lanl.gov/

As a place for further research and study by its member physicists, engineers, chemists, materials scientists, and other employees, the Los Alamos National Laboratory Research Library features the most extensive collection of scientific reports and literature in the field today, including books, journals, databases, patents and technical reports, and other literature. While the library's subscriber-only databases and FlashPoint multidatabase search tool are off limits to off-campus users, there are still plenty of other resources available for public use. This includes free access to some of the library's 5,612 full-text electronic journals in the fields of agriculture, astronomy, biology and genetics, business, chemistry, computer science, current news, defense/military, earth sciences, engineering, environment, government, health and safety, humanities, and international affairs, among others.

Other useful research tools include Info by Subject, offering some fully accessible electronic references and dictionaries, Reference Resources, including popular and general references, and unclassified Electronic Reports, featuring scientific and technical reports from various federal agencies.

NASA HQ Library: NASA Center Libraries, 300 E Street SW, Room 1J20, Washington, DC 20546, 202-358-0168; http://www.hq.nasa.gov/office/hqlibrary/pathfinders/nasalib.htm

Sponsored by the National Aeronautics and Space Administration, this directory features links to all of NASA's space research libraries, with most offering free access. Each library offers a selection of free online resources for the public, such as NASA documents and technical reports, journals, subject guides, alphabetical title lists, and links to other aeronautics, aviation, and space research agency Web sites.

Smithsonian Institution Libraries, P.O. Box 37012, MRC 154, Washington, DC 20013-7012, 202-357-2240; http://www.sil.si.edu/

The largest cultural and historical complex in the world covering seemingly every facet of American life, the Smithsonian Institution's libraries Web site offers information and resources including a digital library (browsable by subject), access to special collections, and listings and links to Smithsonian Institution libraries.

U.S. National Archives and Records Administration, 8601 Adelphi Road, College Park, MD 20740-6001, 866-272-6272; http://www.archives.gov/
The chief repository of historic documents and information, the U.S. National Archives and Records Administration offers access to archival collections, records and holdings, and exhibits related to the nation's heritage and history. Resources include guides to federal records, archival research catalog and databases, and access to online exhibits.

Presidential Libraries

George Bush Presidential Library and Museum, 1000 George Bush Drive West, College Station, TX 77845, 979-691-4000; http://bushlibrary.tamu.edu/
Covering the history, challenges, and influences of the 41st president (1988–92), this official library and museum features original artifacts and resources for further study, including biographies, photographs, and documents and public papers encompassing Bush's political life.

The Jimmy Carter Library and Museum, 441 Freedom Parkway, Atlanta, GA 30307-1498, 404-865-7100; http://www.jimmycarterlibrary.org/
Paying tribute to the son of a peanut farmer who became the 39th president (1977–81), the Jimmy Carter Library and Museum Web site provides access to a host of materials. They include selected documents and photographs, manuscript collections, audiovisual material, oral histories, selected bibliographies, and Web links to pages related to Carter's presidency, his career before and after the White House, and First Lady Rosalyn Carter.

The William J. Clinton Presidential Center, 1000 La Harpe Boulevard, Little Rock, AR 72201, 501-370-8000; http://www.clintonpresidentialcenter.com/
Located within a 27-acre city park along the south bank of the Arkansas River, the William J. Clinton Presidential Center, named after the 42nd president (1993–2001), provides access to biographies, selected documents, and photos chronicling Clinton's years in the White House and his administration.

The Dwight D. Eisenhower Library and Museum, 200 Southeast 4th Street, Abilene, KS 67410, 1-877-RING-IKE, http://www.eisenhower.utexas.edu/
Featuring 23 million pages of manuscripts, audiovisual materials, and other historical items relating to the 34th president (1953–61), the Dwight D. Eisenhower Library and Museum offers various online resources of interest. An online reference section features biographical facts and information covering Eisenhower's personal life, his presidential years, his service during World War II, and other topics. A manuscript collection and audiovisual archive also contains many online documents and photographs useful to students working on school papers and special projects.

Gerald R. Ford Library and Museum, 1000 Beal Avenue, Ann Arbor, MI 48109, 734-205-0555; http://www.ford.utexas.edu/
Recording and preserving the history of the 38th president (1974–77), through its physical site and official Web site, the Gerald R. Ford Library and

Museum promotes study and research into the life and work of the former president. The Web page offers biographies of Gerald R. Ford and First Lady Betty Ford, online documents such as cabinet meeting minutes, and selected historical and White House photographs of popular and scholarly interest.

Rutherford B. Hayes Presidential Center, Spiegel Grove, Fremont, OH 43420, 800-998-7737; http://www.rbhayes.org/
Recalling the life of the 19th president (1877–81), American's first presidential library features papers, photographs, texts of speeches, and a Civil War database.

The Herbert Hoover Presidential Library and Museum, P.O. Box 488, 210 Parkside Drive, West Branch, IA 52358, 319-643-5301; http://www.hoover.archives.gov/
One of the 11 presidential libraries operated by the U.S. National Archives and Records Administration, the Herbert Hoover Presidential Library and Museum, preserving the life's work of the 31st president (1929–33), offers access to its research collections. Included are historical materials, papers, photos, a daily calendar, and a scholarly articles database.

President Andrew Johnson Museum and Library, P.O. Box 5026, Greeneville, TN 37743, 800-729-0256; http://ajmuseum.tusculum.edu/
Dedicated to the 17th president (1865–69) of the United States, the President Andrew Johnson Museum and Library offers a number of online resources, including a biography, a time line of his life, detailed collection of the papers of his presidency, and a list of related links.

Lyndon Baines Johnson Library and Museum, 2313 Red River Street, Austin, TX 78705 512-721-0200; http://www.lbjlib.utexas.edu/
This official library and museum commemorating the life of the former 36th president (1963–69) offers a wide range of research and memorabilia accessible online. Resources include biographical information about President Lyndon Baines Johnson and Lady Bird Johnson, quick facts, speeches and messages, photographs, audiovisual materials, oral histories, and selected pages from the president's daily diary.

John F. Kennedy Library and Museum, Columbia Point, Boston, MA 02125, 866-JFK-1960; http://www.cs.umb.edu/jfklibrary/
Containing important historical documents, manuscript material, interviews, and other memorabilia of the 35th president (1961–63), the John F. Kennedy Library and Museum offers a number of free resources for students and researchers. Accessible online are archival, manuscript, and audiovisual materials chronicling the personal and political life of JFK, including presidential records, a picture gallery, public papers, texts of news conferences, a complete biography, and resources for teachers and students.

Abraham Lincoln Presidential Library and Museum 1 Old State Capitol Plaza, Springfield, IL 62701, 217-524-7216; http://www.alincoln-library.com/Apps/default.asp
Devoted to the life and work of the 16th president (1861–65), this official Web site offers free access to materials such as a Lincoln chronology, a sec-

tion of things "Lincoln Never Said," selected readings, related articles, and links to related Web sites.

The Richard Nixon Library and Birthplace Foundation, 18001 Yorba Linda Boulevard, Yorba Linda, CA 92886, 714-993-5075; http://www.nixonfoundation.org/
For political and historical scholars and students, the Richard Nixon Library and Birthplace Foundation, offers further opportunities for study and research of the 37th president (1969–74) through its online Research Center. The center includes biographies of the president and of First Lady Pat Nixon, research bibliographies covering Nixon's life and presidency, the Vietnam War, public papers, and related Web sites and links.

The Ronald Reagan Presidential Library, 40 Presidential Drive, Simi Valley, CA 93065, 800-410-8354; http://www.reagan.utexas.edu/
This official Web site of the library honoring the memory of the 40th president (1981–89) features a variety of free resources useful to researchers, including biographical information, selected photographs, audiovisual material, text collections, public papers and speeches, and more.

The Franklin D. Roosevelt Library and Museum, 4079 Albany Post Road, Hyde Park, NY 12538, 800-FDR-VISIT; http://www.fdrlibrary.marist.edu/
Housing 17 million pages of documents, thousands of photographs, and hours of recorded speeches, films and videos, and numerous oral histories, the FDR Library and Museum, dedicated to the 32nd president (1933–45), provides a number of free online resources. They include digitized documents, photographs, recordings, and indexes and finding aids with keyword searching.

Harry S. Truman Presidential Museum and Library, 500 West U.S. Highway 24, Independence MO 64050, 800-833-1225; http://www.trumanlibrary.org/
Through its official Web page, the Harry S. Truman Presidential Museum and Library, honoring the 33rd president (1945–53), offers access to a variety of research and resources of interest to students and researchers. Archival materials, fully accessible online, include public papers, oral histories, online documents and photographs, an audio collection, the president's daily appointment calendar, special subject guides, and student research files, featuring 53 topics and copies of documents for special class projects or papers.

INDEPENDENT RESEARCH LIBRARIES

Throughout the United States and the world, countless independent, privately endowed research libraries collect, research, and provide access to records, materials, and collections covering a variety of subjects. Attracting scholars and researchers from all over the world, they include some of the nation's oldest and most distinguished historic societies, museums, and libraries, such as the Newberry Library, the Folger Shakespeare Library, the Getty Research Library, the Hagley Museum and Library, and the Huntington Library. While offering a rich abundance of primary research material, including publications, catalogs, guides, monographs, journals, books, and Internet-accessible databases, they also serve the public through exhibitions, tours, lecture programs, classes, and other events. Most independent research facilities are open to the public, but some require appointments to view special collections. Examples of leading independent research libraries include:

American Antiquarian Society
185 Salisbury Street, Worcester, MA 01609-1634
508-755-5221; fax: 508-754-9069; http://www.americanantiquarian.org/

American Philosophical Society
105 South Fifth Street, Philadelphia, PA 19106-3386
215-440-3400; fax: 215-440-3423; http://www.amphilsoc.org/

The Folger Shakespeare Library
201 East Capitol Street SE, Washington, DC 20003
202-544-4600; fax: 202-544-4623; http://www.folger.edu/Home_02B.html

The Getty Research Library
1200 Getty Center Drive, Suite 1100, Los Angeles, CA 90049-1688
310-440-7390; fax: 310-440-7780; http://www.getty.edu/research/

The Hagley Museum and Library
P.O. Box 3630, Wilmington, DE 19807-0630
302-658-2400; fax: 302-658-0568; http://www.hagley.lib.de.us/

The Historical Society of Pennsylvania
1300 Locust Street, Philadelphia, PA 19107
215-732-6200; fax: 215-732-2680; http://www.hsp.org/

The Huntington Library, Art Collections, and Botanical Gardens
1151 Oxford Road, San Marino, CA 91108
626-405-2115; fax: 626-405-0225; http://www.huntington.org/

The Library Company of Philadelphia
1314 Locust Street, Philadelphia, PA 19107-5698
215-546-3181; fax: 215-546-5167; http://librarycompany.org/index1.htm

Linda Hall Library of Science, Engineering and Technology
5109 Cherry Street, Kansas City, MO 64110
816-363-4600; fax: 816-926-8790; http://www.lindahall.org/

Massachusetts Historical Society
1154 Boylston Street, Boston, MA 02215
617-536-1608; fax: 617-859-0074; http://www.masshist.org/

The Morgan Library
29 East 36th Street, New York, NY 10016
212-685-0008; fax: 212-685-4740; http://www.morganlibrary.org/

The Newberry Library
60 West Walton Street, Chicago, IL 60610
312-943-9090; http://www.newberry.org/

The New York Academy of Medicine
1216 Fifth Avenue, New York, NY 10029
212-876-8200; fax: 212-722-7650; http://www.nyam.org/

The New-York Historical Society
170 Central Park West, New York, NY 10024-5194
212-873-3400; fax: 212-875-1591; http://www.nyhistory.org/

The New York Public Library, Astor, Lenox, and Tilden Foundations
Fifth Avenue and 42nd Street, New York, NY 10018
212-930-0709; fax: 212-869-3567; http://www.nypl.org/

The Virginia Historical Society
428 North Boulevard, P.O. Box 7311, Richmond, VA 23221
804-358-4901; fax: 804-355-2399; http://www.vahistorical.org/

Winterthur Museum, Garden and Library
Winterthur, DE 19735
302-888-4701; fax: 302-888-4870; http://www.winterthur.org/

To access additional listings and links to North American research libraries, visit the following recommended sources:

Libdex Open Directory (http://www.libdex.com/)
An index of more than 18,000 libraries of every kind, this directory features 307 research libraries accessible on the Web. (To produce this list, use the libraries search engine and enter the phrase "research libraries." Then browse the directory of "libraries," and select "research.")

PUBLIC LIBRARIES

Public libraries provide access to a multitude of online databases, references, searchable catalogs, youth and adult resources, links to local information, local history and local archives, and other Internet-based services for your convenience.

The more than 9,000 public libraries throughout the United States offer a diverse and extensive collection of print and electronic primary and secondary source materials as well, such as books, magazines and newspapers; subject collections; and special collections. Today, most public libraries, big and small, are accessible on the World Wide Web. This includes free and, in some cases, unrestricted access to electronic databases and other popular references and tools.

Even if you don't know the Web page or Web address of your local public library, finding that information is usually simple. You can enter the name of your library into a search engine or consult an online directory that lists public libraries. Online resources include:

lib-web-cats (http://www-librarytechnology.org/libwebcats/)
This database contains information and listings of virtually every library of every type worldwide.

PublicLibraries.com (http://www.publiclibraries.com/),
One of the best guides to public libraries, this site features state-by-state listings of seemingly every public library and Web access.

SCHOOL LIBRARIES

School libraries, also known as school media centers, provide access to all kinds of print and nonprint resources for teachers and students alike. There are 76,000 public school and 17,000 private school libraries in the United States alone. Depending on the grade level of students, services can range from storytelling in elementary school libraries to computer instruction for higher grade levels. Reference materials and resources vary, but most libraries offer certain basic materials. School libraries contain print, nonprint, and electronic resources. Print resources are books, newspapers, magazines, and microforms (microfilm and microfiche); nonprint resources are videotapes, audiotapes, and filmstrips. Electronic resources can range from CD-ROM indexes to online databases. Most school libraries have dedicated Web pages that provide access to the library's online catalog and some popular online references and databases. This substantially improves your opportunities to conduct research efficiently.

Information about your library's holdings, including books by author, title, or subject, and other published materials, can be found in the online catalog. In most cases, you can access the catalog from any location.

As with any academic or public library, your school library may allow you to check out books, photocopy materials, or make an interlibrary loan of a book or magazine from another library in your school district.

Naturally, in addition to using your resources at your school library's Web site, you can also access free resources at many other school libraries via the World Wide Web. The following online directories can serve as gateways to other venues around the world:

School Libraries on the Net (http://www.school-libraries.net/)
This collection, sponsored by the School of Library and Information Science at San Jose University, includes Web pages created or maintained by school librarians, organized by country and state.

School Libraries on the Web: A Directory (http://www.sldirectory.com/index.html)
Maintained by Philadelphia school librarian Linda Bertland, this Web site lists Web pages for K–12 school libraries in the United States and in countries around the world focusing on the content offered through each school's library/media center.

SPECIAL LIBRARIES

Varying greatly in access and public use, nearly 10,000 special libraries, including corporate, association, legal, medical, museum, religious, and other specialized libraries, exist in the United States alone. These libraries can be an additional resource to further research of your topic.

Many libraries in this category are distinguished research and information centers. Many of Fortune 500 companies have library and information centers, as do major hospitals and medical centers. Various religious groups also offer places for further study and research, such as American Baptist Historical Society, Samuel Colgate Historical Library, the Eastern Mennonite University, Hartzler Library, and the Reformed Episcopal Seminary, Kuehner Memorial Library. (For a free listing with links to many other religious and theological libraries in the United States and Canada, visit member directory of the American Theological Library Association [ATLA] at: http://www.atla.com/member/directories/directory_institutional=public.html.)

For subjects such as motion pictures and television, the Academy of Motion Pictures Arts and Sciences's Margaret Herrick Library, the American Film Institute, and the British Film Institute are three leading repositories of research and information. For researching businesses, foundations, or public institutions, the Annual Reports Library fulfills this need. For legal studies and research, leading university libraries, such as the Case Western Reserve University Law Library, the Emory University Hugh F. MacMillan Law Library, or the Georgetown University Law Library, offer extensive sources in this area of study.

(For more information regarding special libraries in all areas of study, see the *Directory of Special Libraries and Information Centers, 28th Ed.* [Detroit: Gale Research Co., 2003], discussed later in this chapter.)

STATE LIBRARIES

Featuring such resources as historical treasures, legal records, and studies conducted by state agencies, state libraries offer free public access to a wealth of local and regional information. The contents of state library Web sites vary from state to state. Some offer a more diverse selection of online resources than others do. They include online catalogs and catalog searching, archives and histories, directories and subject guides, genealogy records and other Web resources. The following is a list of state libraries, state commissions, or state agencies offering Web access:

ALABAMA
Alabama Department of Archives & History (http://archives.state.al.us/)

ALASKA
Alaska State Library (http://archives.state.al.us/)

ARIZONA
Arizona Department of Library, Archives and Public Records
(http://www.dlapr.lib.az.us/)

ARKANSAS
Arkansas State Library (http://www.asl.lib.ar.us/)

CALIFORNIA
California State Library (http://www.library.ca.gov/)

COLORADO
Colorado State Library (http://www.cde.state.co.us/index_library.htm)

CONNECTICUT
Connecticut State Library (http://www.cslib.org/)

DELAWARE
DelAWARE: The Digital Library of the First State (http://www.state.lib.de.us/Collection_Development/Electronic_Resources/DelAWARE/)

DISTRICT OF COLUMBIA
District of Columbia Public Library (http://dclibrary.org/)

FLORIDA
Florida Department of State: Division of Library and Information Services (http://dlis.dos.state.fl.us/index.cfm)

GEORGIA
Georgia Public Library Services (http://www.gpls.public.lib.ga.us/)

HAWAII
Hawaii State Library (http://www.librarieshawaii.org/)

IDAHO
Idaho State Library (http://www.lili.org/)

ILLINOIS
Illinois Library and Information Network (http://library.ilcso.illinois.edu/ilcso/cgi-bin/welcome)

INDIANA
Indiana State Library (http://www.statelib.lib.in.us/index.html)

IOWA
State Library of Iowa (http://www.silo.lib.ia.us/)

KANSAS
Kansas State Library (http://skyways.lib.ks.us/kansas/KSL/)

KENTUCKY
Kentucky Department for Libraries and Archives (http://www.kdla.ky.gov/)

LOUISIANA
State Library of Louisiana (http://www.state.lib.la.us/)

MAINE
Maine State Library (http://www.state.me.us/msl/)

MARYLAND
SAILOR: Maryland's Online Public Information Network (http://www.sailor.lib.md.us/)

MASSACHUSETTS
Massachusetts Library and Information Network (http://www.mlin.lib.ma.us/flash3.html)

MICHIGAN
Library of Michigan (http://www.michigan.gov/hal)

MINNESOTA
Minnesota's State Government Libraries (http://www.state.mn.us/libraries/calco.html)

MISSISSIPPI
Mississippi Library Commission (http://www.mlc.lib.ms.us/)

MISSOURI
Missouri State Library (http://www.sos.mo.gov/library/Default.asp)

MONTANA
Montana State Library (http://msl.state.mt.us/)

NEBRASKA
Nebraska Library Commission (http://www.nlc.state.ne.us/)

NEVADA
Nevada State Library and Archives (http://dmla.clan.lib.nv.us/docs/nsla/)

NEW HAMPSHIRE
New Hampshire State Library (http://www.state.nh.us/nhsl/)

NEW JERSEY
New Jersey State Library (http://www.njstatelib.org/)

NEW MEXICO
New Mexico State Library (http://www.stlib.state.nm.us/)

NEW YORK
New York State Archives (http://www.archives.nysed.gov/aindex.shtml)
New York State Library (http://www.nysl.nysed.gov/)

NORTH CAROLINA
State Library of North Carolina (http://statelibrary.dcr.state.nc.us/)

NORTH DAKOTA
North Dakota State Library (http://ndsl.lib.state.nd.us/)

OHIO
State Library of Ohio (http://winslo.state.oh.us/)

OKLAHOMA
ODL Online: Oklahoma Department of Libraries (http://www.odl.state.ok.us/)

OREGON
Oregon State Library (http://www.osl.state.or.us/home/)

PENNSYLVANIA
State Library of Pennsylvania (http://www.statelibrary.state.pa.us/libraries/site/default.asp)

RHODE ISLAND
Rhode Island Office of Library and Information Services (http://www.olis.state.ri.us/)

SOUTH CAROLINA
South Carolina State Library (http://www.state.sc.us/scsl/)

SOUTH DAKOTA
South Dakota State Library (http://www.sdstatelibrary.com/)

TENNESSEE
Tennessee State Library and Archives (http://www.state.tn.us/sos/statelib/tslahome.htm)

TEXAS
Texas State Electronic Library (http://link.tsl.state.tx.us/)
Texas State Library and Archives Commission (http://www.tsl.state.tx.us/)

UTAH
Utah Library Network (http://library.utah.gov/)

VERMONT
Vermont Department of Libraries (http://dol.state.vt.us/)

VIRGINIA
Library of Virginia (http://www.lva.lib.va.us/)

WASHINGTON
Washington State Library (http://www.statelib.wa.gov/)

WEST VIRGINIA
West Virginia Archives and History (http://www.wvculture.org/history/)
West Virginia Library Commission (http://librarycommission.lib.wv.us/)

WISCONSIN
Wisconsin Division for Libraries and Community Learning (http://www.dpi.state.wi.us/dlcl/)

WYOMING
Wyoming State Library (http://www-wsl.state.wy.us/)

Additional online directories providing links and access to state libraries include:

State Libraries Information (http://web.syr.edu/~jryan/infopro/state.html)
This directory, maintained by Joe Ryan of Information Resources for Information Professionals, offers a complete list of state libraries from A to Z.

LIBRARY DIRECTORIES

To find libraries of any specialty or interest, in addition to consulting your local phone book for libraries nearest you, various directories, in print and on the Web, can help. Online directories also can direct you to the Web pages of libraries in the United States and around the world.

On most Web directories, you can search for libraries by name, by type (academic, public, etc.), or geographic location. Each listing includes links to the library's Web site and online catalog. Regions covered include the United States and Canada, Latin America and the Caribbean, Europe and Asia, Africa and the Middle East, and the Pacific Region.

In Print

American Library Directory, 57th Ed., 2 vols. (New York: R.R. Bowker, 2004)
Updated annually, this definitive guide provides vital information on libraries in the United States categorized by state, then city, and then library in alphabetical order. Also covered are libraries for the blind, the physically handicapped, and the deaf.

Directory of Special Libraries and Information Centers, 31st Ed. (Detroit: Gale Research Co., 2005)
This stunning two-volume set lists thousands of special libraries and information centers from around the globe dedicated to the fields of science and engineering, medicine, law, art, religion, the social sciences, and humanities.

On the Web

LibDex (http://www.libdex.com/)
Searchable directory of more than 16,000 libraries with Web sites.

Libweb (http://sunsite.berkeley.edu/Libweb/)
Provides online searching of libraries of more than 100 countries, including academic, public, national, state, special, and school libraries.

lib-web-cats (http://www.librarytechnology.org/libwebcats/)
Features links to Web pages of more than 5,000 libraries.

Links for Librarians (http://www.sivideo.com/9library.htm)
Compiled by Stan Nicotera, this list features links to basic references, library resource listings for libraries around the world, library servers, medical/health sciences libraries, public library sites, online public access catalogs, school librarian pages, school libraries on the Web, state library Web sites, and much more.

National Libraries of the World (http://www.ifla.org/II/natlibs.htm)
Presented by the International Federation of Library Associations and Institutions, this library and information science portal alphabetically lists Web-accessible national and major libraries by country, from Argentina to Wales.

LIBRARY ONLINE PUBLIC ACCESS CATALOGS

As noted earlier in this book, online catalogs, also known as Online Public Access Catalogs (OPACs), offer computerized access to information on books, periodicals, special collections, and databases that are available at your library or other libraries anywhere in the world.

Requiring keyword searching, these easy-to-use portals organize information by author, title, or subject, including catalogs of other libraries, journal indexes, subject guides to find selected Internet resources, special collections and archives, and other subject-specific resources, as well as resources for special libraries and librarians.

For a complete directory of general resource, individual, and international OPACs accessible on the Web, the Internet Library for Librarians, a popular online resource for librarians since 1984, offers titles, descriptions, and direct Web access to many other OPACs of interest. Its Web site (and links under "Library OPACs" on the main menu) are at: http://www.itcompany.com/inforetriever/opac.htm.

VIRTUAL LIBRARIES

In addition to academic, government, research, school, and public library Web pages, the World Wide Web offers virtual libraries as well. Virtual libraries feature a solid selection of references, periodicals, subject guides, special collections, and links that can be of great value to your research. Popular sites include:

The Internet Public Library (IPL) (http://www.ipl.org/)
Maintained by the University of Michigan School of Information, IPL is a virtual library with subject collections covering practically every discipline, as well as almanacs, calendars, dictionaries, books, newspapers, and magazines, and a special collections section of original resources developed or hosted by IPL. The IPL also has sections dedicated to kids (KidSpace) and teenagers (TeenSpace).

LibrarySpot.com (http://www.libraryspot.com)
Unquestionably the most diverse and comprehensive online library of its kind, LibrarySpot.com offers an impressive array of online tools and links that are well categorized, and easy to navigate. Categories range from "Must See Sites" to shortcuts to searching full-text articles, to recent published lists and rankings, to links to libraries online, academic libraries, film libraries, government libraries, K–12 libraries, law libraries, medical libraries, national libraries, presidential libraries, public libraries, and state libraries. In addition, the site features a very thorough reference desk, covering the gamut of possibilities, in A to Z fashion.

Michigan eLibrary (MeL) (http://www.mel.org/index.html)
Provided the Library of Michigan, this virtual library provides free access to thousands of information resources. As part of its MeL Internet Collection, the library features "best of the Internet" sites recommended by librarians in such subject areas as arts and humanities; business, economics and labor; education; government, politics and law, health, recreation and leisure; reference; science; and social issues.

O'Keefe Library—Best Information on the Net (http://library.sau.edu/bestinfo/Default.htm)
Part of the official Web site for St. Ambrose University's O'Keefe Library, this section is devoted to the "best" resources on the Web. Covered are links to such online references as biographical sources, consumer information, dictionaries and encyclopedias, popular quotations, rankings and awards, statistics and demographic data, and more.

Questia: The World's Largest Online Library (http://www.questia.com)
Designed for users of all ages, this invaluable online resource offers unlimited access to more than 48,000 books and 390,000 journal, magazine, and newspaper articles, each searchable by word, phrase, title, author, or subject.

Journal articles are derived from more than 235 publishers in the fields of humanities and social sciences. More than 5,000 research paper topic ideas are also available in various disciplines, including art history, drama, health, history, psychology, philosophy, and more. In addition, the library features a wide array of online writing tools, from automatically creating footnotes and bibliographies to organizing your work in project folders, to meet students' academic needs.

14

Finding Newspapers, Magazines, Journals, and Radio and Television News

For many years, researchers have understood the value of newspapers, magazines, popular periodicals, and radio and television as major sources of facts and information on any number of subjects. Besides providing critical background and information, these primary sources are a major record of current and past events, and diverse points of view, opinion, and commentary on controversial issues.

Extracting information from hundreds of local, regional, and national publications and radio and television broadcasts is possible in many forms. Libraries around the world routinely preserve and index thousands of publications, everything from weekly newspapers to monthly magazines, for general use. Major microform collections house on microfilm and microfiche complete back issues of popular magazines and newspapers. Countless electronic databases offer access to more exhaustive collections online, including newspapers from all locations. Online directories link you to seemingly every newspaper, magazine, periodical, journal, and newsletter. Transcripts of many major news programs also can be obtained, for a small fee, through different service companies. All of the above options add value to your research.

RESEARCHING NEWSPAPERS, MAGAZINES, AND JOURNALS

Recently published newspapers and magazines are excellent sources when dealing with topical issues. As noted earlier in this book, the periodicals section of your library carries many current periodicals, including local newspapers, magazines, and journals, from around the United States and the world. The locations and availability of publications vary greatly. To save yourself time, research your library's periodicals holdings list or online catalog to see which publications are carried. For titles listed, essential information is provided, including the dates available and the location.

The fastest way to find a newspaper, magazine, or journal covering your topic is to search your library's online catalog, in person or on the Web. If you know the title of publication, simply key in the title (example: *New York Times*), then enter. Your title search will produce a list of holdings and in what format—print, microform, or electronic. Most older newspapers and magazines are generally available on microfilm (discussed later in this chapter).

If you don't know the title of the publication you need, then simply do a subject search combining the type of periodical with your topic. For example, entering "magazines women," your search will search all records in its catalog for magazines devoted to women and women's issues. Any combination of words with your type of publication, whether magazine or journal, will produce similar results. To locate print or electronic periodical indexes that catalog articles in your field of interest or discipline, again you would combine your subject with the words "periodical indexes" in your search ("humanities periodical indexes").

With many newspapers, magazines, and journals available today in electronic format or on the Web, publications generally have a short shelf life. The vast corridors of stockpiled back issues, long a cornerstone of library research, are slowly vanishing. Most libraries keep current or recent issues on hand only for a few weeks before relegating them to reference shelves with other back issues in their collection. Issues that are back-filed may cover only the current year. Libraries lack the necessary storage space to hold onto original back issues much longer than a year.

In this instance, you have two other choices for finding articles that are not readily accessible:

1. Check your library's microfilm and microfiche collection. Complete or partial holdings of a selected group of publications may be available in microform through a library in your area. This includes major daily newspapers, local newspapers, historical newspapers, magazines, and journals of interest to researchers.
2. Check your library's electronic periodical indexes and databases. Several databases discussed later in this chapter provide full access to a broad variety of newspapers and magazines, including full-text articles.

Several general guides and directories can help you look up a newspaper or magazine of interest:

Ethnic Press (Chicago: Center for Research Libraries, 1900–current)
Covers more than 2,000 periodicals and newspapers published by various ethnic minority groups in North America.

Working Press of the Nation (New York: Farrell Pub. Corp., 1947–)
Comprehensive directory featuring newspaper, magazine, radio, and TV station listings, and much more.

MICROFILM AND MICROFICHE PERIODICALS

When introduced for public use, microfilm and microfiche solved two major problems for libraries: lack of space due to the increasing number of publications offered for daily use, and an effective way to preserve back issues of popular periodicals before they turned brittle with age.

Today, despite the onslaught of high technology, microfilm and microfiche collections remain a viable option for research. While not as hip to use as the World Wide Web, they offer several major advantages. Most official newspaper Web sites only offer access to current articles of interest and usually charge a nominal fee for researching articles in their archives—and often not for as many years back as you would like. On the other hand, electronic databases mostly cover recent issues Some databases simply offer citations or abstracts; others give access to full-text versions of originally published articles.

Microfilm and microfiche volumes are split into quarterly or half-yearly portions and filed in chronological order. Microfilm reels are stored in marked boxes in file drawers face up with labels identifying the year in question (Example: "Jan 1993—Aug 1993"), while microfiche is filed in clearly marked envelopes. Some collections cover a publication's complete history; others only partial collections, with certain years omitted. Libraries may also offer different portions of a collection. Their collection may cover certain years of a publication, while another library's collection may cover that publication in its entirety. So it pays to check around.

To locate newspaper holdings on microfilm at other libraries in your area, the best printed resources are *Newspapers in Microform, United States, 1948–1972* (Washington, D.C.: U.S. Library of Congress, 1973). This 1,056-page directory lists microform holdings—approximately 34,289 titles from hundreds of libraries—held by U.S. libraries for U.S. newspapers from 1704 to 1972. Another excellent printed resource is *Newspapers in Microform, Foreign Countries, 1948–1972* (Washington, D.C.: U.S. Library of Congress, 1973). This massive directory features information on microform holdings of foreign newspapers from 1655 to 1972.

In addition, several printed indexes, essential for retrospective research of this kind, index the entire contents of several leading U.S. newspapers. Gale Group publishes a printed and electronic edition of its *National Newspaper Index,* which includes *The Christian Science Monitor, The Los Angeles Times, The New York Times* (including *The New York Times Book Review* and *The New York Times Magazine*), *The Washington Post* and *The Wall Street Journal.*

Additional printed volumes, published by UMI (University Microfilms International), index the microfilm collections of many other major metropolitan newspapers individually. They include the *Atlanta Journal* and *Atlanta Constitution* (1989–); *The Boston Globe* (1974–); *The Chicago Tribune* (1972–); *The Christian Science Monitor Index* (1949–); *The Denver Post* (1976–); *The Detroit Free Press* (1988–); and *The Houston Post* (1988–).

Also indexed are *The Los Angeles Times* (1988–); *The New Orleans Times-Picayune* (1972–); *The New York Times* (1851–); *The St. Louis Post-Dispatch* (1988–); *The San Francisco Chronicle* (1988–); *The Times of London* (1785–); *The Wall Street Journal* (1958–); and *The Washington Post* (1979–). Also published separately, indexing black periodicals, is *The Index of Black Newspapers* (1977–).

To find historical journal microform collections, *American Periodicals, 1741–1900* indexes more than 1,000 American journals of the 18th and 19th centuries in the following microfilm collections: *American Periodicals, 18th*

Century, American Periodicals, 1800–1850, and *American Periodicals, 1850–1900,* Civil War and Reconstruction.

While the world itself has changed dramatically over time, microfilm and microfiche collections remain a steady staple of information. Listed below is a sample of leading newspapers, arranged by state and country, and popular magazines and journals, including the beginning and ending dates of publication. Most are available in microform, though dates of coverage vary, and are perfect for research:

U.S. NEWSPAPERS BY STATE

Alabama

The Birmingham News (Birmingham, Ala.: 1888–)

Alaska

Anchorage Daily News (Anchorage, Alaska: May 1, 1948–)
Anchorage Times (Anchorage, Alaska: June 2, 1917–)
Fairbanks Daily News-Miner (Fairbanks, Alaska: 1909–)

Arizona

Arizona Republic (Phoenix, Ariz.: May 19, 1890—as the Arizona Republican; 1930—as the Arizona Republic)

Arkansas

Arkansas Democrat-Gazette (Little Rock, Ark.: April 11, 1878–)

California

Fresno Bee (Fresno, Calif.: 1922–)
The Los Angeles Times (Los Angeles, Calif.: December 4, 1881–)
La Opinión (Los Angeles, Calif.: September 18, 1926–)
The Orange County Register (Santa Ana, Calif.: 1911—as the Santa Ana Register; 1985–as the Orange County Register)
Riverside Press-Enterprise (Riverside, Calif.: 1883–)
Sacramento Bee (Sacramento, Calif.: 1908–)
The San Diego Union-Tribune (San Diego, Calif.: 1868–)
San Francisco Chronicle (San Francisco, Calif.: January 1, 1865–)
San Jose Mercury News (San Jose, Calif.: 1851–)

Colorado

Colorado Springs Gazette (Colorado Springs, Colo.: January 4, 1873–)
Denver Post (Denver, Colo.: 1895–)
Rocky Mountain News (Denver, Colo., weekly: April 23, 1859–)

Connecticut

The Hartford Courant (Hartford, Conn.: 1764–)

Delaware

The News Journal (Wilmington, Del.: 1875–)

District of Columbia

Washington Post (Washington, D.C.: December 6, 1867–)
Washington Times (Washington, DC: March 18, 1894–)

Florida

Florida Times-Union (Jacksonville, Fla.: 1899–)
Fort Lauderdale Sun-Sentinel (Fort Lauderdale, Fla.: 1960–)
The Miami Herald (Miami, Fla.: December 1, 1910–)
Orlando Sentinel (Orlando, Fla.: 1876–)
Palm Beach Post (Palm Beach, Fla.: 1916–)
St. Petersburg Times (St. Petersburg, Fla.: July 25, 1884–)
The Tampa Tribune (Tampa, Fla.: 1895–)

Georgia

The Atlanta Constitution (Atlanta, Ga.: June 17, 1868–)
Atlanta Daily World (Atlanta, Ga.: 1928–)

Hawaii

Honolulu Star-Bulletin (Honolulu, Hawaii: 1912–)
Honolulu Advertiser (Honolulu, Hawaii: 1929–)

Idaho

The Idaho Statesman (Boise, Idaho: July 26, 1864–)

Illinois

Arlington Heights Daily Herald (Arlington Heights, Ill.: 1901–)
Chicago Sun-Times (Chicago, Ill.: August 21, 1864–)
Chicago Tribune (Chicago, Ill.: April 23, 1849–)

Indiana

The Indianapolis Star (Indianapolis, Ind.: June 6, 1903–)

Iowa

The Des Moines Register (Des Moines, Iowa: June 2, 1915–)

Kansas

The Wichita Eagle (Wichita, Kans.: 1886–)

Kentucky

The Courier-Journal (Louisville, Ky.: November 1868–)
Lexington Herald-Leader (Lexington, Ky.: June 16, 1901–)

Louisiana

The Times-Picayune (New Orleans, La.: January 25, 1837–)

Maine

The Bangor Daily News (Bangor, Maine: January 1, 1900–)

Maryland

The Sun (Baltimore, Md.: 1837–)

Massachusetts

The Boston Globe (Boston, Mass.: 1872–)
Boston Herald (Boston, Mass.: 1848–)
The Christian Science Monitor (Boston, Mass.: 1908–)

Michigan

Detroit Free Press (Detroit, Mich.: January 1, 1871–)
Detroit News (Detroit, Mich.: 1873–)
Grand Rapids Press (Grand Rapids, Mich.: 1893–)
Michigan Chronicle (Detroit: Mich.: February 1943–)

Minnesota

Rochester Democrat and Chronicle (Rochester, Minn.: December 17, 1870–)
St. Paul Pioneer Press (St. Paul, Minn.: December 22, 1909–)
Star Tribune (Minneapolis, Minn.: April 5, 1982–)

Mississippi

Clarion-Ledger (Jackson, Miss.: January 3, 1883–)

Missouri

The Kansas City Star (Kansas City, Mo.: September 21, 1885–)
St. Louis Post-Dispatch (St. Louis, Mo.: March 10, 1879–)

Montana

Great Falls Tribune (Great Falls, Mont.: January 11, 1921–)

Nebraska

Omaha World-Herald (Omaha, Nebr.: August 18, 1890–)

Nevada

Las Vegas Review-Journal (Las Vegas, Nev.: April 3, 1949–)
Las Vegas Sun (Las Vegas, Nev.: July 1, 1950–)

New Hampshire

The Union Leader (Manchester, N.H.: 1863–)

New Jersey

Asbury Park Press (Asbury Park, N.J.: 1876–)
Bergen Record (Hackensack, N.J.: 1895–)

Star-Ledger (Newark, N.J.: 1917–)
Times (Trenton, N.J.: 1882–)

New Mexico

Albuquerque Journal (Albuquerque, N.M.: January 31, 1882–)

New York

The Buffalo News (Buffalo, N.Y.: October 11, 1880–)
Daily News (New York: April 1855–)
Journal News (White Plains, N.Y.: 1852–)
Newsday (Melville, N.Y.: 1940–)
New York Post (New York: 1801–)
The New York Times (New York: September 18, 1851–)
Syracuse Newspapers (Syracuse, N.Y.: 1964–)
Village Voice (New York: 1955–)
The Wall Street Journal (New York: July 8, 1889–)

North Carolina

The Charlotte Observer (Charlotte, N.C.: 1886–)
Raleigh News & Observer (Raleigh, N.C.: 1872–)

North Dakota

The Forum (Fargo, N. Dak.: November 17, 1891–)

Ohio

Akron Beacon Journal (Akron, Ohio: 1839–)
The Cincinnati Enquirer (Cincinnati, Ohio: 1841–)
Columbus Dispatch (Columbus, Ohio: 1871–)
Dayton Daily News (Dayton, Ohio: 1898–)
The Plain Dealer (Cleveland, Ohio: 1842–)
Sporting News (Marion, Ohio: October 22, 1892–)
Toledo Blade (Toledo, Ohio: 1835–)

Oklahoma

The Daily Oklahoman (Oklahoma City, Okla.: February 29, 1894–)
Tulsa World (Tulsa, Okla.: World Pub. Co., September 14, 1905–)

Oregon

The Oregonian (Portland, Oreg.: December 4, 1850–)

Pennsylvania

Allentown Morning Call (Allentown, Pa.: 1883–)
The Philadelphia Inquirer (Philadelphia, Pa.: April 2, 1860–)
Pittsburgh Post-Gazette (Pittsburgh, Pa.: 1786–)
Pittsburgh Tribune-Review (Pittsburgh, Pa.: October 8, 1955–)

Rhode Island

Providence Journal-Bulletin (Providence, R.I.: January 26, 1863–)
Worcester Telegram & Gazette (Worcester, R.I.: October 19, 1888–)

South Carolina

Charleston Post & Courier (Charleston, S.C.: 1803–)
The State (Columbia, S.C.: February 18, 1891–)

South Dakota

Argus-Leader (Sioux Falls, S. Dak.: April 7, 1890–)

Tennessee

The Commercial Appeal (Memphis, Tenn.: 1841–)
Knoxville News-Sentinel (Knoxville, Tenn.: 1896–)
Nashville Tennessean (Nashville, Tenn.: 1866–)

Texas

Austin American-Statesman (Austin, Tex.: May 31, 1914–)
The Dallas Morning News (Dallas, Tex.: October 1885–)
Fort Worth Star-Telegram (Fort Worth, Tex.: January 1, 1909–)
The Houston Chronicle (Houston, Tex.: October 14, 1901–)
Houston Post (Houston, Tex.: August 19, 1880—as the Houston Daily Post)
San Antonio Express-News (San Antonio, Tex.: 1865–)

Utah

The Salt Lake City Tribune (Salt Lake City, Utah: January 1, 1875–)

Vermont

The Burlington Free Press (Burlington, Vt.: June 15, 1827–)

Virginia

Richmond Times-Dispatch (Richmond, Va.: January 27, 1903–)
USA Today (Arlington, Va.: January 3, 1989–)

Washington

Seattle Post-Intelligencer (Seattle, Wash.: 1874–)
Seattle Times (Seattle, Wash.: May 3, 1867–)
Spokane Spokesman-Review (Spokane, Wash.: 1883–)
Tacoma News Tribune (Tacoma, Wash.: April 7, 1883–)

West Virginia

The Charleston Gazette (Charleston, W. Va.: 1887–)

Wisconsin

Milwaukee Journal Sentinel (Milwaukee, Wis.: January 1, 1883–)

Wyoming

Casper Star Tribune (Casper, Wyo.: 1891–)
Wyoming Tribune-Eagle (Cheyenne, Wyo.: September 8, 1968–)

FOREIGN NEWSPAPERS

Canada

Globe and Mail (Toronto, Ont.: 1844–)
Montreal Gazette (Montreal, Que.: 1785–)
Vancouver Sun (Vancouver, B.C.: 1886–)

England

Guardian (London: 1821–)
The Times of London (London: 1785–)

France

Le Canard Enchaine (Paris: 1915–)
Le Monde (Paris: 1944–)

Soviet Union and Russia

Moscow News Weekly (Moscow: 1934–)
Pravda (Moscow: 1913–)

MAGAZINES AND JOURNALS

Advertising

Advertising Age (January 1930–)

Aeronautics and Space Flight

Aviation (January 1922–June 1947)
(renamed *Aviation Week*)
Aviation Week (July 1947–February 1958)
(changed to *Aviation Week Including Space Technology*)
Aviation Week Including Space Technology (February 1958–January 1960)
(renamed *Aviation Week & Space Technology*)
Aviation Week & Space Technology (January 1960–)
Space World (January 1967–December 1988)

African Americans

Black Enterprise (August 1970–)
Ebony (November 1945–)
Jet (1951–)
Negro History Bulletin (October 1937–December 2001)
Journal of Negro History (January 1916–)

Aging

Aging (June 1951–1996)

Agriculture

Farm Journal (August 1945–)

Anthropology

American Anthropologist (January 1888–)
Current Anthropology (January 1960–)

Archaeology

Archaeology (1982–1990)

Architecture

Architectural Record (1891–)
House Beautiful (December 1896–)

Art

American Artist (January 1940–)
ArtForum (June 1962–)
Art in America (1913–)
ARTnews (February 1923–)

Astronomy

Astronomy (August 1973–)
Sky and Telescope (November 1941–)

Automobiles

Car & Driver (April 1961–)
Hot Rod (January 1948–)
Motor Trend (September 1949–)
Popular Mechanics (August 1959–)
Road and Track (September 1977–)

Aviation—see Aeronautics and Space Flight

Biology

BioScience (January 1964–)

Broadcasting

Broadcasting (October 15, 1931–)
Broadcasting & Cable (March 1, 1993–)

Business

American Economic Review (March 1911–)
Barron's (May 9, 1921–)

Business Week (September 1929–)
Economist (September 1843–)
Forbes (September 1917–)
Fortune (February 1930–)
Harvard Business Review (October 1922–)
Monthly Labor Review (January 1958–)
Nation's Business (September 1912–)

Camping—see Recreation

Chemistry

Journal of Chemical Education (January 1965–)

Children and Youth

Child Development (March 1966–)
Children Today (January–February 1972–1996–)
Parents (1968–)

Communication

Journal of Communication (May 1, 1951–)

Computers

Byte (January 1983–July 1998)

Conservation—see Ecology

Consumer Education

Changing Times (January 1960–June 1991)
(renamed *Kiplinger's Personal Finance*)
Consumer Bulletin (January 1958–May 1973)
(continued as *Consumers' Research Magazine*)
Consumer Reports (June 1942–)
Consumers' Research Magazine (June 1973–)
Home Mechanix (January 1985–July/August 1996)
(now called *Today's Homeowner*)
Kiplinger's Personal Finance (July 1991–)
Money (October 1972–)
Today's Homeowner (September 1996–)
(formerly titled *Home Mechanix*)

Dance

Dance Magazine (September 1942–)

Drama—see Theater

Ecology

Audubon (1899–)
The Conservationist (April/May 1960–April 1995)
Environment (October 1958–)
International Wildlife (January/February 1971–January/February 2002)
National Parks (January 1955–)
National Wildlife (1962–)
Natural History (January 1919–)
Sea Frontiers (1975–1993)
Sierra (October 1977–)

Economics—see Business

Education

American Education (December 1964/January 1965–1985)
Current (May 1960–)
Education Digest (November 1935–)

Electronics

Popular Electronics (January 1959–)
Electronics Now (July 1992–December 1999)
(formerly titled *Radio Electronics*)
Radio Electronics (October 1948–June 1992)

Engineering

Civil Engineering (October 1930–December 1964)

Environment—see Ecology

Fashion

Glamour (1941–)
Mademoiselle (February 1935–November 2001)

Film—see Motion Pictures

Finance—see Business

Foreign Language

Americas (1949–)

Foreign Policy—see Political Science

Forestry

American Forests (January 1931–)

Future

The Futurist (February 1967–)

Gardening and Horticulture

HG (House and Garden) (June 1901–)
Horticulture (1960–)
Organic Gardening (1954)
(formerly *Organic Gardening and Farming*)

General Interest

Atlantic Monthly (1932–)
(formerly called *Atlantic*)
Commonweal (November 1924–)
Cosmopolitan (April 1952–)
Esquire (Autumn 1933–)
Life (January 1936–December 1972, October 1978–May 2000)
Look (January 1953–October 1971)
Maclean's (March 1911–)
Newsweek (February 1933–)
New Yorker (February 1925–)
People Weekly (March 1974–)
Reader's Digest (August 1821–)
Saturday Evening Post (1897–)
Time (March 1923–)
U.S. News and World Report (March 1948–)

Geography

Focus (October 1950–)
Geographical Review (January 1916–)
National Geographic (1888–)

Health and Medicine

American Journal of Public Health (January 1971–)
(formerly titled *American Journal of Public Health and the Nation's Health*)
American Journal of Public Health and the Nation's Health (January 1928–December 1970)
(now called *American Journal of Public Health*)
Current Health 2 (September 1982–)
Health (January 1974–)
JAMA: Journal of the American Medical Association (July 14, 1883–)
New England Journal of Medicine (1812–)
Prevention (June 1950–)

History

American Heritage (January/February 1947–)
American Historical Review (October 1895–)
American History (June 1994–)
(formerly titled *American History Illustrated*)

American History Illustrated (April 1966–Mar./Apr. 1994)
(now called *American History*)
Journal of American History (1907–)
Smithsonian (April 1970–)

Home Economics

Better Homes and Gardens (1922–)
Sunset (May 1898–)

Law

Harvard Law Review (1887–)

Literature and Language

Modern Fiction Studies (February 1955–)
The Writer (April 1887–)

Literature and Politics

Harper's Magazine (March 1913–)
The Humanist (1941–)
Saturday Review (January 1951–1972)
(Published thereafter as four titles: *Saturday Review of Education, Saturday Review of the Arts, Saturday Review of the Sciences, Saturday Review of the Society*)
Saturday Review of Education (February 1973–May 1973)
Saturday Review of the Sciences (February 1973–May 1973)
Saturday Review of the Society (February 1973–May 1973)

Motion Pictures

American Film (October 1975–January/February 1992)
Film Comment (1962–)
Film Quarterly (Summer 1946–)

Music

Billboard (1896–)
Down Beat (July 1934–)
Rolling Stone (November 1967–)

Nursing

American Journal of Nursing (October 1900–)
Nursing (November 1971–)

Photography

Popular Photography (May 1937–)

Physical Fitness—see Health

Political Science

American Political Science Review (November 1906–)
Annals of the American Academy of Political and Social Science (1890–)
Atlas (March 1961–April 1972)
(renamed *Atlas/World Press Review*)
Atlas/World Press Review (May 1974–February 1980)
(now titled *World Press Review*)
Congressional Digest (February 1922–)
Congressional Quarterly Weekly Report (January 6, 1956–April 11, 1998)
(now called CQ *Weekly*)
CQ Weekly (April 18, 1998–)
(formerly known as *Congressional Quarterly Weekly Report*)
Current History (September 1941–)
Foreign Affairs (September 1922–)
Foreign Policy (Winter 1970–71–)
Nation (July 6, 1865–)
National Review (November 19, 1955–)
New Statesman (April 2, 1913–February 21, 1931; July 6, 1957–June 3, 1988; June 14, 1996–)
(previously titled *New Statesman and Nation*)
New Statesman and Nation (February 28, 1931–June 29, 1957)
(renamed *New Statesman*)
New Statesman & Society (June 10, 1988–June 7, 1996)
(formerly called *New Statesman*)
The New Republic (November 7, 1914–)
The Progressive (December 7, 1929–)
Public Opinion Quarterly (January 1937–)
Public Interest (Fall 1965–)
UNESCO Courier (February 1948–)
United Nations Chronicle (April 1975–1996)
U.S. Department of State Dispatch (September 1990–)
Washington Monthly (March 1973–)
World Press Review (March 1980–)
(formerly titled *Atlas/World Press Review*)
The World Today (1960–)

Population

American Demographics (January 1979–)

Psychiatry

American Journal of Psychiatry (July 1921–)

Psychology

The American Behavioral Scientist (September 1960–)
The American Journal of Psychology (November 1887–)
The American Psychologist (January 1946–)
Journal of Applied Psychology (March 1917–)
Journal of Clinical Psychology (January 1945–)
Psychology Today (May 1967–89, 1991–)

Recreation and Sports

Field and Stream (February 21, 1874–)
Motor Boating & Sailing (October 1970–)
Outdoor Life (1897–)
Parks & Recreation (January 1966–)
Sport (1978–1990)
Sporting News (March 3, 1886–)
Sports Illustrated (January 1954–)

Religion and Theology

America (April 17, 1909–)
Christian Century (January 4, 1900–)
Christianity Today (October 15, 1956–)
Commentary (January 1945–)

Science

American Scientist (April 1942–)
Bulletin of the Atomic Scientists (1960–99)
Nature (November 4, 1869–)
Science (July 1938–)
Science Digest (January 1937–September 1986; April 1988–April/May 1990)
Science News (1878–)
Scientific American (August 1845–)

Social Sciences

Social Work (January 1956–)
Society (February 1972–)
(called *Trans-Action* before January 1972)

Sociology

American Journal of Sociology (July 1895–)
American Sociological Review (February 1936–)
Journal of Marriage and the Family (February 1964–)
(formerly *Marriage and Family Living*)
Journal of Social Issues (February 1945–)
Marriage and Family Living (Winter 1941–November 1963)
Social Forces (September 1921–)
Social Problems (June 1953–)

Sound Recordings

Audio (March 1954–February/March 2000)
(formerly *Audio Engineering*)
Audio Engineering (May 1947–February 1954)
Stereo Review (November 1968–January 1999)
(became *Stereo Review's Sound & Vision* in 1999)
Stereo Review's Sound & Vision (February/March 1999–)

Speech

Vital Speeches of the Day (October 1934–)

Technology

Popular Science (January 1959–)
Technology Review (January 1889–January 1997)
(renamed *MIT's Technology Review*)
Technology Review: MIT's Magazine of Innovation (May/June 1998–)
(formerly *MIT's Technology Review*)
MIT's Technology Review (February/March 1997–March/April 1998)
(previously *Technology Review*)

Theater

The Drama Review: TDR (Spring 1968–Winter 1987)
(renamed *TDR*)
TDR (Spring 1988–)
(formerly *The Drama Review: TDR*)
Opera News (December 1936–)

Travel

Travel Holiday (February 1979–)
(formerly *Travel, Incorporating Holiday*)
Travel, Incorporating Holiday (November 1977–January 1979)
(renamed *Travel Holiday*)

Women's Periodicals

Cosmopolitan (March 1886–March 1925; April 1952–)
Good Housekeeping (July 1959–)
Harper's Bazaar (January 1964–)
Ladies' Home Journal (June 1889–)
McCall's (October 1965–)
Ms. (January 1972–)
Redbook (May 1933–April 1961; May 1961–October 1978; November 1983–)
Seventeen (January 1967–)
Vogue (January 1968–)
Working Woman (November 1976–)

Zoology

American Zoologist (February 1961–2001)

NEWS DIGESTS

When looking for specific details and general highlights recapping the major news events, national and international news and news from all major subject areas, several published digests, available in electronic and printed editions, can help you achieve this goal. They include:

Editorials On File (New York: Facts On File News Services, 2005)
This twice-a-month publication contains 200 full-text editorials and editorial cartoons from more than 150 U.S. and Canadian newspapers. Each issue covers around 10 topics, or nearly 5,000 editorials a year. Includes a cumulative index with each issue to find information by subject, key name, or newspaper.

Facts On File: A Weekly World News Digest with Cumulative Index (New York: Facts On File News Services, 2005)
Delivering accurate, concise news information since 1940, this publication digests key world and U.S. news events derived from more than 200 different newspapers, periodicals, journals, and government online sources. Featured are charts and graphs, biographies of major news figures, financial information, statistics on sports, business, and other areas of interest, story chronologies, and year in review listings.

Facts On File News Digest (New York: Facts On File, 2005)
Available in print and online by library subscription, *Facts On File News Digest* is published 52 weeks a year, highlighting current news events from real news accounts.

Issues & Controversies On File (New York: Facts On File, 2005)
Published twice a month and offered online by subscription, this critically acclaimed reference features authoritatively written, balanced and accurate essays, covering 70 timely topics a year.

NEWSPAPER AND MAGAZINE INDEXES, DATABASES, AND DIRECTORIES

Various electronic and online databases, discussed earlier in this book, make it possible for you to retrieve abstracts and full-text articles, culled from hundreds of popular newspapers, magazines, and scholarly journals published worldwide. Besides such traditional forms of research as microfilm and microfiche, electronic indexes and databases have become the standard by which periodical literature is accessed by a growing number of students, researchers, and general enthusiasts. In addition to databases previously covered, many other sources offer access to a broad range of material. Most beneficial in this case are:

Accessible Archives (Accessible Archives, Inc., 1728–) WEB
Full-text database of 18th- and 19th-century American newspapers, including *The Charleston Mercury, The New York Herald, The Pennsylvania Gazette,* and *The Richmond Enquirer.*

British Newspaper Index (Primary Source Media/Research Publications International, 1990–) CD, WEB
Indexed are citations and abstracts to major British newspapers and their supplements, including *The Times, The Times Literary Supplement, The Times Higher Education Supplement, The Times Education Supplement, The Sunday Times, The Financial Times, The Observer, The Independent,* and *The Guardian.*

Canadian News Disc (Southam Electronic Publishing, 1992–) CD
This CD-ROM delivered database features full-text articles from several Canadian newspapers, in both English and French versions.

DIALOG OnDisc Papers (Dialog, 1986–) CD
Updated quarterly, this CD-ROM database provides text of articles from major metropolitan newspapers, including:

The Boston Globe 1986–present
Detroit Free Press 1986–present
The Los Angeles Times 1986–present
Miami Herald 1986–present
Newsday/New York Newsday 1986–present
The Philadelphia Inquirer 1986–present
San Francisco Chronicle 1986–present
San Jose Mercury News 1986–present

DataTimes Newspaper Index (OCLC FirstSearch, 1996–) WEB
Covers nearly 150 U.S. regional newspapers.

EBSCO Host Academic Search Elite (EBSCO Publishing, 1985–)
Includes abstracts and full-text articles from 450 general magazines.

Facts On File World News Digest (Facts On File News Services; 1940–) WEB
Online digest of full-text newspaper and journal articles, plus biographies, chronologies, government documents, speeches, statistics, and more, covering current world events and political news from around the world.

Federal News Service (LexisNexis, 1988–) WEB
This federal news database offers transcripts of presidential statements; briefings at the White House, State, Defense and Justice Departments, speeches and press conferences of major political leaders and spokespersons; and congressional hearings.

FindArticles.com (http://www.findarticles.com/PI/index.jhtml) WEB
Claiming honors as "the Web's largest free article database," FindArticles.com provides searching of more than 3.5 million articles from more than 700 publications. Publications are also listed by name from A–Z and can be browsed by topic. Publications range from arts and entertainment, to business and finance, to computers and technology, to health and fitness, to home and family, to news and society, to reference and education, and sports.

General Periodicals OnDisc (UMI, 1986–97) CD
Contains abstracts and more than 350 scanned images from more than 1,000 popular periodicals with monthly updates.

Global NewsBank (NewsBank; 1996–) WEB
Full access to international articles, translated into English, from newspapers, magazines, wire services, government documents, and news agencies.

Globe and Mail/Financial Times of Canada (Globe Information Services, 1991–)
This Canadian news database offers full-text articles of Canada's top newspapers.

InfoWeb: Newsfile with Popular Periodicals (NewsBank) CD
Provides full-text news articles from regional, national, and international sources plus full-text articles from 120 leading magazines.

The Los Angeles Times (ProQuest; 1985–) WEB
This Web version provides extensive coverage of national, international, and local news in current past editions of this major daily newspaper.

National News 5 (ProQuest; 1986–) CD, WEB
Collectively, this database offers full-text access to *The New York Times, The Los Angeles Times, The Washington Post, The Wall Street Journal,* and *The Christian Science Monitor.*

National Newspaper Index (InfoTrac/GaleGroup, 1986–) CD, WEB
CD-ROM and online companion to the popular printed index of five popular periodicals: *The Christian Science Monitor, The Los Angeles Times, The New York Times* (including *New York Times Book Review* and *New York Times Magazine*), *The Washington Post* and *The Wall Street Journal.* Coverage includes news reports, articles, editorials, letters to the editor, obituaries, biographies, and reviews..

NewsBank CD-News (NewsBank, 1983–) CD
The most comprehensive resource of news coverage, with full-text articles, from the following newspapers, updated quarterly:

Arizona Republic/Phoenix Gazette
Arizona Business Gazette 1987–present
Atlanta Journal/Atlanta Constitution 1983–present
Austin American-Statesman 1989–present
(Baltimore) Sun 1991–present
(Baton Rouge) Advocate 1986–present
The Boston Globe 1985–present
Buffalo News 1992–present
Chicago Tribune 1985–present
The Christian Science Monitor 1989–present
Cincinnati Enquirer 1990–present
Cincinnati Post/Kentucky Post 1990–present
Columbus Dispatch 1985–present
Daily Oklahoman 1981–present
The Dallas Morning News 1984–present
Dayton Daily News 1993–present
Denver Post 1989–present
(Denver) Rocky Mountain News 1989–present
Des Moines Register 1991–present
Detroit News 1991–present
Evansville Courier 1991–present

(Fort Lauderdale) Sun-Sentinel 1986–present
Fort Worth Star-Telegram 1991–present
Greensboro News and Record 1993–present
(Hackensack) Record 1984–present
Hartford Courant 1991–present
The Houston Chronicle 1985–present
Indianapolis Star/Indianapolis News 1993–present
Knoxville News-Sentinel 1990–present
(Louisville) Courier Journal 1988–present
The Los Angeles Times 1985–present
(Memphis) Commercial Appeal 1990–present
Milwaukee Journal/Milwaukee Sentinel 1990–present
(Minneapolis) Star Tribune 1986–present
Newsday/New York Newsday 1986–present
Orange County (California) Register 1987–present
Orlando Sentinel 1985–present
Palm Beach Post 1989–present
(Portland) Oregonian 1987–present
(Raleigh) News & Observer 1990–present
Sacramento Bee 1984–present
San Francisco Chronicle 1985–present
San Diego Union-Tribune 1984–present
Seattle Times 1985–present
St. Louis Dispatch 1989–present
St. Petersburg Times 1987–present
Tampa Tribune 1990–present
Tulsa World 1987–present
USA Today 1987–present
The Washington Post 1986–present
Washington Times 1984–present

NewsBank Comprehensive Newspapers (NewsBank, 1980–) CD, WEB
Complete coverage of local and regional news and national and international news, with full-text access to individual newspaper titles. Includes staff-written articles, news features, special interest stories, editorials, daily columns, letters to the editor, sports reports, and much more.

NewsBank Newsfile (NewsBank; 1980s–) WEB
Indexes more than 70,000 articles, some full text, from more than 500 newspapers and news wire services, including regional, national, and international sources.

Newspaper Abstracts Complete (ProQuest, 1985–) CD, WEB
Fully indexes 27 newspapers worldwide, including such prominent publications as the *Chicago Tribune* and the *Denver Post,* and smaller newspapers, such as the *Amsterdam News* (New York, N.Y.) and *The Guardian* (Manchester, N.H.)

Newspaper Abstracts National (ProQuest, 1986–) CD, WEB
Indexes, with full-text articles, several major U.S. newspapers: *The Atlanta Journal and Constitution; The Boston Globe; The Christian Science Monitor;*

The New York Times; The Los Angeles Times; USA Today; The Wall Street Journal; and *The Washington Post.*

Newspaper Abstracts Major Papers (ProQuest, 1986–) CD, WEB
Includes the full text of five national newspapers: *The New York Times, The Los Angeles Times, The Washington Post, The Wall Street Journal,* and *The Christian Science Monitor.*

Newspaper Abstracts with Full Text (ProQuest; 1989–) WEB
Features selected full-text articles, reviews, editorials, and more from leading newspapers, such as *The New York Times* and *The Wall Street Journal.*

Newspaper Source (EBSCO Publishing; 1984–) WEB
Provides full-text coverage for more than 140 U.S. and international newspapers.

The New York Times (ProQuest; 1851–three years before current date) CD, WEB
Complete articles and images covering national, regional and international news starting with the first issue of this major metropolitan daily

Polling the Nations (ORS Publishing, 1986–93) CD
This comprehensive database contains polls, surveys, and public opinion culled from various sources, including Gallup Polls, *Good Housekeeping* surveys, and others. Content corresponds to the *American Public Opinion Index* and data microfiche, updated annually.

Poole's Plus (1802–1906) WEB
This pioneering index features more than 3 million citations to 19th-century American and British publications, including books, journal and newspaper articles, and government publications. The database includes separate indexes to *The New York Times* (1863–1905), the *New York Daily Tribune* (1875–1906) and *Harper's Magazine* (1876–97).

Popular Periodical Index (Camden, N.J.: Rutgers University, 1973–current)
This index covers dozens of American periodicals.

ProQuest Historical Newspapers (ProQuest; 1851–2001) WEB
Cover-to-cover digital reproductions in downloaded PDF files of every page from every issue of *The New York Times, The Wall Street Journal, The Washington Post, The Christian Science Monitor, The Los Angeles Times,* and the *Chicago Tribune.*

ProQuest News and Magazines (ProQuest; 1986–) WEB
This news and magazine database offers current information on popular magazines, journals, national, and local newspapers.

ProQuest Newspaper Abstracts (ProQuest, 1985–) CD, WEB
Indexes thousands of newspaper articles, in leading international, national, and regional newspapers, such as *The New York Times, USA Today, The Wall Street Journal, The Atlanta Journal Constitution, Barron's, The Boston Globe, The Guardian,The Christian Science Monitor, The Chicago Defender,*

and *The Washington Post*. Archival coverage dates from 1989, back files from 1985 to 1988.

SIRS Discoverer (ProQuest; 1988–) CD, WEB
Includes full-text articles and images from more than 1,600 national and international newspapers, magazines, and government documents.

UMI Newspapers OnDisc (UMI, 1988–) CD
Presents full-text versions of articles from four major newspapers, as follows, updated monthly:

The New York Times 1988–present
USA Today 1990–present
The Wall Street Journal 1989–present
The Washington Post 1989–present

The Washington Post (ProQuest; 1989–) CD, WEB
Complete electronic and Web version of one of America's most respected newspapers.

World News (Dialog; current) WEB
Covers hundreds of news items daily from around the globe.

USA Today (ProQuest; online: 1987–; CD: 1990–) CD, WEB
Entire online editions of this popular newspaper are abstracted and indexed.

PUBLICATION WEB SITES

Most newspapers and trade and specialty publications have Web sites or online editions that are archived and updated regularly. One advantage of using these sources is that most publishers make some, if not all, of the articles in an issue accessible the day they are published, free of charge. The availability of material, however, varies from a few weeks to several years. Some publications provide limited archived articles online; others require users to register, or charge a nominal fee to access older material.

To determine if a publication offers Web access, you can search for it online or check out a Web directory that features links to newspapers, trade journals, magazines, and other sources. Examples include:

AllYouCanRead.com (http://www.allyoucanread.com/)
Calling itself "the largest database of magazines and newspapers on the Internet," this site features listings for about 26,500 newspapers and magazines, in virtually every conceivable category, and media sources from around the world.

BizJournals.com (http://www.bizjournals.com/search.html)
This rich business resource indexes articles from 42 local business journals across the country that can be searched by city or all markets simultaneously.

Cyber Newsstand (http://broadcast-live.com/newspapers/)
Features links to major newspapers and periodicals—American, Australian, British, French, German, European, Asian, and Latin American—from around the world, including leading financial, sports, science and technology newspapers.

Cyber Paperboy (http://www.cyberpaperboy.com/)
Indexes more than 4,500 newspapers by state and country.

DailyEarth (http://www.dailyearth.com/)
Global directory of online newspapers organized by state and country.

Directory of Electronic Journals and Newsletters (http://www.arl.org/scomm/edir/archive.html)
Compiled by the Association of Research Libraries, this searchable database covers electronic journals in the fields of arts and humanities, general interest, life sciences, people and places, physical sciences, social sciences, and technology. Records display journal or newsletter title, publication summary, and Web address.

Electronic Journal Miner (http://ejournal.coalliance.org/)
This searchable directory covers thousands of electronic journals and magazines by subject or title. Search results include title of publication, Web address, abstracts about the publication, frequency of publication, and more.

Internet Public Library: Online Newspapers (http://www.ipl.org/div/news/)
Offers links to international newspapers by title and geographic location.

NewJour—Electronic Journal and Newsletter Archive (http://gort.ucsd.edu/newjour/)
Created by Ann Shumelda Okerson of Yale University and James J. O'Donnell of Georgetown University, this archive lists, from A to Z, new journals and newsletters available on the Internet. The archive contains more than 13,000 items, including recent issues.

NewsDirectory (http://www.newsdirectory.com)
Lists newspapers and magazines by region and magazines by subject.

NewsLibrary.com (http://www.newslibrary.com)
Billed as "the world's largest archive," this news research site contains 341 newspapers and other news sources, all searchable by region, state, or a specific topic, with the ability to search millions of articles at one time from a single source. While access to this vast collection of news archives is free, a fee is charged to purchase any articles from this site. Single articles can be purchased, as can monthly and yearly passes good for a specific number of purchases.

NewsLink (http://newslink.org/)
This comprehensive directory features links to national newspapers, newspapers by state for all 50 states, major metropolitan newspapers (dailies and non-dailies), business, alternative, specialty, and campus publications, international publications, press associations, and popular magazines.

Newspapers.com (http://www.newspapers.com)
Featuring more than a dozen categories, this site offers links to state and national press associations, news services, syndicates, newspaper groups, college and university newspapers, and the "Top 10" and "Top 100" newspapers in the United States.

Newspapers Galore (http://www.wcow.com/html/news.html)
Searchable directory of more than 3,000 newspapers arranged by city.

News Paradise (http://www.newsparadise.com/)
Presents more than 120 English-language newspapers from around the world.

NewsVoyager (http://www.newspaperlinks.com/voyager.cfm)
Called "the ultimate newspaper portal," this site, hosted by the Newspaper Association of America, provides links to U.S. daily and weekly newspaper home pages and sections, Canadian and international daily newspapers, newspaper groups and associations, other media organizations, and other sites with links to college newspapers and newspaper archives.

SmallTownPapers (http://www.smalltownpapers.com/)
Online directory of small-town newspaper archives and local newspapers presented exactly as they were printed.

The World Press (http://www.theworldpress.com/)
Features links to newspapers around the world.

RESEARCHING RADIO AND TELEVISION NEWS

With the dramatic buildup and expansion of cable television networks and talk radio stations, featuring news and interviews 24 hours a day, seven days a week, one should never overlook the potential of those media as a source of information.

Many radio and television stations today offer around-the-clock coverage of local state, national, and international news on their Web sites. Reporting is usually up-to-date, and is a mix of staff-written and wire service stories. Some stations archive articles that you can access at a later date. To find radio or television station Web sites, one of the best directories on the Web is NewsLink (http://newslink.org) which, as discussed earlier, features links to not only newspapers and magazines, but also seemingly every radio and television station by state.

Transcripts of current and past news broadcasts, both domestic and international, may be useful as you research your essay, term paper, or written project. Many major news networks publish transcripts of news programs and interviews in a number of formats, including Web and CD-ROM databases, microfilm, and printed sources. In addition, transcript service and document delivery companies also provide this material, usually for a fee. Networks with transcripts of news programming include:

ABC (American Broadcasting Co., 1968–)
ABC (Australian Broadcasting Co., 1995–)
BBC Worldwide (1979–)
CBC News (Canada, 1936–)
CBS (Columbia Broadcasting System, 1968–)
C-SPAN (current)
FOX News Network (1997–)
NBC (National Broadcasting Corp., 1968–)
PBS (including National Public Radio, 1990–)
Voice of America (VOA, 1953–80)

Usually, transcripts can be obtained one of three ways: from the source, from translation service, or via archival sources. The following is a partial list of electronic and online sources:

ABC Australia (Australian Broadcasting Corporation, current–)
(http://www.abc.net.au/rn/tranlist.htm)
Offers links to recent transcripts of network's Radio National programs.

Broadcast News (Primary Source Media, 1992–95) CD
Provides access to full-text transcripts of more than 80 North American news programs from the major broadcast networks, ABC, CNN, PBS, and National Public Radio.

CBC News (Canadian Broadcasting Corp., 2001–) WEB
(http://archives.cbc.ca/index.asp?IDLan=1)
Features a growing collection of digitized radio and television material. Archival material dates back to 1936, but most items currently offered are from recent programming.

CBS News (Columbia Broadcasting System, 2000–) WEB
(http://www.cbsnews.com/sections/home/main100.shtml)
Offers free access to transcripts of news programs broadcast since January 2000.

C-SPAN (Cable Satellite Public Affairs Network, current) WEB
(http://www.c-span.org.)
Unlike other networks that routinely transcribe news and public affairs broadcasts, C-SPAN offers only transcripts of its popular series *Booknotes*.

Global Newsbank (NewsBank, 1996–) WEB
Provides translated and English-language news articles from more than 1,000 broadcasts, news agency transmissions, wire services, newspapers, magazines, and government documents around the world.

LexisNexis Guided News Search (LexisNexis, 1982–) WEB
Source of full-text transcripts from the English-language and foreign-language press, wire services, radio, and TV news. Covered are programs produced by BBC (1979–), mostly daily news service material broadcasts from other countries over radio, TV, press, Internet, and news agencies, ABC News (1986–97), including broadcasts of *Nightline, 20/20,* and *PrimeTime*

Live; CBC (Canadian Broadcasting Corporation) News (1982–97), CBS News (1990–present), including *CBS This Morning, CBS Evening News,* and *60 Minutes,* CNN (1992–2001), and Fox News Network. Also other network programs by NBC News (1997–) including *Dateline, Meet the Press, NBC Nightly News,* and *Today,* NPR (National Public Radio, 1992–), including *Morning Edition, All Things Considered,* and *Weekend Edition,* and PBS's *Newshour* with Jim Lehrer.

NBC (National Broadcasting Corp, current)
This network's official Web site offers some free transcripts online from current news programs, such as *Meet the Press.* For *Meet the Press,* transcripts are offered for the past three weeks; also an archive of the preceding four weeks.

NPR (National Public Radio, 1996–) WEB
Transcripts can be keyword-searched for NPR programming dating back to 1996. Tapes and printed transcripts from programs produced since September 1990 are available for purchase.

PBS (Public Broadcasting Service, 1970s–) WEB (http://www.pbs.org.)
This official site offers written transcripts and Real Audio excerpts of the network's news and public affairs programs, including *The NewsHour with Jim Lehrer* and *Washington Week in Review.*

PAIS (Public Affairs Information Service, 1972–) WEB
By subscription, this online library database includes some foreign newspaper and wire service transcripts.

TV and Radio Transcripts Daily (Dialog, current) WEB
Produced by the Federal Document Clearing House (FDCH), this service, offered by subscription, contains complete verbatim transcripts of news events affecting business and financial markets, and interviews with corporate chief executives from ABC News, CNBC/Dow Jones Desktop Video, CNNfn, Fox News, *Nightly Business Report,* and *Wall Street Corporate Reporter.*

Voice of America (Voice of America, current) WEB (http://www.voanews.com/index.cfm)
Offers transcripts of current programs only.

In addition to the above sources, several microform collections, featuring transcripts of television news broadcasts along with printed indexes, are also available, mostly through university libraries with dedicated communications and journalism programs, for the following networks and programs only:

ABC Public Affairs Broadcasts (Microfiche: 1986–March 1997)
Consists of written transcripts of ABC television news broadcasts, organized by title of each program. A published quarterly guide, *ABC News Index,* indexes the programs by subject and names of the personalities interviewed.

CBS News (Microfilm: 1977–September 1988; CD-ROM: February 1990–May 1996)

Features transcripts of news broadcasts on microfilm, and the *CBS News Index*, a printed index of the contents of this serial collection. Later transcripts of CBS news broadcasts are available on CD-ROM. Another microform collection, *Columbia Broadcasting System Monitoring Reports*, which contains reports of foreign broadcasts from August 28, 1939, to May 23, 1945, published by the Library of Congress, is available through the Library of Congress and the Center for Research Libraries in Chicago.

PBS Public Affairs/News Transcripts (Microfiche: October 1973–95)

Accompanied by a printed guide, this microfiche collection contains complete transcripts of PBS television news and public affairs broadcasts, including the following programs: *Adam Smith's Money World, Bill Moyers' Journal, MacNeil/Lehrer Hour, Currents, Healthline, Innovation,* and *Metroline (Metro Week in Review).*

Researching on the Web

Hundreds of thousands of academic, not-for-profit and for-profit groups, companies, organizations, and institutions exist around the country for the purpose of disseminating up-to-date information on topics of special interest. The World Wide Web offers endless amounts of sites to research. This chapter is devoted to those Web sites that are considered the best in their field by scholars, librarians, researchers, and other professionals, who have recognized these sites in published articles and Web lists.

By no means is the list in this chapter complete. It is not meant to be. Instead, it is designed to provide additional tools and additional sites suitable for research that will produce useful material for your paper.

NARROWING YOUR FOCUS

Conducting your research on the Web involves the same strategy as researching other forms. First, you need to ask yourself what you are really searching for. The Web contains an estimated 3 billion documents not indexed in any standard vocabulary or by standard Library of Congress subject headings, so if you don't know what you want, you won't get very far.

Searching for information on the Web is like a guessing game: You're always wondering which combination of words will work best. Part of the problem is that you are never certain of the key terms that have been used to index or organize their page by topic, and which terms are stored in search engines. Therefore, there is no one best way to do research. Analyze your topic and determine which distinctive words or phrases more aptly focus your search. For example, if you enter the keywords "affirmative action," into a search engine, your search results will be too broad. But if you narrow your focus, for instance, by adding the word "unconstitutional" to your search, then combining these words will direct to you countless Web pages discussing this topic.

Whatever you do, don't get frustrated. Play with words in your search until you find the most Web sites relevant to your subject or topic. Then go from there.

RESEARCH SITES BY CATEGORY

Naturally, with something so large as the World Wide Web, you would expect to find not only single pieces of information, but also fully devoted Web sites on many different subjects. Whether you are researching the retraining of older workers or newly discovered planets, the Web is home a virtual menagerie of Web sites just for you, including:

African-American Studies

African and Afro-American Studies (http://www.brockport.edu/~library5/wafro.htm)
This site, created and maintained by the SUNY Brockport Drake Memorial Library, provides bibliographic and research links, including electronic and historical texts.

Soul Search: The Search Engine for the World's People of Color (http://www.soulsearch.net/)
Distinctive collection of more than 1,000 sites covering culture, such as art, dance, and history.

Aging

Center for the Advanced Study of Aging Services (http://cssr.berkeley.edu/aging)
Part of the University of California's School of Social Welfare, the center researches programs and services designed to improve the lives of older persons. It also works to improve the training of social workers to meet the needs of a growing population of older Americans.

Duke University Center for the Study of Aging and Human Development (http://geri.duke.edu)
More than 100 Duke scientists and scholars from disciplines as varied as biochemistry, economics, and sociology, conduct research in affiliation with the center. Major areas of study include depression in later life, Alzheimer's disease, the cellular and molecular biology of aging, family relationships in later life, and the economic status of older adults.

Jean Mayer U.S. Department of Agriculture Human Nutrition Research Center on Aging at Tufts University (http://hnrc.tufts.edu/)
Studies the effect of human nutrition on health. Experts on antioxidants, high carbohydrate/high fiber diets, body composition, calcium metabolism and more.

Agriculture

AgNIC (http://laurel.nal.usda.gov:8080/agnic/)
Created by the National Agricultural Library, AgNIC (Agricultural Network Information Center) is a collection of quality information on a variety of agricultural, food and environmental topics, searchable or browsable by topic.

U.S. Department of Agriculture (http://www.usda.gov/)
The U.S. Department of Agriculture's official Web site offers searchable information on topics including agriculture, education, food and nutrition, laws and regulation, natural resources and the environment, and research and science.

Art History

Academic Info—Art and Art History (http://www.academicinfo.net/artlibrary.html)

Another excellent Web directory with links to art databases, art publications, journals, and museum exhibits generally not found at other sites.

ArtSource (http://www.ilpi.com/artsource/welcome.html)

Originally launched as a service for art librarians, this Web page, developed by Mary Molinaro of the University of Kentucky, offers a comprehensive list of links and resources on art history.

IRIS (http://opac.pub.getty.edu/)

This online catalog, also known as the Integrated Research Information System (IRIS) at the Getty Research Library, contains more than 500,000 bibliographic records for the 800,000 volumes of books, serials, and auction catalogs in the general and special collections. The catalog also includes descriptive records of approximately 3,000 archival and photograph collections with more than 2 million photographs documenting works of art and architecture.

The Mother of All Art History Pages (http://www.umich.edu/~hartspc/histart/links.html)

This Web site features searchable sites on all aspects of art history.

Perseus Project (http://www.perseus.tufts.edu/)

A collaborative nonprofit enterprise located in the Department of the Classics at Tufts University, this evolving digital library for the study of ancient Greek culture features a wide range of primary and secondary sources. The site includes illustrated art catalogs, essays on various related topics, ancient texts and translations, maps, and pictures of art objects from other museums.

Timelines of Art History (http://www.art-and-archaeology.com/timelines/tl001.html)

Organized by civilization and period, this educational Web site dedicated to art history provides selected links about the art and archaeology of ancient civilizations, including Egypt, Greece and Rome, Asia, and the Middle East.

Yahoo Art and Art History (http://dir.yahoo.com/Arts/art_history/)

Extensive Web directory offering summaries and links to other art and related sites.

Associations and Organizations

ASAE's Gateway to Associations (http://info.asaenet.org/gateway/OnlineAssocSlist.html)

Using the American Society of Association Executives' online directory, associations can be searched by association name, category, and location, with direct links to each association's Web site.

Associations on the Net (http://www.ipl.org/div.aon/)

To find information on a variety of professional and trade associations, cultural and art organizations, political parties, advocacy groups, labor unions, academic societies and research institutions, this online resource features abstracts on more than 2,220 related Web sites.

Internet Public Library: Associations on the Net (http://www.ipl.org/div/aon/)
The Internet Public Library publishes this online directory of Web sites of prominent associations and organizations, covering many fields of interest, including arts and humanities, business and economics, computers and the Internet, education, entertainment and leisure, health and medical sciences, law, government and political science, and more.

Astronomy

AstroWeb (http://www.stsci.edu/astroweb/astronomy.html)
Maintained by a consortium of nine individuals and seven astronomical institutions, this collection lists astronomy-related information available on the Web by subject.

Center for Earth and Planetary Studies (http://www.nasm.edu/ceps)
In association with the Collections and Research Department of the National Air and Space Museum, the Center for Earth and Planetary Studies provides access through its homepage to a variety of research materials and image collections related to Mars, Venus, Mercury, Earth, the Moon, and planetary science and geophysics.

Education Index: Astronomy Resources (http://www.educationindex.com/astro/)
Fully searchable educational site, arranged alphabetically by subject, offering direct links to a large number of good astronomy resources for all ages.

Educational Observatory Institute—Astronomy Resources (http://www.edu-observatory.org/eo/eo/html)
Appropriate for K–12 and college-level students, this site, created and maintained by Samuel Worley of Iowa State University, provides a host of educational materials for astronomy students and researchers, including links to online atlases, books, bibliographies, catalogs, map indexes, sky maps and charts, and more.

History of Astronomy Resources (http://www.astro.uni-bonn.de/~pbrosche/hist_astr/ha_general.html)
Maintained by Wolfgang R. Dick of Bonn University in Germany, this site, suitable for students and researchers, provides full access to a wide variety of astronomy information, including biographical information, oral histories, astronomy libraries, and online resources.

Spaceweather.com (http://www.spaceweather.com/)
Sponsored by NASA, this site covers news and information on space weather and other celestial activity, including solar flares, spots, and other near-Earth phenomenon, such as asteroids and meteors.

Business, Economics, and Finance

Bureau of Economic Analysis (http://www.bea.doc.gov/)
This federal agency, whose stated aim is to promote a better understanding of the U.S. economy, provides accurate and reliable economic data offering

analysis of national, international, regional, and industry-related economic estimates and statistics.

Bureau of Labor Statistics (http://www.bls.gov/)
A federal fact-finding agency in charge of labor economics and statistics, the U.S. Department of Labor, through its Bureau of Labor Statistics, offers information and data on social and economic conditions relevant to working and the workplace.

Corporate Information (http://www.learnwebskills.com/company/over09.html)
Requiring registration for first-time visitors to use for free, this comprehensive directory provides U.S. and international company information, including research reports, company profiles, earnings information, and analyst reports, searchable by company, by country, by industry, or by state. Companies are also listed alphabetically for easy use.

County Business Patterns (http://www.census.gov/epcd/cbp/view/cbpview.html)
A service of the U.S. Census Bureau since 1993, Country Business Patterns publishes annual reports that analyze economic activity, changes, and data by county, state, or zip code, available for download.

Federal Reserve (http://www.federalreserve.gov/)
The Federal Reserve, which oversees U.S. monetary policy and its effects on the U.S. economy, offers a variety of economic research and data in several forms, free of charge. They include historical data and statistics, surveys and reports, staff studies, and working papers covering a wide range of economic and financial subjects.

Chemistry

Chemistryweb (http://www.ssc.ntu.edu.sg:8000/chemweb/htmlj/)
Covering a broad range of topics, this online directory contains many useful resources for students and researchers, including information and links to chemistry directories, online journals, reference materials, and selected bibliographies.

Librarians' Index to the Internet—Chemistry (http://www.lii.org)
Designed for library professionals, this searchable index includes a subject directory of more than 6,600 resources on the Web, evaluated and recommended by librarians, for finding valuable facts, information, and research in the field of chemistry.

Computers and Cyberspace

Annenberg Public Policy Center of the University of Pennsylvania (http://www.annenbergpublicpolicycenter.org/)
The center focuses on information and society, children and television, the "dialogue of democracy" and "health communication." Recent studies have looked at the Internet's influence on children, the child television audience, and television in the home.

Cyberspace Policy Institute (http://www.cpi.seas.gwu.edu/about/people.html)
Part of George Washington University. List of experts on the changing nature of telecommunications delivery systems, computer networks, electronic intellectual property, privacy, security (including "telemedicine" security), and related issues, such as ethics and values among providers and users of computer and communications networks.

Massachusetts Institute of Technology Media Laboratory (http://www.media.mit.edu/research/index.html)
The lab conducts advanced research into a broad range of information technologies, such as news in the future, digital life, and interactive cinema.

Stanford Computer Industry Project (http://www.stanford.edu/group/scip/intro.html#i2)
Areas of research include network platforms, intranets, software development, multimedia, and Information Age organizations.

Consumer Issues

Consumer Law Briefings (http://www.consumerlaw.org/)
Concerned with consumer justice and consumer issues, the National Consumer Law Center features current and detailed information covering legal and consumer issues on such topics as bankruptcy, credit discrimination, debt collection abuse, immigrant justice, and others, written by experts in the legal industry.

Consumer WebWatch (http://www.consumerwebwatch.org/)
A grant-funded project of Consumers Union, the nonprofit publisher of *Consumer Reports* magazine and ConsumerReports.org, this Web site features expertly written investigative and informative articles covering a myriad of consumer protection issues. Included is a news archive of past articles and research archives of studies and research collaborations.

Country Directories

Altapedia Online (http://www.altapedia.com/index.html)
This virtual resource features facts and statistics on geography, climate, people, religion, language, history, economy, and full-color physical maps and political maps on countries around the world.

Background Notes (http://www.state.gov/r/pa/ei/bgn/)
These are full-text publications, published by the U.S. State Department, offering details and insight into all countries of the world. Facts covered include the history, government and political conditions, economy, foreign relations, basic travel information, and U.S. relations with other countries.

CountryWatch (http://www.countrywatch.com/)
Available only by subscription, CountryWatch provides current information on each of the 192 countries of the world, including news wires, population,

currency, maps, and brief summaries on history, economy, agriculture, and environment.

Exploring Countries and Regions (http://www.worldbank.org/)
The World Bank Group offers information about countries and regions. Factual overviews include growth domestic product rates, population and mortality rates, infant mortality and life expectancy rates, school enrollment figures, adult literacy rates, and more.

International Resources (http://www.nsu.newschool.edu/internationalaffairs/05_resources.htm)
Provided by New School University in New York, this directory features a section of online sources that includes descriptions and links to dozens of Web sites related to international affairs. Subject areas include cities and urban policy, economics and trade, environment and natural resources, health, human rights, immigration and migration, international law, international organizations, and many others.

Demographic Data

American Fact Finder (http://factfinder.census.gov/home/saff/main.html?_lang=en)
Maintained by the U.S. Census Bureau, this site is a source for population, housing, economic, and geographic data. Fast access is provided to community profiles, age, education, income and race demographic data, foreign trade and housing data, and detailed census data.

American Religion Data Archive (http://www.arda.tm/)
Funded by Lilly Endowment, Inc., the American Religion Data Archive (ARDA) collects and publishes reports and surveys relevant to different churches, religious professionals, and religious groups. More than 220 surveys are downloadable, and abstracts can be browsed of past reports in an archive.

Bureau of Justice Statistics (http://www.ojp.usdoj.gov/bjs/)
Provided by the U.S. Department of Justice, this site offers an impressive collection of statistics about crime and crime victimization, criminal offenders, criminal record systems, law enforcement and court sentencing, and special topics, including drugs and crime, homicide trends, firearms and crime, and international statistics.

Center for Environmental Statistics (http://www.epa.gov/)
For the latest information on environmental quality and environmental topics such as air and water pollution, the U.S. Environmental Protection Agency offers a number of printable resources, including publications, reports, newsletters, and databases.

Crime in the United States (http://www.fbi.gov/ucr/ucr.htm)
With data provided by 17,000 law enforcement agencies, each year the FBI collects, publishes, and archives special studies, reports, and publications reporting crime statistics in the United States. This official site features current and past crime reports, from 1995 to the present, covering crime offenses

for the nation, the states, and individual agencies; hate crimes; and law enforcement officers killed and assaulted.

National Center for Education Statistics (http://nces.ed.gov/)
The National Center for Education Statistics features facts, figures, statistics, surveys, tables, and other information related to education in the United States and other nations around the world.

Population Reference Bureau (http://www.prb.org/)
This Web site provides objective data and information regarding social, economic, population, and political trends issues by focus area and by region, featuring population bulletins, population data sheets, and world population estimates.

Population Studies Center, University of Michigan (http://www.psc.isr.umich.edu/research/)
Founded in 1961, the Population Studies Center, one of the oldest population centers in the United States, has carved out a distinguished record in both domestic and international population research. Accessible through the center's Web site is demographic research in the following areas: fertility and family planning, marriage and family, race and ethnicity, aging and disability, and education.

Education

Digest of Education Statistics (http://nces.ed.gov/pubs2001/digest/)
Provided by the National Center for Education Statistics, this free service offers statistical information such as tables and figures, covering a variety of education statistics, including the number of schools and colleges, teachers, enrollments, graduates, and much more, published since 1995.

U.S. Department of Education (http://www.ed.gov/)
Promoting equal access to education and educational excellence, the U.S. Department of Education includes on its Web site a broad range of materials covering the field of education. They include current and archived press releases, speeches and transcripts of congressional testimony (since 2002), and research and statistics provided by various support organizations.

Environment

Agency for Toxic Substances and Disease Registry (http://www.atsdr.cdc.gov)
An agency of the U.S. Department of Health and Human Services, the Agency for Toxic Substances and Disease Registry offers the latest news, toxicological profiles, and information on health effects and disease related to toxic substances. Online sources include a hazardous substance database, science page, maps of hazardous waste sites, and information center.

Environmental and Occupational Health Resource Guide (http://www.eohsi.rutgers.edu/)
A service of the Environmental and Occupational Health Sciences Institute at Rutgers University, this guide was compiled to help the media and others find experts on environmental and occupational health.

KidsHealth (http://www.kidshealth.org/)
Designed for parents, kids, and teens, this keyword-searchable site covers a broad spectrum of environmental topics and provides access to full-text articles and other resources by topic.

Scripps Institution of Oceanography (http://sio.ucsd.edu/)
A searchable database of research activity at the Scripps Institution, one of the world's oldest, largest, and most important centers for global science research. Find experts on climate prediction, earthquakes, the physiology of marine animals, beach erosion, and so on.

Sea Grant (http://www.seagrantnews.org/experts/)
The national Sea Grant network is a 30-year-old partnership between universities and the National Oceanic and Atmospheric Administration. This directory can lead you to experts from more than 300 universities and institutions on beaches, marine mammals, hurricanes, tourism, seafood, and all things coastal.

World Resources Institute (http://www.wri.org/)
With a staff of more than 100 scientists, economists, policy experts, business analysts, statistical analysts, and other experts in their respective fields, this independent nonprofit organization publishes a number of free publications and reports on global environmental trends, environmental changes, and environmental resources authoritatively written and researched.

Worldwatch Institute Resource Center (http://www.worldwatch.org/topics/)
Examining the complexities of the world economy and the environment, Worldwatch, established in 1974, offers this online resource center featuring comprehensive information on a wide range of environmental topics. Research areas cover people, energy, nature, and the economy in relationship to the environment. Press releases are archived, as are links to other sites and organizations, and Worldwatch reports.

Ethics

Center for the Study of Society and Medicine (http://www.societyandmedicine.columbia.edu/index.shtml)
Located at Columbia University, the center offers a list of specialists on the history of medicine, medical ethics, and human rights and medicine.

The Hastings Center (http://www.thehastingscenter.org/)
The center studies ethical issues in the areas of health, medicine, and the environment. It's the only center for the study of bioethics that's not connected to a university or medical school.

Film and Theater

All-Movie Guide (http://www.allmovie.com/)
Provided by New Age Voices, this virtual movie database offers a wide spectrum of information, trivia, and subject essays chronicling movies and the people who make them. Content is searchable using the site's main search engine or subject-specific search engines, such as Film Finder or People Finder. The site contains a section of comprehensive essays chronicling the history of different eras and genres of movies as well.

Internet Movie Database (http://www.imdb.com)
The largest online database of film information, this site chronicles more than 140,000 movies, as well as popular television series. Included are filmographies, plot summaries, character names, movie ratings, year of release, genres, reviews, Academy Awards information, and more.

Film Studies (http://www.uark.edu/~aca/studies/film.html#gen)
Maintained by M. Norden for the American Communication Center, this site links to dozens of general film studies databases, and other film resources for scholars and researchers.

Live Broadway (http://www.livebroadway.com/)
Produced by the League of American Theatres and Producers, this Web site provides access to news and information on major Broadway shows, and research and reports on the business, demographics, and economic impact of Broadway theater.

Movie-STAR (http://www.cuadra.com/demos/moviestar.html)
This site covers virtually every Academy Award winner and nominee since 1927, in all major categories, for more than 2,798 motion pictures and 4,460 individuals.

Playbill Online (http://www.playbill.com/index.php)
Serving the theater community since 1884, *Playbill* has been a favorite publication for the latest news and information on the stage. This Web site comprehensively covers U.S. and London theater, including news, the week in review, Broadway grosses, feature articles, and a who's who of theater.

Forensic Science

Forensic Science Resources—Summary (http://www.ncjrs.org/forensic/summary.html/)
In association with the U.S. Department of Justice, the National Criminal Justice Reference Service provides this Web site, with a wealth of information and links related to the study of forensic science, including background, history, the latest facts and figures, recent legislation, and forensic publications. The site also includes access to a searchable abstracts database with summaries of more than 180,000 criminal justice publications, including federal, state, and local government reports, books, research reports, journal articles, and unpublished research.

Zeno's Forensic Page (http://forensic.to/forensic.html)
Created and regularly updated by Zeno Geradts, a forensic scientist at the Netherlands Forensic Institute, this site offers useful resources and links to general information, forensic science, forensic medicine, and forensic psychiatry Web sites.

General Reference Sources

Fast Facts: Almanacs/Factbooks/Handbooks and Related Reference Tools (http://www.freepint.com/gary/handbook.htm)
Compiled by Gary Price of George Washington University, this directory features links to virtually every type of almanac, factbook, handbook, reference, and subject guide available online.

Ready Reference: Selected Internet Sites (http://www.winsor.edu/pages/sitepage.cfm?id=426)
Full-text sources suitable for research are listed alphabetically by subject on this site created by Ellen Berne and modified by Carla Bosco of the Virginia Wing Library at the Winsor School in Boston, Massachusetts.

Research Guides A–Z (http://lib.mansfield.edu/subjects.html)
Created by Mansfield University of Pennsylvania's librarian Larry Schankman this annotated directory offers direct links to selected general references on the Web covering everything from acronyms and abbreviations to the weather.

xrefer.com (http://www.xrefer.com/)
This searchable, subscription-only database features reference books from the world's leading publishers, including dictionaries, encyclopedias, subject specific titles, and more, accessible by subscription. An enhanced version, xreferplus, offers access to 150 reference books by more than 35 publishers, also by subscription.

Geology and Earth Science

EROS Data Center (Earth Resources Observation Systems) (http://edc.usgs.gov/)
This archive provides a myriad of digital maps, including aerial, elevated, and satellite views of Earth.

Geology Resources on the World Wide Web (http://www.colby.edu/geology/otherresources.html)
This multifaceted directory offers links on a variety of related geology subjects, such as volcanoes and earthquakes, geological images on the Web, government agencies, and miscellaneous sites.

National Geophysical Data Center (http://www.ngdc.noaa.gov/)
The National Geophysical Data Center provides access to global geophysical data describing the sea floor, solid earth, and solar-terrestrial environment, including Earth observations from space.

Government and Politics

Center for the American Woman and Politics (http://www.cawp.rutgers.edu/)
Located at Rutgers University, the center compiles information about women in government and politics and maintains the National Information Bank on Women in Public Office, a database of current and past women officeholders and candidates.

The Center for Congressional and Presidential Studies (http://www.american.edu/academic.depts/spa/ccps/)
Located at American University, in Washington, D.C., the center focuses on Congress and the presidency and interactions between the two.

John F. Kennedy School of Government (http://www.ksg.harvard.edu/research.shtml)
Harvard's graduate school of public policy, planning, and administration houses experts on everything from affirmative action to corporate law to welfare in a searchable list.

Health and Medicine

AMA Health Information (http://www.ama-assn.org/ama/pub/category/3158.html)
Provided by the American Medical Association, this page contains links to health information (click on "Patient Education Resources") that take you to the AMA's award-winning Medical Library, voted one of the top 10 consumer health sites by the Medical Library Association. The site provides reliable, quality information, including introductory and advanced text, from the AMA's partner medical societies on the full range of health issues for patients and consumers, covering diseases and conditions, therapies and health strategies, and more.

Healthfinder (http://www.healthfinder.gov/)
Produced by the U.S. Department of Health and Human Services, Healthfinder is a comprehensive guide to reliable health information. Material ranges from articles on the latest health news to a complete health library that covers health information from A to Z, plus links to selected publications such as medical dictionaries, an encyclopedia, and journals. In addition, there is a directory of Web sites of clearinghouses, government agencies, nonprofits, and universities.

MayoClinic.com Diseases and Conditions (http://www.mayoclinic.com/findinformation/diseasesandconditions/index.cfm)
This site presents comprehensive overviews, listed from A to Z, on various diseases and conditions, plus helpful guides on the prevention and treatment of certain diseases.

MEDLINEPlus (http://medlineplus.gov)
A service of the U.S. National Library of Medicine and the National Institutes of Health, MEDLINEPlus is one of the best resources of medical information on the Web today. The site includes information on more than 650 health topics, including conditions, diseases, wellness, prescription and over-the-counter drug information, a medical encyclopedia and dictionary, health news from the past 30 days, and other resources, including links to medical libraries, health organizations, and more.

The Merck Manual (http://www.merck.com/pubs/mmanual_home/)
Published by the drug manufacturer Merck, this online version of the printed edition offers excerpts and details covering the fundamentals of the human body, aging, drug therapies and treatment, health disorders and disease, accidents and injuries, and special sections on children's, men's, and women's health issues.

National Cancer Institute (http://www.cancer.gov/)
This online information center provides a host of resources, including expertly written overviews about the types of cancer, treatment, prevention, genetics and causes, screening and testing, and literature.

National Health Information Center (http://www.health.gov/nhic/)
Established in 1979 by the Office of Disease Prevention and Health Promotion (ODPHP), the U.S. Department of Health and Human Services, and other federal agencies, the National Health Information Center is a health information referral service. The site features a comprehensive Health Information Resource Database that includes 1,800 organizations and government offices that provide health information upon request, as well as downloadable fact sheets and publications.

WebMD Health (http://my.webmd.com/webmd_today/home/default)
One of the Web's most recognized health resources, WebMD features a large amount of resources online for consumers and patients, including detailed medical information on diseases and conditions, drug and herbal therapies, health and wellness, diet and nutrition, and family, pregnancy, and lifestyle issues.

WholeHealthMD.com (http://www.wholehealthmd.com/)
Covering alternative medicine, WholeHealthMD.com provides the latest information on new approaches to healing, covering a myriad of ailments and conditions. The site offers free online access to an extensive reference library containing informative articles on chronic conditions, integrative medicine, supplements, and foods, and various other resources offering dietary advice, self-care techniques, and lifestyle tips.

History and Culture

African-American History: A Guide to Resources and Research on the Web (http://web.uccs.edu/history/ushistory/afroam.html)
Maintained by the University of Colorado at Colorado Springs' Department of History, this Web site covers every major subject area related to African-American history. Contents include general sources, culture, black nationalism, civil rights, history of slavery and slave narratives, online journals, African-American women's history, and biographical links to major figures from the 20th century.

American and British History Research Guides (http://www.libraries.rutgers.edu/rul/rr_gateway/research_guides/history/history.shtml)
Created by the Rutgers University Libraries, this well-organized subject directory features annotated links to reference resources, archival and manuscript guides, general history portals, sites organized by subject or by period, full-text documents, and history associations, among others devoted to American and British history.

American Cultural History: The Twentieth Century (http://kclibrary.nhmccd.edu/decades.html)
Examining the cultural and historical achievements of the 20th century, this reference site presents a series of informative and illustrated overviews,

prepared by Peggy Whitley and her fellow reference librarians at Kingwood College. Highlighted are accomplishments in art and architecture, books and literature, fads and fashion, education, historic events, music, persons and personalities, technology, and theater and film.

The American Civil War Homepage (http://sunsite.utk.edu/civil-war/warweb.html)
Begun as a class project at the University of Tennessee at Knoxville and first launched in 1995, this is a collection of hypertext links and electronic files about the American Civil War (1861–65). Divided into 12 categories covering the historical and political issues of the war, it lists battles and campaigns, bibliographies and histories, biographical information, documentary records, and more.

The American Revolution: National Discussions of Our Revolutionary Origins (http://revolution.h-net.msu.edu/)
Primarily designed for students, scholars, and the public, created by H-Net to complement the official companion site to PBS's *Liberty!* documentary series, this Web site is a place for discussions and research sources on the American Revolution. The site includes bibliographies, documents, maps, images, scholarly essays, and other sources, as well as links to sites about colonial American history.

Ancestors in the Americas (http://www.pbs.org/ancestorsintheamericas)
The official site for the PBS series of the same name, this Web page covers Asian-American history, including time lines, individual stories, resources and site links to other Asian-American ethnic groups, such Chinese, Filipino, Indian, Japanese, Korean, Pacific Islander, and Southeast Korean.

H-AMINDIAN (American Indian History and Culture) (http:/www.asu.edu/clas/history/h-amindian/index.html)
A joint project between Arizona State University and H-NET, this site covers the history, culture, ideas, and events of American Indians, with links to online sources, bibliographies, and nearly 30 categories of historical links.

Latino American History: A Guide to Resources and Research on the Web (http://web.uccs.edu/history/ushistory/latino.html)
Devoted to all aspects of Latino-American history, this well organized and comprehensive site provides many useful resources and links for students and researchers. Contents include general resources, archives, Hispanic women's history, political movements, popular culture, religion, and sources listed in chronological order.

Making of America (MOA) (http://cdl.library.cornell.edu/moa and http://moa.umdl.umich.edu)
Made possible by a grant from the Andrew W. Mellon Foundation, the MOA collection is comprised of more than 4 million digitized pages of books and journals derived from more than 13,000 volumes of primary source materials housed at the Cornell University and the University of Michigan libraries. This major collaborative effort provides direct access to 267 monograph volumes, 22 journals, and more 100,000 journal articles on Cornell's Web site, and 8,500 books and 50 journal articles—focusing on the areas of American

history, education, psychology, religion, science, sociology, and technology—on Michigan's Web site.

The National Park Service Links to the Past (http://www.cr.nps.gov/)
Sponsored by the National Park Service, this Web site features links exploring people, places, objects, and events in U.S. history and culture. Subjects covered include archaeology, architecture, engineering, cultural groups, landscapes, historic buildings and structures, laws/regulations/standards, mapping, maritime history, military history, museums and collections, registered historic places and landmarks, and more.

International Affairs/International Studies

Carnegie Endowment for International Peace (http://www.ceip.org/)
Established in 1910, the Carnegie Endowment conducts research in international affairs and U.S. foreign policy. It also publishes the quarterly magazine *Foreign Policy.* It is a good source for experts on post-Soviet states, democratization in Russia, and international migration.

Center for Strategic and International Studies (http://www.csis.org/)
CSIS is a public-policy research institution that claims to be the only institution of its kind to maintain resident experts on all the world's major geographical regions.

East-West Center (http://www.eastwestcenter.org/)
Established by the U.S. Congress more than 30 years ago, the center is a good source for experts on trade, politics, development, population, and culture of the Asia-Pacific region.

The Middle East Center (http://mec.sas.upenn.edu/)
The center's faculty, at the University of Pennsylvania, specializes in Middle East languages, sociology, folklore, history, political science, and economics.

Paul H. Nitze School of Advanced International Studies (http://www.sais-jhu.edu/)
Since its founding in 1943, this leading international affairs school, a division of Johns Hopkins University since 1950, has prepared graduate students for professional careers in government, business, journalism, international law, and nonprofit organizations. The school's Web site offers links to various research centers on foreign policy and access to its library catalog.

Sources Select Online (http://www.sources.com/)
This is one of the key source guides used by Canadian journalists and a great resource for reaching 5,000 experts on all things Canadian—health care, Parliament, Canadian unity, and more.

Woodrow Wilson School of Public and International Affairs (http://www.wws.princeton.edu/research/resources.html)
Located at Princeton University, the school is a major center for research on public and international affairs. Faculty members are experts in urban land use, industrial regulation and pricing, nuclear power, international trade policy, and health services.

Law and Criminal Justice

American Law Sources Online (http://www.lawsource.com/also/)
This comprehensive directory covers links to easily accessible online sources of the law for the United States and Canada, including court decisions, constitution, legislation, bills, and resolution, among others, by state or province.

FindLaw (http://www.findlaw.com)
Designed for legal professionals, businesses, students, and individuals, FindLaw considers itself the most comprehensive legal resource on the Internet. Resources include Web search engines, access to legal cases, case law and codes, legal news, and general legal information on a variety of topics.

Internet Law Library (http://www.lawguru.com/ilawlib/)
Formerly the U.S. House of Representatives Internet Law Library, this site offers direct links to a growing number of legal resources searchable by source and by agency; U.S. state and territorial laws; laws of other nations; treaties and international law; laws of jurisdictions by subject, and more.

Law Library of Congress (http://www.loc.gov/law/public/law.html)
The Law Library of Congress provides free access to several useful digital resources and links for researchers. They include the Guide to Law Online, an annotated guide to sources of information on government and law available online prepared by the Law Library of Congress Public Services Division, and the Global Legal Information Network (GLIN), a database of laws, regulations, and other legal sources.

Legal Information Institute (http://www.law.cornell.edu/)
A directory of legal Internet sites maintained by the Law School of.Cornell University, this directory of legal Internet sites covers constitutions and codes, court opinions, law by source or jurisdiction, topical libraries, and directories.

LexNotes (http://www.lexnotes.com/index.shtml)
This online resource categorizes links to research sources, bibliographies, pathfinders, articles, reviews, papers, and legal news.

National Archive of Criminal Justice Data (http://www.icpsr.umich.edu/NACJD/index.html)
Established in 1978, the National Archive of Criminal Justice Data distributes crime and justice data compiled by federal agencies, state agencies, and investigators for analysis. Data can be keyword searched or browsed by subject.

National Criminal Justice Reference Service (http://www.ncjrs.org/)
This online clearinghouse houses library abstracts and full-text publications on many subjects of interest, including the courts, drugs and crime, juvenile justice, law enforcement, victims of crime, statistics, and many other issues.

Nolo.com (http://www.nolo.com)
Nolo is a leading publisher of legal books, forms, and software. Its Web site features a collection of free information and tools, including a legal encyclo-

pedia with hundreds of articles, a law dictionary of legal terms defined in plain English, a legal research center providing details on the U.S. Constitution, U.S. laws and regulations, state laws, Supreme Court cases, and federal, state and local court information.

Sourcebook of Criminal Justice Statistics (http://www.albany.edu/sourcebook/)
Available in print, on CD-ROM and online, this annual sourcebook features data culled from more than 100 sources about many aspects of criminal justice in the United States, including public attitudes toward crime, known offenses, the characteristics of people arrested, and the judicial processing of defendants, to name but a few.

Media Studies

Annenberg Public Policy Center of the University of Pennsylvania (http://www.annenbergpublicpolicycenter.org/)
The center focuses on information and society, children and television, the "dialogue of democracy," and "health communication." Recent studies have looked at the Internet's influence on children, the child television audience, and television in the home.

Freedom Forum Media Studies Center (http://www.freedomforum.org/templates/document.asp?documentID=13087)
The center can provide expert commentary on media and journalism issues, and publishes reports, both in print and online, on various media-related topics.

Joan Shorenstein Center on the Press, Politics and Public Policy (http://www.ksg.harvard.edu/presspol/)
This Harvard University research center is concerned with campaigns and elections, journalism and public policy, and race, gender, and the press.

Military and Defense

Center for Defense Information (http://www.cdi.org/issues/)
Experts in military, intelligence, and defense issues, this independent watchdog group, founded in 1972 by recently retired senior U.S. military officers, features a host of resources available online on a variety of topics, such as arms trade issues, defense, and foreign policy.

DefenseLINK (http://www.defenselink.mil)
Sponsored by the U.S. Department of Defense, DefenseLINK presents news and information about defense policies, organizations, functions and operations, and military information. Resources include press articles, radio and TV reports, briefings, press advisories, and speeches and transcripts.

Department of Homeland Security (http://www.whitehouse.gov/homeland/)
Established following the terrorist attacks on September 11, 2001, the U.S. Department of Homeland Security covers national, economic, and homeland

security issues. Its Web site features current news, press briefings, and archived radio addresses and radio interviews with federal officials.

The Pentagon (http://www.defenselink.mil/pubs/pentagon/)
The Web site of the headquarters of the U.S. Department of Defense offers general information, history, and facts and figures of interest.

Physics

PhysicsWeb (http://physicsweb.org/resources/home)
The Institute of Physics' Web site is home to a rich collection of research and reference materials for students. Journals and historical references are offered, as is a section called "Best of Web," featuring articles from *Physics World* magazine as well as new stories and links to related Web sites on modern physics.

Physlink.Com (http://www.physlink.com/)
Up-to-date research and resources in physics and astronomy are available through this site. Under the Education category, students can access links to the history of physics and astronomy, essays, and other astronomy links and resources.

SciCentral—Physics Web (http://www.scicentral.com/)
Comprehensive directory of scientific news sources featuring breaking research news from hundreds of professional sources and more than 100 specialties in the fields of science and engineering.

Public Opinion Surveys

American Public Opinion and U.S. Foreign Policy (http://www.ccfr.publications/opinion/main.htm/)
Surveys conducted every four years since 1974 on behalf of the Chicago Council on Foreign Relations focus on the concerns of Americans regarding economic, political, and military engagement in foreign affairs. Full-text reports are accessible on the site.

The Gallup Organization (http://www.gallup.com)
One of the leading polling companies in the United States, Gallup posts on its Web site results of recent political and economic surveys, plus "special reports" examining social and consumer attitudes. Free access is limited to current published material; access to archived material is by subscription only.

Pew Center for the People and the Press (http://people-press.org/)
An independent opinion research group, the Pew Center studies attitudes toward press, politics, and public-policy issues. The group's official Web site offers summaries of all surveys published since 1989. It also provides access to surveys by topic, and an index of public responses to surveys from 1986 to 2002.

Polling Report (http://pollingreport.com)
This independent, nonpartisan resource indexes current polls and surveys from news and polling organizations highlighting trends in American public opinion on such important subjects as politics and public policy, business, and the economy.

Public Agenda (http://www.publicagenda.org)
Exploring critical issues since 1975, this nonpartisan opinion research organization probes Americans on what they think about important issues and publishes their findings in research studies available online. Recent studies are accessible free of charge, and can be downloaded.

Roper Center for Public Opinion Research (http://www.ropercenter.uconn.edu/)
A leader in the field of public opinion research, the Roper Center collects and distributes information about public opinion surveys on topical and timely issues of national importance. Not all of Roper's survey results are accessible without charge. Mostly recent poll results can be browsed, printed, and downloaded. Archived material is accessible by subscription only.

Washington Post Poll Vault (http://washingtonpost.com/wp-srv/politics/polls/vault/vault.htm)
This special section of the *Washington Post* Web site contains results of selected polls since 1993 that represent samples of public opinion on topics of national and regional interest.

Rankings and Awards

Gary Price's List of Lists (http://www.specialissues.com/lol/)
This directory indexes lists and rankings by subject. Featured under each subject heading, in alphabetical order, are articles, with direct links, including publisher name, article title, and year published.

Lists on the Web (http://207.21.203.96/list.html)
This directory features rankings and listings for all kinds of topics. The site links to articles ranking the top companies and corporations, the top advertisers and advertising agencies, the top magazines and newspapers, the top restaurants and travel destinations, the top books and music, the top movies and television shows, and the top sports teams and athletes. Everything in between is covered as well, from the most wanted criminals to the richest people in America.

Religion and Theology

Finding God in Cyberspace (http://sim74.kenrickparish.com/)
One of the best Web guides to religious studies, this provides numerous annotated links on all aspects of religion, including print resources, people resources, digital resources, academic disciplines, religious traditions, and more.

Religions of the World (http://www.mnsu.edu/emuseum/cultural/religion)
Created and maintained by Minnesota State University's Emuseum, this Web page presents a series of useful and informative overviews on Islam, Judaism,

Buddhism, Animism, Christianity, and Hinduism. Covered under each religion are history, basic beliefs, terms, and links to other sites of interest.

Wabash Center for Teaching and Learning Theology and Religion (http://www.wabashcenter.wabash.edu/Internet/front.htm)
This annotated Web guide features a wide variety of electronic resources covering the study and practice of religion, including bibliographies, electronic texts, electronic journals, histories, liturgies, philosophies and traditions, reference resources, and other related Web sites.

Science and Technology

NASA (http://www.nasa.gov/)
For kindergarten through post-secondary students, this home page of the National Aeronautics and Space Administration (NASA) offers an impressive array of educational materials, including articles, multimedia resources, and links to related sites dedicated to space exploration, biotechnology, space biology, and more.

SciCentral (http://www.scicentral.com/E-02engi.html)
Maintained by professional scientists, this site provides centralized access to thousands of valuable online resources and news and feature articles in 120 science and engineering subject areas, including biosciences, Earth and space sciences, health sciences, and physics and chemistry.

U.S. Geological Survey (http://www.usgs.gov/)
A federal source for Earth science, natural and living resources, natural hazards and the environment, the U.S. Geological Survey (USGS), through its official Web site, offers the latest news and information, including related regional studies and state information. Other resources include publications and products, such as biological information on the Web, a publication warehouse containing more than 60,000 citations of USGS series publications, national weather data, and map locators and atlases.

Social Issues

Carter Center (http://www.cartercenter.org/)
Founded by former president Jimmy Carter and his wife, Rosalynn, in 1982, the Carter Center focuses on issues related to fighting disease, hunger, poverty, and conflict around the world. Affiliated with Emory University.

Center for Law and Social Policy (http://www.clasp.org/)
The center works in the areas of family policy and access to civil legal assistance for low-income families. Family policy projects include welfare reform, workforce development, child care, child support enforcement, and reproductive health.

Center on Budget and Policy Priorities (http://www.cbpp.org/staff.html)
Focusing on government policies and programs that affect low- and moderate-income people, the center is a good source of experts on welfare reforms, state income trends, and the effects of government benefit programs on poverty.

Columbia University School of Social Work (http://www.columbia.edu/cu/ssw/faculty/fac_interests.html/)
The birthplace of formal social work education in the United States.

Families and Work Institute (http://www.familiesandwork.org/about/bios/index.html)
Features experts on how to create stronger families, more supportive communities, and more effective workplaces, who can talk about low-income employees, what employers are doing for new and expectant parents, the future of fatherhood, and balancing productivity with a life at home.

The Maxwell School Center for Policy Research (http://www-cpr.maxwell.syr.edu/)
The Maxwell School Center, at Syracuse University, conducts a broad range of research in the areas of aging, disability, income security, domestic, urban, and regional issues, public finance, and problems of economic development in less industrialized countries.

National Center for Children in Poverty (http://www.nccp.org/)
Part of Columbia University, this is a good source for statistics about child poverty, early childhood care and education, and child health.

Public Agenda Online (http://www.publicagenda.org/)
This public opinion research organization was founded in 1975 by social scientist and author Daniel Yankelovich and former secretary of state Cyrus Vance. They publish guides for journalists on social issues, including abortion, the federal budget, gambling, race, welfare, and more. Each guide includes links to experts and authors of relevant studies.

University of Chicago Center for the Study of Race, Politics and Culture (http://csrpc.uchicago.edu/)
A center for African-American studies that also focuses on race and U.S. society.

University of North Carolina Frank Porter Graham Child Development Center (http://www.fpg.unc.edu/)
Experts in development, care, and the well-being of children can discuss children with disabilities, high-risk students, ear and upper respiratory infections, and so on.

Urban Institute (http://www.urban.org/)
The institute investigates social and economic problems and programs designed to alleviate them and features experts on federalism, economics, social welfare (children, the elderly, health, etc.), and community building.

Speeches

American Rhetoric Online Speech Bank (http://www.americanrhetoric.com/speechbank.htm)
The Online Speech Bank contains more than 5,000 full-text transcripts, audio and video versions of public speeches, debates, interviews, legal proceedings and other recorded media events of current and historical figures in business,

culture, politics, and science. The site features nearly 450 active links, arranged alphabetically by first name.

Great American Speeches (http://www.pbs.org/greatspeeches/)
Maintained by PBS, this site hosts a large collection of speeches, including audio and video excerpts as applicable, from 1881 through the 1990s.

History and Politics Out Loud (http://www.hpol.org/)
Funded by the National Endowment for Humanities in partnership with Michigan State University, this site offers a small searchable archive for scholars, teachers, and students of transcripts and recordings of significant speeches in American history maintained by Northwestern University. Its oldest speeches date to 1931, but the majority of speeches are from the 1960s and 1970s.

History Channel: Speeches (http://www.historychannel.com/speeches/index.html)
This free online archive contains audio files of hundreds of speeches that can be searched by speaker, topic, or time period. A complete index of speeches, arranged alphabetically, is available, as well as speeches, listed by category, in the areas of politics and government, science and technology, arts, entertainment, and culture, and war and diplomacy. Historical text is provided with each speech.

Presidents of the United States (http://odur.let.rug.nl/~usa/P/)
This site contains transcripts of selected speeches, writings, biographies, and anything else related to every U.S. president. The site also includes useful links to other Web sites dedicated to the lives of American presidents.

Subject Guides and Directories

Academic Info (http://www.academicinfo.net)
Intended for high school and college students, this educational subject directory contains annotated listings of the best general Web sites in various disciplines, including area and country studies, the arts, business, education, engineering, health and medicine, humanities, law and government, library and information science, sciences and social sciences. Specialized research tools include links to museums, archives, and selected research and national libraries that make research available online or whose collection warrants special notice.

Argus Clearinghouse (http://www.clearinghouse.net)
No longer maintained, Argus Clearinghouse provides access to a selective collection of topical guides available on the Web. Categories include arts and humanities, business and employment, communication, computers and information technology, education, engineering, environment, government and law, health and medicine, places and people, recreation, science and mathematics, and social sciences and social issues. Each guide listed carries a rating of one to five checks, based on the average score of criteria by which they were evaluated by clearinghouse staff.

BUBL Information Service (http://bubl.ac.uk/)
Based at the University of Strathclyde in the United Kingdom, this online catalog of 12,000 Internet resources covers all academic subject areas, with a special focus on library and information science. Each item is carefully catalogued and described and includes active links to appropriate Web pages. Also listed are current links to U.S. journals and newspapers.

Digital Librarian: A Librarian's Choice of the Best of the Web (http://www.digital-librarian.com/)
Chronicling the "best" subject-specific sites on the Web, this directory, maintained by Margaret Vail Anderson, a librarian in Cortland, New York, covers more than 100 subject areas with links to dozens of Internet resources.

INFOMINE: Scholarly Internet Resource Collections (http://infomine.ucr.edu/)
This virtual library contains information and links to more than 14,000 useful Internet resources including databases, electronic journals, electronic books, online library catalogs, and other university-level research and educational tools.

The Invisible Web Directory (http://www.invisible-web.net/)
This directory of searchable databases covers some of the best resources on the Web. Subject areas include art and architecture, bibliographies and library catalogs, business and investing, computers and the Internet, education, entertainment, government information, health and medical, legal and criminal science, news and current events, public records, reference, science, social sciences, and U.S. and world history.

Internet Resources by Subject Category (http://www.libraries.rutgers.edu/rul/rr_gateway/research_guides/research_guides.shtml)
A superb directory of subject research guides on a variety of topics and related subcategories covering arts and humanities, business, medicine, science, technology and mathematics, and social sciences and law. Included are links to databases and indexes, Internet resources and printed resources. Some databases and indexes are restricted to student use only, while others offer free access.

Librarians Index to the Internet (http://lii.org)
Authored by Carole Leita of the Berkeley Public Library, this searchable directory comprehensively indexes more than 12,000 Internet resources covering a broad range of subjects, chosen for their usefulness for public library users. They include arts and humanities, business and finance, government and law, health and medicine, home and housing, Internet guides and search tools, news, magazines and media, people, ready references and quick facts, science and technology, society and social issues, and sports, recreation and entertainment.

Scout Report Archives (http://scout.wisc.edu/Archives/)
This searchable and browsable database of electronic resources covers subject-specific reports containing more than 16,000 subject headings, based on seven years of evaluations by professional librarians and subject matter experts,

originally published by the *Internet Scout Report*. Subjects can be keyword-searched or browsed. Reports summarize the contents of each subject and include full versions and links to relevant Web pages.

Selected Web Sites By Subject (http://oldsite.library.upenn.edu/resources/subject/subject.html)
Maintained by the University of Pennsylvania Library, this virtual directory lists subjects alphabetically covering a plethora of topics and Internet sites for further research. Topics include African-American studies, African studies, anthropology and archaeology, area studies, art and architecture, Asian/Pacific and East Asian studies, biological sciences, business, chemistry, classical studies, communications, literature and literary theory, computer science, criminology, dental medicine, education, engineering, environment and ecology, film studies, folklore, French studies, gay, lesbian, and bisexual resources, geology and geophysics, German studies, U.S. and foreign governments, health sciences, history, Iberian studies, Italian studies, Jewish studies, language and linguistics, Latin American studies, and law.

UC Berkeley and Internet Resources by Academic Discipline (http://www.lib.berkeley.edu/Collections/acadtarg.html)
This online directory indexes a list of recommended resources, by subject, in the areas of humanities, social sciences, and science. Subject listings include virtual links to databases, indexes, and other resources, some restricted for use by UC Berkeley students, but offering worthwhile and useful information for students and researchers.

The WWW Virtual Library (http://vlib.org/)
The oldest subject catalog of Internet resources on the Web, first created by Tim Berners-Lee, the creator of hypertext markup language and the Web itself, this site, connected to individual indexes on hundreds of services around the world, features links to thousands of subject-specific resources.

Web Searching

Business.com—The Search Engine for Business Information (http://www.business.com)
This business search engine and business directory contains news, research, and information on more than 400,000 listings of companies, products, and services within 25,000 subcategories.

Infopeople Best Search Tools (http://www.infopeople.org/search/tools.html)
This site features major search engines with comprehensive databases, metasearch engines (allowing you to search multiple engines at once), and subject directory searches for the Librarians Index to the Internet and Yahoo!, all in one.

SearchEdu.com (http://www.searchedu.com/)
This giant search engine allows you to search more than 15 million university and education pages from its database, as well as online dictionaries, the *CIA World Factbook*, *Encyclopaedia Britannica*, *Encarta*, and *Information Please Almanac*, and the U.S. Census and the Library of Congress.

SearchGov.com (http://www.searchgov.com/)
From the same people behind SearchEdu.com, this online search engine can search every federal, state, and local government, federal, executive, and independent agency with links to all of the above.

BEST REFERENCES ON THE WEB

With so many thousands of potential references on the Web, it often can be difficult to decide which is the most reliable, or most suitable, for providing the research you need. Fortunately, library professionals and, in particular, members of their trade associations, have taken up the task of documenting the best and most useful Internet resources for researchers.

The American Library Association (ALA), the oldest and largest library association in the world, each year publishes a variety of special features on its Web site that spotlight quality library and Internet references on a variety of topics.

One such Web page, titled "Reference on the Web," highlights the ALA's most recommended Web references by subject. Written by library professionals, this collection of republished articles includes Web addresses and detailed summaries of what each site offers. A complete list of topical references on the Web can be accessed, free of charge, at http:///www.ala.org. To access this section, click on "Periodicals" in the main menu, then on "Booklist." Next click on "Special Lists & Features," and listed among other special features is "Reference on the Web." After clicking on this title, you will be directed to a list of columns.

Major areas of interest covered include advertisements, American ethnicity, ancient Rome, assassination archives and research, black history, computers, desktop references, dictionaries, environmental resources, floods, fire and famine, lives of the presidents, military history, poetry, quotations, women's history, and women in sports.

The Association of College and Research Libraries, established in 1966, also features links to past "Internet Resources" columns written by research librarians and library professionals, published in its *College & Research Library News,* which covers the latest trends and practices in academic and research libraries. Each column thoroughly details its subject with comprehensive listings and summaries of a wealth of resources that include access to full-text documents and a wide range of freely accessible materials. Resources include general, historical, educational, professional, and metasites relevant to each subject.

The following is a complete list, in chronological order, of subjects accessible at ACRL's Web site (http://www.ala.org/ala/acrl/acrlpubs/crlnews/internetreources.htm):

African American Culture (January 1999)
Alternative Assessment (November 2004)
Alternative Energy (January 2005)
Archives and Special Collections (March 2003)
Assessment Student Learning (May 2004)
Astronomy (December 2001)
Authors—20th-Century Authors (December 1999)

Banking Data and Research (November 1999)
Biography Resources (January 2002)
Book Arts (April 2004)
Botany (June 2000)
Career in Academic Leadership (June 2004)
Chemistry (November 2000)
Children's Literature (July/August 2001)
The Civil Rights Movement (September 2004)
Comic Books and Graphic Novel (February 2005)
Communication Sciences and Disorders (February 2001)
Complementary and Alternative Medicine (September 2002)
Computational Science (February 2002)
Criminal Investigation and Forensic Science (October 2003)
Crisis, Disaster, and Emergency Management (November 2002)
Culinary Resources (November 2003)
Dance (December 2002)
Disabilities (February 2000)
Distance Education (May 1998)
Diversity in Higher Education (September 2000)
Drug Information (July/August 2001)
East Asian Studies (July/August 1998)
Educational Technology (January 2003)
The Electoral College, Political Partners, and Elections (July/August 2004)
Electronic Commerce (October 1999)
El Niño (October 1998)
Environmental Engineering (May 2002)
E-Poetry (April 2003)
Fashion and Costume (April 1999)
Foreign Language, Literature, and Culture (May 1999)
Genealogy (June 1999)
Geographic Information Systems (March 1999)
Grant Resources on the Web (July/August 1999)
Gray Literature (March 2004)
Horticulture (May 2003)
Human Rights on the Internet (September 1999)
Indigenous Nations (January 2004)
Information Architecture (October 2000)
Information Literacy Sites (February 1999)
Investments and Personal Finance (February 1998)
Knowledge Management (February 2004)
Latin America (December 2003)
Library Assessment (January 2001)
Literary Theory (March 2002)
Locating Public Domain Images (January 1998)
Maps and Mapping Resources (October 2001)
Mathematics (May 2000)
Medical Resources for the Consumer (December 2000)
Nonprint Media Preservation (September 2003)
Nutrition and Vegetarianism (April 1998)
Outdoor Recreation (May 2001)

Philosophy (April 2000)
Photojournalism (July/August 2003)
Physics (March 2000)
Plagiarism and Cyber-Plagiarism (June 2003)
Publishing/Information Industry (September 2001)
Refugees (September 1998)
Russian Studies (January 2000)
Scholarship of Teaching and Learning (July/August 2002)
Science Fiction and Fantasy (October 2002)
Social Work/Welfare (March 1998)
Southeast Asian Studies (February 2003)
Travel (April 2002)
Travel: Cruising for Travel Information (June 1998)
U.S. History (November 2001)
Western European Literatures (April 2001)
World Religions (June 2002)

FINDING OTHER WEB DATABASES

Given the thousands of online databases flooding the market, it's hard to keep track of all that are available. To obtain more information about available online databases, consult the following:

Gale Directory of Databases (Detroit, Mich.: Gale Group, 2005)
Comprehensive directory profiling more than 4,000 online databases, including product overviews and Web addresses.

16

Finding Search Engines

In today's high-tech world, finding and using search engines is extremely important. Search engines play an important role in providing access to and retrieving key information from Web sites on virtually every subject. A few examples are AltaVista, HotBot, Excite, Google, and Yahoo!.

These software-driven "spiders" or "robots," as they're called, rove through millions of indexed URLs—or Web pages—matching sites to the exact word or phrase of your search with amazing speed and accuracy. In short, search engines are a researcher's dream, minimizing both time and effort for what otherwise would be a laborious and painstaking process.

RESEARCHING SEARCH ENGINES

When researching and working with search engines, one very important fact to understand is that not all search engines are alike. Each has something different to offer, based on the following characteristics:

Size: One big difference between search engines is their size. Some index more Web pages and have larger databases than others, so the results of your search at one site may differ from another.

Search methods: The key to a successful search, as discussed in Chapter 1 (under "Searching Your Topic") is your method of searching. The methods of searching vary from engine to engine. Among the most popular methods are Boolean and proximity searches, truncation and wildcard symbols, or keyword and name phrasing.

Scope: In addition to size and search methods, another distinguishing characteristic is the scope, or comprehensiveness, of each search engine. Certain sites have the capacity to search Web sites, Usenet groups, image databases, and software archives, while others may not.

USING SEARCH ENGINES

With such inconsistencies between search engines—and considering how valuable your time is—here are a few methods used by experienced searchers that may improve your chances of a successful search.

1. **Check Help Sections.** When visiting a search engine site, click on icons for "search help," "tips," or "FAQs" (Frequently Asked Questions). Browse

these sections for tips on the best search methods to apply at each respective site, including how to formulate your search or truncate a term or search for a phrase.

2. Employ a Variety. When conducting your research, you want to find as much credible material as possible for your written paper or project, so don't settle on using just one search engine. Use a variety of sites since no site covers the entire Web. According to experts, smaller search engines are known to store and index sites that larger search engines have missed.

See "Searching for Your Topic" in Chapter 1 for more on how to use search engines.

CATEGORIES OF SEARCH ENGINES

Search engines come in different forms that allow users to search or browse everything from individual Web sites to annotated directories listing potential sites by group or category. Four kinds of search engines exist:

Web Search Engines

Web search engines—also known as "portals" because they are gateways to other sites with information—are the equivalent of "one-stop shopping." They attempt to provide you with a collection of links to other Web sites relevant to the subject you have searched. Remember, if you can't find what you need on one search engine, try another. You may have better luck with another one. The most popular search engines on the Web today are:

AllTheWeb.com (http://www.alltheweb.com)
AllTheWeb, formerly known as FAST or FAST Search, offers customizable Web searching, powered by Yahoo!, plus news, picture, video, MP3, and FTP search capabilities.

Alta Vista (http://www.altavista.com/)
Established in 1995 and for many years the most popular search engine of its time, AltaVista still receives significant amounts of traffic as a major search engine and is a favorite among researchers and students.

AOL Search (http://search.aol.com/)
AOL Search is available in two different versions, one for subscribers and another for nonsubscribers. The nonsubscription edition provides general searches via Google, including cached pages not offered to AOL subscribers.

Ask Jeeves (http://www.askjeeves.com/)
This human-powered search service, founded in Berkeley, California, in 1996, provides searching and retrieval via various Web sites and search-based products, including Ask Jeeves, Ask Jeeves for Kids, Excite, iWon, Teoma, and many others. It first searches within its own database to exactly match pages with your search and, if it fails, then matches Web pages from various other search engines.

Excite (http://www.excite.com/)
This popular search service, established in 1995, allows searching of the Web, listing the most relevant sites with detailed descriptions. In addition, search results can be reprocessed and viewed in order of search engines from which they came.

Gigablast (http://www.gigablast.com)
Among other much smaller indexes of the Web, compared to Google and Yahoo!, this free search engine service provides dependable searching of Internet content.

Go.com (http://www.go.com/)
Formerly known as Infoseek, Go.com, owned by the Walt Disney Company and part of its GoNetwork, provides online search capabilities of virtually any subject or topic, powered by Google.

Google (http://www.google.com/)
The world's largest search engine, Google searches and retrieves with relative ease detailed results with links to relevant sites. Unlike other search engines, Google uses a mathematical algorithm that "rates pages on who links to them," and has won widespread acclaim for high relevancy of results. Besides general searches, Google also maintains the largest archive of Usenet messages—some 845 million posts from 1981 to the present.

HotBot (http://www.hotbot.com/)
Debuting in 1996, HotBot is rated as "one of the best search sites on the Web." Refreshing its entire database every three to four weeks, this site performs searches of three major search engines: Google, Teoma, and Yahoo! Results are listed numerically with detailed descriptions and Web links.

LookSmart (http://www.looksmart.com)
Independently launched in 1996 entirely by volunteer editors, LookSmart searches noncommercial Web pages, in addition to listing sites that pay to be featured in its commercial categories.

MSN Search (http://search.msn.com)
Not the major search engine it once was, but still effective, MSN Search provides searching of listings from Yahoo!.

Netscape Search (http://search.netscape.com)
Like AOL Search, Netscape Search is powered by Google and accesses its database of Web pages through online searching. One major distinction between Netscape Search and Google, however, is that Netscape Search also features content from its own database as part of any search results.

Teoma (http:/www.directhit.com/)
Analyzing millions of searches a week, this crawler-based search engine owned by Ask Jeeves is smaller than its rivals Google and Yahoo! Yet, it produces a collection of relevant Web pages based on your search, along with suggestions to narrow and refine your search and resources, with link collections from other experts and enthusiasts.

WiseNut (http://www.wisenut.com)
This easy-to-use general search engine, owned by LookSmart, produces a numerical list of search results featuring site name, description, and Web address.

Yahoo! (http:www.yahoo.com)
More famous as a premier Web directory, Yahoo! is also a powerful search engine enabling you to search the Internet, plus images, Yellow Pages, and other products.

Web Metasearch Engines

One way to make your searches much more efficient and less time consuming is to use metasites, or metasearches. Metasearch sites work differently than single search engines. They query multiple search engines at once, producing the best results from leading search engines. Some of the best metasites on the Web include:

Dogpile (http://www.dogpile.com/)
Calling itself "the Top Dog of the search industry," Dogpile searches the Internet's top search engines, including AskJeeves, FindWhat, Google, Look Smart, and Yahoo!. Results from your search are "fetched" from a customizable list of search engines, directories, or specialty search sites. Searches can be easily refined to make your searches most meaningful. With Dogpile, you can search the Web, images, audio, multimedia, news, and shopping sites.

InfoGrid (http://www.infogrid.com)
This site provides direct links to major search engines and topical Web sites in many different categories, plus metasearches and news searching.

Ithaki (http://www.ithaki.net/)
Available in 14 languages, this global metasearch engine allows you to search more than 35 different categories, and offers country-specific searches that query search engines in that area or region only.

Ixquick (http://www.ixquick.com/)
Established in 1999, Ixquick bills itself as "the world's most powerful metasearch engine." With a reported 1.4 million pages processed per day, this site provides multiple searching of the Web, in addition to MP3s, news, and pictures in all languages.

KartOO (http://www.kartoo.com)
A unique metasearch engines, KartOO provides a visual display of your results, presenting them in a series of interactive maps and topics related to your query. The site is offered in many different languages.

Mamma (http://www.mamma.com/)
Claiming to be the "mother of all search engines," Mamma offers powerful metasearching of the Web, as well as news, images, and yellow and white pages.

Meceoo (http://www.meceoo.com/)
Customizable search engine that performs metasearches of Alta Vista, AllTheWeb, and Inktomi allowing users to exclude certain Web pages from search results, such as .org sites.

MetaCrawler (http://www.metacrawler.com)
Developed in 1994 and therefore one of the oldest search engines around, Metacrawler, owned by Infospace (owners of Dogpile), searches as many as 16 different search engines simultaneously, including Ask Jeeves, Google, Yahoo!, and LookSmart.

MetaEureka (http://www.metaeureka.com)
Powerful metacrawler-based search engine that searches listings of several major search engines and paid listings services.

1Blink (http://www.1blink.com)
A lesser-known search engine that metasearches the databases of several major search engines and also searches within subject categories.

ProFusion (http://www.profusion.com/)
Unlike most metasearch sites, ProFusion offers multiple searching of leading Web search engines, but also the ability to target your search under one of many "search groups" by category and subcategories. Main categories include arts and humanities, business, career, education, entertainment, finance, government, health, legal, news, reference, science, sports, technology, travel, and the Web.

Query Server (http://www.queryserver.com/web.htm)
Performs metasearching of major search engines, and offers news, health, money, and government search services.

Search.com (http://www.search.com/)
Set up differently from other metasites, Search.com allows multiple keyword-searching of topics. The site also enables you to search in any of 200 special-subject collections by topic.

SurfWax (www.surfwax.com)
Bestowed an honorable mention for the "Best Meta Search Engine Award" by Search Engine Watch in 2002, this metasearch site offers "seamless searching" and allows pages to be previewed (using the "SiteSnaps" feature) and results or documents to be saved.

Turbo10 (http://turbo10.com)
Fast and efficient metasearch engine that combs traditional search engines and invisible Web databases with instantaneous results.

ZapMeta (http://www.zapmeta.com)
Officially launched in 2003, this powerful metasearch tool provides simultaneous multiple searches of several leading search engines in one place, and a variety of options to sort results retrieved by popularity, title, source, or domain. Besides Web searching, ZapMeta also offers a Web directory and product search powered by Open Directory and Pricegrabber, respectively.

Web Directories

What is a Web directory? These sites organize topics by category, from A to Z. Some directories feature main categories and subcategories as well. Most directories feature an annotated list with the name of the site, Web address, and a brief description. Simply by clicking on the link, you will be transferred to the site you have chosen.

Web directories are useful for locating articles, reports, studies, and organizational Web sites offering a myriad of resources relevant to your subject or topic. Among the most popular are:

About.com (http://www.about.com/)
Attracting a reported 20 million visitors a month, this powerful network and directory of subject guides on the Internet includes more than 475 topics, certified by company subject specialists who are responsible for site review, feature articles, and discussion areas.

Google Directory (http://directory.google.com/)
Well-organized, alphabetical directory similar to Yahoo! Search Directory, listing more than 15 searchable categories and subjects.

LookSmart's Directory (http://search.looksmart.com/)
LookSmart's Directory features Web sites grouped by category, offering a diverse collection on each subject, including computer, entertainment, hobbies and interests, reference and education, science and health, society and politics, sports, travel, and work and money.

Lycos (http://www.lycos.com/)
Founded in June 1995, Lycos started out as a search engine, depending on listings that came from spidering the web. In April 1999, it shifted to a directory model similar to Yahoo!.

Netscape Network Search (http://channels.netscape.com/ns/search/default.jsp)
Offering more categories than LookSmart's Directory, much like Yahoo!, Netscape Network Search offers a browsable directory of subjects. The site features more than a dozen categories, listed in alphabetical order, with subcategories including arts, business, computers, games, health, home, kids and teens, news, recreation, reference, regional, science, society, sports, and travel.

Open Directory (http://dmoz.org/)
Billed as "the largest, most comprehensive human-edited directory of the Web," this site catalogs more than a dozen subject directories with hundreds of subcategories completely constructed and maintained by volunteer editors. This widely visited database actually powers the directory services of the Web's largest and most popular search engines and portals, including AOL Search, Google, HotBot, Lycos, Netscape Network Search, and many others.

Super Searchers (http://www.infotoday.com/supersearchers/ssmo.htm)
Features detailed descriptions with links to 239 Internet sites, search engines, and online resources.

Yahoo! Search Directory (http://dir.yahoo.com/)
One of the best-known Web directories is Yahoo! A popular resource for students, the Yahoo! Search Directory offers directories on a wide range of subjects, each with subcategories, covering arts and humanities, business and economics, computers and the Internet, entertainment, government, health, news and media, recreation and sports, science, and social science.

TOPICAL SEARCH ENGINES

Besides a variety of general and metasearch engines, the World Wide Web is home to many useful topical search engines—also called "specialty" and "vertical" search engines—that provide subject-specific searching of many different subject areas. Some examples follow:

Arts and Entertainment Search Engines

A field as wide ranging as arts and entertainment can often be difficult to research, unless you consult a search engine that cross-references articles and documents specific to this industry in film, literature, music, visual, and performing arts. Choices include:

Art and Culture (http://www.artandculture.com/)
A cross-disciplinary search engine that covers the world of contemporary arts, featuring thousands of artist biographies, essays, and overviews of the full range of artistic disciplines, including design arts, film, literature, music, visual, and performing arts.

Business and Financial Search Engines

The Web has plenty of search engines that specifically index business and financial-related Web pages and offer searching of their own databases. Some of the best in this category are:

Business.com (http://www.business.com/)
Extensively lists both commercial and noncommercial listings of business Web sites.

Business 2.0 Web Guide (http://www.business2.com/webguide/)
Developed and maintained by professional research librarians, this is a business-oriented directory of Web sites.

DailyStocks.com (http://www.dailystocks.com/)
This searchable site offers access to stock symbols, news stories, quotes, and other information.

eBizSearch (http://www.ebizsearch.org)
An experimental search engine retrieves both academic and popular articles and reports about e-business.

Hoover's Online (http://www.hoovers.com/)
Provides online searching of information on more than 12 million companies in 30 different industries.

MoneyWeb Financial Search Directory (http://www.moneywebsearch.com/)
Searchable directory of Web sites on business, finance, and money.

MSN Money's Stock Research Center (http://moneycentral.msn.com/investor/research/welcome.asp)
Financial research center offering searches and access to stock research and new developments.

TradingDay.com (http://www.tradingday.com/)
Offers stock quotes with links to company research and more.

Zapdata (http://www.zapdata.com/)
Enables users to retrieve real-time industry reports using Dun and Bradstreet business data free of charge.

Computers and Technology Search Engines

Information on computers and technology is not hard to come by, but some research questions may require the use of search engines that specialize in computer and technology-related subjects. Recommended are:

HotWired (http://hotwired.wired.com/)
Search for technology information to other documents indexed in *Wired News, Webmonkey, Wired Magazine,* and *HotWired Archives.*

Webopedia (http://www.pcwebopedia.com/)
Online dictionary and search engine covering computer and Internet technology terms and definitions.

Country and Region Search Engines

While most search engines are international in scope, should you want to search a specific country, you can do that, too. Outside of the United States or the United Kingdom (the latter mostly offering versions of U.S. brand-name search engines), many countries offer their own specific-search engines based on the contents of their databases and devoted to a particular country or region of the world. It helps to be multilingual, since not many of these sites are offered in English. Some of the best in the category are:

AUSTRALIA AND NEW ZEALAND

Being Seen in New Zealand: The Lowdown on Kiwi Search Engines (http://www.traffick.com/story/vortals/0203nzsearch.asp)
Web article that features a brief directory of search engines in New Zealand.

High Search Engine Ranking (http://www.high-search-engine-ranking.com/)
Operated by Australian search engine marketer Kalena Jordan, this site lists both Australian and New Zealand search engines and related news.

EUROPE

European Search Engine (http://www.webmasterworld.com/forum18/)
Online directory of "the largest collection of Euro search information on the Internet."

FRANCE

Abondance (http://www.abondance.com/)
Provides Web searching only in French.

GERMANY

German Search Engine Resources (http://searchenginewatch.com/sereport/02/09-german.html)
Provides a complete list of German search engines with discussion of techniques for search engine marketing in Germany.

Government Search Engines

You can search for official government information from any number of government-sponsored and commercial sites. Highly recommended are:

FirstGov (http://www.firstgov/)
A well-organized and searchable site of federal and local governments and information that can be browsed by category.

Google U.S. Government Search (http://www.google/unclesam)
Powered by Google, this Web page offers limited searches of U.S. government Web sites from a single source.

SearchGov.com (http://www.searchgov.com/)
This metacrawler-based search engine combs through U.S. and state government Web sites.

usgovsearch (http://usgovsearch.northernlight.com/)
Much like a metasearch site, usgovsearch searches across a variety of U.S. government Web pages and information provided by the NTIS (National Technical Information Service).

Health and Medicine Search Engines

Health and medicine search engines can help you find information quickly. Several leading sites include:

Go Ask Alice! (http://www.goaskalice.columbia.edu/search.html)
Web database of almost 2,600 previously posted questions and answers on health and medicine topics, searchable by subject, title, keyword, or question.

MedHunt (http://www.hon.ch/MedHunt/MedHunt.html
Searches medical Web sites for general medical information using subject, terms, or keywords.

Kid-Safe Search Engines

So-called kid-safe search engines claim to filter out offensive sexual or violent content while providing the same search capabilities as "regular" search engines. Three kid-safe search engines are:

Ask Jeeves For Kids (http://www.ajkids.com/)
A question-and-answer search engine that directs children to appropriate Web pages. Like the adult version of *AskJeeves,* it will then cross-search various other search engines until better results are found. Includes CyberPatrol blocking of objectionable Web pages.

KidsClick! (http://www.kidsclick.org/)
Highly recommended by librarians, this general search engine covers 5,000 Web sites in various categories.

Yahooligans! (http://www.yahooligans.com/)
The oldest major directory for children, Yahooligans!, powered by Yahoo!, provides searching and access to "hand-picked" appropriate Web sites for children ages seven to 12.

Legal Search Engines

Many search engines are designed to provide the legal information you need, among them:

Law.com (http://www.law.com/index.shtml)
Law.com is more than a search engine that provides searching and access to legal-related Web pages: It also offers links and many other services, such as free e-mail assistance.

LawCrawler (http://lawcrawler.findlaw.com/)
Powerful search engine sponsored by Google that retrieves information from various Web sites covering the law and legal issues.

News Search Engines

Every now and then in the course of your research, you may need a search engine that indexes hundreds of current and older news stories on the Web culled from a variety of different sources. For timely searching of news content, try the following news search engines:

MAJOR NEWS SEARCH ENGINES

AllTheWeb News (http://www.alltheweb.com/?cat=news)
Keyword-searches news sites on the Web and offers advanced news searching to refine or narrow your choices to particular categories.

AltaVista News (http://news.altavista.com/)
Offering drop-down options for searching to narrow your results by topic, AltaVista News provides keyword searching of news indexed by its sister search engine AllTheWeb based on the contents of many major newspapers

and news organizations, including *The New York Times*. In addition, the site features the latest news headlines that can be browsed by category.

Daypop (http://www.daypop.com/)
Keyword-searchable site that combs through literally thousands of news Web sites every single day.

Google News (http://news.google.com/)
Google News enables users to keyword-search thousands of major news sources and to browse news by category.

Yahoo News (http://news.yahoo.com/)
Much like Google News, Yahoo News offers keyword searching of many national news sources, fed by major wire services and news organizations. Another option is *Yahoo Full Coverage,* which features news, articles, and news resources assembled by category and "hand-picked" by Yahoo! editors.

OTHER NEWS SEARCH ENGINES

Ananova (http://www.ananova.com/)
Covers hundreds of different news sources, all completely searchable.

Net2one (http://www.net2one.com)
Offers limited free keyword searching of the news across the Web besides offering e-mail service for a small fee. Paying members are provided full access to another news search engine that produces better results.

NewsNow (http://www.newsnow.co.uk/)
Provides global searching of new sources around the world by country, besides featuring news headlines organized by category.

NewsTrawler (http://www.newstrawler.com/)
Metasearch site that provides multiple searching of more than one news site from a single location. In addition, the site lists hundreds of news sites by country or by category.

NewsTrove.com (http://www.newstrove.com/)
From this single resource, you can keyword-search or browse news by category.

Rocketinfo (http://www.rocketnews.com)
Formerly called RocketNews, this site enables you to search news on the Web via several resources at once, in addition to saving your searches.

World News Network (http://www.wn.com/)
Searchable international news site drawn from hundreds of Web news sources in 20 different languages. Stories are also grouped by subject (with some 500 subjects to pick from), and by geographical location.

Question-and-Answer Search Engines

The Web contains a plethora of question-and-answer search engines designed to provide answers and/or information regarding almost any subject. Some services are free, while others charge a small fee.

AllExperts.com (http://www.allexperts.com)
Possibly the oldest and largest free question-and-answer service on the Internet, AllExperts enables visitors to access thousands of volunteer "experts" able to answer almost any question, selected by category.

Ask Jeeves (http://www.askjeeves.com/)
Besides being a major general search engine, AskJeeves allows searching for answers to popular questions.

Information Please (http://www.infoplease.com/)
A great source for facts and information, Information Please offers reliable answers and searching of various almanacs, an encyclopedia, and a dictionary.

Google Answers (http://answers.google.com)
Users can search for answers from professional researchers for a small fee.

SwapSmarts (http://www.swapsmarts.com/)
Fee-based service that connects users to experts who can answer most topical questions. The site also maintains a collection of articles on various subjects offered free of charge or for a small fee.

Science Search Engines

Science is also well represented on the Web with several search engines that providing searching of documents, including books, peer-reviewed articles, and reports, plus links to scientific journals, organizations, and many other resources. Some sites worth visiting include:

BioView (http://www.bioview.com/bv/servlet/BVHome)
Scientific search engine producing categorized results with links to journals, organizations, and more.

CiteSeer.IST (http://www.researchindex.com)
Computer science research search engine that includes citation indexing, bibliographic coupling, and links to related documents.

Scirus (http://www.scirus.com/srsapp/)
A comprehensive science-oriented search engine, able to search more than 167 million science-specific Web pages to quickly locate scholarly, technical, and medical data, reports, and peer-reviewed articles and journals drawn from Elsevier Science's massive library of books and journals, for scientists and researchers.

SciSeek (http://www.sciseek.com/)
Finds documents of interest on the Web in a specific scientific area.

Search4Science (http://www.search4science.com/)
Norwegian science search engine run by "scientists for scientists," offering keyword searching of thousands of scientific words and expressions.

WEB SEARCH ENGINE TUTORIALS

Even the most inexperienced beginner can find searching the Web frustrating, and may require a little outside help. If this is the case, several credible tutorial Web sites offer free assistance and free guides that can make your searching experience both worthwhile and meaningful. They include:

Search Engine Math (http://searchenginewatch.com/facts/math.html)
Covers the basic commands needed to improve your searches, no matter what your subject or needs.

Search Engine Showdown (http://www.searchengineshowdown.com/)
Evaluates and compares various search engines and offers advice and tips for searching.

Power Searching for Anyone (http://searchenginewatch.com/facts/powersearch.html)
For experienced users, this site provides instruction on advanced search commands and how to better control your searches.

Section III

FINDING SOURCES BY SUBJECT

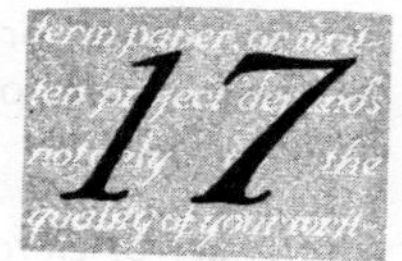

Aging

As a subject area for your paper, report, or written project, few topics are as interesting as aging. Whether you are writing about serious health issues or the latest demographic and statistical trends, countless resources are available on all areas and categories of aging. They include comprehensive A–Z encyclopedias and information handbooks, relevant indexes and abstracts, timely full-text articles from leading journals, newspapers, and magazines, general online databases, and specific Web sites, organizational subject directories, as well as detailed studies, position papers, and reports. Any one can be a good starting point for your research no matter your topic.

To put you on the right course, this chapter contains a list of selected references and sources highly recommended by librarians and researchers in this specialty.

SELECTED BOOKS AND REFERENCES

Aging in America A to Z, by Adriel Bettelbaum, 300 pages (Washington, D.C.: CQ Press, 2001)
Written by a reporter for *Congressional Quarterly* magazine, this encyclopedic volume provides direct answers to questions, terms, and concepts affecting older citizens, with emphasis on political and policy issues. This well-written compendium contains more than 250 in-depth articles, arranged alphabetically, about public policy and real-world concerns of seniors, from Alzheimer's disease to the privatization of Social Security. The book is extensively cross-referenced for easy access.

Aging Sourcebook: Basic Information on Issues Affecting Older Americans, edited by Dan R. Harris and Laurie L. Harris, 889 pages (Detroit, Mich.: Omnigraphics, Inc., 1997)
An insightful reference that examines a wide range of issues facing older Americans, including health and safety, legal, financial and end-of-life issues. The book also discusses at length demographic trends, Social Security, Medicare, estate planning, and retirement lifestyle options.

Americans 55 and Older: A Changing Market, 3rd Ed., edited by Sharon Yntema, 482 pages (Ithaca, N.Y.: New Strategist Publications, Inc., 2001)
This useful guide to demographics of older Americans offers information, statistics, and demographic variables, presented by age, race, origin, sex, region

of residence, and more, about attitudes and behavior, education, health, income, labor force, living arrangements, population, spending, and wealth of those 55 and over. The book also covers projections of the labor force to 2006.

Dictionary of Gerontology by Diana K. Harris, 216 pages (Westport, Conn.: Greenwood Publishing Group, 1988)
This book offers hundreds of precisely defined terms and concepts applied to the field of aging, explained clearly and understandably for any student, scholar, or practitioner. The book not only covers well-known and common terms but also specialized theories, studies, terms, and organizations in the field of gerontology and vocabulary related to medical research methods encompassing all different disciplines of gerontology.

Encyclopedia of Adult Development, edited by Robert Kastenbaum, 592 pages (Phoenix, Ariz.: Oryx Press, 1993)
An excellent source of information and knowledge about lifespan development of adults, this multidisciplinary encyclopedia examines issues of persons 18 years and older with insights from specialists in various fields, including anthropology, history, education, nursing, health sciences, and psychology. The book also features many informative and in-depth articles for further reading.

Encyclopedia of Aging, edited by David J. Ekerdt, 4 vols., 2,000 pages (New York: Macmillan Reference USA/Gale Group, 2002)
A 2002 *Booklist* Editors' Choice for "best reference," this four-volume set discusses the causes and ramifications of aging in an engaging way. This encyclopedia covers biological, medical, psychological, and sociological topics, as well as social and public policy issues. Other issues explored include economics, law, religion, spirituality, and ethics among the aging.

Encyclopedia of Elder Care: The Comprehensive Resource on Geriatric and Social Care, by Mathy D. Mezey, 824 pages (New York: Springer Publishing Co., 2004)
This resource covers important clinical issues in the care of the elderly. The book contains nearly 300 articles written by medical experts, addressing all aspects of clinical care and health issues, including acute and chronic disease, home care, nursing-home care, rehabilitation, health promotion, disease prevention, education, case management, social services, assisted living, advance directives, palliative care, and much more. Following each article is a list of Web resources for readers.

Encyclopedia of Gerontology: Age, Aging and the Aged, edited by James E. Birren, et al., 1,474 pages (San Diego, Calif.: Academic Press, 1996)
Edited by gerontology researcher James Birren and others, this two-volume set contains articles and research on the biology, psychology, and sociology of aging, reflecting all major topics of research and areas of public interest. The 139 entries cover five areas of aging; each article depicts the development and changes of aging and includes theories and summaries of empirical findings, definitions, a glossary of unfamiliar terms, and a bibliography of suggested readings.

Older Americans Almanac: A Reference Work on Seniors in the United States, edited by Ronald J. Manheimer, 881 pages (Detroit: Gale Group, 1998)
This comprehensive volume features explanatory essays on the history of aging, the physical, mental, and social processes of aging, and legal, financial, and end-of-life issues supported by tables, figures, and charts.

SELECTED ARTICLE INDEXES AND ABSTRACTS

Printed Indexes and Abstracts

Social Work Abstracts (Washington, D.C.: National Association of Social Workers, 1972–)
Published quarterly, in March, June, September, and December, the printed volume extracts its information from the quarterly publication *Social Work Abstracts,* which reviews more than 400 U.S. and international journals and publishes approximately 450 abstracts in each issue. Also available in an online version, the series was originally titled *Social Work Research and Abstracts* from 1972 to 1994, at which time it was renamed.

Web Indexes and Abstracts

AgeLine (AARP, 1966–) (http://research.aarp.org/ageline/home.html)
A free service of the American Association of Retired Persons (AARP), this online guide indexes books, research reports, articles from more than 600 journals and magazines, and videos related to aging and life over the age of 50. Searchable by subject, author, title, or journal name or year, the database covers research, policy, and professional and general interest publications in the fields of gerontology, health care, business, consumer affairs, psychology, sociology, and economics, as well as a wide variety of other related topics.

AskERIC (Educational Resources Information Center, 1966–) (http://www.eduref.org/Eric/)
ERIC is a comprehensive information database that contains more than 1 million abstracts of journal articles and education-related literature from 1966 to the present. Topics are keyword searchable, and many aging-related subjects can be searched, such as aging, aging education, Alzheimer's disease, geriatric education, and long-term care. Charges may apply for obtaining full-text documents.

Social Science Citation Index (Thomson ISI, 1980–)
This multidisciplinary database provides access to current and retrospective bibliographic information, author abstracts, and cited references found in more than 1,700 of the world's leading scholarly social sciences journals covering more than 50 disciplines. Also covered are selected items from approximately 3,300 of the world's leading science and technology journals.

Social Services Abstracts (Cambridge Scientific Abstracts, 1980–)
Bibliographic database providing abstracts and some full-text coverage of current research focused on social work, human services, and related disciplines, including social welfare, social policy, and community development.

The database abstracts and indexes more than 1,406 publications and includes abstracts of journal articles and dissertations, and citations to book reviews. Major subject areas covered include community and mental health services, crisis intervention, family and social welfare, gerontology, poverty and homelessness, social and health policy, social work, violence, abuse, and neglect, and welfare services.

Social Work Abstracts (National Association of Social Workers, 1977–)
This Web version of the popular printed index of the same name, produced by the National Association of Social Workers, contains abstracts of more than 35,000 records, spanning 1977 to the present, from social work and other related journals, including aging and gerontology from hundreds from scholarly journals.

Sociological Abstracts (Sociological Abstracts, Inc./Cambridge Scientific Abstracts, 1963–)
Sociological Abstracts is a primary resource for accessing the latest research sponsored in sociology and related disciplines in the social and behavioral sciences. It includes abstracts of journal articles from more than 2,600 journals in 30 different languages and from about 55 counties, abstracts of conference papers presented at various sociological association meetings, relevant dissertation listings from Dissertations Abstracts International, enhanced bibliographic citations of book reviews, and abstracts of selected sociology books.

SELECTED FULL-TEXT ARTICLE DATABASES

Contemporary Women's Issues (OCLC/Gale Group, 1992–)
Provides full-text access to worldwide information on women from more than 150 countries, bringing together such disciplines as sociology, psychology, health, education, and human rights. Updated biweekly, this database indexes books, journals, newsletters, research reports from nonprofit groups, government and international agencies, and fact sheets, with links to full-text articles.

GenderWatch (ProQuest, 1970–)
This unique full-text database, with archive material dating back to 1970, provides international coverage of women's and gender issues, including aging, body image, childbirth, child care, eating disorders, family, sexual harassment, social roles, the impact of gender and gender roles on the arts, business and work, crime, family, health care, politics, popular culture and media, religion, research and scholarship, and sports.

Human Nutrition (Cambridge Scientific Abstracts/SilverPlatter, 1982–)
Combining selected information from 14 databases, including MEDLINE, the Food Science and Technology Abstracts, and Cambridge Scientific Abstracts, this specialized database indexes scholarly journals targeting human nutrition and its impact on human health. Topics covered include food allergies and nutrition, food production, agriculture and meat industries, chemistry of food additives, nutritional evaluation of food products, and the effects of nutrition on human health.

Lexis/Nexis Academic Universe (LexisNexis, 1980s–   )
Covering a wide range of news, business, legal, and reference information, LexisNexis Academic also covers general medical and health topics. Searchable are full-text medical journals and newsletters including information on drug interactions, cancer, poison, disease, trauma, and medical administration, and medical abstracts from the National Library of Medicine's MEDLINE for more than 3.500 worldwide clinical and research journals dating back to 1966.

Wilson OmniFile Full Text (H.W. Wilson, Indexing: 1982; full text: 1994–   )
Multidisciplinary index providing abstracts and full text from five H.W. Wilson full-text databases: General Science Full Text, Humanities Full Text, Readers' Guide Full Text, Social Sciences Full Text, and Wilson Business Full Text. Indexing is from 1982, with full-text coverage from 1994 to the present. Beginning dates for abstracting, indexing, and availability of full-text articles varies by database. General science subjects covered include biology, food, genetics, health and medicine, nutrition, and physiology. In the area of social sciences, the database indexes such topics as community health and medical care, family studies, gender studies, and gerontology.

SELECTED PERIODICALS

In addition to consulting indexes and abstracts and full-text databases, you may also find the need to peruse academic journals specializing in a particular field of study. The following is a sample listing of top journals in their specialty available in print or online.

Abstracts in Social Gerontology: Current Literature on Aging (New York: The National Council on the Aging, 1963–90; Newbury Park, Calif.: SAGE Publications, 1990–   , quarterly)
Compiled by the National Council on the Aging (NCOA) and published by Sage Publications, this leading quarterly journal offers abstracts and bibliographies of major articles, books, government reports, legislative research studies, and other materials. Contents of each publication cover all aspects of gerontology, including demography, economics, family relations, institutional care, mental health, societal attitudes, work, and retirement.

Age and Ageing (London: Oxford University Press/British Geriatrics Society, 1972–   , bi-monthly)
A publication of the British Geriatrics Society, this international journal features expertly written articles and reviews on geriatric medicine and gerontology. Coverage includes such subjects as research on aging, and clinical, epidemiological, and psychological aspects of later life. Free articles are available at the Oxford Journals Online Web site (http://ageing.oupjournals.org/). Articles also can be searched, and records include table of contents from May 1972 to August 1974, abstracts from November 1974 to December 1998, and full-text articles from January 1999 to the present. Contents of the journal are covered by several major online indexing services, including BIOSIS, MEDLINE, and Science Citation Index.

Ageing and Society (Cambridge; New York: Cambridge University Press/The Centre for Policy on Aging/The British Society of Gerontology, 1981– , bi-monthly)
The official journal of the Centre for Policy on Ageing and the British Society of Gerontology, this world-renowned interdisciplinary journal, published by Cambridge University Press, features scholarly papers on a broad range of subject areas advancing the understanding of the social and cultural aspects of human aging. Available by subscription through Cambridge Journals Online, the journal also includes an extensive section of book reviews and regular updates on research in the field. Issued six times yearly, occasional special issues on important topics are likewise published.

Archives of Gerontology and Geriatrics (Amsterdam: Elsevier Biomedical Press, 1982– , bi-monthly)
Launched in May 1982, the *Archives of Gerontology and Geriatrics* is a leading professional journal published six times yearly that publishes papers by specialists dealing with experimental gerontology and clinical and social geriatrics. Papers offer new information and results from clinical studies pertaining to social aspects of geriatrics, the epidemiology of aging, health care of the elderly, and the aging of human cells, tissues, and organs. Available online through Elsevier Science Direct, a popular information database, articles are also abstracted and indexed through many other leading library databases, including BIOSIS, Chemical Abstracts, PsycINFO, and Psychological Abstracts.

Educational Gerontology (London: Taylor & Francis, Ltd., 1976– , eight times a year)
This international journal offers authoritative articles on the most current research in the fields of gerontology, adult education, and the social and behavioral sciences for those in the field of educational gerontology. Published eight times per year, abstracts and full-text articles can be found in Academic Search Premier (1993–), Ingenta Select (1999–), and abstracts only in Educational Research Abstracts (ERA) online.

Geriatrics (Cleveland, Ohio: Advanstar Communications, 1946– , monthly)
Published by Advanstar Communications since January 1946, *Geriatrics* is a peer-reviewed journal dedicated to providing primary care physicians with the latest articles on the care of patients over the age of 45. This award-winning monthly journal features in-depth clinical reviews, current abstracts from the top 50 medical research journals, Continuing Medical Education articles, and much more. Past journals are referenced in the Index Medicus (1966–), with full-text articles available through Academic Search Premier (1993–).

Journal of Aging Studies (Greenwich, Conn.: JAI Press, 1987– , quarterly)
In existence for more than 13 years, this scholarly journal highlights new interpretations, findings, theories, and innovations pertinent to aging. Full-text articles and summaries of previously published articles are available by subscription through Elsevier Science Direct from 1995 to the present. Articles are also cited and/or indexed in several leading indexes and databases

available through most libraries, including Abstracts in Social Gerontology; Age-Line; Articles 1st; Arts & Humanities Citation Index; Psychological Abstracts; Social & Behavioral Sciences; Social Science Citation Index; Social Science Index; and Sociological Abstracts.

Journal of Mental Health and Aging (New York: Springer Publishing Co., 1995– , quarterly) (http://www.springerpub.com/)
Designed for mental health professionals engaged in research, training, clinical care, and social services, as well as law and policy, this peer-reviewed quarterly journal is a major source of timely information, including current research findings, aging studies, policy analysis and innovations in mental health care. The journal and its current and past content are indexed and abstracted in many popular library indexes and databases, including Abstracts in Social Gerontology, Current Literature on Aging, AgeLine, CINAHL, PsycINFO, PsycLIT, Public Affairs Information Services (PAIS), Social Gerontology Abstracts, Social Services Abstracts, Social Work Abstracts, and Sociological Abstracts.

Journal of Nutrition for the Elderly (New York: Haworth Press, Inc., 1980– , quarterly)
This peer-reviewed journal, published quarterly, features lots of useful information about the importance of nutrition and nutrition education for older adults. Articles are based on published research papers from experts in a variety of fields in the biological and social sciences examining the role of nutrition in disease prevention and management, functional performance, and quality of life for older adults.

Journal of Women & Aging (New York: Haworth Press, 1989– , quarterly)
This multidisciplinary quarterly of psychosocial practice, theory, and research shares the knowledge of professionals who are concerned about aging and women. Full-text access and abstracts and indexing of past issues are provided by several library databases, including Academic Search Elite, AgeLine, CINAHL, Expanded Academic ASAP, and many others.

The Journals of Gerontology Series A: Biological Sciences and Medical Sciences (Springfield, Ill.; Washington, D.C.: The Gerontological Society of America, 1946– , monthly)
The Gerontological Society of America publishes two monthly peer-reviewed electronic journals devoted the study of different fields of gerontology, the *Journal of Gerontology: Biological Sciences,* and the *Journal of Gerontology: Medical Sciences.*

Biological Sciences covers all aspects of aging, such as biochemistry, endocrinology, exercise, genetics, nutrition, physiology, and biological underpinnings of late-life diseases.

Medical Sciences publishes articles discussing various medical sciences pertaining to aging, such as clinical epidemiology, clinical research, and health services research for professions including medicine, dentistry, allied health sciences, and nursing. Articles share original research pertinent to human biology and disease as well.

The contents of each journal are accessible without charge from the society's Web site (http://biomed.gerontologyjournals.org/contents-by-date.0.

shtml). This includes the most recent editions, as well as searchable abstracts of journals from January 1995 to December 1999, PDF and abstracts from January 2000 to February 2000, and full-text articles and abstracts from March 2000 to April 2004.

Psychology and Aging (Arlington, Va.: American Psychological Association, 1986– , quarterly)
Published quarterly by the American Psychological Association, Inc., this psychological journal reports on applied, biobehavioral, clinical, education, experimental and psychosocial research concerning adult development and aging. Besides emphasizing original research, articles also offer theoretical analyses, practical clinical problems, or policy as well as critical reviews of a content area.

Research on Aging (Thousand Oaks, Calif.: SAGE Publications, 1979– , bimonthly)
For more than two decades, this outstanding journal has covered the most current knowledge on critical issues facing the elderly of interest to scholars, researchers, and professionals alike. Peer-reviewed articles in each issue examine a wide range of issues, practical research findings, future directions in the field, age demographics, age discrimination, age and inequality, aging and social stress, Alzheimer's disease, and migration patterns of the elderly. Full-text articles and abstracts are available through EBSCOHost (1999–) and Ingenta (1999–).

SELECTED WEB SITES

The Age Concern Institute of Gerontology (http://www.kcl.ac.uk/kis/schools/life_sciences/health/gerontology/index.php)
Founded in 1986, the Age Concern Institute of Gerontology (ACIOG) promotes the study of aging and old age with particular emphasis on interdisciplinary research. The institute's Web site offers free access to the latest reports from experts and gerontology data.

HCFA: Health Care Financing Administration (http://www.cms.hhs.gov/default.asp?fromhcfadotgov=true)
The Centers for Medicare and Medicaid Services (CMS) is a federal agency within the U.S. Department of Health and Human Services. It is responsible for such programs as Medicare and Medicaid. Available through the CMS's Web site is a host of information related to aging, including coverage, quality initiatives, and statistics and data.

Resources in Social Gerontology (http://www.trinity.edu/~mkearl/geron.html)
This online directory features a large variety of resources with links covering all aspects of gerontology, including general references, academies, institutes, centers of study, and other vital sources of knowledge and information.

SeniorNet (http://www.seniornet.org/php/default.php)
Providing education for and access to computer technologies for senior citizens and older adults, this international nonprofit organization, based in San

Francisco, was born out of a research project funded by the Markle Foundation in 1986. It supports more than 240 learning centers throughout the United States and abroad. The group's Web site features instructional materials, research, and hundreds of discussion topics on older adults and technology.

Senior Women Web (http://www.seniorwomen.com/)
One-stop source of information covering news and issues, culture and arts, health, fitness, and style, and relationships related to senior women.

Business and Economics

In the vast field of business and economics, finding timely background information and data is vitally important. Your quest for information may include researching a major Fortune 500 company, basic concepts and strategies of business or economics, or current business or economic trends. No matter what your purpose is, a wealth of business sources is available in a variety of formats on all aspects of business, economics, finance, and related disciplines.

Among the potential list of sources are printed references and directories, periodical indexes with citations and abstracts of published articles, full-text scholarly and popular journals, and electronic sources, including online databases and Web sites. Each is useful for finding pertinent facts and histories, profiles of key business figures, historical and economic data, terms and definitions, details about concepts and practices, emerging markets and developing countries, and information on practically any for-profit or nonprofit corporation or other business throughout the world. You can also find comparative market share information and market data on products and brands, demographic information, research about economic conditions and market conditions, corporate and investment news, and annual reports of major publicly held companies. Based on the recommendations of librarians, researchers, and specialists in their fields, the following lists highlight some good sources of information in the study of business and economics today.

SELECTED BOOKS AND REFERENCES

General Resources

Fitzroy Dearborn Encyclopedia of Banking and Finance, 10th Ed., edited by Charles J. Woelfel, 1,220 pages (Chicago: Fitzroy Dearborn, 1998)
This revised edition includes 4,200 entries, including 2,000 new additions, providing complete definitions of thousands of basic banking, business, and financial terms, and other relevant information such as analyses of recent trends, historical background, and statistical data, as well as laws and regulations.

Encyclopedia of Business Information Sources, 19th Ed., 1,234 pages (Detroit: Gale Research, 2004)
Alphabetically arranged by subject, this useful resource lists primary sources for business information—electronic, print, and live sources—under indus-

tries and business concepts and practice. This encyclopedia covers a wealth of resources within each subject, including databases, directories, indexes, newsletters, and research centers. E-mail addresses and Web page addresses are provided with most entries.

International Encyclopedia of the Stock Market, edited by Michael Sheimo, 2 vols. (Chicago: Fitzroy Dearborn, 1998)
The first authoritative work of its kind, this encyclopedia provides relevant information and definitions on more than 2,000 terms covering the history and practices of the international stock market. Entries pertain to industrialized and developing countries, individuals, banks, brokerage and leveraged buyout firms, events, and slang terms.

Handbooks, Directories, and Yearbooks

Directory of Corporate Affiliations, 8 vols. (Skokie, Ill.: National Register Publishing, 1973–2001; New Providence, N.J.: LexisNexis, 2002–)
Billing itself as "the most trusted guide to corporate linkage in the U.S. and worldwide," this comprehensive source, in print for more than 30 years, provides extensive details on more than 131,000 parent companies, affiliates, subsidiaries, and divisions. The eight-volume set makes it easy to research public and private firms in the United States, companies around the globe and their links to U.S. companies, and manufacturers and parent companies of products or services. With this directory, you also can research a given industry, individual executives of a specific company, the net worth and sales data of businesses, key contact information and personnel, and much more. In 2002, LexisNexis acquired the series, offering it online by subscription under the name LexisNexis Corporate Affiliations.

Dun & Bradstreet Million Dollar Directory (New York: Dun & Bradstreet, Inc., 1959–)
This annual directory provides a wealth of information about America's leading corporations, including the names, addresses, and phone numbers, annual sales volume, total number of employees, names, titles, and functions of officers and directors, sticker symbol and stock exchange information, and more.

The Europa World Yearbook, 44th Ed. (London: Europa Publications, 2003)
An excellent source for social, political, and economic information, this international yearbook covers more than 250 countries and territories and more than 1,650 international organizations. Individual surveys offer historical, governmental, and economic data on countries and territories. Contents are also accessible online through the publisher's Web site (http://www.europaworld.com/) by subscription.

Financial Yellow Book, 900 pages (New York: Leadership Directories, 2005)
Up-to-date directory, first published in 1992, that contains information on leading U.S. financial institutions, including brokerage firms, consumer finance companies, mortgage companies, private investment firms, and securities underwriters and venture capital firms.

Hoover's Handbook of American Business, 15th Ed., 1,005 pages (Austin, Tex.: Hoover's Business Press, 2005)
This comprehensive volume contains in-depth coverage of 750 of the largest and most influential U.S. companies, from corporate giants to more than 50 of the largest privately owned companies. This valuable reference covers personalities, events, and strategies that have made each company tops in its field. In addition, it includes 60 pages of business lists, including the Fortune 500 list of the largest U.S. corporations, *Software Magazine*'s top 50 software companies and *Advertising Age*'s top 50 media companies.

Hoover's Handbook of Private Companies 2005, 10th Ed., 558 pages (Austin, Tex.: Hoover Business Press, 2005)
Hoover's Handbook of Private Companies presents information about 900 nonpublic U.S. enterprises, including large industrial and service corporations, hospitals and health care organizations, charitable and membership organizations, mutual and cooperative organizations, joint ventures, government-owned corporations, and major university systems. Entries range from 200 in-depth profiles to 700 shorter entries. The book also lists companies ranked by sales and by number of employees, plus the fastest-growing private companies.

Hoover's Handbook of World Business 2004, 10th Ed., 486 pages (Austin, Tex.: Hoover's, 2004)
Hoover's Handbook of World Business profiles hundreds of the most influential public, private, and state-owned companies headquartered in Canada, Europe, and Japan and in emerging countries, such as Brazil, China, and Taiwan. This handy reference offers detailed profiles of 300 companies from these regions, and includes lists of the top global companies from *Fortune* and other publications.

International Directory of Company Histories, 74 vols. (Detroit: St. James Press/Gale Group, 2005)
Unrivaled in its breadth of coverage, this 74-volume work, first published in 1988, brings together detailed histories of the world's 4,550 largest and most influential companies. Each entry provides a complete overview, from three to five pages, of the subject, based on popular magazines, academic periodicals, books, annual reports, and the archives of the companies themselves. Discussed in detail are the company founders; major milestones, including expansions/losses and labor/management actions; principal competitors; statistics; names of key players; and more. Volumes 1 through 6 cover major industries arranged alphabetically; Volumes 7 through 74 cover companies by name, listed alphabetically within each volume. A cumulative index is included in each volume.

Moody's Industrial Manual (New York: Moody's Investor Service, Inc., 1954–2000; New York: Mergent, 2001–)
Annually updated manual offering full financial reports for every industrial corporation listed on the New York Stock Exchange, American Stock Exchange, and regional exchanges. Entries also feature company histories, background, and information regarding mergers and acquisitions, subsidiaries, principal plants and properties. Published as *Moody's Industrial*

Manual by Moody's Investor Service from 1954 to 2000, the title was changed to the *Mergent Industrial Manual* beginning in 2001.

Nelson's Directory of Investment Research, 2 vols. (Port Chester, N.Y.: Nelson Research, 2000)
This annual two-volume directory profiles more than 19,000 publicly traded companies around the world. Also includes information on investment research firms and investment analysts.

Standard & Poor's Corporation Records (New York: Standard & Poor's Corp., 1941–99)
Published annually since 1941, this authoritative reference offered comprehensive financial histories of 9,000 public companies. Standard & Poor's ceased publication of this reference in 1999.

Standard & Poor's Register of Corporations, Directors, and Executives, United States and Canada, 3 vols. (New York: Standard & Poor's Corp., 1973–)
Three-volume set featuring corporate profiles, brief biographical information about corporate directors and executives, and SIC listings, updated annually.

Standard & Poor's Stock Reports: New York Stock Exchange, American Stock Exchange, Nasdaq Stock Market and Regional Exchanges (New York: Standard & Poor's Corp., 1998–)
Authoritative reference featuring two-page reports on 4,000 public companies and actively traded stocks for all stock exchanges. Entries include business summaries, financial and historical data, trends, and prospects for actively traded stocks. Includes seven-year income and balance sheet data for each company as well. Beginning in 1998, Standard & Poor's combined the information for all public companies and stock exchanges into one reference. Previously, they were published as separate annuals. Titles include *Standard & Poor's Stock Reports: American Stock Exchange* (February 1973–October 1997); *Standard & Poor's Stock Reports: Nasdaq and Regional Exchanges* (June 1994–December 1997); *Standard & Poor's Stock Reports: New York Stock Exchange* (January 1977–November 1997); and *Standard & Poor's Stock Reports: Over the Counter* (March 1973–March 1994).

Thomas Register of American Manufacturers, 90th Ed., 31 vols. (New York: Thomas Publishing Company, 2000)
First published in 1905, this 31-volume reference provides complete contact information, including addresses, phone, fax, and toll-free numbers, names of subsidiaries, sales offices and corporate affiliations, on more than 165,000 U.S and Canadian manufacturers, including separate product and service headings that make it easy to track brand names of manufacturers. Also available on CD-ROM and DVD-ROM.

The U.S. Industry and Trade Outlook 2000, 960 pages (New York: McGraw-Hill, 2001)
Also offered on CD-ROM, this foremost reference on business and economics, prepared jointly by the International Trade Administration of the U.S. Department of Commerce and the publisher, offers a comprehensive and

revealing snapshot of U.S. trade and industry as of 1999. Combining industry-specific data and detailed studies from the government and private sector, this latest edition features analyses of the major U.S. industries and sectors, industry-specific outlooks for international trade, and discussions of domestic and global economic actions. Also included are 650 easy-to-read tables and charts, hundreds of industry reviews, analyses, and forecasts, and geographical snapshots of industry and trade trends.

Ward's Business Directory of U.S. Private and Public Companies, 48th Ed., 8 vols. and supplement (Detroit: Gale Group, 2005)
An invaluable eight-volume reference that features thousands of updated company and industry profiles, including analyses of market position, specific data on companies, and parent company and subsidiary relationships.

SELECTED ARTICLE INDEXES AND ABSTRACTS

Printed Indexes and Abstracts

Business Periodicals Index (New York: H.W. Wilson, 1958–)
First printed in 1958, this index covers nearly 350 journals in business, finance, investment, accounting, insurance, labor and management, and economics. Titles indexed include general business magazines, financial publications, and trade journals.

Economic Literature Index (Nashville, Tenn.: American Economic Association, 1969–)
Another popular printed source, this index cites articles from more than 340 journals in economics.

Index of Economic Articles (Homewood, Ill.: R.D. Irwin, Inc., 1961–)
Annual reference, formerly called *Index of Economic Journals* and prepared under the auspices of the American Economic Association, that indexes 350 research and scholarly journals on economics from 1886 to 1983. An online version from 1969 to the present is also offered.

NewsBank Index (New Canaan, Conn.: NewsBank, Inc., 1982–)
Indexes articles available in microform focusing on socioeconomic, political, international, and scientific topics from more than 100 U.S. newspapers.

New York Times Index (New York: New York Times Co., 1899–)
This index lists stories available on microfilm under subject heading and uses phrases instead of article titles.

The Wall Street Journal Index (New York: Dow Jones & Co., 1957– ; Wooster, Ohio: Newspaper Indexing Center, Micro Photo Division, Bell & Howell Co., 1976–)
Principally used to find older articles on microfilm published since 1955, this large hardbound volume—divided into two sections, corporate news and general news—indexes articles by subject using phrases to describe each entry.

Web Indexes and Abstracts

ABI/Inform (OCLC First Search, 1971–)
Index of citations on business and management topics in U.S. and international publications.

Business Source Elite (EBSCOHost, 1985–)
This subscriber database indexes more than 1,100 journals in the fields of business, management, economics, banking, finance, and accounting.

Expanded Academic Index (InfoTrac, 1980–)
This Web-delivered database indexes business and related articles published in a variety of professional and newsstand publications searchable by journal title, scholarly, and full-text articles.

PAIS International (OCLC Public Affairs Information Service, 1972–)
Indexing the international literature of public and social policy, this database is a useful source of information on business, demographics, government, international relations, and more.

Periodical Abstracts (ProQuest, 1987–)
Indexes general and academic journals, some full text, covering business, current affairs, economics, literature, religion, psychology, women's studies, and others. Database is contained within ProQuest Direct.

SELECTED FULL-TEXT ARTICLE DATABASES

ABI/Inform (ProQuest, 1971–)
Covering nearly every aspect of business, including company histories and new product development, this database cites, with some full text, scholarly articles about research in business and management from almost 1,800 international business publications, including full text of *The Wall Street Journal.*

Academic Search Elite (EBSCOHost, Indexing: 1980– , full text: 1990–)
Devoted to all subject areas Academic Search Elite offers full-text sources for business and business-related articles from professional and popular publications.

Business NewsBank (NewsBank, 1993–)
This subject-specific database contains selected full-text articles from the business sections of almost 500 local, regional, and national business news publications in the U.S. and Canada, daily newspapers, and local business weeklies, including information on small companies generally available elsewhere. In addition, this electronic database provides complete coverage of selected business newswire services.

Business Source Elite (EBSCOHost, 1984–)
Indexes citations and full-text articles from 930 journals and magazines covering banking, business, economics, finance, management, and more. Includes full-text access to previously published articles in *Business Week, Forbes, Harvard Business Review,* and *The Wall Street Journal.*

Business Source Elite (NewsBank, 1996–)
Covering global news, this database provides direct access to some 400,000 fully indexed full-text articles from more than 1,000 news sources, including international newspapers and wire services, broadcasts, news agency transmissions, magazines, and government documents.

EconLit (American Economic Association, 1969–)
Produced by the American Economic Association, this database features citations and abstracts for journals, books, dissertations, and working papers related to economics, and full-text of the *Journal of Economic Literature.*

Factiva (Dow Jones, current)
This Internet-based database (formerly known as Dow Jones Interactive) provides in-depth business and financial research, including full-text information from major newspapers and business magazines.

Investext Plus (Gale Group, 1998–)
Provides access to analytical research reports on companies and industries from more than 500 major investment banks and brokerage firms worldwide. Also includes Mergent company and history and debt reports and trade association reports from more than 50 major industries.

LexisNexis Academic Business (LexisNexis, 1972–)
Extensively covers U.S. and international business news and trade publications, including company, industry, and market news, financial information, accounting literature, country reports and country analyses, and biographical information on leading business executives from popular references. Also searchable by company name and SIC code are international company reports, stock reports, bankruptcy reports, Hoover's company reports, Standard & Poor's corporate descriptions, disclosure reports, and annual reports (from 1972 to 1995).

LexisNexis Academic Universe (LexisNexis, 1977–)
Fully indexed full-text database covering a variety of categories, including business, industry, and market news, accounting, financial filings, and trade show information directory, and components of the LexisNexis Business database.

Mergent Online (LexisNexis, 1993–)
Formerly called FIS Online, this subject-specific database offers detailed, full-text business and financial information for 23,000 U.S. and international companies, including fact sheets with business descriptions and company overviews, financial statements (downloadable to spreadsheet software), SEC filings (real-time and archived to 1993), and prospectuses for 2,000 U.S. companies. This database also provides easy access to current and historical annual reports, hard-to-get, timely annual reports on international companies, fully illustrated research reports from over 500 brokerage and independent research firms, and much more.

Periodical Abstracts Research II Edition with Full Text (UMI ProQuest, 1986–)
This reference source provides abstracts and some full-text articles from more than 1,600 academic journals, popular magazines, and key business

publications, including 239 general-interest publications and 212 business titles.

ScienceDirect (Elsevier Science, 1995–)
This large full-text electronic collection of science, technology and medical journals published by Elsevier Science also includes many journals in the fields of business and finance since 1995, as well as back files to older articles.

Wall Street Journal (Wall Street Journal, 1986–)
In-depth coverage of national and international finance with access to full-text articles from this leading financial publication from 1986 to the present.

SELECTED PERIODICALS

American Banker (New York: American Banker, 1887– , daily)
A "must read" for those studying banking and related disciplines, this daily newspaper, aimed at professionals in American banking, features current news and timely articles covering all levels and all areas of banking and financial services. Coverage includes banking regulations, mergers and acquisitions, investment products and services, profiles of banks, and commentary and analysis.

Barron's National Business and Financial Weekly (Boston, Mass.: H. Bancroft, 1921–42; Barron's, 1942–94; Chicopee, Mass.: Dow Jones & Co., 1994– , weekly)
Covering U.S. business and financial markets, *Barron's* is a useful source of information for investment statistics and analysis of companies, market trends, and market conditions for personal investors and investment professionals

Business Week (New York: McGraw-Hill, 1929– , weekly)
This popular business magazine provides well-researched and well-written articles including profiles of companies, analysis of company performance and industries, and more. Full text is accessible through LexisNexis and Dow Jones News/Retrieval (1993–).

The Economist (London: Economist Newspaper Ltd., 1843– , weekly)
Established in 1843, *The Economist,* published weekly, covers all aspects of free trade and free markets with expertly written articles that are easy to understand.

Forbes (New York: Forbes, Inc., 1917– , biweekly)
This influential financial magazine covers a wide range of business and economic news, focused mostly on the industry leaders, with articles written for a general business audience. Full-text coverage is available through LexisNexis (1983–).

Fortune (New York: Time, Inc., 1930– , biweekly)
Known for its annual rankings of the "top 500" companies, the highest-paid executives, and more, *Fortune* magazine, first published in February 1930, covers business, investing, and personal finance. Articles include profiles of

companies and executives, current management trends, and the performance of smaller companies and market segments. Full text is accessible through LexisNexis (1983–).

Harvard Business Review (Boston: Graduate School of Business Administration, Harvard University, 1922– , bimonthly)
Published since 1922, this leading bimonthly business journal emphasizes articles about management strategies, practices, policies, and techniques written by leading academic and business writers.

Money (New York: Time, Inc., 1972– , monthly)
Written for the consumer, *Money* provides helpful articles and information devoted to personal investing and retirement, and advice and tips on all types of investments, tax saving plans, and more for readers of all income levels.

Monthly Labor Review (Washington, D.C.: Government Printing Office, 1915– , monthly)
First published in 1915, this journal of fact, analysis, and research from the U.S. Bureau of Labor Statistics reports on everything concerning labor and the U.S. work force, bringing together top economists, statisticians, and experts from the private sector and others. Each issue covers a broad range of subjects, including the economy, employment, inflation, productivity, occupational injuries and illnesses, wages, prices, and many more.

Occupational Outlook Quarterly (Washington, D.C.: U.S. Department of Labor, Bureau of Labor Statistics in cooperation with the Veterans Administration, 1958– , quarterly)
Identifies labor trends for occupations and industries. Jobs with strong growth potential are regularly highlighted.

The Wall Street Journal (New York: Dow Jones & Co., 1889– , weekdays)
Known for its investigative reporting, *The Wall Street Journal,* the longest-running business journal in the United States today, is an excellent source of in-depth coverage of business, economic, and political news. Each issue offers expert analysis, opinions, and timely information about major and emerging companies, plus special features on a wide array of relevant topics.

SELECTED WEB SITES

Bureau of Economic Analysis (http://www.bea.doc.gov/)
An agency of the U.S. Department of Commerce, the Bureau of Economic Analysis publishes national, industry, international, and regional economic data.

Current Economic Conditions (http://www.federalreserve.gov/FOMC/BeigeBook/2004/)
This report, known as the "Beige Book" and published eight times a year, summarizes the current economic conditions in each district of the Federal Reserve Bank. Each report features interviews with economists, market experts, and other sources of each region. Reports from 1996 to the present are accessible at this site.

Econ Data and Links (http://zimmer.csufresno.edu/~johnsh/econ/econ_EDL.htm)
Extensively covers current U.S. and world economic data in table format, with links to related data, as well as a directory of other Web sites covering a wide range of subject areas.

Federal Reserve Economic Data (FRED) (http://research.stlouisfed.org/fred2/)
Created by St. Louis Federal Reserve District, the Federal Reserve Economic Data, also known as FRED, presents a myriad of historical U.S. economic and financial data. Items include daily U.S. interest rates, exchange rates, business and monetary indicators, regional economic data, and the balance of the Federal Reserve.

The Library of Congress Country Studies (http://lcweb2.loc.gov/frd/cs/cshome.html)
This site offers detailed analysis about the economic, political, national, and social security systems and institutions of countries around the world.

Monthly Labor Review (http://stats.bls.gov/opub/mlr/mlrhome.htm)
Online version of the printed journal of the same name containing abstracts, excerpts, and full-text articles, in PDF form, plus monthly statistics on employment and earnings nationwide.

Resources for Economists on the Internet (http://econwpa.wustl.edu/EconFAQ/EconFAQ.html)
Sponsored by the American Economic Association, this directory lists more than 1,487 resources in 97 sections and subsections available on the Internet for those interested in or studying economics.

Statistical Abstract of the United States (http://www.census.gov/statab/www)
Indexes a wide range of statistics and economic indicators in tabular format, including basic statistics, specific table numbers, plus the source of the statistics for further reference.

Survey of Current Business (http://www.bea.doc.gov/bea/pubs.htm)
This statistical series covers monthly, quarterly, and annual statistics for the previous two years, cyclical for such areas as business sales and inventories, commodity prices, earnings, industrial productivity, labor force, personal income, and much more.

Treasury Bulletin (http://www.fms.treas.gov/bulletin/index.html)
Reporting on the fiscal operations of the federal government, this site offers vital statistics on the federal debt, bonds, notes, market yield, and other federal financial obligations. In addition, the report fully details positions of major foreign currencies, the state of the domestic economy, the most current growth rate of the gross domestic product, the latest rate of personal savings, and the federal deficit.

World Development Indicators (http://www.worldbank.org/data/countrydata/countrydata.html)
Compiled for World Bank member countries, this site contains timely statistics on national accounts, international transactions, manufacturing, and monetary indicators around the world.

Criminal Justice

The administration of justice includes criminal law, constitutional law, individual rights, and procedures and evidence. Sources of information on criminal justice can include dictionaries, encyclopedias, handbooks, and general references. The following is a list of selected books, article indexes and abstracts, full-text databases, periodicals, and Web sites suitable for your use.

SELECTED BOOKS AND REFERENCES

The Encyclopedia of American Crime, 2nd Ed., by Carl Sifakis, 2 vols., 1,204 pages (New York: Facts On File, 2001)
This revised and updated illustrated reference features 2,000 A-to-Z entries detailing crimes, criminals, and law enforcement figures from the Salem, Massachusetts, witchcraft trials to more recent court cases and crimes such as the O. J. Simpson trial, the Jean Harris trial, the Oklahoma City bombing, and more. Entries include biographies, terms and definitions, and summaries of criminal activities, ranging from a paragraph to more than a page in length.

Encyclopedia of Crime and Justice, 2nd Ed., edited by Joshua Dressler, 4 vols., 1,780 pages (New York: Macmillan Reference USA, 2001)
This revised second edition of the 1982 first edition is an authoritative, interdisciplinary source of information covering the legal, sociological, psychological, historical, and economic aspects of crime and justice worldwide. Highly recommended for college and university libraries, law schools, and students studying criminology, each entry in this worthwhile reference covers a myriad of relevant topics, including such civil and criminal issues as rape, domestic violence, and terrorism. Entries discussing legal cases also include a bibliography of sources for further study. Among the appendixes is a glossary of terms.

Encyclopedia of Crime and Punishment, edited by David Levinson, 4 vols., 2,104 pages (Thousand Oaks, Calif.: SAGE Publications, 2002)
This unique hefty four-volume set features 430 signed entries, based on numerous sources, about a wide range of topics of interest to students and teachers alike. Volume 1 covers "Careers in Criminal Justice," Volume 2, "Web Resources," Volume 3, "Professional and Scholarly Organizations," and Volume 4, "Selected Bibliography," as well as a chronology of events in criminal justice from 1795 to the present.

The Encyclopedia of Serial Killers, by Michael Newton, 400 pages (New York: Facts On File, 2000)
Including case histories, individual essays, and exhaustive overviews, this volume examines the world of serial killers. Entries provide in-depth coverage of related topics, including contributing factors to the development of serial killers, law enforcement techniques, court cases, major criminal activities, popular myths depicted in film and television, key law enforcement figures, current practices of punishment, and much more.

The Encyclopedia of World Crime: Criminal Justice, Criminology, and Law Enforcement, edited by Jay Robert Nash, 6 vols. (Wilmette, Ill.: CrimeBooks, 1989, 1990)
This illustrated six-volume reference set features 23,000 entries that cover "the most noted and historically significant crimes and criminals." Included with the set are a biographical and subject names index, and a subject index for the 341 categories of criminal activity.

The Oxford Handbook of Criminology, 3rd Ed., edited by Mike Maguire, Rod Morgan and Robert Reiner, 1,350 pages (New York: Oxford University Press, 2002)
The third edition of this authoritative and comprehensive source, substantially revised and updated since the previous edition, expertly covers many key topics of criminology and includes references for further research. Providing critical and theoretical discussion, the book, featuring articles written by many leading writers in the field, surveys a broad spectrum of criminology and criminal justice topics, from crime statistics and the criminal justice system to the media and crime. Each chapter includes not only a bibliography of sources but also links to other criminal justice sites.

Research Methods in Criminal Justice and Criminology, 6th Ed., 528 pages (Boston, Mass.: Allyn & Bacon, 2003)
Considered a classic in its field, the latest edition of this best-selling textbook features examples of research in criminal justice, teaching students the art of research with readings that include a variety of actual research studies on the subject of criminal justice and criminology.

SELECTED ARTICLE INDEXES AND ABSTRACTS

Printed Indexes and Abstracts

Criminal Justice Abstracts (Monsey, N.Y.: Willow Tree Press, 1977–)
Print equivalent of the Web database indexing hundreds of journals in the field of criminal justice since 1977.

Index to Canadian Legal Periodical Literature (Montreal: Canadian Association of Law Libraries, 1956–)
Fully bilingual (English and French) bibliographic reference that comprehensively indexes secondary legal periodicals, articles related to law in non-legal Canadian journals, articles published in topical law reports, collected essays, and cassettes. Features author and subject indexes with complete bibliographic information, a book review index, and a table of cases.

Index to Foreign Legal Periodicals (Berkeley, Calif.: University of California Press/American Association of Law Libraries, 1960–)
First published by the Institute of Advanced Legal Studies at the University of London in 1960, this annual index covers articles and book reviews published in 520 English-language legal journals worldwide. Coverage also includes collections of legal essays, congress reports, and such areas as public and private international law, foreign law, and jurisdictions other than the United States, the United Kingdom, Canada, and Australia. Indexed by author, subject, country, or region since 1958.

Index to Legal Periodicals and Books (New York: H.W. Wilson, 1908–)
The most significant index of legal periodical literature from 1908 to 1980, this print companion (originally called the *Index to Legal Periodicals*) to the online database indexes more than 600 legal journals and periodicals by subject. Excluded are legal newspapers, newsletters, and some journals covered in other popular Web databases, such as Current Law Index and LegalTrac. The index is also available on CD-ROM and online with coverage from 1981 to the present.

Index to Periodical Articles Related to Law (Dobbs Ferry, N.Y.: Glandville, 1958–)
Since publication of its first volume in September 1958, this annual compendium has indexed periodicals in subject areas related to law, such as social science and business.

An Index to Legal Periodical Literature (Boston: Boston Book Co.; Los Angeles: Parker and Baird Co.; Buffalo: Dennis, 1786–1937)
Also known as the *Jones-Chipman Index to Legal Periodical Literature* (named after its editors), this six-volume set was the first to comprehensively index American legal periodicals from the early 19th century to 1937. The reference series includes 98,254 citations from 590 general periodical titles, 236 legal periodical titles, and 67 law report titles, in 11,000 volumes. Four volumes of *An Index to Legal Periodical Literature,* from 1786 to 1922, are now available in a searchable format online through the 19th Century Masterfile database.

Shepard's Law Review Citations, 2 vols. with supplements (Colorado Springs, Colo.: Shepard's Citations, 1968–)
Updated with annual supplements, *Shepard's Federal Law Citations* covers citations to articles from legal periodicals of federal court cases since 1957. Articles published in state and regional reporter systems and some major law reviews are also cited. Law reviews and legal periodicals cited in the index are listed in alphabetical order by title. Articles are indexed from 19 law reviews, such as the *California Law Review* and the *Yale Law Journal.* Material from 1957 to 1993 is contained in two hardcover volumes, with additional citations featured in bound softcover supplements since 1994.

Web Indexes and Abstracts

Criminal Justice Abstracts (SAGE Publications, Inc., 1966–)
This Web-delivered database indexes 184 journals, including 45 with full-text articles, primarily focused on criminal justice topics, such as juvenile justice,

juvenile delinquency, crime prevention, police, courts, punishment, and sentencing. Criminal Justice Abstracts is available through several online database providers, including Cambridge Scientific Abstracts and Ovid.

Current Law Index (Information Access Corp., 1980–)
Arranged by subject, author, title, and case and statute name, Current Law Index provides citations to legal articles published since 1980, the same as LegalTrac. Cumulated every other year, the index does not include legal newspapers and some legal newsletters.

Index to Foreign Legal Periodicals (RLG, 1960–)
Similar to the print edition, this online version—part of the RLG Citation Resources database—indexes articles and book reviews from more 550 legal periodicals, the contents of 80 individually published collections of legal essays, festschrifts, melanges, and congressional reports, and a wide range of legal journals. Excluded are materials related to the laws of the United States and the United Kingdom.

Index to Legal Periodicals Full Text (H.W. Wilson, 1981–)
This reference resource, originally begun as a printed index more than 50 years ago, offers full-text coverage of all aspects of the law. With coverage of periodicals from the United States, Canada, Great Britain, Northern Ireland, Australia, and New Zealand, this database provides access to books, book reviews, court decisions, jurisdictional surveys, scholarly articles, symposia, and more. That includes full text of more than 200 selected periodicals, indexing of 1,000 legal journals, law reviews, institutes, statutes, bar association publications, university publications, and government publications, and nearly 300 law reviews—more than any comparable database.

Legal Resource Index (LexisNexis/Westlaw, 1980–)
Available through LexisNexis and Westlaw, this database indexes approximately 850 law journals and periodicals published in the United States, Canada, the United Kingdom, Australia, and other major English-speaking countries. Featuring some of the same material as LegalTrac, coverage dates for most periodicals is since 1980. For periods before 1980, use the hardcover reference *Index to Legal Periodicals.*

LegalTrac (InfoTrac, 1980–)
This Internet database, available by subscription, offers indexing for all major law reviews, legal newspapers, specialty law publications, bar association journals, and thousands of law-related articles from general interest publications published in the United States. References are searchable by subject, author, and case and statute names. Selected full-text articles are included.

LexisNexis Statistical Universe (LexisNexis, 1973–)
Subject-specific bibliographic database that indexes and abstracts more than 100,000 state and federal government, association, research institute, international, and nongovernmental organization statistical publications. Some sources contain the full text of statistical tables or links to agency Web sites. The index is based on three statistical indexes: *American Statistical Index* (1973), covering U.S. government publications, *Statistical Reference Index* (1980–), featuring state, business and association publications, and the

Index to International Statistics (1983–), focusing on intergovernmental publications.

NCJRS Abstracts Database (National Criminal Justice Reference Service Abstracts, 1972–)
Key source for summaries of articles and reports on criminal justice. Provides summaries of criminal justice publications, including federal, state, and local government reports, books, research reports, journal articles, and unpublished research.

PAIS International (OCLC Public Affairs Information Service, 1972–)
Abstracts journal articles, books, statistical yearbooks, directories, conference proceedings, research reports, and government documents about domestic and international public policy with topics that include criminal justice and law.

PsycINFO (American Psychological Association, 1887–)
Indexes and abstracts articles about the psychological aspects of criminal social deviance from social and behavioral science journals. Includes full-text articles from more than 40 journals published by the American Psychological Association (1988–).

Social Services Abstracts (Cambridge Scientific Abstracts, 1980–)
This major sociology database abstracts and indexes journal articles, dissertations, and current research on criminal justice, social services, and related areas, including such issues as social welfare, social policy, and community development, from more than 1,600 periodicals.

Sociological Abstracts (Sociological Abstracts, Inc./Cambridge Scientific Abstracts, 1963–)
Leading bibliographic database that abstracts and indexes international literature in sociology and related disciplines in the social and behavioral sciences, including abstracts of journal articles and citations of book reviews from more than 1,809 publications, and abstracts of books, book chapters, dissertations, and conference papers. Records from k[illegible] journals in sociology (since 2001) include a list of references cited. Covers theoretical and applied sociology, social science, and policy science, plus sociological aspects of anthropology, gender studies, gerontology, family studies, health, race and ethnicity, psychology, social work, urban studies, and more.

SELECTED FULL-TEXT ARTICLE DATABASES

Academic Search Elite (EBSCOHost, indexing: 1980– , full text: 1990–)
Covers a wide range of academic areas, including general academic, general reference subjects, and the social sciences, including current and previous articles published in leading scholarly journals and newspapers, including *The Wall Street Journal, The New York Times,* and *The Christian Science Monitor.*

CQ Researcher (Congressional Quarterly, 1983–)
Provided by Congressional Quarterly, this online database features comprehensive full-text reports, complete with bibliographies, devoted to current

and controversial events and political or social issues. Each report presents a fair and balanced examination of all sides of the issues. Topics range from mandatory sentencing to school violence. Past articles are searchable by keywords, dates, and other criteria.

Criminology: SAGE Full-Text Collection (SAGE Publications, 1982–)
Full text of 15 journals published by SAGE and its affiliated companies, encompassing more than 4,100 articles covering such topics as corrections, criminal justice, family and domestic violence, forensic psychology, juvenile delinquency, juvenile justice, penology, and policing. This searchable database provides indexed summaries or abstracts, plus complete text of each journal article (in PDF format), from such publications as *Crime and Delinquency* (1984–), *Criminal Justice* (2001–), *Criminal Justice and Behavior* (1982–), *Criminal Justice Policy Review* (2000–), *Homicide Studies* (1997–), and many more.

Expanded Academic ASAP (InfoTrac, 1980–)
Offering balanced coverage of all academic disciplines, including the arts, humanities, social sciences, business, science, and technology, besides indexing more than 2,700 scholarly, trade, and general-interest journals, magazines, and newspapers with full-text coverage for 1,400 full-text titles, this database also covers a variety of criminal justice journals. They include *Crime and Delinquency* (1984–), *Crime and Justice* (1998–), *Crime, Law and Social Change* (1999–), *Criminal Justice and Behavior* (1997–), *Criminal Justice Ethics* (1983–) *Criminal Justice Review* (1998–), and *Criminology* (1984–).

HeinOnline (William S. Hein & Co., 1808–)
Produced by William S. Hein & Co., Inc., an American legal publisher for more than 80 years, HeinOnline provides full-text access to more than 400 international law journals, both current and historical. The subscription database is very useful for researching articles and journals from the early 19th century to the present that are not covered by Legal Resource Index, LexisNexis, or Westlaw. The collection includes core U.S. law journals, international law journals, treaties and agreements, U.S. Supreme Court literature, and more.

LexisNexis Academic Universe (LexisNexis, 1977–)
Especially strong in the area of law, this full-text database covers news, business, medical, and legal information from more than 5,000 sources, including major newspapers, magazines, federal and state court decisions, and law reviews.

Periodical Abstracts Research II Edition with Full Text (UMI ProQuest, 1986–)
Providing abstracts, indexing, and full-text articles from more than 1,600 academic journals, popular magazines, and leading business publications, the contents of this database also contain complete coverage of 635 periodicals related to the social sciences and 239 general-interest publications with articles on criminal justice and behavioral science.

PsycINFO (American Psychological Association, 1887–)
Indexes more than 1,300 psychology and psychological journals, books, dissertations, and technical reports in more than 25 languages, on such related disciplines as sociology, linguistics, law, physiology, and psychiatry.

UMI Dissertation Abstracts (UMI/Oryx Press, abstracts, 1980– , full text, 1997–)
With more than 1.4 million entries, the UMI Dissertation Abstracts database indexes seemingly every doctoral dissertation produced at accredited universities in the United States since 1861, with abstracts from 1980 to the present, and full-text material since 1997 on a variety of scholarly topics.

WilsonWeb (H.W. Wilson, 1982–)
Indexes approximately 3,800 periodicals, including many journals available in full text.

SELECTED PERIODICALS

The British Journal of Criminology (London: Stevens; Chicago, Ill.: Quadrangle Books, 1960– , bimonthly)
Considered one of the world's premier criminology journals, *The British Journal of Criminology,* in print since 1960 and available online, features peer-reviewed articles for professionals concerned with crime, law, criminal justice, politics, and penology that cut across all areas of criminology. Coverage includes an extensive book review section listing articles and official publications in criminology and related fields.

Full-text articles from September 1998 to the present and abstracts from January 1996 to June 1998 only are searchable through Oxford University Press Journals online (http://bjc.oupjournals.org/search.dtl). Abstracting and indexing of previous articles are also available through several leading library databases, including British Humanities Index, Criminal Justice Abstracts, Psychological Abstracts, PsycINFO, Social Sciences Citation Index, Sociological Abstracts, and many others.

Canadian Journal of Criminology and Criminal Justice (Ottawa, Ont.: Canadian Criminal Justice Association, 1958– , quarterly)
Published quarterly since 1958 by the Canadian Criminal Justice Association, this leading scientific journal, with subscribers in more than 35 countries, discusses all aspects of criminology through in-depth articles based on research and experimentation. Designed for justice administrators, researchers, practitioners, and academics, each issue covers criminological findings and opinions. Since its debut, this journal has experienced several name changes. For the first 12 issues, it was titled *Canadian Journal of Corrections*. Then, from volume 13 to volume 19, it was retitled *Canadian Journal of Criminology and Criminal Justice and Corrections*. The title changed again with volume 20, to the current title, *Canadian Journal of Criminology and Criminal Justice*. Tables of contents and abstracts of past issues and articles (1997–) can be found at the publisher's Web site (http://www.ccja-acjp.ca/en/cjc.html).

Corrections Today (Laurel, Md.: American Correctional Association, 1954– , seven times a year)

Originally titled the *American Journal of Correction* (1954–78), this professional journal, published seven times a year, covers every sector of the corrections and criminal justice fields. Some full-text articles are available through such popular library article databases and indexes as *Expanded Academic ASAP* (February 1993–) and *Reference Center Gold* (February 1993–).

Crime Times (Mesa, Ariz.: Wacker Foundation, 1995– , quarterly) (http://www.crime-times.org/)

Published quarterly by the Wacker Foundation, a nonprofit organization based in Mesa, Arizona, this newsletter shares the latest research and news regarding medical and scientific discoveries about "the biological aspect of crime and violence," including causes and treatment. Articles since the first issue, published in 1995, can be accessed online free of charge by title, subject, author, issue number, and full-page listing.

Crime and Delinquency (New York: National Council on Crime and Delinquency, 1960– , quarterly)

Published quarterly (January, April, July, and October) in association with the National Council on Crime and Delinquency, this thought-provoking professional journal for policy makers, scholars, administrators, and researchers addresses specific policy or program implications in the criminal justice field. Articles feature outstanding, balanced analysis of the social, political, and economic contents of criminal justice. Discussion also focuses on the victims, criminals, courts, and sanctions, research findings, program and policy implication, new directions in the field, and reviews of current criminal justice literature. Archived issues, including previous journal articles, are available through Ingenta (1999–).

Criminal Justice and Behavior (Beverly Hills, Calif.: SAGE Publications, 1974– , bimonthly)

The official publication of the American Association of Correctional Psychology, this bimonthly journal promotes scholarly discussion and evaluations, based on timely and theoretical research, of assessment, classification, intervention, prevention, and treatment programs designed to help correctional professionals. Articles are mostly aimed at advancing the knowledge and expertise of academic scholars and professionals involved in forensic psychology, with an emphasis on correctional psychology. Content also includes a wide range of insightful opinions and commentaries in response to previous published articles, and book reviews of important and related sources in the field. The journal is also available through several article databases, including ingenta (1999–).

Criminal Justice Ethics (New York: John Jay College of Criminal Justice, Institute for Criminal Justice Ethics, 1982– , semiannual)

This semiannual journal emphasizes ethical issues of interest to criminal justice professionals, lawyers and judges, philosophers, and the general public. Topics cover important issues in the courts, corrections, the police, and legal philosophy. To see a sample issue or its contents, visit: http://www.lib.jjay.cuny.edu/cje/.

Criminal Justice Policy Review (Indiana, Pa.: Indiana University of Pennsylvania, 1986– , quarterly)
Written by scholars and professionals, this multidisciplinary journal, published quarterly in association with Indiana University of Pennsylvania's Department of Criminology in the College of Humanities and Social Sciences, features articles, essays, research notes, interviews, and book reviews on the study of criminal justice policy based on experimental and nonexperimental approaches. Suited for criminologists, criminal justice researchers, sociologists, public administrators, scholars, practitioners, and students with an interest in criminal justice policy. A collection of article abstracts from the most recent issues can be found at the publication's Web site (http://www.chss.iup.edu/cr/CJPR/Abstract.htm).

Criminal Justice Review (Atlanta, Ga.: College of Health and Human Sciences, Georgia State University, 1976– , biannual)
Biannual scholarly journal devoted to a broad range of criminal justice matters, with attention given to all aspects of crime and the justice system, and local, state, or national concerns. This peer-reviewed journal features comprehensive articles, commentaries, essays, and research notes of interest examining a variety of justice-related topics.

Current and past articles from *Criminal Justice Review* are indexed and abstracted in such popular databases as Criminal Justice Abstracts, Criminal Justice Periodical Index, PsycINFO, Psychological Abstracts, PAIS International, Sociological Abstracts, and Social Sciences Index. Tables of contents of past issues are accessible only through the College of Health and Human Sciences' Web site (http://www.gsu.edu/~wwwcjr/tables.html).

Criminal Law Bulletin (Boston: Warren Gorham & Lamont, 1965– , six times a year)
Published six times a year, this authoritative source features insightful articles, written by renowned experts, about the latest trends and developments in criminal law, including updates on all major federal, state, and Supreme Court decisions. Each issue also contains feature columns examining the latest in corrections law, ethics, forensic science, and law enforcement.

Criminology: An Interdisciplinary Journal (Columbus, Ohio: American Society of Criminology, 1970– , quarterly)
This official publication of the American Society of Criminology is published four times annually (February, May, August, and November). It is devoted to a thorough review of crime and deviant behavior associated with sociology, psychology, design, systems analysis, and decision theory as applied to crime and criminal justice. Articles focus on empirical and original research and scientific methodology, as well as theoretical and criminal investigation issues. Abstracts of *Criminology: An Interdisciplinary Journal* can be accessed on the society's Web site (http://www.asc41.com/absbyear.html) from 1980 to the present, with full-text versions are available through EBSCOHost and ProQuest databases.

FBI Law Enforcement Bulletin (Washington, D.C.: Federal Bureau of Investigation, 1932– , monthly)
Published monthly by the Federal Bureau of Investigation (FBI) since 1932. Each issue features a collection of criminal justice stories, reports, and project findings. Past full-text issues of the *FBI Law Enforcement Bulletin* from 1989 to the present are accessible through the FBI's Web site (http://www.fbi.gov/publications/leb/leb.htm).

Federal Probation (Washington, D.C.: Administrative Office of the United States Courts, 1937– , three times a year)
Published by the Administrative Office of U.S. Courts three times a year (June, September, and December), this professional journal deals with the current thought, research, practice, and philosophy in corrections and criminal justice. Selected versions of past issues, from 1998 to 2002, are available on the Federal Judiciary's Web site (http://www.uscourts.gov/library/fpcontents.html); full-text versions through Academic Search Elite (May 1990–) and WilsonWeb (December 1976–).

Journal of Crime and Justice (Jonesboro, Tenn.: Pilgrimage, Inc., biannual)
Published by the Society of Police and Criminal Psychology in association with the Midwestern Criminal Justice Association, this biannual interdisciplinary journal includes editorial commentary, theoretical empirical studies, and book and media reviews for criminal justice academicians and professionals. Tables of contents of current and previous issues are accessible on the association's Web site (http://www.mcja.org/); full-text articles are available through LexisNexis Academic.

The Journal of Criminal Justice and Popular Culture (Albany: SUNY Albany School of Criminal Justice, 1993– , six times a year)
Issued six times a year by the University at Albany School of Criminal Justice, *The Journal of Criminal Justice and Popular Culture,* an electronic journal, publishes scholarly research and opinion. Each issue features peer-reviewed original articles, essays, and book reviews examining the intersection of crime, criminal justice, and popular culture in society today. Full-text articles published since 1993 can be accessed without charge at the journal's Web site (http://www.albany.edu/scj/jcjpc/).

The Journal of Criminal Law and Criminology (Chicago: Northwestern University School of Law, 1910– , quarterly)
One of the most read and widely cited publications in the world, *The Journal of Criminal Law and Criminology,* first published in 1910 by Dean John Henry Wigmore, prints serious dialogue and debate about criminal law and criminology. Written for judges, academics, criminologists, police officers, and practitioners, topics in this quarterly journal include constitutional questions, international law, evidence, jurisdiction, white-collar crime, and securities regulation.

Journal of Quantitative Criminology (New York: Plenum/Kluwer Academic Publishers, 1985– , quarterly)
This unique online journal, published by Kluwer Academic Publishers, presents articles that apply quantitative techniques, including original research,

critiques, and papers, and that explore new directions in the field of criminology. Available only by subscription, the journal is part of a licensed Web collection at Kluwer Online (http://www.kluweronline.com/). Articles published in the *Journal of Quantitative Criminology* are abstracted and indexed in several key library databases, including Criminal Justice Abstracts, Psychological Abstracts, PsycINFO, Social Sciences Citation Index, Social SciSearch, and Sociological Abstract.

The Journal of Research in Crime and Delinquency (Beverly Hills, Calif.: SAGE Publications, 1964– , quarterly)
For more than 40 years, this respected international journal has presented a wide range of research and analysis of new advancements and the latest contemporary issues and controversies in the fields of criminology and criminal justice. Each issue is packed with in-depth articles, research notes, and essays examining the social, political, and economic aspects of criminal justice. Full-text articles are available through many leading library article databases, including Ingenta (1999–).

Justice Quarterly (Omaha, Neb.: The Academy of Criminal Justice Sciences, 1984– , quarterly)
The official journal of the Academy of Criminal Justice Sciences, an international association established in 1963 to promote professional and scholarly activities in the field of criminal justice, each edition features articles on criminal justice and related issues. Quarterly published articles range from theoretical and empirical studies to qualitative and quantitative research to book reviews in the areas of crime and justice. *Justice Quarterly* is indexed in many popular library databases, including Criminal Justice Periodical Index and Criminal Justice Abstracts.

Western Criminology Review (San Bernardino, Calif.: Department of Criminal Justice, California State University, San Bernardino, 1998– , biannual)
Published by the Department of Criminal Justice, California State University, San Bernardino, *Western Criminology Review* is dedicated to scholarly discussion of policy, practice, research, and theory, reflecting national, international, and local concerns, in the fields of criminology and criminal justice. Articles review historical and contemporary perspectives, as well as a variety of methodologies related to this rapidly growing industry. Current and past issues are available in html and PDF format (http://wcr.sonoma.edu/).

SELECTED WEB SITES

General Information

Crime Library (http://www.crimelibrary.com/)
This continually growing collection features more than 500 nonfiction stories on current and historical crimes, criminals, criminal profiling, forensics, and trials. The collection covers recent crimes and the world's most notorious criminal characters from the 1400s to the present. The Crime Library was originally founded by Marilyn J. Bardsley in January 1998 and, in September 2000, was purchased by Court TV as a joint venture of AOL-Time Warner and Liberty Media, Inc.

FindLaw Legal News: Crime (http://news.findlaw.com/legalnews/crime/)
Features crime news and commentary from current headlines, including a list of related criminal justice Web sites.

Internet Legal Resource Guide (http://www.ilrg.com/)
Founded in 1995 as a comprehensive online resource of legal information, this searchable directory indexes more than 4,000 Web sites listed by category, including thousands of Web pages, legal forms, and downloadable files.

Law.com (http://www.law.com)
Provides links and direct Web connections to more than 20 award-winning national and regional legal publications online, including *The American Lawyer, The National Law Journal, New York Law Journal,* and *Legal Times.*

Librarians' Index to the Internet—Law Topics (http://lii.org/search/file/law)
Alphabetically arranged index of librarian-selected Internet resources for law topics, including crimes and criminal court cases.

Mega Links in Criminal Justice (http://faculty.ncwc.edu/toconnor/)
Compiled by Dr. Thomas R. O'Connor of North Carolina Wesleyan College's Justice Studies Department, this site lists numerous criminal justice Web sites.

National Criminal Justice (NCJRS) Database Service (http://abstractsdb.ncjrs.org/content/AbstractsDB_Search.asp)
The National Criminal Justice Reference Service Abstracts Database contains summaries of more than 180,000 criminal justice publications. To search the NCJRS collection of 7,000+ full-text publications, go to the NCJRS Virtual Library.

NCJRS Virtual Library—Full-Text Publications (http://fulltextpubs.ncjrs.org/content/FullTextPubs.html)
Searchable database of full-text publications by the NCJRS and other related government agencies, including the U.S. Department of Justice, Office of Justice Programs and the White House Office of National Drug Control Policy.

RefDesk.com—Crime and Law Enforcement (http://www.refdesk.com/crime.html)
This site provides fast access to and easy navigation of indexed crime and law enforcement Web sites, covering crime news, crime prevention, criminal justice data and statistics, forensic medicine, hate crimes, homicide trends, and more.

World Criminal Justice Library Electronic Network (http://newark.rutgers.edu/~wcjlen/WCJ/)
Comprehensive source of links to criminal justice sites by country, bibliographies, library catalogs, online periodicals, new publications, publishers' catalogs, and statistical resources in the field of criminal justice.

Statistics—Comprehensive Sources

Bureau of Justice Statistics (BJS) (http://www.ojp.usdoj.gov/bjs)
Sponsored by the U.S. Department of Justice, this site offers a broad spectrum of data and statistics. Areas covered include courts and sentencing, crimes and victims, criminal offenders, federal justice, law enforcement, and prosecution.

International Justice Statistics (Bureau of Justice Statistics) (http://www.ojp.usdoj.gov/bjs/ijs.htm#UNPRI)
This secondary site, also from the U.S. Department of Justice, provides access to Bureau of Justice Statistics publications, justice statistics from the United Nations, and links to official country Web sites.

Statistics—Individual Sources

Homicide Trends in the United States (Bureau of Justice Statistics) (http://www.ojp.usdoj.gov/bjs/homicide/homtrnd.htm)
Contains charts and descriptions of homicide patterns and trends in the United States from 1976 to the present.

National Crime Victimization Survey (NCVS) (http://www.ojp.usdoj.gov/bjs/abstract/cvusst.htm) (http://www.ojp.usdoj.gov/bjs/cvict.htm)
This ongoing household survey—the United States's second largest—features detailed and specific data on the number of household burglaries, rapes, sexual assaults, motor vehicle thefts, and other thefts experienced by U.S. residents, age 12 and older, each year.

National Household Survey on Drug Use and Health (http://www.oas.samhsa.gov/nhsd.htm)
Key source of information highlighting the consequences, patterns, and prevalence of alcohol and drug abuse among U.S. citizens age 12 and older.

Quick Facts—Bureau of Federal Prisons (http://www.bop.gov/fact0598.html)
This collection lists statistics on prisoners by age, ethnicity, gender, race, security level, sentencing, and type of offense.

Sourcebook of Criminal Justice Statistics (http://www.albany.edu/sourcebook/)
Includes data from more than 100 sources about all aspects of criminal justice in the United States displayed in more than 600 tables.

Sourcebook of Federal Sentencing Statistics (http://www.ussc.gov/ANNRPT/2001/SBTOC01.htm)
This federal sourcebook contains detailed statistics on the application of the federal sentencing guidelines and provides selected district, circuit, and national sentencing data.

Uniform Crime Reports (UCR) (http://www.fbi.gov/ucr/ucr.htm)
A nationwide cooperative statistical effort of the Federal Bureau of Investigation (FBI) and almost 17,000 city, county, and state law enforcement agencies voluntarily reporting data on crimes brought to their attention.

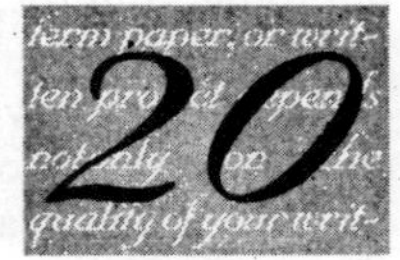

Ecology and the Environment

From the harmful effects of air and water pollution to the hazards of global warming, ecology and the environment are issues hotly debated by activists, politicians, policy makers, scientists, researchers, think tanks, and environmentalists. The issue is one that likely will not go away. Much information is available on the subject.

SELECTED BOOKS AND REFERENCES

AAAS Atlas of Population and Environment, by Paul Harrison and Fred Pearce; foreword by Peter H. Raven, 204 pages (Berkeley, Calif.: University of California Press, 2000)
This atlas colorfully illustrates the relationship between the environment and the world population, and is an excellent source of statistical data. Includes an index by topic.

Earth Almanac: An Annual Geophysical Review of the State of the Planet, 2nd Ed., 568 pages (Phoenix, Ariz.: Oryx Press, 2000)
Arranged by subject area, entries offer a treasure trove of statistical environmental information. Appendices provide additional worthwhile information. Areas covered include abbreviations, conversion formulas, Earth facts, geologic time line, glossary of terms, international and national scientific programs, and treaties and laws.

Encyclopedia of Global Change: Environmental Change and Human Society, edited by Andrew S. Goudie and David J. Cuff, 2 vols., 1,424 pages (New York: Oxford University Press, 2002)
This authoritative guide features 320 essay-length articles, listed from A to Z, covering natural and artificial changes to the Earth's biological, chemical, and physical systems. Highlighting the text are graphs, maps, and photos. Also included is a bibliography of sources.

Encyclopedia of Global Environmental Change, edited by Ted Munn, 5 vols. (New York: Wiley, 2002)
Five-volume set featuring 500 in-depth articles, 100 biographies, and 150 definitions. Articles are arranged by subject, and contain abstracts, bibli-

ographies, photos, and diagrams. Each volume includes an alphabetical list of articles in back. This well-researched and well-written reference series is divided into five volumes: Volume 1, "The Earth System: Physical and Chemical Dimensions of Global Environmental Change"; Volume 2, "The Earth System: Biological and Ecological Dimensions of Global Environmental Change"; Volume 3, "Causes and Consequences of Global Environmental Change"; Volume 4, "Responding to Global Environmental Change"; and Volume 5, "Social and Economic Dimensions of Global Environmental Change."

Encyclopedia of Environmental Science, edited by David E. Alexander and Rhodes W. Fairbridge, 741 pages (Boston: Kluwer Academic Publishers, 1999)
More than 1,000 entries, arranged in alphabetical order, highlight this encyclopedic volume, covering key environmental terms and topics. Most entries include a list of references, including useful print and Web resources. Also provided is a series of worthwhile appendixes, including a directory of environmental organizations, listings of endangered species by state, a time line of environmental history, and Web sites by subject.

Environmental Encyclopedia, 3rd Ed., edited by Marci Bortman et al., 1,641 pages (Detroit: Thomson-Gale, 2003)
Available in print and online via Gale Virtual Reference Library, this fully revised and updated edition includes many well written, nontechnical articles offering critical analysis, current status, and possible solutions to the gamut of environmental issues facing the world today.

Environmental Engineering Dictionary, 3rd Ed., by C. C. Lee, 682 pages (Rockville, Md: Government Institutes, 1998)
Seemingly every technical and regulatory engineering term used in environmental science—more than 14,000 in all—is defined and explained in this dictionary. Definitions provide exact versions as provided by the Environmental Protection Agency (EPA) for statute, regulation, and environmental science terms. Reference sources used for most definitions are also listed. An appendix features an extensive list of environmental acronyms.

Global Environment Outlook, 264 pages (New York: Oxford University Press, 1997)
Region-by-region coverage of current global environmental conditions is contained in this reference source. Policy responses and perspectives on many key environmental issues are discussed. Statistical data as it applies to global environmental conditions are included, along with an index by topic.

International Encyclopedia of Environmental Politics, edited by John Barry and E. Gene Frankland, 513 pages (London; New York: Routledge, 2001)
This A–Z encyclopedia covers environmental political issues around the world with more than 500 insightful entries that include a list of sources for further reading. Also provided is an index of entries arranged by major themes.

Macmillan Encyclopedia of Energy, edited by John Zumerchik. 3 vols. (New York: Macmillan Reference USA, 2001)
Covers a broad spectrum of energy topics with more than 250 illustrated articles written by scholars and experts. Detailed biographies of key figures in the science and energy fields are also included. An electronic version of the entire contents of this three-volume set is available online via Gale Virtual Reference Library.

Macmillan Encyclopedia of the Environment, edited by Stephen R. Kellert, 6 vols. (New York: Macmillan Library Reference USA; London: Simon & Schuster and Prentice Hall International, 1997)
This full-color, beautifully illustrated six-volume reference series provides coverage of virtually everything about the environment, from basic information to recent developments. Detailed entries focus on such topics as biology, chemistry, climate and weather, ecology, endangered species, disasters, evolution, genetics, land use, natural resources, pollution, population growth, waste management, and more.

Pollution A to Z, edited by Richard Stapleton, 2 vols., 757 pages (New York: Macmillan Reference USA, 2003)
Approximately 264 in-depth articles, written by leading scientists, educators, professionals, and other experts, covering all areas of pollution—air, land, space, and water—make up this important volume. Entries discuss current issues, key concepts, research, and legislation. Many topical issues are likewise critically examined, including asbestos, carbon monoxide and CFC pollution, among others. Also reviewed are social movements and organizations leading the fight against pollution, such as Earth First and the Green Party. This volume is also available by subscription online via Gale Virtual Reference Library.

The Wellbeing of Nations: A Country-by-Country Index of Quality of Life and the Environment, by Robert Prescott-Allen in cooperation with International Development Research Centre, et al., 342 pages (Washington, D.C.: Island Press, 2001)
Highlighting this 342-page volume is recent data on the quality of life and the environment in 180 countries worldwide. Indicators examined include air quality, energy use, global atmosphere, land health, protected areas, water quality, resource pressures, and others, of each country. Included in the first section of the book are maps and charts; the second half includes detailed data tables and methodologies used in the assessment of each country.

Wiley Encyclopedia of Energy and the Environment, edited by Attilio Bisio and Sharon Boots, 1,562 pages (New York: Wiley, 1997)
Arranged alphabetically, this acclaimed encyclopedia covers a wide range of energy and environmental topics, with lengthy entries illustrated by diagrams and photos. Bibliographies are listed at the end of each entry for further research in the respective subject area.

World Resources 2000–2001: People and Ecosystems: The Fraying Web of Life, 400 pages (Washington, D.C.: World Resources Institute, 2001)
Published by the World Resources Institute, this printed edition, also available online, reviews global environmental trends as they relate to the world's popu-

lation, food and water supply, consumption and waste, energy use, climate changes, and the well-being of humans. Entries are arranged by ecosystem and include key environmental and social indicators for more than 150 countries. An index offers easy access to specific topics.

SELECTED ARTICLE INDEXES AND ABSTRACTS

Printed Indexes and Abstracts

Applied Science and Technology Index (New York: H.W. Wilson, 1958–)
This annual series indexes articles published in 335 periodicals in many disciplines, including environmental science.

Biological Abstracts (Philadelphia: BioSciences Information Service, 1926–)
Long-running printed series, now also an online database, that indexes and abstracts periodicals in such disciplines as agriculture, biology, and related sciences.

Biological and Agricultural Index (New York: H.W. Wilson, 1964–)
Cumulative subject index to periodicals in the fields of biology, agriculture, and related sciences. The print version lists articles by subject and by author. Entries include subjects, organisms, chemical compounds, biological structures, and research techniques.

Environment Abstracts (Cambridge, Mass.: Environment Information Center, Inc., 1970–99)
Excellent source of citations and abstracts of both print and nonprint materials, including journal articles, reports, and other sources covering environmental and energy-related topics. Subject areas include conservation of natural resources, urban ecology, electric power generation, and environmental impact.

General Science Index (New York: H.W. Wilson, 1978–)
This popular reference indexes approximately 150 periodicals in the sciences and related disciplines, including atmospheric science, biology, environmental science, and oceanography.

Pollution Abstracts (Bethesda, Md.: Cambridge Scientific Abstracts, 1970–)
Combines information on scientific research and government policies in a single resource. Abstracts material from conference proceedings, hard-to-find documents, and published journals. Print version expanded to an online database of the same name.

Water Resources Abstracts (Bethesda, Md.: Cambridge Scientific Abstracts, 1967–)
Also available as an online database, this printed version provides citations and abstracts to literature on water-related topics covering the characteristics, conservation, control, pollution, treatment, use and management of water resources.

Web Indexes and Abstracts

AGRICOLA (AGRICultural OnLine Access) (National Agricultural Library, 1970–)

This Web-delivered database (http://www.nal.usda.gov/ag98/ag98.html), covering every major agricultural subject, features citations, with some full text, to key publications in agriculture and other allied disciplines. Subject areas include animal breeding, entomology, environmental pollution, farm management, feeds, pesticides, rural sociology, veterinary medicine, and water resources.

Applied Science and Technology Index (H.W. Wilson, 1983–)

Indexes 391 journals in such fields as environmental engineering, waste management, and petroleum and gas. Database is also available on CD-ROM and in print.

Biological Abstracts (Thomson BIOSIS, 1969–)

This online bibliographic reference offers millions of citations to life science journal literature.

Biological Sciences (Cambridge Scientific Abstracts, 1982–)

Provides countless citations and abstracts to journal articles in the life sciences. Topics include ecology and environmental biotechnology. Includes some full-text articles from BioOne.

Energy Citation Database (U.S. Department of Energy Office of Scientific and Technical Information, 1948–)

This Web-based database (http://www.osti.gov/energycitations/), designed and developed by the U.S. Department of Energy Office of Scientific and Technical Information, offers full bibliographic records from 1948 to the present of primary and secondary energy-related literature. Regularly updated, records include literature in such disciplines as chemistry, physics, materials, environmental science, geology, engineering, mathematics, climatology, and oceanography. Periodicals cited include literature, conference papers, journals, books, dissertations, and patents.

Environment Abstracts (LexisNexis, 1975–)

Extensively indexes journal articles, conference proceedings, and other sources of information on important and controversial environmental issues. Most abstracts include links to accompanying full-text documents. Database combines information from three printed indexes: *Acid Rain Abstracts, Energy Information Abstracts* and *Environment Abstracts,* each of which ended publication in 1995.

Environmental Sciences and Pollution Management (Cambridge Scientific Abstracts, 1967–)

Abstracts worldwide periodicals covering air, land, water and noise pollution; bacteriology; ecology; toxicology; risk assessment; environmental biotechnology and engineering; waste management; water resources, policies and regulations. Updated monthly, with more than 76,000 abstracts added annually.

General Science Index (H.W. Wilson, 1984–)
Available in print and on CD-ROM as well, this online version indexes more than 140 science periodicals covering such subjects as conservation, the environment, and oceanography.

GEOBASE (Elsevier Science, 1980–)
Bibliographic databases that index worldwide research literature in Earth and environmental sciences, ecology, geography, geology, ecology, international development, and related disciplines. Nearly 2,000 journals are indexed from cover to cover, with abstracts to an additional 3,000 archived journals.

Physical Sciences Digest (Plexus Publishing, 1987–)
This companion database to Biology Digest contains comprehensive abstracts covering all the physical sciences. Available only online, Physical Sciences Digest provides immediate access to current and past scientific developments. Individual digests summarize articles and research reports from international publications, such as *Discover, Scientific American, Astronomy,* and *Geotimes,* and academic journals, including *Science, Nature, Physics World, Environmental Science and Technology,* and *Geophysical Research Letters.*

Physical Sciences Digest, along with Biology Digest and Plexus companion databases, is also offered as part of NewsBank Science Source Collection. Cambridge Scientific Abstracts likewise offers Physical Sciences Digest (as Science and Technology Digest) on the Web by subscription, and through EBSCO Publishing's database collections.

Pollution Abstracts (Cambridge Scientific Abstracts, 1981–)
Based on the printed version, this primary database of fast, reliable environmental information extensively abstracts literature covering the subject areas of air, land, marine, noise, and water pollution, plus related topics, such as environmental action, toxicology and health, sewage and wastewater treatment, and waste management.

TOXLINE (Cambridge Scientific Abstracts, 1998–)
Searchable database that provides more than 4 million citations and abstracts of the worldwide literature in all areas of toxicology, including chemicals, pharmaceuticals, pesticides, and environmental pollutants. Sources include journals, books, reports, and theses. The database contains records from the past five years, plus the current year.

SELECTED FULL-TEXT ARTICLE DATABASES

Academic Search Elite (EBSCOHost, indexing: 1980– , full text: 1990–)
Indexing a wide range of subjects, this premier academic database also includes general environment and environment-related journals, including *Audubon, Ecology, Environmental Ethics, Environmental Science and Technology, Environment, Journal of Environmental Health, Oceanus,* and *Sierra.*

Annual Reviews (Annual Reviews, 1932–)
Current collection of critical reviews written by leading scientists, published yearly. Subjects explored include energy and the environment, ecology and systematics, genetics, and many more.

Biological and Agricultural Index Plus (H.W. Wilson, 1983–)
More than 225 peer-reviewed journals in agriculture and the life sciences are abstracted and indexed, including full-text articles, from such disciplines as ecology, environmental science, and forestry. Also available online and on CD-ROM.

Expanded Academic Index (InfoTrac, 1980–)
Like Academic Source Elite, this popular InfoTrac library database also indexes articles published in many leading general environment and environment-related journals, including some of the same titles, such as *Audubon, Ecology, Environmental Ethics, Environmental Science and Technology, Environment, Journal of Environmental Health, Oceanus,* and *Sierra.*

JSTOR (Journal Storage Project, 1996–)
Full-text journal collection that offers direct access to numerous ecology reference sources, including the *Journal of Ecology,* the *Journal of Animal Ecology,* and *Ecology.*

LexisNexis Environmental (LexisNexis, 1970–)
Contains abstracts and full-text news from a large variety of sources, including scholarly and professional journals, conference papers and proceedings, federal and state government reports, major daily newspapers, consumer and trade magazines, newsletters, law reviews, administrative codes, case law, regulatory agency decisions, waste sites, and hazardous material data.

Wilson Select Plus (H.W. Wilson, 1994–)
Web accessible through OCLC FirstSearch, this searchable collection includes abstracts and full-text articles from more than 1,300 publications. Includes selected full-text articles from H.W. Wilson's *Business Abstracts, General Sciences Abstracts, Humanities Abstracts, Readers' Guide,* and *Social Sciences Abstracts.*

SELECTED PERIODICALS

Audubon Magazine (New York: National Audubon Society, 1899– , bimonthly)
Published by the National Audubon Society, one of the oldest and largest conservation societies in the United States, this bimonthly magazine covers a broad spectrum of conservation and environmental topics in each issue. The magazine is beautifully photographed and illustrated, and the primary focus of articles is on birds and wildlife and their habitats.

The Ecologist (Wadebridge, U.K.: Ecosystems Ltd., 1970– , monthly)
Possibly the most widely read environment magazine, *The Ecologist,* read by some 200,000 subscribers in 150 countries, features authoritative articles on issues related to the environment. It examines such major environmental challenges as rain forest destruction, climatic changes, and environmental and political agendas around the world.

Ecology (Washington, D.C.: Ecological Society of America, etc., 1920– , annually)
Published annually since 1920 by the Ecological Society of America, a Washington, D.C.–based nonpartisan, nonprofit organization of scientists, *Ecol-*

ogy magazine pays particular attention to all aspects of ecology in its wide-ranging articles. Included are statistical reports, features, articles, notes, comments, and data papers covering new concepts, and analytical, experimental, historical, and theoretical approaches applicable to species, populations, communities, or ecosystems. Offered in print and electronic form, full-text articles from past issues are accessible through JSTOR from the first volume through 1998.

Electronic Green Journal (Moscow, Idaho: Electronic Green Journal, 1994– , biannual)
Web-based (http://egj.lib.uidaho.edu/index.html) peer-reviewed professional journal devoted to international environmental topics. Subjects covered include assessment, conservation, development, disposal, education, hazards, pollution, resources, technology, and treatment in the fields of ecology and environmental sciences.

Environmental Science and Technology (Easton, Pa.: American Chemical Society, 1967– , annual)
Published by one of the oldest scientific associations in the world, *Environmental Science and Technology* delivers authoritative and comprehensive articles about the latest technological advances, regulations, policies, and scientific research in the environmental arena. Topics in past issues have included everything from air quality modeling, to risk from fine particles, to dioxin risk assessment, to recycled wastewater.

EPA Journal (Washington, D.C.: Environmental Protection Agency, 1975–95, bimonthly)
First published in 1975, this bimonthly journal, published by the Environmental Protection agency (EPA), offered a national and global perspective on key environmental issues. Articles focused on work within the EPA and federal government and private sector to solve environmental problems. Publication was discontinued with the winter 1995 issue. Contents of each previously published journal are featured on the EPA's Web site (http://www.epa.gov/history/collection/aid10.htm). Full-text articles are available of past journals through WilsonWeb beginning with the September/October 1982 issue.

National Wildlife (Washington, D.C.: National Wildlife Federation, 1962– , monthly)
Since publication of its first issue in December 1962, this monthly magazine has covered such topics as nature and the environment for conservation-minded readers. Issues feature natural history and outdoor adventure articles, ecological news items, and full-color photo galleries.

Sierra (San Francisco, Calif.: Sierra Club, 1893– , bimonthly)
One of the oldest environmental journals in the United States, this award-winning, general-interest environmental magazine, published by the Sierra Club, a San Francisco–based nonprofit group, celebrates the wonders of nature through expertly written and strikingly photographed adventure and travel features. Showcased in each issue are travel destinations in natural settings, products, services, lists of Sierra-sponsored trips, and much more.

Worldwatch (Washington, D.C.: Worldwatch Institute, 1988– , bimonthly)
Published by the Worldwatch Institute, a Washington, D.C.–based nonprofit environmental advocacy group, this bimonthly magazine focuses on current developments in many related areas. Issues contain articles discussing current environmental trends worldwide, such as climate change, deforestation, population growth, species extinction, and economic and environmental policies.

SELECTED WEB SITES

EarthTrends: The Environmental Information Portal (http://earthtrends.wri.org/)
Developed and maintained by the World Resources Institute, this site is a great source of environmental data on countries, ecosystems, energy, agriculture, population, and more.

Energy Trends: Energy Research and Development, Global Trends in Policy and Investment (http://energytrends.pnl.gov/)
Another excellent site sponsored by the Pacific Northwest Laboratory that examines trends in energy research, development, and investment around the globe.

EnviroLink Network (http://envirolink.org/)
This site, developed by the nonprofit organization EnviroLink, is one of the most comprehensive resources on the Web on the subject of the environment. Access is provided to literally thousands of online environmental resources.

Environmental Defense (http://www.edf.org/)
Founded to "protect human health, restore our oceans and ecosystems, and curb global warming," this New York–based nonprofit environmental group offers current information on environmental topics.

Environmental News Network (http://www.enn.com/)
Online newspaper featuring environmental news stories, in-depth accounts, press releases, and other information.

Environmental Quality Statistics (http://ceq.eh.doe.gov/nepa/reports/statistics/)
Features statistical tables created by the U.S. Department of Energy and published in its annual report of the Council on Environmental Quality.

Global Trends 2015 (http://www.cia.gov/cia/reports/globaltrends2015/index.html)
Position paper by the National Intelligence Council that covers future trends regarding the environment.

Global Warming: Early Warning Signs (http://www.climatehotmap.org/)
This online map illustrates the consequences of global warming and climate changes. Maps are available by region, and the site includes various indicators, references, and teaching resources on the subject.

Know Your Environment (http://www.acnatsci.org/education/kye/index.html)
Published by the Environmental Associates in association with the Academy of Natural Sciences of Philadelphia, this extensive database offers direct

access to articles about natural resources, human influence, public policy, and technology and environment.

MapCruzin.com (http://www.mapcruzin.com/index.html)
The home page of the Clary Meuser Research Network, this site provides tools and resources devoted to improving social and environmental conditions.

Pew Center on Global Climate Change (http://www.pewclimate.org/)
Established in 1998 as a nonprofit, nonpartisan, independent organization to address global climate change, the Pew Center offers news, basic information, and in-depth reports about global warming and related environmental issues.

Second Time Around (http://www.epa.gov/seahome/housewaste/src/recycle.htm)
EPA generated Web site that describes the benefits of recycling aluminum, batteries, glass, motor oil, paper, plastic, steel, yard waste, and more.

U.S. Environmental Protection Agency (http://www.epa.gov/)
This official home page of the U.S. Environmental Protection Agency (EPA) offers an abundance of resources, including an excellent data source called EnviroFacts (http://www.epa.gov/enviro/index_java.html).

Water Quality Information Center (http://www.nal.usda.gov/wqic/)
The National Library of Agriculture Water Quality Information Center page provides electronic access to information about water and agriculture. The site includes links to bibliographies, databases, discussion lists, environmental news, and much more.

World Resource Institute: Research Topics (http://www.wri.org/wrisites.cfm)
This Web page provides links to topical environmental research facts and figures, special reports, and comprehensive data on a broad array of environmental, economic and social issues.

The World's Water (http://www.worldwater.org/)
Developed and maintained by the Pacific Institute for Studies in Environment, Development and Security, this Web page presents current information and data on the world's freshwater resources. Includes links to many organizations, institutions, and individuals working on a wide range of global freshwater problems and solutions.

The Yearbook of International Cooperation on Environment and Development (http://www.greenyearbook.org/)
This independent publication from the Fridtjof Nansen Institute in Norway, published by EarthScan, features a variety of links to international agreements, nongovernmental organizations, country profiles, and environmental performance articles, to name but a few.

21

Film and Television

Thanks to an abundance of printed and electronic sources, you can locate production credits, plot summaries, biographical data, filmographies, literature, critical essays, and serious studies of well-known performers, producers, directors, and others, for virtually every film or television show. Information is also widely accessible on worldwide societies and organizations and research centers and archives dedicated to film and television history and preservation. As with any other category, sources can be books, indexes, Web sites, or abstracts of serious and scholarly journals discussing a myriad of topics. Described in this chapter is a selected list of information on the subject of film and television.

SELECTED BOOKS AND REFERENCES

General Sources

The Complete Directory to Prime Time Network and Cable TV Shows, 1946–present, 8th Ed., by Tim Brooks and Earle Marsh, 1,592 pages (New York: Ballantine Books, 2003)

This comprehensive guide covers programs from all major commercial broadcast networks—more than 60. Each entry provides a complete broadcast history, cast, and plot summaries about each show and its stars. This fully revised and updated eighth edition includes more than 500 new listings, plus more than 800 entries with descriptions of cable network programming. Special features include annual program schedules for the past 57 years, listings of top-rated shows by season, Emmy Award winners, longest-running series in TV history, spin-off series, theme songs, and more.

Contemporary Theatre, Film, and Television: A Biographical Guide Featuring Performers, Directors, Writers, Producers, Designers, Managers, Choreographers, Technicians, Composers, Executives, Dancers, and Critics in the United States and Great Britain, 58 vols. (Detroit: Gale Group, 2004)

Now available electronically through Gale Virtual Reference Library, this popular printed reference series features detailed biographical and career information on more than 11,000 entertainment professionals. Coverage includes birth dates, education, background (including professional training), marriage information, political and religious affiliations, and much more.

Encyclopedia of Movie Special Effects, by Patricia Netzley, 304 pages (Phoenix, Ariz.: Oryx Press, 2000)
This subject-specific volume features 366 entries covering special effects in the American movie industry, including brief biographies, studio terms and definitions, descriptions of special effects techniques, lists of special effects used in certain films, and concise biographies of major special effects people.

The Film Encyclopedia: The Most Comprehensive Encyclopedia of World Cinema in a Single Volume, 4th Ed. by Ephraim Katz, Fred Klein, and Ronald Dean Nolen, 1,520 pages (New York: Harper Resource, 2001)
Authoritatively written reference guide featuring more than 7,000 entries on "the artistic, technical, and commercial aspects of movies." Entries include biographical information on many famous actors, cinematographers, directors, editors, producers, and screenwriters in motion picture history, motion picture studio histories, and overviews of such subjects as film genres and film style.

Halliwell's Film and Video Guide 2004, 19th Ed. by Leslie Halliwell, 1,012 pages (New York: Harper Resource, 2003)
Listing more than 20,000 English-language films and videos, this well-done compendium features concise information, including running time, date of release, credits, and reviews.

Halliwell's Filmgoer's Companion, 12th Ed., edited by Leslie Halliwell and John Walker, 864 pages (New York: HarperCollins, 1997)
This edition of the long-running film reference series chronicles American and foreign directors, writers, and actors, and film themes, terms, and techniques.

History of American Cinema, 10 vols. (New York: Charles Scribner's Sons, 1990)
"A major achievement in film history, unlikely to be surpassed for many years" (*American Historical Review*), this award-winning, 10-volume reference series chronicles the complete history of American cinema from its beginnings in the 19th century to 1990. Each volume is copiously illustrated and chronicles the evolution and development of films by decade, complete with indexes, notes, a bibliography, and a myriad of appendixes.

International Directory of Films and Filmmakers, 2nd Ed., 5 vols., edited by Christopher Lyon and Susan Doll (Detroit; New York; San Francisco: St. James Press, 1990–93)
Now out of print, this five-volume reference set is an invaluable source of bibliographies on American and foreign-made films and documentaries (pre-1993), and well-known actors, actresses, directors, filmmakers, production artists, and writers. Volume 1 chronicles American and foreign films, silent films, and documentaries in alphabetical order. An extensive list of reviews, plot summaries, and critical commentary is provided for each entry. Subsequent volumes offer biographical information and expository essays on directors and filmmakers (Volume 2), actors (Volume 3), and writers and production artists (Volume 4). Volume 5 contains a title index to cross-reference entries in all volumes.

International Motion Picture Almanac (Chicago, Ill; New York: Quigley Pub. Co., 1929– , annual)
Called *The Motion Picture Almanac* from 1929 to 1935–36, then renamed *The International Motion Picture Almanac* beginning with the 1936–37 edition. A separate edition, *The Motion Picture and Television Almanac,* launched with the 1952–53 edition.

Magill's Cinema Annual, edited by Frank Magill, et al. (Englewood Cliffs, N.J.: Salem Press, 1982– ; Detroit: Gale Group, 1983–)
First published by Salem Press in 1982, then by the Gale Group beginning in 1983, this annual reference offers detailed retrospective coverage of major domestic and foreign films released in the United States from 1981 to the present. Early editions, published by St. James Press, were split into three parts: silent films, foreign films, and English-language films. Current editions published by Gale Group chronicle films released from the previous year. In both past and current volumes, essential details are provided with each entry, including complete cast and credits, awards and nominations, MPAA ratings, and critical reviews with author bylines. Eight indexes cross-reference subjects in the entire volume.

Screen World (New York: Greenberg, 1949–65, Vols. 1–16; New York: Crown, 1966– , Vols. 17–42; New York: Applause Books, 1992– , Vols. 43–)
Each volume of this definitive reference series, first published in 1949, covers every significant United States and international film released during the previous year. Each entry includes complete plot summaries, cast, credit, and production company information, month released, rating, and running time. Also contains biographical information on more than 2,250 living stars, including real name, place and date of birth, and educational background.

Total Television: The Comprehensive Guide to Programming from 1948 to the Present, 4th Ed., by Alex McNeil, 1,251 pages (New York: Penguin Books, 1996)
A great companion to *The Complete Directory to Prime Time Network and Cable TV Shows, Total Television* exhaustively chronicles more than 7,000 daytime, prime time, syndicated, and cable programs. Supplementary material includes a year-by-year, night-by-night grid of each network's prime-time line-up of shows from 1948 through the end of the 1995–96 season. Indexes cross-reference nearly every network, cable, and syndicated series that aired. All performers, writers, directors and producers are conveniently indexed for easy cross-referencing.

Variety International Film Guide, 41 vols. (London: Tantivy Press; New York: A.S. Barnes, 1964–88; London: Andre Deutsch; Hollywood: Samuel French, 1989–98; Los Angeles: Silman-James Press, 1999–)
This popular annual reference series is a veritable "who, what, where, and when" of cinema. Includes news, reviews, and 240 color and black-and-white illustrations covering film productions from some 70 countries, plus information about film archives, film festivals, film schools, top-grossing films, and worldwide box-office figures.

VideoHound's Golden Movie Retriever 2005, 14th Ed., edited by Jim Craddock, 1,655 pages (Detroit: Gale Group, 2004)
This reference source contains listings of movies available on video, rated from one to four "bones" for quality. Included are nine primary indexes for easy cross-referencing of material.

Film and Television Studies and Criticism

Film Review Index: Volume I: 1882–1949, Volume II: 1950–1985, by Patricia King Hanson and Stephen L. Hanson (Phoenix, Ariz: Oryx Press, 1986–1987)
Indexes approximately 8,000 major film reviews from newspapers, magazines, trade journals, reference works, and monographic surveys. Provides review sources for silent films and films produced before 1950. Includes an index of directors.

A Guide to Critical Reviews: Part IV: The Screenplay from Jazz Singer to Dr. Strangelove, 3rd Ed., 2 vols, by James M. Salem (Metuchen, N.J.: Scarecrow Press, 1984–)
This two-volume set indexes reviews from selected newspapers and popular magazines for nearly 12,000 American and foreign screenplays and full-length movies from 1927 to 1980.

Index to Critical Film Reviews in British and American Periodicals, by Stephen E. Bowles, 3 vols. (New York: B. Franklin, 1975)
Comprehensive three-volume reference that lists more than 20,000 film reviews, including documentaries and shorts, from selected periodicals from the 1950s to 1973.

International Index to Film Periodicals, 1972– (New York, R.R. Bowker Co., 1973–)
Indexes articles of "aesthetic or critical value" from approximately 90 film periodicals, arranged in sections by category. To find film reviews, look under the film's title in the "Individual Films" section. This source is one of the main components of the online FIAF International FilmArchive Database (1972–2001), which also includes biographies of film stars and information about film archives and collections.

Leonard Maltin's Movie Guide 2005, 1,637 pages (New York: Signet, 2004)
Written by film critic and historian Leonard Maltin and a staff of contributing reviewers, this annually updated, best-selling home reference offers capsule reviews on almost 19,000 American and foreign films, including recent video, DVD, and laserdisc releases. Also includes several bonus features, such as a list of "100+ Recommended Family Films" on video, "Fifty Films That Got Away, Movies You Really Ought to See," and a list of specialty video mail-order companies.

Los Angeles Times Index (Ann Arbor, Mich.: UMI, 1972–)
Published eight times a year with quarterly and annual accumulations, the *Los Angeles Times Index* provides abstracts of news items, feature articles, editorials, editorial cartoons, obituaries, commentaries, and reviews of movies and television programs through the 1996 edition. Beginning in 1997,

the publisher of this print index series revamped the format, eliminating the abstracts. Instead, each entry lists the headline, author, and article type (such as editorial or feature article) and also includes subject terms under which the article is indexed.

Magill's American Film Guide, edited by Frank N. Magill; associate editors, Stephen L. Hanson and Patricia King Hanson, 5 vols., 3,691 pages (Englewood Cliffs, N.J.: Salem Press, 1983)
Lists in alphabetical order in-depth critical essays of approximately 1,000 major American films, from three to eight pages in length, examining the film and its relationship to film history.

Magill's Survey of Cinema: English Language Films, First Series, edited by Frank N. Magill; associate editors, Patricia King Hanson and Stephen L. Hanson, 4 vols. (Englewood Cliffs, N.J.: Salem Press, 1980)

Magill's Survey of Cinema: English Language Films, Second Series, edited by Frank N. Magill; associate editors, Stephen L. Hanson and Patricia King Hanson, 6 vols. (Englewood Cliffs, N.J.: Salem Press, 1981)
In-depth analyses of more than 1,200 major English-language films produced from 1927 to 1980. Critical evaluations and detailed plot summaries cover all aspects, including acting, directing, editing, screenwriting, and production. This resource is also offered online through DIALOG.

Magill's Survey of Cinema: Foreign Language Films, edited by Frank N. Magill, 8 vols. (Englewood Cliffs, N.J.: Salem Press, 1985)
Eight-volume set encompassing more than 700 foreign-language films released between 1929 and 1985. Detailed plot summaries and reviews accompany each entry. A cumulative index cross-references films in the preceding volumes. Also offered as online database through DIALOG.

Magill's Survey of Cinema: Silent Films, edited by Frank N. Magill; associate editors, Patricia King Hanson and Stephen L. Hanson, 3 vols., 1,280 pages (Englewood Cliffs, N.J.: Salem Press, 1982)
Critically examines and summarizes major silent films produced between 1902 and 1936, with a cumulative index included. Also available online through DIALOG.

Media Review Digest (Ann Arbor, Mich.: Pierian Press, 1973–)
Published annually, this reference features citations of more than 375,000 reviews and links to more than 300,000 full-text reviews and related sources on the Internet of films, videos, videodiscs, audio tapes, compact discs, CD-ROMs, DVDs, and other media with an emphasis on educational and other nontheatrical titles.

New York Times Film Reviews (New York: New York Times, 1913/1968–1999/2000)
Organized by year, with indexes in each volume, the *New York Times Film Reviews* reprints more than 17,000 films (1913–82 and 1985–86) as published in *The New York Times*. Contains reviews of American films, foreign films, documentaries, independent films, and experimental films. The 1913–68 edition also features a beautifully illustrated portrait gallery with

photos of famous film stars; subsequent editions include illustrated movie reviews.

The New York Times Index (New York: New York Times, 1851–)
Cumulative index to *The New York Times,* including film reviews by *Times* critics, located under the subject heading, "Motion Pictures—Reviews and Other Data on Specific Productions." Films are listed individually in alphabetical order after a chronological list of articles. The index lists reviews of all kinds of motion pictures—documentaries, foreign and American films, and independent films.

Reader's Guide to Periodical Literature (New York: H.W. Wilson, 1901–)
One of the best references for reviews published in newspapers and magazines, *Reader's Guide to Periodical Literature* is a good source of information, particularly on older films. The popular compendium indexes both American and foreign films. Reviews are indexed under the subject heading, "Moving Picture Plays—Criticisms, Plots, etc.—Single Works," in alphabetical order by film title.

Retrospective Index to Film Periodicals, 1930–1971, by Linda Batty, 425 pages (New York: R. R. Bowker Co., 1975)
This retrospective index, which predates the *Film Literature Index,* covers the contents of 14 English-language film journals from 1930 through 1971, along with film reviews and film-related articles published in *The Village Voice.*

Selected Film Criticism, 7 vols. (Metuchen, N.J.: Scarecrow Press, 1982–85)
Offers selected movie reviews, reproduced in their entirety, that were originally published in magazines and trade journals from 1896 to 1960. Each film has an average of two reviews. Volumes 1–5 and Volume 7 index American and foreign film reviews (1896–1960). Volume 6 features reviews of foreign-language films released in the United States (1930–50). Volume 7 is a cumulative index to the previous volumes in the set.

Variety Film Reviews, 1907–1996, 24 vols. (New York: Garland Pub., 1983–96)
Similar to the *New York Times Film Reviews,* this reference series, encompassing 24 volumes, reprints film reviews published in *Variety.* Reviews are arranged chronologically and are good sources of information on American and foreign films, as well as obscure films and those that premiered at international film festivals. Cumulative title indexes, 1907–80 (Volume 16) and 1981–84 (Volume 18), cross-reference films reviewed in each volume. Title and director indexes for 1985–86 are in the back of each volume. Publication of the series ceased with Volume 24.

Video Librarian (Seabeck, Wash.: Video Librarian, 1986–)
Annual index to this monthly video review magazine for public, school, academic, and special libraries featuring hundreds of reviews each month of current theatrical and nontheatrical videos. Originally published as a newsletter beginning in 1986, the publication shifted to a magazine format in 1996. Also offered as searchable database called Video Librarian Plus! with access to more than 12,000 full-text video reviews.

Filmographies

American Film Institute Catalog of Motion Pictures Produced in the United States: Feature Films, 1911–1920, edited by Patricia King Hanson, 2 vols., 1,504 pages (Berkeley: University of California Press, 1989)

American Film Institute Catalog of Motion Pictures Produced in the United States: Feature Films, 1921–1930, edited by Kenneth W. Munden, 2 vols. (New York: Bowker, 1979; Berkeley: University of California Press, 1997)

American Film Institute Catalog of Motion Pictures Produced in the United States: Feature Films, 1931–1940, edited by Alan Gevinson and Patricia King Hanson (Berkeley: University of California Press, 1993)

American Film Institute Catalog of Motion Pictures Produced in the United States: Feature Films, 1941–1950, edited by Amy Dunkleberger and Patricia King Hanson, 3 vols., 1,115 pages (Berkeley: University of California Press, 1999)

American Film Institute Catalog of Motion Pictures, 1961–1970, edited by Richard P. Krafsur, 2 vols. (New York: Bowker, 1976; Berkeley: University of California Press, 1997)
The most authoritative work of its kind, this five-part set covers only American films—feature films that were four reels or longer. Includes title, credits, date of release, literary source (if known), and complete synopsis.

The Holt Foreign Film Guide, by Ronald Bergan and Robin Karney (New York: Henry Holt, 1989)
Guide to 2,000 foreign films from more than 50 countries selected by the authors—classics, box-office successes, and more unusual films. Provided with each entry are credits, plot summary, critical commentary, and running time. Entries include both the original foreign language title and U.S. release title.

The Motion Picture Guide, 1927–1984, by Jay Robert Nash and Stanley Ralph Ross, 12 vols. (Chicago: Cinebooks, 1985–86)
Indispensable, 12-volume reference set that offers complete descriptions, including cast and credits, for more than 50,000 English-language and notable foreign feature films released between 1927 and 1984. Entries include production information, synopsis, analysis, and ratings, ranging in length from two sentences to several pages. Documentaries, X-rated, or unrated films are excluded. A cumulative index (Volumes 11 and 12) accompanies the set. Also available on CD-ROM.

SELECTED ARTICLE INDEXES AND ABSTRACTS

Printed Indexes and Abstracts

The Alternative Press Index (College Park, Md.: Alternative Press Center, 1969–)
Provides comprehensive coverage of mainstream American films, foreign films, documentaries, and independent films reviewed by alternative and radical

periodicals. In the index, reviews are listed by title under "Film Reviews," and also under "Films, Documentary," "Films, Independent," and "Films, Political." The index is also available as an online database from 1991 to the present.

Art Index (New York: H.W. Wilson, 1929–).
Indexes many key film journals by author and subject, as well as publications in the fields of art history, graphic arts, photography and films, and related subjects.

Arts and Humanities Citation Index (Philadelphia: Institute for Scientific Information, 1976–)
This multidisciplinary index covers more than 6,000 journals of the arts and humanities, including film.

Biography Index (New York: H.W. Wilson, 1946–)
Cumulative index to biographical material found in books and magazines from 1946 to present, including profiles of film personalities.

Film Literature Index (Albany, N.Y.: Filmdex, 1973–)
Complete author and subject index to more 300 well-known international periodicals, covering film criticism from 1974 to the present, as well as topics related to film, television, and video. Part I contains an index of film reviews; Part II, an index to television and video reviews. This edition also includes film title, personal name, and subject indexes.

Film Review Annual (Englewood, N.J.: Jerome S. Ozer, 1981–)
With the 2004 edition covering films of 2001, this multivolume set, though one or two years out of date, is still a good source of citations and reproductions of complete reviews of major feature films distributed in the United States, from 1982 to the present. Reprints of reviews are derived from a broad range of periodicals, including newspapers, magazines, and scholarly film journals. Covers mostly American films and some foreign films. The titles of films featured are listed in the front of each volume.

Film Review Index, edited by Patricia K. Hanson and Stephen L. Hanson, 2 vols. (Phoenix, Ariz: Oryx Press, 1986–87)
This selective guide cites reviews from more than 7,000 feature films made between 1914 and 1986 from popular magazines and trade journals, including *Hollywood Reporter, Variety,* and *Motion Picture Herald Product Digest.* Each listing contains many unique or hard-to-find sources.

Humanities Index (New York: H.W. Wilson, 1947–)
Covers a broad range of subjects, including folklore, history, language and literature, and performing arts. Also indexes reviews from scholarly journals of American and foreign films (listed under "Moving Picture Reviews—Single Works") with some of the best coverage of foreign-language films.

The Left Index (Santa Cruz, Calif.: Left Index, 1982–)
A quarterly index to extreme leftist, marxist, or radical periodicals, this reference is helpful in locating citations of reviews of American films and foreign films, and documentaries and independent films (in the Subject Index

under "Motion Picture Reviews") included in such publications. Citations are listed by film title. Following each citation are numbers that correspond with the author list in the front of each volume.

Web Indexes and Abstracts

Art Abstracts and Art Index Retrospective (1929–)
Indexes international journals in a wide range of fields, including film, television, and video. Popular film journals indexed include: *American Film, American Cinematographer, Cineaste, Cinema Journal, Film Comment, Film Quarterly, Films and Filming, Films in Review, Journal of Popular Film and Television,* and *Sight and Sound.*

Arts and Humanities Citation Index (Web of Science, 1978–)
International interdisciplinary index features citations to literature of the arts and humanities. More than 6,100 journals are indexed—1,000 fully and nearly 5,000 selectively (in the latter, mostly science and social science journals). About 15 leading film journals are included, from *American Film* to *Wide Angle.*

FIAF International FilmArchive Database (International Federation of Film Archives, 1972–)
Published by the International Federation of Film Archives (FIAF), the International FilmArchive Database is the online companion to the *International Index to Film Periodicals* and the *International Index to Television Periodicals.* Both indexes combined contain more than 300,000 article references from more than 300 periodicals, with in-depth coverage of the world's foremost academic and popular film journals. Each entry has a full bibliographic description, an abstract, and comprehensive headings (such as biographical names, film titles, general subjects, etc.) for easy reference. The database, which cumulates citations to the annual printed volume, also contains a list of information on film archives and a bibliography of FIAF member publications.

Film Index International (ProQuest, 1930–)
Compiled by the British Film Institute, this CD-ROM database contains key information on more than 100,000 feature films, short subjects, documentaries, and made-for-television movies released between 1930 and 1993. Entries include biographical information on more than 30,000 film industry figures, and 330,000 references to articles on movies and film and television personalities.

Humanities Abstracts (H.W. Wilson, 1984–)
Coverage overlaps with Wilson's *Art Abstracts,* but it does index a few journals not indexed elsewhere.

International Film Archive (International Federation of Film Archives, 1972–)
Updated semiannually, this outstanding electronic database indexes more than 200 international film and television journals with more than 375,000 individual entries from 1972 to the present. Items are fully searchable, including articles, bibliographies, discographies, filmographies, interviews, obituaries,

and more on specific films, television programs, personalities, and other related subjects.

International Index to the Performing Arts (ProQuest, 1998–)
A good source for reviews and film-related articles, this international index features citations of more than 210 scholarly and popular performing arts journals. Also indexed are biographical profiles, conference papers, discographies, interviews, obituaries, and reviews. Retrospective citations cover 46 periodicals dating back to 1864. An expanded version, IPA Full Text, provides full-text indexing to 34 titles. Indexed are dozens of respected film journals and periodicals, including *American Cinematographer* (1994–), *Cinema Journal* (1996–), *Classic Images* (1998–), *Film Comment* (1994–), *Film Quarterly* (1945–2000), *Film Review* (1998–), *Historical Journal of Film, Radio and Television* (1998–), *Millimeter—The Magazine of Motion Picture and Television Production* (1998–), and many others.

MLA International Bibliography (EBSCOHost/InfoTrac, 1963–)
This is an excellent source for citations of articles, critical reviews, and analyses in scholarly film journals and monographs such as *Cinema Journal, Creative Screenwriting, Journal of Popular Film and Television, Modern Drama,* and books by film critics. Subjects are keyword searchable.

Periodical Contents Index (PCI) (ProQuest, 1770–1995)
Indexes more than 6 million articles in 3,651 journals, including thousands of international humanities periodicals, from their first issues to 1995. Contains abstracts and full-text articles for such prominent film journals as *Cineaste, Cinema Journal* (1962–), *Film History* (1987–), and the *Journal of Popular Film and Television* (1972–).

Reader's Guide to Periodical Literature (H.W. Wilson, 1983–)
Popular index to 240 general interest magazines, some full text, including movie reviews.

SELECTED FULL-TEXT ARTICLE DATABASES

Academic Search Elite (EBSCOHost, indexing: 1980– , full text: 1990–)
Covering a variety of disciplines, Academic Search Elite is a good source for reviews and general articles on movies and movie personalities culled from scholarly journals and some popular magazines.

Academic Search Premier (EBSCOHost; indexing: 1980, full text: 1992–)
This major database contains full-text articles from many academic journals, such as *Cineaste* and *Journal of Performance and Art,* and popular magazines, including *People, Time,* and *Rolling Stone*. Coverage varies by title.

Art Full Text (H.W. Wilson, 1984–)
Indexes many scholarly film journals, including reviews and film criticism.

Expanded Academic ASAP (InfoTrac, 1980–)
Considered by some as one the best places to find reviews of recent films, Expanded Academic ASAP contains citations and full-text reviews from

selected popular magazines, scholarly journals, and some major American newspapers. Updated daily, coverage includes American and foreign films, and subjects are keyword searchable. Enter the film's title and "reviews" in the search box for best results.

JSTOR (Journal Storage Project, 1996–)
This electronic archive contains scholarly journal articles covering the arts and humanities. Options allow users to browse journals online or retrieve full-text through title or subject search.

LexisNexis Academic Universe (LexisNexis, 1977–)
Full-text index of articles from thousands of newspapers, magazines, newswires, media transcripts, trade journals, and other industry publications in the United States and abroad. Content includes newspaper reviews of motion pictures released within the past 10 years. Reviews are searchable under the "General News Topics" category, and under "News/Arts & Sports/Book, Movie, Music & Play Reviews."

Magill's Survey of Cinema (DIALOG, 1902–)
Contains the entire contents of the print editions of *Magill's Survey of Cinema* and *Magill's Survey of Cinema: Foreign Language Films*—full-text articles covering more than 1,800 notable films released since 1982. Entries consist of abstracts and credit listings for hundreds of films. Full-text listings include film title, release date, country of origin, extensive cast and credit listings, color or black-and-white indicator, abstract, critical essay, citations to noteworthy reviews, a list of significant awards, qualitative rating, and running time. Available through DIALOG, the database is updated monthly.

Periodical Abstracts Research II Edition with Full Text (UMI ProQuest, 1986–)
Another excellent source that features abstracts and some full-text articles to reviews and general articles about movies. Indexes articles from academic journals, popular magazines, and key business publications—some 1,600 general-reference publications in all, including 396 humanities periodicals. The full-text edition includes ASCII full-text articles from approximately 600 of the indexed titles,

ProjectMUSE (Johns Hopkins University Press, 1990–)
Electronic collection of full-text film criticism and film, television, and mass media studies from more than 100 journals published by major universities, including *American Imago, Cinema Journal, MLN, Modernism/Modernity, Postmodern Culture, Theatre Journal,* and many more. Coverage is for the most recent 10 years but also varies by journal.

ProQuest Direct (ProQuest, 1986–)
This full-text database indexes more than 1,100 general interest and scholarly periodicals and newspapers, including many film journals, such as *Film Comment, Historical Journal of Film, Radio and Television,* and many others, and popular publications, including *Premiere, The Village Voice,* and *Video Magazine.* Coverage is one month to two months behind, but reviews are searchable by movie title.

SELECTED PERIODICALS

American Film: Film, Video, and Television Arts (New York: BPI Communications; Los Angeles: American Film Institute: 1975–92, monthly)
This monthly magazine, published by the American Film Institute, offered in-depth coverage of the Hollywood film industry, including movies, profiles of movie legends, and their impact on popular culture. Bound periodical and microform collections, available through university and public libraries, provide access to the entire run of issues.

Camera Obscura: A Journal of Feminism and Film (Berkeley, Calif.: Camera Obscura Collective; Durham, N.C.: Duke University Press, 1976– , three times a year)
From the first to the most current issue, this unique printed scholarly journal has offered a feminist perspective on film, television, and other visual media. Each issue features information, essays, interviews, and summary pieces exploring feminist work and media practices, from avant-garde to mainstream. Now published online by Duke University Press. Current and past issues are indexed and abstracted by such popular library databases as The Alternative Press Index, Art Index, Arts and Humanities Citation Index, Film Literature Index, International Bibliography of the Social Sciences, International Index to Film Periodicals, and Women's Studies Index. Full-text articles are also available through LexisNexis Academic Universe (1993–), and ProjectMUSE (2000–).

Cineaste (New York: Cineaste Publishers, 1967– , quarterly)
Billing itself as "America's leading magazine on the art and politics of the cinema," this internationally recognized scholarly journal covers a myriad of topics and issues. Written by acclaimed writers, critics, and scholars, it features in-depth articles, reviews of the latest Hollywood movies, independent productions, and foreign films, critical analyses of controversial films, and informative interviews with directors, screenwriters, performers, and others who make films. Full-text articles are accessible through ProQuest Direct (1994–).

Cinema Journal (Norman, Okla.: Society for Cinema Studies, 1966/1967– , quarterly)
Published quarterly the University of Texas Press and the Society for Cinema and Media Studies, this scholarly journal presents myriad essays from various perspectives written by university educators, filmmakers, historians, critics, scholars, and others devoted to the study of the moving image. Contents are indexed or abstracted in *Arts and Humanities Citation Index, Extended Academic Abstracts, Film Literature Index, International Index to Film Periodicals,* and *PMLA*. Online issues have been available through Johns Hopkins University Press's ProjectMUSE since 1999.

Film Comment (New York: Lorien Productions, 1962– , bimonthly)
This bimonthly journal, published by the Film Society of Lincoln Center, contains scholarly articles on recent feature films, interviews with top filmmakers, and retrospective film studies on American and foreign films. Full-text articles from 1988 to the present are searchable through the online database ProQuest Direct.

Film and History: An Interdisciplinary Journal of Film and Television Studies (Cleveland, Ohio: Historians Film Committee, 1970– , biannual)
Published by the Historians Film Committee, an affiliated society of the American Historical Association, *Film and History* surveys feature films and documentaries that represent and interpret history and historical events. Articles range from analysis of individual films and television programs historical in nature to critical examinations of history as portrayed in films. Tables of contents from 1997 to the present are accessible through the publisher's Web site (http://www.h-net.org/~filmhis/). Current and past full-text articles are available through ProQuest Direct (1998–).

Film Quarterly (Berkeley: University of California Press, 1958– , quarterly)
Film Quarterly publishes in-depth, peer-reviewed articles, detailed reviews of current movies, avant-garde and experimental films, documentaries, and major film books, as well as interviews with important filmmakers and much more. Content also deals with film history, film theory, and the impact of film, video, and television on culture and society. Issues are available in print and electronic form by subscription.

Historical Journal of Film, Radio and Television (Oxford: Carfax Publishing/International Association for Media History, 1981– , quarterly)
This academic journal documents the history of audiovisual media and its impact on culture, politics, and society in the 20th century. Published quarterly by the International Association for Media and History, each issue features articles, conference reports, book reviews, essays, histories, and debates of current issues. Content also includes reviews of films, radio, and television programs of historical or educational importance, audiovisual media, and listings of archival materials and dissertations. *Historical Journal of Film, Radio and Television* is abstracted in such library databases *as Annotated Bibliography for English Studies, Communication Abstracts, Current Contents Arts and Humanities, EBSCO Academic Search Elite, Film Literature Index, International Index to Film and Television Periodicals,* and *Media Review Digest.*

Journal of Film and Video (Champaign, Ill.: University Film and Video Association, 1984– , three times a year)
The official publication of the University Film and Video Association, this internationally respected journal probes film and video production, history, theory, criticism, and aesthetics. Articles cover film and related media and their function in society, and the teaching and study of film and video. Offered in full-text form in ProQuest Direct (1997–).

Journal of Popular Film and Television (Washington, D.C.: Heldref Publications, 1978– , quarterly)
Quarterly peer-reviewed scholarly journal examines the social and cultural aspects of commercial films and television. Essays discuss at length a wide range of subjects, such as networks, genres, series, and audiences, in addition to film and TV personalities, directors, and studios. Regular features include book and video reviews, filmographies, and bibliographies. Available in full-text form in ProQuest Direct (1988–), Expanded Academic ASAP (1992–), and others.

The Moving Image (Minneapolis: University of Minnesota Press, 2001– , biannual)
Published twice a year, in the spring and fall, *The Moving Image,* the official journal of the Association of Moving Image Archivists, examines important issues involving preservation and restoration of film, television, video, and digital images. The journal is intended for archivists, librarians, technical specialists, scholars, and academics interested in the field of moving-image archiving. Articles cover ethics, techniques, and theory of restoration, and are written by leading scholars and archivists. Tables of contents of back issues (2001–) are accessible at the following Web site: http://www.upress.umn.edu/journals/movingimage/default.html.

Sight and Sound (London: British Film Institute, 1932– , monthly)
Published by the British Film Institute since 1932, this monthly magazine, which merged in 1991 with *Monthly Film Bulletin,* features critical, in-depth articles about major motion pictures and classic cinema, reviews of new feature films and new video releases, international film news, and coverage of television. Film reviews include complete cast and credit information.

Variety (New York: Variety Pub. Co., 1905– , weekly)
First published in 1905, this weekly trade paper of the motion picture, television, and theater industry features articles, columns, features, news briefs, obituaries, and special issues.

The Velvet Light Trap (Madison, Wisc.: University of Wisconsin at Madison; Austin, Tex.: University of Texas, 1971– , quarterly)
Edited by graduate students at the University of Wisconsin at Madison and the University of Texas at Austin, this scholarly journal, published quarterly, investigates and evaluates the historical questions and meanings of film, television, and other media with articles and interviews. Critical, theoretical, and historical discussion usually relates to a common theme in each issue. *The Velvet Light Trap* is indexed or abstracted in *Communication Abstracts, Film Literature Index, International Index to Film Periodicals, Sociological Abstracts, America: History and Life,* and *Historical Abstracts.*

Wide Angle (Baltimore, Md.: Johns Hopkins University Press, 1976– , quarterly)
This scholarly film studies journal features copiously illustrated articles, book reviews, and interviews with major filmmakers and numerous other film subjects suitable for students studying film or cinema history. Full-text issues are available online through ProjectMUSE (1996–99).

SELECTED WEB SITES

Academy Awards Database (http://www.oscars.org/awards_db/index.html)
This official database of the Academy of Motion Picture Arts and Sciences contains complete records of Academy Award nominees and winners in all categories.

Academy of Television Arts and Sciences (http://www.emmys.com/)
Offers complete information on current daytime and prime-time Emmy Awards winners and nominees and recent Hall of Fame inductees.

All-Movie Guide (http://www.allmovie.com/)
Features biographies of famous actors and directors, film finder and people finder databases, lengthy essays about film genres from action movies to westerns, information about current movies, and more.

BOXOFFICE Online (http://www.boxoff.com/)
The home page of BOXOFFICE *Magazine*, a trade magazine, this site contains articles, interviews, news, reviews of current movies, and previews of upcoming films. Of value to researchers are special sections accessible without charge or authorization: "Classic Reviews," which critiques 75 films from the 1930s to the 1990s, and "Review Archive," a complete database of more than 900 film reviews since 1995.

Cinema Sites (http://www.cinema-sites.com/Cinema_Sites_REV.html)
Compiled by and maintained by David R. Augsburger, this comprehensive directory lists various sources of film reviews.

Film.com (http://www.film.com/)
Provides full-text access to reviews, recent film releases, and movie news.

FilmCritic.com: Movie Reviews on Internet Time (http://www.filmcritic.com/)
Established in 1995 as The Movie Emporium, FilmCritic.com houses more than 41,000 movie reviews and features written by 20 critics throughout the country.

Internet Movie Database (http://www.imdb.com/)
Perhaps the most significant database of movies available on the Web today, this site contains complete production information, reviews, plot summaries, and more for more than 100,000 domestic and foreign films in all genres. IMDB also features listings, production, and credit information for many popular television programs, and more than 1.5 million filmographies and biographies of people from all levels of the film and television industry.

Internet Press: Movies (http://www.wwideweb.com/movies.htm)
Hundreds of links to studios, film magazines, and newspapers, movie information, old films, archives, reviews, box-office results, movie music, international film festivals, and more.

Movie Review Query Engine (http://www.mrqe.com/)
Searchable database that accesses full text of reviews of popular movies culled from a variety of sources.

New York Times Movie Reviews
(http://movies.nytimes.com/ref/movies/reviews/index.html)
Every movie review in *The New York Times* archive from 1983 to the present—more than 5,000 reviews in all—is accessible.

Roger Ebert Movie Reviews (http://www.suntimes.com/index/ebert.html)
Reviews of movies since 1985 by *Chicago Sun-Times* and TV critic Roger Ebert are available. Films are searchable by title, actor, director, producer, or writer; results are sortable by star rating, title, or date of publication.

Rotten Tomatoes: Movie Reviews and Previews (http://www.rottentomatoes.com/)
Critical reaction from the nation's top print and online film critics of movies deemed "rotten tomatoes" makes up this fun site.

TV Guide Movie Database (http://www.tvguide.com/movies/database/)
Based on Cinebooks' acclaimed 23-volume reference, *The Motion Picture Guide,* and Ephraim's Katz's comprehensive *Film Encyclopedia,* this searchable database contains cast and credits, awards won, and critical reviews for more than 30,000 movies released in the United States. (Registration is required for full access.) Other key features include movie industry news, interviews, video charts, filmographies, and biographical data on thousands of actors, directors, and other people who make films. For reviews of current films, check the "In Theaters" section in the index.

22

Health and Medicine

Many people would like to be better informed about the diseases and conditions that may threaten their health and well-being. Of paramount importance is finding accurate information on symptoms, procedures, tests, and treatments for common health issues; the effectiveness or side effects of certain prescription drugs; specific aspects of human anatomy; and the best techniques for staying fit and healthy. Vast resources are available, and some are listed below.

SELECTED BOOKS AND REFERENCES

American Medical Association Encyclopedia of Medicine, edited by Charles B. Clayman, 1,184 pages (New York: Random House, 1989)
Despite many new advances and breakthroughs in medicine since its publication, this comprehensive illustrated A–Z guide still has much to offer. It exhaustively covers common and uncommon disorders and diseases, including symptoms, diagnosis, drugs, and treatments. Some 5,000 entries list 2,800 drugs, describe more than 2,200 illnesses, explain 600 tests and operations, and much more, in language written for the layperson.

Drug Facts and Comparisons 2005, 59th Ed., 2,533 pages (St. Louis: Facts & Comparisons, 2004)
First published in 1953, this annual reference, organized by therapeutic drug class, contains facts and information for quick comparison on more than 600 generic drugs and more than 2,000 representative trade names, including charts and tables and numerous cross-references within each entry.

Encyclopedia of Human Nutrition, edited by Michele J. Sadler, 3 vols., 2,200 pages (San Diego: Academic Press, 1999)
This encyclopedia, also available as an online edition, contains signed articles with bibliographies written by an international group of distinguished academics, research scientists, and food-industry professionals. Alphabetical entries cover all aspects of nutrition—scientific, political, and social—and a wide range of other subjects, including anatomy and physiology, nutritional management, nutritional therapies, religious customs, and more. Accompanying this three-volume set are appendices with charts of weights and measures, nutritional allowances, and nutritional content of foods.

Ferri's Clinical Advisor 2005: Instant Diagnosis and Treatment, 7th Ed., by Fred Ferri, M.D., 1,568 pages (St. Louis: Mosby, Inc., 2004)
Revised annually, this latest hardcover edition, first published in 1999, features more than 1,000 topics with basic information on more than 600 disorders, including signs and symptoms, and diagnostic and therapeutic information. Divided into five sections, this easy-to-use reference also offers key information on preventive medicine, patient and disease management, and laboratory and diagnostic tests.

Gale Encyclopedia of Medicine, 3rd Ed., 5 vols., 3,956 pages (Detroit: Gale, 2005)
Compiled with the help of an advisory board of physicians, librarians, health care professionals, and writers, this five-volume reference set encompasses more than 1,700 entries, in alphabetical order, covering 965 conditions, 235 procedures and tests, and 325 therapies and treatments, including alternative and drug treatments. Signed entries run from one to three pages in length. Content includes brief bibliographies, definitions of key terms, and lists of organizations. Each volume is illustrated with black-and-white photographs, line drawings, and charts.

Mayo Clinic Family Health Book, 3rd Ed., edited by Scott C. Litin, 1,448 pages (New York: HarperResource, 2003)
This well-documented single-volume reference features detailed information on more than 1,000 diseases and disorders, human growth and development, and modern medical methods for first aid and emergency medical care.

Physicians' Desk Reference, 58th Ed., 3,200 pages, (Montvale, N.J.: Thomson Healthcare, 2003)
Annual compilation of Food and Drug Administration–approved prescription drugs with manufacturers' labeling information on more than 4,000 drugs, including some dietary supplements and other products. This latest volume was combined with an electronic version on CD-ROM.

SELECTED ARTICLE INDEXES AND ABSTRACTS

Printed Indexes and Abstracts

Abstracts of Hospital Management Studies (Ann Arbor: Health Administration Press for the Cooperative Information Center for Health Care Management Studies, the University of Michigan, 1965–87)
Also known as *Abstracts of Health Care Management Studies,* this index was actually an international journal with abstracts of studies dealing with hospital management, planning and public policy, and the delivery of health care. Launched in 1965, this publication, found today mostly at university and medical school libraries, changed its name to *Abstracts of Health Care Management Studies* in 1979 until ceasing publication in July 1987.

The Alternative Press Index (College Park, Md.: Alternative Press Center, 1969–)
Published quarterly and cumulated annually, this comprehensive subject index, considered the most up-to-date guide to alternative sources, features citations to more 250 alternative periodicals. Each article is listed and cross-

referenced by subject, and citations contain the title, author, and information about the publication. Annual editions contain a selection of abstracts from 50 research journals.

Consumer Health and Nutrition Index (Phoenix, Ariz.: Oryx Press, 1985–97)
Published quarterly from July 1985 to April 1997, this index describes articles from more than 60 newspapers and magazines found in most public libraries, including *Prevention, Harvard Medical School Letter, New England Journal of Medicine,* and *The New York Times.* Index is also available on CD-ROM.

Cumulated Index to Nursing and Allied Health Literature (CINAHL) (Glendale, Calif.: Seventh-Day Adventist Hospital Association, 1956–76; Glendale Adventist Medical Center, 1977–2000)
A comprehensive and authoritative index to current periodical literature for nurses, allied health professionals, and others interested in health care issues. Approximately 640 nursing, allied health, and health-related journals are regularly reviewed and indexed for inclusion. Five bimonthly issues and one cumulative bound volume per year. Formerly titled *Cumulative Index to Nursing Literature* (Volumes 1–21) from 1956 to 1976; renamed *Cumulative Index to Nursing and Allied Health Literature* in 1977 (Volume 22). Publication ended in 2000.

Hospital Literature Index (Chicago: American Hospital Association, 1950–2000)
This primary subject and author index, produced by the Chicago American Hospital Association and the National Library of Medicine, indexes English-language journals stressing the administration, planning, and delivery of services in hospitals and other health care institutions. First called the *Cumulative Index of Hospital Literature* (1950–74), the index became known as the *Hospital Literature Index* in 1974, then as the *Hospital and Health Administration Index* in 1995. Under the name of the *Hospital Literature Index,* contents were published quarterly and cumulated annually. As the *Hospital and Health Administration Index,* the index was published three times yearly, with the third issue an annual accumulation, until 2000, when it ceased publication. The index is now part of the online database MEDLINE, published by PubMed.

Index Medicus (Bethesda, Md.: National Library of Medicine, 1966–)
Physicians, medical editors, and medical librarians consider this a most useful reference. Published by the National Library of Medicine, it is the most comprehensive index of the world's biomedical literature. It features citations to articles from 3,100 biomedical journals worldwide. Issued monthly in two-volume sets with contents arranged by subject and author, and a bibliography of medical reviews. The cumulated contents of published issues from each year comprise the annual *Cumulated Index Medicus.* The index is available electronically through the MEDLINE database, which provides direct access to citations and abstracts to articles from 3,400 journals.

International Nursing Index (New York: American Journal of Nursing Co., 1966–2000)
Produced by the American Journal of Nursing in cooperation with the National Library of Medicine from 1966 to 2000, this subject-author index

includes nursing journal articles also covered in the online database MEDLINE.

Nursing Studies Index, 4 vols. (Philadelphia: Lippincott, 1963–72; New York: Garland Pub. Co., 1984)
Print index compiled by the Yale University School of Nursing covering nursing literature published between 1900 and 1959. This four-volume annotated guide cites studies, historical materials, research/search methods in periodicals, books, and pamphlets published in English. Virginia A. Henderson, a research associate at the Yale University School of Nursing, was funded to direct the project—then called the *Nursing Studies Index Project*—from 1959 to 1971, producing the first annotated index of nursing research.

Physical Education Index (Cape Girardeau, Mo.: BenOak Pub. Co., 1970–97)
Annual index providing citations abstracts to journal articles about physical education and related disciplines (sports, sports medicine, dance, coaching, fitness, motor learning, etc.) from 303 core scholarly journals and numerous other publications from between 1970 and 1997. Now available as an online database through Cambridge Scientific Abstracts.

Physical Fitness/Sports Medicine (Washington, D.C.: The President's Council on Physical Fitness and Sports, 1978–94)
The *Physical Fitness/Sports Medicine* index consisted of citations to more than 3,000 periodicals, including *Physical Fitness/Sports Medicine,* a publication of the President's Council on Physical Fitness and Sports, and papers presented at selected sessions of Congress. Citations of the President's Council *Physical Fitness/Sports Medicine* periodical began with the winter 1978 issue and ended with the spring 1994 issue.

Science Citation Index (Philadelphia: Institute for Scientific Information, 1961–95)
Published by the Institute for Scientific Information, this index, now also offered online, features citations to published journals in the fields of chemistry, mathematics, medicine, biology, engineering, and physics. Also offered on CD-ROM and on microfiche.

Web Indexes and Abstracts

AgeLine (American Association of Retired Persons, 1966–)
Compiled by the Research Information Center of the American Association of Retired Persons (AARP), AgeLine contains citations to published literature on health services, technology, research, and consumer information for and about adults age 50 and older. Abstracted are books, journal and magazine articles, research reports, and videos focusing on clinical and nonclinical aspects of health care delivery. Publications featured in this database are from 1978 to the present, with selected coverage from 1966 to 1977. This database can be accessed free of charge at http://research.aarp.org/ageline/home.html.

The Alternative Press Index (OCLC/Alternative Press Center, 1991–)
Online version of this guide to the alternative press in the United States and around the world from 1991 to the present. Includes citations and abstracts

of articles, editorials, book reviews, and columns found in more than 250 alternative journals, newsletters, and newspapers. Each article is cross-referenced by subject.

Biological Sciences (Cambridge Scientific Abstracts, 1982–)
This interdisciplinary database features abstracts and citations to research, literature, conference proceedings, technical reports, monographs, and selected books, including 20 separate subfiles covering a variety of biological and medical issues.

Consumer Health and Nutrition Index (National Services Corp., 1985–97)
This CD-ROM companion to the print index contains more than 94,000 records and 5,600 subject headings with abstracts from more than 70 consumer health and medical publications. Journals indexed include: *American Family Physician, Longevity, Men's Health Letter, JAMA, Medical Abstracts Newsletter, Diabetes Forecast, Healthline, Nutrition Today, Consumer Reports on Health, Executive Good Health Report, Environmental Nutrition Newsletter, Vegetarian Times, Prevention, American Baby, Arthritis Today, New England Journal of Medicine, Health,* and *Vibrant Life.*

Cumulative Index to Nursing and Allied Health (CINAHL) (CINAHL Information Systems, 1982–)
Outstanding online index of articles from more than 1,200 nursing and allied health journals. Also indexes selected books, dissertations, proceedings, and audiovisual materials. While CINAHL is mostly citations of articles, full text is provided for 27 nursing journals. Index is available in print as well, under the titles *Cumulative Index to Nursing Literature* (1956–76) and *Cumulative Index to Nursing and Allied Health Literature* (1977–2001)

Dissertation Abstracts (FirstSearch, 1861–)
Covering a variety of subject areas, this index contains information on dissertations accepted at U.S. institutions of learning, with limited coverage given to international institutions. Printed edition offers indexing from 1955 to 1982.

ISI Current Contents Connect (Thomson ISI, past five years plus current year)
Powered by ISI Web of Knowledge, this multidisciplinary Web database, updated daily, provides complete access to abstracts, tables of contents, and bibliographic information from more than 8,000 leading scholarly journals and more than 2,000 books, with links to full-text articles, documents, and additional Web resources.

MEDLINE (PubMed/National Library of Medicine, 1950–)
Compiled by the National Library of Medicine, this premier medical database provides bibliographic citations and abstract references to more than 4,000 professional and scholarly journals. Articles cover all aspects of health care and medicine and are fully searchable. This database is the electronic version of the print *Index Medicus*, the *Index to Dental Literature*, and the *International Nursing Index*. An expanded version, MEDLINEPlus, includes medical dictionaries, information clearinghouses, organizations, publications, and consumer health libraries.

Physical Education Index (Cambridge Scientific Abstracts, 1970–)
Physical Education Index contains citations from peer-reviewed journals, conference proceedings, patents, reports, trade magazines, and articles from popular and other relevant publications. Covers such topics as biomechanics and kinesiology, health, measurement and evaluation, motor learning, physical education, physical fitness, physical therapy, and more.

Science Citation Index (Web of Science/Institute for Scientific Information, 1995–)
Published by the Institute for Scientific Information, this index covers the fields of chemistry, mathematics, medicine, biology, engineering, and physics. Content is searchable by title, author, or subject.

Social Sciences Index (H.W. Wilson, 1974–).
This electronic author-subject index provides bibliographic references to periodicals in the fields of anthropology, area studies, community health and medical care, economics, family studies, minority studies, social work, sociology, and related subjects.

TOXLINE (Cambridge Scientific Abstracts, 1994–)
Produced by the National Library of Medicine, TOXLINE provides abstracted information on chemicals, pharmaceuticals, pesticides, and pollutants.

SELECTED FULL-TEXT ARTICLE DATABASES

Academic Search Premier (InfoTrac, indexing: 1984– , full text: 1990–)
A good source for scholarly journals, this database offers full-text access to nearly 3,180 scholarly publications in all academic disciplines. Coverage varies by publication, but most full-text articles are from 1990 to the present.

Health and Wellness Resource Center (InfoTrac, 1980–)
Full-text indexing and access to articles on a myriad of health and medicine issues from nearly 400 newspapers and periodicals. Database also offers full-text encyclopedias, directories, medical dictionaries, and pamphlets, and Web links. Newspaper and magazine content is similar to that of Health Reference Center—Academic.

Health Periodicals Database (Gale Group, 1976–)
This single resource, available through DIALOG, offers timely, in-depth information on a wide range of health, fitness, nutrition, and specialized medical topics. Indexed are citations and abstracts and full text of 130 consumer health periodicals and 110 core health publications, including professional medical journals and pamphlets from medical associations. Coverage includes such topics as AIDS, biotechnology, cardiovascular disease, dieting, drug abuse, environment and public health, gerontology, health care costs, medical ethics, mental health, occupational health and safety, sports medicine, and toxicology.

Health Reference Center—Academic (InfoTrac, 1980–)
Health Reference Center—Academic has nearly the same magazine and newspaper coverage as *Health and Wellness Resource Center.* It provides indexing of medical, nursing, and consumer-oriented information from more than 200 medical journals and consumer health magazines since 1980. This

includes more than 150 full-text articles, selective indexing of 1,500 general interest titles, and the full text of six medical reference books and more than 500 pamphlets. Book references include the *Columbia University College of Physicians and Surgeons Complete Home Medical Guide* and *The Consumer Health Information Source Book*.

LexisNexis Academic Universe (LexisNexis, 1977–)
Providing up-to-date coverage of a variety of subjects, including news and current events, from more than 5,600 sources, LexisNexis Academic Universe is also a good place for finding full-text articles in the field of medicine. Years covered varies but most go back at least ten years.

Nursing Journals (ProQuest, 1984–)
Contains the full text of articles from more than 275 key nursing journals, some of which are duplicated in CINAHL.

Periodical Abstracts Research II Edition with Full Text (UMI ProQuest, 1986–)
Provides abstracts, indexing, and full text of articles from academic journals, popular magazines, and key business publications. It is a full-text resource providing complete coverage of high-demand sources. The database covers more than 1,600 general-reference publications, including 635 periodicals related to the social sciences, 169 in the general sciences, and 239 general-interest publications. The full text edition includes ASCII full-text articles from approximately 600 of the indexed titles.

SELECTED PERIODICALS

FDA Consumer (Rockville, Md.: U.S. Department of Health, Education, and Welfare, Public Health Service, Food and Drug Administration, 1967– , bimonthly)
Published bimonthly by the U.S. Food and Drug Administration, *FDA Consumer,* formerly known as *FDA Papers* (1967–72), offers informative, in-depth articles on food, drugs, and health-related issues of interest to consumers. Articles focus on ways to get healthy and stay healthy and include reports on current FDA activities to regulate products, such as food, human and animal drugs, medical devices, cosmetics, radiation-emitting products, biologics, and more.

Harvard Health Letter (Stamford, Conn.: Consumer Health Publishing Group, 1975– , monthly)
The Harvard Health Letter is a source of authoritative health information, research news, and the latest developments in treatments and medications. With more than 180,000 subscribers, each issue features articles reviewed and approved by Harvard's editorial board on such health issues as Alzheimer's disease, depression, diabetes, heart disease, preventive medicine, and more.

Health (Birmingham, Ala.: Health Publishing, Inc., 1967– , 10 times a year)
This glossy consumer magazine for women features current news and informative feature articles on health and beauty and ways to live and keep healthy.

JAMA: Journal of the American Medical Association (Chicago: American Medical Association, 1848– , weekly)
The official journal of the American Medical Association, this flagship publication, published weekly online, features original, well-researched, and peer-reviewed articles on a wide range of medical topics and multiple areas of medicine. Articles focus on clinical science, controversial issues, disease prevention, new developments, ethical and legal concerns, public health, quality of medical care, and more. Contents also include medical news, opinion papers, and book reviews. Subscribers to this journal also have full access to current and past issues, full text and abstracts from January 1998 to the present; abstracts only from January 1975 to December 1997; and tables of contents only from January 1966 to December 1974. To access the JAMA archives, visit http://jama.ama-assn.org/ (click on "Past Issues").

New England Journal of Medicine (Boston: Massachusetts Medical Society, 1812– , weekly)
First published in 1812, this leading weekly peer-reviewed medical journal reports on the latest medical breakthroughs and research findings of interest to professionals in the fields of biomedical science and clinical practice. Each issue contains research findings, opinion papers, and book reviews on a variety of topics. Most articles published in the journal deal with internal medicine and specialty areas, including allergy/immunology, cardiology, endocrinology, gastroenterology, hematology, kidney disease, oncology, pulmonary disease, rheumatology, HIV, and infectious diseases. Abstracts summarizing articles published in current and past issues are available through the journal's Web site from 1975 to the present (http://content.nejm.org/).

Prevention (Emmaus, Pa.: Rodale, 1950– , monthly)
Prevention magazine discusses the latest ways to achieve a healthy lifestyle. Each issue features articles stressing the importance of exercise, nutrition, mental health, and other issues with an emphasis on the prevention of illness.

SELECTED WEB SITES

AMA Health Info (http://www.ama-assn.org/ama/pub/category/3158.html)
This Web page of the American Medical Association (AMA) features the AMA's Patient Education Resource (Medem) database, with access to medical information from leading U.S. medical societies.

Biomedicine and Health in the News (http://library.uchc.edu/bhn/)
A free service of the Lyman Maynard Stowe Library at the University of Connecticut Health Center, this unique Web site provides quick access to citations of biomedical, scientific, and health journal literature reported in *The New York Times* from 1994 through March 2004. Each citation is accompanied by a brief summary of the article and, in some cases, the full citation to the published journal literature is included.

1stHeadlines-Health (http://www.1stheadlines.com/health.htm)
Continuously updated 24 hours a day, 1stHeadlines is a comprehensive directory of stories from top online news sources, including newspapers and tele-

vision news networks. Stories are listed by category—U.S. and world, business, health, lifestyles, sports, technology, and weather. The health section provides access to the latest news in this field.

healthfinder (http://www.healthfinder.gov/)
This federal gateway to reliable health information offers visitors a variety of choices, including a health library organized from A to Z; "Just for You" health topics organized by age, race, and ethnicity; information about doctors, dentists, hospitals, health insurance, and more; and a directory of selected health information Web sites such as those of government agencies, information clearinghouses, nonprofit organizations, and universities.

MayoClinic.com (http://www.mayoclinic.com)
Home page of the world-renowned Mayo Clinic with a directory of health resources. Direct access is provided to A-to-Z online database of diseases and conditions, information about healthy living, a searchable drug database with brand names, descriptions, purposes, and common side effects, and health decision guides on a wide range of health issues.

Medical Breakthroughs (http://www.ivanhoe.com/home/p_home.cfm)
Published by Ivanhoe Broadcast News, Inc., this site contains the latest medical news from leading medical centers and research labs, browsable or searchable by topic.

MEDLINEPlus (http://medlineplus.gov/)
A public service of the National Library of Medicine and the National Institutes of Health, MEDLINEPlus is a database covering 650 topics on conditions, diseases and wellness, drug information, and much more.

Merck Manual (http://www.merck.com/mrkshared/mmanual/home.jsp)
Provides full online searching of the popular medical reference *The Merck Manual of Diagnosis and Therapy*, offering detailed descriptions of virtually every disease and condition, including symptoms, signs, and forms of treatment.

National Center for Health Statistics News Releases and Fact Sheets (http://www.cdc.gov/nchs/releases.htm)
Offers statistical fact sheets on a diverse range of public health issues, including contraceptive use, infant mortality, teen pregnancy, and youth suicide published from 1994 to the present. Fact sheets include references to reports and telephone numbers for follow-up information.

Newswise (http://www.newswise.com/nwhome.htm)
A comprehensive database of current news, plus a searchable archive, Newswise features the latest news releases from major institutions in the fields of scientific, medical, and business research. News sections include science, medical, and business news, searchable or browsable by date.

WebMD (http:/www.webmd.com)
WebMD offers free access to information on conditions or diseases on seemingly every topic.

History

The birth of civilization, the invention of the first gas-powered automobile, the outbreak of the Civil War, the new developments in culture, fashion, and technology, and the passing of time itself all share something in common: They are all major moments in American and world history. Literally hundreds of historical references are accessible in print or electronic form, each providing a unique perspective on history. A bevy of general references, illustrated histories, historical periodicals, and electronic resources, including CD-ROM and online databases, is available at most libraries. Selected sources in this category as recommended by librarians and researchers are:

SELECTED BOOKS AND REFERENCES

General Sources

Handbook for Research in American History: A Guide to Bibliographies and Other Reference Works, 2nd Ed., by Francis Paul Prucha, 214 pages (Lincoln: University of Nebraska Press, 1994)
Although slightly outdated, this handbook, first published in 1987 and revised in 1994, remains a useful tool for locating many print and electronic sources for historical research. The book is divided into two sections. The first section highlights bibliographies, indexes to periodical literature, maps and atlases, and government publications. The second section incorporates chapters discussing various other reference sources for broad-subject areas, such as military history, and more specialized topics, such as diplomatic history. An author-title-subject index offers easy cross-referencing of subjects.

U.S. History

Dictionary of American History, 3rd Ed., edited by Stanley I. Kutler, 10 vols. (New York: Charles Scribner's Sons, 2003)
Originally published in 1940, this fully revised edition of the 10-volume library reference offers quick access to more than 4,000 definitive articles, ranging from 100 to 800 words in length, on a broad spectrum of topics in American history. The new edition includes more than 800 new entries. Incorporated in text for the first time are more than 1,500 illustrations and 300 maps.

Encyclopedia of American History, edited by Gary B. Nash, 11 vols., 4,864 pages (New York: Facts On File, 2003)
This 11-volume reference offers in-depth coverage of the most important individuals, events, and topics in U.S. history. Unlike most encyclopedias, this reference is arranged chronologically and organized by era. The encyclopedia was developed and supervised by Gary B. Nash, a professor of American history at the University of California, Los Angeles, and author of the *National Standards for United States History*. Each volume was edited by leading scholars and specialists in the field.

Encyclopedia of American Military History. 3rd Ed., by Spencer C. Tucker, 1,200 pages (New York: Facts On File, 2003)
Written by military historian Spencer C. Tucker, this well-organized and easy-to-use encyclopedia presents more than 1,200 entries on the subject of American military history from the colonial era to the "war on terror" beginning with the events of September 11, 2001. Illustrated by more than 200 black-and-white photographs and 50 maps, this three-volume set documents seemingly every aspect of military history—military leaders, wars, campaigns, battles, events, famous soldiers, military branches, key technological developments, overviews of weapons systems, and more. Includes a glossary, bibliography, and index.

Encyclopedia of the American Civil War: A Political, Social, and Military History, edited by David S. Heidler and Jeanne T. Heidler, 5 vols., 2,733 pages (Santa Barbara, Calif.: ABC-CLIO, 2000)
With a foreword written by Pulitzer Prize–winning author James M. McPherson, this five-volume reference set chronicles the Civil War in an easy-to-read A-to-Z format. Combining the efforts of editors and more than 250 contributors, this remarkable reference offers more than 1,600 concise articles—ranging from a few paragraphs to several pages—on seemingly every aspect of this period in American history. Supplementing the entries are more than 500 black-and-white illustrations, 75 maps, and more than 250 primary source documents that bring to life every battle, military life, and the war's impact on society.

Encyclopedia of the Vietnam War: A Political, Social and Military History, edited by Spencer C. Tucker, 3 vols., 1,196 pages (Santa Barbara, Calif.: ABC-CLIO, 2001)
This three-volume encyclopedia, written by the author of the *Encyclopedia of American History*, comprehensively covers the military, social, and political aspects of the Vietnam War. Content includes detailed articles on military tactics and weapon systems, biographies of communist leaders, and critical overviews of the antiwar movement, military strategy, and various nations. Following each entry is a bibliography of references. Volume 3 documents the history of the Vietnam War, highlighted by government memos, military telegrams, speeches, policy statements, and more.

The Oxford Companion to American Military History, edited by Richard Holmes, 1,408 pages (New York: Oxford University Press, 2003)
Featuring more than 1,000 entries, this book examines the American military history with factual and extensive essays, written by more than 500 leading scholars, on the major wars and battles, weapons, and leaders.

Reference Sources in History: An Introductory Guide, 2nd Ed., by Ronald H. Fritze, Brian E. Coutts, and Louis A. Vyhnamek, 334 pages (Santa Barbara, Calif.: ABC-CLIO, 2004)
This annotated and updated volume exhaustively catalogs and summarizes more than 1,000 atlases, bibliographies, chronologies, encyclopedias, dictionaries, handbooks, and sourcebooks on practically every conceivable subject in history. More than 900 references are included, with bibliographic information cited for an additional 400 sources. This master reference work also includes guides to many history Web sites of interest to undergraduates, graduate students, academic researchers, and the general public.

The Timetables of American History, edited by Laurence Urdang, 516 pages (New York: Touchstone Books, 2001)
One of the best sources of its kind, this fascinating, updated single-volume reference provides a comprehensive account of American happenings—the people and events—in the arts, history, politics, science, technology, and more while simultaneously relating them to world events.

World History

Chronicle of the 20th Century, edited by Daniel Clifton, 1,438 pages (Liberty, Mo.: JL International Publishing, 1994)
This lavishly illustrated, entertaining reference, written in a newspaper-style format, chronicles everything about the 20th century—the people, places, events, fads and fashions, politics, personalities, wars, sports, science, and cinema.

Dictionary of Historic Documents, Revised Edition, by George C. Kohn, 656 pages (New York: Facts On File, 2003)
The only reference of its kind, the *Dictionary of Historic Documents, Revised Edition* describes and explains more than 2,400 major historic documents in world history, including their historical and social importance. Covered are key acts, agreements, bills, constitutions, court decisions, historic treaties, laws, letters, proclamations, speeches, and other writings, from the Code of Hammurabi to President George W. Bush's "Freedom and Fear Are at War" speech. Includes a list of entries by category, a timetable of documents, an extensive bibliography, and index.

Dictionary of Wars, Revised Edition, by George C. Kohn, 624 pages (New York: Facts On File, 1999)
Spanning some 4,000 years, this book offers detailed summaries of all wars from the earliest in history to the present day. It contains more than 1,800 extensively cross-referenced entries, dealing with civil wars, global conflicts, mutinies, punitive expeditions, rebellions, revolutions, and undeclared wars throughout the world.

The Encyclopedia of World History: Ancient, Medieval, and Modern,Chronologically Arranged, 6th Ed., 1,243 pages (Boston: Houghton Mifflin, 2001)
Perhaps the best single-volume reference available on the subject, this fully revised and updated edition, written by renowned historian Peter N. Stearns and 30 prominent historians, features a year-by-year and region-by-region

chronicle of the history of the world. More than 20,000 authoritatively written entries span the millennia from prehistoric times to the year 2000. Entries cover civilizations, rulers, and historical figures, people, places, and trends, and much more.

Hammond Concise Atlas of World History, 6th ed., edited by Geoffrey Barraclough, 184 pages (Union, N.J.: Hammond, 2002)
Uniquely combines the visual details of a standard atlas with well-written, lively narrative of world history from ancient history through 2001.

A History of the Twentieth Century: The Concise Edition of the Acclaimed World History, by Martin Gilbert, 832 pages (New York: Perennial, 2002)
An extraordinary volume that chronicles in year-by-year fashion world events that shaped the 20th century. Documenting the cultural developments, disasters, religious and social movements, scientific advances, technological innovations, wars, and personalities of the century.

The Random House Timetables of History, 2nd Ed., 360 pages (New York: Random House, 1996)
This pocket-sized reference provides a chronology of 7,000 years of world history, from the first civilization (4000–2000 B.C.) to the present. More than 5,000 significant moments in history are highlighted—in the arts, history, religion, and science—for easy reference.

20th Century Day by Day, edited by Daniel Clifton, 1,560 pages (New York: DK Publishing, 1999)
Ideal for students, researchers, and history buffs, this fully updated edition covers the important people, places, and events of the 20th century. Features thousands of color and black-and-white illustrations.

SELECTED ARTICLE INDEXES AND ABSTRACTS

Printed Indexes and Abstracts

America: History and Life (Santa Barbara, Calif.: ABC-CLIO, 1964–99)
Abstracts articles on the history of the United States and Canada published throughout the world, from 1450 to the present. Web version also available.

American Periodicals, 1741–1900: An Index to the Microfilm Collections—American Periodicals, 18th Century, American Periodicals, 1800–1850, American Periodicals, 1850–1900, Civil War and Reconstruction, edited by Jean Hoornstra and Trudy Heath, 341 pages (Ann Arbor, Mich.: University Microfilms International, 1979)
Comprehensive guide to the three-part microfilm series, *American Periodicals Series, 1741–1900 (APS I, II, III)* covering some 1,000 periodicals—and more than 150 years of American journalism—indexed by subject, title, editor, and reel number. Indexed are the contents to *Series I: 1741–1800—Beginnings, Series II: 1800–1950—Growth and Change*, and *Series III: 1850–1900—Crisis and Reconstruction.*

Series I is devoted to 18th-century publications, beginning with Ben Franklin's *General Magazine* and Andrew Bradford's *American Magazine* and including 80-some other titles. *Series II* features pre–Civil War periodicals, including such abolitionist journals as *The Genius of Universal Emancipation* (1821–39) and William Lloyd Garrison's *Liberator* (1831–65), and counterpoint publications such as *Southern Quarterly Review* (1842–57). *Series III* contains more than 118 periodicals from the Civil War and Reconstruction eras and from the last half of the 19th century. Full text and digitized images of the entire microfilm collection are also offered online.

Combined Retrospective Index to Journals in History, 1838–1974 (Washington, D.C.: Carrollton Press, 1977)
Eleven-volume set offering comprehensive, retrospective indexing of 243 historical periodicals by subject and author from 1838 to 1974.

Humanities Index (New York: H.W. Wilson, 1974–)
This handy volume indexes articles covering all of the humanities, including history. Popular historical journals abstracted include *Civil War History, History, Journal of Asian History, Journal of Family History, Journalism History, Labor History,* and many others.

Web Indexes and Abstracts

The Alternative Press Index (OCLC/Alternative Press Center, 1991–)
Provides Web access to citations with abstracts of 300 alternative, radical, and leftist periodicals.

America: History and Life (ABC-CLIO, 1960–)
This Web companion to the printed index offers complete bibliographic references to the United States and Canada including U.S. and Canadian history, area studies, current affairs, literature, and history-related topics in the social sciences and humanities. Article abstracts are from approximately 2,100 international journals in the social sciences and humanities, including local, state, and special-interest journals. AHL also cites book, film, and video reviews from 142 scholarly journals, and dissertations from *Dissertation Abstracts International.*

Arts and Humanities Citation Index (ISI Thomson, 1975–)
Offering keyword searching of citations to articles published in journals or used in particular books in the humanities, this index is very useful in researching the history of a subject. Cited abstracts are from 1999 to the present, with archived material since 1975. Also available is Arts and Humanities Search (1980–) via DIALOG, DataStar, and OCLC, updated weekly.

Historical Abstracts (ABC-CLIO, 1450–)
Historical Abstracts indexes the world's periodical literature in history and the related social sciences and humanities from 1450 to the present, excluding the United States and Canada, which are covered by *America: History and Life.* The database corresponds to two companion publications, *Historical Abstracts: Part A, Modern History Abstracts (1450–1914)* and *Historical Abstracts: Part B, Twentieth Century Abstracts (1914 to the Present).* Included are article abstracts and bibliographic citations of books and dissertations, covering all aspects of world history, from more than 2,100 leading journals published since 1971 in more than 50 languages, of special

interest to researchers and students of history. Cultural, diplomatic, economic, military, political, religious, and social issues, as well as the history of medicine, science, and technology, are also covered.

With more than 20,000 new citations added annually, this leading bibliography for history study is searchable by subject, descriptors, author, title, date, journal name, time period, document time, and language. Published since 1954, *Historical Abstracts* is also available via the World Wide Web and in print format through an online service company called Dialog. The printed edition covers more years than the CD-ROM version.

Humanities Index (H.W. Wilson, 1984–)
While other indexes provide more extensive research, this index, produced by the H.W. Wilson Company, cites articles from major and lesser-known English-language scholarly journals in the humanities, including such historical journals as *The American Historical Review* and *Victorian Studies,* from 1984 to the present. For research in earlier years in history, consult the printed version of this index.

Index to American Periodicals 1700–1935 (Computer Indexed Systems, 1741–)
Including all known publications from 1741 to 1935, this database combines two *Indexes to Early American Periodicals.*

International Medieval Bibliography (International Medieval Institute, University of Leeds)
Leading interdisciplinary bibliography of the Middle Ages and the most unique and comprehensive index on the subject. Featured are more than 300,000 articles published in over 4,000 journals and periodicals and 5,000 miscellaneous volumes, including conference proceedings and essay collections, related to the European Middle Ages (c. 400–1500). Produced by members of the editorial team at the University of Leeds and 30 contributors worldwide, publications dating from 1967 to the present and published in Australasia, Brazil, Europe, North America and Japan are represented. Updated yearly, a printed edition is published twice yearly, and this database is also available online.

Social Sciences Index (H.W. Wilson, 1984–)
Covering some historical topics, this major bibliographic database and companion to H.W. Wilson's Humanities Index covers major scholarly journals in anthropology, geography, political science, and social sciences since 1984. Titles include *The British Journal for the History of Science, Business History Review, History Today, The Journal of American History, Journal of World History,* and many others. When researching subject matter from earlier years, it's best to consult the printed version of this index instead.

SELECTED FULL-TEXT ARTICLE DATABASES

Academic Search Elite (EBSCOHost, indexing: 1980– , full text: 1990–)
Offers citations and some full text in wide range of academic areas, including business, social sciences, humanities, general academic, general science, education, and multicultural issues.

America Periodicals Series (UMI, 1741–1900)
Full-text and digitized images of more than 1,000 American magazines and journals published between 1741 and 1900. Periodicals include special interest and general magazines, literary and professional journals, children's and women's magazines, and many other historically significant periodicals. Many historical topics of interest are covered, including the American Revolution, Reconstruction, and independence; slavery and emancipation; the changing role of women; advances in medicine and technology, and changes in politics, science, and religion.

HarpWeek (Harper's Weekly, 1857–)
A primary source for examining 19th-century American history on a week-by-week basis, *HarpWeek* contains scanned images, with interactively linked indexes, of *Harper's Weekly* from the antebellum and Civil War eras (1857–1865) and Reconstruction period (1866–1871). Covering everything from front-line Civil War reports to the election of President Lincoln, full-text contents include editorials, news stories, illustrations, cartoons, and even advertisements.

History of the World (Bureau of Development, Inc., 1994–)
This CD-ROM database contains six highly recognized reference sources on one disk—*The Hutchinson Compact Chronology of World History, The Hutchinson Dictionary of World History, The Hutchinson Dictionary of Ideas, The Helicon Book of Days, J. M. Roberts' Shorter History of the World,* and *Bing History of the World.* The people, ideas, trends, and events that influenced the world since 10,000 B.C. are featured. There are more than 10,000 entries, quotations, tables, and feature articles, 600 illustrations, a chronology of 11,000 events, and more than 1,200 thematic chronologies. Books can be searched separately or collectively, and can be searched directly from your word processor or through Windows applications. "On This Day" anniversaries and history quizzes are among the added features.

JSTOR (Journal Storage Project, 1996–)
This comprehensive online archive includes important scholarly journal literature covering many academic fields, including history.

MilitaryLibrary FullTEXT (EBSCOHost, indexing: 1975, full text: 1990–)
Includes citations and some full-text access to more than 350 military and general-interest publications, 245 pamphlets, and indexing and abstracts for more than 380 magazines. Military publications indexed include *Army Times, Defense, Military Review,* and *Parameters.*

Palmer's Full Text Online 1785–1870 (ProQuest, 1785–)
Palmer's Full Text Online provides access for students, researchers, and the general public to 1 million articles from *The Times* covering almost a century of British and world history.

ProjectMUSE (Johns Hopkins University, 1990–)
Provides worldwide, networked subscription access to full-text articles from more 100 scholarly journals in the arts and humanities, social sciences, and mathematics.

SELECTED PERIODICALS

American Heritage (New York: Forbes, Inc., 1947– , bimonthly)
This popular bimonthly magazine focuses on a wide range of issues related to American history and the American experience, discussing the arts, business, current and international affairs, changing lifestyles, and politics.

American Historical Review (Bloomington, Ind.: American Historical Association, 1895– , five times a year)
The official publication of the American Historical Association, this major historical journal is published five times yearly (February, April, June, October, and December). It includes scholarly articles and critical reviews of current publications in all fields of history. Each issue contains articles by leading scholars, and reviews of books and films.

Chronicon: An Electronic History Journal (Cork, Ireland: University College Cork, 1997– , annually) (http://www.ucc.ie/ucc/chronicon/)
Published annually by the History Department of the University College Cork since 1997, this free e-journal features articles on all aspects of history with a particular focus on Irish history.

The English Historical Review (Oxford, England: Oxford University Press, 1886– , quarterly)
First published in 1886, *The English Historical Review,* the oldest English-language scholarly historical journal in the world today, deals with all aspects of British, European, and world history since the classical era. Published quarterly, each issue includes articles and lively debates on medieval and modern themes, book reviews, and summaries of international literature. *The English Historical Review* is abstracted and indexed by such leading library databases as America: History and Life, Historical Abstracts, British Humanities Index, CSA Worldwide Political Science Abstracts, Periodicals Contents Index, and Sociological Abstracts. The full text and tables of contents of current and past journals are available online by subscription through JSTOR and Oxford Journals Online.

Essays in History (Charlottesville, Va.: Corcoran Department of History, University of Virginia, 1954– , annually)
Founded as a print journal in 1954, this annual peer-reviewed journal is sponsored by the Corcoran Department of History at the University of Virginia and has been published solely in electronic format since 1994. It features articles on all areas of history, including book reviews. *Essays in History* is indexed in the Historical Abstracts and America: History and Life databases. Current and past electronic editions and full-text articles are accessible at the journal's main Web site (http://etext.lib.virginia.edu/journals/EH/). Copies of past issues that are not available online are obtainable from Bell & Howell Information and Learning (formerly UMI) at http://www.umi.com/.

The Historian (Kensington, R.I.: Phi Alpha Theta, 1938– , quarterly)
Found in libraries and institutions around the world, this distinguished journal features articles, interviews, and books by historians and graduate students in all fields of history. Continuously in print since the winter 1938

issue, the journal is sponsored by Phi Alpha Theta, an international society of history at the University of South Florida that promotes the study of history and encourages its student members to publish their scholarly works.

Journal of American History (Bloomington, Ind.: Organization of American Historians, 1914– , three times a year)
Published for more than 80 years by the Organization of American Historians, this leading print journal includes scholarly articles, reviews of current books, films, exhibitions, and Web sites of interest to historians, and historical essays on a wide range of topics. Full text of current issues of the *Journal of American History* is available online through History Cooperative.

SELECTED WEB SITES

American Studies Web (http://www.georgetown.edu/crossroads/asw/)
Created by David Phillips of the American Studies program at Yale University, this Web page offers links to Web sites on all aspects of American culture.

Electronic Texts Collections (http://history.hanover.edu/etexts.html)
This large collection of links, developed by the History Department at Hanover College, features indexes and other resources on European, American, and world history.

Historical Text Archive (http://historicaltextarchive.com/)
Originally founded in 1990 in Mississippi as an anonymous FTP site, Historical Text Archive offers easy access to a collection of high-quality articles, books, essays, historical photos, and links to information on a wide range of historical subjects.

History Cooperative (Champaign, Ill.: The Cooperative, 2000–) (http://www.historycooperative.org/home.html)
This site, created for history scholars and students alike, offers full-text access to current issues of many leading historical journals, including the *American Historical Review, The History Teacher, Journal of American History, Law and History Review, Western Historical Quarterly,* and many others.

Internet Library of Early Journals (http://www.bodley.ox.ac.uk/ilej/)
A joint project completed in 1999 by the Universities of Birmingham, Leeds, Manchester, and Oxford under the auspices of the eLib (Electronic Libraries) Programme, this Web site provides direct access to digital versions of 18th- and 19th-century journals together with bibliographic data. Among the 18th-century journals represented are *Annual Register, Gentleman's Magazine,* and *Philosophical Transactions of the Royal Society;* from the 19th century, *The Builder, Blackwood's Edinburg Magazine,* and *Notes and Queries.*

Medieval Review (Kalamazoo, Mich.: Medieval Institute, Western Michigan University, 1993–) (http://www.hti.umich.edu/t/tmr/)
Formerly known as *Bryn Mawr Medieval Review,* this all-electronic journal publishes reviews of current work in all areas of Medieval Studies since 1993. Published by the Medieval Institute at Western Michigan University, the pub-

lication offers searchable archives of past issues of interest to students and scholars around the world.

Michigan Electronic Library: History (http://mel.org/viewtopic.jsp?id=12978&pathid=1907)
The Michigan Electronic Library Web page features a wealth of general history resources, beneficial to students and historians, listed by geographic area, time period, and type of history.

World History Archive (http://www.hartford-hwp.com/archives/index.html)
For quick access to documents about specific topics or periods in history, this archive, arranged by geographical area and covering all regions of the world, features a collection of documents focusing on contemporary history, complete with search engine.

WWW Virtual Library: Military History (http://vlib.iue.it/history/mil/index.html)
Contains a vast collection of research tools with Web links to general and chronological resources, military history, journals, bibliographies, biographies, military museums, and more.

Yahoo Links to U.S. History (http://dir.yahoo.com/Arts/Humanities/history/)
Online directory featuring thousands of history links by region, by subject, and by time period, and additional U.S. history categories.

24

Law

Laws are enacted for the purpose of governing society. These include local, state, and federal codes, legislation, regulations, and court decisions that have either upheld or rewritten longstanding laws. There are also various consumer laws, labor laws, family laws, bankruptcy laws, laws for renting and selling a home, or leasing and purchasing a used car, and city ordinances banning smoking in public places or the use of certain trash receptacles.

Fortunately, many legal resources have been published, including hundreds of indexed and full-text articles in major law reviews, legal newspapers, bar association journals, and international law publications delivering authoritative and critical accounts on notable people, trials, and legal topics.

Available in both print and electronic form, most of the above resources can be found at your local public and college and university library, or university law library, as well as on the World Wide Web. Recommended references include:

SELECTED BOOKS AND REFERENCES

Black's Law Dictionary, 7th Ed., edited by Bryan A. Garner, 1,738 pages (St. Paul, Minn.: West Group, 1999)

The most up-to-date authoritative legal dictionary of its kind, *Black's Law Dictionary* covers in easy-to-understand language more than 24,000 terms and definitions, including 4,500 new additions. Besides offering brief and clear definitions, this book, first published in 1891, includes guides on legal maxims, the U.S. Constitution, the Universal Declaration of Human Rights, a time chart of the U.S. Supreme Court, a Federal Circuit map, and much more. Unlike previous editions, this latest edition does not feature references to court cases the definitions were derived from.

Burton's Legal Thesaurus, 3rd Ed., by William C. Burton, 1,032 pages (New York: Macmillan Library Reference, 1998)

This fully updated and revised thesaurus contains more than 7,000 terms, synonyms, definitions, and parts of speech related specifically to the legal profession—including more than 1,000 terms not in previous editions. Terms added to the third edition cover such critical subjects as electronic commerce, intellectual property, and other new developments and related laws. A thorough index is included.

Constitutional Rights Sourcebook, by Peter G. Renstrom, 770 pages (Santa Barbara, Calif.: ABC-CLIO, 1999)
Thoroughly covers virtually everything related to constitutional rights—nearly 175 Supreme Court cases and individual amendments to the U.S. Constitution—by chapter. Many hot-button legal issues are spotlighted, including affirmative action, drug testing, physician-assisted suicide, capital punishment, parental rights, hate crimes, and much more. Content is extensively cross-referenced throughout each chapter and to other cases and information discussed in subsequent chapters.

Encyclopedia of the American Constitution, 2nd Ed., edited by Leonard W. Levy and Kenneth L. Karst, 6 vols., 3,200 pages (New York: Macmillan Reference USA, 2000)
This encyclopedia contains synopses of hundreds of court cases related to constitutional law, and biographies of every Supreme Court justice and U.S. president. Volume 6 features many appendixes with full text of the Articles of Confederation and the U.S. Constitution, chronologies relating to American constitutional law, a glossary of legal terms, case index, name index, and subject index.

Encyclopedia of the American Legislative System: Studies of Principal Structures, Processes, and Policies of Congress and State Legislatures Since the Colonial Era, edited by Joel H. Silbey, 3 vols., 1,738 pages (New York: Charles Scribner's Sons; Toronto: Maxwell Macmillan Canada; New York: Maxwell Macmillan International, 1994)
This excellent three-volume reference features 91 individually authored essays covering Congress and the state legislatures from the colonial era to the present, complete with a subject index in Volume II.

Great American Court Cases, edited by Mark Mikula and L. Mpho Mabunda, 4 vols., 2,644 pages (Detroit: Gale Group, 1999)
This four-volume set, appropriate for students studying government, civics, U.S. history, and law, chronicles major U.S. court decisions—approximately 800 cases in all. Cases are organized by broad legal principles, then arranged under specific legal issues. Approximately 100 illustrations are featured in the volumes, along with an appendix with guidelines to reading legal citations, a listing of U.S. Supreme Court justices, a cumulative general index in all volumes, cross-reference lists within each volume, and a glossary of terms.

Volume 1 is devoted to individual liberties and high-profile cases such as *Gitlow v. New York* (1925) and *Hustler Magazine v. Falwell* (1988). Volume 2 explores criminal justice and such major court cases as *California v. Acevedo* (1991), *Escobedo v. Illinois* (1964), and *Mapp v. Ohio* (1961). Volume 3 examines the issue of equal protection and covers cases specific to this topic, including *Brown v. Board of Education of Topeka* (1954), *Frontiero v. Richardson* (1973), and *Roe v. Wade* (1971). Finally, Volume 4 deals exclusively with business and government court cases, such as the *Dred Scott* case (1856), *Maryland v. Wirtz* (1968), and *United States v. Nixon* (1974).

The Guide to American Law: Everyone's Legal Encyclopedia, 12 vols. with a 6-vol. supplement (St. Paul, Minn.: West Publishing Co., 1983–85; 1990–95)
Published from 1983 to 1995, this guide covers a wide range of topics and is written for a general audience. Extensively cross-referenced with name and subject indexes, this series contains many other useful elements for researchers, such as tables of legal abbreviations, acronyms, cases cited, and maps of the judicial circuits.

Martindale-Hubbell International Law Digest (New Providence, N.J.: Martindale-Hubbell, 1993–)
Leading legal resource, formerly published as part of the *Martindale-Hubbell Law Digest,* that provides summaries of statutory law for more than 60 countries. Content of the print edition is searchable through the online database LexisNexis.

Martindale-Hubbell Law Digest, 3 vols. (Summit, N.J.: Martindale-Hubbell, 1990–)
Martindale-Hubbell Law Digest offers detailed summaries of statutory laws in the United States, Canada, and the European Union, compiled and updated each year by leading legal scholars and law firms. This three-volume reference is available by itself, or as part of the multivolume *Martindale-Hubbell Law Directory,* and is also accessible in full-text form through LexisNexis.

The Martindale-Hubbell Law Directory, 24 vols. (New York: Martindale-Hubbell Law Directory, Inc., 1931–)
Perhaps the most widely consulted biographical directory in the legal community, *The Martindale-Hubbell Law Directory,* in print since 1931, features more than 900,000 entries for lawyers and law firms in the United States and 140 other countries. Information listed includes attorney and law firm names, bar admission dates, branch office locations, practice areas, and more. This popular reference is also accessible and searchable through LexisNexis.

The Oxford Companion to American Law, 912 pages (New York: Oxford University Press, 2002)
Possibly the best single encyclopedia of American law ever published, this definitive reference features nearly 500 entries written by some 300 legal and historical scholars, law school faculty members, judges, and legal writers with a minimum of legalese.

The Oxford Dictionary of American Legal Quotations, compiled by Fred R. Shapiro, 582 pages (New York: Oxford University Press, 1993)
This source boasts more than 3,500 quotations. It includes a comprehensive collection of famous excerpts from writings of American judges and legal commentators and sayings from literature, humor, motion pictures, and even some song lyrics relating to American law. A CD-ROM edition was published in 1999.

Shepard's Acts and Cases by Popular Names: Federal and State (Colorado Springs, Colo.: Shepard's Citations, Inc., 1968–)
Lists in alphabetical order all federal and state acts and cases cited by popular names. Citations to the U.S. Constitution, U.S. Code or U.S. Statutes cited

by the U.S. Supreme Court and the lower federal courts or as cited in subsequent acts of Congress. U.S. Supreme Court reports, state codes or statutes, and other legal sources are included.

West's Encyclopedia of American Law, 2nd Ed., edited by Jeffrey Lehman and Shirelle Phelps, 12 vols., 7,000 pages (Detroit: Thomson/Gale, 2004)
Written in nontechnical and nonlegal language, this well-organized 12-volume reference set features easy-to-follow explanations of more than 5,000 legal topics, including legal terms and events. In addition to defining important legal terms, this encyclopedia also contains biographies of key figures responsible for shaping U.S. law.

In addition to the above general reference sources, many law encyclopedias have been published covering various laws, codes and statutes for many different states, written more with legal professionals in mind using more technical language and legalese. Should you be interested in researching this area of the law, consult your reference library staff for a list of recommended reference titles.

SELECTED ARTICLE INDEXES AND ABSTRACTS

Printed Indexes and Abstracts

Criminal Justice Abstracts (Monsey, N.Y.: Willow Tree Press, 1977–)
A print companion to the Web database that indexes several hundred journals related to criminal justice published since 1977.

Current Law Index (Los Altos, Calif.: Information Access Corp., 1980–; Detroit: Gale Group, 2002–)
Monthly publication produced in association with the American Association of Law Libraries that indexes law-related articles about cases, statutes, legal trends, and law firm management from more than 900 law journals, legal newspapers, and specialty publications from the United States, Canada, Australia, Ireland, New Zealand, and the United Kingdom. Publications include academic reviews, bar association journals, and selected journals in the fields of accounting, business, criminal justice, criminology, estate planning, international law, and taxation. The index is divided into four separate sections: subject, author/title, case, and statute name. *Current Law Index* is also available as electronic databases called LegalTrac or Legal Resource Index.

Index to Canadian Legal Periodical Literature (Montreal: Canadian Association of Law Libraries, 1956–)
Fully bilingual (English and French) bibliographic reference that comprehensively indexes secondary legal periodicals, articles related to law in nonlegal Canadian journals, articles published in topical law reports and collected essays, and cassettes. Features author and subject indexes with complete bibliographic information, a book review index, and a table of cases.

Index to Foreign Legal Periodicals (Berkeley: University of California Press/American Association of Law Libraries, 1960–)
First published by the Institute of Advanced Legal Studies at the University of London in 1960, this annual multilingual index covers articles and book

reviews published in 520 English-language legal journals worldwide. Coverage also includes collections of legal essays, congress reports, and such areas as public and private international law, foreign law, and jurisdictions other than the United States, the United Kingdom, Canada, and Australia. Author, subject, country or region indexes items since 1958.

An Index to Legal Periodical Literature (Boston: Boston Book Co./Los Angeles: Parker and Baird Co./Buffalo: Dennis, 1786–1937)
Also known as the *Jones-Chipman Index to Legal Periodical Literature* (named after its editors), this six-volume set was the first to comprehensively index American legal periodicals from the early 19th century to 1937. The reference series includes 98,254 citations from 590 general periodical titles, 236 legal periodical titles and 67 law report titles, covering 11,000 volumes. Four volumes of the Index to Legal Periodical Literature, from 1786 to 1922, are now available in a searchable format online through the *19th Century Masterfile* database.

Index to Legal Periodicals and Books (New York: H.W. Wilson, 1908–)
The most significant index of legal periodical literature from 1908 to 1980, this print companion—originally called the *Index to Legal Periodicals*—to the online database, indexes more than 600 legal books and periodicals by subject. Publications cited include yearbooks, bar association journals, university publications and law reviews, and government publications from the United States, Puerto Rico, Great Britain, Ireland, Canada, Australia, and New Zealand. The database also indexes some 1,000 books per year. Excluded are legal newspapers, newsletters, and some journals covered in the print version of *Current Law Index* and popular Web databases, such as LegalTrac. The index is also available on CD-ROM and online with coverage from 1981 to the present.

Index to Periodical Articles Related to Law (Dobbs Ferry, N.Y.: Glandville, 1958–)
Since publication of its first volume in September 1958, this annual compendium indexes periodicals in subject areas related to law, such as aspects of social science and business.

Shepard's Law Review Citations, 2 vols. with supplements (Colorado Springs, Colo.: Shepard's Citations, 1968–)
Updated with annual supplements, Shepard's Law Review Citations extensively covers citations to articles from legal periodicals of federal court cases since 1957. Articles published in state and regional reporter system and some major law reviews are also cited. Law reviews and legal periodicals cited in the index are listed in alphabetical order by title. Articles are indexed from 19 law reviews. Material from 1957 to 1993 is contained in two hardcover volumes, with additional citations featured in bound softcover supplements since 1994.

Web Indexes and Abstracts

Criminal Justice Abstracts (SAGE Publications, Inc., 1966–)
Extensively indexes 184 journals, including 45 with full-text articles, mostly dealing with criminal justice topics, including courts, punishment, and sen-

tencing. A Web-based database is also available through Cambridge Scientific Abstracts and Ovid.

Index to Foreign Legal Periodicals (RLG, 1960–)
Similar to the print edition, this online version—part of the RLG Citation Resources database—indexes articles and book reviews from more than 550 legal periodicals, the contents of 80 individually published collections of legal essays, festschrifts, melanges, and congressional reports, and a wide range of legal journals. Excluded are materials related to the laws of the United States, and the United Kingdom, with the countries in the British Commonwealth.

Index to Legal Periodicals Full Text (H.W. Wilson, 1981–)
Originally begun in print more than 50 years ago, this index offers full-text coverage of all aspects of the law. International in scope with coverage of periodicals from the U.S., Canada, Great Britain, Ireland, Australia, and New Zealand, it provides access to books, book reviews, court decisions, jurisdictional surveys, scholarly articles, symposia, and more. That includes full text of more than 200 selected periodicals, indexing of 1,000 legal journals, law reviews, institutes, statutes, bar association publications, university publications, and government publications, and nearly 300 law reviews—more than any comparable database.

Legal Resource Index (LexisNexis/Westlaw, 1980–)
Published by LexisNexis and Westlaw, this online database, based on the Current Law Index, covers some 850 law journals and periodicals published in the United States, Canada, the United Kingdom, Australia, and other English-speaking countries. Although similar content is covered in LegalTrac, coverage dates for most periodicals is since 1980. To research legal subjects before 1980, consult the hardcover reference *Index to Legal Periodicals.*

LegalTrac (InfoTrac, 1980–)
Subscription database, also derived from the Current Law Index, that indexes all major law reviews, legal newspapers, specialty law publications, bar association journals, and law-related articles published by U.S. general interest publications. Topics are searchable by subject, author, and case and statute names. Selected full-text articles are also available.

LexisNexis Statistical Universe (LexisNexis, 1973–)
Abstracts and indexes more than 100,000 state and federal government, association, research institutes, international, and nongovernmental organization statistical publications. Some full-text statistical tables are accessible, as well as direct links to agency Web sites to browse, download, or print the entire content of publications. The database combines three statistical indexes: *American Statistical Index* (1973), covering U.S. government publications, *Statistical Reference Index* (1980–), featuring state, business, and association publications, and the *Index to International Statistics* (1983–), focusing on intergovernmental publications.

NCJRS Abstracts Database (National Criminal Justice Reference Service Abstracts, 1972–)
Features summaries of federal, state, and local government reports, books, journal articles, research reports, and other criminal justice publications,

including previously unpublished research. Users also are able to search and browse the National Criminal Justice Research Service collection of more than 7,000 full-text publications.

PAIS International (OCLC Public Affairs Information Service, 1972–)
Abstracts many criminal justice and law-rated journal articles, books, statistical yearbooks, directories, conference proceedings, research reports, and government documents covering domestic and international public policy.

PsycINFO (American Psychological Association, 1887–)
Covers the psychological aspects of criminal and social behavior with abstracts and full-text articles from more than 40 journals published by the American Psychological Association (1988–).

Social Services Abstracts (Cambridge Scientific Abstracts, 1980–)
Abstracts and indexes articles on criminal justice from more than 1,600 periodicals.

Sociological Abstracts (Sociological Abstracts, Inc./Cambridge Scientific Abstracts, 1963–)
In the areas of sociology and social behavioral sciences, this bibliographic database abstracts and indexes international literature, such as books, conference papers, dissertations, and journal articles. Some 1,800 publications are referenced.

SELECTED FULL-TEXT ARTICLE DATABASES

Academic Search Elite (EBSCOHost, 1990–)
A leading general reference database, Academic Search Elite provides access to current and previously published articles from all disciplines in leading scholarly journals and newspapers.

CQ Researcher (Congressional Quarterly, 1983–)
Highlights comprehensive and detailed reports, with bibliographic references, published by Congressional Quarterly, focusing on a wide variety of current events and major political and social issues. Subjects are searchable by keyword and date.

Criminology: SAGE Full-Text Collection (SAGE Publications, 1982–)
Published by SAGE Publications, this popular criminology database covers 15 criminal justice journals with access to more than 4,100 articles on related subjects. Summaries or abstracts are provided with each searchable entry, along with full-text PDF versions of each article. Journals represented in this collection include *Crime and Delinquency* (1984–), *Criminal Justice* (2001–), *Criminal Justice and Behavior* (1982–), *Criminal Justice Policy Review* (2000–), *Homicide Studies* (1997–), and many more.

Expanded Academic ASAP (InfoTrac, 1980–)
Covering a wide variety of subjects and disciplines, Expanded Academic ASAP indexes more than 2,700 scholarly, trade, and general-interest journals, magazines, and newspapers with full-text coverage of 1,400 titles. Included are many leading law journals, such as *Law and Contemporary Problems*

(1984–), *Law in Context* (1999–) *Law, Medicine and Health Now: Journal of Law, Medicine and Ethics* (1982–), and *Law and Policy in International Business* (1980–).

HeinOnline (Buffalo, New York: William S. Hein & Co., 1808–)
Produced by William S. Hein & Co., Inc., an American legal publisher for more than 80 years, *HeinOnline* provides full-text access to more than 400 international law journals, both current and historical. The subscription database is very useful for researching articles and journals from the early 19th century to the present that are not covered by Legal Resource Index, LexisNexis, or Westlaw. The collection includes U.S. law journals, international law journals, treaties and agreements, U.S. Supreme Court literature, and more.

LexisNexis Academic Universe (LexisNexis, 1982–)
Especially strong in the area of law, this full-text database covers news, business, medical, and legal information from more than 5,000 sources, including major newspapers, magazines, federal and state court decisions, and law reviews.

Periodical Abstracts Research II Edition with Full Text (UMI ProQuest, 1986–)
Abstracts and indexing, with full-text articles, of more than 1,600 academic journals, popular magazines, and leading business publications, some of which include social science and general-interest publications reporting on criminal justice and behavioral science.

PsycINFO (American Psychological Association, 1887–)
PsycINFO indexes more than 1,300 psychology and psychological journals, books, dissertations, and technical reports in 25 different languages, including such subjects as sociology, law, physiology, and psychiatry. Law journals cited focus on the psychological and social aspects of law and human behavior. Journals include *Law and Human Behavior* (1977–) *Law and Psychology Review* (1975–), and *Law and Society Review* (1983–).

UMI Dissertation Abstracts (UMI/Oryx Press, Abstracts, 1980–; full text, 1997–)
Abstracts seemingly every doctoral dissertation since 1861—more than 1.4 million of them—produced at accredited U.S. colleges and universities on a variety of scholarly topics. Abstracts are from 1981 to the present, and full-text material since 1997.

WilsonWeb (H.W. Wilson, 1982–)
Indexes approximately 3,800 periodicals, with full text of many journals.

SELECTED PERIODICALS

National Law Journal: The Weekly Newspaper for the Profession (New York: American Lawyer Media, 1978– , weekly)
This leading professional journal reports the latest news and legal developments of interest to attorneys, including federal circuit court decisions, legal verdicts, legal news from the business and private sectors, and a host of

important legislative issues. Online full-text articles are available through LexisNexis and Westlaw.

The Practical Lawyer (Philadelphia, Pa.: American Law Institute–American Bar Association, Committee on Continuing Professional Education, 1955– , 6 times yearly)
Published six times a year by the American Law Institute–American Bar Association, this journal offers information on legal topics. Articles offer practical solutions to problems in commercial and corporate law, real estate, litigation, tax and estate planning, and more.

SELECTED WEB SITES

American Bar Association Periodicals (Chicago: American Bar Association, current) (http://www.abanet.org/abastore/index.cfm)
One of the most respected legal publishers, the American Bar Association publishes more than 60 magazines, journals, and newsletters. The Web site provides a complete A to Z list of titles. Links provide descriptive information about the background, history, and content of each publication.

The Constitution of the United States (http://www.law.cornell.edu/constitution/constitution.table.html)
Sponsored by the Legal Information Institute at Cornell University Law School, this site contains the entire U.S. Constitution, section by section.

FedLaw (http://www.thecre.com/fedlaw/default.htm)
Extremely useful online collection of legal references regarding federal legal issues, indexed by title or topic, by federal statutes and regulations, and by federal and legislative branch. Also provides lists of general legal research and references and professional associations and organizations.

FindLaw.com (http://www.findlaw.com)
One of the Web's leading legal authorities, FindLaw.com is a great source for researching local, U.S., foreign, and international legal issues.

Internet Legal Resource Guide (http://www.ilrg.com/)
Categorized directory of more than 4,000 Web sites from around the world concerning the law and legal profession, with a primary emphasis on the laws and legal sources in the United States.

The Legal Information Institute (http://supct.law.cornell.edu/supct/)
Online resource containing full text of every U.S. Supreme Court opinion since 1990, and court decisions for all 50 states.

Legal Periodicals Online (http://library.lsuc.on.ca/GL/research_periodicals.htm)
Developed and maintained by the Law of Society of Upper Canada Great Library, this Web site features an annotated list of dozens of law journals and other legal periodicals available on the Internet, listed in alphabetical order and by state and province or category. Includes periodicals with full-text online access or access to abstracts or tables of contents of current and past

issues. Publications include state law journals, such as *Akron Law Review* (1967–), and law society or law association periodicals, such as *The Young Lawyer* (1997–).

U.S. Supreme Court Decisions (http://www.findlaw.com/casecode/supreme.html)
Offered by FindLaw.com, this Web page has a searchable full-text database of U.S. Supreme Court decisions from 1893 to the present.

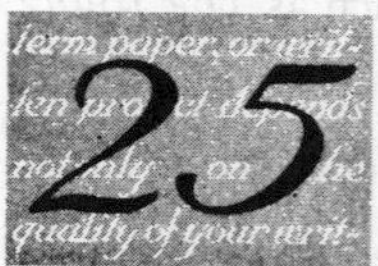

Literature and Literary Criticism

When it comes to the study of literature or critical examination of famous authors, novelists, poets, and literary works, leading scholars and historians have compiled countless volumes of analysis, criticism, and research. For any study devoted to the analysis, interpretation, evaluation, or comparison of literature, you can find many resources to help you understand and interpret the work you are studying. In print or electronic form, and on the Web, you can find articles, essays, book reviews, scholarly and popular journals, dictionaries, encyclopedias, and handbooks. With so many available resources, you may not know where to start. The following list of sources will assist you in your quest for research and information on any subject, or literary figure:

SELECTED BOOKS AND REFERENCES

Anthologies

Norton Anthology of American Literature, 6th Ed., 5 vols., edited by Nina Baym and Judith Tanka (New York: W.W. Norton, 1998)

Classic, broadly focused anthology of American literature featuring the works of 212 well-known writers, including 38 new additions—many in their entirety—from Native American to postmodern women writers. Thirty complete works are included in this two-volume set, among them *The Awakening, A Streetcar Named Desire,* and newer entries, such as Allen Ginsberg's *Howl,* and David Mamet's *Glengarry Glen Ross.*

Oxford Companion to American Literature, 6th Ed., edited by James David Hart and Philip Leininger, 779 pages (New York: Oxford University Press 1995)

This anthology encompasses more than 5,000 scholarly entries treating all areas of American literature. Among the entries are more than 2,000 biographical profiles of U.S. and foreign authors examining each author's style, subjects, and major literary works. In addition, 1,100 summaries discuss major American novels, biographies and autobiographies, essays, plays, poems, and stories. Many other subjects related to writing in America are highlighted as well, such as literary awards, literary and social history, and all are extensively cross-referenced and indexed for easy use.

Biography and Literary Criticism

Contemporary Authors, 202 vols. (Detroit: Gale Research, 1962–)

Published since 1962, this multivolume source supplies biographical and bibliographic information on more than 120,000 modern fiction and nonfiction writers from many countries and fields, including novelists, poets, playwrights, scriptwriters, journalists, biographers, and essayists. This popular reference series is also available on the Web separately and as part of Gale's Literary Index by subscription.

Contemporary Literary Criticism, 178 vols. (Detroit: Gale Research, 1973–)

First published in 1973, this ongoing reference series offers critical essays of authors now living or deceased since 1960 originally published in books, scholarly and popular periodicals, and newspapers with bibliographical citations to the full critical study for further reference. A separate cumulative title index accompanies the set.

Contemporary Novelists, 7th Ed., edited by Josh Lauer and Neil Schlager, 1,200 pages (Detroit: St. James Press, 2000)

This encyclopedic reference, originally published in 1972, includes biographies, bibliographies, and critical essays on approximately 650 contemporary English-language novelists, including 100 new entries. Includes nationality and title indexes. Also offered online as part of Gale's Literary Index, a master index of literary references published by Gale.

Contemporary Poets, 7th Ed., 1,443 pages (Detroit: St. James Press, 2000)

Fully revised and updated reference featuring biographical and bibliographical data on 787 contemporary English-language poets, with 120 new entries added. Coverage includes personal and career information, critical essays, and detailed bibliographies covering each poet's works. Nationality and title indices are provided for cross-referencing of subjects. Written by noted experts, this reference is also accessible online as part of Gale's Literary Index, featuring 130 literature references from Gale and other publishers' imprints.

Dictionary of Literary Biography (Detroit: Gale Group, 2004)

With nearly 300 volumes published since 1978, this reference series provides detailed biographical and critical information on more than 10,000 authors grouped by period, genre, or movement from a wide range of historical periods and nationalities written by more than 8,000 editors and contributors. Each entry includes a biography, a complete listing of the author's writings, and a selection of critical sources for further study. Mostly focusing on English or American authors, the series also covers 20th-century American and British science fiction and fantasy writers prior to World War I. Yearbooks, published annually since 1980, feature updates of previously included authors and new authors. The final volume indexes the authors by name and corresponds with entries to all volumes. The entire contents of the series are available as a single online database and also as part of Gale's Literary Index.

Magill's Bibliography of Literary Criticism: Selected Sources for the Study of More Than 2,500 Outstanding Works of Western Literature, edited by Frank N. Magill, 4 vols., 2,380 pages (Englewood Cliffs, N.J.: Salem Press, 1979)
This four-volume set indexes criticism in books and periodicals and all types of literature from biblical times through 1979. Each volume contains an author-title index, and Volume 4 is a title index.

Magill's Critical Survey of Long Fiction, 2nd Rev. Ed., edited by Carl Rollyson and Frank N. Magill, 8 vols., 4,392 pages (Pasadena, Calif.: Salem Press, 2000)
Revised in 2000, this multivolume series, formerly edited by Frank N. Magill and first published in 1983, supplies critical studies and in-depth overviews of major authors of long fiction.

Magill's Critical Survey of Poetry, 2nd Rev. Ed., edited by Philip K. Jason and Frank N. Magill, 8 vols., 5,352 pages (Pasadena, Calif.: Salem Press, 2002)
Revised version of the original 1982 edition edited by Frank N. Magill featuring scholarly articles and in-depth essays on 368 English-language poets, including 27 new entries, examining the work of major and minor poets. Each entry, averaging 10 pages each, surveys subjects' backgrounds and achievements combined with critical analysis of their major works. Updated and annotated bibliographies accompany all entries.

Magill's Guide to Science Fiction and Fantasy Literature, edited by T. A. Shippey and A. J. Sobczak, 4 vols., 1,126 pages (Pasadena, Calif.: Salem Press, 1996)
Provides a plot summary and brief critical analysis for several hundred works of science fiction and fantasy, arranged by the title of the work. Volume 4 includes bibliographies, lists of prizewinners, and much more.

Magill's Literary Annual, edited by Frank N. Magill, et al. (Englewood Cliffs, N.J.: Salem Press, 1977–)
Each edition of this annually published two-volume set contains critical essays, reviews, and sources for further study of 200 major literary works published in the United States each year. In addition, the set includes four cumulative indexes—biographical works by subject, a category index, a title index, and an author index—listing titles reviewed in past editions from 1977 to 2004 in Volume 2. Updates *Magill's Masterplots* annual.

Magill's Masterplots, edited by Frank N. Magill, 11 vols. (Englewood Cliffs, N.J.: Salem Press, 1954–)
First launched in 1954, This multivolume work offers critical essays and synopses with principal characters drawn from world literature arranged by title. An author index accompanies the series. Also since 1954, Salem Press publishes an annual series called *Masterplots Annual* that includes reviews of 100 outstanding books each year. A cumulative print index, *Index to Masterplots: Cumulative Indexes 1963–1990*, also indexes many volumes in the series.

Magill's Masterplots II, edited by Frank N. Magill, 30 vols. (Englewood Cliffs, N.J.: Salem Press, 1986–)
Newer series of interpretive essays and criticisms with summaries and brief bibliographies on the works of 20th-century authors, published as four- to

six-volume sets on different genres of literature published around the world. Titles in the series include *Masterplots II: African-American Literature Series* (1994–); *Masterplots II: British and Commonwealth Series* (1989–); *Masterplots II: Drama Series* (1990–); *Masterplots II: Juvenile and Young Adult Fiction Series* (1991–); *Masterplots II: Nonfiction Series* (1989–); *Masterplots II: Short Story Series* (1986–); and *Masterplots II: World Fiction Series* (1987–). Salem Press's *Index to Masterplots: Cumulative Indexes 1963–1990* also indexes the series.

Magill's Survey of American Literature, edited by Frank N. Magill, 8 vols., 2,896 pages (New York: Marshall Cavendish Corp., 1991–94)
Features critical surveys of major American writers from the 17th to the late 20th century representing all forms of literature.

Magill's Survey of Contemporary Literature, edited by Frank N. Magill, 19 vols. 13,701 pages (Englewood Cliffs, N.J.: Salem Press, 1971, 1977)
This major multivolume literary series contains 500 updated reprints of 2,000 reviews from *Masterplots* annuals from 1954 to 1976 on authors of contemporary literature. Each essay includes brief biographical data about the author and publication data about the work, a brief description of the work and a critical essay.

Magill's Survey of Modern Fantasy Literature, edited by Frank N. Magill, 5 vols., 2,589 pages (Englewood Cliffs, N.J.: Salem Press, 1983)
Featuring 500 critical essays covering individual works, collections, series, trilogies, and short fiction, this five-volume set includes biographical information about each author, dates of publication, descriptions of their work, and criticisms. The fifth and final volume features 19 critical essays on theories of fantasy, eroticism, witchcraft, fantasy poetry, and other forms of fantasy.

Magill's Survey of Science Fiction Literature: Five Hundred 2,000-Word Essay Reviews of World-Famous Science Fiction Novels with 2,500 Bibliographical References, edited by Frank N. Magill, 5 vols., 2,542 pages (Englewood Cliffs, N.J.: Salem Press, 1979–)
A five-volume set providing lengthy and detailed essays and plot summaries of science fiction with critical analysis of each author's style, content, and individual works covering some of the most significant science fiction novels ever written. In 1982, Salem Press published a bibliographical supplement to the series.

Magill's Survey of Short Fiction, 2nd Ed., edited by Charles E. May and Frank N. Magill, 7 vols. 2,900 pages (Pasadena, Calif.: Salem Press, 2001)
Part of Salem Press's award-winning Critical Survey series, this seven-volume set examines the work of 500 short fiction writers, including such diverse writers as Hans Christian Andersen, Woody Allen, Ursula Le Guin, and Alice Walker. Entries offer biographical information, critical analysis of specific works, a list of literary works, dates of publication, and an annotated bibliography for each author reviewed.

Twentieth-Century Literary Criticism, 140 vols. (Detroit: Gale Research Co., 1978–)
Features excerpts from criticism of the works of more than 500 novelists, poets, playwrights, short story writers, and other creative writers living

between 1900 and 1960. Every fourth volume in the series is devoted to literary topics that could not be covered under the author approach.

World Authors, 8 vols. (New York: H.W. Wilson, 1975–)
First published in 1975, this eight-volume reference set—a companion volume to H.W. Wilson's now outdated biographical dictionary *Twentieth Century Authors* (1942–79)—features biographical sketches on internationally known authors. The first volume in the set spans 20 years (1950–70), with each subsequent volume covering a five-year period, including 1970–75, 1975–80, 1980–85, 1985–90, 1990–95, and 1995–2000.

Encyclopedias

Benét's Reader's Encyclopedia of American Literature, 5th Ed., edited by Bruce Murphy, 1,144 pages (New York: HarperCollins, 1996)
This classic, fully revised and updated, explores all aspects of world literature. Entries encompass biographies of poets, playwrights, novelists, and belletrists, plot summaries and character sketches from major works, historical information on literary schools, movements, terms, and awards, myths and legends, and much more. Coverage is given to African, African-American, Eastern European, Middle Eastern, South American, and women's literature, and more.

Encyclopedia of American Literature, edited by Jay Parini, 2,280 pages (New York: Oxford University Press, 2003)
Suitable for high school and university students and literature enthusiasts, this multivolume reference examines American literature from colonial times to the present. Throughout this outstanding resource are 350 historical and topical articles discussing all genres of literature. Includes an extensive index and bibliographies for further reading.

Encyclopedia of Folklore and Literature, edited by Mary Ellen Brown and Bruce A. Rosenberg (Santa Barbara, Calif.: ABC-CLIO, 1998)
Authoritatively surveys the connections between folklore and literature in 350 alphabetically arranged entries. Divided into four categories, entries explore writers who used folklore as a source in their literary works, concepts, themes, and characters with folklore origins found in written literature and studies in the field of folklore and literature by leading scholars. Major emphasis is given to European and Western themes, including classical Greek and Roman mythology.

Encyclopedia of the Novel, edited by Paul Schellinger, 2 vols., 1,613 pages (Chicago: Fitzroy Dearborn, 1998)
Designed for more advanced literature students, this highly recommended encyclopedia comprehensively covers the history and development of the novel in 650 scholarly essays. All aspects of novel are explored, including classic novels, famous novelists, novels, novels about a specific country or region, and other subjects, such as theory, influence, and criticism. Each entry includes brief biographies, lists of works, and additional readings.

Encyclopedia of World Literature in the 20th Century, 3rd Ed., edited by Steven R. Serafin, 4 vols. 3,000 pages (Detroit, Mich.: St. James Press, 1998)

This widely acclaimed four-volume encyclopedic set offers in-depth criticisms of more than 2,000 individual authors discussing "genres, movements, and trends in literature" of authors from around the world, including Chinua Achebe, James Baldwin, Samuel Beckett, William Faulkner, Ernest Hemingway, Gertrude Stein, and Virginia Woolf, and entries on numerous other topics. Bibliographies are included.

The Facts On File Companion to the American Short Story, edited by Abby H. P. Werlock (New York: Facts On File, 2000)

This guide, written in a clear, easy-to read style, discusses American short fiction from the 19th century to the 1990s. Approximately 675 entries, listed in alphabetical order, cover author biographies, famous characters, influential events, themes and theories, and detailed summaries of major stories. Author entries provide personal and career information, including important dates, biographies, lists of stories, critical reaction, and a list of references. Also included are appendixes, covering short story awards and winners, stories by subject and setting, and a selected bibliography of critical histories and theoretical approaches to short story writing. Other useful references include *The Facts On File Companion to American Drama, The Facts On File Companion to Classical Drama,* and other titles in the Facts On File literature list.

General References

Literary Research Guide: A Guide to Reference Sources for the Study of Literatures in English and Related Topics, 4th Ed., edited by James L. Horner (New York: Modern Language Association of America, 2002)

Complete bibliographic reference of sources available for study of literature and related topics. Items covered in this revised fourth edition include databases, dissertations, guides to manuscripts and archives, indexes, literary genres, periodicals, and American, English, Irish, Scottish, and Welsh literature.

World Literature and Its Times, edited by Joyce Moss and Lorraine Valestuk, 6 vols. (Detroit: Gale Group, 1999–)

Each volume of this highly acclaimed academic reference set spans 50 entries of major fiction, nonfiction, and poetry from countries listed in alphabetical order by title. Each entry combines literary and historical information and discusses the social and political background, plot or contents, social, political or literary events of the author's life and influences on each work. The six-volume set covers the literatures of Africa, Asia, India, Italy, France, England, Ireland, Latin America, the Middle East, Portugal, and Spain.

SELECTED ARTICLE INDEXES AND ABSTRACTS

Printed Indexes and Abstracts

Book Review Digest (New York: H.W. Wilson, 1905–)

Indexes selected excerpts of book reviews published in about 75 humanities, social sciences, and general interest periodicals from the United States,

Canada, and Great Britain. Covers English-language juvenile and adult literature, both fiction and nonfiction, except publications, textbooks, and technical books in the fields of science and law (reviews of science books for the general reader are included). All reviews are arranged in two sections: review listings, arranged alphabetically by author's last name; and a combined subject and title index, listed by subject headings, by genre, or by title. Includes cross-references. H.W. Wilson also offers this resource online covering reviews from 1983 to the present.

Book Review Index (Detroit: Gale Research Company, 1965–)
Indexes citations of reviews of books, reference works, periodicals, and audiobooks (the last only if based on a published book) from 1965 to the present. Lists reviews from more than 600 periodicals, including general interest and scholarly publications. Entries are alphabetically arranged, usually by author's last name. Published quarterly with semiannual and annual cumulations, this printed reference includes a title index.

Book Review Index to Social Science Periodicals, edited by Arnold M. Rzepecki with the assistance of Paul Guenther, 4 vols. (Ann Arbor, Mich.: Pierian Press, 1978–81)
Precursor to *Social Sciences Index* listing reviews of books, arranged alphabetically by author's last name, covering area studies, consumer affairs, criminology, economics, education, environmental science, geography, history, international relations, political science, public administration, social work, and sociology from 1964 to 1974. Includes an index with a list of periodicals.

Combined Retrospective Index to Book Reviews in Humanities Journals, 1802–1974, 10 vols. (Woodbridge, Conn.: Research Publications, 1982–84)
Ten-volume set comprising nine author volumes and one title volume featuring comprehensive citations of more than 500,000 book reviews published in more than 150 humanities journals between 1802 and 1974. Includes book reviews, notes, and briefs. Entries in author volumes are arranged alphabetically by the author's last name. The title volume list entries alphabetically by the first word in the title cross-referenced to the main entry in the author volumes.

Combined Retrospective Index to Book Reviews in Scholarly Journals, 1886–1974, 15 vols. (Arlington, Va.: Carrollton Press, 1979–82)
An outstanding compilation that cites more than 1 million book reviews found in 459 scholarly journals in the fields of history, political science, and sociology published between 1886 and 1974. Features book reviews, notes, and briefs. Set includes 12 author volumes and three title volumes, with author entries arranged alphabetically by last name and titles listed alphabetically by first word in the title.

Index to Book Reviews in the Humanities, 31 vols. (Williamston, Mich.: P. Thomson, 1960–90).
Annually indexes book reviews in humanities periodicals; arranged by author's last name. Entries provide such vital information as book title, reviewer's name, and a numeric code that identifies the periodical in which

the review was published. Includes is a list of periodicals indexed each year.

The New York Times Book Review Index (New York: Arno Press, 1968–)
Five-volume index listing reviews published in *The New York Times Book Review* (excluding the weekday editions of *The New York Times*) from 1896 to 1970. Covered are "full-length reviews and essays, brief reviews and biographical sketches, letters to the editor and brief commentaries and notes and anecdotal items." The set lists reviews alphabetically by author (by the author's last name and byline), subject (arranged by topic and chronologically under subject headings), or category. Categories include anthologies, article and essay collections, children's fiction and nonfiction, criticism, drama, humor and cartoons, mystery, detective and spy fiction, nature and wildlife books, poetry, reference works, science fiction, self-help books, short stories, travel books, and westerns. Entries for reviews list title, author(s) of item, and reviewer's name. An online database provides book review coverage from 1980 to the present.

Times Literary Supplement Index, 1902–1980 and 1940–1980, 5 vols. (Reading, England: Newspaper Archive Developments, 1978, 1982)
Lists by personal name, title, or subject book reviews, articles, and poems published in *The Times Literary Supplement* from 1902 to 1980; also available online from 1902 to the present.

Web Indexes and Abstracts

Book Review Digest (OCLC FirstSearch/H.W. Wilson, 1983–)
Web version of the print edition that cites and excerpts book reviews published in the past 18 months of current English-language fiction and nonfiction from 100 leading periodicals in the United States, Canada, and Great Britain. Searchable by author, subject, and title.

Books in Print (R.R. Bowker, current)
Weekly updated companion to the printed library edition listing more than 840,000 books currently in print and 85,000 book reviews. Contains complete bibliographic and ordering information for more than 2.9 million books, audiocassettes, and videos in print from U.S. publishers and provides the complete text of book reviews. Also includes information from Books out of Print and Forthcoming Books.

The New York Times Book Review Index (The New York Times, 1980–)
Fully searchable online database of book reviews from *The New York Times Book Review* published since 1980. Published reviews are searchable by author, subject, or category. Printed reference indexes reviews published between 1896 and 1970 that are not included in the electronic edition.

Times Literary Supplement Index (Gale Group, 1902–present)
Archives and indexes complete facsimile editions, including book reviews, articles, and biographical information on contributors, searchable by name, title, or subject, published in this weekly and most respected London literary journal since 1902.

ARTICLES AND LITERATURE

Print Indexes

Essay and General Literature Index (New York: H.W. Wilson, 1900–)
Often referred to as the *Essay Index,* this hardcover reference indexes essays published as parts of collections covering the arts, drama, economics, education, history, linguistics, philosophy, religion, science, and social and political science since 1900 listed by author or subject. Most volumes cumulate four years of material. This index is also offered online.

The Columbia Granger's Index to Poetry in Anthologies, 12th Ed., edited by Tessa Kale, 2,219 pages (New York: Columbia University Press, 2002)
Each volume of this series, first published in 1904, provides bibliographic information on poem anthologies and selected works. Includes indexes for title, first line, author, subject, and last line. In 1999, an online version known as *The Columbia Granger's World of Poetry* became available.

Humanities Index (New York: H.W. Wilson, 1974–)
Indexes articles published in more than 500 of the most important and widely read academic journals published since 1974 in the fields of archaeology and classical studies, area studies, folklore, history, language and literature, performing arts, philosophy, religion, theology, and related subjects.

English Literary Periodicals, 4 vols. (Ann Arbor, Mich.: University Microfilms, 1951)
Indexes microfilm periodicals available in special collections published in Great Britain between the 17th and 19th centuries, including political, religious, theatrical, satirical, and women's magazines and literary reviews based on a bibliography compiled by Professor Richmond Bond of the University of North Carolina. Each title list includes a brief bibliographic description, place and date of publication, and more. Periodicals are also cataloged in an online database of the same name.

Index to Black Periodicals (Boston, Mass.: G.K. Hall & Co., 1950–99; Detroit: Gale Group, 2000–)
The only dedicated reference to black periodicals, this printed reference, formerly known as the *Index to Selected Periodicals, Index to Periodical Articles By and About Negroes,* and *Index to Periodical Articles By and About Blacks,* indexes 30 to 40 general interest and scholarly African-American periodicals per annual issue. Covers poetry, short stories, and reviews of books, film, music, records, and theater, arranged by author or subject from 1950 the present. An Internet version called International Index to Black Periodicals Full Text, is also available, covering black literature and periodicals published from 1902 to the present.

International Index to Periodicals, 18 vols. (New York: H.W. Wilson, 1907–65)
Eighteen-volume set, originally published as the *Readers' Guide to Periodical Literature Supplement* (1907–19) then retitled in 1920, indexing periodicals published throughout the world through April 1964/March 1965.

Literary Criticism Index, 2nd Ed., edited by Alan R. Weiner and Spencer Means, 559 pages (Metuchen, N.J.: Scarecrow Press, 1994)
An excellent source for tracking down criticism on a specific or individual piece of literature, this revised single volume reference indexes bibliographies listing sources of literary criticism.

MLA International Bibliography (New York: Modern Language Association of America, 1921–)
Fully indexes by subject, author, or title newly published or revised internationally published scholarly books, reference works, articles, films, sound recordings, and microforms on modern languages and literature, including literary criticism, literature, drama, folklore, and linguistics, and other materials from 1921 to the present. Also features book reviews of multiple scholarly works. This five-volume set extensively covers U.S., African, English, Spanish, French, German, Italian, Asian, and Latin American literature and folklore. The entire index is also available online with coverage from 1963 to the present.

Poetry: Index 1912–1997, by Jayne Marek, 832 pages, (Chicago: Poetry Press, 1998)
Indexes by author poetry published in anthologies from 1912 to 1997.

Poole's Index to Periodical Literature, 1802–1906, 7 vols. (Boston; New York: Houghton Mifflin Co., 1891–1906)
Subject index, arranged alphabetically, to literary articles and book reviews published in 479 American and English general periodicals for the years 1802 to 1906. A separate volume, *Cumulative Author Index for Poole's Index to Periodical Literature 1802–1906* published in 1971, contains a cumulative index to the authors and articles listed in the main volumes. An online version of the index is also offered.

Readers' Guide to Periodical Literature (New York: H.W. Wilson, 1890–)
Thoroughly indexes literature published in English-language, general-interest periodicals from the 19th century to the present. Published annually. Citations cover nonfiction, fiction, poems, short stories, and reviews of ballet, books, compact discs, dance, motion pictures, musicals, operas and operettas, phonograph records, products, radio programs, tape recordings, television programs, theater, videodiscs and videotapes by subject or author. Reviews are arranged alphabetically by author. Includes a list of periodicals indexed in each volume. H.W. Wilson offers access to the same indexed material via an online version.

Short Story Index (New York: H.W. Wilson, 1956–)
First published in 1956, this long-running reference series indexes short stories by author, subject, or title of the collection.

Web Indexes and Abstracts

American Humanities Index (Whitson Publishing, 1975–)
Provides in-depth coverage of the humanities with bibliographic references to more than 1,000 creative, literary, and scholarly journals published in the

United States and Canada from 1975 to the present. Citations cover articles, essays, reviews, poems, fiction, paintings and illustrations, and photographs.

The Columbia Granger's World of Poetry (Columbia University Press, current)
This online database indexes a series of poetry references, including *The Classic Hundred Poems,* a fully annotated anthology; *The Top 500 Poems; The Columbia Granger's Index to Poetry in Anthologies; The Columbia Granger's Index to Poetry in Collected and Selected Works;* and *The Columbia Granger's Index to African-American Poetry.*

Essay and General Literature Index (H.W. Wilson, 1985–)
An online database that cites nearly 65,000 essays contained in more than 5,000 anthologies and collections published since 1985 in the United States, Great Britain, and Canada. More than 300 volumes, with an additional 20 annuals and serial publications, are indexed annually. Primarily focuses on the field of humanities and social sciences, including economics, political science, history, criticism of literary works, drama, and film. Indexes essays and chapters in book collections as well.

Gale's Literary Index (Gale Research, current)
Master index providing quick and easy access to author and title listings via the World Wide Web from 130 literary references published by Gale, Charles Scribner's Sons, St. James Press, and Twayne Publishers, including *Contemporary Authors, Contemporary Literary Criticism, Contemporary Novelists,* and *Contemporary Poets.* Cross-references more than 110,000 author names, including pseudonyms and pen names, and more than 120,000 titles in one source.

MLA International Bibliography (Modern Language Association, 1963–)
Provides direct Web access to citations and indexing of more than 1.2 million scholarly journal articles, book chapters, monographs, and dissertations on all areas of modern language and literature based on the printed index of the same name from 1963 to the present.

Poole's Index to Periodical Literature (Paratext, 1802–1922)
Brings together several indexes of 19th and early 20th century periodicals, including books, newspapers, magazines, and government documents, plus date and title information not available in the print version. Includes indexes of *The New York Times* (1863–1905) and *Harper's Magazine* (1850–92), U.S. and British government documents, *Stead's Index to Periodicals* (1890–1902), and *Jones and Chipman's Index to Legal Periodicals* (1786–1922).

The Readers' Guide to Periodical Literature (H.W. Wilson, 1890–1982)
Online version of the classic library reference indexing popular general interest magazines published in the United States and Canada on all subjects, including business, current events, education, history, politics, sports, and science. An expanded version, called *Readers' Guide Full-Text Mega Edition,* provides index and some full-text articles from 1983 to the present.

SELECTED FULL-TEXT ARTICLE DATABASES

ABELL: Annual Bibliography of English Language and Literature (Modern Humanities Research Association, 1920–)
Indexes citations of journal articles on all aspects and periods of English literature, with full-text availability of articles from 120 scholarly journals.

Academic Search Elite (EBSCOHost, indexing: 1980– , full text: 1990–)
Indexes more than 2,700 journals with full-text coverage of 1,530 academic titles in the fields of humanities, education, and general science. Full text extends back to January 1990, while indexing and abstracts is from January 1984 to the present. This subscription database is an ideal place to look up book reviews, criticisms, and reviews of creative works, from poems to short stories.

Contemporary Authors (Gale Group, current)
Web edition of this reference series includes biographical and bibliographical information on more than 100,000 contemporary writers. Covers novelists, poets, essayists, journalists, and other writers. Includes full text of journals on literature and literary criticism.

Expanded Academic Index ASAP (InfoTrac, 1980–)
Indexes more than 2,600 journals, magazines, and newspapers, with full text available for selected literary journals.

Humanities Full Text (H.W. Wilson, 1984–)
Provides online indexing of journal articles, some full text, from 400 major humanities periodicals in the fields of archaeology, classical studies, film, folklore, gender studies, history, journalism, communications, language, literature, literary and political criticism, performing arts, philosophy, and religion.

International Index to Black Periodicals Full-Text (Chadwyck-Healey, 1902–)
Web adaptation of the printed volume offering current and retrospective bibliographic citations and abstracts from 150 scholarly and popular journals, newspapers, and newsletters from the United States, Africa, and the Caribbean since 1902, and full-text coverage of 40 black studies periodicals from 1988 to the present. Coverage spans cultural, economic, historical, religious, social, and political issues in the area of black studies.

JSTOR (Journal Storage Project, 1996–)
Full-text collection of more than 300 scholarly journals covering the arts and sciences, including such literature journals as *African American Review, Comparative Literature, ELH, Modern Language Journal, New Literary History, Review of English Studies,* and *Shakespeare Quarterly.*

LION: Literature Online (ProQuest, current)
This subscription-based library bills itself as "the world's largest cross-searchable database of literature and literary criticism." It covers more than 330,000 works of English and American poetry, drama and prose, 400

author bibliographies, 1,000 biographies of the most studied authors, 200 journals (with 30 in full text), and links to author Web sites and *ABELL (Annual Bibliography of English Language and Literature).*

Literature Resource Center (Gale Group, current)
Online database providing direct access to biographical, bibliographical, and critical analysis, based on Gale's library of literary references, including *Contemporary Authors, Dictionary of Literacy Criticism,* and articles from more than 130 literary journals. Areas covered include drama, history, journalism, nonfiction, and poetry. Also includes a link to the full-text version of Merriam-Webster's *Encyclopedia of Literature* and links to 5,000 Web sites focusing on major authors and their works.

NewsBank Newsfile Collection (NewsBank, 1991–)
Besides covering current events, this fully searchable collection includes full-text articles from 500 U.S. regional and national newspapers, news broadcasts, and wire services from 1991 to the present. Coverage includes newspaper book reviews and literary news topics found under the category "General News: Arts and Sports Reviews."

Periodical Abstracts Research II Full Text (UMI ProQuest, 1986–)
Offers complete citations with abstracts to some 1,600 periodicals, including the current six months of *The New York Times* and *The Wall Street Journal.* Publications index includes 396 humanities and 239 general-interest periodicals with full-text article searchable from approximately 600 titles.

Periodical Contents Index Full Text (Chadwyck-Healey, 1770–1995)
This major online periodical database offers full text and retrospective coverage of of the content (including book reviews) of thousands of humanities and social science periodicals since their first issues from 1770 to 1995.

ProjectMUSE (Johns Hopkins University Press, 1990–)
Full-text collection of more than 100 scholarly journals in arts and humanities, mathematics, and social sciences, including 31 literature titles.

SELECTED PERIODICALS

American Literature: A Journal of Literary History, Criticism, and Bibliography (Durham, N.C.: Duke University Press; published in cooperation with the Modern Language Association 1929– , quarterly)
Regarded as "the preeminent journal in its field," this quarterly scholarly journal features criticisms of a broad spectrum of literary periods and literary genres. Each issue contains articles written by leading scholars and critics covering the works of American authors, and a large book review section. The journal is indexed and abstracted in such leading references as *America: History and Life, Historical Abstracts, Humanities Index, Index to Book Reviews in the Humanities, MLA International Bibliography,* and many others. Links to full text of recent articles is available through *JSTOR* (1929–99) and ProjectMUSE (2003–).

Comparative Literature (Eugene: University of Oregon, 1949– , quarterly)
Founded in 1949, this official publication of the American Comparative Literature Association is devoted to the worldwide exploration of important issues of literary history and theory. Published quarterly by the University of Oregon, each issue typically contains scholarly articles covering a broad range of theoretical and critical approaches. EBSCOHost's Academic Search Premier (1975–) and Wilson Select Full Text Plus (1995–) are among the online databases that offer full-text indexing of articles from past issues. Online access to the first 50 volumes is available through JSTOR (1949–98).

Contemporary Literature (Madison: University of Wisconsin Press, 1968–)
Written by leaders in their field and some of the most respected writers today, this quarterly journal focuses on the study of contemporary American, British, and Continental literature. Available in print and online, content typically includes interviews with emerging authors, articles on contemporary literature, and reviews of recently published critical works. Articles are indexed in such popular online databases as Biography Resource Center (1993–99), EBSCOHost's Academic Search Premier (1975–) and Expanded Academic ASAP (1992), excluding the most recent 12 months. Back issues of *Contemporary Literature* are available in full-text form through JSTOR, and also accessible through ProjectMUSE.

ELH: Journal of Literary History (Baltimore, Md.: Johns Hopkins University Press, 1934– , quarterly)
This quarterly academic journal offers "superior studies that interpret the conditions affecting major works in English and American literature." Articles offer a scholarly view of historical, critical, and theoretical concerns relative to its subject. One of the first journals offered in electronic form by ProjectMUSE, *ELH* is available as part of its online collection starting with the winter 1993 issue, and through JSTOR (1934–94) with links to full-text recent issues (1995–2003).

Journal of Modern Literature (Philadelphia: Temple University; Bloomington: Indiana University Press, 1970– , quarterly)
More than 30 years after its founding, the *Journal of Modern Literature* is widely recognized as "the journal of record on modern literature." Each issue addresses contemporary writing and literature written from 1900 to the present. Contents include essays, interviews, position papers, and political manifestos on related subjects. Full-text articles are available through Academic Search Premier (1975–), Wilson Select Full Text Plus (1997–), and ProjectMUSE (1998–present)

The New York Review of Books (New York: Arno Press, 1963– , biweekly)
Widely regarded as "the premier literary intellectual magazine in the English language," this biweekly magazine founded during a New York newspaper publishing strike in 1963 features informative and critical essays on culture, current affairs, and literature. Articles from recent editions are accessible online at http://www.nybooks.com/.

The New York Times Book Review (New York: Arno Press, 1896–; Chicago: Fitzroy Dearborn Publishers, 2001– , weekly)
Distributed separately or as part of Sunday's *New York Times,* this weekly literary tabloid reviews new nonfiction and fiction books, and includes essays on literary culture, previews of upcoming books, discussion of publishing trends, and more. Visitors can browse recent articles online at http://www.nytimes.com/pages/books/.

PMLA (Publications of the Modern Language Association) (New York: Modern Language Association of America, 1884– , 6 times a year)
Published six times yearly since 1884, this journal of the Modern Language Association of America offers a variety of articles geared toward university and college scholars and teachers of English and foreign languages. Four issues per year (January, March, May, and October) feature a collection of essays written by association members on language and literature. A directory is published in September listing all members, including names and addresses, and a program is published in November for the association's annual convention. A collection of past issues is accessible to subscribers at JSTOR (1889–1990).

Publishers Weekly: The International News Magazine of Publishing (New York: F. Leypoldt, 1872– , weekly)
The longest-active trade publication of its kind, this weekly newsmagazine offers international coverage of book publishing, including interviews with authors, industry news, and a list of the latest nonfiction and fiction bestsellers. Every issue covers all segments of publishing, from the creation and production of books to sales and marketing. The Web site offers current and past articles, including news, features, book reviews, and special reports, at http://www.publishersweekly.com/. Full access is restricted to subscribers only.

TLS: The Times Literary Supplement (London: Times Newspapers Ltd., 1902– , weekly)
Weekly literary supplement published by the Times Newspapers of London featuring comprehensive and entertaining essays on new and forthcoming books, both hardcover and paperback, on the arts, history, politics, and world literature. Full-text images of previous issues from 1902 to 1994 are available as part of a subscription database, TLS: Times Literary Supplement, offered by the Gale Group.

World Literature Today (Norman: University of Oklahoma, 1927– , quarterly)
Founded in 1927 by Oklahoma scholar Roy Temple House, this quarterly scholarly journal upholds his original vision, featuring interviews, reviews, and essays on authors and literature from around the world. Content includes reviews of fiction, poetry, and criticism, divided by language, and articles and columns discussing global and regional trends, children's literature, and writers' conferences. Full-text articles of *World Literature Today* are available at InfoTrac's Expanded Academic ASAP (1994–).

For a complete and current list of literature journals, not including newsletters, see:

MLA Directory of Periodicals: A Guide to Journals and Serials in Language and Literature, 2nd Ed. 2 vols., (Modern Language Association, 1991–96)
Produced by the Modern Language Association of America, this second edition, two-volume directory lists periodicals, indexed in the *MLA International Bibliography,* in the fields of literature, language, linguistics, culture, and folklore. All entries provide such basic information as title, publisher, editor name, and language. In 2000, the directory was offered online via subscription through EBSCO Publishing. Content is keyword-searchable by subject, title, and more.

SELECTED WEB SITES

English Literature on the Web (http://www.lang.nagoya-u.ac.jp/~matsuoka/EngLit.html)
Large online directory of literature sites on the Web.

English Literature Reference Sources (http://www.library.cornell.edu/olinuris/ref/lit/engbib.html)
Compiled by Lance J. Heidig and revised by Teresa Demo and Fred Muratori of Cornell University libraries, this Web page features a selected bibliography of library resources, such as chronologies, handbooks, indexes, and sources of literary criticism on English literature.

Literary Sources on the Net (http://andromeda.rutgers.edu/~jlynch/Lit/)
A comprehensive collection of electronic sources for the study of literature covering such areas as classical, biblical, medieval, Victorian, and more with links.

Voice of the Shuttle: English Literature (http://vos.ucsb.edu/)
Provides access to both primary and secondary resources for students and instructors from elementary school, high school, and the general public on all academic disciplines, including English literature.

26

Music

For serious study or research, thousands of reliable resources chronicle everything there is to know about music: the distinctive styles and movements, the world-famous composers, performers, and musical groups, the top-charting songs and recordings, the historical periods and major events, and more. Most of it is available at a library in print or electronic form or on the Internet. This chapter offers some recommended sources for music research.

SELECTED BOOKS AND REFERENCES

Baker's Biographical Dictionary of Musicians, 9th Ed., edited by Nicolas Slonimsky, 6 vols., 4,220 pages (New York: Schirmer Books, 2001)
One of the most comprehensive biographical dictionaries ever written, this extensively updated and expanded, six-volume edition contains more than 15,000 brief biographies of composers, musicians, and performers from every genre, including more than 3,000 new additions contributed by editors and leading specialists. Famed music writer Theodore Baker originally wrote this popular reference in 1900, followed by esteemed musicologist and editor Nicolas Slonimsky—from the fifth through eighth editions—who died in 1995.

Baker's Biographical Dictionary of Popular Musicians since 1990, 2 vols. (Detroit: Gale Group, 2004)
Chronicles personalities in rock, pop, hip-hop, blues, electronica, musical theater, soundtrack, classical, country, R&B, jazz, folk, Latin, and world music. Includes selective discography, bibliography, and Web sites.

Baker's Biographical Dictionary Of 20th-Century Classical Musicians, edited by Nicolas Slonimksy, Laura Kuhn, and Dennis McIntire, 1,595 pages (New York: Schirmer, 1997)
An important single-volume reference work, this solidly written and researched volume, first published in 1900 and written and edited by Nicolas Slonimsky, follows the same format as *Baker's Biographical Dictionary of Musicians*, but profiles the most influential musicians of the 20th century.

Concise Oxford Dictionary of Music, 4th Ed., edited by Michael Kennedy, 828 pages (New York: Oxford University Press, 1996)
Derived from the *Oxford Dictionary of Music*, this outstanding, fully updated reference—perhaps the most authoritative dictionary of its kind—features

more than 14,000 comprehensive entries covering the gamut of musical arts—musical terms, works, composers, librettists, musicians, singers, and orchestras. Areas of interest include works lists for major composers, histories of musical instruments, and coverage of living composers and performers.

Contemporary Musicians: Profiles of the People in Music, 49 vols. (Detroit: Gale Group, 2004)
With 49 volumes and counting, this cumulative reference series thoroughly profiles more than 2,000 important musicians from all genres of music—blues, classical, country, folk, gospel, jazz, New Age, rap, rock, and more. A cumulative index accompanies the set.

The Encyclopedia of Popular Music, 3rd Ed., edited by Colin Larkin, 8 vols. (New York: Grove, 1998).
Praised by *The Times of London* as "absolutely invaluable . . . a work of almost frightening completeness," this eight-volume reference, compiled by music expert Colin Larkin, is regarded as the most authoritative volume ever produced covering rock, pop, and jazz artists. It features biographies of more than 14,000 artists. Each entry includes vital information of interest to music scholars, music lovers, and researchers—critical discographies, record titles and release dates, and assessments of each artist's contributions. Also provided is an extensive index of song titles for easy reference.

The Garland Encyclopedia of World Music, edited by Bruno Nettl and Ruth M. Stone, 9 vols. (New York: Garland, 1997–1978)
This ambitious 10-volume reference series fully examines the cultural appeal of music around the world by topic, by region, and by ethnic group. Each entry gives detailed treatment of its subjects, with discussion of the social aspects of music and the different musical traditions of ethnic groups or countries. Included with each volume are CDs of previously unrecorded music, reference lists of bibliographic sources, and resource guides.

The Great Song Thesaurus, 2nd Ed. by Roger Lax and Frederick Smith, 774 pages (New York: Oxford University Press, 1999)
First published in 1984, this revised second edition offers immediate access to information on more than 11,000 American and English songs, alphabetically arranged. Divided into 10 sections, entries list the composer, lyricist, year of popularity, and recording artists of each song. Includes a song lyric line index.

International Dictionary of Black Composers, edited by Samuel A. Floyd, 2 vols., 2,000 pages (Chicago: Fitzroy Dearborn, 1999)
This indispensable single-subject dictionary features 185 authored entries, including analysis and full-page portraits, of famous black composers from the past 300 years. Entries offer a diverse range of information, including complete discographies and lists of compositions (by genre) and print works.

The New Grove American Dictionary of Music, 4th Ed., edited by H. Wiley Hitchcock and Stanley Sadie, 4 vols. (New York: Grove, 1993)
Focusing on American music, this music dictionary contains a wide range of articles on American composers, groups, ensembles, popular styles, genres, and uniquely American instruments.

The New Grove Dictionary of Music and Musicians, 2nd Ed., edited by Stanley Sadie, 29 vols., 25,000 pages (New York: Grove's Dictionaries, 2001)
With more than 29,000 entries, this 29-volume set offers comprehensive coverage of world and popular music, information on 20th-century artists, composers, musical history, and much more.

The New Harvard Dictionary of Music, edited by Don Michael Randel, 942 pages (Cambridge, Mass.: Belknap Press of Harvard University Press, 1986)
This scholarly, single-volume reference, features more than 6,000 concise articles on music of the 20th century. Included are discussions of all styles and forms of music and musical instruments written by more than 70 experts in each field. More than 220 drawings and 250 musical examples complement the text.

Popular Musicians, edited by Steve Hochman, 4 vols., 1,253 pages (Pasadena, Calif.: Salem Press, 1999)
Nicely organized and well-written four-volume set featuring more than 500 alphabetically arranged biographies of a wide range of contemporary artists. Profiles discuss each artist's musical style, debut album, band members, and awards, complete with discography. Also includes a bibliography, index of album and song titles, and a glossary of terms.

SELECTED ARTICLE INDEXES AND ABSTRACTS

Printed Indexes and Abstracts

Humanities Index (New York: H.W. Wilson, 1974–)
Indexes all subjects from the field of humanities, including classical and area studies, folklore, history, and the performing arts.

The Music Index: A Subject-Author Guide to Music Periodical Literature (Warren, Mich.: Harmonie Park Press, 1949–)
Published annually with quarterly updates since 1949, *The Music Index* provides authoritative bibliographic coverage of more than 700 international music periodicals. Entries offer researchers access to a wealth of information and data covering current and past music personalities, the history of music, musical genres, and musical instruments. Other items indexed include book reviews, reviews of music recordings, tapes, and performances, debuts, and obituaries. A complete online version of the index was introduced in 1999.

Web Indexes and Abstracts

Arts and Humanities Search (Thomson ISI, 1980–)
Updated weekly, this online citation database indexes the world's leading arts and humanities journals—more than 2.5 million records and 1,300 sources—from 1980 to the present. Cites articles, bibliographies, editorials, letters, reviews, and more. For ease of use, cited references are keyword searchable.

Canadian Music Periodical Index (National Library of Canada, 1999–)
A free service of the National Library of Canada, the Canadian Music Periodical Index indexes 475 Canadian music journals, newsletters, and magazines from the late 19th century to the present. Featuring some 30,000 entries, the database also covers news and articles about international music and musicians published in Canadian periodicals since 1999. Users can search entries by author, date, geographical area, name, periodical, subject, and type of article (interview, obituary, review, etc.). To access, visit the National Library of Canada Web site at http://www.collectionscanada.ca/cmpi-ipmc/index-e.html.

Humanities Abstracts (H.W. Wilson 1984–)
This bibliographic database includes citations and abstracts to articles from well-known scholarly journals and specialized magazines in all areas of humanities, including music and the performing arts. For indexing prior to 1984, consult the print edition that indexes articles since 1974. In 1996, H.W. Wilson introduced a CD-ROM version of this same title.

Humanities and Social Sciences Retrospective (H.W. Wilson, 1907–84)
Provides retrospective indexing of nearly 1,200 journals and more than 1.3 million articles in humanities and social sciences as far back as 1907. Content includes book reviews and many important scholarly journals, with coverage of the entire range of humanities, including music and the performing arts.

Iter (University of Toronto, 1842–)
This nonprofit research project, supported by the University of Toronto Libraries, indexes every issue of 400 scholarly journals on the Middle Ages and Renaissance, including many music journals, such as *Acta Musicologica, Archiv für Musikwissenschaft,* and *Musical Quarterly.* More than 15,000 new citations were added as of February 2004. The database is accessible free of charge at http://www.itergateway.org/journal_titles.cfm.

International Index to Musical Periodicals (ProQuest, 1874–)
Offers citations and abstracts, with some full text, to more than 400 current music periodicals from more than 20 countries covering all aspects of music. Content ranges from scholarly studies to discussion of the latest musical trends. Combines current and retrospective coverage with more than 30,000 records from 1996 to the present, and records from 99 periodicals as far back as 1874.

IIPA—International Index to the Performing Arts (ProQuest, 1864–)
This database, updated monthly, offers abstracts and some full text in dance, drama, film, musical theater, and television, drawn from 199 current periodicals from 1998 to the present, and 93 other periodicals published since 1864.

MUSE (MUsic SEarch) (National Information Services Corporation, 1960–)
Regarded as the world's most extensive collection of bibliographic records on music reference and research materials, this searchable CD-ROM database combines *RILM Abstracts of Music Literature,* the RILM thesaurus, the Library of Congress Music Catalog and other records from the U.S.

Library of Congress. Worldwide coverage of reference and research materials indexes all music genres and other related subjects, including composers, history, music theory, reviews and analyses, sound recordings, and liturgy. In addition, users have full-text access to scholarly journals and magazines, including *Essays in Sound, Music Theory Online,* and *Strings.* Includes more than 550,000 citations from the *RILM Abstracts of Music Literature,* from 1969 to the present, and the Music Catalog of the Library of Congress since 1960.

The Music Index Online: A Subject-Author Guide to Musical Periodical Literature (Harmonie Park Press, 1979–)
Like the print edition, it indexes every aspect of classical and popular music from more than 700 international music periodicals and journals categorized and organized by subject.

OCLC Music Library (OCLC, through 1999)
CD-ROM database that contains bibliographic records of sound recordings on cylinders, phonograph records, reel-to-reel tapes, audiocassettes, and CDs from national and international libraries.

RILM Abstracts of Music Literature (Repertoire International de Litterature Musical, 1969–)
Produced by the Repertoire International de Litterature Musical (RILM), this continuously updated online version corresponds with the printed *RILM Abstracts of Music Literature.* It features citations and abstracts (150 words or less) of articles, books, catalogs, and more. Included are records in more than 202 languages from 3,700 scholarly journals, including *Clavier, Instrumentalist, Journal of Band Research,* and *Musical Quarterly,* with abstracts published in the original language, often with English or partial English translation.

RIPM: International Index to Nineteenth-Century Music Periodicals (National Information Services Corp., 1800–1950)
Based on the printed index, this Web-accessible database updated every six months indexes more than 60 19th-century journals in 13 languages. Titles include specialized music journals, daily newspapers, articles in literary periodicals, theatrical journals and magazines, plus engravings and lithographs in the illustrated press. With content provided by the International Musicological Society; International Association of Music Libraries, Archives and Documentation Centres; UNESCO International Council for Philosophy and Humanities Studies; and NISC, this product contains more than 350,000 records referencing writings about composers, performers, and musical compositions and musical events. It also corresponds to the printed volumes *Répertoire International de la Press Musicale.*

RISM: International Inventory of Musical Sources after 1600 (National Information Services Corporation, 1600–)
Semiannually updated database that identifies international musical sources and writings about music after 1600. Covers manuscripts, printed music, works on music theory, archives, and music collections from schools and private collectors.

SELECTED FULL-TEXT ARTICLE DATABASES

Academic Search Premier (EBSCOHost, indexing: 1980– , full text, 1992–)

Provides full-text access to more than 2,340 scholarly publications covering all areas of academic study. Enables keyword searching of words within the titles of articles, subject headings, author names, and abstracts. Popular journals covered include *American Music* (1993–), *Black Music Research Journal* (2002–), and *Perspectives of New Music* (1993).

Expanded Academic Index ASAP (InfoTrac, 1980–)

Offers indexing, abstracts, and full text of many scholarly journals embracing all disciplines, including such music journals as *Dance Magazine, Down Beat, Notes: Quarterly Journal of the Music Library Association,* and *Opera News.*

General Reference Center (InfoTrac, 1980–)

Indexes popular and general magazines, reference books, and newspapers with information on current events, popular culture, the arts and sciences, sports and more, with full text access. Magazines referenced include *Down Beat* (1980–) and *Rolling Stone* (1980–).

JSTOR (Journal Storage Project, 1996–)

Consists of more than 730,000 full-text scholarly journal articles.

ProjectMUSE (Johns Hopkins University Press, 1990–)

Offers worldwide subscription access to the full text of more than 100 scholarly journals in the arts, humanities, and more, including literature and criticism, histories, and studies of the visual and performing arts.

SELECTED PERIODICALS

American Music: A Quarterly Journal Devoted to All Aspects of American Music (Pittsburgh, Pa.: Society for American Music, 1983– , quarterly)

Published quarterly by the Society for American Music and the University of Illinois Press, this journal covers all aspects of American music and music in the United States. Each issue contains scholarly reviews of books, music, recordings, and other media. Tables of contents of current and past issues, from 1983 to the present, can be found under the heading "Publications" at the society's Web site (http://www.american-music.org/).

American Record Guide (Washington, D.C.: Helen Dwight Reid Educational Foundation; Cincinnati, Ohio: American Record Guide, 1935– , bimonthly)

Established in 1935, *American Record Guide* is the oldest record review magazine of classical music and music in concert. Each issue features more 500 reviews, written by more than 80 freelance writers and independent critics, and overviews surveying the recordings of various composers.

Down Beat (Elmhurst, Ill.: Maher Publications, 1934– , monthly)

This popular magazine contains everything of interest to contemporary musicians and educators, including news, articles, how-to features, interviews, and reviews. Content of current issues and an archive of previously published issues are searchable and retrievable online at the publication's Web site: http://www.downbeat.com/.

Fanfare: The Magazine for Serious Record Collectors (Tenafly, N.J.: J. Flegler, 1977– , bimonthly)
Launched in 1977 by publisher Joel Flegler, this bimonthly magazine is for serious aficionados of classical music. Each issue features reviews of classical recordings, industry articles, and profiles and interviews with artists and composers. Current reviews and the table of contents of the most recent issue are accessible online at http://www.fanfaremag.com/.

Goldmine (St. Clair Shores, Mich.: Arena Magazine Co., 1974–85; Iola, Wisc.: Krause Publications, 1985– , biweekly)
First published in 1974, *Goldmine* focuses on collecting and the history of modern music in all genres—alternative, big band, blues, classical, country, folk, rock, and more. Published biweekly, each issue is packed with the latest collecting news, discographies, histories, interviews, reviews, and calendar of upcoming events. Subscribers have complete online access to the content of current issues and archived material.

Notes: Quarterly Journal of the Music Library Association (Baltimore, Md.: Johns Hopkins University Press, 1934– , quarterly)
Intended for music librarians, this quarterly journal, published since 1934, offers well-written, scholarly articles covering all areas of music librarianship but also various subject areas useful to student researchers, including book reviews, bibliographies, discographies, music histories, and reviews of sound recordings and digital media. Content of past journals is covered in JSTOR from 1934 through 1998, and other educational library databases, including Expanded Academic ASAP.

Rolling Stone (San Francisco: Straight Arrow Publishers, 1967– , monthly)
Rising to fame in the late 1960s and 1970s, this popular monthly magazine, founded in San Francisco in 1967 by Jann Wenner and music critic Ralph J. Gleason, features timely and topical articles on current events, music, and the music industry, including interviews and music reviews.

SELECTED WEB SITES

All-Music Guide (http://www.allmusic.com/)
This definitive source offers keyword searching of information about artists, albums, songs, styles, and record labels, and subsections on every music genre with overviews by decade.

American Memory Project: Performing Arts (http://memory.loc.gov/ammem/collections/finder.html)
Online collection of the Library of Congress featuring various memorabilia and music collections, such as sheet music, folk music recordings, jazz photography, and the Leonard Bernstein collection.

Cyberspace Music Resources (http://thunder1.cudenver.edu/cam/cmr/)
Compiled and maintained by Dr. Judith A. Coe, a singer, songwriter, educator, composer, and synthesist, this site contains an annotated list of subject areas for music research, including bibliographies, books and dissertations, discussion forums, and other Internet resources.

Essentials of Music (http://www.essentialsofmusic.com/)
A good starting point for beginning research about classical music, Essentials of Music, created by Sony Music Entertainment, provides basic information and overviews of western music history covering Middle Ages, Renaissance, baroque, classical, romantic, and 20th century. Other features include brief biographies of more than 70 composers, a glossary of musical terms, and more than 200 audio excerpts of classical music.

Grovemusic.com (http://www.grovemusic.com)
Full-text access to Grove's library of highly acclaimed music dictionaries and encyclopedias, with advanced searching of subjects. Integrates the entire contents of *The New Grove Dictionary of Opera, The New Grove Dictionary of Music and Musicians,* and *The New Grove Dictionary of Jazz.* Source material includes authoritative articles, biographies, and background information covering all aspects of music.

Internet Resources for Music Scholars (http://hcl.harvard.edu/loebmusic/online-ir-intro.html)
Maintained by the Harvard University Music Library, this site features a variety of tools and links for music research. Direct access is provided to online journals, music departments and libraries, music information metasites, newsletters, scholarly societies, and much more.

Kathy Schrock's Guide for Educators (http://school.discovery.com/schrockguide/)
Principally designed to enhance curriculum and professional growth of educators, this directory of online guides, a part of the online Discovery Channel School, offers a categorized list of many useful Web sites on a variety of subjects, including performing arts and music.

Librarians' Index to the Internet: Music Topics (http://www.lii.org/search/file/music)
General resource list covering music topics from A to Z.

Open Directory Project: Arts: Music (http://dmoz.org/Arts/Music/)
This extensive collection of music Web sites compiled and organized by category includes sites on bands and artists, instruments, people, regions, and styles of music.

Worldwide Internet Music Resources (http://www.music.indiana.edu/music_resources/)
This comprehensive music resource list, offered as a service of the William and Gayle Cook Music Library at Indiana University, features a variety of links arranged by subject covering such subjects as genres, performance, composition, research, the music industry, and music journals.

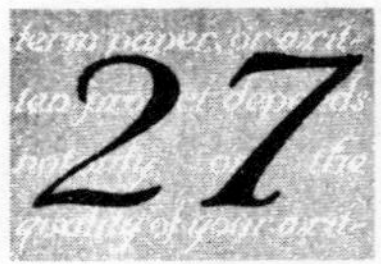

Nursing

Nursing is one of the fastest-growing professions today. Increasingly, research and literature is being published that discusses the administration, policies, principles, practices, ethics, methodologies, values, and effectiveness of nursing. Heading the list are literature indexes and computer databases containing bibliographic records and full-text newspaper and journal articles, conference proceedings, pamphlets, scholarly dissertations, and other printed or nonprinted sources. They include databases that are fully searchable by subject, author, keyword, or title enabling researchers to locate clinical articles by experts and scholars, original studies by researchers, and consumer-oriented material. This chapter highlights selected references on nursing.

SELECTED BOOKS AND REFERENCES

Encyclopedia of Bioethics, 3rd Ed., edited by Stephen G. Post, 5 vols. (New York: Macmillan Reference USA, 2003)
This five-volume revised edition provides informative articles about all aspects of health care ethics in modern medicine, science, and technology. Some 460 in-depth articles cover a wide range of complex issues facing health care professionals today, including abortion, animal research, death and dying, fertility and reproduction, genetics, organ donation and transplant, public health, mental health, and much more.

The Encyclopedia of Infectious Diseases, 2nd Ed., by Carol Turkington and Bonnie Lee Ashby, 397 pages (New York: Facts On File, 2003)
This easy-to-understand encyclopedia is written in plain language for laypeople and nonhealth-care professionals. It covers a wide range of infectious diseases and their causes. More than 600 entries discuss common diseases in detail, including their symptoms, prevention, drug therapies, and medical treatment. Written by medical writer Carol Turkington and physician Bonnie Lee Ashby, this fully revised and updated second edition covers childhood diseases, foodborne diseases, and many others. Six appendixes offer more information regarding drug treatments and known side effects, guidelines for home remedies for disinfection, a directory of health organizations, medical hot lines, health publications, and infectious disease Web sites. An extensive bibliography rounds out this title.

Encyclopedia of Nursing Research, edited by Joyce J. Fitzpatrick, 736 pages (New York: Springer Pub. Co., 1998)
Written by 200 contributing experts, this encyclopedia describes and explains key terms and concepts in nursing research. Entries cover a wide range of topics, such as nursing care, nursing education, nursing services, cultural, historical, and philosophical issues, key nursing organizations, and publications extensively cross-referenced to help readers find information.

The Gale Encyclopedia of Medicine, 3rd Ed., 5 vols., 3,956 pages (Detroit, Mich.: Gale Group, 2005)
An encyclopedia suitable for doctors, nurses, health care workers and non-professionals, offering in-depth coverage and easy-to-read articles on more than 1,700 medical topics such as diseases, disorders, tests, and treatments on major and minor medical issues. This revised third edition features more than 200 new entries and 300 fully updated articles. Articles range from one to 10 pages in length. Besides a short glossary of terms, each article includes a list of additional references, including articles, books, tapes, Web sites, and associations with contact information.

Magill's Medical Guide, 3rd Rev. Ed., edited by Anne Chang, M.D., et al. 4 vols., 2,900 pages (Pasadena, Calif.: Salem Press, 2004)
This revised third edition provides 960 articles on a wide range of medical topics, including 89 new topics and 148 newly commissioned updated essays. Essays ranging from 500 to 3,000 words address a myriad of important and emerging health subjects, including AIDS, anthrax, Botox, cloning, fetal surgery, and gene therapy.

The Merck Manual of Diagnosis and Therapy, 17th Ed., edited by Mark H. Beers and Robert Berkow, 2,833 pages (New York: John Wiley & Sons, 1999)
Classic print reference for physicians, residents, and nurses, also available in electronic form, offering information about the diagnosis and treatment of common human diseases, disorders, and injuries, including symptoms and recommended treatments, arranged by etiology, organ system, or specialty.

Mosby's Medical, Nursing and Allied Health Dictionary, 6th Ed., edited by Kenneth N. Anderson, Patricia D. Novak, and Jeff Keith, 2,134 pages (St. Louis: Mosby, 2001)
This fully revised sixth edition of the nursing dictionary provides detailed definitions with more than 2,300 color illustrations on more than 6,000 key medical terms. Alphabetically arranged entries offer practical reference information on such topics as human anatomy, major diseases, disorders, and procedures, and drug therapies.

SELECTED ARTICLE INDEXES AND ABSTRACTS

Printed Indexes and Abstracts

Abstracts of Hospital Management Studies (Ann Arbor, Mich.: Health Administration Press for the Cooperative Information Center for Health Care Management Studies, the University of Michigan, 1965–87)
Available at university and medical school libraries, this index, first published as an international journal in 1965, abstracted studies focused on hospital

management, planning and public policy, and health care delivery. Formerly known as *Abstracts of Health Care Management Studies,* it was later renamed *Abstracts of Hospital Management Studies* until ceasing publication in July 1987.

Consumer Health & Nutrition Index (Phoenix, Ariz.: Oryx Press, 1985–97)
A popular reference source found in most public libraries, this quarterly reference indexes articles from newspapers, magazines, and journals, including such well-known publications as *Prevention, Harvard Medical School Letter, New England Journal of Medicine,* and *The New York Times* from July 1985 to April 1997. A CD-ROM version is also available.

Cumulated Index to Nursing and Allied Health Literature (CINAHL) (Glendale, Calif.: Seventh-Day Adventist Hospital Association, 1956–76; Glendale, Calif.: Glendale Adventist Medical Center, 1977–2000)
The most comprehensive index to periodical literature for nurses and allied health professionals, with citations to 640 nursing, allied health, and health-related journals. Five bimonthly and one cumulative bound volume were issued from 1956 to 2001. Formerly called the *Cumulative Index to Nursing Literature* (Volumes 1–21) from 1956 to 1976, this popular reference was renamed *Cumulative Index to Nursing and Allied Health Literature* in 1977 (Volume 22). It remained in print until 2000.

Hospital Literature Index (Chicago: American Hospital Association, 1950–2000)
Produced by the American Hospital Association and the National Library of Medicine, this subject-author index abstracts articles that appeared in hospital journals focused on administration, planning, and delivery of services in hospitals and other health care institutions. Originally titled the *Cumulative Index of Hospital Literature* (1950–74), the index was renamed *Hospital Literature Index* in 1974, then *Hospital and Health Administration Index* in 1995. As *Hospital Literature Index,* contents were published quarterly and cumulated annually, whereas the *Hospital and Health Administration Index* was published three times yearly, with the third issue an annual cumulation until it ceased publication in 2000. PubMed integrated the entire contents of this reference set into its online database, MEDLINE.

International Nursing Index (New York: American Journal of Nursing Co., 1966–2000)
Subject-author index to nursing journals produced by the American Journal of Nursing in cooperation with the National Library of Medicine, also covered in the online database MEDLINE.

Index Medicus (Bethesda, Md.: National Library of Medicine, 1966–)
Highly regarded print index, perhaps the most comprehensive index to biomedical literature, containing citations to articles from more than 3,000 biomedical journals throughout the world. Published by the National Library of Medicine, the index is issued monthly in two-volume sets arranged by subject and author, including a bibliography of medical reviews. The full contents of the monthly volumes comprise the annual *Cumulated Index*

Medicus. The index is available electronically through the MEDLINE database, which provides direct access to citations and abstracts to articles from 3,400 journals.

Nursing Studies Index, 4 vols. (Philadelphia: Lippincott 1963–1972; New York: Garland Pub., 1984)
Compiled by Yale University School of Nursing, covering nursing literature published between 1900 and 1959, this four-volume annotated guide cites reported studies, historical materials, and research methods in periodicals, books, and pamphlets published in English.

Physical Education Index (Cape Girardeau, Mo.: BenOak Pub. Co., 1970–97)
Provides citations and abstracts of journal articles about physical education and related disciplines (sports, sports medicine, dance, coaching, fitness, motor learning, etc.) from 303 scholarly journals and numerous other publications. Also offered online through Cambridge Scientific Abstracts.

Physical Fitness/Sports Medicine (Washington, D.C.: The President's Council on Physical Fitness and Sports, 1978–94)
Consists of citations to more than 3,000 periodicals, including *Physical Fitness/Sports Medicine* (from 1978 to 1994), a publication of the President's Council on Physical Fitness and Sports, and papers presented at selected Congresses.

Science Citation Index (Philadelphia: Institute for Scientific Information, 1961–95)
Published by the Institute for Scientific Information, this index offers citations to published journals in the fields of chemistry, mathematics, medicine, biology, engineering, and physics. The index is also produced on CD-ROM and microfiche.

Sociological Abstracts (San Diego, Calif.: Sociological Abstracts, Inc., 1953–)
Bibliographic reference featuring abstracts to literature of sociology and the related social sciences that covers such areas as health care, medicine, public health, and rehabilitation from sources in more than 30 languages.

Web Indexes and Abstracts

AgeLine (American Association of Retired Persons, 1966–)
Extensive collection produced by the Research Information Center of the American Association of Retired Persons (AARP) containing citations with abstracts of health literature in the areas of health services, research, technology, and consumer information geared for adults over age 50. Abstracts cover recent and previously published books, journal and magazine articles, research reports, and videos dealing with the clinical and nonclinical aspects of health care delivery. Publications included are from 1978 to the present, with selected coverage of archived material from 1966 to 1977. This database is available to the public free of charge. To access, visit http://research.aarp.org/ageline/home.html.

Biological Sciences (Cambridge Scientific Abstracts, 1982–)
Interdisciplinary database that cites and abstracts research, literature, conference proceedings, technical reports, monographs, and some books, including 20 separate subfiles, related to biological and medical issues.

CancerLit (National Cancer Institute, 1983–)
Leading bibliographic database produced by the National Cancer Institute that covers biomedical and cancer literature. Records contain citations with abstracts of all aspects of cancer therapy, including experimental and clinical cancer therapy, biochemistry, growth factor studies, immunology, and physiology of cancer.

Consumer Health & Nutrition Index (National Services Corp., 1985–97)
Electronic version delivered on CD-ROM of print edition featuring more than 94,000 records and 5,600 subject headings with abstracts from more than 70 consumer, health, and medical publications. Titles indexed include *American Baby, Arthritis Today, Consumer Reports on Health, Diabetes Forecast, Environmental Nutrition Newsletter, Health, Healthline, New England Journal of Medicine, Nutrition Today,* and *Prevention.*

Cumulative Index to Nursing and Allied Health (CINAHL) (CINAHL Information Systems, 1982–)
Superb source of indexed articles from more than 1,200 nursing and allied health journals based on the print edition. Indexing covers some books, dissertations, proceedings, and audiovisual materials, and includes full text of 27 nursing journals and some state nursing acts as well. Print equivalent called the *Cumulative Index to Nursing Literature* (1956–76) and *Cumulative Index to Nursing and Allied Health Literature* (1977–2001).

Dissertation Abstracts (FirstSearch, 1861–)
Indexes a diverse collection of dissertations from U.S. institutions of learning with limited coverage of institutions abroad. Printed edition offers indexing from 1955 to 1982.

HealthSTAR (National Library of Medicine/American Hospital Association; Ovid Technologies, 1975–)
Formerly produced as a separate database by the National Library of Medicine and the American Hospital Association and ceasing production in December 2000, HealthSTAR features citations with abstracts of published literature on health services, administration, research, and technology emphasizing the clinical and nonclinical aspects of health care delivery. Now produced by Ovid Technologies, the database is updated monthly with new journal citations culled from MEDLINE.

ISI Current Contents Connect (Thomson ISI, past five years plus current year)
Multidisciplinary database offering abstracts, tables of contents, and bibliographic records of articles published in some 8,000 scholarly journals and 2,000 books. Updated daily, it also includes links to full-text articles and documents and other resources accessible on the Web.

MEDLINE (PubMed/National Library of Medicine, 1950–)
World's leading medical database compiled by the National Library of Medicine featuring citations with abstracts to more than 4,000 professional and scholarly journals, including nursing and biomedical journals, on all aspects of health care and medicine. This fully searchable database encompasses information from *Index Medicus,* the *Index to Dental Literature,* the *International Nursing Index,* and other sources in the areas of allied health, biological and physical sciences, humanities and information science as they relate to medicine and health care, communication disorders, population biology, and reproductive biology. More than 8.7 million records from more than 3,600 journals are indexed, plus selected monographs of congresses and symposia from 1976 to 1981. Abstracts are included for about 67 percent of the records. A new and expanded version called MEDLINEPlus offers additional resources in nursing, including medical dictionaries, information clearinghouses, organizations, publications and consumer health libraries. MEDLINE is available through the National Library of Medicine, as well as other library database providers, including EBSCOHost, FirstSearch, and Ovid.

Physical Education Index (Cambridge Scientific Abstracts, 1970–)
Contains citations culled from peer-reviewed journals, conference proceedings, reports, trade magazines, and articles from popular and related publications. Records cover a host of relevant topics, including biomechanics and kinesiology, health, measurement and evaluation, motor learning, physical education, physical fitness, and physical therapy.

PsycINFO (American Psychological Association, 1887–)
Comprehensively abstracts journals, books, and book chapters in psychology and related disciplines from 1887 to the present. Nursing-related topics cover psychological aspects of counseling, health personnel issues, health promotion, mental health services, and rehabilitation.

Science Citation Index (Web of Science/Institute for Scientific Information, 1995–)
Multidisciplinary electronic index published by the Institute for Scientific Information that includes citations to journal articles and book chapters in health science and many other fields of study, including biology, chemistry, and medicine. Content is searchable by title, author, or subject.

Social Sciences Index (H.W. Wilson, 1974–).
Provides author-subject indexing to popular and scholarly periodicals in the fields of anthropology, community health and medical care, family studies, minority studies, social work, and sociology.

Sociological Abstracts (Sociological Abstracts, Inc./Cambridge Scientific Abstracts, 1963–)
Indexes the latest research in sociology and social and behavioral sciences with abstracts of articles from more than 2,600 journals, conference papers, dissertations, book reviews, and selected books from 1963 to the present. Covers topics such as sociology of health and medicine, human biology, and gerontology. The print version covers material published since 1953.

TOXLINE (Cambridge Scientific Abstracts, 1994–)
Produced by the National Library of Medicine in association with Cambridge Scientific Abstracts, TOXLINE abstracts information on chemicals, pharmaceuticals, pesticides, and pollutants.

SELECTED FULL-TEXT ARTICLE DATABASES

Academic Search Premier (InfoTrac, 1990–)
General, multidisciplinary database and good source of information with full-text articles from scholarly journals—more than 3,000 publications in all academic disciplines—from 1990 to the present.

Clinical Pharmacology (EBSCOHost, current)
Offers current and concise clinical drug monographs for all U.S. prescription drugs, hard-to-find herbal and nutritional supplements, new and investigational drugs, and over-the-counter products.

Expanded Academic ASAP (InfoTrac, 1980–)
Indexes literature, with access to some full-text articles, in many academic disciplines, including nursing. Indexes up to 2,600 scholarly journals, magazines, and newspapers.

Health and Wellness Resource Center (InfoTrac, 1980–)
Offers indexing and full-text articles on health and medicine, including encyclopedias, directories, medical dictionaries, periodicals, newspapers, pamphlets, and Web links. Similar in scope to Health Reference Center —Academic.

Health Periodicals Database (Gale Group, 1976–)
Containing a wealth of information on health, fitness, nutrition, and specialized medical topics, this electronic database, delivered on the Web via DIALOG, features citations and abstracts and full-text articles from 130 consumer health periodicals and 110 core health publications, as well as professional medical journals and pamphlets from medical associations. Covers the gamut of health science topics, including AIDS, biotechnology, cardiovascular disease, dieting, drug abuse, environment and public health, gerontology, health care costs, medical ethics, mental health, occupational health and safety, sports medicine, and toxicology.

Health Reference Center—Academic (InfoTrac, 1980–)
Provides timely and reliable indexing of medical, nursing, and current health issues published in more than 200 medical journals and consumer health magazines. Contains full-text articles from 150 periodicals and six medical reference books, including the *Columbia University College of Physicians and Surgeons Complete Home Medical Guide* and the *Consumer Health Information Source Book*. Also indexes 1,500 general interest titles and more than 500 pamphlets. Coverage of magazines and newspapers is nearly identical to that of Health and Wellness Resource Center.

Health Source: Consumer Edition (EBSCOHost, indexing: 1984– , full text: 1990–)
Good source of information on general health topics and health sciences that abstracts and indexes more than 205 publications, with full-text for more than 190 journals.

Health Source: Nursing/Academic Edition (EBSCOHost, indexing: 1960s– , full text: 1975–)
Abstracts and indexes more than 850 journals and full-text articles in nursing and allied health fields, including more than 450 peer-reviewed journals on many medical disciplines.

Kluwer Online (Kluwer Academic Publishers, 1997–)
Provides online access to the complete contents of more than 700 Kluwer journals, covering a wide array of subjects, including medicine, science, and technology.

LexisNexis Academic Universe (LexisNexis, 1977–)
Up-to-date electronic database that indexes more than 5,600 sources on a myriad of subjects, including news and current events, and provides access to full-text articles on many medical topics and related fields.

Periodical Abstracts Research II Edition with Full Text (UMI ProQuest, 1986–)
Complete access to citations and abstracts with full text to more than 1,600 academic journals and popular magazines, many in medicine and health sciences.

ProQuest Nursing Journals (ProQuest, 1984–)
This searchable database indexes 287 nursing and allied health periodicals, offering full text and images from such journals as *Nursing, Nursing Management, Nursing Economics, Nursing Forum, RN, Journal of Nursing Education, Nurse Practitioner, Nurse Researcher,* and *Nursing Diagnosis.* Other publications covered include *Alternative Therapies in Health and Medicine, American Journal of Sports Medicine, Occupational Therapy International, Physical Therapy,* and *Patient Care Management.* Some journals are similar to those indexed in CINAHL.

PubMed (National Library of Medicine, 1960s–)
A service of the National Library of Medicine, PubMed provides access to more than 11 million MEDLINE citations and additional life science journals. PubMed includes links to many sites providing full text articles and other related resources.

ScienceDirect (Elsevier Science, 1995–)
Multidisciplinary collection, emphasizing medicine, science, and technology, that provides access to more than 1,200 journals, 735 of them in full-text format, from 1995 to the present. Subjects include biochemistry, biological sciences, chemistry, clinical medicine, microbiology and immunology, neurosciences, pharmacology and toxicology, physics, and social sciences.

SPORTDiscus (SIRC, 1949–)
Leading sport, fitness, and sports medicine bibliographic database offering more than 500,000 citations and abstracts to serial and monographic literature, with links to full-text articles, covering all aspects, including recreation, exercise physiology, sports medicine, coaching, physical fitness, the psychology, history, and sociology of sport, training, and conditioning.

Wiley Interscience Journals (Wiley Interscience, 1997–)
Contains abstracts, tables of contents, and full-text articles from more than 450 journals published by Wiley Interscience, including 360 current titles on such subjects as chemistry, life sciences, medicine, and social sciences.

SELECTED PERIODICALS

AJN: American Journal of Nursing (Philadelphia, Pa.: J.B. Lippincott Co., 1900– , monthly)
The oldest nursing journal in the world, this peer-reviewed monthly journal provides in-depth coverage of the nursing profession and issues related to the education and practice of nursing. Each issues contains clinical and evidence-based news, analysis, and commentary and research reports discussing practical applications in acute care, critical care, long-term care, primary care, and rehabilitation.

Critical Care Nursing Quarterly (Philadelphia, Pa.: Lippincott, 1973– , quarterly)
This topical quarterly journal focuses on current clinical procedures in critical care. Coverage includes the latest developments, strategies, and techniquesin intensive and critical care, patient management, and pharmacological and technological advances. Also available in electronic form, full-text articles of past issues of *Critical Care Nursing Quarterly* are available through InfoTrac's Health and Wellness Reference Center (1996–) and EBSCOHost's Health Source: Nursing/Academic Edition (1999–), among others.

Journal of Advanced Nursing (Oxford; Boston: Blackwell Scientific Publications, 1994– , monthly)
Published monthly, this scholarly journal is dedicated to exploring the critical global challenges and nature of nursing in all fields of health care, including all aspects of nursing care, nursing education, management, and research. Articles in each issue mostly reflect "the diversity, quality and internationalism of nursing" including new advancements and developments, and scientific and philosophical theories. Past editions and articles are indexed and abstracted in such leading references as *Applied Social Science Index and Abstracts, Cumulative Index to Nursing and Allied Health Literature, Current Contents, MEDLINE,* and *Social Sciences Citation Index.*

SELECTED WEB SITES

ANA: The American Nurses Association (http://www.ana.org/index.htm)
Representing more than 2.6 million registered nurses nationwide, the American Nurses Association's Web site offers useful information and resources of

interest to professional nurses and nursing students, including news, information, and position papers on nursing, nursing ethics, and nursing careers.

Free Medical Journals List (http://www.freemedicaljournals.com/)
Offers free access to a wide assortment of medical journals on the Web, sorted alphabetically by name or by specialty.

Galaxy Nursing Index Page (http://www.galaxy.com/cgi-bin/dirlist?node=25254)
Free, fully browsable, fully searchable Web directory featuring extensive listings on sources for nursing in such areas as nursing administration, education, evaluation, nursing theories, and nursing specialties. Directories and nursing guides are included.

HealthWeb: Nursing (http://www.healthweb.org/browse.cfm?subjectid=60)
Contains links to the best health information in nursing on a broad range of subjects, such as AIDS or rehabilitation nursing.

Medscape (WebMD, 1994–) (http://www.medscape.com/)
An online journal of health news for health care professionals featuring full-text articles covering such areas as cardiology, family medicine, pulmonary medicine, and radiology, access to the online information database MEDLINE, and a medical dictionary.

Nursing Center—Journal Articles (http://www.nursingcenter.com/library/index.asp)
Contains articles from nearly 40 trusted nursing journals, including *AJN* and *Nursing 2004*, available in both HTML and .PDF formats.

Research in Nursing (http://library.west.asu.edu/subjects/nur/index.html)
Lists a variety of journal indexes and abstracts, print reference sources, and additional Internet sites, with direct links, related to the profession of nursing.

Virtual Nursing Center (Martindale's Health Science Guide) (http://www.martindalecenter.com/Nursing.html)
Virtual reference center featuring case studies, continuing education materials, medical dictionaries and glossaries, online nursing journals, and more.

Yahoo! Nursing (http://dir.yahoo.com/Health/Nursing/)
Well-organized collection and one of the most extensive listings of Web sites on nursing, with information about conferences, history, nursing specialties, and student nursing.

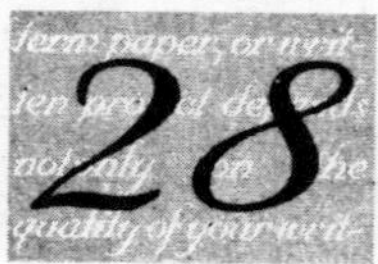

Politics and Public Policy

From current legislation to public policy decisions affecting every city, state, or nation, politics is a fact of life that has been around for centuries. And yet, issues and challenges never seem to go away, and politics remains at the core of public policy and public administration in all that embodies society. This chapter details an abundance of source material that has aided political science students, researchers, and scholars in the research of this field. Plenty of print and electronic sources are available for research.

SELECTED BOOKS AND REFERENCES

Almanacs

Activist's Almanac: The Concerned Citizen's Guide to the Leading Advocacy Organizations in America, by David Walls, 431 pages (New York: Simon & Schuster, 1993)

This 431-page guide features detailed descriptions of many national activist organizations throughout the United States. Each entry provides specific information about each group, including its purpose, priorities, members, structure, resources, publications, and services.

The Almanac of American Politics 2004, by Michael Barone and Richard E. Cohen, 1,800 pages (Boston: Gambit, 1972–; National Journal Group, 1999–).

Published annually since 1972, *The Almanac of American Politics* has become a leading source of information on politics and elected officials. This latest edition, cowritten by political reporter and Fox News analyst Michael Barone and Richard E. Cohen, follows the same format as previous editions. It features brief overviews of all 50 states, including congressional districts and profiles of governors, senators, and state representatives. Biographical details are provided on each elected official, along with their voting records, election results, and ratings by 11 interest groups and *The National Journal.*

Encyclopedias

Citizen Action Encyclopedia: Groups and Movements That Have Changed America, by Richard S. Halsey, 385 pages (Westport, Conn.: Oryx Press, 2002)

This encyclopedia thoroughly details the people, organizations, events, and movements behind citizen activism in the United States, covering the broad spectrum of American activism in the 20th century, including ultraliberal and ultraconservative activists and organizations.

Encyclopedia of Interest Groups and Lobbyists in the United States, by Immanuel Ness, 2 vols., 800 pages (Armonk, N.Y.: M.E. Sharpe, 2000)
This two-volume encyclopedia covers seemingly every major interest group and lobbyist in the United States. Part I offers detailed profiles of 172 such groups organized into 13 categories, including banking, environment, health, human rights, and many others. Each entry offers complete information on each group, such as history, general legislative interests, successes and failures, membership, annual budget, table summaries of donations made to political candidates in the 1996 and 1998 elections, and lobbying activities. Part II of the set highlights political action committees (PACs) and lobbyists.

Encyclopedia of the United States Cabinet, by Mark Grossman, 3 vols., 1,137 pages (Santa Barbara, Calif.: ABC-CLIO, 2000)
Devoted entirely to the history of the U.S. cabinet and its secretaries, this award-winning three-volume set profiles every cabinet department. Examined in detail is the history of each department with biographical information, as well as historical overviews of cabinet members.

A chronological list of cabinet members by department is featured at the beginning of each volume. Cabinet profiles cover not only the history but also the origin of each department, even those departments that have merged into other departments or ceased operation. An extensive bibliography and general index accompany this fact-filled reference source, which is also available as an electronic book.

International Encyclopedia of Public Policy and Administration A–Z, edited by Jay M. Shafritz, 4 vols., 2,504 pages (Boulder: Westview Press, 1998)
Covering the concepts, practices, issues, and theories that define public policy making, from analysis to implementation, this four-volume encyclopedia offers some 900 articles penned by more than 400 leading scholars and practitioners from throughout the world. Offered are basic definitions, thorough descriptions, explanations of historical significance, and bibliographies for each topic.

General References

Congress and the Nation X: 1997–2001, 1,232 pages (Washington, D.C.: Congressional Quarterly Service, 2002)
The 10th edition of this renowned series published since 1945 chronicles congressional legislation and the second term of President Bill Clinton. Coverage includes key legislation, detailed chronologies of congressional action, selections with texts of presidential speeches, key voting records of the 105th and 106th congressional sessions, detailed tables and charts, and much more.

Directory of Congressional Voting Scores and Interest Group Ratings, 3rd Ed., by J. Michael Sharp, 2 vols., 1,676 pages (Washington, D.C.: CQ Press, 2000)
This two-volume compilation features voting study comparisons and interest group rating data on every U.S. congressman and woman elected to office, 1947–99.

Public Interest Profiles, 2001–2002 by Congressional Quarterly editors (Washington, D.C.: Congressional Quarterly, 2000)
First published in 1977, this annual reference fully details some 200 national nonprofit interest groups in the United States, indexed by name, subject, and group.

U.S. Energy and Environmental Interest Groups: Institutional Profiles, by Lettie McSpadden Wenner, 358 pages (Westport, Conn.: Greenwood Press, 1990)
This A–Z companion offers complete overviews of every major energy and environmental interest group in the United States. Each entry provides important information about each group, including policy issues, resources, and tactics.

U.S. Religious Interest Groups: Institutional Profiles, by Paul J. Weber and W. Landis Jones, 240 pages (Westport, Conn.: Greenwood Press, 1994)
This alphabetically arranged compendium details every major religious interest group in the United States. Contents of each entry include origin and history, mission statement, funding source, policy concerns, and religious affiliations. Also provided are appendixes of groups by policy area, religious affiliation, political identification, and more.

U.S. Women's Interest Groups: Institutional Profiles, edited by Sarah Slavin, 688 pages (Westport, Conn.: Greenwood Press, 1995)
This general reference title highlights major women's interest groups in the United States, covering their origin and development, electoral activities, funding, and policy concerns.

Vital Statistics on American Politics, 2005–2006, by Harold W. Stanley and Richard G. Niemi, 400 pages (Washington, D.C.: CQ Press, 2005–)
This essential resource, published annually since 1988, contains more than 200 tables and charts on many aspects of American politics and government. Each volume features data relating to campaign finance, political action committees, elections, political parties, public opinion, voting, the media, Congress, the presidency, the judiciary, federal and state finance, foreign policy, military, and social and economic policy.

Washington Information Directory 2004–2005, 1,050 pages (Washington, D.C.: CQ Press, 2004)
Since publication of the first edition in 1975–76, this widely distributed annual directory has offered detailed descriptions of hundreds of government agencies, congressional committees, nonprofit organizations, and special interest groups located in the U.S. capital. Includes an alphabetical index.

Washington Representatives 2001, by Mark Francis, Valerie S. Sheridan, Natacha Leonard, and Diane R. Murphy, 1,400 pages (Washington, D.C.: Columbia Books, Inc., 2001)
Originally called the *Directory of Washington Representatives of American Associations and Industry* (1977–), this popular political reference features two alphabetical listings of more than 17,000 lobbyists, public and government affairs representatives, and special interest advocates and the causes

they represent. Entries provide key contact information, including name, address, phone and fax numbers, e-mail and Web addresses, and a brief description. Listings are organized by client and by representative, and indexed by subject/industry, foreign interest, and legislative issue.

SELECTED ARTICLE INDEXES AND ABSTRACTS

Printed Indexes and Abstracts

The Alternative Press Index (College Park, Md.: Alternative Press Center, 1969–)
For news and opinion on politics and public policy decisions from the alternative press, this printed edition indexes articles of some 200 so-called leftist and radical periodicals dating back to 1969. An online database version of the same name is also available, indexing material from 1991 to the present.

America: History and Life (Santa Barbara, Calif.: ABC-CLIO, 1964–1999)
This print index abstracts and indexes journal articles, dissertations, and book or media reviews from more than 2,400 journals in 40 different languages on American history, including social and cultural history. The first 10 volumes, titled *America: History and Life,* index material from July 1964 to winter 1973. Four other 15-volume sets cover material from 1974 to 1988. They include *America: History and Life, Part A: Article Abstracts and Citations; America: History and Life, Part B: Index to Book Reviews; America: History and Life, Part C: American History Bibliography, Books, Articles and Dissertations;* and *America: History and Life, Part D: Annual Index.* In 1989, the series was returned to its original title, *America: History and Life,* with Volume 26. The entire series is also available online from 1982 to the present.

Historical Abstracts (Santa Barbara, Calif.: ABC-CLIO, 1955–2000)
This predecessor to the online version (1960–) abstracts both scholarly journals and dissertations on world history (except U.S. and Canadian history) from 1450 to the present, including social and cultural history.

International Political Science Abstracts (IPSA) (Montreal: International Political Science Abstracts, 1951–)
Published bimonthly by the International Political Science Association since 1951, this long-running series abstracts articles selected from political science journals and yearbooks published worldwide. In addition to the printed version, *IPSA* is offered online. Coverage is from 1989 to the present.

PAIS Bulletin (New York: Public Affairs Information Service Inc., 1939–)
This interdisciplinary, international index provides quick access to citations of articles, books, and other documents covering important political, economic, and social issues affecting world communities, countries, people, governments, and public policy issues by subject. From 1939 to 1990, the index was called the *PAIS Bulletin.* It was renamed *PAIS International in Print* in 1991. A Web version, PAIS International, is also available through libraries.

Social Sciences Index (New York: H.W. Wilson, 1974–)
Quarterly author-and-subject index with abstracts covering 550 journals in the social sciences, including area studies, community health and medical care, economics, family studies, minority studies, policy sciences, political science, and urban studies.

Web Indexes and Abstracts

The Alternative Press Index (OCLC/Alternative Press Center, 1991–)
Internet subject index based on the print edition to nearly 300 alternative, radical, and leftist English-language periodicals from 1991 to the present.

America: History and Life (ABC-CLIO, 1960–)
Web edition with complete bibliographic citations and abstracts covering the history of the United States and Canada.

Historical Abstracts (ABC-CLIO, 1955–)
Features citations and abstracts of scholarly journals and dissertations on the history of the world from 1450 to the present, published since 1955. Adapted from the printed edition. Coverage does not include the United States and Canada, which are covered in the index *America: History and Life.*

International Political Science Abstracts (International Political Science Association, 1989–)
This Web adaptation of the printed version abstracts approximately 900 journals and yearbooks in the fields of political science, international relations, public administration, and public law. Most abstracts are in English, although some are in French. Coverage is from 1989 to the present.

PAIS International (OCLC Public Affairs Information Service, 1972–)
Like the printed index, this bibliographic Web version covers literature of public affairs, public policy, social policy, and general social sciences from local, national, and international perspectives. The database provides citations of journal articles, books, committee reports, directories, government documents, statistical compilations, and reports of public, intergovernmental, and private organizations.

Social Sciences Index (H.W. Wilson, 1984–)
This electronic equivalent to H.W. Wilson's printed edition indexes journals in area studies, geography, international relations, political science, public administration, policy sciences, and other disciplines.

Social Services Abstracts (Cambridge Scientific Abstracts, 1980–)
Online database that contains more than 78,000 records, including bibliographic citations and abstracts of articles from more than 1,500 journals publishing current research on social work, human services, and related areas, including social welfare, social policy, and community development.

Worldwide Political Science Abstracts (Cambridge Scientific Abstracts, 1975–)
Extensively provides citations, abstracts, and indexing of the international serials literature in political science and its complementary fields, including

international relations, law, and public administration/policy. Contents include back files of *Political Science Abstracts,* published by IFI/Plenum, 1975–2000, and *ABC POL SCI,* published by ABC-CLIO, 1984–2000.

SELECTED FULL-TEXT ARTICLE DATABASES

Alt-Press Watch (1970–)
A good source of different viewpoints and perspectives from beyond the mainstream media, this database provides full-text access to 170 newspaper, magazine, and journal titles of the alternative and independent press.

CQ Researcher (CQ Researcher, 1991–)
Ideal for finding timely overviews and critical analyses of current issues, CQ Researcher features information and full-text research reports on major controversial topics of national and international importance. Varying in length, each report includes complete and balanced summaries and analysis representing both sides of the issues. Often paired with this popular database is *CQ Weekly,* an independently published political magazine, with access to full-text articles published since 1983. The weekly journal provides in-depth reporting of activities of the U.S. Congress, including the status of bills, votes and amendments, floor and committee decisions, and major public policy issues.

Ethnic Newswatch (ProQuest, 1985–)
Full-text access to 240 newspapers, magazines, and journals of the ethnic, minority, and Native press covering local, national, and international news, culture, and history. Indexed are articles covering all areas of politics and political science, as well as arts and media, education, environment, journalism, sociology, Spanish, and ethnic and cultural studies (African American, Arab and Middle Eastern, Asian American, European, Jewish, Native Peoples, etc.).

LexisNexis Academic Universe (LexisNexis, 1977–)
Contents include full-text documents on all topics from more than 5,600 news, business, legal, medical, and reference publications, such as national and regional newspapers, wire services, broadcast transcripts, international news, and non-English language sources, U.S. federal and state case law, codes, regulations, legal news, law reviews, and international legal information, business news journals, company financial information, and industry and market news, and more.

LexisNexis Congressional (LexisNexis, 1789–)
Useful for researching legislative histories, major policy issues, and general information about the U.S. Congress, this subject-specific database provides comprehensive indexing and abstracting of congressional publications and legislative histories. It includes the full text of congressional reports, documents, bills, the *Congressional Record,* selected testimony in hearings before Congress, laws, statutes, U.S. Code Service, the *Federal Register,* the Code of Federal Regulations, and *The National Journal,* as well as information about members of Congress. Congressional publications are indexed from 1789 to the present. Coverage dates of other items varies.

ProQuest Newspapers (ProQuest, 1984–)
Full-text searchable current events database includes citations of nine national newspapers, including *The Atlanta Journal and Constitution* (1990–); *Boston Globe* (1985–); *Chicago Tribune* (1985–); *Christian Science Monitor* (1990–); *Los Angeles Times* (1985); *The New York Times* (1999–); *USA Today* (1987–); *Wall Street Journal* (1984–); and *The Washington Post* (1987–).

SELECTED PERIODICALS

The American Political Science Review (Washington, D.C.: American Political Science Association, 1906– , quarterly)
The longest-running publication of the American Political Science Association (APSA), this scholarly journal, first published in November 1906, offers the latest research from the fields of political science and extensive book reviews from all fields of political science. Published in print and online, access to past issues is available through JSTOR (1906–2000), and full-text articles and abstracts downloadable in .PDF form through Cambridge University Press Online (http://www.journals.cambridge.org).

CQ Weekly Report (Washington, D.C.: Congressional Quarterly, 1946– , weekly)
A good source for keeping up with what's happening on Capitol Hill, this weekly journal, published since 1946 by *Congressional Quarterly*, includes comprehensive legislative news and analysis, and recounts congressional activities of the week. *CQ Weekly* is also published on the Web with access to full-text articles since 1983 by subscription.

Dissent (New York: Foundation for Study of Independent Ideas, Inc., 1954– , quarterly)
A magazine of the liberal left, this independent-minded quarterly journal, in the words of *The New York Post*, "ranks among the handful of political journals read most regularly by U.S. intellectuals." Each issue features articles about politics in the United States, provocative social and cultural commentaries, and coverage of European politics. Archives of past issues from 1999 to the present are browsable at http://www.dissentmagazine.org/.

Foreign Affairs (New York: Council of Foreign Relations, 1922– , five times yearly)
This well-known journal, published by the Council of Foreign Relations since 1922, bills itself as "America's most influential publication on international affairs and foreign policy." Read by business leaders, government figures, journalists, and scholars, each issue contains articles on international relations, including in-depth analysis and debate of the most significant issues in the world today. Back files of *Foreign Affairs* magazine can be browsed back to 1973, including the text of articles.

Human Events (Washington, D.C.: Eagle Publishing, 1944– , weekly)
This weekly journal, founded in 1944, offers news and commentary with a conservative perspective. Articles include columns by top conservative colum-

nists such as Ann Coulter and Robert Novak, and features on important social and cultural issues such as immigration, taxes, and spending.

Journal of Public Affairs (London: Henry Stewart Publications, January 2001– , quarterly)
This international scholarly journal focuses specifically on the area of public affairs, providing expert analysis, case studies, research, and articles on current issues. Each issue focuses on different themes, such as government relations and lobbying, corporate social responsibility, issues management, and political strategy and marketing. Tables of contents and full-text articles are accessible through Ingenta (2001–).

The Nation (New York: The Nation, 1865– , 47 times a year)
Established by abolitionists in 1865, *The Nation* is the oldest journal of liberal opinion in America today. Each issue covers such subjects as politics, economics, education, foreign policy, labor, law, social issues, and the arts. Published 47 times a year, the journal often features pieces written by the country's most respected liberal thinkers.

National Journal (Washington, D.C.: National Journal Group, 1969– , weekly)
Published by the National Journal Group, Inc., a leading Washington, D.C., publisher of political books, directories, magazines, and newsletters, this weekly print and online journal offers in-depth coverage of politics, Congress, and federal agency activities. Selected stories and columns are available online at http://nationaljournal.com/about/njweekly/stories/. Full-text articles also indexed by LexisNexis Academic Universe.

National Review (New York: National Review, 1955– , biweekly)
First published in 1955, this esteemed biweekly political journal offers in-depth news, analysis, and opinion with a conservative bent. Content includes articles, essays, and interviews offering conservative views on social and political issues across the United States and the world. Selected full-text articles published from 2002 to the present can be obtained online at http://www.nationalreview.com/full_coverage/article.asp.

The New Republic (Washington, D.C.: The New Republic, 1914– , weekly)
This weekly opinion journal published since 1914 is geared toward readers interested in politics and domestic and international affairs. Issues contain in-depth reports and essays on topics such as economics, politics, theater, motion pictures, music, and the arts written from a liberal viewpoint. Editions of *The New Republic* starting in 2003 are available for print or digital subscribers in .PDF format at http://www.tnr.com/pdf_archive.mhtml.

Political Science Quarterly (New York: Academy of Political Science, 1886– , quarterly)
Published by New York's Academy of Political Science since 1886, *Political Science Quarterly* is reportedly "the most widely read and accessible scholarly journal covering government, politics and policy." Written for political scientists and the general public, each issue of this nonpartisan journal

consists of five to six articles on politics, emerging trends, and world affairs, with an emphasis on American politics. Tables of contents and full-text articles are available through such online journal databases as Ingenta (1998–) and JSTOR (1886–1998/99).

The Washington Post (Washington, D.C.: The Washington Post Co., 1877– , daily)
The Washington Post is a major daily source of news and investigative articles providing extensive coverage of national politics. Articles range from general news stories to feature stories on the latest legislative activities to policy decisions and politics in the White House. Full-text articles available through LexisNexis Academic Universe and other library databases.

SELECTED WEB SITES

Public Policy Organizations

American Enterprise Institute for Public Policy Research (http://www.aei.org/)
Founded in 1943, the American Enterprise Institute for Public Policy Research is one of America's largest think tanks. Based in Washington, D.C., the institute focuses its research in the areas of economics and trade; social welfare; government tax, spending, regulatory, and legal policies; U.S. politics; international affairs; and U.S. defense and foreign policies. Its Web page offers access to news and commentary, highlights of current research, and publications.

Brookings Institution (http://www.brookings.org/)
One of Washington's oldest think tanks, this independent, nonpartisan organization is dedicated to research, analysis, and public education concerning economic, foreign policy, and governing issues. The institution's Web site features a variety of resources for students, including news, an index of research topics by category with full-text links, and related publications.

Cato Institute (http://www.cato.org/)
Founded in 1977 and headquartered in Washington, D.C., this nonprofit public policy research foundation engages in research in the public policy arena emphasizing a libertarian philosophy. The foundation's Web site offers plenty of useful resources, in particular, an extensive research area of public policy topics, such as budget, taxes, welfare, and the workforce.

Heritage Foundation (http://www.heritage.org/)
This conservative research and educational institute, founded in 1973, devotes itself to "public policies based on the principles of free enterprise, limited government, individual freedom, traditional American values, and a strong national defense." The foundation's home page includes a wide variety of public policy resources, including one of the largest Web collections of research issues with full-text links on varying subjects.

RAND Corporation (http://www.rand.org/)
The RAND Corporation is a nonprofit research organization, or "think tank." The home page of this nonprofit corporation offers many quick links

to resources, including overviews and full-text documents of core research in the areas of children and adolescents, civil justice, education, energy and environment, health and health care, international affairs, pollution and aging, public safety, and many more.

Urban Institute (http://www.urban.org/)
A nonpartisan economic and social policy research organization, the Urban Institute chiefly focuses on complex national and local issues, such as poverty, educational achievement, and community building. The institute's Web site provides direct access to new reports, research, issues in focus, and policy centers.

Federal Organizations

FirstGov: U.S. Government Official Web Portal (http://www.firstgov.gov/)
Official federal government gateway to a wide variety of Web resources in one place, including links to federal agencies, legislative and federal branches, state and local governments, information by topic, a reference center offering current data and statistics, and much more.

GPO Access (http://www.gpoaccess.gov/)
A free service of the U.S. Government Printing Office, GPO Access offers official information and full-text documents from all three branches of the federal government. Resources can be accessed by branch or by topic. Several other online databases are featured as well, including an A–Z list of federal resources and a locator for federal depository libraries.

International Organizations

United Nations (http://www.un.org/english/)
Main Web page of this international humanitarian and peacekeeping organization providing opportunities to learn more about the United Nations, its history and mission, its agenda and current issues, current actions against terrorism, and upcoming conferences and events.

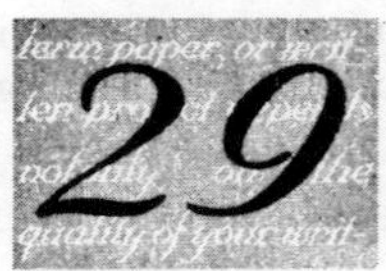

Psychology

In a field as vast and rapidly changing as psychology, many leading authorities, scholars, researchers, and psychological professionals have chronicled everything about the history, technique, and applications of psychiatry for further study and research. Whether you want to find up-to-date information about difficult psychological terms or concepts, thousands of psychological conditions, psychological drugs, or prominent specialists in the fields of psychiatry and psychology, every possible source on these and countless other subjects await you.

Credible published research, facts, and evidence, including case studies, family histories, journal articles, popular references, and print and electronic sources can provide answers. This chapter summarizes selected references and resources.

SELECTED BOOKS AND REFERENCES

Beginning Research in Psychology: A Practical Guide to Research Methods and Statistics, by Colin Dyer, 482 pages, Oxford, UK; Cambridge, Mass.: Blackwell, 1995, 1999)
Republished in 1999, this introductory volume covers research methods and statistics for beginning students of psychology and related disciplines. This 482-page handbook features interviews and case studies, survey methods, observational research, working with numerical data and statistics, hypothesis testing, and much more.

Comprehensive Clinical Psychology, edited by Alan S. Bellack and Michel Hersen, 11 vols. (New York: Pergamon, 1998)
Also published online, this 11-volume reference set covers all aspects of clinical psychology. Each volume is dedicated to a single subject area, including (in order), foundations, professional issues, research methods, assessment, children and adolescents, adults, clinical geropsychology, health psychology, applications in diverse populations, and sociocultural and individual differences in people with clinical psychology disorders. The final volume is an index to the entire series.

A Dictionary of Psychology, edited by Andrew M. Colman, 844 pages (Oxford: Oxford University Press, 2003)
Edited by the author of *What Is Psychology?*, this fully revised and updated dictionary includes more than 10,000 entries detailing all aspects and areas

of psychology. Explained in simple language are definitions of countless terms and concepts in the field of psychology, plus relevant technical words from related disciplines used by many psychologists. Further coverage is provided on psychoanalysis and terms introduced into the profession by Freud, Jung, Adler, Erikson, Kohut, Lacan, Reich, and many others. Likewise highlighted are phobias, phobic stimuli, and mental disorders, and more than 700 commonly used abbreviations and symbols in psychology.

Encyclopedia of Psychology, edited by Alan E. Kazdin, 8 vols. (Washington, D.C.: American Psychological Association; New York: Oxford University Press, 2000)
An exceptional A-to-Z source on psychology, this eight-volume set, produced under the editorial direction of Alan Kazdin and the American Psychological Association, contains some 400 biographies and more than 1,500 articles in the fields of psychology, allied fields, and other disciplines. Each major topic includes a lengthy essay and brief articles about each subject along with a list of sources.

International Encyclopedia of the Social and Behavioral Sciences, edited by Neil J. Smelser and Paul B. Baltes, 26 vols. (New York: Elsevier, 2001)
This outstanding reference set—called "the single largest social and behavioral sciences reference set ever published"—features about 4,000 well-written articles on everything related to social and behavioral sciences. The set includes a comprehensive name index and subject index.

Magill's Encyclopedia of Social Science: Psychology, edited by Nancy A. Piotrowski, 4 vols., 1,200 pages (Hackensack, N.J.: Salem, 2003)
Based on Frank N. Magill's six-volume *Survey of Social Science: Psychology Series* (1993), this revised four-volume set features 452 comprehensive overviews, including 177 newly commissioned and 103 updated entries, covering disorders, popular concepts, tests, theories, treatment, key figures, and issues in the field of psychology. Each ranges from one to eight pages in length, and all are cross-referenced in the fourth volume, which includes an index.

SELECTED ARTICLE INDEXES AND ABSTRACTS

Printed Indexes and Abstracts

Combined Retrospective Index to Journals in Sociology, 1895–1974, 6 vols. (Washington, D.C.: Carrollton Press, 1978)
Complete six-volume set providing retrospective coverage of sociology periodicals. Articles are searchable by subject or keyword in the first five volumes, then by author in the sixth and final volume. The print reference series also lists articles chronologically under subject or author headings.

Psychological Abstracts (Washington, D.C.: American Psychological Association, 1927–).
Comprehensively indexes more than 1,200 psychology periodicals and literature; also available in electronic format as PsycAbstracts and PsycINFO.

Social Planning, Policy and Development Abstracts (San Diego, Calif.: Sociological Abstracts, 1979–96)
Offered in print only, this index provides international abstract coverage of journal articles, book reviews, and dissertations. From 1997 to the present, abstracts appear in *Sociological Abstracts.*

Social Sciences and Humanities Index (New York: H.W. Wilson, 1966–74)
Nine-volume index of citations to numerous journals in humanities and social sciences published between 1965 and 1974.

Social Sciences Citation Index, 3 vols. (Philadelphia, Pa.: Institute for Scientific Information, 1956–90)
This international, interdisciplinary three-volume resource indexes citations to more than 4,700 scholarly journals, with 1,400 titles fully covered, in social, behavioral, and related sciences published from 1956 to 1990. Journals in biomedical, natural, and physical sciences are selectively indexed as well. Includes source, citation, subject, corporate, and geographic area indexes to entries in all three volumes. Also available on CD-ROM is an online edition, published by Web of Science, that indexes material from 1956 to the present.

Social Sciences Index (New York: H.W. Wilson, 1974–)
This popular reference provides author and subject indexing of 342 English-language periodicals. Citations cover biographies, book reviews, feature articles, review articles, and interviews in the fields of anthropology, area studies, community health and medical care, economics, family studies, minority studies, social work, sociology, and related subjects.

Social Work Research and Abstracts (New York: National Association of Social Workers, 1972–)
Indexes more than 400 English-language and international scholarly journals on social work, social welfare, and related fields derived from each issue of the quarterly publication, *Social Work Abstracts.* In 1994, the name of the index was changed to *Social Work Abstracts.*

Sociological Abstracts (San Diego: Sociological Abstracts, Inc., 1953–)
Print index featuring abstracts from international sources on sociology and related disciplines, also available in a Web version (1963–) from Cambridge Scientific Abstracts.

Web Indexes and Abstracts

Current Contents Connect (Thomson ISI, 1994–)
Popular multidisciplinary resource offers access to bibliographic records of more than 8,000 scholarly journals and more than 2,000 books from 250 disciplines in the sciences, social sciences, and arts and humanities. Available on CD-ROM and the Internet, this database is distributed separately and packaged with the Web of Science, which connects users to three fully searchable periodical indexes, including Arts and Humanities Citation Index, Citation Index Expanded, and Social Science Citation Index.

Family and Society Studies Worldwide Database (NISC, 1970–)
This comprehensive source includes more than 198,000 citations and abstracts of more than 1,000 books, conference papers, journal articles, popular literature, and government reports on family science, human ecology, and human development. Records combine material from the discontinued print version, *Inventory of Marriage and Family Literature,* and the online *Australian Family and Society Abstracts.*

MEDLINE (PubMed/U.S. National Library of Medicine, 1950–)
One of the best sources of biomedical literature, this free Internet database produced by the National Library of Medicine provides more than 4 million citations, many with abstracts, to more than 3,900 current international journals published in more than 70 countries in the fields of health care, medicine, and preclinical sciences.

Mental Health Abstracts (IFI Claims, 1967–2000)
Featuring more than 500,000 bibliographic records, this online database, available through DIALOG, covers all aspects of mental health and mental illness, providing abstracts of some 1,200 journals from 41 different countries and in 21 different languages. Also referenced are books, conference proceedings, monographs, technical reports, symposia, Far Eastern literature, and nonprint media from 1967 to June 2000. Coverage includes such related topics as child development, epidemiology, mental health services, psychiatry, psychology, psychopharmacology, sexology, and social issues. From 1969 to 1982, the National Clearinghouse of Mental Health Information of the U.S. National Institute of Mental Health originally produced this database. In 1983, IFI Plenum Data Corporation began updating the database on a regular basis.

PsycINFO (American Psychological Association, 1887–)
Also available in print as *Psychological Abstracts* (1927–), this online version features abstracts of every kind of English-language psychology or journal publication. Abstracted are book chapters, journal articles, dissertations, reports, scholarly documents, technical reports, and other psychologically relevant material. The coverage list includes more than 1,900 journals, including *Academic Psychiatry* (1997–) and *Zoo Biology* (1982–), updated monthly. A wide array of related disciplines are covered as well, including anthropology, business, education, law, linguistics, medicine, nursing, pharmacology, physiology, psychiatry, and social work.

PsycLIT (American Psychological Association, 1974–)
Compiled by the American Psychological Association, this CD-ROM version of the print edition, *Psychological Abstracts* (1927), contains citations and abstracts of articles from more than 1,300 psychology journals from 50 countries, and summaries of English-language books and chapters in psychology and related fields. Journal articles are indexed from 1974, and books and chapters from 1987 to the present. Material from this index is also available online as PsycINFO (1967–), updated monthly.

Social Science Citation Index (Thomson ISI, 1978–)
This fully searchable Web-adapted version of the print edition offers comprehensive citations of thousands of leading journals in many fields, includ-

ing anthropology, area studies, demography, ethnic group studies, family studies, health policy, history, law, linguistics, psychiatry, psychology, sociology, substance abuse, and women's studies.

Social Work Abstracts (National Association of Social Workers, 1977–)
Corresponding to the print index *Social Work Research and Abstracts*, this Web version covers literature on counseling and psychiatric social work.

SocioFile (SilverPlatter, 1974–)
Electronic resource providing abstracts of international sociology literature, including articles, dissertations, conference papers, and books. This electronic edition corresponds to the print version of *Sociological Abstracts* (1963–).

Sociological Abstracts (Cambridge Scientific Abstracts, 1963–)
Provides comprehensive international coverage of journal articles, books, conference papers, dissertations, and other materials in sociology and related disciplines.

SELECTED FULL-TEXT ARTICLE DATABASES

Periodical Abstracts Research II Edition with Full Text (UMI ProQuest, 1986–)
Covers periodical abstracts with some full-text articles from academic journals, popular magazines, and general-interest publications, including 635 periodicals related to the social sciences and 169 in the general sciences. Full-text articles are available from approximately 600 of the indexed titles.

PsycARTICLES (American Psychological Association, 1987–)
Comprehensive database of full-text articles from a wide range of related journals published by the American Psychological Association and other selected publishers such as the APA Educational Publishing Foundation, the Canadian Psychological Association, and Hogrefe and Huber. Full-text coverage begins in 1987; titles include *American Psychologist, Behavioral Neuroscience, Journal of Comparative Psychology, Journal of Experimental Psychology, Prevention and Treatment,* and many more. Articles can be viewed and printed from any Web browser.

Psychology and Behavioral Sciences Collection (EBSCOHost, 1990–)
Worldwide database providing access to nearly 515 full-text titles, including 490 peer-reviewed journals, covering such topics as anthropology, emotional and behavioral issues, mental health, observational and experimental methods, and psychiatry and psychology.

Social Sciences Full Text (H.W. Wilson, 1984–)
This online resource extensively indexes citations with abstracts of more than 415 English-language journals plus some full text, in such fields as anthropology, criminal justice, economics, family studies, geography, international relations, policy sciences, political science, psychiatry, psychology, social work and public welfare, sociology, urban studies, and women's studies. Indexed are a wide array of journals including *Addictive Behaviors* (1994–), *Ageing and Society* (1987–), *The American Journal of Psychiatry* (1982–),

The British Journal of Psychology (1982–), *Canadian Journal of Psychiatry* (1982–), and many more. Also available in print form as *Social Sciences Index* (1974–).

SELECTED PERIODICALS

The American Journal of Drug and Alcohol Abuse (New York: Marcel Dekker, 1974– , quarterly)

This interdisciplinary journal serves researchers and other professionals for timely discussions of "the pre-clinical, clinical, pharmacological, administrative, and social aspects" of substance abuse. Topics are wide ranging in nature but focus on ideas and modalities in the study and treatment of drug abuse and alcoholism. The publisher offers access to a fully searchable database of the tables of contents of recent and previous issues. To view or search, visit http://www.dekker.com/servlet/product/productid/ADA.

American Psychologist (Washington: American Psychological Association, 1946– , monthly)

First published in January 1946, this official monthly journal of the American Psychological Association covers all aspects of psychology. Issues contain articles about the practice of psychology, public policy, surveys of membership, and events. Abstracts and citations of articles from current and past issues are referenced in several leading print and electronic indexes, including *PsycINFO Social Sciences Citation Index, Social Sciences Index,* and *Social Work Research and Abstracts*. Tables of contents of issues can be viewed online at http://www.apa.org/journals/amp/abstracting.html.

Community Mental Health Journal (New York: Human Sciences Press; Kluwer Academic Publishers, 1965– , bimonthly)

This bimonthly journal is the only periodical devoted exclusively to community mental health. Sponsored by the American Association of Community Psychiatrists, this publication distinguishes itself from others by publishing specific and relevant articles on the research, theory, and practice of this specialty. Subjects covered include crisis intervention, planned change, suicide prevention, social system analysis, early case finding, family therapy, milieu therapy, human ecology, high-risk groups, and social welfare. Tables of contents of past issues are accessible at Ingenta (1997). For further information on the journal, visit the publisher's Web page at http://www.kluweronline.com/issn/0010-3853/contents.

Journal of Counseling Psychology (Arlington, Va.: American Psychological Association, 1954– , quarterly)

This quarterly scholarly journal publishes empirical research on counseling activities, career development and vocational psychology, the development of new measures used in counseling, and professional issues in counseling psychology. Past issues and articles are indexed and abstracted in *Current Contents, PsycINFO, Social Sciences Index,* and many others.

Journal of Drug Issues (Tallahassee, Fla.: Journal of Drug Issues, 1971– , quarterly)

Offers professional and scholarly discussion of national and international problems directly related to drugs, particularly illicit drugs. The content of this peer-reviewed publication is aimed at research scholars, public policy analysts, and others dealing with the widespread problem of drug abuse. Selected samples of past articles from the journal can be read online at http://www2.criminology.fsu.edu/~jdi/.

Journal of Alcohol and Drug Education (Lansing, Mich.: Education Section of the North American Association of Alcoholism Programs, 1955– three times a year)
Published three times a year by the American Alcohol and Drug Information Foundation, this educational journal covers different philosophies and viewpoints about alcohol and drugs. Issues usually contain case studies, empirical studies, original research, review and theoretical articles, and some educational and ecological intervention studies discussing teacher experiences, experiments, techniques, procedures, and programs. The journal and its contents are indexed by *CINAHL (Cumulative Index in Nursing and Allied Health Literature).*

Psychology Today (New York: Sussex Publishers, 1967– , monthly)
Written from a clinical and an academic perspective, this widely respected print journal features articles on popular psychology and psychological research. Articles in each issue contain timely and helpful information on many related subjects, including family issues, relationship difficulties, and psychological conditions. Also available in electronic form, the contents of current and past issues can be accessed and searched online at http://www.psychologytoday.com/.

SELECTED WEB SITES

All About Depression (http://www.allaboutdepression.com/)
Launched in July 2000 as part of a doctoral dissertation by Dr. Prentice Price, this Web page features a great deal of current and relevant information about clinical depression. Subjects covered include causes, diagnosis, treatment, antidepressant medications, special topics, and resources, including a list of national mental health organizations.

American Psychological Association (http://www.apa.org)
The official home page of the largest association of psychologists worldwide, this site offers free access to an assortment of psychology materials and information. Contents include topical overviews on such subjects as Alzheimer's disease, depression, emotional health, obesity, personality disorders, stress, and trauma, plus countless publications for students and its members. Also featured is information about the association's journals and databases, including PsycARTICLES, PsycINFO, and PsycLIT.

American Psychological Society (http://www.psychologicalscience.org)
Founded in 1988, this nonprofit organization is dedicated to promoting "the interests of scientifically oriented psychology in research, application, teaching, and the improvement of human welfare." Its Web site offers an extensive list of leading psychology journals and resources for students interested in psychology.

Classics in the History of Psychology (http://psychclassics.yorku.ca)
Developed by Christopher D. Green of York University, Toronto, Ontario, this electronic resource offers unfettered access to the full texts of a large inventory of public domain documents, including more than 25 books, 200 articles and chapters, and other scholarly literature online.

The Encyclopedia of Psychology (http://www.psychology.org)
Created and maintained by William Palya of the Department of Psychology at Jacksonville State University, this browsable online encyclopedia covers every area of psychology, featuring original information provided by various researchers and practitioners, with links to credible Web sites offering additional information about scientific psychology.

Mental Help Net (http://mentalhelp.net/)
First developed in 1995, this information network bills itself as "the most comprehensive source of online mental health information." A winner of numerous awards for design and content, Mental Help Net features news, articles, features, advice columns, editorials, topical overviews on mental health subjects, and links to many other behavioral science Web sites.

Policy Information Exchange (http://mimh200.mimh.edu/mimhweb/pie/)
In association with the Missouri Institute of Mental Health, this leading center for policy, research, and training offers this comprehensive Web site of information on mental health, substance abuse, and more. The site includes a searchable database of more than 5,000 related full-text documents judged to be of special interest to the mental health community.

Positive Psychology Center (http://www.psych.upenn.edu/seligman/)
Under the guidance of Martin E. P. Seligman, Ph.D., this not-for-profit organization, based on the University of Pennsylvania campus, conducts scientific research to "solve real-world problems, alleviate suffering, and help individuals and institutions achieve a high quality of life." The alliance's Web site features articles, columns, research, archived materials, and links on positive psychology.

PsychologyGateway.com (http://www.psychologygateway.com)
A Web site of Elsevier Science, one of the world's leading publishers of scientific periodicals, this Internet resource offers access to journal abstracts, full-text journal articles, books, news, and links to many resources of interest to researchers and psychology professionals.

The Psychology Virtual Library (http://www.clas.ufl.edu/users/gthursby/psi)
Part of the World Wide Web Virtual Library, this online resource, maintained by a psychologist at the University of Florida, features an A-to-Z directory of psychology Web pages indexed by topic with links to relevant sites. Subjects covered include basic academic psychology, clinical social work, directories of psychology sites, e-mail lists and newsgroups, history of psychology, journals, library resources online, and much more.

PsychWeb (http://www.psywww.com/index.html)
Designed for psychology practitioners and students, this comprehensive directory offers access to a bevy of psychology resources on the Web, including

full-text classic books online, brochures, scholarly resources by topic, self-help resources with information about psychology disorders, and sports psychology resources.

Social Psychology Network (http://www.socialpsychology.org/)
Maintained by Scott Plous of Wesleyan University, this online network, which calls itself "the largest social psychology database on the Internet"—features more than 5,000 links related to psychology.

Religion and Theology

Religious study has grown in popularity in recent years, particularly at schools of religion and colleges and universities with religion programs.

Whether reading biblical passages or considering the inherent meanings of religious artifacts, enormous opportunities exist today for students, researchers, and believers to more fully explore the common characteristics, conceptions (and misconceptions), methods, practices, and traditions of religions from around the world.

To satisfy your strong desire to explore traditional and nontraditional religions, differences between one religion over another, laws separating church and state, or deeply rooted religious theories or changing attitudes towards religion, almost everything in the world related to this specific field of study is accessible in some form. This chapter surveys a large selection sources on religion and theology.

SELECTED BOOKS AND REFERENCES

Contemporary American Religion, by Wade Clark Roof, 2 vols., 861 pages (New York: Macmillan Library Reference, 2000)

This highly recommended reference features more than 500 well-written articles on contemporary religion, religious personalities, and other popular topics, such as fundamentalist Christianity, feng shui, Elvis cults, and temptation. Each article is followed by a list of references for further study. Approximately 200 black-and-white photos and graphics complement the text.

Dictionary of American Religious Biography, 2nd Ed., by Henry Warner Bowden, 720 pages (Westport, Conn.: Greenwood Press, 1993)

This revised and enlarged second edition offers 550 biographical sketches, including 125 new entries, of the most prominent religious figures in history "reflecting America's cultural and religious diversity." Each entry summarizes the subject's personal history and his or her contributions to religious life, followed by a list of sources. Appendixes provide easy cross-referencing of subjects by religious denomination and place of birth.

Encyclopedia of American Religions, 7th Ed., by J. Gordon Melton, 3 vols., 1,253 pages (Detroit: Gale Research, 1999)

This three-volume reference, last updated in 1999, features descriptive essays on 1,588 prominent and obscure American religious groups, from Adventists to Zen Buddhists, and 22 religious families. Entries focus on the origins and traditions of each major religious group.

The Encyclopedia of Christianity, edited by Erwin Fahlbusch, 912 pages (Grand Rapids, Mich.: Wm. B. Eerdmans; Leiden, Netherlands: Brill, 1999–)
This first of five volumes, and an English version of the German edition, *Evangelisches Kirchenlexikon,* thoroughly surveys the 2,000-year history of Christianity from a global perspective. Articles discuss religions and their philosophies and include statistical information from more than 170 countries in context. Relevant social and cultural issues are also discussed, including armaments, genocide, and racism, as well as biblical and apostolic traditions.

Eerdmans Dictionary of the Bible, edited by David Noel Freedman, 1,425 pages (Grand Rapids, Mich: W.B. Eerdmans, 2000)
Written by 600 leading scholars of all theological persuasions, this first-rate illustrated dictionary covers nearly 5,000 books, persons, places, and major terms noted in the Bible. Each entry critically analyzes each biblical book and related writings, as well as their cultural, natural, geographical, and literary importance.

HarperCollins Concise Guide to World Religions: The A to Z Encyclopedia of All the Major Religious Traditions, by Mircea Eliade and Ioan P. Culianu, 320 pages (New York: HarperCollins, 1999)
Fascinating A–Z guide that explores 33 major religions and religious traditions around the world, from Buddhism to the religions of Africa and Oceania. Entries also cover religious figures, histories, mythologies, mystical techniques, and sacred texts in context.

Religions of the World: A Comprehensive Encyclopedia of Beliefs and Practices, edited by J. Gordon Melton and Martin Baumann, 4 vols., 1,507 pages (Santa Barbara, Calif.: ABC-CLIO, 2002).
Religions of the World features core essays on major religious traditions, and also 1,000 religious groups and 276 recognized nations and territories, principally focusing on the development and practice of those religions covered.

Religious Sites in America: A Dictionary, by Mary Ellen Snodgrass, 508 pages (Santa Barbara, Calif.: ABC-CLIO, 2000)
Comprehensively explores some 160 worship groups and religious centers in the United States, including their origin, history, location, and purpose.

SELECTED ARTICLE INDEXES AND ABSTRACTS

Printed Indexes and Abstracts

Catholic Periodical and Literature Index (Haverford, Pa.: Catholic Library Association, 1888–)
Originally called *The Guide to Catholic Literature* through 1967, this popular reference series features citations and abstracts of articles concerning Catholic issues and theology from 1888 to the present. Most reference collections begin with the July/August 1968 edition. The collection is also available on CD-ROM.

The Christian Periodical Index (Cedarville, Ohio: Association of Christian Librarians, 1956–)

First published in 1956 by the Association of Christian Librarians, this reference series, printed twice yearly with the second issue serving as an annual cumulation, indexes articles and reviews in more than 130 publications with an evangelical Christian perspective. Provides indexes by subject, author, and review. Titles indexed range from the *Africa Journal of Evangelical Theology* to *Youth Worker.*

Guide to Social Science and Religion in Periodical Literature (Flint, Mich.; Clearwater, Fla.: National Periodical Library, 1964–)

First called the *Guide to Religious and Semi-Religious Periodicals,* this print edition, published semiannually, indexes nearly 100 periodicals by subject on social science and religion. Every item indexed includes the title of the periodical, date published, volume and issue numbers, author, and page number. Periodicals indexed include *American Journal of Pastoral, Biblical Archaeology Review, Christian Standard, Commonweal, Current History, History of Religions, Jewish Spectator,* and many others.

Historical Abstracts (Santa Barbara, Calif.: ABC-CLIO, 1955–2000)

This print version of the online database (1960–) abstracts both scholarly journals and dissertations on world history (except U.S. and Canadian history) from 1450 to the present, including social and cultural history.

Humanities Index (New York: H.W. Wilson, 1947–)

Multidisciplinary subject index covering all of the humanities.

Index Islamicus (London: Mansell, 1977–85; East Grinstead, West Sussex, U.K.: Bowker-Saur, 1994–)

This 17-plus-volume set cites Islamic and Middle Eastern literature and periodicals, including some 2,000 journals, along with conference proceedings, monographs, multiauthor works, and book reviews. Citations cover written works about the Middle East and also other Muslim areas of Asia, Africa, and elsewhere. An online database produced by the Islamic Bibliography Unit at Cambridge University Library and distributed by Cambridge Scientific Abstracts is also available. Records included in the database cover nearly a century of publications, from 1906 to the present. A CD-ROM database of the same name is also produced and distributed by Bowker-Saur. It contains more than 190,000 records searchable by author, database, free text, keyword, publication date, subject, title, and record type.

Index to Jewish Periodicals (Cleveland Heights, Ohio: Index to Jewish Periodicals, 1963–)

Beginning with the June/August 1963 edition, this 40-plus-volume reference set—the only English-language publication of its kind for the study of Jewish and Middle Eastern affairs—covers current Jewish topics that appear in periodicals published in the United States, Canada, England, Israel, South Africa, and Australia. The set features citations arranged by subject and author.

Index to Religious Periodical Literature (Chicago: American Theological Library Association, 1949–)

Continued under the title of *Religion Index One: Periodicals* (1977–), this author-subject index covers 150 periodicals, with special emphasis on

English-language scholarly authors. Some book reviews are also listed by author name.

International Medieval Bibliography (Leeds, U.K.: University of Leeds, 1968–)
Indexes bibliographic citations of journal articles and miscellaneous publications on the Middle Ages published worldwide starting in 1967. An online database is also offered that is similar in content.

New Testament Abstracts (Cambridge, Mass.: Weston School of Theology, 1956–)
With more than 45 volumes in print, this reference series offers abstracts from more than 500 periodicals in numerous languages from 1956 to the present. Published three times yearly by Weston Jesuit School of Theology in cooperation with the Catholic Biblical Association of America, the set also features summaries of more than 800 current books on religious topics. Abstracts and summaries are arranged by subjects, such as New Testament, General, Gospel-Acts, Epistles-Revelation, Biblical Theology, New Testament World, etc.

Old Testament Abstracts (Washington, D.C.: Catholic Biblical Association of America, 1978–)
Published thrice yearly by the Catholic Biblical Association, this bibliographic reference, also offered on CD-ROM, features citations and abstracts of articles on Old Testament subjects from 1978 to the present.

The Philosopher's Index (Bowling Green, Ohio: Philosopher's Information Center, 1967–)
Cumulative index with informative author-written abstracts covering scholarly research in 15 fields of philosophy culled from books and journals published since 1940. Entries are arranged by subject and include author and titles of articles under subject headings. Citations of articles are listed in the Author Index and include publication name, year, volume, number, and pages. An electronic version is available through Ovid Technologies.

Religion Index One: Periodicals (Chicago: American Theological Library Association, 1977–)
Continuation of the *Index to Religious Periodical Literature* (1949–) featuring citations of serials and journal articles. Components have since been incorporated into several online databases, including the ATLA Religion Database (1993–) and an electronic version of the same name.

Religion Index Two: Multi-Author Works (Chicago: American Theological Library Association, 1976–)
Now part of the ATLA Religion Database (1993–), this reference indexes multiauthor works, published conference proceedings, and individual essays within a multiauthor work by subject, author/editor, and scriptural name.

Religious and Theological Abstracts (Myerstown, Pa.: Religious and Theological Abstracts, 1958–2001)
This popular reference series, available in more than 40 volumes, provides brief, nonsectarian English-language abstracts of articles in English, Hebrew,

Afrikaans, and most major European languages published in more than 400 periodicals in all fields of religion and theology from 1958 to 2001. Included is a wide array of periodical literature, including Christian, Jewish, and other world religions and some denominational and popular religious magazines. Abstracts provide author, subject, and scriptural indexes.

Web Indexes and Abstracts

America: History and Life (ABC-CLIO, 1960–)
Helpful for performing historical research in religion, this bibliographic reference features citations and abstracts of publications about the history of the United States and Canada.

Arts and Humanities Citation Index (Thomson ISI, 1980–)
Provides subject and cited reference indexing and searching of 1,300 leading arts and humanities journals, including selected indexing of social science and science journals, from 1980 to the present.

Catholic Periodical and Literature Index (Theological Library Association [ATLA] and the Catholic Library Association [CLA], 1981–)
Indexes citations to more than 160 Catholic periodicals, as well as to papal documents, books about the Catholic faith, book reviews, and monograph literature.

The Christian Periodical Index (CPI) (Association of Christian Librarians, 1976–)
Electronic version of the *Christian Periodical Index*, via the Web or on CD-ROM, including most titles indexed in the printed version from 1976 to the present. The Web edition is updated quarterly, the CD-ROM annually.

Historical Abstracts (ABC-CLIO, 1955–)
A complete reference guide to the history of the world since 1450, this Web database of the print edition features citations with abstracts to scholarly journals and dissertations from 1955 to the present. Excluded from coverage is the United States and Canada, which are covered in the index *America: History and Life.*

Index to Book Reviews in Religion (American Theological Library Association/Cambridge Scientific Abstracts/ATLA, 1949–)
Published by the American Theological Library Association in cooperation with Cambridge Scientific Abstracts, this index incorporates book reviews from the *Index to Religious Periodical Literature, Religion Index One,* and *Religion Index Two,* plus reviews not included in these databases.

Iter (University of Toronto, 1842–)
A nonprofit research project underwritten by the University of Toronto Libraries, Iter indexes citations of articles, bibliographies, catalogs, and literature of more than 400 scholarly journals on European Medieval and Renaissance history and culture from 1842 to the present. Records in the database cover only the years 400 to 1700.

Religion Index One: Periodicals (Cambridge Scientific Abstracts, 1949–)
Incorporating the contents of the printed *Index to Religious Periodical Literature* beginning in July 1977, Religion Index One indexes more than 500 periodicals by subject and author. Includes denominational and popular magazines as well as scholarly journals from 1949 to the present.

Religion Index Two: Multi-Author Works (Cambridge Scientific Abstracts, 1970–)
Electronic version of the printed series providing subject, author/editor, and scriptural access to indexed books, published conference proceedings, and more since 1970.

SELECTED FULL-TEXT ARTICLE DATABASES

Academic Search Elite (EBSCOHost, indexing: 1980– , full text: 1990–)
Provides access to full-text articles on current and past events and a broad range of academic disciplines. Abstracts are indexed since 1980, full-text articles from 1990 to the present.

ATLA Religion Database (American Theological Librarian Association, 1949–)
This premier database indexes more than 400,000 citations, with some full text, of journal articles, book reviews, and essay collections from the past 50 years in all fields of religion. Subcategories include religious research in such fields as anthropology, business, history, law, medicine, sociology, and psychology.

ATLA Serials Online (American Theological Librarian Association, 1924–)
Offered individually and as part of the ATLA Religion Database, this full-text collection covers 50 religion and theology journals, including more than 50,000 articles and book reviews, from 1924 to the present in the fields of archaeology, Bible study, ethics, missions, pastoral ministry, philosophy, religion, society, and theology. Journals include *Arts, Archaeology, Catholic Biblical Quarterly, Christian Century, Eastern Buddhist, International Bulletin of Missionary Research*, and many others.

International Medieval Bibliography (IMB) (International Medieval Institute, University of Leeds, 1967–)
Indexes full-text articles from more 4,000 periodicals and 5,000 miscellaneous volumes, including conference proceedings, essay collections, and Festschriften, on the Middle Ages in Europe, the Middle East, and North Africa from c. 400 to 1500. IMB online is the electronic version.

LexisNexis Academic Universe (LexisNexis, 1977–)
Current events database offering full-text articles on a broad spectrum of fields and subjects, including news, business, legal information, country and state profiles, federal case law, the U.S. Code, the Constitution, and court rulings.

Periodical Abstracts (ProQuest, 1986–)
Offered as part of ProQuest Direct, this online database indexes citations to articles from hundreds of general and academic journals in all fields of study,

50 percent of which is full text. Disciplines covered include culture, current events, history, literature, psychology, religion, sociology, and women's studies.

The Philosopher's Index (Ovid Technologies/Philosopher's Information Center, 1940–)
This online index cites journal articles, books, contributions to anthologies, and book reviews from nearly 570 journals of philosophy from 43 countries. Topics covered include aesthetics, epistemology, ethics, metaphysic logic, political philosophy, and the philosophy of law, religion, science, history, education, and language, with links to full-text where available. *The Philosopher's Index: A Retrospective Index to Non-U.S. English Language Publications from 1940* is the print equivalent to this electronic edition.

ProQuest Religious Periodicals (ProQuest, indexing: 1986– , full text: 1990s–)
Updated daily, this Web-based database features a fully searchable index of nearly 100 full-text religious periodicals, including *Catechist, Cistercian Studies Quarterly, Journal of Biblical Literature, Old Testament Abstracts, Spiritual Life, Theological Studies,* and 85 other English-language religious publications. Indexing is for items published since 1986, with full-text material from the early to mid-1990s. Articles are available in different formats (text or image).

Religion and Philosophy Collection (EBSCOHost, 1975–)
This essential tool for researchers and students of theology and philosophical studies features abstracts and full-text articles from nearly 300 journals, including almost 250 peer-reviewed titles. Subjects covered include biblical studies, epistemology, major denominations, philosophy, religious history, and world religions. Journals indexed in the collection include *Archaeology, Biblical Interpretation, British Journal for the History of Philosophy, Catholic Historical Review, Christianity Today, Comparative Sociology, Ethics, Greek Orthodox Theological Review, Islamic Law and Society, Journal of Jewish Thought and Philosophy, Method and Theory in the Study of Religion,* and many more.

Wilson Select (H.W. Wilson, 1994–)
High-quality indexed and abstracted articles, all in full text, culled from the following H.W. Wilson databases: *Readers' Guide Abstracts, Humanities Abstracts, General Science Abstracts, Social Sciences Abstracts,* and *Wilson Business Abstracts.*

SELECTED PERIODICALS

America (New York: America Press, Inc., 1909– , weekly)
Published and edited by lay Roman Catholics, this national Catholic weekly, founded by Jesuits of the United States in 1909, offers commentary and opinion from various standpoints on many social and political issues, written by well-known writers and theologians. Contents include timely and thought-provoking articles, book, film or art reviews, and special issues on crucial topics and prominent individuals. Articles from earlier published volumes are referenced in such major print and online indexes as *Catholic Index, Guide*

to Social Science and Religion Periodical Literature, New Testament Abstracts, Old Testament Abstracts, and *The Reader's Guide to Periodical Literature.* Back issues of *America* are available online through ProQuest Religious Periodicals from 1983 to the present.

Christian Century: An Ecumenical Magazine (Chicago: Christian Century Co., 1884– , biweekly)
Established in 1884, this biweekly nondenominational journal has offered a moderate to liberal viewpoint on matters of religion, politics, and society. For more than 100 years, the publication has published articles by some of the most respected theologians, historians, and church leaders examining ethical and social issues, contemporary concerns, and religious and moral issues. In addition, the staff-written and contributed articles and editorials have focused on such topics as poverty, human rights, economic justice, international relations, national priorities, and popular culture from a religious perspective.

Christianity Today (Carol Stream, Ill.: Christianity Today, 1956– , biweekly)
Founded by Protestants more than 40 years ago, *Christianity Today* features in-depth news, articles, editorials, and reviews on Christian life of interest to ministers and other religious professionals. Each issue explores the major challenges facing Christians today, including education, family, life ethics, money and business, persecution, politics and law, sexuality and gender, and social justice, all written from an evangelical Christian perspective. Issues from 1999 to the present are accessible through the publisher's archives page at http://www.christianitytoday.com/ct/main/archives.html.

Commentary (New York: American Jewish Committee, 1945– , monthly)
Adhering to its mission to "clarify public opinion on problems of Jewish concern," this monthly journal focuses on major Jewish issues in United States and abroad. Published since 1945 by the American Jewish Committee, each issue provides commentary and opinion on political topics and problems of bigotry, human rights, and Jewish cultural interests. Full-text of the journal is available via the online databases PCI Full Text (1945–90), and Expanded Academic ASAP (1992–).

Commonweal (New York: Calvert Pub. Corp., 1924– , 22 times yearly)
Reflecting a largely Roman Catholic perspective, this award-winning, independent opinion journal, edited and managed by lay Catholics, focuses on contemporary and social issues of interest to Roman Catholics. Each issue comprises columns, editorials, essays, letters to the editors, and reviews of books, movies, plays, and other media. Tables of contents with selected links to articles in current and past issues, from 1997 to the present, are retrievable online at http://www.commonwealmagazine.org/inside.htm.

Journal of the American Academy of Religion (Oxford University Press, 1933– , quarterly)
One of the top academic journals in its field, *Journal of the American Academy of Religion* features scholarly articles exploring a variety of theological

issues. In addition to provocative and insightful articles, each issue includes a large section of reviews of current literature. The journal is indexed and abstracted in such popular databases as ATLA Religion Database, Guide to Social Science and Religion in Periodical Literature, Humanities Index, ISI: Current Contents, New Testament Abstracts, Religion Index One: Periodicals, Religious and Theological Abstracts, and Religious Periodical Index. To browse full text .PDF (2001–) and HTML articles (2000–) from past issues, visit the publication archives at http://www3.oup.co.uk/jaarel/contents.html.

Journal of Early Christian Studies (Baltimore, Md.: Johns Hopkins University Press/North American Patristics Society, 1993– , quarterly)
The official publication of the North American Patristics Society (NAPS), this quarterly scholarly journal principally focuses on the study of Christianity and late ancient societies and religions from C.E. 100–700. Contents of each issue include engaging articles about traditional patristics scholarship, new themes, and methodologies, plus an extensive book review section. Previously published issues are indexed and abstracted in several leading databases, including Arts and Humanities Citation Index, ISI: Current Contents, Humanities Index, MLA International Bibliography, and New Testament Abstracts.

Modern Judaism: A Journal of Jewish Ideas and Experience (Baltimore, Md.: Johns Hopkins University Press, 1981– , three times yearly)
This interdisciplinary scholarly journal discusses the modern Jewish experience. Articles address topics relevant to "the understanding of Jewish life today and the forces that have shaped that experience." *Modern Judaism* is indexed and abstracted in a variety of online databases, including ATLA Religion Database, America: History and Life, Arts and Humanities Citation Index, Historical Abstracts, Humanities Index, Index to Jewish Periodicals, and many others. Full-text access of past issues is offered online through ProjectMUSE (1996–).

Religious Studies Review (Hanover, Pa.: Council on the Study of Religion, 1975– , quarterly)
Published by the Council of Societies for the Study of Religion in association with Valparaiso University since September 1975, this scholarly journal reviews more than 1,000 publications annually in the field of religious studies and related disciplines. Each issue includes lengthy essays on recent books or single-topic articles. In addition, the journal publishes bibliographies and a registry of religious dissertations completed or currently in progress.

SELECTED WEB SITES

Adherents.com (http://www.adherents.com/)
Reportedly the second most frequently visited general religion site on the Internet, this independently operated Web site features 57,000 adherent statistics and religious geography citations of published membership/adherent statistics and congregation statistics for some 4,200 religions, churches, denominations, and more worldwide.

American Studies Web: Religion and Religious Cultural Studies (http://cfdev.georgetown.edu/cndls/asw/aswsub.cfm?head1=Religion%20and%20Religious%20Cultural%20Studies)
Maintained at Georgetown University as part of the American Studies Crossroads Project, this site directs users to a variety of religious and religious-related Web sites.

Facets of Religion (http://www.facetsofreligion.com/)
Lists some 300 categories covering all major religions and such subjects as ancient religions, ethics, and historical studies.

Finding God in Cyberspace (http://sim74.kenrickparish.com/)
Comprehensive guide to religious studies resources on the Web developed and maintained by John L. Gresham.

Glossary of Religious Terms (http://www.religioustolerance.org/glossary.htm)
This Web page offers a helpful glossary of important terms for various religious groups around the world.

Religions of the World (http://www.mnsu.edu/emuseum/cultural/religion/)
Introductory site to major religions and religious groups that includes histories, geographic information, maps, basic beliefs and terms, and links to other related Web sites.

Religious Movements (http://religiousmovements.lib.virginia.edu/)
Part of the Religious Movements Homepage Project at the University of Virginia, this Web site offers detailed profiles of more than 200 different religious groups and movements in the world today, as well as essays, articles, and other valuable resources.

Religious and Sacred Texts (http://davidwiley.com/religion.html)
This online collection of religious and sacred texts covers a variety of traditions and historical periods for such faiths as Christianity, Islam, Judaism, Hinduism, Confucianism, and Taoism.

Virtual Religion Index (http://religion.rutgers.edu/vri)
Global directory cataloging a myriad of religion-related Web pages with links from the Rutgers University Religion Department.

31

Science and Technology

Scientific discoveries throughout history have dramatically shaped the world as people know it today. From the invention of the first telegraph to the Hubble space telescope, countless men and women of every scientific discipline have explored the vast unknown. Such discoveries have resulted in cures for formerly untreatable diseases, broken the human genetic code, and accomplished many other scientific and technological feats.

Whether you are a mathematical wizard, the top chemist in your class, or a regular student wanting to do better in your math or science class, you can find substantial material in both print and electronic form on practically any topic. The following sources include literature across a broad range of sciences that is recommended for students of every age.

SELECTED BOOKS AND REFERENCES

Dictionaries

The Facts On File Dictionary of Astronomy, 4th Ed., by Valerie Illingworth and John O. E. Clark, 496 pages (New York: Facts On File, 2000)

The Facts On File Dictionary of Atomic and Nuclear Physics, by Richard Rennie, 256 pages (New York: Facts On File, 2002)

The Facts On File Dictionary of Biochemistry, by John Daintith, 256 pages (New York: Facts On File, 2002)

The Facts On File Dictionary of Biology, 3rd Ed., edited by Robert Hine, 368 pages (New York: Facts On File, 1999)

The Facts On File Dictionary of Biotechnology and Genetic Engineering, by Mark L. Steinberg and Sharon D. Cosloy, 240 pages (New York: Facts On File, 2000)

The Facts On File Dictionary of Botany, 2nd Ed., edited by Jill Bailey, 256 pages (New York: Facts On File, 2002)

The Facts On File Dictionary of Cell and Molecular Biology, by Robert Hine, 256 pages (New York: Facts On File, 2002)

The Facts On File Dictionary of Chemistry, 3rd Ed., edited by John Daintith, 272 pages (New York: Facts On File, 1999)

The Facts On File Dictionary of Computer Science, by Valerie Illingworth and John Daintith, 256 pages (New York: Facts On File, 2000)

The Facts On File Dictionary of Earth Science, by John O. E. Clark and Stella Stiegeler, 368 pages (New York: Facts On File, 2000)

The Facts On File Dictionary of Ecology and the Environment by Jill Bailey, 256 pages (New York: Facts On File, 2003)

The Facts On File Dictionary of Environmental Science, by Bruce Wyman and L. Harold Stevenson, 464 pages (New York: Facts On File, 2001)

The Facts On File Dictionary of Evolutionary Biology, by Elizabeth Owen and Eve Daintith, 256 pages (New York: Facts On File, 2003)

The Facts On File Dictionary of Forensic Science, by Suzanne Bell, Ph.D., 288 pages (New York: Facts On File, 2004)

The Facts On File Dictionary of Geology and Geophysics, edited by Dorothy Farris Lapidus, 347 pages (New York: Facts On File, 1987)

The Facts On File Dictionary of Inorganic Chemistry, by John Daintith, 256 pages (New York: Facts On File, 2003)

The Facts On File Dictionary of Marine Science, by Barbara Charlton, 384 pages (New York: Facts On File, 2001)

The Facts On File Dictionary of Mathematics, 3rd Ed., edited by John Daintith and John Clark, 241 pages (New York: Facts On File, 1999)

The Facts On File Dictionary of Organic Chemistry by John Daintith, 256 pages (New York: Facts On File, 2003)

The Facts On File Dictionary of Physics, 3rd Ed., edited by John Daintith and John Clark, 256 pages (New York: Facts On File, 1999)

The Facts On File Dictionary of Science, 6th Ed., edited by E.B. Uvarov Alan Isaacs, 468 pages (New York: Facts On File, 1986)

The Facts On File Dictionary of Space Technology, Revised Ed., by Joseph A. Angelo Jr., 480 pages (New York: Facts On File, 2003)

The Facts On File Dictionary of Weather and Climate, by Jacqueline Smith,. 256 pages (New York: Facts On File: 2001)
With more than 20 volumes in print, this critically acclaimed, attractively illustrated series of Facts On File dictionaries is geared toward students in grades 9 and up. Each volume contains basic vocabulary terms and definitions, with information that is concise and to the point.

McGraw-Hill Dictionary of Scientific and Technical Terms, 6th Ed., 2,380 pages (New York: McGraw-Hill, 2003)
Written for the layperson, this revised sixth edition provides definitions in clear, simple language, covering 100 areas of science and technology and accompanied by more than 3,000 illustrations. Included is a helpful pronunciation guide, an index of scientific and technical terms, and appendixes with biographical listings, conversion tables, and more.

Ultimate Visual Dictionary of Science, 448 pages (New York: DK Publishing, 1998)
For students in grade 6 and up, this easily understandable, well-written and beautifully illustrated volume offers informative descriptions of various scientific concepts and phenomena in nine major fields of science, including astronomy, biology, computer science, earth science, electronics, life sciences, mathematics, medicine, and physics.

Encyclopedias

Encyclopedia of Earth System Science, edited by William A. Nierenberg, 4 vols. (San Diego: Academic Press, 1992)

Encyclopedia of Human Biology, 2nd Ed., edited by Renato Dulbecco, 9 vols. (San Diego: Academic Press, 1997)

Encyclopedia of Microbiology, 2nd Ed., edited by Joshua Lederberg, 4 vols. (San Diego: Academic Press, 2000)

Encyclopedia of Physical Science and Technology, 3rd Ed., edited by Robert A. Meyers, 18 vols. (San Diego: Academic Press, 2002)
This series of university- and professional-level encyclopedias covers an amazing amount of information about each discipline with complex technical articles of varying lengths about a variety of subjects. An online version of the *Encyclopedia of Physical Science and Technology*, all 18 volumes, is available through ScienceDirect.

Grzimek's Animal Life Encyclopedia, edited by Bernhard Grzimek, 13 vols., 6,500 pages (Detroit: Gale Group, 2002)
Acclaimed by critics as "the best reference work on animals ever published," this revised and updated version of the original 13-volume set, originally edited by famed zoologist and animal lover Bernhard Grzimek, is a complete reference for researchers and students studying the animal kingdom. Updated with the help of prominent advisors and contributors from the international scientific community, this republished series, for students of every academic level, details animals around the globe, including their food systems, life cycles, predators, ecology, and more.

McGraw-Hill Encyclopedia of Science and Technology: An International Reference Work in Twenty Volumes Including an Index, 9th Ed., 20 vols., 15,600 pages (New York: McGraw-Hill, 2002)
This 20-volume reference is intended for those with a science background. It has 7,500 articles written by more than 9,000 contributors, including 25

Nobel Prize winners, covering more than 80 fields of science and technology. An older single-volume concise version of the entire set, the *McGraw-Hill Concise Encyclopedia of Science and Technology* (1998), is also available.

Gale Encyclopedia of Science, 3rd Ed., edited by K. Lee Lerner and Brenda Wilmoth, 6 vols., 4,495 pages (Detroit: Gale, 2004)
This six-volume reference covers all major all fields of science and technology, including science, engineering, mathematics, medical and health sciences, and technology with alphabetically arranged entries discussing various terms, concepts, and scientific areas. A list of sources accompanies most entries.

Kirk-Othmer Concise Encyclopedia of Chemical Technology, 4th Ed., 2,196 pages (New York: Wiley, 1999)
Also available in a 27-volume set, this abridged edition, helpful to chemists and nonchemists, incorporates more than 1,000 entries, featuring basic and advanced information, including illustrations, tables, and graphs covering the entire field of chemical technology. Some of the subjects include analytical techniques, biotechnology, environmental concerns, patents and licensing, process development and design, regulations, solid-state chemistry, and many more.

Van Nostrand's Scientific Encyclopedia, 9th Ed., 2 vols., 3,936 pages (New York: Van Nostrand Reinhold, 2002)
Suitable for both students and professionals, this substantially revised two-volume set covers a broad range of scientific disciplines, including engineering, math, and technology. Highlighted by numerous charts and illustrations, this encyclopedia features comprehensive articles on a host of subjects. They include animal science, anatomy, astronomy, atmospheric science, chemistry, chemical engineering, civil engineering, computer science, earth science, energy sources, information science, life science, materials, mathematics, mechanical engineering, medicine, mining, physics, physiology, planetary science, plant science, power technology, space science, structural engineering, and numerous others. In 1999, an electronic edition was released on CD-ROM.

General References

History of Modern Science and Mathematics, edited by Brian S. Baigrie, 4 vols., 1,040 pages (New York: Charles Scribner's Sons, 2002)
Recommended for high school level students and above, this highly useful multivolume encyclopedia offers topical coverage on the historical development of 23 scientific disciplines focused more on natural than applied sciences. Organized by topic and by disciplines of science and mathematics, entries cover a variety of related subjects, such as algebra, anthropology, astronomy, paleontology, physics, and trigonometry. Informative sidebars and historical photographs are included, along with an extensive bibliography, subject index, and interdisciplinary time line.

Information Sources in Science and Technology, 3rd Ed., by C. D. Hurt, 346 pages (Englewood, Colo.: Libraries Unlimited, 1998)
Part of the Libraries Unlimited Library and Information Science Text Series, this fully revised reference lists a selection of more than 1,500 sources—abstracts and indexes, bibliographies, dictionaries, encyclopedias, handbooks,

and Web sites—in 21 subject areas, organized by subject with titles arranged alphabetically in each section. Major disciplines covered include chemistry, geology, medicine, and others.

Instruments of Science: An Historical Encyclopedia, edited by Robert Bud and Deborah Jean Warner, 725 pages (New York: Science Museum, London, and National Museum of American History, Smithsonian Institution, in association with Garland Pub., 1998)
Written by 223 scientists, instrument designers, historians, and Nobel laureates from 15 countries, this encyclopedia features approximately 327 entries describing historically significant instruments used in testing, monitoring, and research science, from "Abacus" to "X-ray machine." This well-done volume describes many instruments relating to applied and engineering sciences, life sciences, mathematical sciences, natural philosophies, and physics.

Reader's Guide to the History of Science, edited by Arne Hessenbruch, 934 pages (Chicago: Fitzroy Dearborn, 2000)
Fully covers the history of science and science literature with 600 detailed entries focusing on all aspects, including individuals, institutions and disciplines, themes, and concepts, including Einstein and Galileo, astronomy and mathematics, religion and romantic science, paradigm and fact. A brief bibliography follows each essay, critically discussing the titles listed on each topic.

Science and Technology Desk Reference: Over 1,700 Answers to Frequently-Asked and Difficult-to-Answer Reference Questions in Science and Technology, 2nd Ed., by James E. Bobick, 795 pages (Washington, D.C.: Gale Research, 1996)
This ready reference assembles more than 1,700 commonly asked or difficult reference questions and answers arranged by subject, covering such fields as chemistry, computer science, earth science, health science, mathematics, and space science.

SELECTED ARTICLE INDEXES AND ABSTRACTS

Printed Indexes and Abstracts

Applied Science and Technology Index (New York: H.W. Wilson, 1958–)
This annual reference indexes 335 periodicals in many fields of science and technology, including aeronautics and space science, automation, chemistry, computer technology, electricity, mathematics, physics, and telecommunications. The print reference is also offered as a Web database indexing material from 1983 to the present.

Biological Abstracts (Philadelphia: BioSciences Information Service, 1926–)
Also offered online, this outstanding print series features citations and abstracts from worldwide life sciences journals in research biology, botany, zoology, microbiology, clinical and experimental medicine, and more, from December 1926 to the present. An electronic version, BIOSIS Previews, provides abstracts from 1980 to the present.

Biological and Agricultural Index (New York: H.W. Wilson, 1964–)
Originally called *The Agricultural Index* (1916–), this retitled cumulative subject index—also available online—covers more than 300 journals in the fields of agriculture, biology, and related sciences.

Chemical Abstracts (Columbus, Ohio: American Chemical Society, 1907–)
Abstracts literature from chemical publications in more than 50 languages.

The Engineering Index (New York: Engineering Magazine, 1896–1906; American Society of Mechanical Engineers, 1907–68; Engineering Index, Inc., 1969–86)
Discontinued in 1986, this annual series offers citations and abstracts of engineering literature, including books, conference papers, journals, and other publications, arranged by subject and indexed by author.

General Science Index (New York: H.W. Wilson, 1978–)
Indexes more than 100 general science periodicals not covered in other indexes. H.W. Wilson also produces this index in an electronic format offering coverage from 1984 to the present.

INSPEC (London: Institution of Electrical Engineers, 1967–)
Conveniently indexes in a single source mostly computer, electrical engineering, and physics literature. The Institution of Electrical Engineers, publishers of the print index, also produces a Web version indexing science literature from 1969 to the present.

Science Abstracts (London: Institution of Electrical Engineers, 1967–)
Provides abstract coverage of books, conference papers, dissertations, patents, and periodicals across the fields of science.

Science Citation Index (Philadelphia, Pa.: Institute for Scientific Information, 1961–94)
Interdisciplinary index published from 1961 to 1994 offering citations of literature in the fields of science, medicine, agriculture, technology, and the behavioral sciences. Several electronic versions of the index are also available.

Web Indexes and Abstracts

AGRICOLA (AGRICultural OnLine Access) (National Agricultural Library, 1970–) (http://www.nal.usda.gov/ag98/ag98.html)
This major bibliographic database contains citations describing agricultural publications and resources created by the National Agricultural Library (NAL) and its cooperators. While the database covers records in electronic form since 1970, it cites materials in all formats, including printed works from the 15th century. Records include all aspects of agriculture and allied disciplines, such as animal and veterinary sciences, entomology, plant sciences, forestry, aquaculture and fisheries, farming and farming systems, agricultural economics, extension and education, food and human nutrition, and earth and environmental sciences.

Applied Science and Technology Index (H.W. Wilson, 1983–)
Updated monthly, this online version of the print index conveniently provides citations of articles published in more than 390 English-language journals in

all fields of engineering, applied science, technology, and related industries and trades. They include chemistry, computer technology, engineering, geology, meteorology, and telecommunications. Indexed are feature articles, interviews, book reviews, product reviews and announcements, reports, and much more.

Aquatic Sciences and Fisheries Abstracts (ASFA) (Cambridge Scientific Abstracts, 1971–)
With more than 3,500 new records added monthly, this database indexes abstracts of more than 5,000 serial publications, books, reports, conference proceedings, translations, and limited-distribution literature in the field of aquatic science. Major subject areas covered include aquatic organisms, aquatic pollution, brackish water environments, conservation, environmental quality, fisheries, freshwater environments, marine biotechnology, marine environments, meteorology, oceanography, policy and legislation, and wildlife management.

Biological Abstracts (Thomson BIOSIS, 1969–)
The first choice for many biology researchers, this database indexes articles from more than 4,000 publications each year, and provides direct access to more than 7.7 million citations, including 370,000 new citations annually on articles from journals around the world. Items listed cover topics in every life science discipline, including botany, microbiology, and pharmacology.

Biological and Agricultural Index (H.W. Wilson, 1983–)
The Web version of the long-running printed index provides thorough indexing of 258 common periodicals, including a wide range of scientific journals in the fields of agriculture, biochemistry, biology, biotechnology, entomology, genetics, microbiology, and zoology. Nearly half of the index's content is devoted to agriculture. Materials indexed include abstracts and summaries of papers, biographical sketches, book reviews, feature articles, reports of symposia and conferences, review articles, selected letters to the editor, and special issues or monographic supplements.

Biology Digest (Cambridge Scientific Abstracts, 1989–)
Specifically designed to meet the academic needs of college undergraduates and high school students, this bibliographic compilation—a companion database to the monthly scholarly journal of the same name—abstracts and indexes leading technical journals in all of the life sciences. Featuring more than 20,000 records, with more than 300 new abstracts added monthly, key subject areas covered include air and water pollution, anatomy, biochemistry, botany cell biology, climatology, crop science, ecology, energy resources, entomology, forestry, genetics, and much more.

Chemical Abstracts Online (Chemical Abstracts Service, 1967–)
Available through various licensed database providers, such as DIALOG, this online resource includes more than 17 million citations to international literature of chemistry and its applications from 1967 to the present. The Web version corresponds to the bibliographic information listed in the print index of the same name.

Environment Abstracts (Lexis-Nexis, 1975–)
Dealing mostly with subjects in the area of the environment and conservation, this bibliographic database indexes abstracts of journal articles, conference proceedings, government documents, research reports, and other key sources. Many abstracts also include links to the corresponding full-text document. This reference is the Web companion to three printed indexes, including *Energy Information Abstracts* and *Environment Abstracts,* both of which ceased publication in 1995.

General Science Index (H.W. Wilson, 1984–)
Also available in print, this Web database indexes articles from 140 leading English-language periodicals published in the United States and Great Britain, including popular science magazines and professional journals. Subjects covered are astronomy, atmospheric science, biology, botany, chemistry, conservation, earth science, environment, food, genetics, health, mathematics, medicine, microbiology, nutrition, oceanography, physics, physiology, and zoology.

INSPEC (Institution of Electrical Engineers, 1969–)
Leading bibliographic index of English-language scientific and technical literature in such fields as communications, computers and computer science, control engineering, electronics, electrical engineering, and information technology dating back to 1969. An online provides access to abstracts from 1898 to 1968 at http://www.iee.org/Publish/INSPEC/.

ISI Current Contents Connect (ISI Thomson, 1983–)
Multidisciplinary Web resource offering bibliographic records of more than 8,000 leading scholarly journals and more than 2,000 books. Includes access to many scholarly Web sites with links to full-text journal articles in science and technology.

Life Sciences Collection (Cambridge Scientific Abstracts, 1982–)
Features more than 2 million citations and abstracts of 25 life science disciplines compiled from more than 5,000 articles, books, journals, monographs, and other sources, from 1982 to the present. This invaluable database covers such subject areas as biochemistry, biology, biotechnology, cell and molecular biology, ecology, entomology, genetics, human genome, microbiology, virology, and more. Many aspects of agriculture, AIDS research, and veterinary science are also included.

MEDLINE (PubMed/U.S. National Library of Medicine, 1950–)
Produced by the U.S. National Library of Medicine (NLM), this database is the premier source for bibliographic citations and abstracts to all aspects of the health sciences including environmental health, microbiology, and toxicology.

Physical Sciences Digest (Plexus Publishing, 1987–)
Created as a companion database to Biology Digest, Physical Sciences Digest provides summaries of articles and research reports covering all the physical sciences from publications worldwide. Adding 225 new digests every month, the digest covers such titles as *Discover, Scientific American, Astronomy, Geotimes, Science, Nature, Physics World, Environmental Science and Tech-*

nology, and *Geophysical Research Letters. Physical Sciences Digest* is available online within *NewsBank Science Source Collection,* through Cambridge Scientific Abstracts (offered as *Science and Technology Digest*), and through EBSCO Publishing's database collections.

Science Citation Index (SCI) (ISI Thomson, 1945–)
Citing references found in 3,700 of the world's leading scholarly science and technical journals covering more than 100 disciplines, the Science Citation Index, also available in an expanded format through the Web of Science and SciSearch, provides direct access to current and retrospective bibliographic information. The index covers approximately 3,500 scientific and technical journals. The online SciSearch edition, available via DIALOG, archives citations back to 1974; the CD-ROM-delivered Science Citation Index, back files to 1980; and the Internet version, Web of Science, citations from 1945 to the present.

Web of Science (Thomson ISI, 1983–)
Similar in scope to ISI Current Contents Connect, this Web database indexes more than 8,500 scholarly and technical research journals in all areas of science and technology, including some full-text.

SELECTED FULL-TEXT ARTICLE DATABASES

Academic Search Elite (EBSCOHost, index: 1980– , full text: 1990–)
This comprehensive database covers a wide range of academic areas, including biology and health sciences. Coverage includes full text for more than 1,200 journals, with many dating back to 1980; abstracts and indexing for more than 3,000 scholarly journals (including more than 1,700 peer-reviewed journals); and coverage of *The Wall Street Journal, The New York Times,* and *The Christian Science Monitor.* Some of the science journals featured include *Annals of Human Biology* (1999–), *Astronomy* (1984–), *Bioscience* (1992–), *Nature* (1997), *Scientific American* (1995–), and *Weatherwise* (1984–).

Academic Search Premier (EBSCOHost, index: 1980– , full text: 1992–)
Academic Search Premier, an upgraded version of Academic Search Elite, is the world's largest scholarly academic multidisciplinary database, and covers a broad range of disciplines including general academic, business, social sciences, humanities, general sciences, education, and multicultural topics. Offers full-text coverage of more than 3,600 journals, and indexing and abstracts for all 4,500 journals.

The ACM Digital Library (Association for Computing Machinery, varies by title)
Subscription database providing online access to full-text articles in every periodical published by the Association for Computing Machinery, including an archive of articles since the mid-20th century.

Annual Reviews (Annual Reviews, 1932–)
For students conducting science and social science research, *Annual Reviews* is a useful source. It indexes timely critical reviews written by leading scientists in

the biomedical, physical, and social sciences fields. Coverage varies by individual journal title, ranging from 1932 to the 1980s. Indexed articles are available in full text format from the mid-1990s for most journals, including *Anthropology, Astronomy and Astrophysics, Biochemistry, Fluid Mechanics, Genetics, Immunology, Microbiology, Neuroscience, Plant Biology* and *Psychology.*

Biological and Agricultural Index Plus (H.W. Wilson; index: 1983– , full text: 1997–)
Biological and Agricultural Index Plus offers convenient online access to the core literature of biology and agriculture with full text articles from peer-reviewed journals. Full-text citations include links to PDF versions of articles, featuring graphs, charts, diagrams, photos, and illustrations. This Web index cites biology, agriculture, and related science articles published in 359 periodicals, including *Advances in Applied Microbiology* (1983–), *Behavioral and Neural Biology* (1982–), *The Biological Bulletin* (1983–), *Biochemistry and Cell Biology* (1986–), and *Microbiological Reviews* (1983–). Indexing of articles published between 1916 and 1991 is available in the print version of *Agricultural Index* and *Biological and Agricultural Index.*

General Science Full Text (H.W. Wilson, 1984–)
This online edition, available to libraries by subscription, provides access to citations and abstracts of articles from popular and professional science journals and *The New York Times'* science section on biological, environmental, medical and physical sciences, and related subjects. Subjects covered include atmospheric science, earth science, conservation, food and nutrition, genetics, nursing and health, physiology, and zoology.

Ingenta (Ingenta, Inc., 1988–)
Contains tables of contents and more than 14 million full-text articles from some 26,000 leading journals, 1988 to the present.

MathSciNet (American Mathematical Society, 1940–)
This fully searchable database covers mathematical reviews and publications, including more than 1,700 journals and 427,000 original articles, from 1940 to the present.

NewsBank ScienceSource Collection (NewsBank, 1987–)
This comprehensive Web science resource for both novice and experienced users covers life, earth, physical, medical, health, and applied sciences. Besides featuring abstracts from the journal *Biology Digest* from 1987 to the present, this database also includes computer and physical science abstracts, as well as full-text encyclopedia entries and scientist biographies.

Periodical Abstracts Research II Edition with Full Text (UMI ProQuest, 1986–)
Powerful database that provides abstracts, indexing, and full text of articles from more than 1,600 academic journals, business periodicals, and popular magazines, including 169 periodicals in general sciences and 239 general-interest publications. Some of the science journals covered are *Ecology, Environmental Science and Technology, New Scientist,* and *Science.* This premier database offers ASCII full-text articles from approximately 600 of the indexed titles.

ScienceDirect (Elsevier Science, 1995–)
ScienceDirect is billed as the world's largest electronic collection of science, technology, and medical journals—some 1,800 and counting—published by Elsevier Science. This online database contains bibliographic information and more than 5.8 million full-text articles, mostly from 1995 to the present, in the above disciplines. Back files are available for chemistry journals as well.

SELECTED PERIODICALS

Discover (New York: Time, Inc; Disney Magazine Publishing, 1980– monthly)
Published since 1980, this handsomely illustrated, monthly science newsmagazine covers "the wonders, mysteries and challenges of modern science." Articles focus on all areas of science, including ancient life, the environment, medicine, and technology, and are written for a general audience. Each issue also contains book reviews, stories of amateur scientists and their experiments, puzzles, and Web links. Articles from current issues, and archives of older articles for members only from 1992 the present, are accessible online at http://www.discover.com/.

Natural History (New York: American Museum of Natural History, 1900– 10 times a year)
Published since 1900 by New York's American Museum of Natural History, this award-winning general interest magazine celebrates Earth's natural beauty combining authoritative articles and spectacular close-up photography of the wonders of nature. Each issue examines subjects in such fields as biology and natural and earth sciences.

Nature (London: Macmillan Journals Ltd., 1869– , weekly)
First published on November 4, 1869, this international weekly journal of science is intended for professional scientists. In each issue, articles are devoted to rapid changes and advances in all branches of science, including news, research reports, and discussion of important scientific issues. Tables of contents of recent and past issues are available online at http://www.nature.com/nature/.

Science (New York: s.n., 1880–82; Cambridge, Mass: Moses King, 1883– , weekly)
This weekly peer-reviewed publication published by the American Association for the Advancement of Science emphasizes discussion of current research and science policy. Read by scientists and nonscientists alike, each issue contains a mix of original research articles, reports, technical comments, letters, essays on science and society, and reviews of books, film, and multimedia of interest to readers. Current issues and archives of older issue are posted online at http://www.sciencemag.org/.

Science News (Washington, D.C.: Science Service, 1922– , weekly)
Debuting in 1922 as the *Science News-Letter* edited by Watson Davis, this award-winning illustrated magazine, renamed *Science News* in 1966, covers "the most important research in all fields of science." Each issue features articles about important events in science and technology, plus book reviews.

Scientific American (New York: Munn & Co., 1845–1948; Scientific American Inc., 1948–; monthly)
Founded by Rufus Porter in 1845, this general science journal is the oldest continuously published magazine in the United States today. Published monthly in 15 different languages, each issue covers the latest news and events in science and technology across a broad range of fields, including biotechnology, ecology, information technology, molecular engineering, and planetary science, for the general public. A selection of articles from current issues can be read online at http://www.sciam.com/.

SELECTED WEB SITES

Homework Help—Girl Power! Science and Technology Section (http://www.girlpower.gov/girlarea/sciencetech/links.htm)
This site features the "coolest" Web sites on science. Examples of sites include "Adventures in Science and Technology," "Chem for Kids," "Cool Science for Curious Kids," "Girl Zone's TechKnow Girl," "Mad Sci Network," and many others.

The Internet Public Library: Science and Technology (http://www.ipl.org/div/subject/browse/sci00.00.00)
Subject collection featuring Web sites on natural and physical sciences and their practical applications, such as agriculture and aquaculture, and science and technology libraries, plus an annotated directory of Internet resources listed in alphabetical order.

SciTechResources.gov (http://www.scitechresources.gov/)
Managed by the U.S. Department of Commerce National Technical Information Service, this Web page catalogs an extensive list of government science and technology sites that are searchable and browsable by topic. Subjects covered include agriculture, applied science and technologies, astronomy and space, biology and nature, computers and communication, earth and ocean sciences, energy and energy conservation, and many more.

SciTech Web (http://www.sciam.com/article.cfm?articleID=000E2B4F-3BAD-1CF5-93F6809EC5880000)
Features an extensive collection of science Web sites that are winners of *Scientific American's* annual SciTech Web Awards, as well as links to current science and technology articles in archaeology and paleontology, astronomy and astrophysics, biology, chemistry, computer science, earth and environment, engineering and technology, mathematics, medicine, and physics.

Science and Technology Refdesk (http://www.refdesk.com/science.html)
Lists from A to Z a diverse collection of science and technology Web sites featuring loads of facts and information on virtually every discipline or subject.

Virtual Center Science and Technology (http://echo.gmu.edu/center/)
Incorporating material from the WWW Virtual Library for the History of Science, Technology, and Medicine, founded in 1994, the Virtual Center Science and Technology features a large variety of sites on the history of science, technology, and medicine arranged by category and in alphabetical order.

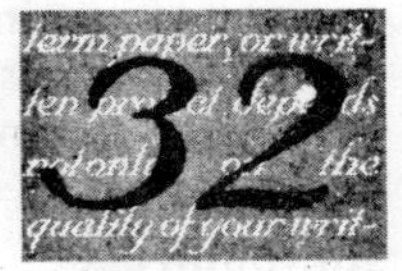

Sports

To many sports enthusiasts, the echoing crack of the bat or the resounding body slam of an opponent in the ring embodies the true spirit of sports. In reality, there's more to this popular past time than a few home runs or cracked vertebrae. Sports are the stuff of legends and players of every caliber, of grit, determination, and heart pumping action, of athleticism, psychology, and individual performance, and, more importantly, love and appreciation for the sport itself.

Today, the sports business is a billion-dollar industry and an integral part of American and world culture. Interest in sports has hardly waned from the most watched Super Bowls, to the greatest World Series, to record-breaking accomplishments of sports stars. Yet there is a dark side; widespread controversies about steroid use, long-term contracts ruining the sport, and franchises relocating to other cities when the revenues dry up.

Whether you love sports, have a difficult research question or a desire to learn more about a particular sport, athlete, or controversial issue, many sources provide information to suit your needs. Among them are almanacs and general reference works, abstract and citation indexes, popular periodicals and journals, and countless print and electronic sources.

The following list describes the selected references in the above categories to get you started.

SELECTED BOOKS AND REFERENCES

Almanacs

Sports Illustrated 2005 Almanac, by the editors of Sports Illustrated, 896 pages (Boston: Little, Brown, and Co., 2004)

Published annually by Little, Brown & Co. since 1991, this book provides extensive coverage of the year in sports for 19 major sports, including baseball, football, biathlon, and figure skating. Included is a wealth of statistics, records, and essays by *Sports Illustrated* writers.

2005 ESPN Sports Almanac, edited by Gerry Brown and Michael Morrison, 960 pages (New York: Hyperion, 2004)

Called by its publisher "the most authoritative sports reference book ever published," this best-selling almanac annually recaps the major sports stories and sports moments of the previous year. Featuring hundreds of photographs and thousands of graphics and tables, it offers year-by-year and sport-by-sport coverage, including facts and statistics, "Top Ten Moments" from each sport, plus essays and analysis by popular ESPN on-air personalities including Chris Berman, Dan Patrick, Stuart Scott, Linda Cohn, and others.

Dictionaries

Dictionary of the Sport and Exercise Sciences, edited Mark H. Anshel, 176 pages, (Champaign, Ill.: Human Kinetics Books, 1991)
Easy-to-use dictionary that covers all sports and exercise sports sciences. Entries feature clear and concise definitions of terms for such areas as adapted physical education, biomechanics, exercise physiology, motor control, motor development, motor learning, sport pedagogy, sport psychology, and sport sociology.

The Oxford Dictionary of Sports Science and Medicine, 2nd Ed., compiled by Michael Kent, 567 pages (Oxford; New York: Oxford University Press, 1996)
Written for athletes, coaches, medical professionals, and students, this second revised and updated edition includes more than 7,500 cross-referenced terms in all major areas of sports science and medicine. Subjects covered include anatomy, exercise physiology, nutrition, sports sociology, sports injuries, and scientific and training principles.

Encyclopedias

Encyclopedia of World Sport: From Ancient Times to the Present, edited by David Levinson and Karen Christensen, 488 pages (New York: Oxford University Press, 1999)
Information about hundreds of sports from around the world since ancient times is well detailed and nicely chronicled in this informative encyclopedia. Entries cover not only each individual sport and how it's played but also the history and evolution, human experience, emotion, and influences that shaped them.

International Encyclopedia of Women and Sports, 3 vols., edited by Karen Christensen, Allen Guttmann, and Gertrude Pfister (New York: Macmillan Library Reference, 2001)
In the words of one critic, "No other encyclopedia treats the field of women in international sports with such currency, depth, and detail" as this three-volume reference set does. It features more than 130 biographies, 170 individual and group sports overviews, and 75 country profiles, all related to women and sports. Articles up to 4,000 words long examine cultural, ethical, health, and societal issues, as well as non-Western sports, extreme sports, and outdoor recreation, generously supplemented by photographs, charts, informative sidebars, and bibliographies.

Rules of the Game: The Complete Illustrated Encyclopedia of all the Sports of the World, by the Diagram Group, 320 pages (New York: St. Martin's Press, 1995)
This concise, color-illustrated volume details the rules and procedures, equipment required, and methods of scoring for more than 150 sports—including darts and jai alai—for over 400 related events.

General Reference

Sports: The Complete Visual Reference, by François Fortin (Buffalo, N.Y.: Firefly Books, Ltd., 2000)

Color-illustrated reference guide to more than 125 sports played around the world, such as baseball, basketball, hockey, golf, BMX, and diving, grouped by category. Clear, concise explanations detail the origin, method of play, the kinds of equipment and environments, and physical and training requirements of each sport. Charts of world records and legendary competitors of the past are also included.

Handbooks

Handbook of Sport Psychology, 2nd Ed., edited by Robert N. Singer, Heather A. Hausenblas, and Christopher M. Janelle, 896 pages (New York: John Wiley & Sons, 2001)

Authored by leading experts, this second, revised edition, featuring 11 new chapters, documents the psychological aspects, discipline, and training of competitive sports, including new research and approaches to exercise, motivation, pain management, and performance.

Sports Nutrition, edited Ronald J. Maughan and Louise Burke, 187 pages (Malden, Mass.: Blackwell Science, 2002)

This book offers practical nutritional information. Subjects covered include nutrition needs, exercise and energy demands, recovery time between training sessions, and nutritional strategies for training, as well as other related topics, such as weight management, limitations to exercise performance, sports foods, and other supplements vital to training and performance.

SELECTED ARTICLE INDEXES AND ABSTRACTS

Printed Indexes and Abstracts

America: History and Life (Santa Barbara, Calif.: ABC-CLIO, 1964–88)

Perfectly suited for researching sports from a historical and cultural perspective, this retrospective print index references American history research in the form of journal articles, dissertations, and book or media reviews from some 2,400 journals in 40 different languages. Coverage begins with published materials from 1964. Twenty-six volumes of this print series were originally published. The first 10-volume index was called *America: History of Life,* from July 1964 to winter 1973. Four additional 15-volume sets that followed were *America: History and Life, Part A: Article Abstracts and Citations; America: History and Life, Part B: Index to Book Reviews; America: History and Life, Part C: American History Bibliography, Books, Articles and Dissertations;* and *America: History and Life, Part D: Annual Index.* These volumes covered published material from 1974 to 1988. Beginning in 1989, with Volume 26, the index returned to its original title, *America: History and Life.* The complete series is also offered online from 1982 to the present.

Biological Abstracts (Philadelphia: BioSciences Information Service, 1926–   )

This printed reference abstracts articles from life sciences journals worldwide in the areas of biological and biomedical research. Interdisciplinary fields such as biochemistry, biophysics, and bioengineering, and references to books, book chapters, and patents are also included. The electronic version, BIOSIS Previews, is based on the printed series, and offers similar abstract coverage from 1980 to the present.

Index Medicus (Bethesda, Md.: National Library of Medicine, 1966–)
Index Medicus is the comprehensive index in the field of health and medicine. Highlighted are citations with abstracts to more than 3,000 international journals issued monthly in two-volume sets, arranged by author and subject. The full contents of issues from each year are featured in the annual *Cumulated Index Medicus* (1879–present). The index is available throughout the online database MEDLINE (1966–present).

Physical Education Index, 26 vols. (Cape Girardeau, Mo.: BenOak Publishing, 1978–2003)
Published through December 2003, this 26-volume subject index abstracts 200 physical education periodicals covering dance, physical education, physical therapy, recreation, sports, and sports medicine. The first volume, published in 1978, covered published material from 1970 to 1977. Subsequent volumes offered added coverage of periodical literature since 1978.

Physical Fitness/Sports Medicine (Washington, D.C.: The President's Council on Physical Fitness and Sports, 1978–94)
Consists of citations of more than 3,000 periodicals, including *Physical Fitness/Sports Medicine* (winter 1978–spring 1994), a publication of the President's Council on Physical Fitness and Sports, and papers presented at selected congresses.

The Sports Periodicals Index, 2 vols. (Ann Arbor, Mich.: National Information Systems, 1985–86)
Subject and name index to 100 sports journals, including the most popular magazines in virtually all sports, since January 1985. The two-volume print index ceased publication in 1986.

Web Indexes and Abstracts

America: History and Life (ABC-CLIO, 1960–)
Indexes and abstracts scholarly literature on the history and culture of the United States and Canada, including sports, and citations to book reviews, media reviews, and dissertations; based on the printed series of the same name.

BIOSIS Previews (Thomson ISI, 1969–)
Indexes journals, books, and conference proceedings—some 5,000 sources throughout the world—in the life sciences. Look here for research articles on biomechanics, kinesiology, and physiology. Online coverage extends back to 1969. See the print equivalent, *Biological Abstracts,* for research prior to 1969.

ERIC (U.S. Department of Education, 1966–)
Provides citations and abstracts to all aspects of educational research and resources taken from professional journals and education related reports,

conference proceedings, and other nonjournal literature (ERIC Documents) from 1966 to the present. Indexes more than 750 journals, as well as research and technical reports, curriculum and teaching guides, conference papers, dissertations, and books.

MEDLINE (U.S. National Library of Medicine, 1966–)
Accessible through PubMed, this major online bibliographic database for health sciences offers information on research articles on human physiology, fitness and health, nutrition, and sports medicine from journals indexed back to 1966.

PCI: Periodicals Contents Index (Chadwyck-Healey, 1770–1995)
Abstracts and indexes more than 200 years of articles in virtually thousands of periodicals in the arts, humanities, and social sciences with access to more than 10 million citations published since 1770. Scope of coverage is worldwide, and covers foreign and most Western languages.

Physical Education Index (Cambridge Scientific Abstracts, 1970–)
Based on the printed index of the same name, this online database indexes citations to peer-reviewed articles, conference proceedings, journals, report literature, and many other publications on such subjects as dance, physical education, and sports medicine. Topics covered include business and marketing, coaching and training, kinesiology, motor learning, recreation, standardized fitness tests, sport law, sport sociology/psychology, and sports equipment. Health education and physical therapy are also covered.

PsycINFO (American Psychological Association, 1887–)
This popular online database abstracts the world's professional and academic literature, including books and articles, in psychology and related disciplines. Indexes more than 1,400 journals in 27 languages from 50 countries from 1887 to the present. Great database for finding research on sports psychology.

SIRS Researcher (Social Issues Resource Series, 1988–)
Produced by Social Issues Resource Series and sold by ProQuest and OCLC, SIRS Researcher is a popular general reference database. It indexes thousands of full-text articles from more than 1,200 domestic and international newspapers, magazines, journals, and government publications on a variety of social, scientific, historic, economic, political and global issues. Many charts, maps, diagrams, and illustrations are included.

Social Sciences Citation Index (Thomson ISI, 1990–)
Multidisciplinary database that provides online access to current and retrospective bibliographic information, author abstracts, and cited references in more than 1,700 leading scholarly social sciences journals searchable by subject, author, or journal name.

Social Sciences Index (H.W. Wilson, 1983–)
Bibliographic database offering citations only of 353 English-language periodicals published in the United States and throughout the world covering a broad array of social sciences journals and a wide range of interdisciplinary fields. Corresponds to printed publication of same name.

SELECTED FULL-TEXT ARTICLE DATABASES

Academic Search Premier (EBSCOHost; index: 1980, full text: 1992–)
Full-text articles from more than 3,400 publications, including an index of articles found in 900 other academic publications, for information on a wide range of topics in art, computer science, education, engineering, ethnic studies, humanities, language, literature, medical sciences, social sciences, and more.

Education Abstracts Full Text (H.W. Wilson, 1983–)
Indexes, abstracts, and provides selected full text of articles in more than 400 education-related periodicals and yearbooks. Includes journals that cover physical education and sports in schools. Indexing begins in 1983, and abstracts and full-text articles in 1994, with most full-text articles beginning in 1996.

Health Source: Consumer Edition (EBSCOHost, indexing: 1984– , full text: 1990–)
Provides citations with abstracts of 325 consumer-health, international health and nutrition periodicals—largely English-language materials—including journals, newsletters, pamphlets, reference books, and other information. Useful for researching topics such as biomechanics, food sciences, physical fitness, sports and sports medicine, and wellness. Dates of coverage vary by title; full text from 1990 to the present.

InfoTrac OneFile (InfoTrac, 1980–)
Features citations, abstracts, and full-text articles from more than 6,000 scholarly journals, popular magazines, and newspapers in nearly every academic discipline, including the arts and humanities, social sciences and science and technology, as well as business, law, current affairs and general interest topics, from 1980 to the present updated daily.

LexisNexis Academic Universe (LexisNexis, 1977–)
Good source for finding current articles and information on professional and amateur sports and athletes featuring full-text newspaper and journal articles more than 5,600 news, business, legal, medical, and reference publications. Includes national and regional newspapers such as the *San Francisco Chronicle* and *The New York Times,* broadcast transcripts, wire services, international news and non–English language sources. Stories are searchable under the "General News Topics" category, and under "News/Arts and Sports."

ProQuest Research Library (ProQuest, index: 1971– , full text: 1988–)
Useful for researching such as topics as athletes, exercise, physical fitness, and sports injuries, ProQuest Research Library indexes current articles, some full text, in nearly every academic discipline, as well as current affairs and general interest topics. Citations and abstracts are from selected publications since 1971, with more complete coverage beginning in 1996. Updated daily, this multidisciplinary database mixes scholarly and popular journals, with full-text coverage of nearly 15 exercise and sport science titles from 1988 to the present.

PsycARTICLES (American Psychological Association, 1987–)
Online database of full-text articles published by the American Psychological Association, APA Educational Publishing Foundation, the Canadian Psychological Association, and Hogrefe and Huber Publishers covering all aspects of psychology. Covers such areas as sports psychology, leisure, and rehabilitation.

Sport Business Research Network (Sports Business Research Network, 1993–)
Major online research database featuring articles, consumer surveys, government data, market research reports, and news releases, some in full text, covering all facets of the sports industry, from archery to youth sports. This comprehensive database provides immediate access to market research from the National Sporting Goods Association, the U.S. Department of Commerce, and sports governing bodies, full-text articles from 14 magazines and newsletters published by Miller Freeman, the world's largest sporting goods trade publisher, and newsletters provided by leading independent industry experts. In mid-1999, SBRNet added buyTRACK, a new database created by Harris Interactive, which tracks the sporting goods purchasing habits of consumers on the Internet.

SPORTDiscus (SIRC, 1949–)
Contains more than 500,000 citations and abstracts, with links to full-text articles, to periodical literature in physical fitness, recreation, sport management, sport science, and related areas. Coverage includes worldwide scientific and practical literature, such as articles, audiovisual material, conference proceedings, dissertations, monographs, and research reports for both individual and team sports. Also indexed is literature on coaching, conditioning, officiating, and training, and additional sport- and fitness-related topics, including biomechanics, exercise physiology, exercise psychology, international sports history, sport psychology, and much more. Most sources are in English and French.

SELECTED PERIODICALS

American Track and Field (Madison, Wisc.: Shooting Star Media, 1994– , five times yearly)
Aimed principally at high school, college, and club track and field and cross-country coaches, this professional periodical is a source of training information, new techniques, and approaches meant to improve "the performance of American athletes in the disciplines of track and field, cross country, and race walking." An official partner with the U.S.A. Track and Field organization, American Track and Field was first published in 1994 and is issued five times yearly. Each issue profiles top athletes and coaches, reviews major world athletic events, reports on U.S. championships, and offers informative articles on related topics, including individual event training, sports nutrition, and sports psychology.

Baseball America (Durham, N.C.: American Sports Pub., 1981– , weekly)
Perhaps the best baseball weekly in its class, this popular tabloid provides complete coverage of high school, college, and professional baseball. Highlighting each issue are expertly written articles, columns, and features cov-

ering the latest news, the top names and up-and-coming players in the game, plus statistics and scores of the most recent games. Past issues are available in microform from January 1991 through the end of the previous year.

Basketball Digest (Evanston, Ill.: Century Pub. Co., 1973– , six times yearly)
Published six times yearly since November 1973, this entertaining tabloid provides an insider's perspective on NBA, NCAA, and WNBA basketball, and the world of hoops in general. Every issue contains informative and timely features, player profiles, statistics, schedules, and more. The editors also publish special sections every year featuring their selections of the "NBA Player of the Year," "All-NBA Teams," "All-Rookie Teams," and "All-American Teams."

Football Digest (Evanston, Ill.: Century Pub. Co., 1971– , eight times yearly)
From the publisher of *Basketball Digest* and *Hockey Digest,* this photo-packed magazine has since 1971 delivered comprehensive coverage of happenings in NFL and college football, including in-depth season previews, informative interviews with players and coaches, the latest news, NFL and college schedules, NFL rosters and directories, and relevant statistics on players and teams. Special issues are also devoted annually to the "NFL All-Pro" and "College All-American" teams.

Golf Digest (Evanston, Ill.: Golf Digest, 1950– , monthly)
Published monthly since 1950, this glossy magazine provides practical advice and in-depth coverage of the game of golf for both amateur and semi-professional golfers alike. Coverage includes "how-to" articles and lessons, feature stories, and reviews of the most recent championship opens, equipment reviews, and much more. An archive of articles published since 2000 is accessible online at http://www.golfdigest.com/features/index.ssf?/features/golfdigestarchive.html.

Hockey Digest (Evanston, Ill.: Century Pub. Co., 1972– , six times yearly)
Since its first issue, published in November 1972, for more than 30 years this popular tabloid has provided the most extensive coverage of hockey, from the game's top stars and Stanley Cup championships to college hockey. A wide range of articles is included in each issue, including interviews with professionals, in-depth features, and expert analysis of the latest trends and game action.

Journal of Sport History (Radford, Va.: North American Society for Sport History, 1974– , quarterly)
A project of the Amateur Athletic Association of Los Angeles and the North American Society for Sport History, this scholarly publication offers articles in each issue devoted to the study of all aspects of sport history. Most articles and back issues of the journal are available online as PDF files from 1974 to 2001, and are fully searchable. To access, visit http://www.aafla.com/search/search_frmst.htm.

The NCAA News (Shawnee Mission, Kan.: National Collegiate Athletic Association, 1900– , biweekly)
The NCAA News is the official publication of the National Collegiate Athletic Association (NCAA), a voluntary organization with members from nearly 1,200 colleges and universities, athletic conferences, and sports organizations nationwide. Published biweekly in print and online, this leading authority on college athletics covers the latest news regarding the business and administration of college athletics throughout the year. Unlike most periodicals, the NCCA provides unfettered access to its archives of past issues and articles dating back to 1964. Editions prior to April 29, 1996, are offered in .PDF format. To access, visit http://www.ncaa.org. Click on "News and Publications," then The NCAA News, followed by the title of the publication under "Archive."

Pro Football Weekly (Chicago, Ill.: Pro Football Weekly, Inc., 1967– , weekly)
Devoted exclusively to pro football, this weekly tabloid newsmagazine provides complete coverage of the NFL, Canadian, Arena, and European football leagues. Each issue features award-winning columns and features, inside information, game previews, scouting analysis, investigative reporting, rosters and injury reports, and complete scores and statistics of the previous week's action. Some content is published online and accessible at http://www.profootball.com.

Runner's World (Emmaus, Pa.: Rodale Press, 1970– , monthly)
First introduced nationally in 1970, this long-running monthly magazine publishes informative and helpful articles of interest to runners of all ages. Issues contain timely articles on medical and training advice, sports medicine and nutrition, shoe evaluations, profiles of running personalities, and coverage of important races and upcoming events designed to educate and inform its readers.

The Sporting News (St. Louis, Mo.: Sporting News, 1886– , weekly)
Long known as the "bible of baseball" and "America's sport authority," this weekly sports publication, published since 1886, provides weekly analysis and reviews of every major sport, including baseball, basketball, football, and hockey. Every issue combines in-depth articles, team-by-team capsules, and the latest news and statistics covering American professional and college sports. *The Sporting News* also provides online access to archival material covering all sports through its Web page called The Vault. Included are sports histories, virtual scrapbooks of legendary sports figures, special features on sports anniversaries, and other resources. To access, visit http://www.sportingnews.com/archives/.

Sports Illustrated (New York: Time, Inc., 1954– , weekly)
Perhaps "the most recognized periodical of American sports," this popular weekly magazine has provided coverage of American sports since 1954. Combining commentary and analysis with action-packed photography, every week articles include profiles of past and current sports legends, weekly wrap-ups of recent competitions in professional and college sports, major sport news, and primers of upcoming college and pro sport seasons.

Tennis (Trumbull, Conn.: Miller Sports Group LLC, 1965– , 10 times yearly)
In print since 1965, this popular publication is a primary source of information and instruction for fans and avid tennis players of all levels of expertise. Articles cover every facet of the game with a primary emphasis on improving skill and enjoyment of the game. Contents of past issues from 1998 to the present are retrievable online at http://www.tennis.com/archives/archives.sps?itype=2662.

USA Today Sports Weekly (Arlington, Va.: Gannett Co., 1991– , weekly)
Formerly known as *Baseball Weekly,* this newspaper-style tabloid, first published on April 11, 1991, in partnership with *USA Today,* provides comprehensive coverage of current sports in season. Each publication includes articles, features, commentaries, photos, statistics, and box scores of the previous week's games. An electronic version is available by subscription. To subscribe and access, visit http://www.usatodaysportsweekly.newsstand.com/.

SELECTED WEB SITES

All Sports (http://www.allsports.com)
Provides news and scores from all major professional sports, including the Canadian Football League (CFL), National Basketball Association (NBA), National Collegiate Athletic Association (NCAA), National Football League (NFL), National Hockey League (NHL), Professional Golf Association (PGA), racing, tennis, and more.

American Statistics Association—Official Team Websites (http://www.amstat.org/sections/sis/teams.html)
Comprehensive online directory provided by the American Statistics Association featuring links to official team Web sites for baseball, basketball, football, hockey, and soccer.

CBS SportsLine (http://www.sportsline.com)
A free service of CBS Broadcasting, Inc., offering full-text articles, scores, columns, and a search engine for information on baseball, NFL, NBA, NHL, golf, tennis, auto racing, and other sports.

CNN/SI (http://sportsillustrated.cnn.com)
Delivers full-text articles daily from the sports desks of CNN and *Sports Illustrated,* plus individual sections on baseball, pro and college football, pro and college basketball, golf, hockey, motor sports, soccer, tennis, and women's sports, and scoreboards and team pages.

ESPN SportsZone (http://espn.go.com/)
Offers regularly updated full-text articles on the NFL, college football, the NHL, the NBA, college basketball, and other sports.

Scholarly Sports Sites, University of Calgary (http://www.ucalgary.ca/library/ssportsite/)
A-to-Z subject directory of sports-related Web sites, including archives and special sports collections, associations, bibliographies, databases, directories,

local organizations, museums and halls of fame, and much more. A keyword search engine is also provided.

Sport Information Resource Centre—Resource Guide (http://www.sportquest.com/resources/sportscience.cfm)
Complete resource guide to sports information and sports-related Web sites, arranged alphabetically, covering all areas and subjects.

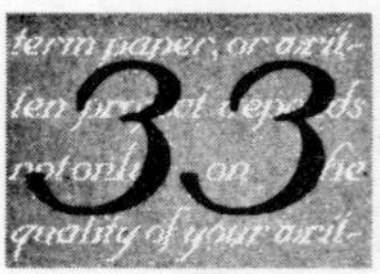

Theater and Dance

With an arsenal of print and electronic material at your disposal, you can delve into the history, literature, acting, choreography, design, and management of theater and dance. You can study a specific period, a particular artist's or playwright's style, theater and dance culture, or theater and dance performances based on a specific literary work. You also can examine theater and dance's history; production companies and individual productions; technical and theatrical aspects; the best plays of the modern ages; excerpts from critically-acclaimed plays; and the most notable names in theater and dance worldwide, or the present state of affairs for academic, children's, community, ethic, experimental, and regional theater.

In addition to combing through general humanities and arts sources, the focus of your research can include books, periodicals, and videos, art history and studio art materials, music, sound recordings, and musical scores, and special collections of theatrical manuscripts and rare print materials, all specific to your topic or subject of interest. Described in this chapter are selected sources and references for research.

SELECTED BOOKS AND REFERENCES

General References

American Musical Theatre—A Chronicle, 3d Ed., by Gerald Bordman, 840 pages (New York: Oxford University Press, 2000)
Written by Gerald Bordman, author of Oxford University Press's acclaimed American Theatre series, this exhaustively researched guide offers detailed summaries of musical theater productions, including musical comedies, operettas, reviews, and one-man and one-woman shows, from 1866 to 1960. A detailed show, song, and people index is included.

American Theatre—A Chronicle of Comedy and Drama 1869–1914, by Gerald Bordman, 802 pages (New York: Oxford University Press, 1994)
The first of four volumes, this well-written and researched book examines American theater history, from post–Civil War era to the start of World War I. Every Broadway show is fully chronicled by season, including plot summaries, details of the production and its stars, and other characteristics.

American Theatre: A Chronicle of Comedy and Drama 1914–1930, by Gerald Bordman, 464 pages (New York: Oxford University Press, 1995)
This second volume in Oxford's American Theatre series chronicles every American theater production in chronological order from1914 to 1930, what many historians believe to be the richest period in American theater. Covering the works of such noted playwrights as George Kaufman, Eugene O'Neill, and Elmer Rice and the era's biggest stars, such as John and Ethel Barrymore and Alfred Lunt, entries include plot summaries, production details, cast and character names, and critical reviews.

American Theatre: A Chronicle of Comedy and Drama 1930–1969, by Gerald Bordman, 472 pages (New York: Oxford University Press, 1996)
In the third volume of Oxford's American Theatre series, Gerald Bordman once again surveys American theater, this time focusing on nonmusical theater—comedy and drama—between 1930 and 1969. Following the same format as previous editions, Bordman vividly details Broadway productions offering plotlines, historical context, cast and credits, critical response, and more. This premier history also chronicles the best work of playwrights from this era, including Arthur Miller (*Death of a Salesman*), Eugene O'Neill (*Long Day's Journey into Night*), Tennessee Williams (*A Streetcar Named Desire*), and many others.

American Theatre: A Chronicle of Comedy and Drama 1969–2000, by Thomas S. Hischak, 520 pages (New York: Oxford University Press, 2001)
This last edition and final volume of Oxford's American Theatre series, written by State University of New York professor of theater Thomas S. Hischak, coauthor of *The Oxford Companion to American Theatre,* offers a fascinating look at Broadway productions through the end of the 20th century.

Cambridge Guide to American Theatre, edited by Don B. Wilmeth with Tice L. Miller, 477 pages (New York: Cambridge University Press, 1996)
This alphabetically arranged chronicle offers extensive coverage of American theater history, including major plays and all forms of theater, including burlesque, circuses, and vaudeville, from their beginnings through 1996. Featuring the contributions of more than 80 experts, this book covers some 2,300 subjects, including biographical sketches of theater personalities, entries for individual plays, essays on production companies and theaters, historical sketches of theater, and related subjects, from overviews of Asian-American theater to Shakespearean stage productions. This volume includes a list of 1,000 additional sources for further reading, and a biographical index of more than 3,000 names.

A Chronology of American Musical Theater, by Richard C. Norton, 3 vols. (New York: Oxford University Press, 2002)
Named an Outstanding Reference Source for 2003 by the American Library Association, this three-volume reference set surveys more than 3,000 musicals by year and by season, from the 1860s through 1997. Each entry provides considerable detail about the productions, including information about the cast and crew, composers, lyricists, set designers, and songs, and every kind of production—Broadway and off-Broadway musicals, operettas, revues, and other stage works. Contents are extensively indexed.

Contemporary Dramatists, 6th Ed., edited by Thomas Riggs, 897 pages (Detroit: St. James Press, 1998)
This fully revised and updated sixth edition offers 450 entries examining the lives and works of the most famous living playwrights in the English language. Entries include biographies, bibliographies, and critical essays on the most studied dramatists in the world of theater.

Contemporary Theatre, Film, and Television: A Biographical Guide Featuring Performers, Directors, Writers, Producers, Designers, Managers, Choreographers, Technicians, Composers, Executives, Dancers, and Critics in the United States and Great Britain, 58 vols. (Detroit: Gale Group, 2004)
This first-rate biographical reference, also available in eBook format through Gale Virtual Reference Library, details the lives and careers of some 11,000 entertainment industry professionals, such as choreographers, critics, designers, directors, executives, producers, technicians, and writers from the United States and Great Britain. Entries provide personal and career vitals, including birth dates, education and professional training, and political and religious affiliations. This series was published as a supplement to *Who's Who in Theatre,* which ceased publication in 1981.

International Encyclopedia of Dance, edited by Selma Jeanne Cohen, 6 vols., 4,000 pages (New York: Oxford University Press, 1998)
This heavily illustrated six-volume encyclopedia features more than 2,000 topical essays exploring all forms of dance throughout the world and its cultural and social significance.

The New Penguin Dictionary of the Theatre, edited by Jonathan Law, David Pickering, and Richard Helfer, 668 pages (New York: Penguin USA, 2001)
An invaluable reference guide for students and aficionados of drama, containing more than 5,000 articles exploring all aspects, styles, and developments in theater.

The Oxford Companion to American Theatre, 2nd Ed., by Gerald Bordman, 744 pages (New York: Oxford University Press, 1992)
Fully updated and expanded, this encyclopedia is a useful source of information about all aspects of American theater, from its beginnings to the late 20th century. More than 3,000 entries highlight great American playwrights, producers, and directors, Broadway stage productions, composers and lyricists, theater companies and organizations, performers, and some foreign plays. Entries include such celebrated plays as *Cat on a Hot Tin Roof, Cats, The Iceman Cometh, Arsenic and Old Lace, My Fair Lady,* and *Who's Afraid of Virginia Woolf?,* and the greatest names in theater, such as Clifford Odets, Lillian Hellman, George Gershwin, Neil Simon, Florenz Ziegfeld, Mae West, Lee Strasberg, and Jessica Tandy.

Theatre Backstage From A to Z, 4th Ed., by Warren C. Lounsbury and Norman C. Boulanger, 231 pages (Seattle: University of Washington Press, 1999)
An ideal source for amateurs and professionals alike, this copiously illustrated revised and expanded manual covers the technical aspects of theater production, including construction, design, lighting, painting, stage managing, and more.

Theatre World, by John Willis, et al., 59 vols. (New York: Daniel C. Blum, 1945–50; Crown Publishers, 1966–91; Applause Theatre and Cinema Books, 1992–)
Annual survey of the American theater offering brief summaries and cast lists for Broadway, off-Broadway, and regional theater productions. Information covered includes awards, biographies, and obituaries for the previous year. Between 1944 and 1965, the series was published by various publishers, including its first, Daniel C. Blum, which issued the first six volumes in the series through 1950. Eighteen additional annual volumes followed. Publication continued under the Crown Publishers imprint in 1966, when the seventh volume in the series was released. Crown became the principal publisher of this series, continuing publication through the 1989–90 season (Volume 46). In 1973, the publication was renamed after its author *John Willis' Theatre World* before returning to its former title in 1982. In 1992, Applause Theatre and Cinema Books acquired the series, publishing its first edition, Volume 47 (1990–91), that same year.

Variety Obituaries, 15 vols. (New York: Garland Pub. Co., 1905–94)
This 15-volume set reprinted show business obituaries of well-known celebrities in the performing arts from 1905 through 1993–94.

Who's Who in Theatre: A Biographical Record of the Contemporary Stage, 17th Ed., 4 vols. (London: Pitman; Detroit: Gale Research, 1981–)
No longer in print but still available at some school and public libraries, this important four-volume set was the first reference of its kind featuring biographies of people from all aspects of theater from 1912 to 1981. Largely emphasizing London theater in earlier volumes, the entire set offers biographical entries on leading actors, composers, critics, dramatists, designers, and historians from both the London and New York stage. In addition, playbills from various productions are included.

Who Was Who in the Theatre, 1912–1976: A Biographical Dictionary of Actors, Actresses, Directors, Playwrights, and Producers of the English-Speaking Theatre, 15 vols., 2,664 pages (Detroit: Gale Research, 1978)
Now out of print but still useful, this 15-volume reference is a "who was who" of noted theater actors, actresses, directors, producers, and playwrights. Biographical sketches offer personal and career information on each subject.

The World Encyclopedia of Contemporary Theatre, by Don Rubin, 6 vols., 544 pages (London; New York: Routledge, 1994–2000)
This six-volume set, called by its publisher "the largest international co-operative publication in the history of world theater," covers the theater productions and performances of 30 countries around the world. Coverage includes dramatists, plays, and theatrical companies and the cultural, political, and religious impact of their work and performances.

Reviews/Criticism

Critical Survey of Drama, 2nd Ed., edited by Frank N. Magill, revised edition edited by Carl Rollyson, 8 vols. (Pasadena, Calif.: Salem Press, 2003)
Eight-volume set of alphabetically arranged articles about major playwrights and their plays comprises the original seven volumes edited by Frank N. Magill, formerly called *Critical Survey of Drama: English Language Series*

(1985) and *Critical Survey of Drama: Foreign Language Series* (1986). This acclaimed reference series features biographical and critical essays on important English-language dramatists from ancient times to the present and such areas as Africa, Australia, Britain, Canada, West Indies, and the United States. Each entry discusses the subject's achievements and principal dramas combining critical analysis and bibliographies for further reading. Additional essays also focus on other aspects of the development and presentation of drama, such as acting, costumes, lighting, and more. Cumulated author and title indexes accompany the set.

Critics' Theatre Reviews, 3 vols. (New York: Critics Theatre Reviews, 1940–42)
This three-volume set offers full text of critical reviews for stage productions from 1940 to 1942. The series continued publication under two different names: *New York Theatre Critics' Reviews* and *National Theatre Critics' Reviews,* each containing full-text reviews from 1943 through 1996.

Dramatic Criticism Index: A Bibliography of Commentaries on Playwrights from Ibsen to the Avant-Garde, compiled and edited by Paul F. Breed and Florence M. Sniderman, 1,022 pages (Detroit: Gale Research Co., 1972)
A good source of criticism and lists of plays by modern playwrights from Ibsen to the early 1970s, this comprehensive index includes approximately 12,000 critical articles, essays, and books on individual plays, arranged alphabetically by playwright. Indexed are both American and foreign 20th-century playwrights. Title and critic's name indexes are provided for cross-referencing of subjects.

A Guide to Critical Reviews, 3rd Ed., by James M. Salem, 2 vols. (Metuchen, N.J.: Scarecrow Press, 1984–91)
This two-volume, three-part series indexes in alphabetical order critical reviews published in magazines, newspapers, and theater journals by subject. Following the name of each entry, the title of the production, debut date, number of performances, and reviews are listed by publication and date published. Part I of the series indexes reviews of American drama from 1909 to 1982; Part II, musicals from 1909 to 1989, and Part III, foreign dramas from 1909 to 1977.

International Bibliography of Theatre, by Benito Ortolani (Brooklyn: Theater Research Data Center, 1998–)
Updated annually, this popular reference is considered by librarians as one of the best indexes in theatre. This annual lists international publications in theater and performing arts and more than 5,000 entries in all, covering all time periods and geographic areas of theater arts. Coverage includes books, articles in scholarly journals, articles in literary and theater magazines, criticism and interviews, and reviews published around the world and in several languages. This directory is divided into two parts: a list of resources and a subject index. Unlike the *MLA International Bibliography* and other arts and humanities indexes, this publication does not list reviews in newspapers and popular media.

Modern Drama Scholarship and Criticism 1966–1980: An International Bibliography, by Charles A. Carpenter, 587 pages (Toronto; Buffalo: University of Toronto Press, 1986)
Suitable for researching international criticism on contemporary and modern playwrights, this first of two volumes covers nearly 25,000 international publications arranged by topic. Books and articles are arranged by geographic area, and playwrights' names are conveniently indexed in the front of the book. Content includes criticism and interviews through 1980.

Modern Drama Scholarship and Criticism, 1981–1990: An International Bibliography, by Charles A. Carpenter, 632 pages (Toronto; Buffalo: Published in association with Modern Drama by University of Toronto Press, 1997)
This follow-up volume to *Modern Drama Scholarship and Criticism, 1966–1980* adheres to the same format as its predecessor, chronicling 25,200 additional periodicals since 1981, including books, articles, criticisms, and interviews on contemporary and modern playwrights.

National Theatre Critics' Reviews, 2 vols. (Woodside, N.Y.: Critics' Theatre Reviews, 1995–96)
Formerly known as *Critics' Theatre Reviews, 1940–1942* and *New York Theatre Critics' Reviews, 1943–1994,* this two-volume set reproduces full-text reviews from 1995 to 1996.

New York Theatre Critics' Reviews, 52 vols. (New York: Critics' Theatre Reviews, 1943–95)
The best source for Broadway and off-Broadway show reviews, this 52-volume index features full-text New York theater critic reviews from 1943 to 1995. The last volume indexes actors, choreographers, directors, and other personnel from the shows reviewed.

The New York Times Index (New York: New York Times Co., 1851–1999)
Indexes citations from 1857 to the present (under the subject heading "Theater") of articles about theater and reviews of individual plays listed alphabetically by title corresponding with the *The New York Times* microfilm collection.

The New York Times Theater Reviews (New York: New York Times, 1870–2001)
Ceasing publication with the 1999–2000 edition, this set of indexes contains the full texts of theater reviews published in *The New York Times* since 1870.

SELECTED ARTICLE INDEXES AND ABSTRACTS

Printed Indexes and Abstracts

Applied Science and Technology Index (New York: H.W. Wilson, 1958–)
Includes citations and abstracts to nearly 600 key English-language periodicals covering the trades, technology, and related topics. This index is a good source of information on such subjects as lighting, special effects, stage

setting, and other technological innovations that affect the theater. Online version provides coverage from 1983 to the present.

Art Index (New York: H.W. Wilson, 1929–)
Indexes citations of articles in some 450 major international arts publications by author and subject. Topics covered include acting, costumes, make-up, set design, and theater.

Arts and Humanities Citation Index (Philadelphia: Institute for Scientific Information, 1976–)
This multidisciplinary index covers more than 6,000 journals in the arts and humanities.

Biography Index (New York: H.W. Wilson, 1946–)
This cumulative index provides more than 272,000 bibliographies from books, pamphlets, and more than 2,800 periodicals arranged by subject from 1946 to the present. An expanded electronic version is also offered through libraries.

Essay and General Literature Index (New York: H.W. Wilson, 1900–)
Indexes hundreds of thousands of essays contained in anthologies and collections spanning the entire range of the humanities and social sciences, including literary works, art history, drama, and film, since the turn of the 20th century. H.W. Wilson also produces this index as an online database offering coverage from 1985 to the present.

Humanities Index (New York: H.W. Wilson, 1947–)
Covers a broad range of subjects, including area studies, folklore, history, language and literature, and performing arts, indexing more than 500 publications. Also indexes reviews from scholarly theater journals. Look under "Theater" for a list of related subject headings, followed by the listing of articles; for reviews, look under "Theater reviews," where plays are listed alphabetically.

Play Index (New York: H.W. Wilson, 1949–2002)
Indexes annotated entries on more than 30,000 individual plays and plays in collections from 1949 to 2002. Coverage includes full-length stage plays, radio, television, and one-act plays, classic dramas, puppet plays, and plays for children and young adults. Entries include author, title, subject, and dramatic style information, and a brief synopsis. Each volume contains an author, title, and subject index for easy use.

Readers' Guide to Periodical Literature (H.W. Wilson, 1901–)
Launched in 1901, this long-running index provides citations of reviews published in popular U.S. magazines. To find citations to reviews, look under the playwright's name.

Web Indexes and Abstracts

Applied Science and Technology Index (H.W. Wilson, 1983–)
Online database adapted from the print index featuring citations and abstracts to 562 trade and professional periodicals published since 1983.

Art Abstracts (H.W. Wilson, 1929–)
Offering "the most sweeping coverage of arts and artists available," this electronic version of the *Art Index* (Volumes 1–32) features citations listed in the print version to international journals published throughout the world. Coverage includes English-language periodicals, museum bulletins, and yearbooks, as well as periodicals published in French, Italian, German, Japanese, Spanish, Dutch, and Swedish. Theater journals indexed include *Entertainment Design* (1999–), *TCI: Theatre Crafts International* (1994–), and *TD&T: Theatre, Design & Technology* (1998–).

Arts and Humanities Citation Index (Web of Science, 1978–)
Interdisciplinary index offering good coverage of theater and related periodicals worldwide, featuring citations of articles in more than 6,000 journals. Citations are searchable by topic, author, or reference. About 15 leading film journals are included, including *American Film* and *Wide Angle.*

Essay and General Literature Index (H.W. Wilson, 1985–)
Based on the print index of the same name, this online version offers information on some 65,000 essays from more than 5,000 anthologies and collections published in the United States, Canada, and Great Britain. Approximately 320 volumes are indexed annually, in addition to 20 selected annuals and serials. Articles are searchable by keyword, author, subject, title, date of publication, or any combination. Retrospective coverage is from 1985 to the present.

Humanities Abstracts (H.W. Wilson, 1983–)
Considered one of the most comprehensive resources in its field, Humanities Abstracts offers abstracts and bibliographic indexing of well-known scholarly journals and lesser-known periodicals in the humanities. Indexes many more journals not indexed in Art Abstracts, including *American Drama* (2001–), *American Theatre* (1995–), *Canadian Theatre Review* (1995–), *Drama* (1983–), *The Drama Review* (1983–), *New Theatre Quarterly* (1988–), *Performing Arts Journal* (1983–), *Plays and Players* (1983–), *TDR* (1988–), *Theatre History Studies* (1995–), and *Theatre Journal* (1983).

International Index to the Performing Arts (IIPA) (Chadwyck-Healey, 1864–)
Popular index covering a broad spectrum of arts and entertainment periodicals and such related fields as broadcast arts, comedy, circus performance, dance, drama, film, magic, musical theater, opera, puppetry, storytelling, and more. Citations cover the contents of more than 225 scholarly and popular performing arts periodicals from 1998 to the present. It also indexes other published items, such as biographical profiles, conference papers, discographies, interviews, obituaries, reviews, and events. Retrospective citations for 46 periodicals begin with 1864. An alternate version, IIPA Full Text, features full-text indexing to 34 performing arts titles. Both IIPA and IIPA Full Text cover such respected theater and dance journals as *American Drama, Dance Chronicle, Opera News, Shakespeare Quarterly,* and *Theatre Journal.*

International Index to Music Periodicals (IIMP) (Chadwyck-Healey, 1874–)
Abstracts of articles from more than 300 international music periodicals. Focuses on articles in journals, magazines, and newspapers (including *The New York Times* and the *Washington Post*). Coverage starts with the first issues of leading musical journals, such as *Anuario Musical, Early Music, Music and Letters,* and *Journal of the Royal Musical Association.* Retrospective coverage of some titles goes back to 1874, with most coverage from 1996 to the present. The database is also offered in a full-text format called IIMP Full Text.

MLA International Bibliography (Modern Language Association, 1963–)
Available through EBSCOHost and InfoTrac, this international index, formerly known as the print index *PMLA Bibliography* (1921–68), offers citations only to critical scholarship literature on folklore, language, and linguistics, including articles, analyses, and reviews in journals and monographs. Subjects are keyword searchable.

Periodical Contents Index (PCI) (ProQuest, 1770–1995)
Indexes citations with abstracts of more than 14 million articles in more than 4,000 humanities and social sciences periodicals, many dating back to the 1800s, and some even earlier. Contains abstracts and full-text articles from dance and theater journals, such as *Dance Magazine* and *Shakespeare Quarterly.*

Readers' Guide Full Text (H.W. Wilson, 1983–)
A source of information on cultural history for more than 100 years, this electronic version of the popular print index provides high-quality indexing of more than 375 periodicals and general interest magazines, with full-text articles, including theater reviews.

SELECTED FULL-TEXT ARTICLE DATABASES

Academic Search Elite (EBSCOHost, index: 1980– , full text: 1990–)
Covering a variety of disciplines, Academic Search Elite is a good source for reviews and general articles on theater and stage personalities culled from popular magazines and some scholarly journals.

Academic Search Premier (EBSCOHost; index: 1980– , full text: 1992–)
Another good source of entertainment reviews, this major database contains full-text articles from many academic journals, such as *Cineaste* and *Journal of Performance and Art,* and popular magazines, including *People, Time,* and *Rolling Stone.* Coverage varies by title.

Art Full Text (H.W. Wilson, index: 1984– , full text: 1997–)
Abstracts and indexes, with some full text, a wide array of peer-reviewed journals that are international in scope, plus links to Web sites of many articles, from 1997 to the present. As with the print version, this online edition indexes only a handful of journals, mostly geared towards the technical side of theater arts.

Expanded Academic ASAP (InfoTrac, 1980–)
One of the best sources for theater reviews and theater criticism, Expanded Academic ASAP contains citations and full-text articles from selected popular magazines, scholarly journals, and major newspapers. Articles cover a wide range of theater topics, as well as related subjects in the arts, humanities, and sciences. Subjects are keyword searchable; to search, combine the name of the production with the phrase "theater reviews." This database includes full-text access to the following magazines and journals: *American Theatre, Back Stage, Dance Magazine, Down Beat, Early Music, Opera News, Performing Arts Journal, TDR, Theatre Journal, Theatre Research International*, among others, from 1994 to the present.

JSTOR (Journal Storage Project, 1996–)
This electronic archive contains the complete back files of 117 scholarly journals in the arts, humanities, and the social sciences, with many titles extending back to the 1800s. Options allow users to browse journals online or retrieve full text using title or subject search. The journals in this collection have been digitized back to the first issue published, and more than 4 million pages are available.

LexisNexis Academic Universe (LexisNexis, 1977–)
LexisNexis Academic Universe includes full-text articles from virtually thousands of newspapers, magazines, trade journals, industry publications, and more published in the United States and abroad. This easy-to-use database is a good source for finding current information on actors, performers, and reviews of performances. Reviews are searchable under the "General News Topics" category, and under "News/Arts and Sports/Book, Movie, Music and Play Reviews."

Periodical Abstracts Research II Edition with Full Text (UMI ProQuest, 1986)
Another solid source is this full-text edition of Periodical Abstracts Research featuring abstracts and some full-text articles to reviews and general articles about stage and theater. Out of some 1,600 general reference publications represented, PAR indexes articles from approximately 396 humanities periodicals in the field.

ProjectMUSE (Johns Hopkins University Press, 1990–)
One of the best collections on the Web today, with more than 100 electronic journals published by major universities, including film, television, mass media, and theater arts studies. Coverage dates back 10 years but varies by journal. Users can browse or search journals by title or subjects. Among the full-text journals featured are *Asian Theatre Journal* (1999–), *Discourse* (2000–), *Performing Arts Journal* (1996–), *TDR: The Drama Review* (1999–), *Theater Journal* (1996–), and *Theatre Topics* (1996–).

ProQuest Direct (ProQuest, 1986–)
ProQuest Direct indexes more than 1,100 scholarly periodicals, as well as newspapers and general-interest magazines, from 1986 to the present. In most cases, full-text articles are available from such journals as *American Theater* and *Theatre Journal*.

SELECTED PERIODICALS

American Theatre (New York: Theatre Communications Group, 1984– , monthly)
This highly regarded monthly, published by the nonprofit Theatre Communications Groups of New York, primarily focuses on professional theater. Published in each issue are two or three major features, including actor profiles, articles on legal and professional issues affecting the theater arts community, and articles covering trends and events in theater. Online access is provided to certain articles from back issues since 1999. To access, visit http://www.tcg.org/frames/am_theatre/fs_am_theatre.htm (click on "Archives").

Back Stage (New York: Back Stage Publications, 1960– , weekly)
Providing an inside look into the performing arts since 1960, this weekly trade paper covers East Coast theater. Coverage includes the latest industry news, feature stories, reviews, casting notices, and advice articles for industry professionals and students. A collection of feature stories is accessible online at http://www.backstage.com/backstage/features/index.jsp.

Drama: The Journal of National Drama (Shaftesbury, U.K.: National Drama, 1993– , biannual)
Designed for educators and practitioners in theater arts, *Drama* is the official publication of National Drama in Great Britain. This scholarly journal, published biannually, offers a forum for educators and practitioners worldwide to discuss theories and practices, opinions and criticisms, debate key issues, and share new research in the field.

Early Theatre (Hamilton, Ont.: McMaster University, 1998– , biannual)
A journal associated with the records of early English drama, *Early Theatre* is a peer-reviewed print journal, now published biannually by the Department of English at McMaster University in Hamilton, Ontario, devoted to drama and theater history of England, Scotland, Ireland, and Wales. This scholarly journal publishes research studies, articles, and notes on the performance history, as well as literary and analytical articles about individual performances.

Performing Arts Journal (New York: Performing Arts Journal Publications, 1976–97; Baltimore, Md.: Published for PAJ Publications by the Johns Hopkins University Press, 1998– , three times a year)
Originally titled the *Performing Arts Journal* from 1976 to 1997 (Volumes 1–19), this scholarly journal, renamed *PAJ: A Journal of Performance and Art* in January 1998, explores new directions and new work in dance, film, music, performance, theater, and the visual arts. Published three times yearly, *PAJ* includes essays and critical commentaries, interviews and book reviews, artists' writings and festival reports, and performance texts and plays in the performing arts. Contents of current and past issues are abstracted and indexed in such popular online indexes as Arts and Humanities Citation Index, ISI Current Contents, Film Literature Index, Humanities Index, and International Index to the Performing Arts.

Playbill (New York: American Theatre Press, 1982– , monthly)
This monthly print magazine covers the professional theater, especially New York theater. Each issue contains feature articles and columns by or about theater personalities, engaging editorials, and travel, fashion, and dining news aimed at active theatergoers. In addition, *Playbill* offers free access to information published on its Web site (http://www.playbill.com/), such as news, features, theater listings, and other resources, including box-office grosses and a theater awards database.

Shakespeare Quarterly (Washington, D.C.: Folger Shakespeare Library, 1950– , quarterly)
First published in 1950 by the Shakespeare Association of America, this quarterly journal is the foremost publication covering all aspects of Shakespeare studies, including play criticisms and theater histories. Issues include essays and research studies, reviews of books, films, and stage productions, and criticism and scholarship of Shakespeare-related works.

Stage Directions (West Sacramento, Calif.: SMW Communications; New York: Lifestyle Media, 1988– , monthly)
With members of community, regional, and academic theater including producers, lightning technicians, and set designers among its readers, *Stage Directions* offers practical help to people involved in theater production, featuring articles about new strategies, ideas, and solutions to common problems, as well as book, CD, and play reviews.

TDR: The Drama Review (New York: New York University, School of Arts, 1968–87; Cambridge, Mass.: MIT Press, 1988– , quarterly)
This widely read, highly acclaimed scholarly journal is devoted to serious study and debate on various kinds of performances, including dance, theater, performance art, popular entertainment, and sports. Published by the New York University School of Arts from 1967 to 1997 and by MIT Press since 1988, each issue features articles, commentaries, interviews, texts of performances, and translations of important works on contemporary performing arts and performing theory. Bibliographic citations with abstracts and full-text articles, in some cases, are indexed in such well-known library databases as Arts and Humanities Citation Index, Expanded Academic ASAP, Humanities Index, International Index to the Performing Arts, and MLA International Bibliography.

Theatre Journal (Baltimore, Md.: Johns Hopkins University Press in cooperation with the Association for Theatre in Higher Education, 1941– , quarterly)
The scholarly *Theatre Journal*, published quarterly by Johns Hopkins University Press in association with the Association of Theater in Higher Education, offers a global view of all aspects of theater arts. Issues feature many social and historical studies and critical reviews of productions, written by noted scholars and practitioners. Issues and contents are indexed and abstracted in ProjectMUSE.

Theatre Topics (Baltimore, Md.: Johns Hopkins University Press in cooperation with the Association for Theatre in Higher Education, 1991– , semi annual)
Hailed as "an excellent addition to literature of drama," this scholarly, peer-reviewed electronic journal, accessible through ProjectMUSE (1996–), features timely articles on a vast number of practical, performance-oriented subjects of interest to theater educators and practitioners and scholars and students of theater. First published in March 1991, it offers articles that reflect the theory and practice of acting, community-based theater, design, directing, dramaturgy, performance studies, and theater pedagogy. *Theatre Topics* is indexed and abstracted in several article databases including American Humanities Index, Annual Bibliography of English Language and Literature, Education Index, and MLA International Bibliography.

Variety (New York: Variety Pub. Co., 1905– , weekly)
Published weekly, *Variety*, the longest-running industry trade paper, features news and reviews covering all areas of show business, including Broadway and off-Broadway players and shows abroad, as well as regional and New York theater productions. It is a good source for theater industry news casting and box-office gross information each week.

SELECTED WEB SITES

Artslynx International Theatre Resources (http://www.artslynx.org/theatre/index.htm)
An easy-to-navigate, well-organized resource listing a variety of topics with links to relevant Web sites on acting, awards, books, children's theater, costume design, directing, dramaturgy, ethnic theater, history, journals, libraries, and much more.

A Brief Guide to Internet Resources in Theatre and Performance Studies (http://www.stetson.edu/departments/csata/thr_guid.html)
Celebrating its 12th anniversary in 2005, this Web site is actually one of the most comprehensive listings of content and links on theater and performance studies.

Drama and Theater Connections (http://personal.uncc.edu/jvanoate/theater/)
Compiled by librarian Judith Van Noate of the J. Murrey Atkins Library at UNC-Charlotte, the well-organized, A-to-Z directory features a large collection of drama and theater arts Web sites.

TheaterPedia (http://www.perspicacity.com/elactheatre/library)
A free service of East Los Angeles College Theatre Arts, this online library and directory allows users to search documents and sources and to browse theater-related subject indexes on playwrights, plays by author or title, play texts, theater terms, theater characters, theater people, and other Internet tools.

Theatre Resources—Rhodes (http://www.rhodes.edu/InformationServices/ResearchandCollections/SubjectGuides/Subject-Guide-Theater.cfm)
Maintained and developed at the Rhodes College library, this categorized directory lists a myriad of online resources and databases covering all areas

of theater arts, such as awards, general collections, drama resources, electronic journals, reviews, theater home pages, and technical resources.

Theatre Reviews Limited (http://www.theatrereviews.com)
Online source providing free access to reviews of recent Broadway, Off-Broadway, and Off-Off Broadway shows in New York City.

The WWW Virtual Library Theatre and Drama (http://vl-theatre.com/)
This multicultural, multilingual Web site features resources from more than 50 countries on all aspects of theater, designed for amateurs, professionals, and students of all ages.

Yahoo's Theatre Pages (http://dir.yahoo.com/Arts/Performing_Arts/Theatre)
Comprehensive listing of theater Web pages and an alphabetical directory of potential sites.

Women's Studies

A vast accumulation of timely and historical research on women exists, discussing their changing roles in society, their standards of living, their sacrifices, suffrage, and their accomplishments in various areas and in every period of history. Thanks to a wide array of print and electronic sources, researchers today can learn all about women of the past and women of today.

There is little about the history or psychology of women that isn't researchable via books, articles, newsletters, professional journals, studies by government and nonprofit agencies, and comprehensive reports on policies and practices of and against women. For further study of this expanding discipline, the following is a list of recommended sources.

SELECTED BOOKS AND REFERENCES

Bibliographies

The Columbia Guide to American Women in the Nineteenth Century, by Catherine Clinton and Christine Lunardini, 331 pages (New York: Columbia University Press, 2000)
This book covers its subject matter with engaging biographical essays, a chronology of events, and detailed overviews with lists of primary source materials for further reference.

Reader's Guide to Women's Studies, edited by Eleanor B. Amico, 732 pages (Chicago: Fitzroy Dearborn, 1998)
Easy-to-use subject index to a diverse collection of books about women, with substantial bibliographic essays.

Chronologies, Encyclopedias, and Histories

Chronology of Women's History, by Kirstin Olsen, 506 pages (Westport, Conn.: Greenwood Press, 1994)
Provides international year-by-year coverage of the landmark events in women's history, from 20,000 B.C. to 1993. Areas discussed include athletics and exploration, activism, business and industry, education and scholarship, general status and daily life, government, law, literature, visual arts, military, performing arts and entertainment, science and medicine, and religion.

Encyclopedia of Women's History in America, 2nd Ed., by Kathryn Cullen-DuPont, 418 pages (Facts On File, 2000)
This authoritative encyclopedia covers the full scope of events and issues that affected women throughout American history. Topics include major court cases, significant legislation, important organizations, and influential women. Lists of bibliographic sources follow each entry. An appendix offers complete texts of reports, documents, and recent court cases and legislation.

Feminism: A Reference Handbook, by Judith Harlan, 308 pages (Santa Barbara, Calif.: ABC-CLIO, 1998)
Offered in both print and electronic form, this handbook details a wide range of subjects important to the study of feminism and women's history. Included are biographical sketches of famous feminists, a chronology of important events, facts about feminist issues, a directory of organizations, print sources and nonprint sources, and overviews on such subjects as economics, education, politics, and social changes for women.

Handbook of American Women's History, 2nd Ed., edited by Angela M. Howard and Frances M. Kavenik, 724 pages (Thousand Oaks, Calif.: SAGE Publications, 2000)
This revised and updated edition offers brief articles about significant people, events, books and periodicals, concepts, and organizations in the history of American women. Each entry provides relevant definitions, discussion of significant historical facts, and a brief bibliography of sources. The book's introduction also references other established sources in women's studies, including monographs, and collections of primary sources beneficial to students and researchers.

The Reader's Companion to U.S. Women's History, edited by Wilma Mankiller, 696 pages (Boston, Mass.: Houghton Mifflin Co., 1998)
Offering a strong feminist perspective, this book features 400 in-depth articles by some 300 leading historians examining a broad spectrum of issues.

Routledge International Encyclopedia of Women: Global Women's Issues and Knowledge, edited by Cheris Kramarae and Dale Spender, 4 vols., 2,288 pages (New York: Routledge, 2000)
This four-volume reference set extensively details the concerns, theories, and practices of women from a global point of view. Entries focus on regional topics and feminist ideas but offer no biographical information on leading feminists and pioneers in the women's movement. However, each article-length entry features a list of references for further reading.

Women's Issues, edited by Margaret McFadden, 3 vols., 1,041 pages (Pasadena, Calif.: Salem Press, 1997)
This three-volume encyclopedia has much to offer for students and researchers studying women's issues. Each section features entries extensively cross-referenced to other related topics. Additional entries include annotated bibliographies of major sources, and appendixes offer other useful information, such as directories of research centers for women's studies and women's organizations and a chronology of events in U.S. women's history.

Women's Studies Encyclopedia, 3rd Ed., edited by Helen Tierney, 3 vols., 1,607 pages (Westport, Conn.: Greenwood Press, 1999)
Revised and expanded three-volume set with essay-length entries covering women's contributions to art, literature, philosophy, learning, religion, science, and others. Each article ends with a list of references and suggested sources for further study or more detailed information.

Statistical References

American Women: Who They Are and How They Live, 2nd Ed., 413 pages (Ithaca, N.Y.: New Strategist Publications, 2002)
This impressive reference contains statistical tables, arranged by category, on a variety of subjects relating to women, including attitudes, education, health, income, labor force, living arrangements, spending, and more. Referenced after each table is the source of data in context. Brief summaries introduce each chapter.

Statistical Handbook on Women in America, 2nd Ed., compiled and edited by Cynthia M. Taeuber, 354 pages (Phoenix, Ariz.: Oryx Press, 1996)
Useful for making historical comparisons of the social and historical progress of women, this revised and expanded edition, presented in statistical tables format, offers a portrait of American women based on government sources, including U.S. census data, among others.

SELECTED ARTICLE INDEXES AND ABSTRACTS

Printed Indexes and Abstracts

The Alternative Press Index (College Park, Md.: Alternative Press Center, 1969–)
Indexes the contents of nearly 200 leftist and radical English-language periodicals, some offering feminist perspectives.

America: History and Life (Santa Barbara, Calif.: ABC-CLIO, 1964–88)
Primary print index to materials for research in American history, including social and cultural history. Abstracted and indexed are journal articles, dissertations, and book and other media reviews from more than 2,400 journals in 40 different languages. Coverage begins with July 1964. The first 10-volume index was titled, *America: History of Life,* from July 1964 to winter 1973. Four additional 15-volume sets followed, namely: *America: History and Life, Part A: Article Abstracts and Citations; America: History and Life, Part B: Index to Book Reviews; America: History and Life, Part C: American History Bibliography, Books, Articles and Dissertations;* and *America: History and Life, Part D: Annual Index.* Each set covered material from 1974 to 1988. Beginning in 1989, with Volume 26, the index returned to its original title. The entire series is also available online from 1982 to the present.

The Chicana Studies Index: Twenty Years of Gender Research (Berkeley: Chicano Studies Library Publications Unit, University of California at Berkeley, 1992)
Subject, author, and title index to approximately 1,150 journal articles, book articles, books, dissertations, and reports on the Chicana experience from 1971 to 1991.

Feminist Periodicals: A Current Listing of Contents (Madison, Wisc.: Women's Studies Librarian, 1981–present)
Reprints the tables of contents from more than 100 feminist periodicals, including popular magazines and scholarly journals—such as *Affilia: Journal of Women and Social Work* and *Yale Journal of Law and Feminism*—not covered in other indexes.

Hispanic American Periodicals Index (HAPI) (Los Angeles: UCLA Latin American Center Publications, University of California, 1970–)
For feminist and women's studies research dealing with Latina publications, this hardcover index, also offered as a Web database, features bibliographic citations of more than 400 social science and humanities journals published worldwide. Citations cover articles, book reviews, Latin American studies, Latina/Latino studies, original literary works, analysis of current political, economic, and social issues, and Central and South America, the Caribbean, Mexico, U.S.-Mexico border issues, and Hispanics in the United States.

Historical Abstracts (Santa Barbara, Calif.: ABC-CLIO, 1955–2000)
Also offered online (1960–), this index abstracts scholarly journals and dissertations on world history (except U.S. and Canadian history) from 1450 to the present, including social and cultural history.

Humanities Index (New York: H.W. Wilson, 1974–)
Indexes major scholarly journals in the humanities; also offered as an online database from 1984 to the present.

Index to Black Periodicals (Boston, Mass.: G.K. Hall & Co., 1950–99; Detroit: Gale Group, 2000–)
Published annually, this series, previously titled *Index to Selected Periodicals, Index to Periodical Articles By and About Negroes,* and *Index to Periodical Articles By and About Blacks,* indexes by subject or by author up to 40 general interest and scholarly African-American periodicals in each issue. Coverage includes poetry, short stories, and reviews of books, film, music, records, and theater. Boston-based G.K. Hall & Co. published this series from 1950 to 1999. In 2000, the index was retitled the *G.K. Hall Index to Black Periodicals.* It is now published by the Gale Group.

Journal of Women's History Guide to Periodical Literature, compiled by Gayle V. Fischer, 501 pages (Bloomington: Indiana University Press, 1992)
Index to periodical literature, organized by subject, from 1980 to 1990. Includes a lengthy introduction on the discipline of women's history.

The Lesbian Periodical Index, compiled and edited by Clare Potter, 413 pages (Tallahassee, Fla.: Naiad Press, 1986)
Indexes more than 42 lesbian periodicals by author and subject from 1947 through 1985, with separate sections for lesbian writings, book reviews, and visual art.

SAGE Family Studies Abstracts (Beverly Hills, Calif.: SAGE Publications, 1979–)
Quarterly abstracts of current literature on family studies and related issues from hundreds of books and articles. Provides concise, descriptive summaries

and bibliographic information on a host of subjects including child care, ethnic and cross-cultural relations, family relations, gender roles, individual relations, separation and divorce, sexuality, and much more.

Social Sciences Index (New York: H.W. Wilson, 1974–)
Indexes articles in major English-language scholarly journals in the various social sciences, including such subjects as area studies, family studies, policy studies, and women's studies. The index is also available online (1983 to the present).

Women's Studies Index (Boston, Mass.: G.K. Hall & Co., 1991–99; Detroit: Gale Group, 2000–)
Indexes mostly but not exclusively North American women's journals, including popular, feminist, lesbian, and scholarly publications. G.K. Hall published the original 10-volume set of this series with coverage from 1989 to 1998. The series is known as the *G.K. Hall's Women's Studies Index*, published by the Gale Group, since 1999.

Women Studies Abstracts (Rush, N.Y.: Women Studies Abstracts, 1972–)
Quarterly abstracts that cite both popular and scholarly periodicals from a broad range of disciplines not normally identified in mainstream humanities and social sciences indexes. Indexed are journal articles, book and other media reviews, and special issues of journals and reports.

Web Indexes and Abstracts

The Alternative Press Index (OCLC/Alternative Press Center, 1991–)
Web version of the subject index to more than 200 leftist and radical English language periodicals, some of which are feminist or women's periodicals.

America: History and Life (ABC-CLIO, 1960–)
Online edition with complete bibliographic citations and abstracts of articles on the history of the United States and Canada.

Current Contents (Institute for Scientific Information, 1993–)
Complete tables of contents and holdings information for journals in many fields.

Dissertation Abstracts International (UMI, 1861–)
Provides bibliographic citations and abstracts of doctoral dissertations and masters' theses completed at more than 1,000 accredited colleges and universities worldwide. Abstracts are included for doctoral records since July 1980; coverage is from January 1861 to the present. Covers approximately 3,000 subject areas. Available online and on CD-ROM; both databases are based on the print editions *Comprehensive Dissertation Index, Dissertation Abstracts International* (A, B, and C), *Masters Abstracts International*, and *American Doctoral Dissertations.*

Family Studies Database (National Information Services Corp., 1970–present)
Perhaps the world's most comprehensive database in the fields of family science, human ecology, and human development, containing approximately

181,000 abstracts and bibliographic records drawn from more than 1,000 professional journals, books, conference papers, government reports, and popular literature covering the family and social sciences. Contents include all of the records from the discontinued print index *Inventory of Marriage and Family Literature*. About 9,000 new records are added annually to this CD-ROM database.

GenderWatch (ProQuest, 1978–)
Full-text, keyword-searchable database of articles, booklets and pamphlets, conference proceedings, magazines, newspapers, newsletters, papers, regional publications, and government and special reports from 140 international sources devoted to women's and gender issues since the mid-1970s. Subjects focus on the impact of gender in all subject areas, including business, education, literature and the arts, health sciences, history, political science, public policy, sociology and contemporary culture, gender and women's studies, and much more.

Hispanic American Periodicals Index (UCLA Latin America Center, 1970–)
Web equivalent of the print edition containing bibliographic citations and full-text articles, reviews, and more in more than 400 social science and humanities journals published worldwide, with most articles in Spanish, English, or Portuguese. Searchable by language or keywords, such as author, title, subject, or journal title. Coverage is from 1970 to the present.

Historical Abstracts (ABC-CLIO, 1955–2000)
Complete reference guide featuring citations with abstracts of articles on world history from 1450 to the present, excluding the United States and Canada, which are covered in the America: History and Life database. Contents are derived from the print counterparts *Historical Abstracts: Part A, Modern History Abstracts* (1450–1914), and *Twentieth Century Abstracts* (1914 to present).

International Index to Black Periodicals (Chadwyck-Healey, 1902–)
Comprehensive online index offering abstracts, citations, and full text of more than 150 scholarly and popular periodicals spanning cultural, economic, historical, religious, social, and political issues in the field of black studies. Full text is from more than 24 core periodicals. Retrospective bibliographic records are from 1902 to 1991, with abstracts and citations of current literature from 1998 to the present.

PAIS International (OCLC Public Affairs Information Service, 1972–)
Selected subject index of books, hearings, gray literature, government publications, Internet resources, periodicals, reports, and other publications from 120 countries focused on political science, public policy, international relations, and related subjects. Includes materials in English, French, German, Italian, Portuguese, and Spanish with English-language abstracts and subject headings, plus links to Web resources and publisher Web sites.

Periodical Abstracts (ProQuest, 1986–)
Part of the ProQuest Direct database, this Web version provides comprehensive abstracting, indexing, and full-text articles from more than 1,800 key publications covering a variety of subject areas, including culture, current

events, general interest, history, sociology, and women's studies. Earliest coverage dates back to 1986, with many publications included from the 1990s.

PsycINFO (American Psychological Association, 1887–)
Abstracts and indexes professional and academic literature, such as books, book chapters, dissertations, technical reports, and more than 1,400 journals in psychology and related fields published in 50 countries.

Social Science Citation Index (Thomson ISI, 1980–)
Current and retrospective bibliographic information, author abstracts, and references found in more than 1,700 leading social sciences journals covering more than 50 disciplines.

Social Services Abstracts (Cambridge Scientific Abstracts, 1980–)
Provides citations and abstracts of current research focused on community development, human services, social welfare, social policy, and social work published in more than 1,600 periodicals. Abstracts cover journal articles, dissertations, and citations of book reviews.

Social Work Abstracts (National Association of Social Workers, 1977–)
Abstracts and indexes articles from hundreds of scholarly journals devoted to social work and related fields, including such topics as aging, child and family welfare, homelessness, substance abuse, and more from 1977 to the present.

Sociological Abstracts (Sociological Abstracts, Inc./Cambridge Scientific Abstracts, 1963–)
Indexes and abstracts the international literature in sociology and related disciplines in the social and behavioral sciences. Includes abstracts of books, book chapters, conference papers, dissertations and journal articles from more than 1,700 publications.

Women's Studies International (National Information Services Corp., 1972–)
Combining the contents of *Women's Studies Abstracts, Women's Studies Database, Women's Studies Librarian, POPLINE Subset on Women,* and several bibliographies, this individual database, updated twice yearly, contains citations and abstracts of 2,000 periodical sources in arts and humanities, business, education, history, international relations, political science and economy, and sociology. Content includes books, book chapters, bulletins, dissertations, journals, newspapers, newsletters, proceedings, reports, theses, dissertations, Web sites and Web documents.

Women's Studies on Disc (G.K. Hall & Co.,1988–)
Indexes popular magazines and scholarly journals, including articles, book reviews, women's studies anthologies, women's periodicals and newspapers (1700s to 1981), and women's movement references and resources.

Women Studies Abstracts (Rush Publishing Company/National Information Services Corp. 1972–)
Women Studies Abstracts abstracts articles from 35 journals covering a wide range of subjects in the area of women's studies. Contents include more than 75,330 bibliographic records, with 3,000 more added yearly.

SELECTED FULL-TEXT ARTICLE DATABASES

Contemporary Women's Issues (Gale Group, 1992–)
Contemporary Women's Issues provides full-text Web access to journals, newsletters, and research reports from nonprofit groups, government and international agencies, and fact sheets with global information focused on cultural, social, and human rights issues affecting women in more than 150 countries. Updated biweekly, this database covers such disciplines as business administration, education, health, political science, psychology, and sociology.

Expanded Academic ASAP (InfoTrac, 1980–)
Covers all academic disciplines, including the arts, humanities, social sciences, business, science, and technology.

General Reference Center (InfoTrac, 1980–)
Also known as InfoTrac, General Reference Center features mostly full-text articles and abstracts of articles found in hundreds of magazines, newspapers, and reference books. Updated daily, coverage is from 1980 to the present.

Ingenta (Ingenta, Inc., 1988–)
Online database and comprehensive index of journal literature containing more than 14 million articles from more than 26,000 journals, with coverage back to 1988.

LexisNexis Academic Universe (LexisNexis, 1977–)
Full-text article database covering current events, legal information, and news related to women and women's rights.

ProjectMUSE (Johns Hopkins University Press, 1990–)
Contains the contents of more than 100 electronic full-text journals by a wide array of academic publishers. Covers literature and criticism, history, the visual and performing arts, cultural studies, education, political science, gender studies, and more.

SELECTED PERIODICALS

Feminist Studies: FS (College Park, Md.: Feminist Studies, 1972– , three times a year)
Beginning publication in summer 1972, *Feminist Studies: FS* is dedicated to publishing "serious writing of a critical, scholarly, speculative, and political nature." Each issue includes commentaries, manifestos, position papers, reports, and strategies for change representing a range of disciplines. Tables of contents are viewable online from 1981 to the present. To access, visit http://www.feministstudies.org/.

Journal of Women's History (Bloomington, Ind.: Indiana University Press, 1989–2003)
Originally published three times a year by Indiana University Press, this serious scholarly journal is focused on women's history and women's experience. Tables of contents can be found at http://iupjournals.org/jwh/jwtoc.html. Full-text contents of the journal are available on ProjectMUSE from 1989 to the last issue in 2003.

MS. (New York: Matilda Publications, 1972–89; Lang Communications, 1990–98; Liberty Media, 1998–2001; Arlington, Va.: Feminist Majority Foundation, 2001– , monthly)
Enduring four different owners and sporadic financial instability since its debut in 1972, *MS.* magazine has helped shape contemporary feminism, and advanced issues relating to women's rights, women's status, and women's points of view. Founded by Gloria Steinem and others, *MS.* provides in-depth analysis and reporting of international women's issues. Subjects include environmental feminism, women's work styles, and the politics of emerging technologies.

Psychology of Women Quarterly (New York: Cambridge University Press, 1976– , quarterly)
This scholarly feminist journal features qualitative and quantitative research, critical reviews, theoretical articles, and book reviews focused on the psychology of women and gender. Topics relate to career choice and training, physical and mental health, physical, sexual, and psychological abuse, prejudice and discrimination, violence and harassment, as well as a variety of ethnic and minority issues. Issues are indexed and abstracted in such online article databases as Academic Search Elite, Expanded Academic ASAP, Current Contents, Feminist Periodicals, and others.

Signs: Journal of Women and Culture in Society (Chicago: University of Chicago Press, 1975– , quarterly)
Recognized as a leading international journal in women's studies, *Signs,* first published in 1975, publishes analytical and scholarly articles discussing such issues as class, culture, gender, race, and sexuality with regard to women. Published quarterly by the University of Chicago Press, *Signs* focuses on a wide range of disciplines, theories, and methodologies. Issues are now available in print and online. Tables of contents of past issues since 1996 are viewable online at http://www.journals.uchicago.edu/Signs/home.html.

The Women's Review of Books (Wellesley, Mass.: Wellesley College Center for Research on Women, 1983– , monthly)
Published monthly except August, *The Women's Review of Books* reviews the latest books by and about women, including fiction, nonfiction, and poetry. Each issue includes commentaries and criticisms, interviews, letters, and lists of new books. Back issues are unavailable online, but the tables of contents are, from 2000 to the present. To access, visit http://www.wellesley.edu/WomensReview/.

Women's Studies (New York: Taylor & Francis, Ltd., 1972– , eight times a year)
An interdisciplinary journal published eight times yearly offering a scholarly and critical review of women in all fields, including anthropology, art, history, law, literature, political science, and sociology. Issues also feature book and film reviews and women's poetry. Tables of contents of current issues are available through Ingenta.

Women's Studies Quarterly (New York: Feminist Press, 1981– , quarterly)
Originally published as a four-page newsletter, this leading journal offers scholarly discussions of issues of great importance to educators specializing in the field of women's studies. Published by The Feminist Press at The City University of New York, the journal features articles, bibliographies, classroom teaching aids, essays, sources for course and program development, and various themes of interest to women's studies practitioners with an international perspective.

SELECTED WEB SITES

American Women's History: A Research Guide (http://frank.mtsu.edu/~kmiddlet/history/women.html)
Great site developed by Ken Middleton of the Todd Library at Middle Tennessee State University listing digital collections, bibliographies, book reviews, and links to biographical sources, online journals, and other resources celebrating American women's history.

Ithaca College Women's Studies (http://www.ithaca.edu/hs/wsp/Links.htm)
Features a variety of resources with links concerning feminist theory and women's history.

National Women's History Project (http://www.nwhp.org/)
Recognizing and celebrating women's accomplishments throughout the years, the National Women's History Project, an educational nonprofit organization, provides direct access on its Web site to women's history information, news and events, and other resources.

Women in the United States (http://www.census.gov/population/www/socdemo/women.html)
Offers gender-specific data and information—by geographic location—derived from the 1997 Economic Census, the American Community Survey, the 1990 Decennial Census, and the Census 2000 Dress Rehearsal.

Women's Studies Database (http://www.mith2.umd.edu/WomensStudies/)
Offered by the University of Maryland, this Web site for women's studies researchers and students alike contains links to bibliographies, conferences, history, film reviews, reading and reference rooms, and academic papers, articles, books, and other resources.

Women's Studies Online Resources (http://research.umbc.edu/~korenman/wmst/)
Annotated directory of women's studies with Web links to women- or gender-related discussion lists, and women's studies programs and research centers worldwide. Site is maintained by the University of Maryland Baltimore County's Women's Studies Program.

Women's Studies Resources (http://www.york.ac.uk/services/library/subjects/womenint.htm)
Extensive collection developed by the University of York Library of links to Internet resources on women's studies in the areas of health, history, science and technology, and women's rights.

Women's Studies/Women's Issues Resource Sites (http://umbc7.umbc.edu/~korenman/wmst/links.html)
Highly acclaimed site, maintained by Joan Korenman at Michigan State University, that contains a list of Web sites and other resources with useful information about women's studies and women's issues.

WSSLinks: Women and Gender Studies Web Sites (http://libr.org/wss/WSSLinks/index.html)
Developed and maintained by Women's Studies Section of the Association of College and Research Libraries, this site lists a variety of sites and resources by individual subject devoted to women's studies.

Section IV

USING YOUR SOURCES

35

Citing Your Sources

After completing your research, your most difficult task lies ahead: Writing your paper and incorporating your research into your written document. Your instructor will emphasize the importance of providing documentation when writing your essay, term paper, or written project. This serves two very important purposes: (1) It shows the breadth of evidence you discovered to support your paper; and (2) It adds credibility to your paper by citing documented proof.

Good writers always acknowledge their sources. In other words, they note where their information came from. You must do the same as you develop your paper. Citing your sources gives credit where credit is due for information that you would not be privy to otherwise. As a researcher, your role is not only to share your findings but to show how you uncovered them and through what channels.

AVOIDING PLAGIARISM

One of the biggest problems facing high school and college students today is plagiarism. By properly citing your sources and understanding how to synthesize your information you can avoid plagiarizing.

Simply put, plagiarism is passing off the ideas or words of someone else as your own—committing intellectual theft. This issue has become much more serious with the advent of the Internet. Some students think it is perfectly acceptable to "cut and paste" materials, ideas, or words from work published online into their own.

The New Webster's Encyclopedic Dictionary of the English Language defines *plagiarism* as "the unauthorized use of the language and thoughts of another author and the representation of them as one's own." With the phenomenal growth of Internet "paper mills," companies that sell term papers and essays, schools have begun to crack down on intellectual dishonesty. Serious consequences have resulted, such as failing grades and disciplinary action, including suspension and/or expulsion.

Plagiarism fails to acknowledge the original creator appropriately, and thus creates an act of impropriety or even crime that can easily be avoided. Examples of plagiarism include:

1. Directly reproducing a quotation from a source document without providing quotation marks or giving appropriate credit to the source.

2. Borrowing an idea from a source document and, instead of paraphrasing it, introducing that idea into your paper.
3. Submitting a paper you acquired from another source, student, or company and passing it off as your own.

Remember, your role as a researcher is to share and summarize your findings about your subject from your sources, to paraphrase important passages, and to use direct quotations by key authorities, with your own analysis or interpretation, following the same fundamentals as other researchers and writers have done before you. Blatant or careless misuse of reference sources is no way to demonstrate that you have mastered your subject, or the art of research, by hoping to fool your instructor and your readers.

To avoid plagiarism—even the appearance of plagiarism—the Writing Tutorial Services of Indiana University in Bloomington, Indiana, recommends that you completely and accurately attribute your source when you use:

1. Another person's idea, opinion, or theory.
2. Any facts, statistics, graphs, drawings—any pieces of information—that are not common knowledge.
3. Quotations of another person's actual spoken or written words.
4. Paraphrase of another person's spoken or written words.

Besides these common methods, you should follow six other rules of conduct when synthesizing information from your research:

1. Be sure to identify the source wherever the thought or idea is not your own, or not common knowledge.
2. When extracting words from your source material, use quotation marks, indent long passages, and, above all else, identify your source.
3. Indicate all quoted materials with quotation marks.
4. Make sure material that you paraphrase is rewritten in your own style and language and is not simply a matter of rearranging sentences or altering the main idea of your source.
5. Provide in-text citations for all in-text source material that you use.
6. Include a bibliography or "works cited" at the end of your paper listing every source cited in your paper.

One exception to this case is factual information of a general nature, or "common knowledge." Common knowledge rules apply to generally known facts that appear in many sources. An example of common knowledge would be that John Glenn was the first astronaut to orbit the earth in 1962, or that the Beatles broke up in 1970. But if a writer, researcher, or historian wrote an article or paper documenting new insights of Glenn's historic feat or the reasons for the Beatles' breakup, and you incorporated their findings into your paper, you would need to cite the source and credit them in this case.

There are a few simple steps you can take to identify something as common knowledge in your paper. First, you need to find that same information undocumented in at least five sources. Secondly, and of equal importance, the information you use should be the kind that anyone can locate in general reference sources. The fact that President Richard Nixon resigned from office in 1974 is another example of the type of information that has been common knowledge for years and is generally known to be true. Therefore, citing the source of this information is not necessary.

QUOTING, PARAPHRASING, AND SUMMARIZING

To avoid plagiarizing, three standard methods are commonly used to incorporate information from copyrighted source material into your written document: quoting, paraphrasing, and summarizing.

Quoting from Your Sources

Quoting is using the words stated by the author verbatim from your original source material. The idea of using quoted material in your paper is that it supports your assertions and adds authority to your point of view. Quotations also bring your subject to life, and often provide insights. It's important not to overuse quoted material, but rather to do so sparingly, so that your narrative and your ideas stand out. Your sources, whether they are factual information or quoted material, should be used only to enhance the position and the voice of your paper.

The key to using quotes, as with documented research, is to copy the quotation carefully and reproduce it exactly as it was published—without changing its meaning through editing. When using a direct quotation, always check it to be sure you have copied it and punctuated it correctly, putting quotation marks around the material. To use quoted material effectively, apply the following five methods:

USE SHORT QUOTATIONS

As noted earlier, keep your excerpts of quoted material as short as possible so the material you have chosen does not blur or obstruct the point of view of your paper. Quote only the part of the material that is vital to illustrate your point. The following are two examples of using short quotations differently:

> Throughout Wal-Mart's existence, they have made "billions of dollars in cost efficiencies out of the retail supply chain, passing the larger part of the savings along to shoppers as bargain prices" (Bianco).

> Juries play a major role in the fate of convicted felons in the United States. "In almost all states, the death penalty is limited to cases involving aggravated murder. The U.S. Supreme Court ruled that whenever a sentencing jury has the ability to impose capital punishment, the jury must be informed in advance if the defendant would be eligible for parole" (Robinson).

Notice that at the end of the quotation the source appears in parentheses. This is what is known as an in-text citation, where the name of the source is identified immediately following the quotation or passage. The methods and purpose of in-text citation are discussed later in this chapter.

USE LONG QUOTATIONS

Long quotations are used differently in the context of your paper than direct quotes are. Quotes that exceed four lines or more are indented 10 spaces from the left margin and should be double-spaced. No quotation marks are necessary before or after the quotation.

> It is the responsibility of all drivers in the United States to obey the laws that govern motor vehicles. As Erich Fromm said:
>
> > Hence the obedience which is only rooted in the fear of force must be transformed into one rooted in man's heart. Man must want and even need to obey, instead of only fearing to disobey.

USE DIRECT QUOTES

Direct quotes add flavor, meaning, and substance to your essay, term paper, or written project. The general rule of thumb for using direct quotes, as well as longer quotations, is to include only quotes that will have the greatest impact in your presentation and on your readers. The first example below appeared in a student paper to illustrate the hazards of speeding; the next shows the value of school uniforms in the public schools:

> "Thinking that speed bumps will slow people down is nonsense," said George Williams, a traffic-engineer specialist for Scottsdale (Mascaro).

> School uniforms promote unity, equality, safety, and improvement in discipline and academics. As President Bill Clinton stated in a State of the Union Address, "If student uniforms can help deter school violence, promote discipline, and foster a better learning environment, then strong support should be given to these schools and parents that try them" (AP).

USE QUOTES WITH ELLIPSIS POINTS

Sometimes, especially with long quotations, it may be necessary to purposely omit nonessential words, phrases, clauses, sentences, or paragraphs without distorting or changing the meaning of the original quotation to shorten the quotation to illustrate a point or argument. If this is the case, you should note the fact by adding ellipsis points (. . .) in place of the omitted material, as shown in the examples below:

> Teachers need to remember that their job is about preparing students for the rest of their lives and not putting those students at a disadvantage for a small raise. In one case, "a trial-court judge . . . ordered Detroit teachers back to work based on the finding that the strike caused 'irreparable harm' to students" (Zirkel).

> Tragically, obesity is not just occurring in the adult population, it now has a firm hold on children. For example, "as many as one of every five children aged 6–17 are obese . . . and today, it is estimated that 11 million children are obese" (*Nutrition*).

> Breastfeeding can be called an "effective . . . public health strategy for dealing with the current obesity epidemic" (Creighton), but is not all that needs to be done or considered when parents are trying to prevent obesity in their child.

USE QUOTES WITH BRACKETS

Conversely, when working with quotations, you may find the need to add words to a quoted phrase, clause, sentence, or paragraph to clarify its meaning. When confronted with this task, you should use square brackets in the body of your sentence to insert words inside the quoted matter to signal this change, as follows:

> Schools cannot raise "anywhere near [the] revenue" (Weissman) that would satisfy teachers' demands. Teachers' "demands [are] still so far above the district's ability to pay that [they are] not truly bargaining" (Ahmad).

> The tax credit is used when mothers pay outsiders for the care of their children. A mother who is caring for the child herself should receive credit for it because, as Maggie Gallagher states, "[it] doesn't make sense if we want a good child care system that we're only going to subsidize paid child care" (Ziegler 32).

> Charmaine Yoest states that this is a choice that families make and "[the] more we emphasize the mother's financial penalty, the more the answer comes back to focusing on how the government and the workplace can respond rather than how we can support the family" (Browning 92).

QUOTE KEYWORDS AND PHRASES

Another effective method is to quote keywords or phrases from your source material in your sentences or paragraphs and punctuate them with quotation marks to emphasize a point or argument. As with direct quotes, quoting keywords and phrases can help to emphasis key points in your paper. For example:

> Users of spanking often use the argument of "I got hit as a kid, and I turned out okay," and also believe that as long as a child is spanked on the buttocks, then there's no harm done (Burton 42).

> Telecommuting allows the employee to work from home. These flexible work schedules allow for employers to get the best work from workers and it is "family-friendly" (Hancoch 12).

Paraphrasing Others' Ideas

Paraphrasing is simply restating another author's ideas in your own words. As with quoting material, good paraphrasing does not change the emphasis or original intention of the passage, even though you have restated it in your own words.

Paraphrasing is especially helpful when the source material is rather long or parts of its are unmemorable. The key then is paraphrasing only that information which is critical to your position.

When paraphrasing, it is also critical that you not only interpret the author's ideas correctly but also restate them accurately, and that the words you have chosen capture the essence of what was stated.

To paraphrase correctly, you should read the original source document as many times as you need to be sure that you understand what the author said before writing your own version of the facts. Highlight the key ideas or points in the passage that are important to your paper to make the task of restating them less difficult. After restating the passage in your own words, then carefully review your version against the original to see if your paraphrase faithfully conveys the author's original idea. If so, you have successfully paraphrased the material and can move on to paraphrasing more material as you see fit. To illustrate this point, here is an example of an original passage published in an article in the *Illinois Municipal Review* about concerns about residential speeding, followed by a sample paraphrase of the same material.

Original source:

> Follow-up studies of pedestrian/vehicle accidents have shown that the risk of pedestrian fatality or severe spinal injury in the event of a collision with a motor vehicle increases dramatically when vehicle speeds exceed the 25–30 mph range.

Sample paraphrase:

> Studies on pedestrian/vehicle accidents have proven that the likelihood of pedestrian fatality or severe spinal injury greatly increases when the vehicle speeds surpass 25–30 miles per hour (Montel p. 15).

Summarizing Ideas and Main Points

Summarizing, much like paraphrasing, is the art of saying what another author stated, but more briefly.

When researching your paper, you may uncover long documents loaded with useful facts and information. The trick is successfully incorporating that information into your paper. This is where summarizing can enable you to use words economically.

Summarizing is succinctly restating what you consider to be an author's most important ideas in your own words. Essentially, you are boiling down the ideas or material while carefully maintaining the original emphasis or meaning. To write a good summary, follow these three simple steps:

1. Review the original material as many times as necessary.
2. After reviewing the passage, without looking back at your document, try writing a summary of what you just read.
3. Now review your summary and see if it faithful to the original source document. If not, revise your summary.

CREATING IN-TEXT CITATIONS

Part of citing your sources involves creating in-text citations, routinely used in books, essays, and term papers. In the body of your paper, when incorporating information, quotes, or ideas from a credible source into a paragraph or sentence, you must cite the source that you have used. Usually the citation appears at the end of the sentence or paragraph with the name of the source enclosed in parentheses.

The citation usually contains the first word of your source, as listed in your Bibliography, Works Cited or References section. An in-text citation typically includes either the last name of the author, the title or publication name (in quotations), or the name of the company, organization, or Web site, if no author or article title is known. Each source you cite should correspond with those listed in the Bibliography, Works Cited, or References of your paper.

In-text citations come in many forms and styles. Simply, the author's name only may be cited. Citations may be numbered. Page numbers may be cited. Or you can cite your source as part of your sentence. The following are a few examples of in-text citations generally used by scholars, researchers, and students:

CITING THE AUTHOR

One of the most common forms of in-text citations is simply citing the last name of the author of your source within the sentence or paragraph where it appears:

> When a woman stays home with her children she is able to "give more of herself to her infant at least during the crucial first year, when a child's brain doubles in size, and preferably for the first five years, while the brain trebles in size to attain three-fourths of its final growth" (McCollister).

Notice, in the following example, the above citation corresponds with the first word of the source as listed in the Bibliography, Works Cited, or References:

> McCollister, Betty. "The Social Necessity of Nurturance." *Humanist.* Jan/Feb 2001. Academic Search Elite. 25 Sept. 2003. http://web5.epnet.com/citation.asp

CITING A BOOK OR ARTICLE

If no author name exists and you use source material from a book or publication, list only the first word of the title in parentheses with your in-text citation.

> Scientists have actually found that "about 85 percent of difference between any two average human beings is accounted for by the fact that they're different individuals within the same group, where you only add about 15 percent if you look at individuals within the same group" ("Behavioral").

NUMBERING YOUR CITATIONS

Depending on which style and format you use, some methods call for you to arrange your sources alphabetically and then number them in order, and to subsequently include the number of the citation with each source in the body of the text.

> The future of the job market is in big trouble if employers do not stop hiring illegal aliens. According to the article in *The Phoenix Gazette,* employers knowingly hire illegal immigrants (Sommer 1).

INCLUDING A PAGE NUMBER

If this information is known, you also can include the page number of the source, adding a comma after the name of your source with your citation, as follows:

> Health problems and the care females receive while incarcerated is a major concern inside women's correctional facilities (Watterson, p. 96).

MAKING THE CITATION PART OF YOUR SENTENCE

Additionally, you can incorporate the citation of your source into the body of your sentence, either by name or by number, within a pair of parentheses:

> A 1999 study (4) showed that most Americans save less than five percent of their annual earnings.

> The work of Aristotle (Mendin) supports the theory . . .

MAKING IN-TEXT REFERENCES

Finally, to cite sources in your paper in addition to the above methods, you can identify your source by making an in-text reference at either the beginning or the end of your sentence:

> "An editorial in the July 13, 1998 edition of *The New York Times* took the position . . ."

> Critical errors in President Clinton's handling of the Monica Lewinsky affair surfaced two months after the report was published, according to an article in the eleventh edition of the *Encyclopaedia Britannica.*

FINDING ONLINE GUIDES AND TUTORIALS

Many major universities offer online guides and tutorials providing a wealth of additional tips, examples, and information on acceptable ways of citing your sources, including how to avoid plagiarism and how to quote, paraphrase, and summarize your sources. Highly recommended are:

Arizona State University Library Citation Style Guides
(http://www.west.asu.edu/library/research/reference/gen_ref/style.html)

College of Saint Benedict/Saint John's University's Clemens Library/Alcuin Library
(http://www.csbsju.edu/library/internet/citing.html)

Columbia University's Guide to Online Style
(http://www.columbia.edu/cu/cup/cgos/idx_basic.html)

Indiana University Writing Tutorial Services
(http:///www.indiana.edu/~wts/wts/plagiarism.html)

Purdue University OWL (Online Writing Lab)
(http://owl.english.purdue.edu/handouts/research/r_mla.html)

University of Arizona Library Citation Guide
(http://dizzy.library.arizona.edu/library/type1/tips/data/cite_mla.html)

University of Wisconsin-Madison's Writing Center
(http://www.wisc.edu/writing/Handbook/QPA_paraphrase.html)

Western Washington University Libraries Citation Guides and Style Manuals
(http://www.library.wwu.edu/ref/citn.html)

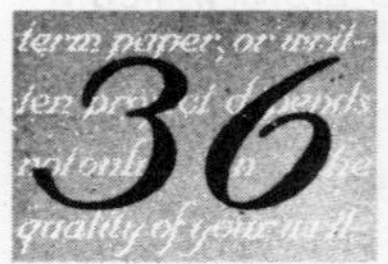

Creating Your Bibliography, Works Cited, or References

Bibliographies, works cited, or references are essential to any project. They illustrate not only the breadth of research you have found but also list all of your sources.

While the purpose of each is the same, Works Cited and References have one distinct difference compared to a Bibliography. Your Works Cited and References lists only sources that you actually cited in your paper, while your Bibliography lists *every* source you consulted for your paper, whether you used it or not.

Creating your Bibliography, Works Cited, or References does not have to be a grueling process. Most students wait until the end to compile their sources, and often do it in makeshift fashion, but the process does not have to be difficult, especially if you plan ahead.

To get a head start, once you have had a chance to evaluate and determine what sources you plan to use to write your paper, start a separate page and begin listing those sources that appear in your first draft. During the course of researching and writing your paper, you may discover additional sources or not use others. That's perfectly fine. Just make sure that any source that you actually cite in your paper is listed in your finished product.

Your task in creating your Bibliography, Works Cited, or References is simple: Gather the primary information for each of the actual sources you used in writing your paper and list them in alphabetical order using either APA (American Psychological Association), MLA (Modern Language Association), or *The Chicago Manual of Style* format. (APA format is used mostly for psychology and social science papers, MLA for humanities and English papers, and *The Chicago Manual of Style* for humanities and scientific documentation.) This, of course, will depend on what format your instructor requires for your project. Be very careful with the way you format the citations, or entries, in your list, and use only one format for your entries, not all three.

Begin your Bibliography, Works Cited, or References on a new page following the last text page of your paper. Starting on the sixth line (approximately one inch) from the top of the page, type and center your title: Bibliography, Works Cited, or References. Double-space after the title and now list all your entries in alphabetical order, as noted earlier. Do not number your entries, and list each citation separately. Each citation should list key information that will enable you, or anyone reading your paper, to check the sources you mention in text against those you have listed. The information listed in your citations should be as complete as possible and follow the prescribed style.

Generally, your entries should provide the following: The name of the author or authors who have written the original source document, starting with their last names first, then first name last, separated by a comma with a period at the end. This is usually followed by the title of the book or article in parentheses or italicized, ending in a period. Listed next is the name of the publication, underlined or italicized, then the date published, in reverse order (in APA style, the date published follows the author's name), also with periods at the end of each. For a book, after the title, the name of the publisher, their location, and the year the book was published are listed next.

Whether you have decided to use APA, MLA, or *Chicago* style, your citations in your Bibliography, Works Cited, or References will appear as follows:

APA STYLE

Bush: U.S. can fight 2 enemies (2002, October 15). *Arizona Republic* [Phoenix, AZ], p. A8

Nicollelis, M. A. L. and Chapin, J. K. (2002, October). Controlling robots with the mind. *Scientific American* 48, 53.

Paloff, R. M. and Pratt, K. (2001). *Lessons from the cyberspace classroom: The realities of online learning*. San Francisco: Jossey-Bass, 164.

Zimmerman, C. B. and Schmitt, N. (2002). Derivative word forms: What do learners know? *TESOL Quarterly* 36, 164.

MLA STYLE

"Bush: U.S. Can Fight 2 Enemies." *Arizona Republic* [Phoenix, AZ] 15 October 2002: A8

Nicollelis, Miguel A. L., and John K. Chapin. "Controlling Robots with the Mind." *Scientific American* Oct. 2002: 48, 53

Palloff, Rena M., and Keith Pratt. *Lessons from the Cyberspace Classroom: The Realities of Online Learning*. San Francisco: Jossey-Bass, 2001.

Zimmerman, Cheryl B., and Norbert Schmitt. "Derivative Word Forms: What Do Learners Know?" *TESOL Quarterly* 74 (2002): 164.

THE CHICAGO MANUAL OF STYLE

Arizona Republic. 2002. Bush: U.S. can fight 2 enemies. October 15, A8.

Nicollelis, M. A. L. and Chapin, J. K. 2002. Controlling robots with the mind. *Scientific American:* 48–53.

Parloff, R. M. and Pratt, K. 2001. *Lessons from the cyberspace classroom: The realities of online learning*. San Francisco: Jossey-Bass.

Zimmerman, C. B. and Schmitt, N. 2002. Derivative word forms: What do learners know? *TESOL Quarterly,* 36, 164.

Please note that, in the above sample citations, the first line of each entry is typed flush left with subsequent lines indented five spaces, with all lines also double-spaced within and between entries. This conforms to APA, MLA, and *Chicago Manual of Style* format, commonly used when creating a Bibliography, Works Cited, or References for any essay or term paper. To ensure that yours passes the test, be sure that you not only follow the examples for what key information should be listed with your entries, but the above format as shown in the sample bibliography in this chapter.

If you are using APA, MLA, or *Chicago Manual of Style,* the format and appearance of your Bibliography, Works Cited, or References will look identical. The following is a sample Works Cited for your use:

WORKS CITED

Albrecht, Susan Fread, and Joles, Candace. "Accountability and Access to Opportunity: Mutually Exclusive Tenets Under a High-Stakes Testing Mandate." *Preventing School Failure* 47.2 (2003): 86–92.

American Psychological Association (APA). *Appropriate Use of High-Stakes Testing in Our Nation's Schools.* APA Office of Public Communications, 2001.

Amrein, Audrey T., and Berliner, David C. "The Effects of High-Stakes Testing on Student Motivation and Learning." *Educational Leadership* 60.5 (2003): 32–39.

High-Stakes Testing in PreK–12 Education. American Educational Research Association (AERA). July 2000. http://www.aera.net/about/policy/stakes.htm.

Rapp, Dana. "National Board-Certified Teachers in Ohio Give State Education Policy, Classroom Climate, and High-Stakes Testing a Grade of F." *Phi Delta Kappan* 84.3 (2002): 215–19.

Townsend, Brenda L. "Testing While Black." *Remedial & Special Education* 23.4 (2002): 222–31.

Even though the information that appears in your citations is the same, the style varies depending on which bibliography format you use—APA, MLA, or *Chicago Manual of Style.* For a more thorough understanding of how to cite your resources, consult the following:

- *MLA Handbook for Writers of Research Papers, 6th Edition,* by Joseph Gibaldi (New York: Beford/St. Martin's, 2003)
- *Publication Manual of the American Psychological Association, 5th Edition* (Washington, D.C.: APA, 2001)
- *The Chicago Manual of Style 15th ed. rev.* (University of Chicago Press, 2003).

For other examples of proper citations, also check the appendixes following this chapter.

ONLINE BIBLIOGRAPHY CREATORS

To take the guesswork—and some of the fun—out of compiling your bibliography, several excellent Web sites offer interactive tools, geared toward K–12 and college students, enabling you to create Bibliographies, Works Cited, or References online that you can cut and paste into your existing Word document. Some sites provide this service at no charge but require you to register; others offer more advanced services for a nominal fee. Additional Web sites also feature style guides and everything you need to independently create your list of references.

Your school's library may offer a similar service. Many K–12 and college libraries offer licensed versions of bibliography creators (also known as citation makers and Works Cited creators) on their Web sites, featuring the same capabilities as many online services listed below.

The following is a partial list of recommended Web bibliography creators and style guides for your use:

Web Bibliography Creators

easybib: MyBib (www.easybib.com/)
This advanced bibliography maker, for students of all ages, processes only MLA-style bibliographies at no charge. To create APA-style bibliographies as well, a customized service, MyBibPro, is offered for a small fee. Two other bibliography creators, available by subscription to schools, teachers, and librarians, are Bib4Class and Bib4School.

Landmarks Citation Machine (http://www.landmark-project.com/citation_machine/index.php)
A free service of David Warlick's Landmark Project, this interactive Web tool generates standard APA and MLA citations and bibliographies for both print and electronic resources.

NoodleBib (www.noodletools.com/)
For grades 1 through 10, this automatic bibliography composer enables you to create, format, and edit printable APA- and MLA-style bibliographies. You simply input your source information for books, articles, and Web sites, and it does the rest. Available by subscription, this service is offered by many elementary, middle school and high school libraries to students at no charge. A similar service, called NoodleBib MLA Starter, is available free of charge to elementary school students at the Web address listed above.

Web Style Guides

APA Style Guide (http://www.lib.usm.edu/research/guides/apa.html)
Sponsored by the University of Southern Mississippi Library, this free site features an extensive APA style guide, based on the fifth edition of the printed reference, covering the ins and outs of citing every kind of source—books, journals, dissertations, other media, and electronic information.

Chicago Manual of Style Citation Guide (http://www.lib.ohio-state.edu/sites/guides/chicagogd.html)
This free online guide, available through Ohio State University's libraries Web site, offers many examples of scientific and humanities style citations used in bibliographies as well as in-text references, based on *The Chicago Manual of Style, 14th Edition.*

Enchanted Learning (http://www.enchantedlearning.com/Citing.shtml)
Designed for elementary school students, this "How to Cite" style guide covers the basics on how to write a bibliography and list references for various types of publications, including books, encyclopedias, magazines or journals, and Web sites.

MLA Style Guide (http://www.dianahacker.com/resdoc/humanities/list.html)
This official Web site in honor of the late Diana Hacker (1942–2004), author of several critically-acclaimed writers' references for Bedford/St. Martin's, features a complete list of sample citations and style for Works Cited entries, adapted from the *MLA Handbook for Writers of Research Papers, 6th Edition.*

APPENDIX I

APA Style

The following style guide covers basic citation examples adapted from *Publication Manual of the American Psychological Association, 5th Edition* (Washington, D.C.: APA, 2001). Examples include citations for books, encyclopedias, periodicals (magazines, newspapers and journals), electronic sources, such as CD-ROM and electronic databases, and Web sites.

Books

A BOOK WITH ONE AUTHOR

Alverex, A. T. (1970). *The savage god: A study of suicide.* New York: Random House.

TWO OR MORE WORKS BY THE SAME AUTHOR

Clemens, Abigail. (1973). *The new world.* Boston, MA: Modern Psychiatry Press.

Clemens, Abigail. (1984). *Post-modern syndrome.* Boston, MA: Modern Psychiatry Press.

A BOOK WITH TWO TO SIX AUTHORS

Natarajan, R., and Chaturvedi, R. (1983). *Geology of the Indian Ocean.* New York: Random House.

A BOOK WITH SIX OR MORE AUTHORS

Rosen, et al. (2000). *History of Death.* New York: Oxford UP.

A BOOK BY A GROUP OR CORPORATE AUTHOR

Physical Endurance Training Center. (1998). *Guidelines to better physical endurance.* Los Angeles, CA: Author.

A BOOK WITH AN EDITOR

Engberg, Robert, ed. (1984). *John Muir summering in the Sierra.* Madison, Wisconsin: University of Wisconsin Press.

A BOOK BY AN UNKNOWN AUTHOR

Computer terminology dictionary (3rd ed.). (1999). New York: Madison Press.

A BOOK TRANSLATION

Buffett, François. (1991). *Childhood speech patterns.* (Young & Charles. Trans.) New York: E.P. Dutton. (Original work published 1988).

AN ARTICLE OR CHAPTER IN AN EDITED BOOK

Potter, Gerald. (2003). Changing attempts at deception. In I. Fein and M. Spalding (Eds.), *Changing habits* (pp. 99–104). Chicago: McGraw-Hill.

A REVISED EDITION OF A BOOK

Owens, Adam. (2002). *Making millions in the futures market* (Rev. ed.). New York: Investment Press.

A MULTIVOLUME WORK

Wayne, Mark (Ed.). (1999–2001). *American civilization: A history* (Vols. 1–3). New York: History Press.

A TECHNICAL OR RESEARCH REPORT

Hall, Thomas, and Klaus, F. (1992). *Children with language disabilities.* (Report No. 999). Washington, D.C.: Early Childhood Education Association.

A REPORT FROM A UNIVERSITY

McGyver, Mark. (1993). *Sexual harassment in the workplace.* (Rep. No. 5). Bloomington: University of Indiana. Human Resources.

Periodicals

A MONOGRAPH

Laslow, T. (2001). Personality disorders. *Monographs of the National Personal Disorder Society,* 42 (2, Serial No. 429).

A BOOK, FILM, OR VIDEO REVIEW

MacNeil, Michael. (2002). New look romantic comedy retread of the past. (Review of the film *The Magillacuddy Sisters*). *Films in Review,* 27, 42–43.

AN ARTICLE IN A JOURNAL THAT IS CONTINUOUSLY PAGED

Wolchik, S. A. (2001) Adolescent Drug Abuse. *American Psychological Bulletin,* 123, 786–792.

AN ARTICLE IN A JOURNAL THAT IS NOT CONTINUOUSLY PAGED

Parmer, S. (2000). Divorce and Children. *Consulting Psychology Journal,* 45(3), 12–21.

AN ARTICLE IN A NEWSPAPER

Rogers, Michael. (2002, November 15). Economy nosedive to bottom out. *The Washington Post,* pp. A3, A24.

AN ARTICLE IN A MAGAZINE

Kandel, T. C. (2000, July 10). Brain Power. *Time,* 34, 23–26.

AN UNSIGNED ARTICLE

New drug therapy for prostate cancer. (1998, January 20). *The Los Angeles Times,* p. 25.

Electronic Sources

A CHAPTER OR SECTION IN AN INTERNET DOCUMENT

Anderson, Todd. Improving the quality of health care. In *Health report, national association of health* (sec. Health Minute). Retrieved September 20, 2002, from http://www.naoh.org/anderson.html.

A MESSAGE POSTED TO A NEWSGROUP

Woodson, H. (1999, August 18). Arizona to hike state property taxes. [Msg. 4]. Message posted to az.tax.central.

A SINGLE DOCUMENT, NO AUTHOR, NO DATE

Military draft. Retrieved September 9, 2000, from http://mmt.sonnn.us/JJJhan/Draft.htm.

A U.S. GOVERNMENT REPORT ON THE WEB

Veterans Administration. Changes approved to VA benefits. Retrieved April 2, 2002, from http://www.va.gov/news/benefits.htm.

AN ARTICLE FROM A NEWSPAPER

Berle, M.G. (2003, October 20). Kerry announces plans to resign. *New York Post*. Retrieved October 21, 2003, from http://www.nypost.com.

AN ARTICLE FROM AN ELECTRONIC JOURNAL

Atkinson, Harold. (1998). New preventative medicine for depression. *Modern Health,* 7. March 5, 1999, from http://www.modernhealth.org/medicine/vol7/98_html.

AN ARTICLE FROM AN INTERNET JOURNAL

Fisher, R. (2000). Scientific breakthroughs in stem cell research. *Scientific Journal,* 4. Retrieved May 4, 2000, from http://sci.org/journal/volume4/breakthrough.html.

AN ARTICLE IN A DATABASE

Parmer, S. (2000), Divorce and Children. [Electronic Version] *Consulting Psychology Journal,* 45(3), 12–21.

AN ELECTRONIC ABSTRACT

Hall, T. S. (2003). Warning signs of teenage depression. Abstract retrieved September 9, 2003, from http://www.bsu.edu/psychology/abstracts.htm.

AN ELECTRONIC DATABASE

Millennium Center for Technology. (2000). *Survey of new technology abroad for personal computers.* Retrieved August 12, 1995, from BIOS database.

CD-ROM

Spiders. (1996). *Grolier's New Multimedia Encyclopedia.* [CD-ROM]. New York: Groliers.

Encyclopedia

AN ARTICLE IN AN ENCYCLOPEDIA WITH ONE AUTHOR

Bergman, P. G. (1998). Relativity. In *The new Encyclopaedia Britannica* (Vol. 26, pp. 501–508). Chicago: Encyclopedia Britannica.

AN ARTICLE IN AN ENCYCLOPEDIA WITH NO AUTHOR

Saide, S. (Ed). (1992). Drugs. In *Encyclopedia of Psychology.* (Vol. 2, pp. 243–250) New York: Dover.

World Wide Web

AN ARTICLE WITH ONE AUTHOR

Anderson, S. (2001, April 10) *Psychiatric Drugs.* Retrieved January 11, 2002, from http: www.Psychdrugs.org

APPENDIX II

MLA Style

The following style guide covers basic citation examples modeled after the *MLA Handbook for Writers of Research Papers, 6th Edition,* by Joseph Gibaldi (New York: Bedford/St. Martin's, 2003). Highlighted in this section are citations for books, encyclopedias, periodicals (magazines, newspapers and journals), electronic sources, such as CD-ROM and electronic databases, as well as the World Wide Web.

Books

A BOOK WITH ONE AUTHOR

Potok, Chaim. *The Chosen.* New York: Fawcett Crest, 1967.

A BOOK WITH TWO TO SIX AUTHORS

Lawrence, Jerome, and Robert Lee. *The Night Thoreau Spent in Jail.* Toronto: Bantam, 1970.

A BOOK WITH MORE THAN SIX AUTHORS

Chafe, William H., et al. *Civilities and Civil Rights.* New York: Oxford UP, 1980.

A BOOK BY A CORPORATE AUTHOR

United States History. *The Story of the United States Capitol.* Washington: Nat'l Geographic Soc., 1975.

A BOOK WITH AN EDITOR

Engberg, Robert, ed. *John Muir Summering in the Sierra.* Madison, Wisconsin: U of Wisconsin Press, 1984.

A BOOK BY AN UNKNOWN AUTHOR

Report of the Commission on Energy. Washington: Energy Commission Board, 1980.

AN ARTICLE IN A REFERENCE BOOK

"Ecology." *The Concise Oxford Encyclopedia.* 1982 ed.

A SECOND OR LATER EDITION OF A BOOK

Lenburg, Jeff. *The Encyclopedia of Animated Cartoons.* 2nd ed. New York: Facts On File, 1999.

AN ARTICLE IN AN ENCYCLOPEDIA WITH ONE AUTHOR

Helms, Ronald. "Electric Light." *World Book Encyclopedia*. 1995 ed.

Periodicals

AN ARTICLE IN A NEWSPAPER WITH ONE AUTHOR

Hunt, Albert R. "Clinton Needs Fewer Reinventions and More Consistency." *The Wall Street Journal*. 10 J1. 1995: A11–12.

AN ARTICLE IN A NEWSPAPER WITH NO AUTHOR

"The City of Baltimore Changes Tax Base." *Baltimore Sun*. 3 Dec. 1977: 2:23.

AN ARTICLE IN A MAGAZINE

Hackworth, Col. David H. "Terms of Forgiveness." *Newsweek* 24 Apr. 1995: 38–40.

Walters, Debra. "Cures for Terrorism Abroad." *Discover.* March 1992: 56–61.

AN ARTICLE IN A SCHOLARLY JOURNAL THAT IS CONTINUOUSLY PAGED

Buffett, Bruce. "Role Reversal in Geomagnatism." *Nature* 401 (1999): 861–62.

Frederick, John. "Alcoholism: Recovery and Rehabilitation." *The Journal of Social Behavior* 47 (1979): 339–53.

AN UNSIGNED ARTICLE

"Trading Places." *Time* 30 December 2002: 67–72.

Electronic Sources

AN ARTICLE ON CD-ROM

"Spiders." *Grolier's New Multimedia Encyclopedia.* CD-ROM. Grolier's, 1996.

AN ARTICLE FROM A DATABASE

Leonard, Tom. "Men and Violence." *Critique: Studies in Contemporary Fiction* 15 (1994): 194–205. *MasterFile.* EBSCO. http://ehostvgw6.epnet.com/....profile=mfp 15 Feb. 2002.

A MESSAGE POSTED TO A NEWSGROUP

Mason, Dan. "Finding New Solutions to Common Everyday Problems." Online posting. 6 Feb. 2003. James Palson Forum for Single Mothers. 10 March 2003. http://www.palson.com/newsgroup/pc/index.cgi

A SINGLE DOCUMENT, NO AUTHOR, NO DATE

"Abortion Ethics."http://ethics.acusd.edu/abortion.html

AN ARTICLE FROM AN ELECTRONIC JOURNAL

Young, Dick. "Notes on the Study of Aquatic Subspecies." Aquatic Monthly. 41:2 (1998). 98–102. 7 May 2003. <http://journal.access.msu.edu/journals/aquatic.monthly/v8890.aquatic.html>

APPENDIX III

The Chicago Manual of Style

This following is based on *The Chicago Manual of Style, 15th Ed.* (University of Chicago Press, 2003). The preferred style for student papers in history and other humanities (such as English, journalism, literature, and fine arts), this style of citations is also used by students writing reports in sciences, including anthropology, astronomy, chemistry, mathematics, medicine, philosophy, physics, political sciences, and psychology. Styles in this case for humanities or scientific citations vary. The following are common examples of humanities style:

Books

A BOOK BY ONE AUTHOR

Burns, George. 1987. *Eighteen again.* New York: Humor Press.

A BOOK BY TWO AUTHORS

Unwin, Liam P., and Joseph Galloway. 1990. *Peace in Ireland.* Boston: Stronghope Press.

A BOOK BY THREE OR MORE AUTHORS

Taylor, John, George Blair, Humphrey Black, and Tim Stanley. 1972. *How to fry a fig.* Boston: You're Kidding Press.

A BOOK BY AN ANONYMOUS AUTHOR

The problems that occur due to anonymity. 1999. Nowhere: Nosuchthing Press.

A BOOK BY AN EDITOR

Tortelli, Anthony B., ed. 1991. *Sociology approaching the twenty-first century.* Los Angeles: Peter and Sons.

Periodicals

AN ARTICLE IN A JOURNAL

Booler, William. "Secrets in the Board room." *Texas Political Review* 29 (1978): 16–21.

When there is no volume number and only an issue number:

Webb, Lisa R. "Completing My Third Degree." *College Times* no. 9 (1989): 9–12.

AN ARTICLE IN A MAGAZINE

Gilman, Mikal. "King of the Titans: Bob Dylan, Van Morrison and Joni Mitchell Triumph on West Coast Tour." *Rolling Stones,* no. 803 (2001): 29–32.

When there is no volume number, issue number, or page numbers:

Schickel, Richard. "Far beyond Reality: The New Technology of Hollywood's Special Effects." *New York Times Magazine,* 18 May 1980.

AN ARTICLE IN A NEWSPAPER

Maslin, Janet. "Johnny Depp with a Don Juan Complex." *New York Times,* 7 March 1995.

Electronic Sources

AN ARTICLE FROM THE INTERNET

Moulthrop, S. A. Traveling in the Breakdown Lane: A Principle of Resistance for Hypertext. http://www.ubalt.edu/www/ygcla/sam/essays/pre_breakdown.html> May 1994.

AN ARTICLE ON CD-ROM

"Pen and Ink." (1997). *Amazing Facts* (Version 3.1). [CD-ROM]. Chicago: Multimedia Productions, Inc.

AN ARTICLE FROM AN INTERNET JOURNAL

Gorr, E. W. and Gorr, Z. W. (1998). The Rhetoric of Video Games. In Rhetorical Theory Quarterly [electronic journal]. [cited 23 February 1998]. http://www.rtquarterly.com/game.html.

A MESSAGE POSTED TO A NEWSGROUP

LeMaster, John. lemasterj@shortstop.com. "POLINEWS: Biological Weapons." In Online Newsgroup. 2 January 1998. Archivedat: http://www.onlinenews.com/archives/January/1998/bioweapons.

AN EMAIL CORRESPONDENCE

Roland, Beth rowland@acns.fsu.edu, "Citation Lecture," private e-mail message to Lisa Webb. 15 September 1998.

SELECTED BIBLIOGRAPHY

Behrens, Laurence, and Leonard F. Rosen. *Writing and Reading Across the Curriculum, 8th Ed.* New York: Longman, 2003.

Booth, Wayne C. *The Craft of Research.* Chicago: University of Chicago Press, 2003.

The Chicago Manual of Style, 15th Edition. Chicago: University of Chicago Press, 2003.

Davis, James. *The Rowman and Littlefield Guide to Writing with Sources.* Lanham, Md.: Rowman & Littlefield, 2003.

Gale Directory of Databases. Detroit: Gale Research, 2003.

Gale Directory of Publications and Broadcast Media. Detroit: Gale Research, 2002.

Gibaldi, Joseph. *MLA Handbook for Writers of Research Papers.* New York: Modern Language Association of America, 2003.

Harmon, Charles. *Using the Internet, Online Services, and CD-ROMs for Writing Research and Term Papers, 2nd Ed.* New York: Neal-Schulman Publishers, Inc., 2000.

Harris, Muriel. *Prentice Hall Reference Guide to Grammar and Usage, 5th Ed.* Upper Saddle River, N.J.: Prentice Hall, 2003.

Kennedy, X. J., Dorothy M. Kennedy, and Sylvia A. Holladay. *The Bedford Guide for College Writers, 6th Ed.* New York: Bedford/St. Martin's, 2002.

King, Dennis. *Get the Facts on Anyone, 2nd Ed.* New York: Macmillan, 1995.

Lester, James D. *Writing Research Papers: The Complete Guide, 6th Ed.* New York: HarperCollins, 1990.

Memering, Dean. *The Prentice Hall Guide to Research Writing, 2nd. Ed.* Englewood Cliffs, N.J.: Prentice Hall, 1989.

Publication Manual of the American Psychological Association, 5th Ed. Washington, D.C.: APA, 2001.

Rodrigues, Dawn. *The Research Paper and the World Wide Web.* Upper Saddle River, N.J.: Prentice Hall, 1997.

Veit, Richard. *Research: The Student's Guide to Writing Research Papers, 4th Ed.* New York: Pearson Longman, 2004.

Veit, Richard, Christopher Gould, and John Clifford. *Writing, Reading, and Research, 5th Ed.* Boston: Allyn and Bacon, 2001.

Whiteley, Sandy. *The American Library Association Guide to Information Access: A Complete Research Handbook and Directory.* New York: Random House, 1994.

INDEX

A

ABI/Inform 20
abstracts 19
academic library 13, 227–228
Academic Search Elite 6, 20
Academic Search Premier 20
accuracy of facts 31
advertising, magazines and journals 256
aeronautics and space flight, magazines and journals 256
aerospace, biographical information 80
African Americans
  archives 44–45
  article indexes and abstracts 321–322
associations on the Web 56–57
  biographical information 86–87
  books and references 319–321
  full-text article databases 322–323
  magazines and journals 256
  periodicals 323–326
  Web sites 277, 326–327
agenda, set for research 10–11
aging
  free electronic journals 145
  magazines and journals 256
  Web sites 277
agricultural and farm
  archives 45
  electronic databases 113
  electronic journals, free 145–146
  magazines and journals 256
  periodical and newspaper indexes 181
  Web sites 277
AlltheWeb 6, 7
almanacs 16, 172–173
Alta Vista 4, 6, 303
alternative medicine associations on the Web 57
Alternative Press Index 18
Alt-Press Watch 20
American Economic Review 17
American History and Life 18, 20
American history archives 45–46
American Jewish archives 46–47
American Psychological Association (APA)
  Publication Manual 533
  style 528–532
    books 533–534
    electronic sources 535
    encyclopedia 535–536
    periodicals 534
    World Wide Web 536
American Small Farm Magazine 17
An Annotated Bibliography of 20th Century Critical Studies of Women's Literature 16
anthropology
  electronic databases 113
  electronic journals, free 145–146
  magazines and journals 257
  periodical and newspaper indexes 181
APA. *See* American Psychological Association
Arabs, biographical information 87
archeology, magazines and journals 257
architecture
  associations on the Web 57–59
  electronic databases 134–135

electronic journals, single subject directories 141
magazines and journals 257
archival collections. *See* archives, find
archives, find 37
finding aids 38–39
Internet 43–52
library catalogs 38
local 42–43
mailing list 165
newsgroups 170
online databases 39–42
research 38
special collections 52–53
types of 37–38
art
archives 47
biographical information 80
electronic journal, single subject directories 142
electronic journals, free 146
magazines and journals 257
periodical and newspaper indexes 182
Web sites 278
Art Index 18, 20
arts and entertainment, search engines 309
Asian Americans, biographical information 87
Ask Jeeves 6
associations and organizations
research 54
on the Web 56
African Americans 56–57
alternative medicine 57
architecture 57–59
chemistry 59
computer science 59–60
criminal investigation/forensic science 60–61
dance 61
disabilities 61
drama 62
environmental health 62–63
gerontology 63
health and medicine 63–65
human rights 65–67
language 67
literature 67–68
mathematics 68
music 69–70
nutrition 70–71
philosophy 71–72
physics 72–73
religion and theology 73
women's studies 73
print and CD-ROM 55
Web 55–56
Web sites 278–279
astronomy
electronic journal, single subject directories 142
magazines and journals 257
Web sites 279
atlases 173–174
author, citing 525
authority of facts 31–32
automobiles, magazines and journals 257

B

Balay, Robert 15
Bibliographic Index 16
bibliographies
general reference 174–175
periodical and newspaper indexes 182
popular reference 16
bibliography, creating 528–529
online creators 531–532
style 529–530
Works Cited sample 530
biochemistry, electronic journals, free 146–147
biographical dictionaries 16
biographical indexes
finding biographical information 75–76
periodical and newspaper indexes 182
biographical information 74
CD-ROM collections 96–97
electronic databases 113–114
electronic form 90–91
indexes 75–76
online 91–94
popular references 76–79
references by subject 80–90
aerospace 80
art 80

business 81
education 81
ethnicities 86–88
film, theater, television 81–82
law 82
literature 82–83
medicine and health care 83
music 83–85
politics 85
science 86
sports 88–89
women 89–90
references for international figures 80
references for regional figures 79
research 74–75
biographical references 16
Biological Abstracts 18
biology
electronic databases 114
electronic journals, free 147–148
electronic journals, single subject directories 142
magazines and journals 256
periodical and newspaper indexes 182
book, citing 525
books and book reviews 183
guides to 180
periodical and newspaper indexes 183
Boolean search 7
The Boston Globe 17
brackets, in quotations 523
British Humanities Index 20
broadcasting, magazines and journals 257
business and economics
article indexes and abstracts 332–333
biographical information 81
books and references 328–332
CD-ROM collections 97–98
electronic databases 114–116
electronic journals, free 148, 149–150
electronic journals, single subject directories 142
full-text article databases 333–335
magazines and journals 257–258
periodical and newspaper indexes 183
periodicals 335–336
search engines 309–310
Web sites 279–280, 336–337
Business Periodicals Index 18

C

catalogs
government information 201–203
library 38
online catalogs 14–15
CD-ROM collections
abstracts 19
associations research 55
library collections 25
locating 95–96
popular titles by subject 96–109
biography 96–97
business and economics 97–98
demographic studies and statistics 98–100
encyclopedias 100–101
general references 101–102
law and government 102–103
health and medicine 103
history 103–105
literature 105–106
performing arts 106–107
phone directories 107
religion 108
science 108–109
women's studies 109
printed editions versus 18
researching 95
chemistry
associations on the Web 59
electronic databases 116
electronic journals, free 148
magazines and journals 258
periodical and newspaper indexes 184
Web sites 280
The Chicago Manual of Style
style 528–532
books 539
electronic sources 540
periodicals 539–540
children and youth, magazines and journals 258

Christian Science Monitor 17, 20
chronicles, by eras and decades 175–176
chronologies 176–177
CINAHL 20
citations, in-text 525
as part of sentence 526
citing author 525
citing book or article 525
in-text references 526
numbering citations 526
online guides and tutorials to 526–527
page numbers 526
citations, styles of 528–532
American Psychological Association
books 533–534
electronic sources 535
encyclopedia 535–536
periodicals 534
World Wide Web 536
The Chicago Manual of Style
books 539
electronic sources 540
periodicals 539–540
Modern Language Association
books 537–538
electronic sources 538
periodicals 538
Columbia Encyclopedia 4
Columbia University, Lehman Library 225
communications
electronic databases 116
magazines and journals 258
Communications Abstracts 18
computer science
associations on the Web 59–60
electronic journals, free 148
magazines and journals 258
periodical and newspaper indexes 184
search engines 310
Web sites 280–281
computing, electronic journals, free 149
congressional archives 47
consumer information
electronic journals, free 149
magazines and journals 258
Web sites 281
country
directories, Web sites 281–282
search engines 310–311
coverage of facts 33–34
CQ Researcher 6, 20
criminal investigation/forensic science
associations on the Web 60–61
electronic databases 117
electronic journals, free 149
periodical and newspaper indexes 184
Web sites 285
criminal justice
article indexes and abstracts 339–342
books and references 338–339
full-text article databases 342–344
periodicals 344–348
Web sites 291–292, 348–350
Criminal Justice Periodicals Index 18
cultural
controversial issues and 116–117
Web sites 288–290
Current Biography 16
current events, electronic journals, free 149
cyberspace, Web sites 280–281

D

dance
article indexes and abstracts 497–500
associations on the Web 61
books and references 492–497
full-text article databases 500–501
magazines and journals 258
periodicals 501–504
Web sites 504–505
databases. *See also* electronic databases
newspaper and magazine 265–270
daybooks 177
define topic 8–9
demographic studies and statistics
CD-ROM collections 98–100
periodical and newspaper indexes 184, 194
Web sites 282–28

departmental libraries (government) 229–231
descriptor search 7–8
Dialog 18
dictionaries
  electronic databases 118–119
  English language 177–178
  popular reference 16
  specialized 178
Dictionary of American Biography 16
directories
  electronic databases 118–119
  general reference 178–179
  mailing list 163–165
  newsgroups 169–170
  newspaper and magazine 265–270
  Web 308–309
direct quotation 522
disabilities associations on the Web 61
discussion groups. *See* e-mail discussion groups
dissertations, periodical and newspaper indexes 184
Dogpile 6
drama associations on the Web 62
DVD resources
  electronic databases 135
  using 25

E

earth and environmental sciences
  electronic databases 119
  electronic journals, free 151
  periodical and newspaper indexes 185–186
  Web sites 283–284, 286
Ebony 17
EBSCOHost 20
ecology
  article indexes and abstracts 354–356
  books and references 351–354
  full-text article databases 356–357
  magazines and journals 259
  periodicals 357–359
  Web sites 359–360
economics. *See* business and economics
Economist 17
education
  biographical information 81
  electronic databases 119
  electronic journals, free 150
  electronic journals, single subject directories 142
  magazines and journals 259
  periodical and newspaper indexes 185
  Web sites 283
Educational Resources Information Center. *See* ERIC
Education Index 18
e-journals. *See* electronic journals
electronic databases
  academic 111
  by subject 113–135
    agriculture 113
    anthropology 113
    biography 113–114
    biology 114
    business and economics 114–116
    chemistry and physical sciences 116
    communications 116
    controversial and cultural issues 116–117
    criminal justice and law 117
    dictionaries, directories, encyclopedias 118–119
    earth and environmental sciences 119
    education 119
    engineering sciences 119–120
    ethics 120
    ethnic and area studies 120
    general references 120–121
    government publications 121–122
    health and medicine 122–123
    history 123–124
    humanities and fine arts 124
    journal and magazine article indexes 124–126
    library science/books and publishing 126–127
    literature 127–129
    newspaper article indexes 129–130

performing arts 130–131
philosophy 131
political science and public administration 131
psychology 132
religion 132
sciences 132–133
social sciences 133
sociology and social work 133
sports and exercise sciences 134
technology 134
visual arts and architecture 134–135
women's studies 135
gathering information 19–21
general 111–112
K-12 111–112
researching 110–111
VHS and DVD collections 135
Web 276–302
electronic journals (e-journals)
free 145–160
aging 145
agriculture 145–146
anthropology 146
art 146
biochemistry 146–147
biology 147–148
business 148
chemistry 148
computer science 148
computing 149
consumer information 149
criminal justice 149
current events 149
economics 149–150
education 150
engineering 150
English 150–151
environment 151
ethnic studies 151
film studies 15–152
foreign languages 152
geological sciences and mining 152
history 152
human development and family studies 152
journalism 152–153
law 153
library science 153–154
mathematics 154
medicine 154–157
military science 157
music 157
nursing 157–158
nutrition 158
philosophy and religion 158
physics 158
political science 158–159
psychology 159
science/technology 159
social work 159
sociology 159–160
speech and communication studies 160
women's studies 160
free article index databases 138
multiple subject directories 139–141
researching 136–137
single-subject directories 141–145
architecture 141
art 142
astronomy 142
biology 142
business and economics 142
education 142
history 143
journalism and the media 143
law 143
medicine 143
music 143–144
philosophy 144
psychology 144
sociology and social sciences 144–145
religion 145
subscription-based article index databases 137–138
electronics, magazines and journals 259
ellipsis points, in quotations 522–523
e-mail discussion groups
deciding to join 162
finding 163–165
further information 165–166
mailing list archives 165

mailing list search engines and directories 163–165
joining 162–163
researching 161
understanding 161–162
understanding for research 165
e-mail newsgroups
deciding to join 168
finding 169
archives 170
directories 169–170
search engines 169
joining 168
researching 166
understanding 166–167
using for research 170
Encyclopedia Americana 16
Encyclopaedia Britannica 4, 16
encyclopedias
CD-ROM collections 100–101
electronic databases 118–119
general reference 179–180
popular reference 16
engineering sciences
electronic databases 119–120
electronic journals, free 150
magazines and journals 259
periodical and newspaper indexes 185
English, electronic journals, free 150–151
English language dictionary 177–178
environmental health associations on the Web 62–63
environmental sciences. *See* earth and environmental sciences; ecology
ERIC 21, 225
Essay and General Literature Index 18
ethics
electronic databases 120
Web sites 284
ethnic and area studies
archives 48
biographical information 86–88
electronic databases 120
electronic journals, free 151
Ethnic Newswatch 20
Excite 6, 303
exercise sciences. *See* sports and exercise sciences
Expanded Academic Index ASAP 20

F

facts, consider 30
accuracy 31
authority 31–32
coverage 33–34
objectivity 33
purpose 30–31
relevancy 32
timeliness 33
The Facts On File Dictionary of Music 16
fashion, magazines and journals 259
federal government information 203–205
film
article indexes and abstracts 367–370
biographical information 81–82
books and references 361–367
electronic journals, free 15–152
full-text article databases 370–371
periodicals 372–374
Web sites 284–285, 374–376
finance
search engines 309–310
Web sites 279–280
finding aids 38
fine arts. *See* humanities and fine arts
FirstSearch 18
foreign government information 207
foreign languages
electronic journals, free 152
magazines and journals 259
foreign newspapers 256
forensic science. *See* criminal investigation/forensic science
forestry, magazines and journals 259
free article index databases 138
free sites, online databases 39–40
full-text articles 19
future, magazines and journals 260

G

gardening and horticulture, magazines and journals 260
general interest, magazines and journals 260
general references
almanacs 172—173
atlases 173–174

bibliographies 174–175
CD-ROM collections 101–102
chronicles, by eras and decades 175–176
chronologies and daybooks 176–177
dictionaries 177–178
English language 177–178
specialized 178
directories 178–179
electronic databases 118–119
encyclopedias 179–180
guides to books and references 180
microform collections 181
periodical and newspaper indexes 181–195
agriculture 181
anthropology 181
arts and humanities 182
bibliography 182
biography 182
biology 182
books and book reviews 183
business and economics 183
chemistry 184
computers 184
criminal justice 184
demography 184
dissertations 184
education 185
engineering 185
environment 185–186
history 186
language and literature 186–187
law 187–188
medicine 188–189
minorities 189
motion pictures 189
music 189
newspapers 190–192
philosophy 192
physical education 192
political science 192–193
psychology 193
public opinion 193
science and technology 194
social sciences 194
sociology 194
statistics 195
women's studies 195
popular quotations 195
public opinion polls 195–196
research 171–172
statistical abstracts 196–197
Web references 198–199
Web sites 285–286
yearbooks 198
General Sciences Index 18
geography, magazines and journals 260
geological sciences and mining
electronic journals, free 152
Web sites 286
gerontology associations on the Web 63
Google 4, 6, 7, 303
government
archives 48
CD-ROM collections 102–103
electronic databases 121–122
publications and agencies 200
federal information 203–205
foreign government information 207
guides and catalogs 201
journals and publications 207–221
research 200
sources online 221–225
state and local information 205–206
search engines 311
Web sites 286–287
government libraries 228–236
departmental 229–231
military 231–232
other 232–234
presidential 234–236
Government Printing Office 17
guides to
books and book reviews 183
citing sources 526–527
government information 201–203
references 180
Guide to Reference Books (Balay) 15

H

handbooks, subject. *See* subject handbooks

health and medicine. *See also* medicine
article indexes and abstracts 378–382
associations on the Web 63–65
biographical information 83
books and references 377–378
CD-ROM collections 103
electronic databases 122–123
full-text article databases 382–383
magazines and journals 260
history 260–261
home economics 261
periodicals 383–384
search engines 311
Web sites 287–288, 384–385
Hispanics/Hispanic Americans, biographical information 87–88
history
archives 48
article indexes and abstracts 389–391
books and references 386–389
CD-ROM collections 103–105
electronic databases 123–124
electronic journals, free 152
electronic journals, single subject directories 143
full-text article databases 391–392
magazines and journals 260–261
periodical and newspaper indexes 186
periodicals 393–394
Web sites 288–290, 394–395
home economics, magazines and journals 261
Hot Bot 6, 303
human development and family studies, electronic journals, free 152
humanities and fine arts
electronic databases 124
periodical and newspaper indexes 182
Humanities Index 18
human rights associations on the Web 65–67
H. W. Wilson 16

I

independent research libraries 236–238
indexes 18
newspaper and magazine 265–270
Index Medicus 18
Index to American Periodicals of the 1700s 21
Index to American Periodicals of the 1800s 21–22
information, gather 10
find sources 13
know when to stop 26–27
other library sources 23–25
plan research 10–13
specialized sources 25–26
use libraries 13–23
Information Please Almanac 16
InfoTrac 6
interlibrary loans 22–23
international affairs/international studies, Web sites 290
Internet
associations research 55–56
check for topic 4
library resource 23–25
references 198–199
Internet archives
African-American studies 44–45
agricultural and farm 45
American history 45–46
American Jewish 46–47
art 47
congressional 47
ethnic 48
find 43–44
government 48
historical 48–49
labor 49
medicine 49
newspaper 49
performing arts 49–50
recordings 50–51
space exploration 51
television news 51
women's history 51
in-text citations 525
as part of sentence 526
citing author 525
citing book or article 525
in-text references 526
numbering citations 526
page numbers 526

Issues and Controversies Opposing Viewpoints 6

J

JAMA: The Journal of American Medical Association 17
journalism and the media
  electronic journals, free 152–153
  electronic journals, single subject directories 143
Journal of Marriage and Family 17
journals
  electronic databases 124–126
  government 207–221
  researching 248–249
  subject headings 256–264
    advertising 256
    aeronautics and space flight 256
    African Americans 256
    aging 257
    agriculture 257
    anthropology 257
    archaeology 257
    architecture 257
    art 257
    astronomy 257
    automobiles 257
    biology 257
    broadcasting 257
    business 257–258
    chemistry 258
    children and youth 258
    communication 258
    computers 258
    consumer education 258
    dance 258
    ecology 259
    education 259
    electronics 259
    engineering 259
    fashion 259
    foreign language 259
    forestry 259
    future 260
    gardening and horticulture 260
    general interest 260
    geography 260
    health and medicine 260
    history 260–261
    home economics 261
    law 261
    literature and language 261
    literature and politics 261
    motion pictures 261
    music 261
    nursing 261
    photography 261
    political science 262
    population 262
    psychiatry 262
    psychology 262
    recreation and sports 263
    religion and theology 263
    science 263
    social sciences 263
    sociology 263
    sound recordings 263
    speech 264
    technology 264
    theater 264
    travel 264
    women's periodicals 264
    zoology 264
  trade and scholarly 17
  Web sites 270–272

K

keyword search
  bibliographical information 74
  CD-ROM collections 95
  common 14
  electronic databases 19, 110, 430
  electronic journals 137
  general databases 111
  general references 171–172
  government guides and catalogs 201
  government publications and agencies 200
  in searching topic 5
  methods of 6–8, 38
  newsgroup 168
  online public access catalogs 245
  on the Web 276
  preliminary research 9
  quotations and 532
  search engines 303
kid-safe search engines 312

L

labor archives 49
Lamm, Kathryn 4
language
  associations on the Web 67
  magazines and journals 261
  periodical and newspaper indexes 186–187
law
  article indexes and abstracts 399–402
  biographical information 82
  books and references 396–399
  CD-ROM collections 102–103
  electronic databases 117
  electronic journals, free 153
  electronic journals, single-subject directories 143
  full-text article databases 402–403
  magazines and journals 261
  periodical and newspaper indexes 187–188
  periodicals 403–404
  search engines 312
  Web sites 291–292, 404–405
Left Index 20
LexisNexis Academic Universe 20
libraries, types of
  academic 13, 227–228
  government 228–236
  independent research 236–238
  public 13, 238–239
  research 13
  researching 226–227
  school 239
  special 240
  state 240–244
  virtual libraries 246–247
library catalogs 14–15, 38, 245–246
library directories 244–245
Library of Congress Subject Heading 7, 14
library resources, using 13–14
  check for topic 4
  electronic databases 19–21
  interlibrary loans 22–23
  Internet 23–25
  microforms 21–22
  online catalogs 14–15, 245–246
  periodicals 17–18
  popular references 15–17
  specialized sources 25–26
  video and DVD resources 25
library science/books and publishing
  electronic databases 126–127
  electronic journals, free 153–154
Linkname: Steve's Online Newspapers 24
literary criticism. *See* literature
literature
  article indexes and abstracts 411–413
  articles 414–416
  associations on the Web 67–68
  biographical information 82–83
  books and references 406–411
  CD-ROM collections 105–106
  electronic databases 127–129
  full-text article databases 417–418
  magazines and journals 261
  periodical and newspaper indexes 186–187
  periodicals 418–421
  Web sites 421
local archives 42–43
local government information 205–206
long quotations 522
The Los Angeles Times 17, 20
Lycos 6

M

magazines 17
  databases 265–270
  directories 265–270
  electronic databases 124–126
  indexes 265–270
  researching 248–249
  subject headings 256–264
    advertising 256
    aeronautics and space flight 256
    African Americans 256
    aging 257
    agriculture 257
    anthropology 257
    archeology 257
    architecture 257
    art 257
    astronomy 257

automobiles 257
biology 257
broadcasting 257
business 257–258
chemistry 258
children and youth 258
communication 258
computers 258
consumer education 258
dance 258
ecology 259
education 259
electronics 259
engineering 259
fashion 259
foreign language 259
forestry 259
future 260
gardening and horticulture 260
general interest 260
geography 260
health and medicine 260
history 260–261
home economics 261
law 261
literature and language 261
literature and politics 261
motion pictures 261
music 261
nursing 261
photography 261
political science 262
population 262
psychiatry 262
psychology 262
recreation and sports 263
religion and theology 263
science 263
social sciences 263
sociology 263
sound recordings 263
speech 264
technology 264
theater 264
travel 264
women's periodicals 264
zoology 264
Web sites 270–272
mailing list
archives 165
search engines and directories 163–165
mathematics
associations on the Web 68
electronic journals, free 154
A Matter of Fact 20
McCormick, Mona 15
media centers. *See* school libraries
media studies Web sites 292
medicine. *See also* health and medicine
archives 49
biographical information 83
electronic journals, free 154–157
electronic journals, single subject directories 143
periodical and newspaper indexes 188–189
Metacrawler 6
metasearch engines 6, 306–307
microfiche 21–22
periodicals 249–252
microfilm 21–22
periodicals 249–252
microforms 21–22, 181
military libraries 231–232
military science
electronic journals, free 157
Web sites 292–293
minorities, periodical and newspaper indexes 189
MLA. *See* Modern Language Association
MLA International Bibliography of Books and Articles on the Modern Languages and Literatures 18
Modern Fiction Studies 17
Modern Language Association (MLA)
style 528–532
books 537–538
electronic sources 538
periodicals 538
motion pictures
magazines and journals 261
periodical and newspaper indexes 189
music
article indexes and abstracts 424–426
associations on the Web 69–70
biographical information 83–85
books and references 422–424
electronic journals, free 157
electronic journals, single subject directories 143–144

full-text article databases 427
magazines and journals 261
periodical and newspaper indexes 189
periodicals 427–428
Web sites 428–429
Music Index 18

N

narrow topic 8–9
National Geographic 17
National News Five 20
National Technical Information (NTIS) 225
Native Americans, biographical information 88
nested search 7
news, search engines 312–313
NewsBank InfoWeb 20
news digests 264–265
newsgroups. *See* e-mail newsgroups
newsletters 136–160
newspapers 17
archives 49
databases 265–270
directories 265–270
electronic databases 129–130
foreign 256
indexes 181–195, 265–270
periodical and newspaper indexes 190–192
researching 248–249
United States 251–256
Newspapers in Microform, United States, 1948–1972 22
Newspapers in Microform, Foreign Countries, 1948–1972 22
The New York Times 18, 20, 21
The New York Times Guide to Reference Materials (McCormick) 15
Northern Light 6
NTIS. *See* National Technical Information
numbering citations 526
nursing
article indexes and abstracts 431–436
books and references 430–431
electronic journals, free 157–158
full-text article databases 436–438
magazines and journals 261
periodicals 438
Web sites 438–439
nutrition
associations on the Web 70–71
electronic journals, free 158

O

objectivity of facts 33
online bibliography creators 531–532
online biographical information 91–94
online catalogs 14–15
online databases 6, 19, 39
free sites, 39–40
overseas sites 41
printed references 42
subscription sites 40–41
online government sources 221–225
Online Public Access Catalogs (OPACs) 14
OPACs. *See* Online Public Access Catalogs
overseas sites, online databases 41
The Oxford English Dictionary 16

P

page numbers, in citations 526
paraphrasing, 523–524
People Magazine 17
performing arts. *See also* dance; drama associations on the Web; film; music; television; theater
archives 49–50
CD-ROM collections 106–107
electronic databases 130–131
periodicals 17–18
gathering information and indexes 181–195
microfilm and microfiche 249–252
philosophy
associations on the Web 71–72
electronic databases 131
electronic journals, free 158
electronic journals, single subject directories 144

periodical and newspaper indexes 192
phone directories, CD-ROM collections 107
photography, magazines and journals 261
phrase search 6–7
phrases, quoting 532
physical education, periodical and newspaper indexes 192
physical sciences. *See* chemistry
physics
associations on the Web 72–73
electronic journals, free 158
Web sites 293
plagiarism, avoiding 519–521
political science and public administration
electronic databases 131
electronic journals, free 158–159
magazines and journals 262
periodical and newspaper indexes 192–193
politics
article indexes and abstracts 443–445
biographical information 85
books and references 440–443
full-text article databases 445–446
magazines and journals 261
periodicals 446–448
Web sites 286–287, 448–449
Popular Periodical Index 18
popular quotations 195
population, magazines and journals 262
preliminary research 9
presidential libraries 234–236
printed references, online databases 42
ProQuest Newspapers 20
psychiatry, magazines and journals 262
psychology
article indexes and abstracts 451–454
books and references 450–451
electronic databases 132
electronic journals, free 159
electronic journals, single subject directories 144
full-text article databases 454–455
magazines and journals 262
periodical and newspaper indexes 193
periodicals 455–456
Web sites 456–458
PsycINFO 20
Publication Manual of the American Psychological Association 533
publications
general interest 17
government 207–221
Web sites 270–272
public library 13, 238–239
public opinion
periodical and newspaper indexes 193
polls 195–196
Web sites 293–294
public policy. *See* politics
purpose of facts 30–31

Q

Questia.com 4
question-and-answer search engines 313–314
quoting 521
direct 522
keywords and phrases 532
long quotations 522
short quotations 521
with brackets 523
with ellipsis points 522–523

R

radio news, researching, 272–275
rankings and awards, Web sites 294
Reader's Digest 17
Readers' Guide to Periodical Literature 18, 19, 21
recordings archives 50–51
recreation, magazines and journals 263
references
best Web, 300–302
guides to 180
in-text 526
popular 15–17

References (listing), creating 528–529. *See also* citations, styles of
online creators 531–532
style 529–530
Works Cited sample 530
region, search engines 310–311
relevancy of facts 32
religion and theology
article indexes and abstracts 460–464
associations on the Web 73
books and references 459–460
CD-ROM collections 108
electronic databases 132
electronic journals, free 158
electronic journals, single subject directories 145
full-text article databases 464–465
magazines and journals 263
periodicals 465–467
Web sites 294–295, 467–468
research, defined 3
research, plan 10
agenda 10–11
timetable/schedule 11–13
tools and strategies 11
research library 13
independent 236–238
research on the Web 276
best references 300–302
sites by category 276–277
African-American studies 277
aging 277
agriculture 277
art history 278
associations and organizations 278–279
astronomy 279
business, economics, finance 279–280
chemistry 280
computers and cyberspace 280–281
consumer issues 281
country directories 281–282
demographic data 282–283
education 283
environment 283–284
ethics 284
film and theater 284–285
forensic science 285
general reference sources 285–286
geology and earth science 286
government and politics 286–287
health and medicine 287–288
history and culture 288–290
international affairs/international studies 290
law and criminal justice 291–292
media studies 292
military and defense 292–293
physics 293
public opinion surveys 293–294
ranking and awards 294
religion and theology 294–295
science and technology 295
social issues 295–296
speeches 296–297
subject guides and directories 297–299
Web searching 299–300
research topic
develop subject 1–9
evaluate sources 28–34
gather information 10–27
research topic, choose 3–5
research topic, develop 3
choose topic 3–5
define and narrow 8–9
preliminary research 9
search topic 5–8

S

scholarly journals. *See* journals
school libraries 239
school media centers. *See* school libraries
science. *See also* technology
article indexes and abstracts 473–477
biographical information 86
books and references 456–473
CD-ROM collections 108–109
electronic databases 132–133

electronic journals, free 159
full-text article databases 477–479
magazines and journals 263
periodical and newspaper indexes 194
periodicals 479–480
search engines 314
Web sites 295, 480
SearchBank 18
search connectors 7
search engine
categories 304
Web directories 308–309
Web engines 304–306
Web metasearch engine 306–307
mailing list 163–165
newsgroups 169
options 6
periodicals and 18
researching 303
topical
arts and entertainment 309
business and financial 309–310
computers and technology 310
country and region 310–311
government 311
health and medicine 311
kid-safe 312
legal 312
news 312–313
question-and answer 313–314
science 314
tutorials 315
using 4, 303–304
search methods 6
Boolean search 7
descriptor search 7–8
nested search 7
phrase search 6–7
subject heading search 7–8
truncated search 7
search options 6
search topic 5
effectively searching 5–6
methods of 6–8
options 6
sentence, citation as part of 526
short quotations 521
Social Change in America: The Historical Handbook 16
social issues, Web sites 295–296
social sciences
electronic databases 133
magazines and journals 263
periodical and newspaper indexes 194
Social Sciences Index 18, 20
sociology and social work
electronic databases 133
electronic journals, free 159–160
electronic journals, single subject directories 144–145
magazines and journals 263
periodical and newspaper indexes 194
sound recordings, magazines and journals 263
sources
consider 28–29
evaluate 28
facts of 30–34
specialized 25–26
understand 28
sources, citing 519
avoiding plagiarism 519–521
in-text citations 525
as part of sentence 526
citing author 525
citing book or article 525
in-text references 526
numbering citations 526
page numbers 526
online guides and tutorials 526–527
paraphrasing, 523–524
quoting 521
direct 522
keywords and phrases 532
long quotations 522
short quotations 521
with brackets 523
with ellipsis points 522–523
summarizing 524
sources, find 13
archives and archival collections 37–53
associations, societies, organizations 54–73

bibliographical information 74–94
by subject
aging 319–327
business and economics 328–337
criminal justice 338–350
ecology and environment 351–360
film and television 361–376
health and medicine 377–385
history 386–395
law 396–405
literature and literary criticism 406–421
music 422–429
nursing 430–439
politics and public policy 440–449
psychology 450–459
religion and theology 459–468
science and technology 469–480
sports 481–491
theater and dance 492–505
women's studies 506–516
CD-ROM collections 95–109
electronic databases 110–135
electronic journals, zines, newsletters 136–160
e-mail discussion groups and newsgroups 161–170
general references 171–199
government publications and agencies 200–225
libraries 226–247
newspapers, magazines, journals, radio, television 248–275
research on Web 276–302
search engines 303–315
space exploration archives 51
special collections 52
specialized dictionary 178
special libraries 240
speech and communication studies
electronic journals, free 160
magazines and journals 264
speeches, Web sites 296–297
sports and exercise sciences
article indexes and abstracts 483–485
biographical information 88–89
books and references 481–483
electronic databases 134
full-text article databases 486–487
magazines and journals 263
periodicals 487–490
Web sites 490–491
Sports Illustrated 17
Standard Periodical Directory 18
state government information 205–206
state libraries 240–244
statistical abstracts 17, 196–197
Statistical Abstracts of the United States 17
statistics. *See* demographic studies and statistics
strategies, list for research 11
style guides 531–532
subject, develop. *See* research topic, develop
subject dictionaries 16
Subject Guide to Books in Print ,16
Subject Guide to Microforms in Print 22
subject guides and directories, Web sites 297–299
subject handbooks 16
subject heading search 7–8
subscription sites
article index databases 137–138
online databases 0–41
summarizing 524

T

technology. *See also* science
article indexes and abstracts 473–477
books and references 456–473
electronic databases 134
electronic journals, free 159
full-text article databases 477–479
magazines and journals 264
periodical and newspaper indexes 194
periodicals 479–480
search engines 310
Web sites 295, 480

television
article indexes and abstracts 367–370
biographical information 81–82
books and references 361–367
full-text article databases 370–371
news
archives 51
researching 272–275
periodicals 372–374
Web sites 374–376
10,000 Ideas for Term Papers, Projects, Reports and Speeches (Lamm) 4
theater
article indexes and abstracts 497–500
biographical information 81–82
books and references 492–497
full-text article databases 500–501
magazines and journals 264
periodicals 501–504
Web sites 284–285, 504–505
theology. *See* religion and theology
Time 17
timeliness of facts 33
timetable/schedule, create for research 11–13
tools, list for research 11
trade journals. *See* journals
travel, magazines and journals 264
truncated search 7
tutorials
citing sources 526–527
search engines 315

U

Ulrich's International Periodicals Directory 18
unabridged dictionaries 16
Union List of Microfilms 22
USA Today 17
U.S. Bureau of the Census 17
U.S. newspapers 251–256
Utility Week 17

V

video resources
electronic databases 135
using 25
Violent Children: Research Handbook 16
virtual libraries 246–247
visual arts, electronic databases 134–135
Vogue 17

W

The Wall Street Journal 20
The Washington Post 18, 20, 21
Web. *See* Internet
Web bibliography creators 531
Webcrawler 6
Web directories 308–309
Web references, best 300–302
Web search engine. *See* search engine
Web searching, Web sites 299–300
Web sites
by category
African-American studies 277
aging 277
agriculture 277
art history 278
associations and organizations 278–279
astronomy 279
business, economics, finance 279–280
chemistry 280
computers and cyberspace 280–281
consumer issues 281
country directories 281–282
demographic data 282–283
education 283
environment 283–284
ethics 284
film and theater 284–285
forensic science 285
general reference sources 285–286
geology and earth science 286
government and politics 286–287
health and medicine 287–288
history and culture 288–290
international
affairs/international studies 290
law and criminal justice 291–292

media studies 292
military and defense 292–293
physics 293
public opinion surveys 293–294
ranking and awards 294
religion and theology 294–295
science and technology 295
social issues 295–296
speeches 296–297
subject guides and directories 297–299
Web searching 299–300
publication 270–272
Web style guides 531–532
Who's Who in America 16
Who's Who in American Art 16
Who's Who in Rock & Roll 16
women's studies
article indexes and abstracts 508–512
associations on the Web 73
biographical information 87
books and references 506–508
CD-ROM collections 109
electronic databases 135
electronic journals, free 160
full-text article databases 513
history archives 51–52
magazines and journals 264
periodical and newspaper indexes 195
periodicals 513–515
Web sites 515–516
Works Cited, creating 528–529
online bibliography creators 531–532
sample 530
style 529–530
The World Almanac and Book of Facts 16
World Wide Web. *See* Internet

Y

Yahoo! 6, 24, 303
yearbooks 198

Z

zines 136–160
zoology, magazines and journals 264